D0777348

# JULIE DANNENBAUM'S COMPLETE CREATIVE COOKING SCHOOL COOKBOOK

*combined with*

## MENUS FOR ALL OCCASIONS

# JULIE DANNENBAUM'S COMPLETE CREATIVE COOKING SCHOOL COOKBOOK

*combined with*

# MENUS FOR ALL OCCASIONS

\*

*Two Volumes in One*

BONANZA BOOKS
NEW YORK

This edition is published by Bonanza Books,
a division of Crown Publishers, Inc.,
by arrangement with Julie Dannenbaum.
a b c d e f g h
BONANZA 1980 EDITION

Manufactured in the United States of America


**Library of Congress Cataloging in Publication Data**

Dannenbaum, Julie.
    Julie Dannenbaum's Complete Creative Cooking School
cookbook, combined with Menus for all occasions.

    Reprint of Julie Dannenbaum's Creative Cooking
School, first published 1971 by McCall Pub. Co.,
New York and of Menus for all occasions, first
published 1974 by Saturday Review Press, New York.
    Includes index.
    1. Cookery. 2. Menus. I. Dannenbaum, Julie.
Menus for all occasions. 1980. II. Title. III. Title:
Complete Creative Cooking School cookbook.
TX715.D186   1980        641.5          80-26194
ISBN 0-517-33488-7

# CONTENTS
## for Volume One

Introduction                                          3

Do It My Way                                          6

Appetizers                                           16

Soup                                                 42

Seafood                                              57

Meats                                                80

Poultry                                             125

Eggs and Crêpes                                     150

Vegetables and Other Accompaniments                 162

Salads                                              191

Desserts                                            202

Stock and Sauces                                    239

Creative Cooking School Menus                       254

Measures                                            258

Index                                               261

# CONTENTS
## for Volume Two

Introduction                          1

Methods and Techniques                5

Breakfasts and Brunches               9

Luncheons                            39

Dinners                              91

Buffets                             181

Suppers                             215

Cocktail Parties                    227

Teas                                243

Outdoor Entertaining                251

Basic Recipes                       277

Index                               291

*Volume One*

# JULIE DANNENBAUM'S CREATIVE COOKING SCHOOL

\*

*Illustrations by Tom Funk*

# CONTENTS
## for Volume One

| | |
|---|---|
| Introduction | 3 |
| Do It My Way | 6 |
| Appetizers | 16 |
| Soup | 42 |
| Seafood | 57 |
| Meats | 80 |
| Poultry | 125 |
| Eggs and Crêpes | 150 |
| Vegetables and Other Accompaniments | 162 |
| Salads | 191 |
| Desserts | 202 |
| Stock and Sauces | 239 |
| Creative Cooking School Menus | 254 |
| Measures | 258 |
| Index | 261 |

*Volume One*

\*

# JULIE DANNENBAUM'S CREATIVE COOKING SCHOOL

# INTRODUCTION

The question I'm most often asked is, How did you get interested in running a cooking school?

The answer goes back to my childhood, for I grew up in a family of cooks and teachers.

My mother, an excellent cook, believed in letting me do anything I was ready for—and willing to clean up after. I could hardly reach the stove when I was turning out towering layer cakes. Under her tutelage, I learned how to smoke ham and bacon, how to make cottage cheese, even how to candy violets.

Home was fifty-six acres in central Pennsylvania, where we grew everything: apples to zucchini. In June my brothers and I roamed the woods picking wild strawberries, which Mother served with a pitcher of cream almost too thick to pour; I remember the marvelous taste whenever I see *fraises des bois* on the menu in France, where in springtime you can still get the tiny, flavorful berries and the thick, thick cream. Our cellar was full of foods "put up" from our garden—vegetables, relishes, jams, fruits, brandied and plain—and always there was hard cider. We baked bread twice a week, and we churned our own butter. I can't remember a meal Mother couldn't stretch for last-minute guests she or my father invited to our table.

Mother taught me to love cooking. My grandfather, who was a chef on the German Line, and my great uncle, a baker, taught me to respect it as both art and career. My professor-father was sure I'd become a home economics teacher, and at his urging, I enrolled at Penn State University.

I stuck out a year and a half in home ec, then I switched courses, but my interest in *food* never wavered. I cooked for family and friends, entertaining frequently. As soon after World War II as European travel was possible again, I took my first lessons at Le Cordon Bleu in Paris. When Dione Lucas came on television a few years after that, I locked my kids in their playroom and sat glued to the set, entranced with her technique. I commuted to New York to take lessons from her, earned her diploma, and eventually became associated with her in the Egg Basket restaurant, where she taught me how to turn out an omelette in thirty seconds. I learned a lot from other teachers as well—among them, Ann Roe Robbins, Michael Field, James Beard, and in Paris, Simone Beck. Then, ten years before I opened my own cooking school, I began to plan how it would be.

I waited until the timing was right. My children obligingly reached their teens just when Americans started to become wildly interested in food and cooking. And I was ready to move, with the wholehearted backing of my family, especially my cooperative husband.

At first, in 1965, I taught two courses in my home, starting with twelve students. By the end of the year, I had eighty names on a waiting list, and I decided to open a real school.

I leased the first floor of a building in Philadelphia's Germantown and began remodeling it to provide a completely equipped demonstration kitchen. A long work counter down the center of the room has twenty-four feet of chopping blocks, cooking tops with ovens below, a deep double sink, and a built-in marble slab for pastry-making. The wall behind is lined with pegboard for hanging pots, pans, and whisks, and with shelves for supplies. A scalloped canopy over the counter shields fans and lights.

My contractor enrolled in the first class—and helped launch the Creative Cooking School, in October, 1966, with champagne toasts.

In each class, I teach a complete meal—at least four recipes, more often five or six. I feel the old classics are great if you have the time. But I'm realistic: no one wants to spend endless hours in the kitchen; everyone wants to be free when guests arrive—yet still serve them a meal they'll remember.

The first step in cooking a successful dinner is to organize a menu that you can manage. In my classes I point out everything that can be done ahead; that way, the students see how to plan their time. There are similar pointers in this book, so you'll know what can be done a week, a day, or a few hours ahead of a party.

But you should consider, when planning a menu, not only your own time but that of the year, for two reasons. First, foods that are in season, fresh foods, are almost always best to cook with (so make the most of strawberries and asparagus in the springtime, green apples and oranges in the fall). Second, heavier foods are more appealing in cold weather; lighter foods belong on summer menus (so chocolate, lemon, and banana desserts are especially good in the winter, while in the summer peaches and berries, which are plentiful then, and sun-ripened and juicy with flavor, are better). My own favorite menu is one I teach in midwinter: Lobster Bisque (see p. 46), Saddle of Lamb (see p. 102), French Green Salad (see p. 194), and for dessert, Pears in Red Wine (see p. 226).

Back to your time: good equipment saves it, and saves drudgery too. Without good sharp knives and a decent-size cutting block, chopping vegetables is much more of a chore than it need be. Heavy pots and pans are easier to cook with and worth the investment; you'll be happiest with professional kinds and sizes. In many of the recipes that follow there are notes about special pieces of equipment I've found particularly useful. Many of the recipes include serving and garnishing directions (no Creative Cooking class is over until each dish is properly garnished and ready for presentation); where needed, there are carving directions too, and here again, I must stress the importance of proper equipment: nothing is more dangerous than trying to carve a roast on a slippery platter or on a board that is too small; nothing is more difficult than carving with a dull knife.

For the benefit of beginners, the recipe directions in this book are detailed: I've tried to include explanations and extra information, along with answers to all the questions I've ever been asked. (This material is set off in separate paragraphs, each identified by a dot [•].) I've already answered one question: How did you get interested in running a cooking school? Anticipating another, also frequently asked—What keeps you interested?—I felt at first, and after five years of teaching, still feel, most rewarded when beginners report back to me about a triumphant dinner, a glorious party. I hope that in the recipes that follow, every other possible question is answered, and that as a result of this book, I'll hear about other good dinners, other successful parties.

# DO IT MY WAY

The best way to learn to cook is to cook: stand yourself in front of the stove and start right in.

Watching a teacher may inspire you, but the lesson won't really sink in until you try it yourself. If your first effort is a disaster, great! You'll learn more from your mistakes than from your successes. I remember trying to make Hollandaise Sauce when I was a child. Time after time, I'd watched my mother and grandmother make it, always with success. But mine curdled. By the time I got it right, I'd learned a lot about working with eggs. If you want to cook, you mustn't be intimidated by a few failures.

Anyone who can read, and who has the intelligence to follow a recipe, can become a competent cook, even a good one. Really fine cooks are blessed with innate ability to season food, to plan menus, and to think up new ideas, but experience can certainly help to fill the instinct gap.

Don't bore yourself with so-called beginner recipes when you start to cook. It is just as easy to teach yourself to make a soufflé as a white sauce—in fact, white sauce is the foundation for a soufflé. I teach soufflés or crêpes in my first lesson. My theory at the Creative Cooking School is that students learning to make interesting and elegant dishes pick up all of the basics of cooking along the way, and because my students are always making something new and exciting, they never have time to lose their original enthusiasm.

After five lessons, they have learned how to make soufflés, crêpes, mayonnaise, basic brown sauce, velouté sauce, and Hollandaise, as well as how to roast a piece of meat, poach fish, and cook vegetables. They have also learned how to prepare five fantastic dinner party menus, and most important, how to prepare them all either easily or with enough ease to present them to guests in a relaxed manner that belies earlier arduous efforts.

Certain cooking techniques—those for beating egg whites and for deglazing pans, for example—are called for again and again in the recipes that follow. My students learn these techniques—the best I've developed, or culled from the many teachers with whom I've studied—in their first five lessons. Each teacher has his or her own methods. Mine may not suit you, but before you decide, do it my way.

### Blanching

This means giving food a quick bath in boiling water. Do it to bacon, for example, to remove its saltiness, to cabbage and onions to weaken their taste, or to peaches, tomatoes, and almonds to loosen their skins.

### Bouquet garni

Bouquets garnis are small packages of herbs used for flavoring soups, sauces, and casseroles; they are removed prior to serving. I use 1 rib of celery, 1 bay leaf, ¼ teaspoon of dried thyme, and 1 tablespoon of parsley for a bouquet garni. I make a celery sandwich by laying the herbs on half the celery, folding the other half over, and tying with a string, one end of which I leave long and tie to the handle of the pot or casserole so the bouquet garni will be easy to remove.

### Bread crumbs

Save bread that's beginning to go stale and use it to make your own excellent dry bread crumbs. Put slices—1 slice will yield ½ cup of crumbs—on a baking sheet and place in a 300° oven for 15 to 20 minutes, or until the bread is very dry and hard, then break it into pieces and put them in a blender. I store dry crumbs in a covered jar on my shelf and use as needed. To make fresh, or soft, bread crumbs, grate bread in a hand grater or tear it apart with your fingers.

### Butter

I feel that unsalted butter gives pastries a richer flavor than does salted butter. In some areas of the country unsalted butter is more expensive than salted, perhaps because it is more perishable (salt in butter helps to preserve it, so that it will keep longer in the store—and in a home refrigerator too). Some of my recipes specify unsalted butter; in those that don't specify, salted is assumed.

### Cooking in a covered casserole

Because the lid of a covered casserole dish gets as hot as the sides of the dish, steam rising from the cooking surface escapes rather than condensing. The escaping steam can change the consistency of a sauce or cooking liquid, often undesirably. To prevent this—to maintain the consistency, that is—cover the casserole with foil before putting the lid on. The dead air space between the foil and the lid will then insulate the lid, making it cool enough to condense the steam.

### Cooking over high heat

Learn to cook on high heat—it saves time, and that's important today. To do it successfully, you must use heavy-bottomed pans. And you must be attentive—*never* turn your back on a pan on high heat. To avoid scorching or burning food, toss it or move it around in the pan with a wooden spatula. The way to save any mixture that suddenly gets too hot is simply to lift the pan off the heat. Don't waste time turning a knob or pushing a button.

### Custards

Custards and dishes of similar consistency—vegetable rings, molds, and mousses—tend to separate and become watery if overcooked. Those that bake in hot-water baths begin to shrink away from the sides of the dish when they're done. Another test for doneness: insert a knife in the custard; if the knife comes out clean, the custard is done.

### Deep frying

Generally I use solid vegetable shortening for deep frying because it gives off less odor than other kinds of fat. When frying, never add too much food to the pan at once or the temperature of the fat will drop.

### Deglazing pans

After you brown meat, salvage the juices and brown bits in the pan for added flavor in your sauce. Remove the meat from the pan and pour off the excess fat—usually, this is all but about 1 tablespoon. To deglaze with wine, stock, or water, add about ¼ cup liquid to the pan, boil it up over heat, and scrape up the brown bits with a wooden spatula. To deglaze with brandy, flame the pan (see Flaming), and when the flames have died down, scrape up the brown bits they have loosened.

### Deveining shrimp

Peel off shrimp shells with your fingers. Fingers are usually faster for most jobs, and never mind the gadgets. For deveining, use a small sharp knife to make a shallow slit along the back of the shrimp, then remove the vein.

## Discoloring

White sauces or custard mixtures that contain egg yolk or white wine are allergic to aluminum pans. If you whisk them smooth in aluminum, you'll see them turn gray before your eyes. Use enamel-on-iron or stainless steel. The chef's professional-weight tin-lined copper saucepan is perfect for sauce-making.

## Eggs

HARD-COOKING: Bring eggs to room temperature, slip them gently into boiling water, wait until boiling resumes, then set a timer for exactly 12 minutes. Early in the cooking time, turn the eggs over to help keep the yolks in the center. When the 12 minutes are up, plunge the eggs into cold water and chill rapidly to prevent the yolks from turning green around the edges, which is harmless, but unsightly. Crack and shell the eggs under cold running water.

BEATING EGG WHITES: Eggs are easier to separate when they're cold from a refrigerator. However, always let egg whites warm to room temperature before beating them. To beat as much air as possible into egg whites, use a piano-wire balloon whisk, and keeping the tip of it in the bowl at all times, swing it round and round—use wrist muscles, not shoulder muscles; or use a rotary beater and move the beater all over the bottom of the bowl. If an electric mixer is used to beat the egg whites, the whites must be watched closely when they start to get stiff, for it's easy to over-beat with an electric mixer. You'll get much more volume (desirable for soufflés) if you beat egg whites in an unlined copper bowl (this is due to the physical reaction caused by the steel of the beater coming into contact with the copper). Clean the bowl with 1 tablespoon of coarse salt and 1 tablespoon of vinegar—rub it out with paper towels. Rinse with *hot* water. Dry thoroughly. The bowl—and the beaters too—must be completely free of grease, for a speck of it, or of egg yolk, which is fatty, in the whites will prevent them from beating up properly. Egg whites are "stiff" when most of them can be scooped onto a whisk or beater at once. Whites should form peaks, but not be dry. If your recipe calls for salt and cream of tartar (cream of tartar helps stabilize beaten egg whites), add them when the egg whites begin to foam.

BLENDING IN EGG WHITES: First, stir a big spoonful of beaten egg whites into your base to lighten it; you don't have to be too careful about this for egg whites are not as fragile as you've probably been led to believe. Then add the remaining egg whites and fold in (see Folding) quickly and lightly. Do not overmix; it is always better to leave a few fluffs showing than to risk deflating the egg whites.

MAKING MERINGUE: Use an electric mixer and a large bowl to make meringue. Be sure that the bowl and beaters are clean—no grease—and that the egg whites are room temperature. When the whites start to foam, add cream of tartar and continue beating until soft peaks form. Add sugar, 1 tablespoon at a time, beating constantly, and continue beating until the mixture looks like marshmallow. It is ready when you can pinch it between your fingers and it doesn't feel grainy.

ENRICHING SAUCES WITH EGG YOLKS: Beat the egg yolks with a fork. Then, to avoid curdling the sauce when adding the yolks, warm the yolks gradually by stirring a little hot sauce into them. Stir the warm yolk mixture into the sauce. Do not boil a sauce after you've added egg yolks— it may curdle. Do not add egg yolks to sauces that will be cooled and reheated before serving.

## Flaming

Heat brandy or liquor in a small long-handled pan just until finger warm. Ignite it—keep your head back—and pour it, flaming, into the pan or over the dish to be flamed, then shake the pan or dish until the flames die.

## Folding

This technique is used to combine a fairly delicate substance with a heavier base. Pour the ingredient to be folded in over the original mixture and, using a large rubber spatula, cut down through the center of the mixture to the bottom of the bowl, across the bottom, up a side, over to the center, then down again. Keep turning the bowl as you fold.

## Freezing foods

When freezing prepared or partly prepared foods (pastry, soups and sauces, desserts, etc.), make sure they are properly wrapped. I generally use aluminum foil to wrap solid pieces of food and special freezer jars for soups and sauces. I bag desserts in huge plastic bags. I try to move foods out of my freezer within 2 months.

### Herbs

I much prefer fresh herbs, but they're not always available. If I can't get fresh tarragon, thyme, basil, or rosemary, I find that substituting 1 teaspoon of the dried herb for 1 tablespoon of the fresh is satisfactory and, if not otherwise specified, assume the herbs in my recipes are dried. However, I *always* use fresh parsley, garlic, and dill, which are readily available and which have a flavor far superior to that of the dried and frozen herbs.

### Mushrooms

CLEANING: Never soak mushrooms. Wipe them clean with paper towels dipped in acidulated water—water with a little lemon juice (1 tablespoon to 1 quart of water) in it—or dip them quickly in acidulated water, then dry them with paper towels.

SLICING: To keep the distinctive mushroom shape, trim the stems, then slice the mushrooms vertically from top to stem.

FLUTING MUSHROOM CAPS: Cut off the stems of the mushrooms even with the caps—don't twist the stems out, or the caps will collapse—then with a small curved knife or a lemon stripper, cut grooves that spiral out from the center of each cap to the edges, all around.

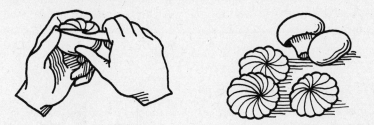

SAUTÉING: Melt butter—use 1 tablespoon for ¼ pound of mushrooms—in a skillet, and when it is hot and foaming, add mushrooms, squeeze on a few drops of lemon juice, sprinkle with salt and freshly cracked black pepper, and toss over high heat for about three minutes.

### Pastry bags and tubes

Invest in a professional pastry bag—one that's big and washable—and a few plain, rose, and star tubes in various sizes. When using a pastry bag, fit on the proper tube, then fold the top of the bag down over your left hand (if you're right-handed), making a cuff, and fill the bag—no more than ¾ full—by scooping whipped cream, batter, or whatever into it with a large rubber spatula, pushing the spatula against the thumb of your left hand. Then unfold the cuff and make 3 pleats to close the top of the bag, twisting it to force the contents down to the tube. Hold the tube close to the surface you want to decorate and squeeze the bag from the top (most amateurs have trouble because they squeeze the tube near the tip rather than from the top of the bag). Practice using the pastry tube by filling the bag with vegetable shortening and piping it out. Fill the bag over and over again, until you learn how to make attractive rosettes

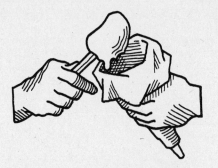

or cream puffs all the same size. To clean a pastry bag, wash it in soap and warm water or drop it in a washing machine. After washing, just stand it up and allow it to dry thoroughly.

### Poaching

Poaching means very gentle simmering in liquid—that is, the liquid should not bubble, just move a bit.

### Reheating French-fried appetizers

Set cake racks on a baking sheet, cover the racks with brown paper, lay the appetizers on the paper, and place in a 350° oven for a few minutes.

### Rolling up cake or vegetable rolls

When the cake or vegetable is ready to be turned out of the pan, tear off 2 sheets of waxed paper 6 inches longer than the pan and lay them out, overlapping lengthwise, on a counter or board. (Dust the paper with sugar or confectioners' sugar if the recipe so directs.) Invert the pan over

the waxed paper, lift it off, and peel off the waxed-paper liner if one was used in baking. Roll up, using the overlapping sheets of waxed paper as an aid. After the first fold, you can align the edges of the overlapping sheets of paper so you have a double thickness of paper to help you as you continue rolling. Cakes should be rolled warm to set their shape, unrolled for filling, and then rerolled. Vegetable rolls may be filled warm or cool.

### Salt

Coarse salt (sea salt or kosher salt) seems saltier than table salt to me. When you rub coarse salt on the exterior of roasts or steaks, an attractive crust will form. Many chefs use coarse salt exclusively. The crystals take longer to dissolve than do those of table salt, which makes coarse salt ideal for salad dressings.

### Seasoning cold food

It's important to overseason any food that will be served very cold, for chilling deadens flavor. There are no hard and fast rules on how much to overseason—just use a little more salt, vanilla, herb, or whatever than you normally would.

### Skimming fat from sauces and stock

Excess fat makes sauces and stock look, and sometimes taste, greasy. The easiest way to remove it—if you have the time—is to chill the sauce or stock; the fat will rise to the top and solidify, and you can lift it off. Or you can tilt the cooking vessel and spoon off the excess fat. If stock or sauce must be absolutely fat-free, finish skimming with a paper towel: lay it on the surface to pick up remaining fat.

### Soufflé dishes

A soufflé collar provides both space and support for a soufflé to puff up properly. To make a collar for a soufflé dish, cut a length of waxed paper long enough to go around the dish with some overlap, fold the paper in half lengthwise, place it around the dish, and tie it on with string so it stands 3 to 4 inches above the dish. If you butter or oil a soufflé dish,

butter or oil the collar too. I find that hot soufflés rise better when the dish and collar are not greased. However, we use both greased and ungreased dishes at the Creative Cooking School. If I grease the dish for a hot soufflé, I usually use butter, because it adds flavor. But because oil is less likely than butter to stick, I recommend oil for cold soufflés, mousses, and any dish that is to be unmolded.

### Tomatoes

PEELING: Spear a tomato on a fork, twirl it in the flame of a gas range for a few seconds, and the skin will loosen. The skin will also loosen if the tomato is blanched—that is, plunged into boiling water for about 30 seconds.

SEEDING: Cut each tomato in half crosswise, hold a half in the palm of your hand and squeeze out the seeds.

SLICING: For salads, slice tomatoes from stem to bottom. They'll lose the least juice that way.

### Unmolding

To make unmolding easier, molds should be oiled before they're filled. Custards and vegetable molds baked in hot-water baths should be removed from the baths and let stand for 5 minutes—to collect themselves—before unmolding. To loosen either baked or chilled molds, run a small knife around the edge—around the center edge too, if it's a ring mold—using a sawing, up-and-down motion. To unmold, place a serving platter over the mold, invert the platter and mold, give both a shake, and lift off the mold.

### Vegetables

REFRESHING: As soon as fresh vegetables have boiled to the tender-crisp stage, drain them and plunge them immediately into cold water. This stops the cooking, and it helps set the color—refreshing the vegetables. Vegetables may be cooked in the morning, refreshed, drained, and covered, and stored in a refrigerator, then reheated at night with butter and seasonings.

SLICING: Use a *mandoline* to slice vegetables. It's speedy, and you'll get nice even slices, which will cook uniformly. The instrument has an adjustable blade so you can make thin or thicker slices. (There is also a ridged blade available for making Waffled Potatoes [see p. 186].)

## Whipping cream

I whip heavy cream in a large metal bowl set in a bowl of ice, and I prefer to use a piano-wire balloon whisk rather than the hand-held electric or rotary beaters some cooks like. Cream whipped over ice (and sweetened with confectioners' sugar) is less likely to turn into butter and will not separate on standing. This means you can assemble a whipped-cream dessert in the morning for dinner that night. Confectioners' sugar (preferable to granulated) for sweetening should be added when the cream is mounding softly.

# APPETIZERS

Nearly every country has its own infinite variety of tempting appetizers. In France it is hors d'oeuvres; in Scandinavia, smorgasbord; in Italy, antipasto; in Russia, zakuska; and so on. In America hors d'oeuvres, cocktail canapés especially, and other appetizers add the touches that transform an ordinary meal into a party and are, for a host or hostess, a delicious way to show off creative talent—which does not mean one should forget that the prime function of an appetizer is to pique the palate.

I do not enjoy satiating my guests with appetizers unless I'm giving a party and they are the mainstay of the menu. Many times I serve only one—Pâté (see p. 17), for example, or Mushrooms à la Grecque (see p. 25)—as a first course at the table or on small plates in the living room.

Casually served, finger foods, such as Crudités (see p. 25)—with thick Greek mayonnaise, Skordalia, for indulgent guests, coarse salt for abstemious ones—are a perfect preamble to a rich dinner. More and more, raw vegetables are the "in" appetizer, for—face it—appetizers in the main are eaten by people who don't need them.

For the "little something to nibble on" that guests expect with cocktails, many party givers have adopted the Continental custom of passing salted almonds along with a variety of olives. (Just sauté blanched almonds in 2 tablespoons of oil, drain on paper towels, and while the almonds are hot, sprinkle them with coarse salt.) Others fill a basket with flaky home-baked Parmesan Sticks (see p. 30).

For cocktail parties it's fun to have as large as possible an assortment of appetizers. Certainly there should be enough so that guests won't have to go on to a dinner. Such a party can end with omelettes and coffee for those who stay late.

Recipes for a variety of party appetizers, all my favorites, are in this chapter, and all of them are geared for advance preparation; most can be made days or even weeks ahead. I've included such perennial pleasers as Quiche Lorraine (see p. 35)—students of mine say that this quiche is the most delectable they've ever tasted—but my fun comes from ferreting out new dishes like Anchovy Rolls (see p. 23) and Roquefort Mousse (see p. 40). All the pâtés must be prepared in advance, ready to be sliced or scooped out and spread on French bread or toast triangles. Terrines improve if made beforehand and served a few days later.

Of course, the grandest appetizer of all is fresh caviar. Serve it in the tin buried in ice and accompany it with hot toast, lemon, and if you must, chopped onion. It will disappear quickly. I've been told that the taste for caviar, like that for olives, is an acquired one; but when caviar and olives are both served, notice that the caviar almost always disappears first.

When serving appetizers, make them look as good as they taste. The recipes suggest garnishes and serving ideas. Put your imagination to work too; but guard against overdecorated appetizers, and remember that all garnishes should be edible. Interesting platters, divided dishes, chafing dishes, all add festive touches to appetizers, which should, ideally, be clean-tasting, even a little sharp, to titillate the palate. If dinner is to follow, they should complement the rest of the meal.

## PÂTÉ

This recipe makes about 2 cups of smooth pâté, delicately flavored. It can be chilled in a crock or a small loaf pan, served in the crock or unmolded from the loaf pan and sprinkled with chopped parsley. Provide thin slices of whole wheat bread, Melba toast, or thick pieces of French bread to spread it on.

| | |
|---|---|
| *1 lb. chicken livers* | *¼ cup dairy sour cream* |
| *1¼ cups unsalted butter* | *1 teaspoon Spice Parisienne* |
| *1½ cups finely chopped Ber-* | *or allspice* |
| *muda onion* | *1 tablespoon Benedictine* |
| *1 teaspoon salt* | *1 tablespoon lemon juice* |
| *½ teaspoon freshly cracked* | *2 tablespoons chopped black* |
| *black pepper* | *truffles, or crushed pista-* |
| *2 tablespoons brandy* | *chios* |

1. Wash chicken livers and dry with paper towels. Melt ¼ cup of butter in a large skillet over high heat, and when foaming subsides, add chicken livers. Sauté quickly over high heat.

• Many people feel compelled to move the chicken livers around in the pan. Don't. Let them hit the pan, take on color, and get a little crusty on the bottom. Then turn them over all at once and brown the other sides.

2. When turning the livers, add chopped onion, and if necessary, a little more butter. Cook until onion is wilted. This whole process takes about 15 minutes. The livers should still be pink inside.
3. Remove from heat. Add salt and pepper and flame with brandy that has been put in a little copper pan with a long handle, heated to luke-warm, and ignited with a match.
4. After flames subside, stir in sour cream, spice, and Benedictine.
5. Purée mixture in a blender, then work it through a fine sieve to make it smooth. Set mixture in refrigerator to chill for at least 30 minutes.
6. Beat 1 cup butter in electric mixer until it is light and creamy. Add cooled liver and continue beating until smooth.

• If liver mixture isn't chilled when it is added to creamed butter, the result will be oily in texture.

7. Taste for seasoning.

• As much as another teaspoon of salt may be needed.
• All foods prepared to be served cold should be slightly overseasoned. Cold foods require more salt than hot foods.

8. Stir in lemon juice and truffles, or pistachios, and mix well.

• Unused truffles from an opened can of them can be transferred to a small jar, and with the addition of truffle juice and enough Madeira or brandy to cover, stored in a refrigerator. They will keep indefinitely.

9. Pour pâté into a crock or loaf pan, cover, and chill in refrigerator until firm—at least 2 hours, preferably overnight.

• This pâté keeps in the refrigerator for 4 to 5 days. Be sure it's covered, since chicken livers tend to darken. The best way is to put a little melted butter, liquid aspic (see p. 243), or buttered wax paper over the top, then cover with a tight lid.
• Let the pâté stand at room temperature for 20 minutes before serving it.
• The pâté can be frozen, but for no longer than 1 month. Frozen pâté should be thawed in a refrigerator for 24 hours, then let stand at room temperature for 20 minutes before it is served. *Makes 6 to 8 servings.*

## PYRAMID OF CHEESE BALLS

2 cups grated Gruyère cheese
2 rounded tablespoons flour
4 stiffly beaten egg whites
¾ cup bread crumbs (see
   p. 7)

½ teaspoon salt
¼ teaspoon freshly cracked
   white pepper
Fat for deep frying
½ cup grated Parmesan cheese

1. Mix Gruyère cheese, flour, and egg whites together and roll mixture, which will be wet, into balls the size of marbles.

•If the balls are made larger they can be served as a first course, or as a luncheon or supper dish with a hot tomato sauce (see p. 250).
• Sharp Cheddar, or any hard, sharp cheese, can be substituted for the Gruyère. Hard cheese is easier to grate.
• For a more piquant flavor, add 1 tablespoon chopped chives or 1 teaspoon freshly grated onion to the cheese mixture.

2. Coat the balls with bread crumbs seasoned with salt and pepper and chill for 15 minutes.
3. Heat fat to 375° in a large heavy saucepan, a deep fryer, or an electric skillet.

• Fat should be at least 2 inches deep. In my classes, we use solid shortening for deep frying.

4. Drop balls into hot fat, 4 or 5 at a time. Brown on all sides, remove with a slotted spoon, and drain on paper towels.

• The reason for frying only 4 or 5 balls at a time is to hold the temperature of the fat. Dump in a dozen chilled balls at once, and temperature plunges.

5. Place a paper doily on a round serving platter, pile balls in a pyramid, and sprinkle them with Parmesan cheese.

• Cheese balls are best when eaten as soon as they are fried. If necessary, they can be held for 15 minutes in a low (150–200°) oven, or they can be frozen, or prepared in the morning and reheated at cocktail time. To reheat, set cake racks on a baking sheet, cover with brown paper, and lay cheese balls on the paper; place in a 350° oven for a few minutes.
*Makes 6 to 8 servings, or about 24 balls.*

## Assorted Hors d'Oeuvres

I like to assemble these when I have omelette parties. Guests like them; they're interesting to serve; and they take the place of a salad. Ideally you should have a collection of *raviers*, the small oblong plates used in Europe for serving hors d'oeuvres. The food can be prepared and arranged in the dishes—be aware of colors when doing the arranging—early in the day, covered with plastic wraps, and refrigerated until serving time. For many hors d'oeuvres, the longer the time spent marinating, the better the taste seems to be.

There is no *recipe*, and the following suggestions do not always give measures by the teaspoonful. Use judgment, some imagination—and what happens to be on hand in the refrigerator.

• Ripe avocado, peeled and cut in thin slices, arranged alternately with pink grapefruit sections, and dressed with Vinaigrette Sauce (see p. 252).
• Genoa salami, rolled into cigarette shapes, garnished with chopped black olives, and dressed with good French olive oil.
• Carrots, finely shredded, mixed with white raisins (2 tablespoons for 4 carrots), and dressed with Vinaigrette Sauce.
• Red radishes, sliced as thinly as possible and mixed with enough sour cream (about 2 tablespoons for 1 bunch of radishes) to hold them together. Season with chopped chives (1 tablespoon per bunch), salt (½ teaspoon per bunch), and freshly cracked white pepper (¼ teaspoon per bunch).
• Celery, finely minced, then mixed with drained chopped anchovies (1 2-oz. can for 4 ribs of celery) and a little Vinaigrette Sauce.
• Cherry tomatoes (with their stems on), washed in ice water just before serving, then sprinkled with coarse salt.
• Swiss cheese, diced, then mixed with caraway seeds (1 tablespoon per ½ lb. of cheese) and enough mustard mayonnaise to bind. (To make mustard mayonnaise, stir about 2 teaspoons Dijon mustard into 2 tablespoons mayonnaise [see p. 251].)
• Cauliflower, divided into flowerets and mixed with sour cream (about 3 tablespoons for a small head) and curry powder, to taste (I use about a teaspoonful for a small head).

## Shrimp Pâté

This pâté has a bland, delicate taste, which is enhanced if the pâté is prepared a day ahead of when it's to be served. It is good as a first course and can be beautifully presented.

2¼ lbs. raw shrimp, in shells
1 teaspoon peppercorns
2 teaspoons salt
2 cups unsalted butter
½ teaspoon mace
½ teaspoon chili powder
2 tablespoons finely
    chopped parsley

2 tablespoons finely chopped
    fresh tarragon, or 2 tea-
    spoons dried
1 tablespoon Pernod, or ani-
    sette
1 tablespoon lemon juice

1. Put shrimp (in shells) in a pot with enough cold water to cover; add peppercorns and salt, and bring to a boil; then reduce heat and cook until the shrimp turn pink (this should take less than 5 minutes). Take pot off heat and let shrimp cool in the liquid. When they are cool enough to handle, remove shells and devein the shrimp.

2. Put shrimp through a food mill, using the finest blade, or chop finely. Set aside.

3. Beat butter with an electric mixer (use the flat whip if the mixer is a heavy-duty one) until it is very creamy; then beat in the shrimp, a little at a time.

• This step can be done by hand, but the result will not be as creamy.

4. Season with more salt, if desired, the mace, chili powder, parsley, and tarragon and beat until mixture is as smooth as possible. Thin with Pernod, or anisette, and lemon juice.

5. Pack the pâté into a crock or a loaf pan and chill it at least 2 hours, preferably overnight.

• Serve from the crock, with toast fingers, crackers, Melba toast, or whole wheat bread. Or for an elegant first course, unmold the pâté from loaf pan, cut it in slices, and serve them on a bed of greens and garnished with thin slices of lemon or with lemon twists (made by cutting thin lemon slices from the center to the edge, then turning the ends to make a twist). *Makes 8 servings.*

## OYSTERS BIENVILLE

These are typically New Orleans. The sauce can be made ahead of time, and baking the oysters takes only minutes. The rock salt keeps the oysters *hot*—a fine serving secret.

4 scallions
6 tablespoons butter

2 tablespoons flour
⅔ cup fish stock (see p. 242),

or bottled clam juice
⅓ cup finely chopped mushrooms
1 egg yolk
⅓ cup dry white wine
¼ teaspoon salt

¼ teaspoon freshly cracked
 white pepper
6 cups rock salt, about
2 dozen oysters on half shell
½ cup bread crumbs (see p. 7)
½ cup grated Parmesan cheese

1. Chop scallions very, very fine, the white part plus three-quarters of the green. Sauté in 2 tablespoons of butter in saucepan over high heat until just wilted. Do not let them burn: keep moving them around with a wooden spatula.

2. Remove pan from heat and stir in flour. Return to high heat and cook for 1 or 2 minutes, to remove the raw flour taste, stirring constantly with a wooden spatula to keep the mixture from burning or browning.

• This butter-flour paste is called a roux. Thorough blending of it helps ensure a smooth, lumpless sauce.

3. Remove pan from heat and add fish stock, all at once. Whisk vigorously to make a smooth mixture.

• I always switch from a wooden spatula to a whisk when I add the liquid. Working with the whisk virtually guarantees smoothness.

4. Squeeze mushrooms in the corner of a clean towel to remove excess juice, then stir into stock.

5. Using the whisk, beat the egg yolk with wine. Remove sauce from heat and stir a few spoonfuls of the hot sauce into the egg-wine mixture, then very gradually stir this egg-wine enriched sauce back into the rest of the sauce.

6. Season with salt and pepper and cook over low heat for 5 to 10 minutes, stirring constantly.

• The recipe can be made the day before up to this point. Plastic wrap pressed on the surface of the sauce will keep a skin from forming when it's refrigerated. Reheat the sauce, stirring, when ready to bake the oysters.

7. Fill an ovenproof serving dish with a layer of rock salt and place it in a 400° oven for 20 minutes, or until it is very hot.

8. Place oysters, on half shell, on the hot rock salt. Return dish to oven and bake for about 3 minutes. Meanwhile melt remaining 4 tablespoons of butter.

9. Remove dish from oven, spoon some of the sauce over each oyster, sprinkle with bread crumbs and grated Parmesan cheese. Dribble generously with melted butter and return to oven for 2 to 3 minutes, or until oysters are lightly browned. **Makes 4 servings as a first course, 6 to 8 servings for cocktails.**

## ANCHOVY ROLLS

8 slices bread
½ cup butter
3 tablespoons Dijon mustard, about
2 2-oz. cans flat anchovy fillets

¾ cup milk
1 egg
¾ cup bread crumbs (see p. 7)
Fat for deep frying

1. Remove crusts from bread and cut into fingers. Roll bread as thinly as possible with a rolling pin.

• Regular store-bought white bread, the light fluffy kind, is best here.

2. Melt butter and brush each bread strip with it and Dijon mustard. Use enough mustard so it can really be tasted.

3. Put anchovy fillets in a sieve, run cold water over them, shake off excess, and lay them on paper towels to dry thoroughly.

4. Lay an anchovy fillet on each finger of bread. Roll up tightly and fasten with a toothpick. Dip rolls into a mixture of milk and beaten egg, then roll in bread crumbs.

5. Heat fat (2″ deep) in saucepan or electric frying pan to 375° and fry anchovy rolls, a few at a time, until brown. Remove with a slotted spoon and drain on paper towels. Serve hot.

• If too many are fried together, they become soggy, as the temperature of the fat drops.
• The anchovy rolls can be fried in the morning and reheated before serving. Or they can be frozen. To reheat, set cake racks on a baking sheet, cover with brown paper, and lay rolls on paper; place in a 350° oven for a few minutes. *Makes 8 servings.*

## EGGS MIMOSA

10 hard-cooked eggs
8 oz. black caviar
1 cup mayonnaise (see p. 251)

1 cup heavy cream
1 bunch watercress

1. Allow 1 egg per person. Shell eggs and cut them in half, crosswise. Cut a slice off the bottom of each half to make it stand up. Remove yolks and set them aside.

• To shell eggs, tap them all over to crack the shell, then peel under running water.

2. Arrange egg whites on a serving dish and fill cavities with caviar, mounding it somewhat.

3. Combine mayonnaise, homemade preferably, with heavy cream whipped to the same consistency. Pour over eggs and caviar, masking them completely.

4. Push reserved yolks through a sieve and sprinkle over masked eggs to resemble mimosa. Garnish with watercress.

• The caviar-filled eggs can be prepared and arranged on a platter in advance. Cover with plastic wrap and store in refrigerator. Add mayonnaise mixture, yolks, and garnish just before serving. *Makes 10 servings.*

## GINGER SAUSAGE ROUNDS

> 1½ lbs. bulk pork sausage
> 1 medium clove minced garlic
> 1 tablespoon finely chopped candied ginger
>
> 3 separated eggs
> Fat for deep frying

1. Mix sausage, garlic, candied ginger, and egg yolks together in a bowl. Beat egg whites until fairly stiff and fold them into sausage mixture.

• There is no salt in this recipe, since most sausage is highly seasoned; if using sausage that is not, sprinkle sausage balls with salt after frying.
• If desired, ¾ lb. ground veal and ¾ lb. finely ground beef may be substituted for the pork sausage. Season meat with 1 teaspoon salt and ½ teaspoon freshly cracked black pepper.

2. Heat fat (2" deep) in a saucepan or electric skillet to 375° and drop sausage mixture from a teaspoon into fat. Don't add too many teaspoonfuls at a time: doing so will lower too much the temperature of the fat, which must be hot to produce crisp sausage balls. Fry for about 5 minutes, or until brown. Remove with a slotted spoon and drain on paper towels. Serve very hot.

• Ginger sausage rounds can be fried in the morning and reheated, or they can be fried and then frozen. To reheat, set cake racks on a baking sheet, cover with brown paper, lay balls on the paper, and place in a 350° oven for several minutes. *Makes 8 to 10 servings, or about 36 rounds.*

## CRUDITÉS WITH SKORDALIA

Skordalia is Greek mayonnaise. It's one of the best dips I know to set out with a colorful assortment of neatly trimmed raw vegetables, arranged on a bed of ice.

### Crudités

Scrub and chill and arrange on a bed of crushed ice any or all of the following:

*Celery ribs, trimmed neatly*
*Green and/or red peppers,*
    *seeded and cut into strips*
*Baby turnips, thinly sliced*
*Zucchini, sliced or cubed*
*Cauliflower flowerets*
*Carrots, sticks or curls*
*Eggplant, cubed*

*White and/or red radishes*
*Cucumber sticks*
*Baby pattypan squash, sliced*
*Black olives*
*Cherry tomatoes*
*Raw snowpeas*
*Fennel, sliced*

### Skordalia

*2 cups mayonnaise (see*
    *p. 251)*
*3 medium cloves chopped*
    *garlic*
*5 tablespoons bread crumbs*
    *(see p. 7)*

*¼ cup ground almonds*
*2 tablespoons chopped pars-*
    *ley*

1. Stir garlic, bread crumbs, ground almonds, and chopped parsley into bowl of mayonnaise. If not seasoned enough, add salt and freshly cracked white pepper, to taste.
2. Chill 2 hours before serving. *Makes 2½ cups.*

## MUSHROOMS À LA GRECQUE

*1 lb. large, firm white mush-*
    *rooms*
*2 tablespoons lemon juice,*
    *plus juice to clean mush-*
    *rooms*

*¾ cup dry white wine*
*1 small bay leaf*
*2 teaspoons minced shallot*
*⅓ cup olive oil*
*¼ teaspoon thyme*

6 *coriander seeds*
¼ *teaspoon chervil, or 1 tea-*
*spoon chopped fresh pars-*
*ley*
½ *teaspoon salt*

¼ *teaspoon freshly cracked*
*white pepper*
1 *tablespoon chopped parsley*
*for garnish*
1 *lemon for garnish*

1. Dip mushrooms quickly in cold water mixed with a little lemon juice (about 1 tablespoon to 1 quart of water) and wipe them with paper towels. Trim off ends of stems and cut mushrooms vertically, through cap and stem, in very thin slices.

• Never soak mushrooms. Cleaning them in lemon water helps keep them white. If mushrooms are small, they can be left whole, or quartered.

2. Put mushrooms into an enameled saucepan with all remaining ingredients except garnishes. Bring to a rolling boil and boil for 5 minutes, covered.

3. Drain mushrooms, reserving the liquid, and put them in an earthenware or enameled serving dish.

4. Boil reserved liquid to reduce it by one-third. Strain it and pour over mushrooms. If desired, store in refrigerator, covered.

5. Bring mushrooms to room temperature and garnish with chopped parsley and very thin overlapping slices of lemon before serving. *Makes 6 servings.*

### GRACE ZIA CHU'S SHRIMP TOAST

Grace Zia Chu is a noted teacher of Chinese cuisine and my favorite Chinese cooking instructor. This recipe is a slight variation from her original. My proportions are a little different, and I use ginger root and scallions.

½ *lb. raw shrimp, in shells*
6 *water chestnuts*
1 *egg*
1 *teaspoon salt*
1 *tablespoon chopped scal-*
*lion, white part only*
1 *teaspoon dry sherry*

1 *tablespoon cornstarch*
1 *teaspoon minced ginger*
*root*
¼ *teaspoon sugar*
6 *slices 2-day-old homestyle*
*bread*
1½ *cups peanut oil*

1. Shell and devein raw shrimp. Wash and drain. Chop them fine along with water chestnuts.

2. Beat egg slightly and mix in shrimp-water-chestnut mixture, salt, scallion, sherry, cornstarch, ginger root, and sugar.

3. Trim crusts from bread, and cut each slice into 4 triangles. Spread shrimp mixture over each triangle.

4. Heat peanut oil (2″ deep) to temperature of 375° on fat thermometer. Lower bread triangles into oil, shrimp side down, and fry about 1 minute; then turn, and fry other side. Fry only a few triangles at a time. Drain on paper towels and serve immediately.

• Shrimp toast can be fried ahead of time, refrigerated or frozen, and reheated. If frozen, it can be reheated without thawing. To reheat, set cake racks on a baking sheet, cover with brown paper, and lay toast triangles on paper; place in a 350° oven for a few minutes; if the toast has been frozen, heat it a little longer—5 to 6 minutes. *Makes 6 servings.*

### BOUREKAKIA

To make Bourekakia—a favorite of Ann Roe Robbins, the well-known New York cooking authority—you will need two possibly unfamiliar ingredients: feta cheese, a strong-flavored Greek goat cheese, best if bought in brine (but be sure to rinse it before using), and filo dough, a pastry as thin as onionskin, which is available in Greek or Armenian grocery stores. The pastry comes in sheets, rolled up in plastic wrap, and it can be stored in the freezer. It is very fragile and dries out rapidly; when it does, it breaks into little bits. Work with it one sheet at a time, keeping the remaining sheets covered with a damp, not wet, towel. If filo dough is not available, substitute commercial strudel leaves and handle them the same way. This appetizer is irresistible with drinks.

½ cup coarsely mashed feta cheese
6 oz. cream cheese
2 eggs
¼ teaspoon freshly grated nutmeg

½ cup melted butter
6 to 8 sheets filo dough, each about 11″ × 15″

1. Beat both cheeses, eggs, and nutmeg together until smooth.

2. Lay a sheet of filo dough on a slightly damp towel and brush it all over with melted butter. With a knife, cut it into strips 2 to 3 inches wide and about 8 inches long. Place a scant teaspoonful of the cheese mixture near one end of each pastry strip. Fold end of strip over cheese, then fold sides in, one over the other, to enclose cheese. Brush folded-over surface with butter and roll up to make a neat little package of pastry with cheese filling inside.

• Work fast. And keep pastry surfaces brushed with butter, partly to prevent their drying out, partly to get a flaky, butter-rich pastry.

3. Bake in a 350° oven for 20 minutes, or until puffed and brown. Serve warm.

• Bourekakia can be prepared 2 days in advance and stored in a refrigerator on a lightly covered tray. Or they can be frozen, then baked, according to the preceding directions, just before you are ready to serve.
• Sometimes I add 2 tablespoons of tarragon or parsley to the filling.
**Makes 8 to 10 servings, or about 36 appetizers.**

## PÂTÉ MAISON

Almost every restaurant in France has a pâté it's proud of. In general, this is a rough country pâté, the kind diners get when they order the "house pâté."

| | |
|---|---|
| 2 lbs. calves' liver | ¼ teaspoon dried thyme |
| 1½ lbs. veal | ¼ cup cognac |
| 2 large eggs | ½ lb. blanched bacon |
| 2 teaspoons salt | 1 tablespoon roughly chopped |
| 2 teaspoons freshly cracked | truffle |
| black pepper | 6 chicken livers, marinated 1 |
| 3 tablespoons dairy sour | hour in 3 tablespoons |
| cream | cognac |
| 1 large clove very finely | 1 cup aspic (see p. 243) |
| minced garlic | |
| 1 tablespoon finely chopped | |
| shallots | |

1. Grind the liver twice, using the finest blade on the meat grinder; since the veal must also be finely ground, grind it twice too, with the same blade. Then, in a large bowl, mix together liver, veal, eggs, salt, pepper (2 teaspoons is correct), sour cream, garlic, shallots, and thyme.

• I mix the ingredients with my hands—it's the fastest, most thorough way.

2. Heat cognac to lukewarm, ignite, and pour it, flaming, over the meat mixture. Let it burn out. Blend well.
3. Line a pâté mold (or a 9-by-5-by-3-inch loaf pan) with overlapping strips of blanched bacon. Let bacon hang over sides of pan.

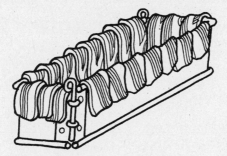

• To blanch bacon: put bacon strips in cold water in a saucepan, bring to a boil, boil 1 minute, drain in a sieve.

4. Fill lined mold with half the liver-veal mixture. Sprinkle chopped truffle down the middle lengthwise and arrange the marinated chicken livers in a row over them. Add rest of the liver-veal mixture and fold bacon ends over the top to cover completely.

5. Wrap the mold completely in heavy-duty aluminum foil and place in a pan of boiling water reaching three-quarters up the mold. Bake on the middle shelf of a 325° oven for 2 hours. Remove from oven.

6. Weight pâté down with a brick and chill overnight in refrigerator.

• The pâté may ooze, so it's a good idea to leave the mold in the second pan (emptied of water) when refrigerating it. Weighting it down makes the pâté compact, and easier to slice.

7. Serve pâté (which is excellent with French bread) chilled and cut in thin slices. Garnish it with chopped aspic.

• This pâté can be stored in the refrigerator for 1 week or frozen for up to 1 month. *Makes 12 to 16 servings.*

## Liptauer Cheese

The classic accompaniment is icicle radishes, but red radishes, cucumber sticks, celery, and finocchio can all be used. The best bread to serve with this dish is thinly sliced caraway rye.

| | |
|---|---|
| *16 oz. cream cheese* | *1 tablespoon paprika* |
| *½ cup unsalted butter* | *1 cup finely chopped onion* |
| *½ cup creamed cottage cheese* | *1 2-oz. can flat anchovy fillets,* |
| *2 tablespoons heavy cream* | *chopped* |
| *1 tablespoon anisette* | *1 3½-oz. jar capers* |
| *2 teaspoons caraway seeds* | *2 bunches white radishes* |

1. With electric mixer, beat cream cheese and butter until very light and creamy. Add cottage cheese and whip until fluffy. Thin with heavy cream and flavor with anisette. Add caraway seeds and mix well.

2. Mound cheese decoratively on a serving plate. Use a spatula to smooth the surface and to make decorative indentations around the sides. Dust top with paprika, preferably medium-sweet Hungarian.

• This recipe may be made up early in the morning and refrigerated until evening; just be sure to cover it. Take it out of the refrigerator about ½ hour before serving time.

3. When serving, set out small dishes containing chopped onion, chopped anchovies, and drained capers as condiments for the Liptauer cheese. Also set out icy-cold white radishes. *Makes 8 to 10 servings*.

## PARMESAN STICKS

*1 recipe of all-purpose puff*    *1 egg white*
    *pastry (recipe follows)*    *4 tablespoons paprika*
*¾ cup Parmesan cheese*

1. Make puff pastry the day before it is to be shaped and baked. Refrigerating it overnight gives the pastry a chance to rest, thus making it easier to handle.

2. Cut the chilled pastry in half from fold to fold. (It's easier to roll out half at a time.) Roll each half on a lightly floured board sprinkled, about ⅛-inch thick, with the grated cheese.

3. Prick pastry all over with a fork and brush it with slightly beaten egg white. Sprinkle with more cheese and a little paprika. Press the cheese into the pastry with a rolling pin.

4. With a pastry wheel, cut pastry into strips ¾ of an inch wide and 5 to 6 inches long.

5. Dampen a baking sheet with water, or line it with baking parchment. Place pastry strips on baking sheet, twisting them if desired, and chill in refrigerator for 30 minutes.

6. Place baking sheet on the middle shelf of a preheated 400° oven and bake the sticks for about 10 minutes. Reduce heat to 300° and bake another 10 minutes, or until crisp. *Makes 12 to 16 servings, or 50 to 60 sticks.*

### All-Purpose Puff Pastry

This is puff pastry made the Scandinavian way, which always works, even on the hottest day.

1⅔ cups loosely packed   ½ teaspoon salt
flour, plus flour to dust on   1 cup chilled unsalted butter
dough and rolling surface

1. Place 1⅔ cups of flour in a bowl and stir in salt.

• If salted butter is used instead of unsalted, add only ¼ teaspoon salt.

2. Cut butter into chips the size of almonds.
3. Turn the chips over in the flour to coat, then with a pastry blender, cut them into the flour. The mixture should look like small peas.

4. Sprinkle the mixture with iced water (use about 5 tablespoons) and stir it with a large fork until it holds together in big chunks.

• Be sure there's ice in the water. It's important to have everything cold or chilled when making puff pastry.
• The amount of water needed will depend on the weather: on dry days more will be required than on humid ones.

5. With your hand, scoop the mixture together and shape it into a dough ball.
6. Dust the ball with flour, wrap it in waxed paper, and refrigerate it for 30 minutes to 1 hour.
7. Place chilled ball on lightly floured marble or on a lightly floured pastry board and roll it out to make a rectangle approximately 8 inches wide by 16 inches long.

• With the first rolling, the dough will look raggedy and will probably be sticky. Use a little flour, if necessary, to keep it from sticking to the marble or board and to the rolling pin.

8. Fold the rectangle into thirds (like a business letter), give it a quarter turn (folds will be on right and left), then roll it into a rectangle and fold it into thirds again.

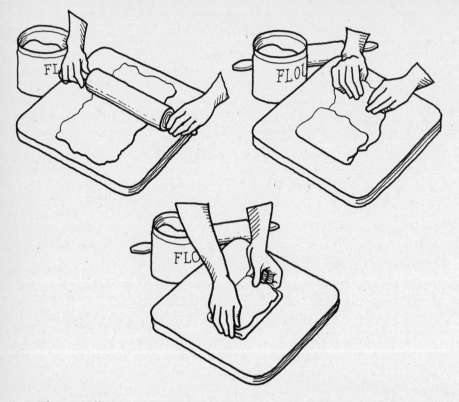

• This is called a *turn*. Each turn consists of 2 rollings, and the dough must be turned 3 times in all—that is, rolled and folded a total of 6 times. Each turn will make the dough smoother, so on the next you'll be able to make the rectangle more exact. Try to be as precise as possible.
• A pastry scraper will help you take dough up from the marble or board, to fold in thirds.

9. Wrap dough in waxed paper and chill in refrigerator for at least ½ hour.

• To keep count of the turns, mark the dough with one finger after the first, two fingers after the second, three after the third.

10. Repeat steps 7, 8, and 9, then repeat steps 7 and 8, wrap dough in waxed paper again, and allow it to rest overnight in a refrigerator before the final shaping and baking.

• The dough can be frozen after the third turn. Wrap it in plastic wrap or foil. Remove it from the freezer the day before it is to be used and thaw it in a refrigerator.

11. Roll out dough and cut it as recipe directs.

• Scraps left over can be stacked on top of each other or bunched together, then rolled out and used.

12. Place dough on a baking sheet that has been dampened with cold water, chill in a refrigerator (the dough should always come to a hot oven from the chill of a refrigerator), then bake in a preheated 400° oven for 5 to 10 minutes. *Makes enough for 1 dozen 3-inch tart shells, 1 9-inch tart shell, 24 Piroshki, or 50 to 60 Parmesan Sticks.*

## PIROSHKI

Piroshki, little meat turnovers, come from Imperial Russia, where they were usually served with clear borscht. This recipe is for bite-size ones, to serve with cocktails. Any kind of pastry, including plain piecrust, can be used, but puff pastry is best.

| | |
|---|---|
| *1 recipe of all-purpose puff pastry (see p. 30)* | *2 chopped hard-cooked eggs* |
| *¾ cup chopped onion* | *½ teaspoon salt* |
| *2 tablespoons butter* | *¼ teaspoon freshly cracked black pepper* |
| *½ lb. beef, ground twice* | *1½ tablespoons dairy sour cream, about* |
| *1 tablespoon chopped parsley* | *1 egg white* |
| *2 tablespoons chopped fresh dill* | |

1. Prepare puff pastry the day before the Piroshki are to be made. It must rest in a refrigerator overnight before final rolling and shaping.
2. Cook onion in butter until transparent, but do not let it brown. Add ground beef and cook until beef is no longer pink. Do not overcook.

• Instead of ground beef, ground veal, chicken, tongue, pork, or ham can be used. The meat should be raw, not leftover.

3. Mix in parsley, dill, hard-cooked eggs, salt, and pepper, and enough sour cream to hold the mixture together.
4. Halve the pastry (after its three turns and overnight chilling); cut through the folds. Roll out one half at a time, rolling it as thin as possible. Cut into rounds with a 2-inch cutter.

• If puff pastry is too thick, the little turnovers will open up when baked.

5. Brush edges of pastry circles with egg white, lightly beaten. Put a scant teaspoonful of filling on each circle. Fold over and seal edges together.

• Don't fill the turnovers too full—it makes the edges difficult to seal. Pinch edges together with fork tines to seal them, pressing all around the edges with determination.

6. Place Piroshki on a damp baking sheet and chill in refrigerator for at least ½ hour, or until ready to bake.

• Piroshki can be made ahead and frozen unbaked. Bake them a few minutes longer if they are still frozen when put in the oven.

7. When ready to bake, move Piroshki from refrigerator to a pre-heated 400° oven for 15 to 20 minutes, or until light brown. Serve hot. *Makes 8 to 10 servings, or about 24 Piroshki.*

## BLINI WITH CAVIAR

Blini are Russian crêpes made with yeast. Usually they contain buck-wheat flour, although authentic Russian blini can be made with all-white flour too.

> ½ package active dry yeast
> ½ teaspoon salt
> 1 separated egg
> 1½ cups lukewarm milk
> 1½ cups flour
> ½ cup buckwheat flour
>
> 1 cup melted, unsalted butter
> 8 oz. red or black caviar
> 2 cups dairy sour cream
> 1¾ cups chopped onion or 1 cup chopped fresh chives

1. Soften yeast in 2 tablespoons of lukewarm water; stir in salt.
2. In a large bowl, beat egg yolk into milk; add the yeast mixture. Add flour and buckwheat flour and beat until batter is smooth. Cover bowl with a cloth and let it stand in a warm place for 2 hours while batter rises.
3. Beat egg white until it forms soft peaks; fold into batter.
4. Drop batter by tablespoonfuls onto a greased griddle or frying pan; cook until the blini are brown on the bottom and little bubbles show on top; turn and brown other side.

• The griddle is hot enough when a drop of cold water will dance on it.
• If the griddle is well seasoned, it won't need greasing each time it's used. Moisten a wadded paper towel with oil and keep it handy to wipe the surface should blini begin to stick.
• Keep finished blini warm in a 200° oven while cooking the rest.

5. Pour hot butter over blini and serve (allow 2 blini per serving) with caviar, very cold sour cream, and chopped onion or chives. *Makes 15 servings or 30 blini, 3 inches in diameter.*

## Quiche Lorraine

A 9-inch quiche can be cut into quarters or sixths and served as a main dish for luncheon or supper. Cut in eighths, it can be served as an hors d'oeuvre or first course. Cut into very thin wedges (it will make 16 to 20), it can be served at a cocktail party. In this event keep the wedges in the original pie shape on a serving platter and let the guests help themselves.

1 lb. bacon
¼ cup fine bread crumbs (see p. 7)
6 tablespoons freshly grated Parmesan cheese
1 9" partly baked pâte brisée shell (recipe follows)
½ cup shredded Gruyère cheese

2 eggs
2 egg yolks
2 teaspoons Dijon mustard
1 teaspoon salt
¼ teaspoon freshly cracked white pepper, or cayenne pepper
1½ cups half-and-half, or milk, or light or heavy cream

1. Cut bacon in little pieces and fry it slowly until crisp. Drain bacon on paper towels and reserve the fat.

• Another way to cook the bacon is in a baking pan, in a 350° oven.

2. Mix bread crumbs with 2 tablespoons Parmesan cheese and sprinkle into partly baked pâte brisée shell.

• The partly baked pastry shell insures a crisp crust. The fine bread crumbs help to seal the shell and prevent sogginess.

3. Sprinkle bacon bits over bread-crumb mixture, reserving a little bacon for garnish. Sprinkle Gruyère cheese over bacon.

• Instead of Gruyère cheese, Swiss or Cheddar may be used.

4. Whisk eggs and egg yolks in a bowl until blended but not frothy. Add mustard, remaining Parmesan cheese, and salt and pepper. Stir in ¼ cup of the reserved bacon fat (it should be liquid, but not hot).

5. Stir in half-and-half and pour the custard mixture over bacon and cheese in the pastry shell.

6. Bake in a 350° oven for about 15 minutes, or until custard is set. To test whether custard is set, insert a silver knife into it; if the custard is set, none will stick to the knife when it's pulled out.

• If quiche is to be baked ahead—but not frozen—and reheated before serving, bake it only 10 minutes and reheat in a 350° oven for 10 minutes. If it is to be frozen, bake it completely and either heat it or let it come to room temperature before serving.

7. Garnish with reserved bacon bits. *Makes 8 servings.*

## Tart Shell

This flaky, buttery crust is ideal for quiches, tarts, and turnovers.

*2 cups loosely packed flour, plus flour to dust on rolling surface*

*1 teaspoon salt*
*½ cup chilled unsalted butter*
*¼ cup vegetable shortening*

1. Place 2 cups of flour in a bowl and stir in salt.

• Lightly salted butter can be used instead of sweet butter. If this is done, use only ½ teaspoon of salt.

2. Cut in butter and shortening with a pastry blender or work them in with fingertips, lifting some up and letting it fall off your fingers. Work quickly (so the mixture stays cool), until the mixture looks like small peas.

• Adding vegetable shortening to the butter makes the pastry flakier.

3. Add just enough iced water (3 to 4 tablespoons), 1 tablespoon at a time, to hold the mixture together in a dough ball.

• Sprinkle the water on the flour mixture while tossing it with a fork to distribute the water as evenly as possible. With cupped hand, try to gather the mixture into a dough ball. If it is still crumbly, add another tablespoon of water. The amount of water needed will depend on the humidity of the day. Use as little as possible to make a manageable dough, for too much water makes pastry tough.

4. Wrap the dough ball in waxed paper and chill it at least ½ hour.

• The dough can be wrapped in foil or plastic wrap and frozen. Or it can be kept in a refrigerator for up to 2 days. Defrost frozen dough in a refrigerator before using.

5. Flatten the ball on a lightly floured pastry board or a lightly floured marble surface and roll it in all directions with a lightly floured pin. Keep turning the dough to roll it into an even circle. Dust the board (or marble) and the pin with more flour, if necessary, to keep dough from sticking.

• The dough can be rerolled if it doesn't come out right. If it cracks, paste it together with a little beaten egg white or water.

6. Using a pastry scraper, roll the dough around the rolling pin, then unroll it over a 9-inch pan or flan ring.

• French quiches and tarts, unlike American ones, come to the table out of the pan. The filling is supported by straight-sided crust, which is shaped in a flan ring that is removed after the shell is baked.

7. Ease the dough into the pan or ring, using care not to stretch it.

8. Trim off excess dough by pushing the rolling pin over the top of the pan or ring; then press the dough over the top edge of the pan or ring to attach it and keep it from shrinking away from pan or ring during baking.

9. With a fork, prick the dough—not all the way through—all over the bottom.

10. Chill in a refrigerator for about 20 minutes before baking.

• At this stage the dough can be frozen. Defrost it in a refrigerator before baking.

11. Before baking, line the shaped dough with waxed paper and fill it with dried beans or rice, the weight of which will prevent it from puffing up while it bakes.

12. For tarts, bake for ½ hour in a preheated 350° oven; then remove beans, waxed paper, and flan ring, reduce heat to 325°, and bake another 20 to 25 minutes, or until pastry is a pale gold color. Remove from oven and cool on a rack at room temperature. For quiches, bake in a preheated 375° oven for 20 to 25 minutes, or until pastry is set, then remove beans, waxed paper, and flan ring, add filling, and continue baking as recipe directs.

• Partly baked pâte brisée shells can be refrigerated or frozen. *Makes 1 9-inch shell.*

## ONION QUICHE

5 cups chopped onions
¼ cup butter
2 eggs

2 egg yolks
½ teaspoon freshly grated
nutmeg

½ teaspoon sugar
1 teaspoon salt
¼ teaspoon freshly cracked
  white pepper
1½ cups half-and-half
¼ cup fine bread crumbs
  (see p. 7)

1 9″ partly baked tart
  shell (see p. 36)
2 to 3 tablespoons chopped
  parsley or chopped chives

1. Sauté chopped onion in butter until transparent but not brown.

2. Whisk eggs and egg yolks in a bowl until blended but not frothy. Add nutmeg, sugar, salt, and pepper. Stir in the half-and-half and slightly cooled onions.

3. Sprinkle bread crumbs into partly baked tart shell and pour in custard.

4. Bake in a 350° oven for about 20 minutes, or until custard is set. Custard is set when a silver knife, inserted into custard, comes out clean.

5. Sprinkle top with chopped parsley or chopped chives. *Makes 8 servings.*


## SPINACH QUICHE

1½ 10-oz. pkgs. frozen
  chopped spinach
2 eggs
2 egg yolks
1 teaspoon salt
½ teaspoon freshly cracked
  black pepper
½ teaspoon freshly grated
  nutmeg

2 tablespoons finely grated
  onion
2 cups dairy sour cream
¼ cup fine bread crumbs (see
  p. 7)
1 9″ partly baked tart
  shell (see p. 36)

1. Thaw spinach, drain it well, and squeeze out any excess moisture.

2. Whisk eggs and egg yolks in a bowl until blended but not frothy. Stir in salt, pepper, nutmeg, onion, and sour cream. Fold in spinach.

3. Sprinkle bread crumbs into the partly baked pâte brisée shell and pour in filling.

4. Bake in a 350° oven for about 20 minutes, or until custard is set—that is, until a silver knife inserted in it comes out clean. *Makes 8 servings.*


## CRAB QUICHE

2 eggs
2 egg yolks
2 cups half-and-half

½ teaspoon salt
¼ teaspoon freshly cracked
  white pepper

¼ *teaspoon freshly grated*
  *nutmeg*
1½ *lbs. crab meat*
¼ *cup fine bread crumbs (see*
  *p. 7)*

*1 partly baked 9" tart*
  *shell (see p. 36)*
*2 tablespoons chopped pars-*
  *ley*

1. Whisk eggs and egg yolks in a bowl until blended but not frothy. Stir in half-and-half, salt, pepper, and nutmeg.

2. Pick over crab meat to remove bits of shell and membrane.

• Use any grade of crab meat. The finest quality is not necessary in this recipe.

3. Sprinkle bread crumbs into partly baked tart shell and arrange crab meat over crumbs. Pour custard mixture over crab meat.

4. Bake in a 350° oven for about 20 minutes, or until custard is set. (Custard is set when a silver knife can be inserted in it and pulled out clean.)

5. Sprinkle top with chopped parsley just before serving. **Makes 8 servings.**

## SMOKED SALMON QUICHE

This quiche must be served as soon as it comes from the oven. If it stands, the salmon toughens.

2 *eggs*
2 *egg yolks*
2 *cups half-and-half*
¼ *teaspoon salt*
¼ *teaspoon freshly cracked*
  *black pepper*
¼ *teaspoon freshly grated*
  *nutmeg*

¼ *cup fine bread crumbs (see*
  *p. 7)*
*1 partly baked 9" tart*
  *shell (see p. 36)*
*1 lb. thinly sliced smoked*
  *salmon*
*2 tablespoons chopped fresh*
  *chives, or chopped parsley*

1. Whisk eggs and egg yolks in a bowl until blended but not frothy. Stir in half-and-half, salt, pepper, and nutmeg.

• A little more salt may be needed, but add it cautiously—smoked salmon can be very salty.

2. Sprinkle bread crumbs into partly baked tart shell and cover with salmon slices. Pour custard mixture over salmon.

3. Bake in a 350° oven for 20 minutes, or until custard is set. When custard is done, a silver knife will come out clean after being inserted in it.

4. Sprinkle top with chopped fresh chives or chopped parsley. **Serve at once. Makes 8 servings.**

## ROQUEFORT MOUSSE

Serve with drinks or as a separate course, with salad.

| | |
|---|---|
| 1½ cups unsalted butter | ¼ teaspoon cayenne pepper |
| 1¼ lbs. Roquefort cheese | 1 tablespoon vegetable oil |
| 3 tablespoons cognac | |
| 1 tablespoon finely chopped parsley | |

1. In mixer, beat butter until light and creamy. Bit by bit, beat in the Roquefort cheese, and continue beating for at least 10 minutes, or until mixture is very, very fluffy. Add cognac, parsley, and cayenne pepper and blend well.

2. Brush a 5-cup loaf mold with oil (don't use too much oil, and be sure to oil the corners) and pour the soft mixture into the mold. Pack it down. Chill mold in refrigerator for at least 2 hours—overnight is better —so flavors blend.

• The mousse can be stored for several days in the refrigerator, or it can be frozen.

3. When ready to serve, run a knife around edges of pan and unmold on a platter. Serve with Melba toast or commercially made water biscuits. **Makes 16 servings.**

## STUFFED EDAM OR GOUDA CHEESE

This spread is best when made the day before it is to be served and refrigerated until serving time. It can also be frozen. Please take note that it is highly seasoned; if you prefer milder foods, I suggest cutting back on the cayenne pepper. Serve it with unsalted warm crackers. I like English water biscuits, or stoned wheat thins.

| | |
|---|---|
| 2 lbs. Edam or Gouda cheese | ¾ teaspoon cayenne pepper, about |
| 1½ cups unsalted butter | |
| 3 tablespoons cognac | |

1. Bring cheese and butter to room temperature. Cut the top off the cheese and hollow it out, leaving the shell about ½ inch thick.

2. Chop all the cheese that has been scooped out, including the top.

3. Put chopped cheese into mixer bowl along with cognac and ¼ teaspoon of cayenne pepper. Beat until the mixture is very creamy. This will

take about 10 minutes. If a heavy-duty mixer is used, beat with the flat whip.

4. Beat in butter, a little at a time, and continue beating until mixture is extremely creamy.

5. Taste for seasoning, and add more cayenne pepper to taste and perhaps a little salt.

6. Use a large rubber spatula to put mixture into a pastry bag fitted with a large star tube. Squeeze mixture into the cheese shell, making a decorative rosette on top.

7. Sprinkle with ½ teaspoon more of cayenne pepper. *Makes 16 servings.*

# SOUP

Soup-making as an art—and it is an art—was almost lost after the advent of the tin can.

Yet nothing is more gratifying than homemade soup ladled from a beautiful tureen into warmed or chilled bowls. Whether it is steaming hot or icy cold, bisque or chowder, clear or thick, soup is unquestionably one of the highlights of a meal.

A heavy soup bolsters an otherwise light entrée. A light soup sharpens the appetite at once. Or soup—served with chunks of French bread and a pot of unsalted butter, a good green salad, and fruit and cheese for dessert—can be the main course, and an excellent way to appease appetites.

Fine soup satisfies the most exacting tastes. It introduces the ability of the cook immediately; it establishes the foundation of the entire meal. Making it demands time, and care in the preparation of basic stocks, but making fine soup can be one of the most individual and creatively satisfying forms of cookery.

Garnishes are essential to soups, and their variety is almost limitless: a light sprinkling of chopped fresh herbs or parsley, of croutons, or of grated cheese, dollops of salted whipped cream or of sour cream, baked custard cut in diamonds or rounds, delicate quenelles, tiny profiteroles, or dumplings, thin slices of lemon, chopped egg, fancy cut vegetables, thin strips cut from crêpes—these are but a few suggestions. Ice cubes may be dropped into some cold soups at the last moment, and shredded or grated fresh vegetables added to cream soups to accent the color and flavor.

Conventions change, but it is difficult to imagine a time when soup will not play an important role in every civilized menu.

## COUNTRY SOUP

This is my favorite soup. It freezes beautifully, and it is the perfect gift to take to someone who appreciates good soup. It is great as a main course or before a light supper.

| | |
|---|---|
| 8 *large, peeled baking potatoes* | 1 *small parsnip* |
| 4 *large, peeled yellow onions* | 2 *medium cloves garlic* |
| 2 *small carrots* | 1 *bay leaf* |
| 6 *ribs of celery* | 2 *tablespoons salt* |
| 4 *leeks, white part only* | 1 *teaspoon freshly cracked white pepper* |
| 3 *tomatoes, unpeeled, but with stem ends removed* | 1 *cup frozen unsalted butter* |
| 2 *peeled turnips* | 2 *sprigs fresh chervil, optional* |
| 6 *large mushrooms* | 2 *lbs. fresh spinach, washed and trimmed of stems* |

1. Cut the first 9 vegetables into medium-size pieces, splitting the leeks lengthwise and holding them under running water to rinse away the sand.

• Don't omit the turnips, whether a lover of them or not, for they combine with the other vegetables to add subtle flavor.

2. Put the cut vegetables into a large heavy saucepan and add enough cold water to cover. Add the garlic and other seasonings.

• The garlic doesn't have to be peeled; just lay the cloves on a chopping board, cover with the flat of a heavy knife, and lean on the knife. This will crush the garlic just enough.

3. Place the frozen butter on top of the vegetables, and add the fresh chervil if it's available. Don't substitute dried chervil. Cover the pan with a tight-fitting lid, and cook over medium heat about 45 minutes, or until vegetables are tender but not mushy.

4. Remove from heat and stir in spinach, stirring until spinach is wilted. This takes only a few minutes.

• Watercress, lettuce, or sorrel may be substituted for the spinach if desired.

5. Purée the mixture through a food mill, using the medium disk, or a coarse sieve. Do not put it in a blender; if blended, this soup comes out an entirely different product.

6. Taste, and, if desired, add more salt. Serve hot.

• A little hot cream may be added to thin the soup and give it added richness. *Makes 12 to 16 generous servings.*

### MINESTRONE ALLA MILANESE

There are as many different kinds of minestrone in Italy as there are vegetable soups in America. Every province has its own. This one, from Milan, is sometimes served cool (not cold), even though it is a thick soup. Genoa flavors minestrone with pesto, a rich paste of fresh basil, pine nuts, garlic, and olive oil pounded together with a mortar and pestle or worked in a blender; the pesto is added to the soup by the teaspoonful. Some minestrones are greener than others; some have more meat in them; some more vegetables. This one has only vegetables, including *cannellini* (white kidney beans). Serve it with bread sticks or good Italian bread.

*½ lb. cubed salt pork*
*1½ cups chopped onions*
*¾ cup chopped carrots*
*½ cup chopped celery*
*2 20-oz. cans cannellini (white kidney beans), rinsed and drained*
*2 cups sliced zucchini*
*1 cup shredded cabbage*
*1 cup tomatoes, peeled, seeded, and diced*
*2 tablespoons tomato paste*
*2½ cups cubed baking potatoes*
*2 quarts chicken stock (see p. 241)*

*3 cloves chopped garlic*
*1 tablespoon chopped parsley*
*2 teaspoons salt*
*½ teaspoon freshly cracked black pepper*
*1 tablespoon chopped fresh basil, or 1 teaspoon dried basil*
*½ lb. fresh green peas, shelled*
*¾ cup elbow macaroni or other pasta*
*1 cup freshly grated Parmesan cheese*

1. Put the salt pork in a deep soup kettle and try it out—that is, cook the cubes over high heat until they are very crisp.

2. Add all remaining ingredients except pasta, peas, and cheese and bring to a boil. Cover, reduce heat, and simmer about 1 hour, or until vegetables are barely tender.

3. Add pasta, peas, and ½ cup of cheese and simmer another 30 minutes.

4. Taste for seasoning and add more salt if desired. Serve hot, or at room temperature, in bowls garnished with the remaining Parmesan cheese, freshly grated. *Makes 12 to 16 servings.*

## CHESTNUT SOUP

Every time I serve chestnut soup my guests rave. Nobody knows what it is.

Instead of garnishing it with parsley, I sometimes add a dollop of salted whipped cream; this makes it pretty rich, but many people like it. Other times I use chopped roasted chestnuts as a garnish.

*¾ cup unsalted butter*
*1 cup diced celery*
*½ cup diced carrots*
*1½ cups diced onions*
*1 teaspoon salt*
*4 lbs. skinned fresh chestnuts, or 3 10-oz. cans cooked chestnuts, or 3 15-oz. cans unsweetened chestnut purée*

*2 quarts strong chicken stock (see p. 241)*
*2 egg yolks*
*¼ cup dry Madeira*
*2 cups light cream*
*2 tablespoons chopped parsley*

1. Melt ½ cup of the butter in a large saucepan until it is hot and bubbly. Add the vegetables and salt. Stir over heat until vegetables are wilted. Do not let them brown.

2. Add chestnuts and chicken stock.

• To skin chestnuts, use a small, sharp knife and cut a strip off one side of the chestnut shell, then coat shell with a little oil; bake nuts in a 350° oven 20 to 30 minutes, until both shells and inner brown skins can be removed easily. Or put chestnuts into cold water, bring them to a boil, and boil 1 minute. The shells and inner skin are easiest to remove while the nuts are still warm.

• If canned chestnuts are used, be sure they're the water-pack variety (chestnuts also come packed in sugar syrup, for use in desserts) and add the liquid along with the nuts.

• If substituting canned purée, be sure it is unsweetened.

3. Cover pan, bring to boil, then reduce heat to a simmer, and cook 45 minutes to 1 hour, or until chestnuts and vegetables are soft.

4. Purée the vegetables and broth through a food mill, using the fine disk, or through a sieve. (Don't use a blender to purée this soup. It makes the texture too fine.)

5. Return ingredients to saucepan, set it over medium heat, and add remaining butter 1 teaspoon at a time, whisking it in.

6. Beat egg yolks in a small bowl, beat in Madeira and cream. Gradually add enough of the hot ingredients to the cream-egg mixture to warm it.

• Warming the mixture gradually helps prevent curdling.

7. Stir warmed mixture into the saucepan and heat until piping hot, *but do not boil.* Serve hot, garnished with chopped parsley.

• If chopped roasted chestnuts are used instead of parsley, bake about one dozen chestnuts in a 350° oven for 20 to 30 minutes, or until soft. Skin, then chop finely. Sprinkle with salt and add a teaspoonful to each serving. *Makes 8 servings.*

## LOBSTER BISQUE

This is a French recipe for making bisque, a very elegant, very rich soup.

| | |
|---|---|
| *1 quart fish stock (see p. 242)* | *3 tablespoons dry Madeira* |
| *2 small uncooked lobsters* | *½ cup light cream* |
| *¾ cup unsalted butter* | *1 tablespoon finely chopped* |
| *¼ cup flour* | *parsley* |
| *1 tablespoon tomato paste* | *1 cup croutons* |
| *¾ cup heavy cream* | |

1. Bring fish stock to a boil and add the lobster. Simmer about 20 minutes, or until lobsters turn red. Let them cool in the stock.

2. When the lobsters are cool, carefully remove all the meat from them, dice it, and set it aside. Save the stock.

3. Because the lobsters are small, the shells can be crushed and used to flavor butter. Cut shells in pieces and put them in a blender, along with the tiny legs. Add ½ cup of butter, push it down, and keep starting and stopping the blender, pushing the mixture down frequently. This takes a little work, but it finally goes through. When the mixture is completely ground, force it through a very fine strainer. None of the shells should come through, just the lobster-flavored butter.

4. Melt ¼ cup of butter in saucepan, stir in flour with a wooden spatula, and cook over high heat, stirring about 2 minutes. The flour should cook but not brown. Add tomato paste and remove from heat. Strain in the

fish stock, and whisk it vigorously. Return to high heat and cook, stirring constantly, until mixture comes to a boil. Turn heat to low and simmer *very* slowly for 10 to 15 minutes.

5. Add lobster-flavored butter, bit by bit, beating it in with a whisk.

6. In a small bowl, beat heavy cream over ice until it begins to thicken. Mix in the Madeira and continue beating until mixture is thick. Stir this and light cream carefully into saucepan.

7. Stir in diced lobster meat and heat through, but do not boil. Stir in chopped parsley and serve hot, with croutons. *Makes 4 to 6 servings.*

### MUSHROOM SOUP ROYALE

The combination of dried and fresh mushrooms gives this consommé-type soup a most interesting flavor. The custard garnish is what makes it *royale.*

*1 small (about 2-oz.) box dried (not freeze-dried) mushrooms*
*1½ quarts veal stock (see p. 242), or chicken stock (see p. 241), or a mixture of the two*
*½ lb. finely diced fresh mushrooms*

*3 tablespoons butter*
*¼ cup Calvados*
*Custard Royale (recipe follows)*
*2 tablespoons chopped parsley*

1. Soak dried mushrooms in cold water to cover for at least 1 hour. Drain, chop, and combine with stock in saucepan. Simmer for 1 hour.

2. Cook the diced fresh mushrooms in butter over low heat for a few minutes, or just long enough to give them a good butter flavor. Add to mixture in saucepan and simmer a few minutes longer.

3. Strain (the soup can be served without straining if desired), stir in Calvados, and serve very hot in soup cups, with a garnish of Custard Royale and chopped parsley.

#### Custard Royale

*1 egg*
*1 egg yolk*
*2 tablespoons milk*
*¼ teaspoon salt*

*Pinch freshly cracked white pepper*
*¼ teaspoon freshly grated nutmeg*

1. Beat egg and egg yolk in a small bowl, then add milk and seasonings. Pour mixture into a greased shallow pan. The custard mixture should be ⅛ to ¼ inch deep. Set loaf pan in a pan of hot water and

place in a 300° oven. Bake for 20 to 30 minutes, or until custard is set. Custard is set when a silver knife, inserted into custard, comes out clean.

2. Cool, then cut in small fancy shapes with truffle cutters—diamond shapes, rounds, and so on—and use as garnish for soup.

• Place a cutout in each soup cup before filling it with hot soup. The custard will float to the top. ***Makes 6 to 8 servings.***

### PUMPKIN SOUP

I feel compelled to serve pumpkin in one form or another at Thanksgiving time. Since pumpkin pie is not one of my favorite foods, we have pumpkin soup. It is a delicious change on a holiday menu.

| | |
|---|---|
| 2 cups pumpkin pulp | 3 tablespoons honey |
| 3 cups strong chicken stock (see p. 241) | ½ teaspoon freshly grated nutmeg |
| ½ cup chopped onion | 1 cup heavy cream |
| ½ cup chopped celery | ½ cup light rum, about |
| 2 tablespoons butter | 2 tablespoons chopped parsley, or sliced boiled chestnuts |
| 1 teaspoon salt | |
| ½ teaspoon freshly cracked white pepper | |

1. Combine pumpkin pulp, chicken stock, onion, and celery in a saucepan. Bring to a boil, turn heat to simmer, cover, and cook about 20 minutes or until vegetables are barely tender.

• Canned pumpkin pulp can be used, but be sure it's unseasoned.

• To make pumpkin pulp, cut pumpkin in half and remove seeds and stringy fibers, then cut pumpkin in small pieces and peel; cook, covered, in a small amount of boiling salted water 25 to 30 minutes, or until tender; drain and mash. A 2-pound pumpkin makes 2 cups of pulp. The pulp can be frozen in pint containers.

2. Purée the cooked vegetables through a food mill, using the finest disk, or a sieve. Return to saucepan and beat in butter, salt and pepper, honey, and nutmeg. Add the heavy cream and bring just to a boil.

3. Pour into soup bowls and add 1 tablespoon light rum to each serving.

4. Garnish with chopped parsley, or sliced boiled chestnuts (see p. 45).

• For a sweeter soup, drained chopped marrons (about one tablespoonful for each serving) can be used instead. *Makes 6 to 8 servings.*

### MANHATTAN CLAM CHOWDER

Just a reminder: Manhattan clam chowder is the one made with tomatoes. New England clam chowder has the milk or cream base.

*4 strips diced bacon*
*1½ cups chopped onions*
*2 cups diced potatoes*
*1 cup diced celery, rib and leaves*
*¾ cup green pepper, seeded and diced*
*1 1-lb. can tomatoes*
*2 cups tomato juice*
*2 cups bottled clam juice*

*1 teaspoon thyme*
*1 tablespoon salt*
*½ teaspoon freshly cracked black pepper*
*2 cups chopped clams (48 fresh clams) with juice, or frozen chopped clams*
*2 tablespoons chopped parsley*

1. In the bottom of a large soup kettle, try out bacon—that is, fry it until it is almost crisp.

2. To the bacon and bacon fat, add chopped onions. Cook until onions are transparent, stirring constantly. Do not let onions brown.

3. Add potatoes, celery, green pepper, canned tomatoes (break them up slightly with a fork), tomato juice, clam juice, 2 cups of water, thyme, salt, and pepper.

•Some markets have a canned mixture of tomato juice and clam juice. This is a convenient combination, usable here.

4. Bring mixture to a boil, then reduce heat to simmer, cover the kettle, and cook about 1 hour, or until vegetables are tender.

5. Add clams, with their juice, and cook for another 10 minutes. Only 10, so clams will not toughen.

6. Before serving, sprinkle chowder with chopped parsley.

• When serving, I usually pass a basket of thick round crackers, an excellent accompaniment for this soup. **Makes 10 to 12 servings.**

## CREAM OF TURTLE SOUP

This soup is often called boula-boula, or just plain boula. It is simple to make—so simple that even a novice cook can prepare it like a professional —but very elegant.

| | |
|---|---|
| *1 10-oz. pkg. frozen peas* | *1 teaspoon salt* |
| *1 2-lb. can turtle soup with* | *3 to 4 drops Tabasco sauce* |
| *meat* | *1 cup stiffly whipped heavy* |
| *½ cup dry Madeira* | *cream* |

1. Cook peas according to package directions, but use a little less water, and cook for only 5 minutes. Drain, then purée them through a food mill or sieve.

2. Heat the turtle soup, add the puréed peas, and whisk to blend well. Add Madeira and season with ½ teaspoon of salt and 3 or 4 drops of Tabasco. Heat to boiling point and pour into oven-warmed soup bowls, the kind that can take a few seconds under a broiler.

3. Add the remaining ½ teaspoon of salt to stiffly whipped cream and put a spoonful on top of each bowl of soup. Put the bowls under broiler just long enough to brown the whipped cream. It takes only a few seconds. Serve immediately. **Makes 5 to 6 servings.**

## CARROT SOUP

There is carrot soup hot, and there is carrot soup cold—and which I serve depends on me and the weather.

| | |
|---|---|
| *3 cups coarsely grated carrots* | *1 teaspoon salt* |
| *¼ cup uncooked rice* | *½ teaspoon cayenne pepper* |
| *1½ quarts strong chicken stock (see p. 241)* | *2 tablespoons chopped parsley for hot soup, or for cold soup, 2* |
| *1 cup light cream for hot soup, or 1½ cups barely whipped heavy cream for cold soup* | *tablespoons chopped parsley or chopped chives or 6 to 8 lemon slices* |

1. Use the coarse side of a 4-sided grater to grate carrots. One bunch should yield about 3 cups.

2. Add carrots and rice to chicken stock and bring to a boil. Reduce heat, cover, and simmer until carrots are barely tender and rice is cooked through.

3. If soup is to be served hot, purée the carrot-rice mixture through a food mill, using the medium disk, then return the mixture to saucepan and add light cream, salt, and cayenne pepper, whisking thoroughly to blend. Heat through, and before serving, garnish with chopped parsley.

If soup is to be served cold, purée the carrot-rice mixture in a blender no more than half full at one time (too much hot mixture will overflow a blender). Chill, and before serving, stir in heavy cream whipped just beyond the foaming stage (but not to the point at which beaters leave a soft mound when lifted). Add salt and cayenne pepper (a few drops of Tabasco sauce can be used instead of cayenne pepper if desired), taste for seasoning. Adjust if necessary; cold foods usually require heavier seasoning than do hot ones. Garnish with chopped parsley or chopped chives, or float a thin slice of lemon on top of each bowl. *Makes 6 to 8 servings.*

### CURRIED AVOCADO SOUP

2 tablespoons diced onion
1 tablespoon butter
1 tablespoon curry powder, about
3 cups chicken stock (see p. 241)
3 avocados, peeled and coarsely mashed

1 teaspoon salt
3 to 4 drops Tabasco sauce
2 cups barely whipped heavy cream
6 to 8 lime or lemon slices
2 tablespoons chopped parsley

1. In a saucepan cook onion in butter over high heat until transparent. Stir in curry powder—a scant tablespoon may be enough, depending on how much curry taste you want—and cook, stirring constantly, for 3 minutes to refine the raw curry taste.

2. Pour in chicken stock.

• As an alternative, 2½ cups of chicken stock and ½ cup of dry sherry or other dry white wine can be used.

3. Bring to a boil, remove from heat, add mashed avocados, salt, and Tabasco.

4. Purée through a sieve or a food mill, or in a blender no more than half full at one time (too much hot mixture will overflow a blender). Cover with plastic wrap and chill in refrigerator.

5. When ready to serve, fold in heavy cream whipped just past the foaming stage (but not to the point at which beaters leave a soft mound when lifted).

• If the soup is to be served hot, use less salt and stir in 2 cups of light cream instead of the heavy cream and heat through.

6. Garnish each serving with a slice of lime or lemon and a sprinkling of chopped parsley. *Makes 6 to 8 servings.*

## SENEGALESE

*¼ cup butter*
*1½ cups very finely chopped onions*
*1 medium clove chopped garlic*
*1 teaspoon curry powder*
*½ teaspoon salt*
*¼ teaspoon freshly cracked white pepper*
*1 10-oz. pkg. frozen peas, thawed*

*¼ teaspoon ground cardamom seed*
*2 tablespoons flour*
*2½ cups chicken stock (see p. 241)*
*1 cup heavy cream*
*6 tablespoons finely diced cooked white meat of chicken*

1. In a saucepan melt butter and cook onions over high heat until transparent, stirring frequently. Do not let onions brown.
2. Add garlic and cook 1 minute longer. Stir in curry powder and salt and pepper and continue cooking a little longer.
3. Add thawed peas and cardamom. Cover and cook, shaking pan frequently, until peas are tender.
4. Remove cover and smooth in flour. Cook for 2 minutes, stirring constantly.
5. Pour in chicken stock, bring to a boil, and boil 2 minutes.
6. Remove mixture from pan and purée in a blender.

• Fill the blender less than half full (several times if necessary), since too much will overflow.

7. If soup is to be served hot, stir in heavy cream, return to heat, and bring just to a boil. If it's to be served cold, chill the puréed mixture, and before serving, stir in cold heavy cream. Adjust seasoning if necessary; cold foods require heavier seasoning than do hot ones.
8. Garnish each bowl of hot or cold Senegalese with a tablespoonful of finely diced chicken. *Makes 4 to 6 servings.*

## Parsley Soup

| | |
|---|---|
| 2 tablespoons diced onion | 1 teaspoon salt |
| 2 tablespoons butter | 3 to 4 drops Tabasco sauce |
| 1½ cups chopped parsley, without stems | 2 cups light cream, or 2 cups barely whipped heavy cream |
| 2 cups chicken stock (see p. 241) | 2 tablespoons chopped parsley |
| ½ cup dry white wine | |

1. In a saucepan cook onion in butter over high heat for 2 or 3 minutes, or until transparent. Add 1½ cups chopped parsley and cook 3 minutes longer, stirring with a wooden spatula.

• Do not use parsley stems. They give this soup a bitter taste.

2. Pour in chicken stock, cover pan, and simmer for 10 minutes.

3. Add wine, salt, and Tabasco, then purée in a blender no more than half full at one time (to prevent overflowing).

4. If soup is to be served hot, stir in light cream and heat through. If it's to be served cold, chill the puréed mixture, and before serving, fold in heavy cream whipped just past the foaming stage (but not to the point at which beaters leave a soft mound when lifted). Adjust seasoning if necessary.

5. Garnish soup (hot or cold) with chopped parsley. **Makes 4 to 6 servings.**

## Cream of Mussel Soup

| | |
|---|---|
| 3 quarts mussels | 3 parsley sprigs |
| 2 cups dry white wine | 2 tablespoons butter |
| 3 tablespoons finely chopped shallots | 1 teaspoon salt |
| 2 tablespoons chopped celery leaves | ¼ teaspoon cayenne pepper, about |
| ½ cup sliced celery | 2 cups heavy cream |

1. Scrub mussels (which in many cities have to be ordered from fish markets in advance) with a stiff brush, using a sharp knife to remove the beards. Scrub thoroughly and rinse in several changes of cold water to remove as much sand as possible. Discard any mussels that are open.

• This is a time-consuming job; it is easier if mussels are soaked in water for an hour before scrubbing.

2. Put the mussels in a deep saucepan, pour in wine, and add shallots, celery leaves and sliced rib, parsley, butter, salt, and ¼ teaspoon of cayenne pepper. Cover and bring to a boil. Let mussels steam over high heat for about 5 minutes, or until they open. Shake pan frequently.

3. Remove mussels. Discard any that haven't opened, and set aside the rest.

4. Strain broth through a sieve lined with a double thickness of dampened cheesecloth. Return broth to pan and reheat. Taste for seasoning; more cayenne pepper may be needed.

5. If soup is to be served hot, add heavy cream and heat just to boiling.

• To further enrich the hot soup, beat 2 egg yolks until frothy, add ¼ cup of the heavy cream to them and warm the mixture by stirring a little broth into it; then stir it and the remaining 1¾ cups of cream into the pan and whisk over heat until the broth thickens slightly.

• If soup is to be served cold, chill the strained broth, and before serving, whip the heavy cream just beyond the foaming stage (but not to the point at which beaters leave a soft mound when lifted) and fold it in. The barely whipped cream gives the soup body. Adjust seasoning if necessary.

6. Add 2 of the set-aside mussels to each bowl of soup.

• Any remaining mussels can be shelled and frozen, to be used later, either in a salad or, with mustard mayonnaise, as appetizers. *Makes 4 to 6 servings.*

## Garlic Soup

A very unusual cold soup. The flavor secret is in blanching the garlic. This gives the soup its unidentifiable, mysterious essence.

> 16 *small cloves peeled garlic*
> 2 *tablespoons butter*
> 2 *tablespoons olive oil*
> 1 *quart strong chicken stock*
>    (*see p. 241*)
> 1 *teaspoon salt*
>
> ¼ *teaspoon freshly cracked*
>    *white pepper*
> 2 *egg yolks*
> 1 *cup light cream*
> 2 *tablespoons chopped*
>    *chives*

1. Put the garlic cloves in a small pan and blanch them by covering them with cold water, bringing to a boil, and boiling 1 minute. Drain, then rinse cloves under cold water.

2. Chop garlic very, very fine.

3. Heat butter and olive oil in a heavy saucepan, then add the chopped garlic and cook very gently until it is golden. Don't burn it; don't even let it really brown.

4. Remove pan from heat and pour in chicken stock. Add salt and pepper, return pan to heat, and bring to a boil. Cover, reduce, heat, and simmer for about ½ hour.

5. Remove mixture from heat and strain it through two thicknesses of dampened cheesecloth.

6. Beat egg yolks, gradually add a little of the hot mixture to warm them, then add them, warmed, to the rest of the hot mixture. Place the egg-enriched mixture over low heat and whisk slowly until it thickens slightly. Don't let it boil or soup will curdle.

7. Chill mixture at least 2 hours, and before serving, stir in the light cream.

8. Serve in chilled bowls—I like to set them in crushed ice—and garnish each bowl with chopped chives.

• Hot crackers, unsalted biscuits especially, are my preferred accompaniment for this soup. *Makes 6 servings.*

## Cold Cream of Cucumber Soup

| | |
|---|---|
| 4 *large cucumbers* | 1 *teaspoon salt* |
| 2 *tablespoons butter* | ½ *teaspoon freshly cracked* |
| 3 *tablespoons chopped scal-* | *white pepper* |
| *lions, white part only* | 2 *cups barely whipped heavy* |
| 2 *tablespoons flour* | *cream* |
| 2 *cups chicken stock (see* | |
| *p. 241)* | |

1. Peel one of the cucumbers, cut off the end, cut 6 thin slices crosswise and set aside for garnish.

2. Peel the other three cucumbers and cut them and what's left of the first cucumber in halves, lengthwise. Scrape out seeds with the tip of a teaspoon, then cut cucumbers into 1-inch pieces.

3. Melt butter in saucepan and cook chopped scallions over high heat for 2 or 3 minutes, or until transparent.

4. Stir in flour and cook, stirring, for 2 minutes.

5. Add pieces of cucumber and continue to cook, stirring constantly, for about 5 minutes or until transparent. Do not let the cucumber pieces brown.

• The cucumber pieces will give off some liquid; nevertheless, they must be watched carefully so that they don't brown.

6. Pour in chicken stock, season with salt and pepper, and bring to a boil, then cover pan, reduce heat to simmer, and simmer for 10 minutes.

7. Purée the mixture in a blender no more than half full (too much hot mixture will overflow a blender), then chill it thoroughly in refrigerator.

8. Before serving, fold in heavy cream whipped just past the foaming stage (but not to the point at which beaters leave a soft mound when lifted), and garnish with the thin cucumber slices.

• Occasionally I top off each serving with tiny sprigs of mint instead. **Makes 6 servings.**

## HERB TOAST FINGERS

These fingers are extremely good with soup.

| | |
|---|---|
| *½ cup butter* | *1 teaspoon chopped parsley* |
| *¼ teaspoon thyme* | *1 small clove chopped garlic* |
| *½ teaspoon salt* | *½ teaspoon chopped shallot* |
| *¼ teaspoon freshly cracked black pepper* | *12 slices day-old homestyle bread* |
| *1 tablespoon lemon juice* | |

1. Put all ingredients except bread in a small saucepan or skillet and heat slowly. Stir until well mixed.

2. Trim crusts from bread, cut bread into fingers, and dip them, both sides, in the heated mixture.

3. Place the fingers on a baking sheet and bake them in a preheated 350° oven for about 20 minutes, or until brown, turning them once. Serve hot, warm, or at room temperature.

• The fingers can be frozen up to 1 month and reheated in a warm (200°) oven 10 to 15 minutes. Or they can be stored 2 weeks in plastic bags (to retain crispness). **Makes 12 to 14 servings, or about 36 fingers.**

# SEAFOOD

At one time only the gods were permitted to enjoy the marvelous flavor of fish: fish was considered far too exquisite for lowly mortals. Not today, however. Today nutritionists and cooking experts urge everyone to eat fish—for nourishment and for sheer deliciousness.

Fortunately the United States has an abundance of excellent fish and shellfish in its oceans, lakes, rivers, and streams. In many cities it is possible, thanks to jet transportation, to get a variety of fresh fish—in excellent condition—every day. Outside the cities, people rely on local streams and lakes for beautiful freshwater fish. It goes without saying that seafood is available in the frozen, smoked, salted, dried, or canned state all over the country.

The United States has about two hundred commercial species of fin and shellfish, ranging in size from baby whitebait to giant tuna and sea bass, from tiny oyster crabs to the Alaskan king crab, which can weigh as much as fifteen pounds. How sad and boring it is when the housewife limits herself to fried fillets! It's especially so since fish is extremely versatile: it can be baked, broiled, steamed, pan fried, sautéed, poached, deep fried, planked, smoked, and baked en papillote. Further, it cooks very quickly, making it perfect for last-minute meals.

Europeans eat far more fish than do Americans, possibly because they are more deft in its preparation. Most of the recipes on these pages are easy. For example, Trout Meunière (see p. 67), meaning "cooked in the style of the miller's wife," is floured, seasoned with salt and pepper, sautéed until beautifully golden, and served with lemon wedges and chopped parsley. It couldn't be easier to prepare, and it constitutes, providing it is not overcooked, pretty elegant fare when accompanied by green salad and a boiled potato.

There are good American substitutes for seafood called for in European recipes. For example, flounder works very well in all sole recipes. Flounder en Papillote (see p. 61) and Ring Mold of Flounder (see p. 63) are both adapted from recipes originally designating sole.

Baked Lobster Nicholas (see p. 69) is one of my favorites, and it's less trouble than fixing a meat loaf. The lobster is simply split, seasoned with butter and lemon juice, baked until red, and served with lemon wedges and melted butter.

For the best seafood dishes, beware of overcooking, the most common error in the preparation of seafood. And use the freshest fish possible. However, frozen fish need not be shunned, for flash freezing of seafood allows much of its fresh flavor to remain. I find the large bags of flash-frozen shrimp indispensable; they are cleaned, and separated, so that few or many can be cooked.

How to identify fresh fish? The eyes are full, bulging, bright, and clear; the gills are clean and odorless. Scales retain their bright sheen and cling tightly to the skin. Fresh fish should smell like the sea or fresh water.

Most of the fish now seen in the markets is already cleaned and dressed, filleted or steaked. However, there is no need to fear cleaning a fish. It's really quite simple. Wash the fish in cold running water; scrape off the scales from tail to head, using a fish scaler or a knife held at a right angle to the fish; gut the fish by slitting the belly open, starting at the tail end and cutting forward to the head; cut around the pelvic fins, near the head, and remove them (I usually leave the head on, and trim the tail neatly); remove dorsal fins; and wash fish well in cold water to remove any blood. If the fish smells fishy, soak it for a few minutes in cold water and lemon juice. After handling fish, I rub my hands with salt and then rinse in cold water; this usually removes any fish odor.

It's ideal, although not necessary, to have a long narrow fish platter, individual fish plates, and fish forks and knives for serving. When lobster and large crabs are served, it's essential to have large platters, small seafood forks, and lobster crackers (nutcrackers).

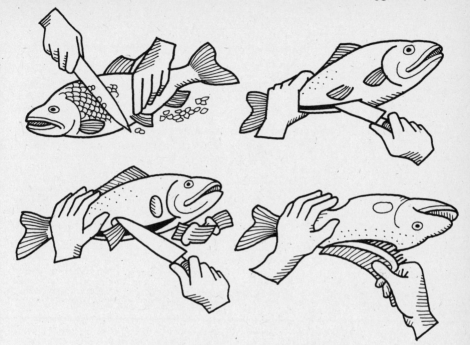

## FLOUNDER WITH CHAMPAGNE SAUCE

8 *flounder filets, about 7 by 3 by ½ inches*
2 *teaspoons lemon juice, plus lemon juice to wash fish*
½ *cup butter, plus butter to grease baking dish and baking paper*
1 *teaspoon salt*
½ *teaspoon freshly cracked white pepper*
1½ *cups thinly sliced white mushrooms*
¼ *teaspoon freshly cracked black pepper*
1 *cup champagne*
1 *tablespoon chopped shallot*
2 *small bay leaves*
6 *peppercorns*
*Champagne Sauce (recipe follows)*
2 *tablespoons roughly chopped truffle, optional*

1. Wash filets in water acidulated with lemon juice (1 tablespoon to 1 quart) to keep the fish white. Dry the fish with paper towels and fold the filets in half, skin side inside; the skin side can be identified by its silvery gray color. Brush with ¼ cup melted butter, add white pepper and ½ teaspoon of salt, and place in a buttered baking dish. An oval ovenproof glass dish is ideal. Set aside.

2. Melt the remaining ¼ cup of butter in a skillet. When foaming subsides, add mushrooms, 2 teaspoons lemon juice, black pepper, and remaining ½ teaspoon of salt. Cook over high heat for 3 minutes only, shaking the pan to toss mushrooms.

• White mushrooms are used for this to keep the mixture light and appetizing-looking.

3. Remove from heat, add the champagne (domestic is fine), return to heat, and bring to a boil. Pour mushrooms and champagne over fish in baking dish.

4. At each end of the baking dish put ½ tablespoon chopped shallot, 1 small bay leaf, and 3 peppercorns. Cover dish with buttered brown paper or foil (to keep fish from drying out) and bake in a preheated 350° oven for about 12 minutes, or until just barely done. Time this step carefully. *Do not overcook the fish.*

• To test for doneness, remove fish from oven and touch with a toothpick to see if it flakes.
• If the fish is to be eaten by dieters or if it's being cooked ahead, stop right now and either serve immediately or let fish cool in the liquid, then cover and refrigerate it.

5. When ready to make sauce, remove and strain liquid (there should be 1¼ to 1½ cups) from fish and set liquid aside.

• To remove the liquid, tip the baking dish enough to spoon it out, or take it up with a bulb baster.

6. Before serving, remove fish filets and mushrooms to ovenproof serving platter, overlapping filets slightly. If some fish liquid has collected during standing, stir it into the sauce, straining it if necessary. Then "nap" the filets with sauce—that is, shake the sauce (use a big spoon and make it quiver as if being held by someone with a case of nerves) over the filets to coat them evenly and completely. Then place the fish under the broiler for a few seconds to brown tops, and if desired, sprinkle chopped truffle down the center of the platter.

• If desired, 1½ cups of white seedless grapes may be heated with the sauce before it is spooned on the fish.

### Champagne Sauce

3 tablespoons butter
3 tablespoons flour
1¼ to 1½ cups fish-champagne liquid
2 egg yolks, optional

2 tablespoons heavy cream, optional
2 tablespoons cognac, optional

1. Melt butter in a saucepan (not aluminum; the sauce would turn gray). Stir in flour with a wooden spatula and cook, stirring constantly, for about 2 minutes, but do not let flour brown. Remove from heat, add fish-champagne liquid, and whisk vigorously; return to heat and bring to a boil, whisking constantly.

• If sauce seems too thick, thin with light cream.
• The sauce can be served at this point, or it can be enriched.
• If sauce must wait, float bits of butter over the top. The butter melts and keeps a skin from forming. When reheating the sauce, add a little light cream if needed. Sauces usually thicken when they stand.

2. To enrich sauce: beat egg yolks with a small whisk and beat in heavy cream and cognac; remove a little hot sauce from pan and stir into the egg-cream mixture to warm it; then stir heated mixture into the pan and cook until sauce thickens slightly, but do not let it boil.

3. Taste for seasoning and add salt and pepper if desired. *Makes 8 servings.*

### FLOUNDER IN PARCHMENT

Fish baked in paper is almost guaranteed to be meltingly tender, rich in flavor.

> 8 *pieces baking parchment,*
>   *10 by 10 inches*
> 8 *flounder filets, about 7 by*
>   *3 by ½ inches*
> *Lemon juice to wash fish*
> *½ cup melted butter, plus but-*
>   *ter to grease baking sheet*
>
> 1 *teaspoon salt*
> *½ teaspoon freshly cracked*
>   *white pepper*
> *Apple and Mushroom Stuffing*
>   *(recipe follows)*

1. Fold the parchment—try not to crease it—and cut out 8 wide hearts with a very slight dip in the center. Set aside.
2. Wash fish in water acidulated with lemon juice (1 tablespoon to 1 quart) to keep fish white. Dry filets and lay them on a tray, skin side up.

• The skin side of fish (or where the skin was) can be identified by its silvery gray color. The flesh side is white.

3. Brush skin side of fish with melted butter, using about ¼ cup, and season with salt and pepper. Set aside while making stuffing.
4. Put a spoonful of stuffing at the broader end of each filet and fold the other end of the fish over the stuffing to cover it.

5. Brush the parchment hearts with melted butter. Lay a folded fish in the center of the right side of each heart. Brush with butter. Bring left sides of parchment hearts over fish, match edges, and fold them over together in two or three narrow folds to lock the fish inside.

• The filets can be stuffed in parchment in the morning, stored in a refrigerator, brought to room temperature, and baked just before they are to be served.

• White or brown paper sandwich bags can be substituted for the parchment. Brush the insides of the bags with butter. Place a stuffed and folded filet in each and close bag.

6. Place the 8 packages on a buttered baking sheet (or an ovenproof serving platter) and bake in a preheated 375° oven for 20 to 25 minutes. Serve en papillote, letting each diner open his own steaming, fragrant package.

### Apple and Mushroom Stuffing

1½ cups peeled, cored, and chopped green apples

¼ cup butter

¾ cup thinly sliced mushrooms

2 teaspoons lemon juice

½ teaspoon salt

¼ teaspoon freshly cracked black pepper

½ lb. cooked shrimp, shelled, deveined, and sliced

1 tablespoon chopped fresh dill or parsley

¼ cup dry white wine

1. Cook the apples in 2 tablespoons of butter 4 minutes, or until tender but not mushy.

2. In another pan, sauté mushroom slices in the remaining 2 tablespoons of butter with lemon juice, salt, and pepper. Shake the pan and cook over high heat for 3 minutes.

3. Combine apples, shrimp, and mushrooms. Stir in fresh dill or parsley.

• Don't use stems of dill. Strip off the feathery heads and chop them.

4. Moisten mixture with dry white wine. **Makes 8 servings.**

### RING MOLD OF FLOUNDER STUFFED WITH SALMON MOUSSE

The beautiful pink salmon mousse is completely encased in white fish fillets—absolutely elegant!

*8 to 10 flounder filets, about 7 by 3 by ½ inches*
*1¾ lbs. fresh salmon, weight after skin and bones are removed*
*Lemon juice to wash fish*
*2 tablespoons vegetable oil to grease mold*
*2 egg whites*
*1 cup light cream*
*2 teaspoons salt*
*1 teaspoon freshly cracked white pepper*
*1 tablespoon chopped fresh tarragon, or 1 teaspoon dry tarragon*
*2 tablespoons chopped parsley*
*Butter to grease baking paper*
*¾ lb. fluted, sautéed mushrooms (see p. 11)*
*8 slices of truffle*
*1 bunch watercress*
*Hollandaise Sauce (see p. 246), Béarnaise Sauce (see p. 248), or Lemon Butter (see p. 253)*

1. Wash flounder in cold water acidulated with lemon juice (1 tablespoon to 1 quart). Dry and set aside.

2. Brush a 10-inch ring mold with oil. Line the mold with the filets, overlapping them at least ¼ inch. Lay them skin side up, with narrow ends in the center of the mold. Ends of fillets will overhang both center and outside edges. Set aside.

3. Work salmon through a meat grinder, using the finest blade, or chop it very finely. Put it in mixer and beat in egg whites at high speed, using the flat whip if the mixer is a heavy-duty one.

• The salmon can be beaten in a bowl over ice, using a wooden spatula, if a mixer isn't available.

4. Slowly beat in cream.

5. Season mixture with salt, pepper, tarragon, and parsley. Beat hard and spoon into the fish-lined mold. Bang the mold to make mixture settle, then fold filet ends over to cover top.

6. Cover mold with buttered brown paper or foil. Set it in a baking pan half filled with boiling water (called a *bain-marie*) and bake in a preheated 350° oven for 25 to 30 minutes, or until done.

• To test for doneness, remove fish from oven and touch filet tops with a toothpick to see if they flake.

7. Remove from oven and let stand at least 5 minutes before attempting to unmold.

• To unmold, run a little knife around the edge of the mold, then place a serving platter over the mold, turn both platter and mold over, and lift mold off. Blot up any juice with paper towels.

8. Fill the center of unmolded ring with fluted, sautéed mushrooms, decorate the top of the ring with thin rounds of truffle and surround with watercress. To serve, cut in wedges. Pass dish of Hollandaise Sauce, Béarnaise Sauce, or Lemon Butter. *Makes 10 servings.*

### Poached Striped Bass with Sauce Gribiche

A fish poacher is handy for cooking a whole fish. It has a rack with handles, so the cooked fish can be lifted out of the court bouillon easily. If you haven't a fish poacher, use a roasting pan—one long enough to accommodate the fish. The fish used in this recipe should be cleaned and split. Ask your fish man to do the work, but not to separate the halves or to remove the head or tail.

| | |
|---|---|
| *1 whole striped bass, sea bass, or salmon, 4 to 6 lbs.* | *1 head Boston lettuce* |
| *Lemon juice to wash fish, if needed* | *Sauce Gribiche (recipe follows)* |
| *1 recipe court bouillon (see p. 242)* | *10 lemon slices* |
| | *4 tablespoons chopped parsley* |

1. Wash the fish well in water and trim the tail neatly.

• If the fish smells fishy, soak it for a few minutes in a mixture of cold water and lemon juice (1 tablespoon to 1 quart).

2. Place the fish in a poacher, or if a poacher isn't available, improvise a hammock for the fish, either by rolling the fish in a few turns of cheese-cloth, leaving enough hanging free at the ends to serve as handles, or by

folding foil to the same width as the fish, but 3 inches longer at each end, and poking a few holes in the foil, then laying the fish on it. Lower the fish into cooled court bouillon, cover, and slowly bring to a boil. Reduce heat—the liquid should barely move—and simmer, covered, for 7 minutes per pound, or until done.

• Test for doneness: touch fish with a toothpick—open the cheesecloth if necessary—to see if it flakes. As a further test (for any fish but salmon): poke down alongside the bone; if it looks pink, the fish is not cooked.

3. When fish is done, turn off heat and let fish cool for 15 to 30 minutes in the liquid.

• This helps to firm the flesh. The fish can be served immediately from the liquid, or chilled.

4. To serve: Peel off skin—I use my fingers to do this—then with a long, thin knife, slice straight down to the bone, making slices 1 inch thick (when the bone is reached, turn the knife to work it under the slice). When the top layer has been sliced, remove bones in one piece and slice bottom layer of fish. Lift the slices onto plates lined with a leaf of Boston lettuce, allowing 3 slices per serving.

• If desired, the fish can be sliced straight through, without removing the bones.

5. Spoon a ribbon of Sauce Gribiche over the fish slices. Or serve spoonfuls beside the fish on the plates. Garnish with serrated slices of lemon edged in chopped parsley.

### Sauce Gribiche

| | |
|---|---|
| 3 hard-cooked eggs | 3 tablespoons wine vinegar |
| 1 teaspoon Dijon mustard | 1 tablespoon minced gherkins |
| ½ teaspoon salt | 1 tablespoon drained capers |
| ¼ teaspoon freshly cracked white pepper | 1 tablespoon chopped parsley |
| 1 cup olive oil | 1 teaspoon dried tarragon |
| | 1 teaspoon dried chervil |

1. Press yolks of hard-cooked eggs—save the whites—through a sieve into a small bowl, and beat with a wooden spatula until smooth; add mustard and salt and pepper.
2. Using the same technique as in making mayonnaise (see p. 251), beat oil into the egg-yolk mixture with a small whisk, adding a few drops at a time at first, then drizzling it in, a tablespoon at a time, whisking constantly.
3. When sauce begins to thicken, add vinegar, a tablespoon at a time,

alternating with oil. Continue whisking until all the vinegar and oil are used and sauce is thick and creamy.

4. Fold in gherkins, capers, parsley, tarragon, and chervil. Chop egg whites and fold them in. Chill. ***Makes 8 to 10 servings.***

## SALMON ROLL

A center cut of salmon is not necessary for this recipe. Any firm fish can be substituted, but *don't* try mackerel, shad, or other oily fish.

*1½ lbs. fresh salmon, weight after skin and bones are removed*
*6 eggs, separated*
*½ cup butter, melted and cooled*
*½ cup flour*
*1 teaspoon salt*
*½ teaspoon freshly cracked white pepper*

*2 tablespoons chopped parsley*
*¼ cup chopped fresh dill*
*3 tablespoons lemon juice*
*2 tablespoons vegetable oil to grease pan and paper*
*2 cups dairy sour cream*
*4 to 6 tablespoons chopped fresh dill*

1. Put salmon through a meat grinder, using the finest blade, or chop it very finely. Set aside.

2. Beat egg yolks well and beat in the cooled melted butter. Add flour 1 tablespoon at a time, mixing constantly with a wooden spatula.

3. Add ground fish to egg-yolk mixture, along with salt, pepper, parsley, dill, and lemon juice. Mix well.

4. Beat egg whites until they form soft peaks. Stir a big teaspoonful of whites into salmon mixture to lighten it, then gently fold in remaining beaten whites.

5. Spread mixture in a jelly-roll pan that has been brushed with vegetable oil and then lined with waxed paper that extends 3 inches at each end, but first, brush paper with vegetable oil. Put pan on middle shelf of a preheated 350° oven and bake for 15 minutes.

6. Turn mixture out of pan onto 2 sheets of waxed paper, the top sheet overlapping the bottom by 3 inches. Remove pan and waxed-paper lining and with the aid of the fresh waxed paper, roll the mixture like a jelly roll.

• If it cracks, don't worry. You can always cover it with chopped parsley.

7. Serve warm, with sour cream mixed with chopped fresh dill to taste.

• To reheat a roll made in advance, let it come to room temperature, then put it in a 200° to 250° oven just long enough to warm through. Before serving, pour ½ cup of *hot* melted butter over it. This will moisten it again. *Makes 8 to 10 servings.*

### TROUT MEUNIÈRE

The trout used in this recipe should be cleaned and split—most fish sellers will do the work—but they should not be separated into halves. The heads and tails should remain intact.

| | |
|---|---|
| 6 *trout, about 1 lb. each* | ¾ *cup butter* |
| ¼ *cup lemon juice, plus lemon juice to wash fish* | 5 *tablespoons finely chopped parsley* |
| 1 *cup flour, about* | 2 *lemons, cut into 8 wedges* |
| 1 *teaspoon salt* | 1 *tablespoon paprika* |
| ½ *teaspoon freshly cracked white pepper* | |

1. Wash the fish in water acidulated with lemon juice (1 tablespoon to 1 quart) and dry them on paper towels.

2. Roll trout in flour, shaking off excess. Sprinkle with salt and pepper.

3. Heat ½ cup of the butter in a skillet until it's hot but not brown. Lay fish in pan and cook over medium high heat for 6 minutes without moving them, then turn carefully and cook 6 minutes on other side. The fish should then be golden brown. Place them on a warm serving dish and keep warm in a low oven.

4. Add the remaining ¼ cup of butter to skillet and heat until it's lightly browned but not burned. Remove skillet from heat, add ¼ cup

parsley and ¼ cup lemon juice, swirl in pan, and pour over fish in platters.

5. Garnish platter with 8 wedges of lemon—4 dipped along the core in remaining chopped parsley, 4 dipped in paprika. **Makes 6 servings.**

### WHITEBAIT WITH CAPER MAYONNAISE

In England, where whitebait are very popular, plates are piled high with dozens of these tiny fish, which are only about an inch long. They are fried in deep fat and eaten whole, usually with thin slices of brown bread made into triangular sandwiches with tartar sauce filling. Whitebait cannot be prepared ahead; they must be fried at the last minute. Look for whitebait (sometimes called shiners) during March and April. If you can find them, and if you have a deep fat fryer with a basket, you will be rewarded with a fine eating adventure.

| | |
|---|---|
| *2 lbs. whitebait* | *2 cups flour, about* |
| *3 cups vegetable shortening,* | *¼ cup drained capers* |
| *for deep frying* | *1 cup mayonnaise (see p. 251)* |

1. Wash the whitebait and dry them carefully on paper towels. Don't press them; they are fragile.

2. In a deep fat fryer, heat shortening to 375° on a fat thermometer. It should be hot and ready to use before the whitebait is floured.

3. Put flour in a baking tray or pan and roll fish in flour to coat. Flour only as many fish as can be fried at one time.

• If too many are fried at once, they tend to stick together, and they're not very attractive.

4. Put floured fish into a coarse strainer and rap it—I do this against my hand—so that excess flour falls off.

5. *Immediately* put fish into frying basket and plunge into hot fat before the flour dampens. Fry only a moment or until golden. Lift out basket and drain fish immediately on paper towels.

6. Flour and fry the next batch of fish, but first, be sure fat temperature is back to 375°.

7. Serve with caper mayonnaise. To make: stir drained capers into homemade mayonnaise. **Makes 8 servings.**

### LOBSTER FLAMBÉ

| | |
|---|---|
| *2 live 1½-lb. lobsters* | *2 tablespoons cognac* |
| *2 tablespoons butter* | *Melted butter, optional* |
| *2 tablespoons vegetable oil* | |

1. The lobsters used in this recipe must be split alive. Lay one lobster on a cutting board, head and claws to the left.

• The claws are usually plugged. If not, lay a towel over them. The safe way to pick up a lobster is by grabbing it right behind the head, where the claws join the body. When a lobster is held this way, its pincers can't reach your hand.

2. On the back of the lobster's head, where it joins the body, there is a cross. Plunge the tip of a large sharp knife into this cross. This severs the spinal cord, and the lobster dies immediately.

3. With the same knife, split the lobster lengthwise, through the head, body, and tail, and open it out flat. Remove the sand bag just behind and between the eyes, and the long intestinal vein.

4. To make it easier to fit lobster pieces in a skillet, remove big and little claws.

5. Repeat steps 1–4 for the second lobster.

6. Heat butter and oil in a skillet. When hot, add lobster pieces and shake skillet back and forth over high heat for about 3 minutes.

7. Pour cognac over lobster pieces and ignite. Shake skillet until flames die.

• If using a gas flame, turn it down before adding cognac; then turn it back up and tip the skillet toward it. The cognac will ignite.

8. Cover skillet and cook lobster pieces over high heat until they turn bright red, about 3 to 5 minutes.

• Frozen lobster tails can be prepared the same way. They don't even have to be defrosted. After they have been buttered and flamed, cover and cook until they turn red. The larger frozen tails will take about 10 minutes. You will need 6 ½-lb. lobster tails for 2 servings.

9. Serve with or without melted butter. *Makes 2 servings.*

## BAKED LOBSTER NICHOLAS

Nicholas owned a fish market at the seashore where I had a house for years. This is the way he taught me to cook plain lobster. Since then, I've rarely done it any other way.

| | |
|---|---|
| 2 *live 2-lb. lobsters* | 8 *lemon wedges* |
| ½ *cup butter* | ¼ *cup melted butter, about* |
| ¼ *cup lemon juice* | |

1. Split and clean lobsters, following steps 1, 2, and 3 in recipe for Lobster Flambé (see p. 68). Do not detach claws.

2. Lay lobster halves on a baking sheet, cut side up. Dot each half with 2 tablespoons butter and sprinkle with 1 tablespoon lemon juice.

• The lobsters can be split and readied to bake 2 to 3 hours before they are to go in the oven. Keep them on ice or refrigerate them, but be sure to bring them to room temperature before proceeding with the recipe. Don't hold them on ice longer than 2 or 3 hours. The sooner the lobsters are baked after being split, the better they are.

3. Place on the middle shelf of a preheated 350° oven and bake 25 to 30 minutes, or until red.

4. Place lobster halves on a large serving plate, garnish with lemon wedges, and serve with hot melted butter.

• If dinner is delayed, the lobsters can be kept for about 15 minutes in a 200° oven. Pour a little melted butter and lemon juice over the halves to keep them from drying out. *Makes 2 servings.*

## COLD LOBSTER MOUSSE

Cardamom seed provides the special, mysterious touch in this recipe, which can, if desired, be prepared a day in advance of when it's to be served.

> 3 cups (1½ lbs.) finely
>   chopped cooked lobster
> ½ cup finely minced celery
> ¼ cup finely minced onion
> 2 tablespoons lemon juice
> ¼ cup chopped parsley
> ½ teaspoon salt
> ½ teaspoon (scant) freshly
>   cracked pepper
> ¼ teaspoon ground cardamom
>   seed
>
> 1½ cups mayonnaise (see
>   p. 251)
> 1½ cups heavy cream
> 2 packages unflavored gela-
>   tin
> ½ cup dry Madeira
> Vegetable oil to grease dish or
>   mold
> 1 small cucumber

1. In a large bowl put lobster, celery, and onion. Sprinkle with lemon juice. Add parsley, salt, pepper, and cardamom. Toss to mix. Fold in mayonnaise and set aside.

• Instead of lobster meat, the same proportion of shrimp or crab meat can be used.

2. Whip cream to the same consistency as the mayonnaise and set aside.

• If cream is whipped too stiffly in making mousses and cold soufflés, it is difficult to mix it smoothly.

3. Sprinkle gelatin in Madeira in a glass measuring cup to soften. Stand the cup in a pan of hot water and stir over heat to dissolve gelatin. Fold it into the cream quickly.

4. Fold the cream-gelatin mixture into the lobster-mayonnaise mixture and pour into an oiled 6- to 8-cup soufflé dish or an oiled ring mold. Cover with waxed paper and put in refrigerator to chill. Chill at least 2 hours before unmolding.

• Before unmolding any soufflé or mousse, run a little knife around the edge with an up and down motion. Place serving dish over mold, invert, give a shake, and lift off mold.

5. Before serving, surround the mousse with a garnish of cucumber ruffles made like this: cut unpeeled cucumber into thin slices; slit them from edge to just beyond the center; hold ends and twist them in opposite directions gently.

• Cherry tomatoes and black olives can be used as an alternate, and very pretty, garnish for the mousse.
• If I've made the mousse in a ring mold and garnished it with cucumber, I like to fill the center with cucumber salad. *Makes 6 to 8 servings.*

## CURRIED SHRIMP WITH CONDIMENTS

The fun of serving curry is the presentation of the condiments. On a huge shiny black tray, I set out white Chinese lotus bowls (with matching porcelain spoons) and fill them with the following: grated coconut, currant jelly, chutney, shredded orange rind, bacon bits, chopped green or red pepper (or both), pine nuts, hard-cooked eggs (white chopped, yolks sieved), crystallized ginger, Bombay duck (fish sautéed in bacon fat), currants or raisins plumped in wine, bits of avocado sprinkled with lime juice, bits of banana sprinkled with lemon juice, chopped scallion tops, chopped fresh pineapple, and sometimes crystallized violets or rose petals. Instead of bread, I serve *pappadoms*, Indian curry biscuits, which I fry on a griddle before serving.

| | |
|---|---|
| 2 *lbs. large raw shrimp, in shells* | ¾ *cup butter* |
| 4 *peppercorns* | 2 *cups chopped onions* |
| ½ *teaspoon salt* | ½ *cup chopped carrots* |
| ⅔ *cup sliced onions* | ½ *cup chopped celery* |
| 1 *bay leaf* | 1 *medium apple, unpeeled but cored, then chopped* |

| | |
|---|---|
| 3 to 4 tablespoons curry powder | 1 cup coconut milk |
| 3 tablespoons flour | Condiments |
| 1 cup light cream | 1 recipe of Saffron Rice (see p. 187) |

1. Shell—save the shells—and devein raw shrimp and set them aside.

2. Put shrimp shells in a saucepan with 6 cups of water, peppercorns, salt, sliced onion, and bay leaf. Bring to a boil, reduce heat to simmer, and cook for at least ½ hour, longer if there is time. Strain stock and set aside to be used in the curry sauce—and also in the Saffron Rice.

3. In a heavy casserole, melt ¼ cup of the butter and sauté shrimp gently, turning them with a wooden spatula, for about 3 minutes. Remove shrimp and set aside.

4. Add remaining ½ cup of butter to casserole and melt, scraping up brown bits. Add chopped onions, carrots, celery, and apple and cook until onions are transparent.

5. With wooden spatula, smooth curry powder and flour into the vegetable mixture. Cook 1 or 2 minutes for flour-and-curry flavor to develop.

• Curry powder is a blend of spices, usually about a dozen different ones, including coriander, cumin, turmeric, various peppers, cloves, mace, allspice, cardamom, and mustard. In India it is freshly made each time it's used, and it varies with each type of dish: sometimes it is quite mild; other times very pungent. Excellent curry can be bought in gourmet shops; many of the curry powders carried in supermarkets are less strong.

6. Stir in 2 cups of the stock made from shrimp shells and cook about 15 minutes, or until vegetables are tender. Add cream and coconut milk and cook until sauce thickens.

• Unsweetened canned coconut milk can be bought, or the milk can be obtained from fresh coconut by piercing the eye of the coconut with an ice pick or skewer and letting the liquid drain out into a cup. Two coconuts may be needed to get enough milk. If necessary, substitute more cream and add a pinch of sugar.

7. Purée the sauce through a food mill, using the medium disk, or blend it in a blender.

• When hot mixtures are put into a blender, keep it less than half full to avoid overflow.
• If the puréed sauce seems too thick, thin it with a little shrimp stock or cream; if not thick enough, cook it until it is reduced.

8. Taste for seasoning, then combine shrimp and sauce and heat 3 or 4 minutes. Take care not to overcook shrimp.

• Sauce can be made ahead, but don't combine shrimp and sauce until serving time. Refrigerate sauce and sautéed shrimp separately, or freeze them, again separately. At serving time, bring them to room temperature, heat the sauce, and add the shrimp to heat through.

9. Serve in a casserole over a spirit lamp. Surround the dish with condiments and Saffron Rice.

• Curry kills the flavor of wine, so plan on serving ale, beer, iced tea, or hot tea. *Makes 6 to 8 servings.*

## SHRIMP À LA KIEV

A friend of mine who spends a lot of time in Asia asked if I could tell him how to make shrimp Kiev. I had never seen a recipe for it. In fact, I had never heard of it. One day Alvin Kerr, a well-known food authority, who had been to Hong Kong recently, told me that shrimp Kiev was frequently served in Hong Kong restaurants. Well, now it's being served in Philadelphia too. I figured out my own way to make it. Filet of flounder or blowfish can be substituted for shrimp.

| | |
|---|---|
| 12 *large raw shrimp, in shells* | ¾ *cup flour* |
| ¼ *cup dry white wine* | 2 *beaten eggs* |
| ½ *cup unsalted frozen butter* | 1 *tablespoon vegetable oil* |
| 3 *tablespoons lemon juice* | ¾ *cup bread crumbs (see* |
| ½ *teaspoon salt* | *p. 7)* |
| ¼ *teaspoon freshly cracked white pepper* | 2 *cups vegetable shortening for deep frying* |
| 2 *tablespoons chopped chives* | 6 *lemon wedges* |

1. Shell the shrimp and slit them lengthwise on the inside curve *but do not cut all the way through.* Lay them out flat, like an open book (this is called butterflying), on waxed paper sprinkled with 2 tablespoons dry white wine. Cover with a second sheet of waxed paper, and pound shrimp flat, using the flat side of a cleaver.

• The larger the shrimp, the easier this is to do. Don't use small shrimp. Sprinkling the waxed paper and shrimp with wine makes it easier to remove the paper when shrimp are pounded.
• Don't worry about the black veins, they're harmless. If you must remove them, do it after shrimp are pounded.

2. Brush flattened shrimp with the remaining 2 tablespoons of wine and lay a thin finger of frozen butter on each shrimp. Sprinkle each with lemon juice, salt, pepper, and chives.

3. Start with the long side and roll shrimp around the butter, tucking in the ends.

• Don't bother fastening these rolls with toothpicks or skewers. Shrimp, like chicken, is very gelatinous and will stick to itself.

4. Coat rolls with flour, shaking off excess, then dip in eggs mixed with oil and roll in bread crumbs. Be sure to coat the ends of the rolls.

5. Lay rolls, seam side down, on a baking sheet and freeze for at least ½ hour, or chill in refrigerator for at least 1 hour.

• Shrimp rolls can be frozen and stored for weeks, wrapped in foil or plastic wrap. Do not thaw before frying. Just take the rolls from the freezer to the hot fat.

6. Before serving, heat shortening in a heavy saucepan or an electric skillet to 375° on a fat thermometer. Fry just 2 rolls at a time. If rolls have come from a refrigerator, fry about 3 minutes; if they are frozen, fry about 5 minutes. Remove from fat with a slotted spoon and drain on paper towels. Serve hot, with lemon wedges.

• It's a good idea to make a few extra shrimp rolls, since one may be troublesome to roll, or one may split open when it's deep fried. *Makes 6 servings of 2 shrimp each.*

## HOT SHRIMP MOUSSE

| | |
|---|---|
| 2 *lbs. raw shrimp, in shells* | ¼ *cup dry Madeira* |
| 4 *egg whites* | 2½ *cups cold heavy cream* |
| 2 *teaspoons salt* | *Oil to grease mold* |
| ½ *teaspoon freshly cracked white pepper* | *Butter to grease baking paper* |

1. Shell, wash, and devein shrimp. Cut them and put in a blender with egg whites, salt, pepper, and Madeira. If blender won't hold the entire mixture, blend in several batches. Blend until smooth and fluffy.

2. Transfer mixture to a bowl and either refrigerate for 2 hours or set

the bowl over ice and stir with a wooden spatula until mixture is very cold.

3. Beat in the cream, a little at a time, and when all of it has been added, pour the mixture into an oiled 1½-quart mold.

4. Set the mold in a pan of boiling water, cover top with buttered brown paper or buttered aluminum foil, place in a preheated 350° oven, and bake 35 to 40 minutes, or until set.

• Another way to set the mousse is to put the mold in its pan of boiling water directly over medium heat and cook for 40 minutes.

5. Remove mold from heat and let stand for 5 minutes before unmolding.

• To unmold, run a little knife around the edge with an up and down motion, then place serving platter over mold, invert, shake, and lift off the mold.

6. Serve at once with Beurre Noir (see p. 253), Lemon Butter (see p. 253), or Hollandaise Sauce (see p. 246). *Makes 8 to 10 servings.*


## MUSSELS MARINARA

This is the Italian version of steamed mussels, with tomato sauce added.

2 quarts mussels
2 cups dry white wine
½ cup finely chopped onions
1 crumbled bay leaf
1 teaspoon thyme

2 tablespoons chopped parsley
Marinara Sauce (recipe follows)

1. Scrub mussels with a stiff brush and remove the beards with a knife. Rinse in several changes of cold water to remove sand. Discard any mussels that are open.

• This is a time-consuming job; it is easier if mussels are soaked in water for an hour before scrubbing.

2. Put mussels in a deep kettle along with wine, onions, bay leaf, thyme, and parsley. Cover the kettle tightly and shake occasionally while steaming mussels over high heat for about 12 minutes, or until they open.

3. Remove from heat, strain off broth, and save it to add to marinara sauce. Discard any mussels that haven't opened.

4. Before serving, combine sauce and mussel broth and pour over mussels in deep soup plates.

### Marinara Sauce

3 lbs. fresh, ripe tomatoes
¼ cup olive oil
3 large cloves finely chopped garlic
1½ cups finely chopped onions
1 teaspoon salt
½ teaspoon freshly cracked black pepper

1 tablespoon chopped fresh basil, or 1 teaspoon dry basil
2 tablespoons chopped parsley

1. Peel and chop tomatoes, then set them aside.

• An easy way to peel tomatoes is to plunge them in boiling water, count slowly to 10, and lift them out with a slotted spoon. Skins will slip off easily with the help of a paring knife. Or spear a tomato (through the stem end) on a fork and hold it over a gas flame, turning to heat it all over. In a few seconds the skin pops and will peel off easily.

2. Heat olive oil in saucepan and cook garlic and onions in oil until transparent. Do not let them brown.

3. Add tomatoes, salt, pepper, basil, and parsley. Bring to a boil, then reduce heat and simmer, stirring frequently, for 20 minutes.

• If this mixture gets too thick (it depends on the juiciness of tomatoes), add a little broth from the mussels. *Makes 4 to 6 servings.*

## SEAFOOD CASSEROLE

An elegant make-ahead party casserole that can be frozen, sauce and all. Defrost in refrigerator. To reheat, bring to room temperature and put in a preheated 350° oven for 10 to 15 minutes. *Always undercook any dish you plan to reheat.*

¾ lb. halibut, or any firm, nonoily white fish
2 egg whites
½ cup light cream
1½ teaspoons salt
1 tablespoon chopped parsley
1 teaspoon chopped fresh tarragon, or ⅓ teaspoon dried

1 teaspoon chopped shallot
1 small clove chopped garlic
6 flounder filets
¼ cup cognac
¼ teaspoon freshly cracked white pepper
12 large raw shrimp, shelled and deveined
½ lb. cleaned and chopped raw shrimp

½ *lb. bay scallops*
¼ *cup melted butter, plus butter to grease baking dish and baking paper*

½ *cup fish stock (see p. 242)*
*Mushroom Sauce (recipe follows)*
¼ *cup chopped parsley*

1. Grind halibut, using the finest blade of meat grinder, or chop it very finely. Put it in a mixer bowl with egg whites and beat at high speed for 5 minutes, or until egg whites are completely beaten into the fish.

• If a mixer is not available, beat fish in a bowl over ice, with a wooden spatula.

2. Slowly add cream, a few drops at a time, using the mixer at low speed, then increasing to high.

3. Add 1 teaspoon of the salt, parsley, tarragon, shallot, and garlic and beat them in. Set aside.

4. On a cutting board cut each flounder filet in half, lengthwise. Pat dry with paper towels and brush the skin side with cognac.

• The skin side can be recognized because it is darker than the flesh side and has a silvery cast to it.

5. Sprinkle flounder with white pepper and remaining salt and spread with the halibut mixture. Lay 1 shrimp on each piece and roll it up. Stand each roll on its end in a buttered baking dish.

6. Over the flounder rolls, scatter the chopped shrimp and the scallops.

• If bay scallops aren't available, use sea scallops. Cut them into quarters or halves, depending on their size.

7. Brush surfaces of rolls generously with melted butter, pour on fish stock, and cover with buttered waxed paper.

8. Place baking dish in a preheated 350° oven and poach the rolls for about 20 minutes, or until done.

• They may take a little longer to cook, depending on the thickness of the flounder. Test rolls for doneness by removing from oven and touching with a fork to see if they flake. If they don't, return to oven for a few minutes more.

9. Pour off excess liquid and use it to thin Mushroom Sauce if it seems too thick. Before serving, pour Mushroom Sauce over the casserole and sprinkle with chopped parsley.

### Mushroom Sauce

1 *tablespoon dried mushrooms*
¾ *cup sliced fresh mushrooms*

2 *tablespoons butter*
1 *teaspoon lemon juice*
½ *teaspoon salt*

¼ *teaspoon freshly cracked*
   *white pepper*
1 *small clove chopped garlic*
1 *tablespoon flour*

½ *teaspoon tomato paste*
1¼ *cups fish stock (see p. 242)*
¼ *cup light cream*

1. Soak dried (not freeze-dried) mushrooms in water to cover for at least 1 hour. Drain, squeeze out excess moisture, chop, and set aside.

2. Sauté the sliced fresh mushrooms in butter over high heat. Sprinkle them with lemon juice and salt and pepper and shake the pan, tossing the mushrooms as they cook. Cook about 3 minutes.

3. Add garlic and dried mushrooms and cook over high heat for 3 more minutes.

4. Mix in flour and tomato paste thoroughly. Add fish stock and light cream. Bring to a boil, then simmer 10 minutes. *Makes 6 servings.*

## CIOPPINO

A West Coast specialty. Frequently called American bouillabaisse.

¼ *cup olive oil*
6 *medium cloves chopped*
   *garlic*
1½ *cups chopped onions*
¾ *cup chopped green pepper*
1 *cup chopped celery*
¼ *cup chopped parsley*
2 *cups dry red wine*
12 *fresh tomatoes, peeled,*
   *seeded, and chopped, or*
   1 *20-oz. can Italian plum*
   *tomatoes*
1 *teaspoon salt*

½ *teaspoon freshly cracked*
   *black pepper*
¼ *teaspoon basil*
¼ *teaspoon oregano*
2 *tablespoons tomato paste*
1 *live 1½-lb. lobster*
1 *dozen clams, in shells*
1 *lb. raw shrimp, shelled and*
   *deveined*
1 *lb. red snapper, cut in*
   *pieces*
1 *lb. bass, cut in pieces*

1. Heat olive oil in a large kettle or saucepan. Stir in garlic, onions, green pepper, celery, and 2 tablespoons of the chopped parsley. Cook, stirring with wooden spatula, until onions are transparent. Do not let vegetables brown.

2. Add wine, tomatoes, salt, pepper, basil, oregano, and tomato paste. Bring to a boil, then cover and simmer for 30 minutes.

3. Split and clean the live lobster, following steps 1, 2, and 3 in recipe for Lobster Flambé (see p. 68). Cut lobster in pieces.

4. Scrub the clams well and rinse them several times in cold water. Throw away any clams with open or damaged shells.

5. After sauce has simmered for 30 minutes, add shrimp, red snapper, bass, lobster, and clams. Cover and bring back to a boil. By the time the clams open, about 5 to 8 minutes, the cioppino is done.

6. Discard clams that do not open.

7. Sprinkle with rest of the chopped parsley and serve in individual bowls. *Makes 4 servings.*

# MEATS

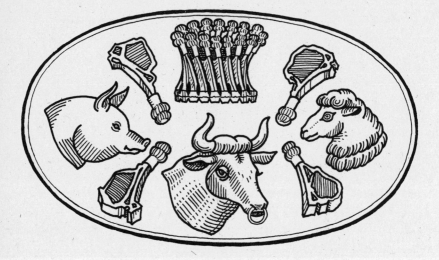

To get good meat, make friends with a good butcher. And don't be surprised at the cost of the friendship. Good meat is expensive. If the price of the best quality seems prohibitive, it is far more sensible to eat eggs, poultry, cheese, and fish.

To be sure of obtaining meat of the best quality, buy government-graded prime. Prime is usually reserved for first-class hotels and restaurants, but many meat markets have it for those who will pay the price.

Beef can be judged by looking at the exposed surface. If the beef is good, the surface will be bright red, firm, and fine-textured, with little visible connective tissue. The bones will be porous and pinkish white. The fat will be creamy in color and flaky, and a network of marbling will be visible. Well-aged beef—that which has been hung the proper length of time—may be dark in color or green from mold before trimming; this is normal, and when the meat is trimmed, the inside will be a good red.

Pork is more likely to be of consistent quality than are other meats. Its color should be grayish pink, the flesh should be firm and well marbled (and it should be cooked to an internal temperature of 170° to kill any trichinae). Hams should be short and plump, with smooth, thin skins.

Lamb has pink flesh, which turns dull red when it reaches the mutton stage. Baby lamb has pink fat, but when the animal ages, the fat is white. Nothing is more succulent than lamb cooked just to the pink stage, the way Europeans cook it. Regrettably, most Americans abuse lamb by overcooking it.

Veal is becoming somewhat more popular than it used to be in the United States, but it is still not as popular as it is in Europe. And good veal, which has flesh that is whitish pink, firm, moist, and fine-grained, is still scarce. The lighter the color of veal the more tender the meat. Veal shows no marbling of fat.

Americans should be able to cook meat to perfection, for they have so many aids. With things like temperature-controlled ovens, meat thermometers, larding devices, roasting pans with adjustable racks, practical oven-to-table equipment, and enamel-on-iron casseroles, there is really no excuse for overcooking roasts or making watery stews or coating chunks of meat with pasty gravy.

Many of the meat recipes, for entertaining and for family meals, found in this chapter can be prepared in advance, and some—particularly stew (which should be undercooked if it is to be reheated later)—even improve with standing.

For serving large pieces of meat, whether roasted or braised, a sturdy carving board and a carving set, with knife honed to razor sharpness, are almost imperative.

### Rib Roast of Beef

Everyone who appreciates beef has very definite ideas about how to do a rib roast. I certainly do: for one thing, I always buy the first 4 ribs of prime beef, and I never have the bones removed. Bones give the meat beautiful flavor. Here is my method.

> 4 ribs of prime beef, with bones
> ½ cup coarse salt
>
> 2 teaspoons freshly cracked black pepper

1. Bring roast to room temperature and rub salt—the coarse salt makes an attractive crust—and pepper on top of the fat but not over the flesh.

2. Stand the roast on its bones, fatty side up, in a shallow roasting pan, and put it into a preheated 350° oven. Time it—calculate 17 minutes cooking time per pound for a roast that is well done on the outside and very rare inside—so it can be allowed to stand for 15 minutes out of the oven before it is carved. This gives the juices a chance to settle and makes carving easier.

• If using a meat thermometer, insert it so that the point is in the center of the meat, not touching bone. For very rare meat, the temperature should read 125°. Remember, the roast continues to cook after it is taken out of the oven.

• Because I like to taste the beef, I do not make any kind of gravy or brown sauce. I do, however, like the English custom of serving horse-radish sauce—made by simply whipping 1 cup of heavy cream and folding in horseradish, preferably fresh horseradish, to taste—with rib roast. And I always serve roast beef with potatoes. Any kind will do, but I'm partial to Potatoes Dauphinoise (see p. 183).

• If dinner is delayed, do not try to reheat a rib roast. Serve it warm, or cool. It's still wonderful. *Makes 10 to 12 servings.*

## ROAST FILET OF BEEF

If you don't like your beef rare, don't serve a roast filet of beef. If it's overcooked, it loses all its flavor and juiciness.

| | |
|---|---|
| 1 *well-trimmed 5- to 6-lb. filet of beef* | 8 *large fluted sautéed mushroom caps (see p. 11)* |
| 1 *tablespoon coarse salt* | 1 *bunch watercress* |
| 1 *teaspoon freshly cracked black pepper* | |

1. If the filet is not a long, well-shaped piece of meat, tie it with a string every 2 inches around so that it is. Bring it to room temperature, rub it all over with salt—the coarse salt makes an attractive crust—and pepper and place it on a rack in a shallow roasting pan.

2. Roast in a preheated 425° oven for 35 minutes. This will give a very rare piece of meat.

• If a meat thermometer is used, the temperature should register 125°.

3. Remove from oven and let stand about 15 minutes before carving.

4. Garnish platter with sautéed mushroom caps and watercress.

• Serve plain or with Béarnaise Sauce (see p. 248), Maître d'Hôtel Butter (see p. 253), or Sauce Périgourdine (see p. 250). If serving with Périgourdine, reserve the pan drippings from the beef to add to the sauce for extra enrichment. *Makes 8 servings.*

## STEAK AU POIVRE

When I was at Le Cordon Bleu in Paris, a long time ago, the chef did Steak au Poivre. When he put it on the platter to present it with the usual flourishes, he said, "I once knew an American who ate the steak pepper and all!" According to him, the pepper should be scraped off before the steak is eaten. This amused me. What's the point of pounding on the pepper if it's not there to enjoy? If you don't love pepper, don't make Steak au Poivre.

| | |
|---|---|
| 6 *1-inch strip or shell steaks* | 2 *teaspoons salt* |
| ¼ *cup melted butter* | ¼ *cup cognac* |
| ¼ *cup freshly cracked black pepper, about* | 1 *bunch watercress* |

1. Trim excess fat from the steaks, then brush both sides with melted butter.

2. With the heel of your hand pound freshly cracked black pepper into both sides of each steak, allowing a good teaspoonful for each side. (Remember, it's not Steak au Poivre unless a lot of pepper is used.)

3. Heat a large heavy frying pan to the smoking point. Put in the steaks—not touching—and sear them over high heat for 5 minutes on each side.

• This timing produces a rare steak. Not raw, but rarer than medium rare.

4. Season the steaks with salt and put them on a hot serving platter.

5. Deglaze the frying pan with a little cognac, either by flaming the cognac or by just letting it boil for 1 or 2 minutes. Scrape up the brown bits and pour the sauce over the meat.

• Some cooks, when they deglaze the pan with cognac, add a little heavy cream, then bring the mixture to a boil before pouring it over the meat. I prefer just cognac.

• As an alternative to the pan sauce, try Béarnaise Sauce (see p. 248).

6. Decorate the platter with lots of watercress. Its good peppery flavor goes well with this steak. And make sure there's plenty of robust red wine with which to wash the steak down. (Men will bless you.) **Makes 6 servings.**

## STEAK DIANE

Pound steaks thin, then cook them individually in a chafing dish while guests watch the show. The following recipe makes just 1 serving.

| | |
|---|---|
| 1 *10-oz. shell, Delmonico, or sirloin strip steak, cut ¼ or ½ inch thick* | 3 *tablespoons butter* |
| | 2 *tablespoons cognac* |
| ½ *teaspoon salt* | 2 *tablespoons dry Madeira* |
| ¼ *teaspoon freshly cracked black pepper* | 2 *tablespoons chopped chives* |

1. Place the steak—if using a ½-inch one, first slit it not quite through and open it up (butterfly it, that is)—between two sheets of waxed paper and pound it as thin as possible. Sprinkle with salt and pepper.

2. Melt 2 tablespoons of butter in a heavy pan or chafing dish. When butter is hot and no longer foaming, sear the steak over high heat for 2 minutes on each side.

3. Add cognac, give it a second to warm, then ignite it either with a match or by tipping the chafing dish toward a flame. Shake the dish until flames die.

4. After removing steak to a warm serving plate, make a quick pan sauce by adding Madeira, boiling for 1 or 2 minutes, swirling in 1 table-spoon of butter, and sprinkling with chopped chives. Pour sauce over steak. *Makes 1 serving.*

### FILET OF BEEF IN CRUST WITH SAUCE PÉRIGOURDINE

This is a sort of compromise beef Wellington—individual filets topped with pâté and baked in a crust of rough puff pastry. It's much easier to serve, since there is no carving. Besides, I think it's a sacrilege to take a whole filet, cook it partially, coat it with duxelles and pâté, wrap it in pastry, and cook it a second time. I prefer my whole filet (see p. 82), plain or with Béarnaise. Note that filets made en croûte must be thick if they are to be rare when the pastry is completely baked.

| | |
|---|---|
| 4 1¼- to 1½-inch pieces filet of beef | 1 recipe of rough puff pastry (recipe follows), made 24 hours in advance |
| 1 teaspoon salt | Flour to dust pastry board |
| ½ teaspoon freshly cracked black pepper | 1 10-oz. can pâté de foie gras |
| 3 tablespoons butter | 1 egg yolk |
| 2 tablespoons cognac | Sauce Périgourdine (see p. 250) |

1. Trim excess fat from filets, then salt and pepper them.

2. Heat butter in a heavy skillet, and when foaming subsides, sear filets—do not let them touch—for 1 minute on each side over high heat.

3. Heat cognac in a small long-handled pan until warm to the touch. Ignite it and pour it, flaming, over the filets. Shake skillet until flames die.

4. Remove filets from skillet, set them in a dish in the refrigerator, and chill for at least one-half hour. Reserve pan juices to add to sauce.

• Filets must be chilled thoroughly before they're wrapped in pastry; if they aren't, the pastry gets soft and sticky. Even more important, chilled meat will stay rare while the pastry bakes.

5. When fillets are chilled, roll out pastry. Cut the folded pastry into 4 equal pieces, roll each piece separately, as thin as possible, on a lightly floured board.

6. Put a slice of pâté de foie gras on each fillet, then lay pastry over the pâté and form it around each fillet. Tuck the pastry around the bottom edge of each fillet, but don't try to cover the whole bottom, for pastry won't bake satisfactorily on the bottom.

7. Place pastry packages in a shallow baking pan, about 2 inches apart, and with a knife, cut 3 slits across the top of each package to let steam escape.

8. Brush pastry with egg yolk thinned with a little water (a mixture called *dorure*), then decorate the top of each package with 2 pastry leaves cut from scraps with a leaf cutter. Mark veins in the leaves with the back of a knife blade and brush leaves with what's left of the egg-yolk mixture.

• The pastry-wrapped fillets can be made in advance of when they're to be baked and either kept in a refrigerator overnight, or frozen for future use. If freezing the fillets, wrap them in plastic wrap or foil, and thaw in refrigerator before baking.

9. Bake in a preheated 450° oven until pastry is a deep golden brown. Check at 20 minutes, and if not brown, bake a few minutes longer.

10. Serve with Sauce Périgourdine. *Makes 4 servings.*

### Rough Puff Pastry

This pastry can be used as a crust for meat pies, as well as for Filet de Boeuf en Croûte.

> 1½ cups lightly packed flour, plus flour to dust on rolling surface
>
> ½ teaspoon salt
> ¾ cup chilled butter

1. Place 1½ cups of flour in a bowl and stir in salt.
2. Cut butter into chips the size of almonds.
3. Turn the chips over in the flour to coat them; then with a large fork, stir in just enough iced water (no more than ⅔ cup) so the mixture can be gathered together in a dough ball.

• Don't worry about the lumps of butter. They are supposed to be visible.
• The amount of water needed will depend on the weather, particularly the humidity.

4. Place the ball on lightly floured marble or pastry board, and knead it just enough to get it together.

• Dough should be kept as cool as possible, so work on a marble surface if you have it.

5. Wrap in waxed paper and chill in a refrigerator for at least ½ hour.

6. Roll dough into a rectangle about 8 inches wide by 20 inches long, fold it in thirds (like a business letter), and give it a quarter turn (folds will be at the sides). Then roll it into a rectangle, fold it, and give it a quarter turn again. And again, for a total of 3 rollings and foldings.

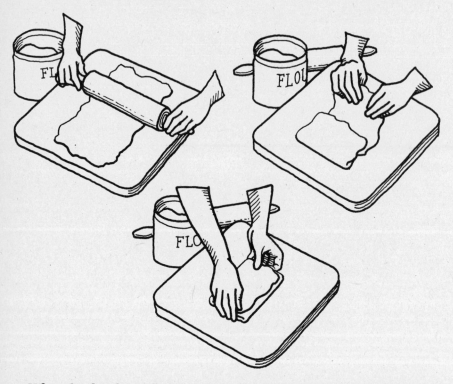

• When the dough is rolled, it will be sticky. Use flour on the rolling surface as needed. If dough is too sticky, return it to refrigerator for more chilling. Scrape dough that sticks to rolling pin and press it back onto rolled dough.

• Butter lumps will still be visible during the first rolling. Don't worry about them.

7. Wrap the rolled dough in waxed paper and refrigerate it to chill thoroughly.

• It's better to make the dough a day or more before it's to be used.

• The dough can be wrapped in plastic wrap or foil and frozen. Put it in a refrigerator to thaw a day before it is to be used.

• If more dough is needed, do not double the recipe. Instead, make it twice. *Makes enough to cover a 4-pound piece of meat or a 10-inch pie.*

### FRENCH POT ROAST

1 4-lb. rump, chuck, bottom round, or top round of beef
3 cups dry red wine
¼ cup wine vinegar
1 tablespoon salt
1 teaspoon freshly cracked black pepper
1 bay leaf
½ teaspoon thyme
¼ cup olive oil
1½ cups sliced onions
2 cloves chopped garlic
¼ cup vegetable oil
1 veal knuckle
18 small white onions
6 medium carrots
18 medium mushrooms
Lemon juice to clean mushrooms
2 tablespoons chopped parsley

1. Place beef in the refrigerator for 24 hours in a marinade made by mixing together—use a bowl large enough to hold the beef—2 cups of the wine, the wine vinegar, salt, pepper, bay leaf, thyme, olive oil, sliced onions, and garlic. Turn beef about every 4 hours while it marinates.

2. After 24 hours remove beef from marinade and drain it, reserving the marinade. Dry beef thoroughly with paper towels.

3. Heat oil in a large heavy casserole until almost smoking, then brown meat on all sides over high heat, turning it with wooden spatulas. This takes about 15 minutes. Remove meat and set aside.

4. Put reserved marinade into the casserole and bring it to a boil. Add the remaining cup of wine and the veal knuckle and return meat to casserole. Cover casserole with foil, put on the lid, and put into a preheated 350° oven to cook for 3 hours.

5. While beef cooks, prepare vegetables: Drop the small onions into boiling water for 30 seconds to loosen skins. Peel, then parboil in water to cover for about 15 minutes. Drain and set aside. Peel carrots, cut them into 3 chunks each, and parboil them in water to cover for about 20 minutes. Drain and set aside. Wipe mushrooms with paper towels dipped in acidulated water (1 tablespoon lemon juice to 1 quart water), cut off stems even with caps—don't twist stems out, or caps will lose their shape when cooking—discard stems, and set caps aside.

6. About ½ hour before beef is done, take casserole out of oven and add parboiled onions and carrots, and uncooked mushroom caps. Cover again with the foil and lid and return casserole to oven to finish cooking.

7. After removing the casserole from the oven, put the beef on a carving board and let it stand for 10 or 15 minutes to give the juices a chance to settle.

8. Discard the veal knuckle and bay leaf. Taste the sauce for seasoning.

9. Carve the meat and arrange it on a serving platter, overlapping the slices. Arrange vegetables in piles around the meat. Sprinkle it all with chopped parsley. Pass the sauce separately.

• Braised beef can also be served chilled, molded in aspic, along with its vegetables. Use a loaf pan or ring mold and oil it with 2 tablespoons of vegetable oil. Into the bottom of the mold, spoon a thin layer of aspic made by straining the sauce in which the meat cooked and bringing it to a boil in a saucepan, then adding 1 tablespoon of gelatin softened in ½ cup of red wine, stirring to dissolve, and after setting pan over ice, continuing to stir until the mixture is syrupy and on the point of setting. Arrange the vegetables, plus some cooked peas (for color), over the aspic. Carve the meat and lay slices over the vegetables. Spoon on the remaining aspic and chill until set. Before serving, run a knife around the edge of the mold (use an up-and-down motion), then place a platter over the mold, invert, give a shake, and lift off the mold. *Makes 6 to 8 servings.*

### HELENE'S SWEET AND SOUR BEEF

| | |
|---|---|
| *1 4-lb. rump, chuck, top round, bottom round, or sirloin tip of beef* | *½ cup butter* |
| | *2½ cups chopped onions* |
| | *1 cup red wine vinegar* |
| *1 tablespoon salt* | *¼ cup sugar* |
| *1 teaspoon freshly cracked black pepper* | *1 cup pitted jumbo prunes, plus 8 for garnish* |

1. Rub the piece of beef with salt and pepper.

2. Melt ¼ cup of the butter in a heavy casserole. When it's hot and the foaming subsides, brown the meat over high heat on all sides, turning it occasionally with wooden spatulas. Don't prick it with a fork. It will take about 15 minutes to brown well.

3. Remove meat and set aside. In the casserole melt the remaining ¼ cup of butter. Add onions, stirring them with a wooden spatula to coat with butter. Cook, stirring frequently, over high heat, until onions are transparent. Do not let them brown. This takes about 10 minutes.

4. Place meat on top of onions in casserole, add vinegar and sugar, and cover top of casserole with foil. Put lid over the foil. Simmer over low heat for about 3 hours, or until meat is tender. Every ½ hour during cooking, remove lid and foil and baste the meat, spooning sauce from bottom of casserole over meat. Halfway through cooking, turn meat over.

5. One half hour before serving, add 1 cup prunes. Replace foil and lid and continue cooking.

6. Before carving, let the beef rest 15 minutes. Carve and arrange slices on a warm platter. Garnish with remaining prunes and serve with pan juices. *Makes 6 to 8 servings.*

## Pot Roast in Beer

1 4-lb. rump, chuck, bottom round, top round, or sirloin tip of beef
3 tablespoons sugar
1 tablespoon salt
1 teaspoon ground cloves
6 peppercorns
1½ cups sliced onions
1 cup sliced carrots
2 cups beer
½ cup olive oil
3 tablespoons vegetable oil
2 tablespoons chopped parsley, or 1 bunch watercress

1. Put the beef in a bowl and sprinkle with sugar, salt, cloves, peppercorns, sliced onions, and sliced carrots. Pour on beer and olive oil. Marinate the meat in this mixture in the refrigerator for 24 hours, turning it about every 4 hours.

2. Remove beef from marinade, drain it—reserve the marinade—and dry it thoroughly.

3. Heat oil in a large heavy casserole. When it's hot, brown the meat over high heat on all sides, turning it occasionally with wooden spatulas. Don't prick it with a fork. It takes 15 minutes to brown thoroughly.

4. Add ¾ cup of reserved marinade to the casserole, cover top with foil, and put on the lid. Cook over low heat for about 3 hours, or until beef is tender. Halfway through cooking, remove lid and foil and turn beef over. If the pot looks dry, add another ½ cup of marinade. The beef should braise throughout the cooking in a small amount of liquid. Cover again and continue cooking.

5. Let the beef rest 15 minutes before carving. Carve it into slices and arrange on a warm platter. Sprinkle with chopped parsley or garnish platter with a bunch of watercress. Serve with pan juices. *Makes 6 to 8 servings.*

## Beef Stew

There are two schools of thought on beef for stews. Some people buy the less expensive cuts and cook them longer. Personally, I prefer good top round or sirloin, and I am very careful to get it off the fire before it is overcooked: good beef, cooked too long, tends to be dry. Ragoût de Boeuf, a change from Boeuf Bourguignon, and an ideal make-ahead dish (it freezes beautifully, or can sit in a refrigerator for 2 days before it's reheated and served), is fairly indestructible, but beware of overcooking: if this stew is cooked too long, it's apt to come out not only with dry beef but also with a generally mushy look.

2 tablespoons dried (not freeze-dried) mushrooms
1½ cups beef stock (see p. 240)
3½ lbs. top round or sirloin of beef, cut in 2-inch cubes
3 tablespoons butter
1 tablespoon vegetable oil
5 tablespoons cognac
3 tablespoons minced shallots
1 clove finely chopped garlic

2 teaspoons arrowroot, potato starch, or cornstarch
1½ tablespoons tomato paste
2 cups dry Burgundy wine
Bouquet garni (see p. 7)
1 teaspoon salt
½ teaspoon freshly cracked black pepper
1 ½-inch piece of lemon peel
2 tablespoons fresh fennel leaves or chopped parsley

1. Soak mushrooms in beef stock for at least 1 hour. Remove mushrooms, squeezing them to remove excess moisture, and chop very fine. Set aside. Reserve beef stock for later use.

2. Pat cubes of meat dry with paper towels and brown them thoroughly, a few at a time—do not let the cubes touch each other—in a mixture of hot butter and oil. Use a 4-quart flameproof casserole or Dutch oven set over high heat, and turn the cubes with tongs to brown all sides. Remove browned cubes to a tray while doing others.

• It's a temptation to dump all the meat in at once and move it around with a wooden spatula. Don't, or the pieces won't get brown and crispy, and may end up as a gray, juicy mess.

3. When all the meat is browned, set it aside, pour off excess fat, leaving about 1 tablespoonful, and deglaze the casserole—remove it from heat first—by warming 2 tablespoons of cognac in a small long-handled pan, igniting it, and while it is flaming, pouring it into the casserole. When flames die down, scrape up with a wooden spatula all the brown bits loosened by the cognac; these will add flavor and color to the sauce.

4. Add shallots and garlic to the casserole, return to high heat, and cook for 1 or 2 minutes.

5. Remove from heat and add reserved mushrooms, then stir in arrowroot (or potato starch or cornstarch) and tomato paste and mix together thoroughly.

• I like to use arrowroot or potato starch as a thickener rather than flour because it keeps the sauce clear, and you need only half the amount of arrowroot that you would need of flour.

6. Stir in wine and reserved beef stock, then return meat to casserole and bring to a boil.

7. Add bouquet garni, salt, and pepper, and lay the lemon peel on top.

8. Lay foil over top of casserole, cover with a tight-fitting lid, and set on the middle shelf of a preheated 350° oven to cook for 1½ to 2 hours, or until beef is tender. (Cooking time depends on the quality of the beef.) Three times during cooking, take casserole out of the oven, remove lid and foil, and baste the meat with 1 tablespoon of cognac.

9. Before serving, remove bouquet garni and lemon peel. Garnish with chopped fresh fennel leaves or chopped parsley.

• I like to serve this stew with Rice Pilaf (see p. 186), little boiled parslied potatoes, potatoes mashed in cream, noodles, green noodles, or pasta seashells. *Makes 6 to 8 servings.*

## HUNGARIAN GOULASH

| | |
|---|---|
| *6 tablespoons butter* | *1 tablespoon flour* |
| *3 lbs. rump, bottom or top round, or sirloin tip of beef, cut in 1-inch cubes* | *1 teaspoon salt* |
| | *½ teaspoon freshly cracked black pepper* |
| *2 cups finely chopped onion* | *1 cup tomato purée* |
| *1 clove finely chopped garlic* | *1 cup beef stock (see p. 240)* |
| *¼ cup sweet Hungarian paprika* | *½ cup dry red wine* |
| | *1 cup dairy sour cream* |

1. Melt ¼ cup of the butter in a large heavy casserole. Dry meat cubes on paper towels. When butter is hot and no longer foaming, brown the meat over high heat, a few pieces at a time, on all sides. Do not let the pieces touch and do not prick them with a fork—use tongs to turn pieces.

• If the meat is moist, or if it is crowded in the pan, the meat will steam instead of brown

2. Remove meat from casserole. Add remaining 2 tablespoons of butter and stir in onion and garlic. Cook until transparent, stirring with a wooden spatula, but don't let mixture brown.

3. Add paprika, working it in with the wooden spatula.

• It must be sweet Hungarian paprika, not hot paprika. I used the hot kind once, and my mouth was on fire for two weeks.

4. Smooth in flour and continue to cook over high heat for 3 minutes more, stirring.

5. Return meat to the casserole and add salt, pepper, tomato purée, beef stock, and wine. Bring to a boil, cover casserole with foil, and put

the lid on. Set casserole in a preheated 325° oven and cook for 2 hours, or until tender.

6. Before serving, stir in sour cream. Serve from casserole with Spaetzle (see p. 181) or with noodles cooked in boiling water until tender, drained, and dressed with melted butter (½ cup to 2 lbs. of noodles), salt and pepper to taste, and 1 tablespoon of caraway seeds. *Makes 6 to 8 servings.*

## HAMBURGERS WITH ICE WATER

Nice little trick here: the ice water keeps the hamburgers very, very moist.

| | |
|---|---|
| 6 tablespoons butter | 1 teaspoon salt |
| ¾ cup finely chopped onion | ½ teaspoon freshly cracked |
| 2 lbs. lean ground beef | black pepper |

1. Melt 2 tablespoons of the butter, stir in chopped onion, and cook over high heat, stirring, until onion is transparent. Do not let it brown.

2. Put beef in a bowl and mix in onion, salt, and pepper.

3. Beat in 1 cup of ice water, 2 tablespoonfuls at a time, with a wooden spatula or with your hand.

4. Scoop up enough beef mixture in a large serving spoon to make a good-size patty; shape it with hands dipped in ice water. Repeat, using the rest of the beef mixture to get 5 more patties.

5. Place patties on a dampened cutting board and smooth with a spatula.

6. Melt the remaining ¼ cup of butter in a large skillet. When it is hot and no longer foaming, sauté patties over high heat for about 2 minutes on each side. *Makes 6 servings.*

## HAMBURGERS WITH CAPER BUTTER

They're good enough for company.

| | |
|---|---|
| 2½ lbs. lean ground beef | 2 teaspoons salt |
| ¾ cup butter | 1 teaspoon freshly cracked |
| ¼ cup capers | black pepper |

1. Shape ground sirloin into 8 patties, about ½ inch thick.

2. Cream butter in a mixer (using the flat whip if the mixer is a heavy-duty one) or with a wooden spatula.

3. Drain and wash capers, then add them to the butter, shaping it into 4 balls. Flatten them a little.

• Instead of caper butter, the hamburgers can be stuffed with Lemon Butter (see p. 253) or Maître d'Hôtel Butter (see p. 253).

4. Lay 1 butter ball on each of 4 patties. Cover with remaining 4 patties and pinch edges together to seal.

5. Season the stuffed hamburgers on both sides with salt and pepper.

6. Heat an ungreased skillet to the smoking point. Put the hamburgers in—do not let them touch—and cook over high heat for 3 minutes on each side. *Makes 4 servings.*

## BRAISED OXTAILS

| | |
|---|---|
| 4 lbs. oxtails, disjointed | 1 teaspoon freshly cracked |
| ¾ cup flour, about | black pepper |
| ¼ cup vegetable oil | 2 cups dry red wine |
| 1 cup chopped carrot | 1 cup beef stock (see p. 240) |
| 1 cup chopped onion | Bouquet garni (see p. 7) |
| 2 cloves finely chopped garlic | 2 tablespoons chopped pars- |
| 2 teaspoons salt | ley |

1. Dredge the oxtails (any butcher will disjoint them) in flour, shaking off excess.

2. Heat oil in a large heavy casserole. Brown the oxtails, a few at a time, over high heat. Turn the oxtails to brown them evenly, and don't let them touch.

3. Return all browned oxtails to the casserole and add carrot, onion, garlic, salt, and pepper. Pour on wine and beef stock. Lay the bouquet garni on top.

4. Bring to a boil, cover the casserole with foil to condense the steam, put on lid, and place in a preheated 350° oven for about 3 hours, or until oxtails are tender.

5. Remove from oven, discard bouquet garni, and skim off fat. Taste sauce for seasoning, adding salt and pepper if desired.

6. Sprinkle with chopped parsley and serve from the casserole. Good with little boiled potatoes. *Makes 6 servings.*

## LIVER WITH ONION-AND-SOUR-CREAM SAUCE

| | |
|---|---|
| ½ cup butter | 1 cup dairy sour cream |
| 1 cup very finely chopped onions | ½ teaspoon salt |
| ¾ cup dry white wine | ¼ teaspoon freshly cracked black pepper |
| ½ cup flour, about | 8 ½-inch slices calves' liver |

1. Make sauce first. Melt ¼ cup of the butter in a saucepan and add chopped onions. Stir until onions are coated with butter and cook over high heat until transparent. Do not let them brown.

2. Add wine and cook, uncovered, over moderately high heat for 20 minutes, or until wine evaporates. At this point the onions will be soft and deliciously flavored with wine.

3. Remove from heat, and sprinkle 1 tablespoon flour over onions, stirring to blend it in. Fold in sour cream, return to heat, and bring to a boil. Turn heat down and cook over low heat for 2 to 3 minutes. Season with salt and pepper.

• Don't worry about the sour cream curdling; sour cream that is combined with flour won't.

4. Dip liver slices in remaining flour, shaking off excess.

5. Melt remaining ¼ cup of butter in skillet. When it's hot and no longer foaming, sauté liver over high heat, a few slices at a time, for 2 minutes on each side. Don't crowd the pan; don't let slices touch.

6. Arrange slices on a serving platter and pour hot sauce over them. *Makes 6 to 8 servings.*

### STUFFED HAM WITH CHAMPAGNE SAUCE AND FROSTED WHITE GRAPES

This unusual recipe for a buffet ham is my very own. Happily my students are wild about the flavor and about how easy it is to serve. Most of all, they like the glamorous look of the handsome ham garnished with frosted white grapes. And note: if you don't want to stuff the ham, the sauce and grape garnish are also elegant on a plain baked ham.

> *½ a boneless precooked ham, about 8 lbs.*
> *1½ cups seedless white grapes*
> *1 beaten egg*
> *4 teaspoons fresh tarragon, or 1⅓ teaspoons dried*
> *4 tablespoons melted butter*
> *2 tablespoons bread crumbs (see p. 7)*
> *½ teaspoon salt, about*
>
> *¼ teaspoon freshly cracked white pepper*
> *2¾ cups champagne*
> *2 tablespoons cognac*
> *¼ cup heavy cream*
> *Few drops lemon juice, optional*
> *1 bunch watercress*
> *Frosted White Grapes (recipe follows)*

1. With a large knife, dig a hole about 4 inches in diameter and 3 inches deep in the center of the ham, on the flat, or cut, side. Chop the removed ham very fine, discarding any fat.

2. Put chopped ham in a bowl along with ¾ cup of the grapes, the

beaten egg, 1 tablespoon of fresh (or 1 teaspoon of dried) tarragon, 2 tablespoons of the melted butter, the bread crumbs, the salt—add this cautiously—and the pepper. Mix together well, then pack into the ham cavity.

• If there is a little stuffing left over, wrap it in foil and bake it along with the ham. Serve as extra stuffing.
• The ham may be stuffed and readied for the oven the day before it is to be baked.

3. Press a large piece of heavy-duty foil against the stuffed end of the ham and shape it around the sides, down far enough so there is room to tie it on with string. Place ham in baking pan, foil side down. (This position holds the stuffing inside the ham.)

4. Brush exposed ham with 2 tablespoons of melted butter. Pour 1 cup of the champagne over the ham and bake in a preheated 325° oven for 10 minutes per pound. Baste the ham 3 times during baking, using ¼ cup champagne each time.

5. Remove ham from oven (do not remove foil until just before serving) and place it on a carving board. Let it rest while making sauce.

6. To make sauce: pour excess fat from pan, leaving about 1 tablespoonful. To lift the flavorful glaze made by champagne and ham juices, flame the pan with cognac—that is, warm the cognac in a small long-handled pan, ignite, then pour it, flaming, into the baking pan. Shake the pan until flames die. Scrape up the brown bits.

7. Stir in heavy cream and remaining 1 teaspoon of fresh (or ⅓ teaspoon of dried) tarragon, bring to a boil, and boil for 3 minutes.

8. Add remaining cup of champagne and boil again until mixture thickens slightly. Taste for seasoning and add a pinch of salt if needed. A few drops of lemon juice won't come amiss.

9. Add the remaining ¾ cup of grapes and heat through.

10. Don't try to slice the ham straight across—the servings will be too large. Carve slices of the ham off the sides, cutting straight down from the outside edge in to the point at which the stuffing begins (see illustration, p. 96). This method of carving will yield individual-size servings. Spoon stuffing onto each serving. Serve sauce separately in a small bowl. Garnish ham platter with watercress and frosted grapes. *Makes 12 to 16 servings.*

## Frosted White Grapes

2 medium bunches seedless
 white grapes
2 egg whites

1 cup crystallized or granulated sugar

1. Remove grapes from the large stem in little bunches.
2. Beat whites until they form soft peaks. Dip the grapes in egg whites (you can be casual about this, each grape doesn't have to be covered).
3. Lay grapes on waxed paper, sprinkle with sugar and chill.

• The grapes can be made in the morning and refrigerated.
• Frosted grapes can also be served as a dessert—and an elegant one it is, too.

## HAM IN CRUST

When I describe this to my classes, I call it "ham tied up in pastry ribbon." It makes a sensational package.

| | |
|---|---|
| *1 10-lb. canned ham* | *Flour to sprinkle on pastry* |
| *1 cup white raisins* | *board* |
| *1 full bottle dry Madeira* | *1 beaten egg yolk* |
| *1 recipe of sour-cream pastry* | *½ cup Dijon mustard* |
| *(recipe follows), chilled* | |

1. The day before the ham is to be baked, remove it from the can and cut little slits all over it with a small sharp knife. Use the knife to poke raisins into the slits. Push some raisins deep into the ham; place others near the surface. The raisins should be distributed through the

ham as evenly as possible; when it is carved, they should form a mosaic design. After adding the raisins, put ham into a large bowl, cover with Madeira, and let soak overnight at room temperature.

2. When ready to bake the ham, remove it from Madeira and dry it thoroughly.

• The Madeira can be saved (store in a refrigerator) and used to soak another ham, or pork or tongue.

3. Roll sour-cream pastry that has chilled for at least 1½ hours about ¼ inch thick on a lightly floured board, then roll out two strips, each 1½ inches wide and 20 to 25 inches long, and a rectangle about 6 inches wide and 10 inches long.

4. Place ham on baking sheet and wrap one long pastry strip around top and sides of ham, lengthwise; tuck the ends securely under the ham. Wrap the second strip around width of ham, again tucking ends under.

5. Brush the pastry all over with beaten egg yolk thinned with a little water. This egg wash, called *dorure*, not only makes the pastry shine but also helps hold the bow to be made next in place. Save some of the wash for the bow.

6. Make bow by pleating the remaining rectangle of pastry in the middle.

7. Lay bow on top of ham, where pastry ribbons cross. Brush bow with the rest of the egg wash. Then place ham in a preheated 350° oven and bake from 45 to 60 minutes, or until pastry crust is done (how long this takes depends on how thick the crust is).

8. Serve with Dijon mustard. *Makes 12 to 16 servings.*

### Sour-Cream Pastry

Use sour-cream pastry for Ham en Croûte and for topping meat and fish pies, and for turnovers. It is not recommended for conventional pies.

> 2 cups lightly packed flour,    ½ teaspoon salt
> plus flour to dust on dough    ¾ cup chilled unsalted butter
> and kneading surface    ½ cup dairy sour cream

1. Place ½ cup of flour in a bowl and stir in salt.
2. Cut butter into chips the size of almonds.
3. Turn the chips over in flour to coat them; then, with a pastry blender, cut them into the flour. The mixture should look like coarse cornmeal.
4. Add sour cream and mix with a fork.

5. Gather together the mixture, which will be soft, with your hand, lay it on a floured board, knead it a few times, then form it into a dough ball, sprinkle it with a little flour, and wrap it in waxed paper.

6. Chill in a refrigerator for 1½ hours or more.

• The dough can be made the day before it is needed, and stored in the refrigerator; it can also be frozen.

• This dough is sometimes a little hard to roll out. To make a nice round circle, don't roll over the edge, just get near the edge. To save steps, keep turning the pastry, moving it instead of walking around the rolling surface. *Makes enough to cover a 4-pound piece of meat or a 10-inch pie.*

## Braised Ham

| | |
|---|---|
| *1 10- to 12-lb. precooked ham, with bone* | *½ teaspoon freshly cracked black pepper* |
| *½ cup butter* | *1 bay leaf* |
| *1 cup chopped onions* | *2 cups dry Madeira* |
| *1 cup chopped carrots* | *1 cup chicken stock (see p. 241)* |
| *1 cup chopped celery* | |
| *½ cup chopped mushrooms* | *2 tablespoons freshly chopped parsley* |
| *½ teaspoon thyme* | |

1. Trim excess fat from ham, leaving about ¼ inch covering the meat.

2. Melt butter in heavy casserole—one large enough to hold the ham—and stir in onions, carrots, and celery. Cook over high heat, stirring, until onions are transparent, but do not let vegetables brown.

3. Place ham on the vegetables. Around it sprinkle chopped mushrooms, thyme, and pepper. Put bay leaf on top, then pour on Madeira and chicken stock.

• As an alternative dry white wine can be substituted for the Madeira.

4. Cover casserole with foil and heavy lid. Set in a preheated 350° oven to braise for about 2 hours. Allow 10 minutes per pound.

5. Remove ham to a serving platter and keep warm. Skim off excess fat from liquid in casserole, discard bay leaf, and prepare sauce either by puréeing the vegetables and the liquid in a blender (which should be no more than half full so the hot mixture doesn't overflow) or by working them through a food mill or sieve.

6. Taste sauce for seasoning and adjust if necessary; if the ham is salty, no additional salt will be necessary.

7. Slice ham on serving platter, pour sauce over it, and sprinkle it with chopped parsley. *Makes 12 to 16 servings.*

## HOT HAM MOUSSE

5 tablespoons butter, plus
  butter for baking paper
3 tablespoons flour
1 cup light cream
2 lbs. ham, any kind (leftover,
  precooked, uncooked,
  baked, or boiled)
3 egg whites

¼ cup dry Madeira
1 teaspoon salt
½ teaspoon freshly cracked
  black pepper
1 tablespoon fresh tarragon or
  1 teaspoon dried
1 tablespoon Dijon mustard

1. Make a *panade* (a thickener to be beaten into the ham mixture) by melting 3 tablespoons of butter in a small saucepan, stirring in flour with a wooden spatula, and cooking over high heat 2 minutes, stirring constantly. Do not let it brown. Remove from heat, add cream, and whisk vigorously. Return to high heat and cook, stirring, until mixture comes to a boil and is very thick.

2. Pour *panade* into a small baking dish and refrigerate for 15 minutes, or until set.

3. Melt the remaining 2 tablespoons of butter and butter a ring mold or soufflé dish generously with it. Set aside.

4. Grind ham in a meat grinder, using the finest blade, or chop with a knife.

5. Put ground ham into mixer bowl and beat in egg whites thoroughly (use the flat whip if the mixer is a heavy-duty one). Add Madeira and season with salt, pepper, tarragon, and mustard.

6. Add the chilled *panade*, beating it in, a spoonful at a time, until thoroughly mixed.

7. Spoon the mixture into prepared mold or soufflé dish, cover it with buttered brown paper or foil, and place the mold in a baking pan half filled with boiling water. Bake in a preheated 350° oven for 30 to 35 minutes, or until mixture is firm to the touch.

8. Remove from oven and let stand 5 minutes. Using an up-and-down motion, run a small knife around the edge of the mold to loosen it, then put serving platter over the mold, invert mold and platter, give them a shake, and lift off the mold. **Makes 6 servings.**

## HAM SLICE WITH MADEIRA

2 tablespoons butter
1 1¼-inch slice precooked
  ham

2 tablespoons chopped shallots
2 tablespoons fresh tarragon,

or 2 teaspoons dried
9 tablespoons dry Madeira
½ cup chicken stock (see
   p. 241)

1 teaspoon potato starch
2 tablespoons chopped parsley

1. Melt butter in a heavy skillet and sauté ham over high heat for 3 minutes on each side. Remove and set aside.

2. Stir shallots into the butter left in the pan, and cook, stirring with a wooden spatula, until transparent. Do not let the shallots brown. Add tarragon and ½ cup of the Madeira and bring to a boil, scraping up the brown bits. Add chicken stock.

3. Make a smooth mixture of potato starch and the remaining 1 tablespoon of Madeira and stir it into the pan. Bring to a boil.

4. Return ham to pan and cook over medium heat, basting with the pan sauce. After 5 minutes turn ham over and continue basting until it is heated through. Taste for seasoning; add pepper, as well as salt if desired.

5. Remove ham to serving platter, pour sauce over it, and sprinkle with chopped parsley. *Makes 4 servings.*

## PORK WITH PISTACHIOS

When buying the pork for this recipe, ask the butcher to remove the chine bone (backbone). Having it out will make carving easier.

1 6-lb. loin of pork
4 cloves garlic, peeled and
   cut into slivers
¼ cup natural pistachio nuts
1 tablespoon coarse salt
1 teaspoon freshly cracked
   black pepper

½ to 1 cup dry Madeira
½ cup chicken stock (see
   p. 241)
1 bunch watercress

1. Trim excess fat from pork, so that there is no more than ¼ inch remaining.

2. With a small sharp knife, make little slits all over the fatty side of the pork. Go deep into the meat with the knife, and using it as a slide, poke a sliver of garlic and a pistachio nut into each slit. When the meat is carved, it will show a mosaic of pistachio nuts.

3. Rub the meat all over with salt and pepper, then put it in a heavy casserole, fatty side up, pour on ½ cup of Madeira, and cover casserole with foil and the lid. Bake in a preheated 350° oven for about 2½ hours or 25 minutes per pound. Halfway through the baking period, take the casserole out of the oven, remove lid and foil, and turn meat over. Add

another ½ cup of Madeira if casserole looks dry. Replace foil and lid and return meat to oven to finish baking with bone ends up.

• If you are using a meat thermometer, the meat will be done when the temperature reaches 170°.

4. When pork is done, put it on a serving platter and keep it warm. Pour off all but 1 tablespoon of the fat from casserole and deglaze with chicken stock—that is, add stock to casserole, place over heat, and stir, scraping up the brown bits. Taste the sauce for seasoning.

5. Carve pork loin between the bones. Garnish platter with watercress and pass sauce separately. *Makes 6 servings.*

## Pork Chops with Sauce Robert

6 ¾-inch loin pork chops  Sauce Robert (see p. 249)
1 teaspoon salt
½ teaspoon freshly cracked
   black pepper

1. Trim excess fat from chops, put it into a large skillet, and cook it over medium-low heat for about 10 minutes, until it melts. This is called rendering. Discard rendered pieces of fat.

2. Season chops with salt and pepper and sauté them in the hot fat over low heat for 15 minutes on each side. Test for doneness by pricking chops near the bone with a fork. If juices run pink, sauté for another 5 minutes.

• Pork chops should always be cooked slowly. When cooked too quickly, over high heat, they toughen.

3. Remove chops to serving platter and keep warm while making sauce.
4. Pour hot sauce over chops before serving. *Makes 6 servings.*

## Pork Chops in Mustard Cream

6 ¾-inch loin pork chops       1 tablespoon Dijon mustard
1 teaspoon salt                1¼ cups heavy cream
½ teaspoon freshly cracked     2 tablespoons chopped pars-
   black pepper                    ley
2 tablespoons dry red wine

1. Trim excess fat from chops, put it into a large skillet, and cook over medium-low heat for 10 minutes, until fat melts. Discard rendered pieces of fat.

2. Season chops with salt and pepper, then put them into the hot fat and sauté slowly, over low heat, for 15 minutes on each side. Test for doneness by pricking chops near the bone with a fork. If juices run pink, sauté for another 5 minutes.

• Cook pork chops slowly, for when they're cooked too quickly, over high heat, they toughen.

3. Remove chops to serving platter and keep warm. Pour off all but 1 tablespoon of the fat and deglaze the pan with red wine, stirring the juices over high heat with a wooden spatula to lift the brown bits. Stir in mustard and heavy cream and bring to a boil. Cook the mixture over moderately high heat to reduce it and thicken it slightly. Adjust seasoning if necessary. Pour over meat.

4. Sprinkle chops with parsley before serving. *Makes 6 servings.*


### BARBECUED SPARERIBS

Try to get ribs that have a lot of meat on them, and ask your butcher to cut them into portions of 2 ribs each.

| | |
|---|---|
| *4 lbs. spareribs* | *6 tablespoons lemon juice* |
| *1 cup finely chopped onion* | *¼ cup brown sugar* |
| *2 tablespoons vegetable oil* | *1½ cups chili sauce* |
| *½ cup vinegar* | *½ teaspoon freshly cracked* |
| *2 tablespoons soy sauce* | *black pepper* |

1. If the butcher hasn't already done it, cut ribs into serving portions of 2 ribs each.
2. Make sauce by mixing all remaining ingredients together in a bowl.

• This sauce can also be used for barbecued chicken. No salt is needed because soy sauce is salty.

3. Lay ribs in a shallow baking pan and pour sauce over them. Bake, uncovered, in a preheated 350° oven for 30 minutes, then take out pan, turn ribs, baste them with sauce, and return them to the oven for another 45 minutes, basting them several times. *Makes 6 to 8 servings.*


### SADDLE OF LAMB

This elegant and costly cut of lamb, called saddle of lamb, must be ordered in advance from most butchers. Ask to have both sides of the loin left still attached to the backbone. The loin should not be cut down the middle; neither should it be boned. The entire saddle, with flaps left on, is what is needed. An 8-lb. saddle is the size I prefer, but the usual 5- to 6-lb. size more than pleases me and will certainly serve up to 8 people. Expensive it is, but happily it goes a long way.

*1 saddle of lamb, 8 lbs. pref-
erably*
*1 tablespoon butter, plus but-
ter to rub on meat*
*2 teaspoons coarse salt*
*¼ teaspoon freshly cracked
black pepper*

*½ cup dry red wine*
*8 large fluted sautéed mush-
room caps (see p. 11)*
*1 bunch watercress*
*1 lemon*

1. Trim any excess fat from underneath the saddle. Roll flaps up underneath, toward the spine. Tie in 4 or 5 places with butcher's cord. Rub lamb with softened butter, coarse salt, and pepper.

2. Place saddle on rack in roasting pan and roast in a preheated 425° oven for 12 minutes per pound, or until a meat thermometer registers 130°. Don't overcook the saddle; it should be served rare.

3. Remove lamb from oven and let stand 5 minutes before carving.

• During this resting period, lamb continues to cook.

4. Make a simple sauce by skimming the excess fat from roasting pan, adding red wine, and boiling for 1 minute to reduce, then scraping up the good brown bits and swirling in 1 tablespoon of butter. Taste for seasoning; it may need a little salt and pepper.

5. Arrange saddle on a carving board with fluted sautéed mushroom caps lined up along the spine. At one end of the board place a bunch of watercress, and in it two fluted lemon cups made by zigzagging around the center of a lemon—cutting at least halfway through—with a small sharp knife, then pulling the lemon halves apart.

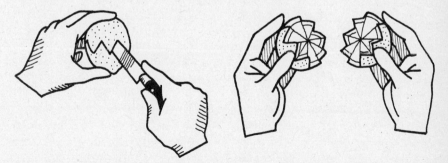

6. Carve the meat, using a long, thin ham slicer if you have one, parallel to the spine, in long thin slices, first one side, then the other.

Then turn the saddle over, cut loose the tenderloins (fillet sections), and carve them in long thin slices too. Serve sauce separately, in a bowl. *Makes 6 to 8 servings.*

## RACK OF LAMB

A rack of lamb requires very little preparation and makes an extremely successful dinner party entrée. Serve it with Minted Hollandaise (see p. 247) or Béarnaise Sauce (see p. 248), Flageolets (see p. 165), Sautéed Cherry Tomatoes (see p. 189), and Stuffed Mushrooms (see p. 179).

*1 rack of lamb, 8 chops*
*1 tablespoon coarse salt*
*1 teaspoon freshly cracked black pepper*

*1 clove garlic, peeled and cut into slivers*

1. Have the butcher trim the rack (or trim it yourself) so that 1½ to 2 inches of bone are exposed on each chop, all gristle and fat is removed, and the chine bone (backbone) at the bottom is taken out. Removing the chine makes the rack easy to carve into chops.
2. Rub the lamb all over with salt—the coarse salt makes an attractive crust—and pepper.
3. Insert the point of a small sharp knife in the fatty side of the meat, and using the knife blade as a slide, push a garlic sliver down into the hole. Repeat with the remaining garlic slivers.
4. Place lamb, fatty side up, on a rack in a baking pan and roast in a preheated 425° oven for 45 minutes, for pink lamb.
5. Before serving, carve between each chop. *Makes 4 servings.*

## LAMB CHOPS IN MINT ASPIC

*8 1-inch rib lamb chops*
*3 cups chicken stock (see p. 241)*
*½ teaspoon salt*
*¼ teaspoon freshly cracked black pepper*
*1 tablespoon tarragon vinegar*

*1½ tablespoons (1½ envelopes) unflavored gelatin*
*6 tablespoons chopped fresh mint leaves*
*2 egg whites*

1. French the bones on the lamb chops—that is, scrape bare the ends (about 1½ inches from the tips). Then trim excess fat from chops.

2. Put the chops in a pan and add 2½ cups chicken stock, salt, pepper, and tarragon vinegar. Bring to a boil, skim off any foam, and simmer, covered, for 25 minutes.

3. Let chops cool in broth; then remove them and chill for 1 hour in refrigerator.

4. Strain broth into a saucepan and set over high heat for 5 minutes.

5. Soften gelatin in the remaining ½ cup of chicken stock and stir into saucepan, then add ¼ cup of the mint leaves and the 2 egg whites and beat with a rotary beater or a whisk over high heat until frothy.

6. Remove pan from heat and let stand 10 minutes, then strain liquid aspic into a bowl through a sieve lined with 2 thicknesses of damp cheesecloth. Taste it for seasoning—more salt and pepper may be necessary—and add the remaining 2 tablespoons of mint leaves.

7. Set bowl of liquid aspic into a bowl of ice and stir until it is thick and syrupy.

8. Remove from ice and pour ⅓ of the aspic, now beginning to set, onto a chilled, very shallow round serving platter. Refrigerate the platter for 10 to 15 minutes, or until aspic is set.

9. Arrange the chilled chops in a circle on the platter of firm aspic, with bones in the center. Spoon another ⅓ of the aspic over chops.

• If aspic in the bowl has set too much, stir it over hot water for a minute.

10. Return chops to refrigerator for another 10 to 15 minutes to set aspic. Bring chops out and spoon remaining ⅓ of the aspic over them. Return to refrigerator to chill ½ hour, or until firm.

• French Potato Salad (see p. 197) is an excellent accompaniment for the chops. *Makes 6 to 8 servings.*

### Noisettes of Lamb

8 *slices of bacon*  
8 *1½-inch loin lamb chops*  
2 *teaspoons salt*  
1 *teaspoon freshly cracked*  
  *black pepper*

2 *tablespoons butter*  
1 *bunch watercress*  
*Hollandaise Sauce (see p. 246)*

1. Blanch the bacon slices—that is, put them in a saucepan, cover with cold water, and bring to a boil, then boil 1 minute. Drain in a sieve.

2. Bone lamb chops, then sprinkle them with salt and pepper and wrap a piece of bacon around the edge of each. Tie the bacon on with heavy string.

• Chops can be boned and wrapped in bacon a day ahead of time and stored in the refrigerator. Do not cook them until ready to serve.

3. Melt butter in a heavy skillet, and when it is hot and no longer foaming, sauté boned chops, or noisettes, over high heat, not letting them touch each other. For rare meat, sauté noisettes 3 to 4 minutes on each side (6 to 8 minutes in all); for medium rare, sauté 4 to 5 minutes on each side (8 to 10 minutes in all); and for well-done, sauté 5 to 6½ minutes on each side (10 to 13 minutes in all).

4. Arrange noisettes on a platter and garnish with watercress. Serve with Hollandaise Sauce.

• Minted Hollandaise Sauce (see p. 247) or Béarnaise Sauce (see p. 248) can be used instead, if desired. *Makes 8 servings.*

### LEG OF LAMB WITH PARSLEY DRESSING

This is baby leg of lamb, encrusted with golden bread crumbs and parsley and roasted the French way, until it's pink.

| | |
|---|---|
| 1 leg of lamb, under 5 lbs. | 10 tablespoons soft butter |
| 2 cloves garlic, 1 cut into slivers, 1 chopped | ½ cup finely chopped parsley |
| ¼ cup olive oil | ½ teaspoon salt |
| 1 tablespoon coarse salt | 1 bunch watercress |
| ¾ teaspoon freshly cracked black pepper | 1 lemon |
| 1½ cups bread crumbs (see p. 7) | White paper for frill |

1. Poke slivers of garlic into the meat by inserting point of a small sharp knife in the fatty side and using the knife blade as a slide to push slivers down into the holes.

2. Rub lamb all over with olive oil, coarse salt, and ½ teaspoon pepper, then set it, fatty side up, on a rack in an open roasting pan and roast in a preheated 325° oven for 18 minutes per pound.

3. To make coating, mix bread crumbs, butter, chopped parsley, chopped garlic, ½ teaspoon of salt, and the remaining ¼ teaspoon of pepper in a bowl. Twenty minutes before roasting time is up, remove lamb from oven and press on coating, then return to oven to finish cooking.

• Of course the lamb can be roasted without the coating, but then it won't be *persillé*, French for parslied.

4. Place lamb on a warm serving platter garnished with watercress, and in it, two fluted lemon cups made by using a small sharp knife to notch cuts around the center of a lemon, with each cut going at least

halfway through, then pulling the lemon halves apart. Cover the bone end of the lamb with a paper frill made by folding in half lengthwise a rectangle (use one about 10 inches wide and 15 inches long) of white paper (parchment or shelf paper), and with scissors, making cuts about 3 inches deep at ½-inch intervals along the folded edge, then unfolding the paper, and refolding it—without creasing—inside out to make the frill puffy. Coil the frill to a diameter of about 1½ inches to fit over the bone and fasten it with staples or cellophane tape. Not only does the frill look pretty, it also helps the carver keep his hands clean.

5. To carve the lamb, place it with the bone end to the right and cut 2 or 3 thin slices opposite the thick meaty portion, then turn the leg to rest on the cut surface, cut a wedge shape at the base of the bulge, and carve thin slices, from right to left, down the leg bone. Slide knife along leg bone to release these slices. *Makes 8 servings.*

### BRAISED BONED LEG OF LAMB

Once learned, the braising technique works with almost any piece of meat. It is especially recommended for less tender cuts. Instead of a leg of lamb, braise a duck or a chicken, a piece of veal, a shoulder of lamb, or a cut of beef. But change the braising liquid. As a rule of thumb, you should use red wine and beef stock for the red meats and white wine and chicken stock for the white meats. You may always vary this, of course.

1 *7-lb. leg of lamb, boned*
2 *tablespoons vegetable oil*
6 *tablespoons butter*
3 *cups chopped onions*
1 *cup chopped carrots*
1 *cup chopped celery*
1½ *cups dry white wine*

1 *cup chicken stock (see p. 241)*
2 *cloves finely chopped garlic*
½ *teaspoon thyme*
1 *bay leaf*
1 *tablespoon chopped pars-*

ley, plus chopped parsley
for garnish
1 cup fresh tomatoes, peeled,
seeded, and chopped, or
canned Italian plum toma-
toes

1 teaspoon salt
½ teaspoon freshly cracked
black pepper
1 teaspoon meat glaze (see
p. 244), optional

1. Brown lamb on all sides—use wooden spatulas to turn it, for if it's pricked with a fork, the juices will escape—in oil and 2 tablespoons of the butter in a heavy casserole. The heat should be high.

2. When lamb is nicely browned, remove it from casserole and add the remaining ¼ cup of butter and the onions, carrots, and celery. Stir vegetables to coat them well with the butter.

3. Lay lamb on top of vegetables. Pour in wine and chicken stock and add garlic, thyme, bay leaf, 1 tablespoon of chopped parsley, and tomatoes (break up canned tomato pieces with a fork). Season with salt and pepper.

4. Cover casserole with foil to condense the steam, put on lid, and bring to a boil.

5. Place casserole on the middle shelf of a preheated 350° oven and cook for about 2 hours—18 minutes a pound, that is—or until lamb is very tender.

• For pink lamb, cook a shorter time, about 1½ hours.

6. When lamb is done, remove it to a warm serving platter and keep it warm. Discard bay leaf. Work the vegetables and liquid through a food mill or sieve or purée them in a blender (filled less than half full, so it won't overflow). Skim to remove all fat, and boil over high heat until mixture is reduced by one-fourth. This reduction intensifies the sauce's flavor. If further intensification is desired, stir in meat glaze.

7. Carve the lamb and arrange it on the platter in overlapping slices. Spoon sauce over meat and garnish with chopped parsley. Serve with Soissons (see p. 166). *Makes 8 servings.*

### BRAISED LAMB SHANKS

When buying the lamb shanks for this recipe do not let the butcher crack the bones, use the shanks as they are.

8 lamb shanks
½ cup flour
¼ cup vegetable oil

1 teaspoon salt
½ teaspoon freshly cracked
black pepper

2 *tablespoons butter*
2 *cloves finely chopped garlic*
1 *cup chopped onions*
1 *cup chopped carrots*
1 *cup chopped celery*
1 *cup dry red wine*

1 *cup chicken stock (see*
  *p. 241), about*
½ *teaspoon rosemary*
1 *tablespoon chopped parsley*
1 *bay leaf*

1. Roll shanks in flour and shake off excess.

2. Heat oil in a large heavy casserole. When oil is hot, brown the shanks over high heat on all sides, doing just 2 or 3 at a time, turning them with tongs, and sprinkling them with salt and pepper as they're turned.

3. Set aside shanks, add butter to casserole and remove from heat, then stir in chopped garlic; the casserole heat is enough to cook it. Return to high heat, stir in onions, carrots, and celery, and cook 3 to 5 minutes—or until vegetables are well coated.

4. Remove casserole from heat and lay shanks on the bed of vegetables. Pour in wine and 1 cup of the chicken stock. Sprinkle with rosemary and parsley; lay bay leaf on top. Cover casserole with foil to condense the steam and put on lid. Bring to a boil, then put casserole in a pre-heated 325° oven and bake for 1½ hours.

5. Remove lamb shanks to a serving platter and keep warm. Discard bay leaf, then make a sauce by puréeing the vegetables and liquid in a blender (filled less than half full, so it won't overflow) or working them through a food mill or sieve. If sauce is too thick, thin it with a little chicken stock. Reheat and pour over shanks. *Makes 8 servings.*

## LAMB STEW

The secret of a superb lamb stew is cooking all the vegetables separately, as in this recipe.

4 *lbs. lamb, cut from the*
  *shoulder or leg into 2-inch*
  *cubes, plus a few cubes of*
  *lamb breast meat*
½ *cup flour, about*
¼ *cup butter*
2 *tablespoons vegetable oil*
½ *teaspoon freshly cracked*
  *black pepper*
1 *teaspoon salt*

2 *cloves finely chopped gar-*
  *lic*
2½ *cups chicken stock (see*
  *p. 241)*
½ *cup dry red wine*
*Bouquet garni (see p. 7)*
1 *cup shelled fresh peas*
24 *small carrots, peeled, or*
  6 *medium carrots, peeled*
  *and sliced on the diagonal*

12 *small turnips, peeled*
12 *small white onions*
 2 *whole tomatoes, peeled, seeded, and quartered*

8 *large sautéed mushroom caps (see p. 11)*
2 *tablespoons chopped parsley*

1. Trim excess fat from meat cubes, then toss them in flour and shake off excess.

2. Heat butter and oil in a large heavy casserole. When mixture is hot and no longer foaming, brown the lamb over high heat, a few cubes at a time, on all sides. Do not crowd the pan; do not let the cubes touch; use tongs to turn them.

3. When all the cubes are browned, return them to the casserole and sprinkle with salt and pepper. Add garlic, pour on chicken stock and wine, and lay the bouquet garni on top.

4. Cover casserole with foil and put on lid. Bring to a boil, reduce heat, and simmer for 45 minutes. Baste several times while cooking.

5. While the lamb cooks, prepare vegetables: put peas in a saucepan with a little cold salted water, bring to a boil, then simmer until almost tender when tasted. Drain and set aside.

6. Put carrots in another saucepan with cold salted water to cover, bring to a boil, then reduce heat and simmer carrots until they are almost tender. Drain and set aside.

7. Put turnips in another saucepan, cover with cold salted water, bring to a boil, and cook until almost tender. Drain and set aside.

8. Drop onions in boiling water for 30 seconds to loosen skins. Drain and peel them, then put them in a saucepan, cover with cold salted water, and cook over high heat until they are almost tender. Drain and set aside.

9. When lamb has cooked 45 minutes, remove bouquet garni, skim off excess fat, and add the prepared vegetables and the mushroom caps. Cover and cook over medium-high heat 15 to 20 minutes or until vegetables are tender. Taste for seasoning. Sprinkle with chopped parsley. Serve from the casserole with hot French bread and green salad. *Makes 6 to 8 servings.*

## ROAST VEAL

Fat adds flavor as well as tenderness to meat, and since veal is not a fatty meat, this particular dish is better when it is larded—when it has strips of fat inserted into it, that is—and barded, or covered with a layer of fat.

1 5-lb. rump or leg of veal, boned and tied
½ lb. salt pork for larding
¼ cup cognac
1 tablespoon coarse salt
½ teaspoon freshly cracked white pepper
Pork fat for barding, if necessary
2 cups mixed chopped carrots, onions, and celery
1½ cups dry white wine
½ cup chicken stock (see p. 241) or veal stock (see p. 242)
½ cup heavy cream
Few drops lemon juice

1. Cut salt pork in thin 5- to 6-inch strips to fit larding needle. Soak strips in cognac for 1 hour, then put them in freezer to stiffen; they'll be easier to work with. Reserve 2 tablespoons cognac to add to sauce later.

2. Lay a strip of salt pork in the hollow of the larding needle and push the needle through the veal, keeping a thumb on the fat in the needle. Hold the strip inside the meat with your fingers while withdrawing the needle. Repeat with other strips, spacing them to make a mosaic design.

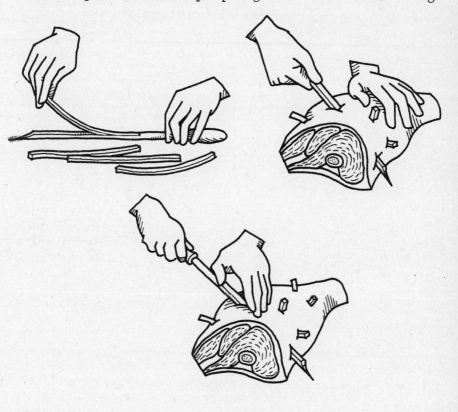

3. Rub veal with salt and pepper. If there is no fat on the outside of the veal, bard it with thin sheets of pork fat (available from most butchers). Lay the fat over the top of the meat and tie it every inch or so.

4. Place chopped vegetables in a roasting pan and lay veal on vege-. tables. Pour on 1 cup wine and roast in a preheated 350° oven for 20 minutes per pound.

• Test veal for doneness by pricking it with a small knife. If juices run pink, cook 20 minutes longer.

5. Remove veal to a serving platter and keep warm. The vegetables in the roasting pan will be brown and glazed. Pour in the remaining ½ cup of wine and bring it to a boil, scraping up the vegetables. Add chicken or veal stock and cook over medium-high heat to reduce. Strain into another pan, add heavy cream and cook until mixture thickens slightly. Taste for seasoning—salt and pepper may be needed—and add a little lemon juice and the reserved cognac.

6. Remove barding fat and strips, carve, and pour sauce over slices. *Makes 8 servings.*

## Stuffed Shoulder of Veal

4 lemons
1 cup raisins
½ teaspoon salt, about
½ teaspoon freshly cracked black pepper, about
2 tablespoons chopped shallots
1 tablespoon butter, plus butter to rub on veal
6 slices white bread, crusts removed and crumbed
¼ cup chopped parsley
5 tablespoons coarsely chopped walnuts or almonds

2 beaten eggs
1½ cups dry vermouth, about
1 5- to 6-lb. shoulder of veal, boned
1 2-oz. can anchovies, drained
2 large cloves garlic
4 bay leaves
1 cup chicken stock (see p. 241) or veal stock (see p. 242)
½ cup heavy cream
1 teaspoon potato starch, optional
1 bunch watercress

1. Make stuffing as follows. Juice 1 lemon and grate its peel. In a large bowl mix together lemon juice, grated peel, raisins, ½ teaspoon salt, ¼ teaspoon pepper, shallots sautéed in 1 tablespoon butter (to

soften them), the bread crumbs, parsley, walnuts or almonds, the beaten eggs, and enough vermouth (about ½ cup) to make a moist mixture.

2. Trim excess fat from veal. With a small sharp knife, make little slits all over the top of the veal. Stuff slits with anchovies and garlic chopped finely and mixed together. Rub veal with butter and ¼ teaspoon freshly cracked black pepper.

3. The boned veal will have a pocket for stuffing. Enlarge it if necessary, then sprinkle it lightly with salt and more freshly cracked black pepper and stuff it with the raisin-bread-crumb mixture. Sew with a trussing needle and string.

4. Place veal in a roasting pan. Cut 2 lemons into thin slices and cover surface of the veal with them.

5. Put bay leaves in pan and pour on ½ cup vermouth and ½ cup chicken or veal stock. Roast in a preheated 350° oven for 2 hours. Baste every ½ hour with a bulb baster. Take the pan from the oven and tilt it back and forth to lift the glaze. Keep 1 cup of liquid in the pan at all times, adding more stock or vermouth when needed.

6. At the end of 2 hours test veal by pricking it with a small sharp knife; if juices run pink, roast ½ hour longer.

7. Remove veal from roasting pan to carving board and keep warm. Strain juices into a saucepan. Deglaze roasting pan with vermouth or stock if needed; bring it to a boil, and loosen brown bits. Add to strained juices.

• Shoulder of veal is not fatty, but skim the mixture if necessary, leaving about 1 tablespoon of fat for flavor.

8. Stir heavy cream into mixture in saucepan and bring it to a boil. Boil until mixture thickens slightly. For a thicker sauce, mix potato starch in 1 tablespoon of cold water and add to sauce.

9. Before serving, remove trussing string and carve veal into neat slices with a portion of stuffing in each. Garnish with watercress and lemon slices cut from the remaining lemon. Pass the sauce separately.

• Potatoes Savoyard (see p. 184) and Whipped Carrots (see p. 170) are excellent as accompaniments for this roast. *Makes 8 servings.*

## STUFFED VEAL

The veal used for this recipe should be about 3 inches thick. It may be prepared ahead if desired—simply stuffed, or stuffed and baked—and stored in refrigerator. Undercook it if it is to be reheated.

1 4- to 5-lb. leg of veal, boned
½ teaspoon salt
¾ teaspoon freshly cracked
   black pepper
¾ cup dry Marsala wine
6 thinly sliced mushrooms
1 large diced truffle
¼ lb. chopped prosciutto
¼ cup grated Gruyère cheese
2 tablespoons melted butter,
   plus melted butter to brush
   on veal

1 tablespoon coarse salt
¼ cup bread crumbs (see p. 7)
¼ cup grated Parmesan cheese
2 tablespoons chopped shallots
½ cup chicken stock (see
   p. 241) or veal stock (see
   p. 242)

1. Lay veal flat on a cutting board, and with a large knife, slit it, lengthwise, not quite all the way through. Open it, like a book, and sprinkle with salt, ¼ teaspoon pepper, and 2 tablespoons of the Marsala.

2. Make stuffing by combining mushrooms, truffle, prosciutto, and Gruyère cheese. Pat it over bottom half of the veal and cover with top half. Sew around the three open sides with a large trussing needle and string.

3. Place veal in a baking pan, fatty side up. Brush it with melted butter and sprinkle with coarse salt and ½ teaspoon pepper.

4. Place in a preheated 350° oven to roast for a total of about 2 hours —25 minutes per pound, that is. During roasting period, baste 3 times with Marsala, using 2 tablespoons each time.

• To do this, take meat pan out of oven, sprinkle wine over the meat, then tilt pan back and forth to lift the glaze. This helps to mix the nice brown bits with the sauce.

5. Twenty minutes before roasting time is up, remove pan from oven, brush veal with more melted butter, and pat on a coating of bread crumbs, grated Parmesan cheese, and 2 tablespoons melted butter.

• The coating can be omitted if desired.

6. Return pan to oven for 20 minutes to finish cooking veal and to set coating.

• Test for doneness by pricking it with a small knife. If juices run pink, cook 20 minutes longer.

7. Remove pan from oven and place meat on a serving platter to keep warm.

8. Make sauce in the roasting pan, as follows. Pour off any excess fat and deglaze pan with the remaining ¼ cup of Marsala. Add chopped shallots and chicken or veal stock. Boil until syrupy. Remove trussing string, carve meat, and pour on sauce.

• Serve the veal with Chestnut Croquettes (see p. 173) and Celery Sticks (see p. 172). *Makes 8 to 10 servings.*

## VITELLO TONNATO

A marvelous cold dish—great for a summer buffet—from the north of Italy, Vitello Tonnato is even better when made ahead. Try to get a long cylindrical piece of veal for it, or have the meat rolled and tied to make this ideal shape. Ask for the bones too.

*1 4-lb. piece of boned veal, shoulder, rack, leg, or rump, and bones from the veal*
*4 chopped anchovy fillets*
*1 clove chopped garlic*
*¾ cup chopped onion*
*½ cup chopped carrot*
*1 teaspoon salt*
*½ teaspoon freshly cracked white pepper*
*Bouquet garni (see p. 7)*

*1½ cups chicken stock (see p. 241)*
*1 cup dry white wine*
*1 13-oz. can white tuna*
*1 cup mayonnaise (see p. 251)*
*2 tablespoons chopped capers*
*1 lemon*
*2 tablespoons chopped parsley*

1. With a small sharp knife, make little slits, about 1 inch deep, all over the veal. Using the knife blade as a slide, stuff bits of anchovy into the slits.

2. Put the veal and the bones into a large heavy casserole and add the garlic, onion, carrot, salt and pepper, and the bouquet garni.

3. Pour on chicken stock and wine, then add the tuna, with its oil. Bring to a boil, skim, cover casserole and reduce heat to simmer. Cook for 2 hours.

4. Remove bouquet garni and veal bones and let veal cool in the stock, which will jell as it cools.

5. Remove veal from casserole, scraping off any jelled stock, and carve the veal in very thin slices. Arrange them, overlapping, on a large oval platter.

6. Make sauce by putting the stock and vegetables through a blender or puréeing them through a food mill or sieve, chilling for 1 hour, then beating in the mayonnaise. Spoon the sauce over the sliced veal and sprinkle the slices with chopped capers.

7. Garnish the platter with chopped parsley and serrated slices of lemon made by using a lemon stripper to carve grooves at ¼-inch intervals from end to end of lemon, then cutting the lemon into thin slices.

• Serve with Rice Salad (see p. 197), either plain or stuffed into hollowed-out tomatoes. *Makes 8 servings.*

## SALTIMBOCCA

I agree with the Romans who gave this dish its name—it means "jump into the mouth." To make the best possible saltimbocca, get the palest pink veal available. By European standards, most U.S. veal is too robust, the pink-to-red color indicating that the animal has already been weaned from milk to grain or grass and that the flesh is less tender than it would otherwise be. Ideally, the slices for saltimbocca should be cut from the leg right above the knee.

*8 ¼-inch slices of veal, cut from leg*
*½ cup grated Parmesan cheese*
*8 paper-thin slices prosciutto*
*¾ cup dry Marsala wine, about*
*8 small sage leaves, or 1 teaspoon dried sage leaves*
*3 tablespoons butter*
*1 tablespoon olive oil*
*1 medium clove chopped garlic*
*¼ teaspoon thyme*

*½ teaspoon salt*
*¼ teaspoon freshly cracked black pepper*
*1 teaspoon tomato paste*
*¾ cup beef stock (see p. 240), about*
*1 tablespoon lemon juice*
*1 teaspoon potato starch or arrowroot, optional*
*8 large fluted sautéed mushroom caps (see p. 11)*
*2 tablespoons chopped parsley*

1. Lay veal slices on waxed paper and sprinkle with grated Parmesan cheese, then cover with another sheet of waxed paper and pound with the side of a cleaver to flatten the veal and work the cheese into it.

2. Remove waxed paper and lay a slice of prosciutto on each slice of veal.

• Prosciutto, an imported air-cured Italian ham, is available in most Italian markets. As a substitute, use Westphalian ham; have it sliced paper thin.

3. Brush ham slices with a little dry Marsala—use about 2 tablespoons in all.

• If dry Marsala is not available, substitute dry Madeira.

4. Lay a small leaf of fresh (⅛ teaspoon of dried) sage on each slice of ham.

5. Roll ham and veal carefully but loosely. Tie with string.

6. Heat butter and olive oil in a skillet, and when mixture is hot and no longer foaming, brown veal rolls over high heat on all sides. Brown a few at a time, and do not crowd the pan—in particular, do not let the rolls touch each other, for if they do touch, the result is braised, not browned, meat.

7. When all the rolls are browned, place them in the pan and flame with 2 tablespoons of dry Marsala—that is, warm the wine in a small, long-handled pan, then ignite it and while it is flaming, pour it over the veal rolls.

8. Remove rolls from pan and stir in garlic, thyme, salt, pepper, and tomato paste. Add beef stock and ½ cup dry Marsala. Stir to loosen brown bits. Return rolls to pan and cook over low heat, covered, for about 15 minutes.

9. When meat is done, remove to serving platter and keep warm. Add lemon juice to pan sauce, then taste for the seasoning.

10. Boil the sauce for a few minutes to reduce it slightly, or thicken it with potato starch smoothed into 1 tablespoon cold beef stock or Marsala.

11. Remove strings from rolls and place them in a serving dish (I like to use an oval one), then pour sauce over and place a mushroom cap on each roll. Sprinkle chopped parsley over all. *Makes 6 to 8 servings.*

## VEAL DECAMERON

Boned chicken breasts can be substituted for the veal in this recipe. The only difference is that chicken breasts must cook in the sauce for 15 rather than 5 minutes.

8 large fresh or canned artichoke bottoms

3 tablespoons butter, plus butter to brush on artichoke bottoms

8 veal scallops, cut from leg, as round as possible and about ¼ inch thick

2 tablespoons Calvados or apple brandy

1 tablespoon lemon juice

1½ cups sliced mushrooms

1 teaspoon salt

½ teaspoon freshly cracked white pepper

2 tablespoons chopped shallots

½ cup dry white wine

2 tablespoons fresh tarragon, or 2 teaspoons dried

1 cup chicken stock (see p. 241)

½ teaspoon tomato paste

1 teaspoon meat glaze (see p. 244)

1¼ cups heavy cream

2 tablespoons grated Parmesan cheese

1 teaspoon potato starch, optional

8 slices of truffle

1. If freshly cooked artichoke bottoms are used, arrange them, still warm, on a serving dish and brush them with melted butter; if canned artichoke bottoms are used, drain, wash in cold water, and pat dry, then

brush with melted butter and put in a low (250°) oven to warm before placing on serving dish. Keep them warm while proceeding with recipe.

2. Melt 2 tablespoons butter in a skillet, and when it is hot and no longer foaming, sauté the veal, a few pieces at a time, over high heat, until lightly browned. This will take about 2 minutes for each side. Do not crowd the pan; do not let pieces touch.

3. When all pieces are sautéed, return them to pan and flame with Calvados—that is, warm the Calvados in a small long-handled pan, then ignite it, and while it is flaming, pour it over the veal. Shake pan until flames die, then remove veal and keep it warm.

4. Add 1 tablespoon butter to the skillet, if needed, and heat until foaming. Add sliced mushrooms and sprinkle over them 2 teaspoons lemon juice, ½ teaspoon salt, and ¼ teaspoon pepper. Sauté by shaking them over high heat for 3 minutes. Remove mushrooms from pan and set aside.

5. Add shallots and wine to pan and cook, stirring, over high heat to lift the glaze, until wine is reduced by half.

6. Remove pan from heat and stir in tarragon, chicken stock, tomato paste, meat glaze, and heavy cream. Season with remaining ½ teaspoon of salt and ¼ teaspoon of pepper. Stir in grated Parmesan cheese and remaining 1 teaspoon of lemon juice. Return to high heat and cook, stirring, until mixture thickens slightly. Or thicken it, if desired, with 1 teaspoon potato starch mixed with 1 tablespoon cold water.

7. Return mushrooms and veal to pan and continue cooking gently for 5 more minutes.

8. Put 1 veal scallop on each artichoke bottom, pour pan sauce over veal, and garnish each piece with a slice of truffle. *Makes 8 servings.*

## VEAL VIENNOISE

The veal cooks in minutes, so have all the garnishes ready and at hand. They make a beautiful platter!

1 lemon
1 2-oz. can flat anchovy fillets
3 hard-cooked eggs
8 veal scallops cut from leg, as round as possible, and about ¼ inch thick
½ teaspoon baking powder
¾ cup flour
1 tablespoon vegetable oil

2 eggs
¾ cup bread crumbs (see p. 7)
9 tablespoons butter
½ cup dry white wine
12 olives, stuffed with pimientos, sliced thin
2 tablespoons chopped parsley

1. Using a lemon stripper, carve grooves from end to end of lemon, making them about ¼ inch apart. Cut lemon into thin slices, making at least 8. The edges will be serrated.

2. Put anchovy fillets in a sieve and rinse them in cold water. Pat them dry on paper towels.

3. Peel hard-cooked eggs, chop the whites, and work the yolks through a sieve.

4. Place the veal scallops between 2 sheets of waxed paper and pound them paper thin with the side of a cleaver or the bottom of a heavy skillet.

5. Stir baking powder into the flour. Beat oil into the eggs. Dip veal pieces in the flour mixture, shake off excess, then dip into egg mixture and roll in bread crumbs.

• Breading is fast and neat done this way: line up 3 bowls, 1 for flour, 1 for egg, 1 for bread crumbs, and next to them place a baking tray; work from bowl to bowl, ending with breaded food on tray.

• Veal can be breaded in the morning, covered loosely with waxed paper, and refrigerated, but because the scallops are thin, they dry out too quickly to be reheated satisfactorily.

6. Melt ½ cup of the butter in a skillet. When it is hot and no longer foaming, sauté breaded veal over high heat 3 minutes on each side. Do a few pieces at a time; do not crowd them—in particular, do not let them touch each other. Remove sautéed veal to serving platter and keep warm.

• The sautéed scallops can be held in a low oven for 15 minutes. But remember, this is really a last-minute dish.

7. Deglaze the pan with wine by boiling it for a minute, then scraping up the brown bits. Swirl in the remaining 1 tablespoon of butter, then pour over veal.

8. Place a serrated lemon slice on each piece of veal, with anchovy fillets crisscrossing the lemon slices. Use the rest of the lemon slices and the egg whites and yolks, the olive slices, and the chopped parsley to fill in spaces between the veal so that the platter doesn't show through.

• The platter looks prettiest if colors are placed symmetrically—i.e., chopped egg whites on opposite sides of it. *Makes 6 to 8 servings.*

## VEAL PICCATA

| | |
|---|---|
| 2 lbs. veal, cut from leg, ¼ inch thick | 2 tablespoons butter |
| ½ cup flour, about | 2 tablespoons olive oil |
| 1 teaspoon salt | 2 tablespoons lemon juice |
| ½ teaspoon freshly cracked white pepper | ¼ cup dry Marsala, optional |
| | 2 tablespoons chicken stock (see p. 241) |

1. Cut veal in 2-inch squares. Place them between 2 sheets of waxed paper and pound paper thin with the side of a cleaver or the bottom of a heavy skillet.

2. Dip veal pieces in flour, shaking off excess, then season with salt and pepper.

3. Heat butter and oil in a skillet. When it is hot and no longer foaming, brown veal over high heat, a few pieces at a time, 2 minutes on each side.

4. Return all pieces to pan, add lemon juice, Marsala (if desired), and chicken stock. Cook 2 minutes over high heat. Remove veal to a warm serving platter and pour pan sauce over it. *Makes 4 to 6 servings.*

## VEAL CASSEROLE

| | |
|---|---|
| 1 cup plump white raisins | 2 teaspoons lemon juice |
| 1 cup white wine | 2 1-lb. cans (about 1½ cups) |
| 4 lbs. veal, cut from the leg | small artichoke hearts |
| into 1-inch cubes | 3 tablespoons flour |
| ¼ cup butter | 1½ cups chicken stock (see |
| ¼ cup cognac | p. 241) |
| 2 cups sliced mushrooms | Bouquet garni (see p. 7) |
| ¼ teaspoon salt | 1½ cups dairy sour cream |
| ⅛ teaspoon freshly cracked | |
| white pepper | |

1. Soak raisins in wine for 1 hour.

2. Dry veal with paper towels. Melt ¼ cup butter in a large heavy casserole, and when foaming subsides, brown veal over high heat, on all sides, a few cubes at a time. Use tongs to turn them. Do not crowd the pan or let the veal cubes touch each other.

3. When all the cubes are browned, place them in the casserole and flame them with cognac—that is, warm the cognac in a small long-handled pan, light it, and pour it, flaming, over the veal.

4. When flames die down, remove veal and set aside. Drain and dry raisins, saving the wine, then add 2 tablespoons butter to casserole and sauté raisins briskly for 2 to 3 minutes. Remove raisins and set aside.

5. Add 2 more tablespoons butter to casserole. When butter is hot and no longer foaming, sauté mushrooms for 3 minutes, first seasoning them with ¼ teaspoon salt, ⅛ teaspoon pepper, and 2 teaspoons lemon juice. Remove and set aside.

6. Add 2 more tablespoons butter to casserole; drain, rinse, and dry artichoke hearts and sauté them for 3 to 5 minutes. Remove and set aside.

7. Add 2 more tablespoons butter to casserole. When it melts, blend in flour smoothly to make a roux. Cook it, stirring, for 2 minutes, but do not let it brown.

8. Remove casserole from heat, add chicken stock and whisk vigorously. Return to heat and cook, stirring constantly, until mixture comes to a boil, then add wine drained from raisins, season with ½ teaspoon salt and ¼ teaspoon pepper, and add the bouquet garni.

9. Return veal to casserole and simmer for 30 to 40 minutes, or until meat is tender. During last 10 minutes of cooking, add mushrooms, raisins, and artichoke hearts.

10. Remove bouquet garni. Blend in sour cream and bring to a boil.

• When sauce is fortified with flour, as this one is, sour cream can be boiled without fear of curdling.

11. Serve with green noodles. Cook them according to package directions, drain, and dress with ½ cup of melted butter and chopped truffle. Season to taste with salt and freshly cracked pepper. *Makes 8 servings.*

## BLANQUETTE DE VEAU WITH RICE TIMBALES

4 lbs. veal cut from the leg, shoulder, or rump into 2-inch cubes, plus a few cubes of lamb breast meat for added flavor
3 teaspoons salt, about
½ teaspoon freshly cracked white pepper, about
6 cups chicken stock (see p. 241), about
2 tablespoons fresh lemon juice
1 bay leaf
1 cup sliced celery
1 cup leeks, whites plus 1 inch of the green, sliced
2 cups sliced carrots
¾ cup sliced onion
6 peppercorns
18 tiny white onions
Velouté Sauce (recipe follows)
2 tablespoons chopped parsley
Rice Timbales (see p. 187)

1. Sprinkle veal cubes with salt and pepper—use about 1 teaspoon of salt and ½ teaspoon of pepper—and let them stand for 1 hour to season well.

2. Put the cubes in a large flameproof casserole or saucepan and cover with 6 cups chicken stock. Bring slowly to a boil and skim the surface.

3. Add lemon juice, bay leaf, celery, leeks, carrots, sliced onion, peppercorns, and 2 teaspoons salt.

• Be sure to clean the leeks carefully: split them lengthwise and hold them under running water, separating the layers to rinse out all the sand.

4. When liquid returns to a boil, reduce heat, cover, and simmer 25 to 45 minutes or until meat is tender.

• Some veal will cook in 20 minutes; other veal will take 1 hour and 20 minutes. Take out a piece to test it.

5. Peel the tiny onions, then with a little pointed knife, cut an X in the root end of each onion (this will help keep the onion whole) and boil the onions in salted water to cover for 5 to 15 minutes, or until barely tender. Cooking time depends on the size of the onions; drain the onions and add them to the casserole when veal is almost done.

• A quick way to peel tiny onions is to put them into boiling water for 20 to 30 seconds, then to drain them, trim the root and stem ends, and rub the skins off under running water.

6. Before serving, drain veal and tiny onions. Add veal to the Velouté Sauce and arrange it on a large heated platter. Sprinkle chopped parsley over the top. Arrange the onions in mounds around the veal, and if it's possible, fish out the leeks and carrots and alternate them around the veal. Arrange Rice Timbales around the platter (tip out the molds onto it), 3 on each side, 1 at each end.

### Velouté Sauce with Mushrooms

| | |
|---|---|
| 5 tablespoons butter | ¼ to ½ cup heavy cream |
| ¼ cup flour | 2 egg yolks, optional |
| 1 teaspoon salt | 1½ cups mushrooms, sliced |
| ⅛ teaspoon cayenne pepper | 1 teaspoon lemon juice |
| ½ teaspoon Dijon mustard | ¼ teaspoon freshly cracked |
| 1 cup stock, strained from | white pepper |
| veal pot | |

1. Melt 3 tablespoons butter in a heavy saucepan, then add flour, ½ teaspoon salt, cayenne pepper, and mustard and work this with a wooden spatula, cooking over high heat for 3 minutes to cook the flour.

2. Remove pan from heat, pour in stock and whisk vigorously.

3. Return pan to heat and cook over high heat, whisking constantly, until mixture is thick.

4. Add ¼ cup heavy cream and simmer 10 minutes.

5. To enrich sauce, if desired, beat egg yolks in a small bowl with ¼ cup heavy cream; add a little bit of the hot mixture from the pan to the egg-cream mixture to warm it gradually; then add warmed egg mixture to pan and heat. Do not boil.

• If you are making the sauce ahead and planning to reheat it, do not enrich it, for when egg-enriched sauces are reheated there is a risk of curdling.

6. Heat remaining butter in skillet until foaming, add mushrooms, sprinkle with lemon juice, ½ teaspoon salt, and white pepper, and cook over high heat, shaking the skillet, for 3 minutes. Add mushrooms to sauce. *Makes 8 servings.*

## VEAL KIDNEYS

8 veal kidneys
1½ cups mushrooms
2 teaspoons lemon juice, plus lemon juice to clean mushrooms
6 tablespoons butter
1 teaspoon salt

¼ teaspoon freshly cracked white pepper
¼ cup cognac
1 tablespoon Dijon mustard
1½ cups heavy cream
¼ teaspoon freshly cracked black pepper

1. Soak kidneys in cold water for 1 hour, then carefully remove membrane, core, and any fat. Cut into 1-inch slices.

2. Wipe mushrooms clean with a paper towel dipped in acidulated water (water with lemon juice) and wipe dry. Trim off ends of stems and slice mushrooms vertically, through cap and stem.

3. Heat 3 tablespoons of butter in a large skillet, and when foaming subsides, add mushrooms and toss them over high heat for 3 minutes, adding 2 teaspoons lemon juice, ½ teaspoon salt, and white pepper. Remove mushrooms and set aside.

4. In the same pan, heat the remaining 3 tablespoons of butter. When it is hot and no longer foaming, sauté sliced veal kidneys over high heat for 2 minutes on each side.

5. Flame kidneys with cognac—that is, warm the cognac in a small long-handled pan, ignite it, and pour it, flaming, over the kidneys. Shake pan until flames die.

6. Stir in mustard and heavy cream and cook over high heat for a few minutes to reduce the sauce. Return mushrooms to pan and heat through. Season with the remaining ½ teaspoon of salt and the black pepper. Serve with rice. *Makes 8 servings.*

## CALVES' SWEETBREADS WITH MADEIRA SAUCE

2 large pairs calves' sweetbreads
¼ cup flour

¼ cup butter
2 tablespoons cognac
Madeira Sauce (see p. 250)

1. Put sweetbreads in a pan and cover them with cold water. Slowly bring them to a boil and cook them slowly, uncovered, for 5 to 7 minutes, depending on their size. Turn them over once during cooking.

2. Drain sweetbreads and plunge them immediately into iced water. This helps to keep them firm. Carefully remove all the skin, sinews, and tubes. Sweetbreads are very delicate.

3. Cut them in half lengthwise and lay them on a plate. Put another plate on top, weight it with something heavy, and place in a refrigerator for at least 1 hour.

4. When ready to cook, dry sweetbreads with paper towels and dust them lightly with flour.

5. Heat butter in a large skillet. When butter is foaming, add sweetbreads—do not let them touch each other—and cover them with a flat lid and weight, to keep them flat. Brown sweetbreads 1 minute on each side.

6. Flame sweetbreads with cognac—that is, warm the cognac in a small long-handled pan, light it, and pour it, flaming, into the skillet. Shake the pan until flames die, and scrape up the brown bits.

7. Arrange sweetbreads on a warm serving platter and spoon Madeira Sauce over them.

• Sweetbreads are good served with Pea Purée (see p. 182). *Makes 4 to 6 servings.*

# POULTRY

From Henri IV to Herbert Hoover, chicken has figured in political life. "A chicken in every pot"—remember the slogan?

Poultry is without doubt the cook's best friend. The number of recipes is almost endless. And most of the dishes in these pages aren't as extravagant as they sound. They may take a little time to make, but it is time well spent.

It helps to know the chicken family. Broilers weigh up to 2½ lbs., fryers are between 2 and 3½ lbs.; roasters start at 3½ lbs. and go to 5 or 6. Then there are stewing hens and capons, which reach the larger weights.

Mass production and artificial feeding make it increasingly difficult to find poultry of real flavor. If possible, poultry should be bought from a farmer or poulterer who specializes in freshly killed birds; next best is frozen.

Some of the recipes that follow involve boning and skinning chicken breasts (butchers and poulterers will bone them, but it's good to know how it should be done), boning a whole chicken or turkey, trussing, and carving. Here are the directions.

### How to Bone and Skin a Chicken Breast

1. Place the whole chicken breast (whole chicken breasts are easier to bone than are split ones) on a cutting board, breastbone up, and, if

you're right-handed, wishbone to the left. Then, with a short sharp boning knife or a 3-inch utility knife, make a slit the full length of the breast-bone.

2. Working first on the side away from you—it's easier to see what you're doing that way—use the knife with a cutting-scraping motion against the breastbone and rib bones, peeling back the flesh with your free hand as you cut.

3. Turn the breast around so that the wishbone is at the right; then free the other side in the same way.

4. Pull off the skin.

• Chicken breasts can be boned the day before they're to be used if, after boning, they're covered with plastic wrap and refrigerated. Bring breasts to room temperature before using.

### How to Bone a Chicken or Turkey

Before trying to bone a chicken or turkey, visualize what it is you're about to do. In boning a bird you work from the top of the bird down —that is from the neck to the vent—completely boning one side before beginning the other. Essentially, you'll open the skin at the back (along the backbone) and then cut and scrape against the rib cage and breastbone to free the flesh all in one piece—hopefully without cutting through the skin except for the original cut. There are a few roadblocks along the way: cutting through the leg and wing joints and freeing the wishbone (the tendons in these areas make them harder to cut through) and, at the very last, scraping flesh free from the ridge of the breastbone which is very close to the skin. But once tried, you'll find the job not at all difficult.

1. Place the bird on a cutting board, breast down, and if you're right-handed, neck to the left. Use a small, very sharp knife to make a slit along the backbone from neck to tail, then cut and scrape against the bones (the cutting edge of the knife should free the flesh by scraping the bones). With the hand that's not holding the knife (the thumb, mostly) push aside the flesh that's scraped loose.

2. The first obstacle to be faced is the bird's equivalent of a shoulder blade—a long, thin, flat bone on the back, floating loose. Scrape it free of flesh and continue on to the wing joint. Cut through it.

3. Now do the lower back. There's a nugget of flesh in a hollow on each side of the backbone, just above the ball joint of thigh. Scrape it out and cut through the thigh joint.

4. Continue down the side of the bird, scraping against the rib bones.

5. You'll come next to the breastbone, which is shaped like the keel of a boat. Scrape against it, but just to the ridge. Do the other side of the bird, again scraping just to the ridge.

6. Getting out the wishbone requires a bit of painstaking work, for this bone is buried in the flesh of the breast, between the "keel" and the neck. Scrape carefully all around this V-shaped bone to free it. Keep your goal in mind: to end with all the bones in one hand, all the flesh in the other.

7. Finally, very carefully, so as not to pierce the skin, scrape right along the ridge of the breastbone. This will free the carcass from the flesh.

• I usually leave the leg and wing bones in, to give the bird more shape, but take out the thigh bones if you wish. They're partly exposed and rather easy to do: scrape the flesh from around each until you can cut through the leg joint and remove the thigh bone.

• Taking out wing bones is harder, for there are several tendons in each wing, and you must virtually turn the flesh inside out until you expose the next joint. Do not remove the second bone of the wing.

• Do not remove the leg bones (drumsticks).

## How to Carve a Duck

INFORMAL METHOD: Place bird on its back and cut from neck to vent right next to breast. You may use poultry shears. Open wide. Turn over and cut back from neck to vent. Cut each half into 2 pieces making 4 pieces of duck in all.

FORMAL METHOD: Lay bird on its back on a carving board. Remove leg from carcass by cutting through skin close to carcass. Bend leg and thigh back to remove. Separate leg from thigh at the joint. Remove other leg in the same way. Carve off breast on one side all the way down to frame of the bird, taking wing off with breast. All breasts and wings should come off together. Lay breast on board and cut across on a diagonal giving 2 pieces of breast, one with wing attached. Repeat on other side.

## How to Truss a Bird (see illustrations, p. 128)

1. Cut a length—about 1 yard—of butcher's cord. Lay the bird on its back, tail toward you. Bring the cord under the tail and legs and loop it, making a half knot, then draw legs close to tail.

2. The string now has two equal ends. Pass each end of the cord between a leg and the body of the bird.

3. Flip the bird over, breast down, then go under the wings with the cord ends and bring the neck flap down over the bird's back.

4. Loop the cord over the flap, making a half knot to hold the flap in place.

5. Turn the bird onto its back again, then bring the cord ends over the wings and tie a knot on the breast.

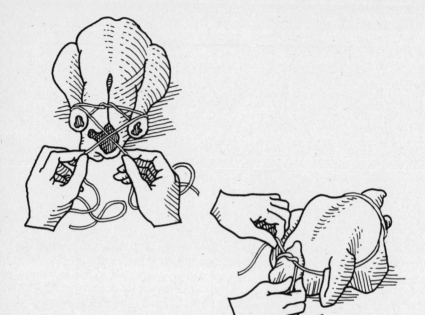

## Chicken Breasts Duxelles with White Wine Sauce

Here is the recipe that made my cooking school famous. It's an original with me, and it's the first entrée that I teach beginning students. When they show off what they learned at Saturday dinner parties, my phone starts ringing early Monday morning.

4 *whole chicken breasts*
2 *tablespoons cognac, plus cognac to brush on breasts*
Salt
*Freshly cracked white pepper*
1 *cup Duxelles (recipe follows*
¼ *cup butter, plus butter to brush on artichoke bottoms*
1 *medium clove finely chopped garlic*
2 *tablespoons finely chopped shallots*
1 *tablespoon chopped truffle*

1 *tablespoon chopped fresh tarragon, or 1 teaspoon dried*
1 *teaspoon meat glaze (see p. 244)*
1¼ *cups chicken stock (see p. 241)*
¼ *cup dry vermouth or other dry white wine*
2 *tablespoons chopped parsley*
8 *fluted and sautéed mushrooms (see p. 11)*
8 *canned artichoke bottoms*

1. Bone and skin chicken breasts (see directions, p. 125) and trim them into neat ovals. These are called *suprêmes;* there will be 8 of them, 2 from each breast.

• Reserve the bones and skin cut from the breast and use them in making chicken stock.

2. Cut pockets in the 8 suprêmes by laying each one flat on a cutting board, placing a hand on top to hold it, and cutting, not all the way through, from the thicker side.

3. Brush the insides of the pockets with a little cognac and sprinkle with salt and a few grains of pepper. Fill pockets with duxelles, but *don't stuff them too full.* Close pockets by pulling the top over the bottom and pressing it with your thumb.

• There's enough gelatin in chicken to hold the edges together, providing the pockets haven't been stuffed too full. Browning the chicken breasts under a weighted lid will also help to keep the pockets closed. It isn't necessary to sew them or to hold them together with toothpicks.

4. Heat butter in a large heavy skillet until it is foaming. Brown chicken quickly over high heat—just enough to be a little crusty (remember, this is not fried chicken)—on both sides, under a flat lid (or flat pan) pressed down with a 2- to 3-lb. weight. Brown what was the skin side first. Don't let suprêmes touch in the pan.

5. Remove the chicken from the pan, pour off all but 1 tablespoon of fat, take the pan off heat, and lift the glaze with 2 tablespoons of cognac heated in a small long-handled pan until it is warm to the touch, then lighted and poured into the chicken pan. When flames die down, scrape up the brown bits that have been loosened by the cognac.

6. Make sauce as follows. Add garlic and shallots to pan and cook for 1 minute over high heat. Stir in truffle and tarragon, then add meat glaze, chicken stock, and wine. Bring to a boil while stirring and boil to reduce the sauce by one third. It will thicken by itself.

• When using dried herbs it's a good idea to rub them between the palms of your hands, over the pan, and drop them in. Rubbing releases their flavor.

• Dried herbs can be substituted for fresh herbs (vice versa) but not in the same amounts. Since dried herbs have more intense flavor than do fresh ones, use one third as much of the dried herbs as you would of the fresh.

7. Return chicken breasts to pan and baste them once with the sauce.

• The recipe can be prepared in advance to this point, with final cooking of chicken breasts done just before serving. Cover the pan and store it in a refrigerator for no longer than 24 hours. Let the chicken breasts and sauce come to room temperature before continuing.

8. Turn heat to simmer and cook chicken breasts, covered, until tender, about 15 to 18 minutes. Don't overcook them.

• The only place you might run into trouble with this recipe is here. Boned chicken breasts don't take long to cook, and once overcooked, they're as hard as rocks. To test for doneness, press them with a fork: if the flesh is still soft, the breasts are not done; if the flesh springs back when touched, they are.

9. Before serving, arrange suprêmes in a large au gratin dish and coat with sauce. Sprinkle with chopped parsley, and in addition, garnish with fluted mushrooms and with artichoke bottoms that have been rinsed and dried, then brushed with butter and heated through in a 325° oven. *Makes 8 servings.*

### Duxelles

Duxelles, which *Larousse Gastronomique* defines as "a kind of mushroom hash," is one of the most useful basics in cooking, worth keeping on hand at all times. Frozen, it can be stored almost indefinitely, and it will keep in a refrigerator for up to 10 days. There are literally dozens of uses for duxelles. Here are a few: when baking a fish, fill it with duxelles; combine duxelles with bread crumbs and use to stuff chicken; hollow out whole tomatoes or (for a sensational hot hors d'oeuvre) little cherry tomatoes, spoon duxelles in the shells, and bake; combine duxelles with mashed hard-cooked egg yolks and pack them back into the whites; or spread duxelles on Melba toast, sprinkle with grated Parmesan cheese and melted butter, and heat under a broiler.

*¼ lb. very finely chopped mushrooms*
*¼ cup butter*
*¼ cup finely chopped shallots*

*½ teaspoon salt*
*¼ teaspoon freshly cracked black pepper*

1. Put the chopped mushrooms in the corner of a tea towel and wring them out to get rid of excess liquid.
2. Melt butter in a skillet, and when it is foaming, add the chopped shallots. Cook over high heat for a few minutes, stirring with a wooden spatula, until shallots are transparent. Don't let them brown.
3. Add mushrooms and cook 15 to 20 minutes, stirring constantly with wooden spatula, until the mushrooms look dry. Season with salt and pepper and cool. *Makes about 1 cup.*

## Petti di Pollo

| | |
|---|---|
| 4 whole chicken breasts | ¾ cup grated Swiss cheese |
| 1 teaspoon salt | ¾ cup chopped prosciutto |
| ½ teaspoon freshly cracked white pepper | ¼ cup dry Marsala wine |
| ¾ cup flour, about | 1 cup Basic Brown Sauce (see p. 248) |
| ¼ cup butter | 2 tablespoons tomato paste |
| 2 tablespoons vegetable oil | |

1. Bone and skin chicken breasts (see directions, p. 125).
2. Lay the 8 pieces of chicken on waxed paper, with what was the skin side facing down. Cover them with another sheet of waxed paper and pound them thin with the flat side of a cleaver.
3. Season with salt and pepper and dip in flour, shaking off the excess.
4. Heat 2 tablespoons butter and the oil in a heavy skillet. When hot and no longer foaming, sauté chicken quickly over high heat for 1 minute on each side.
5. Melt the remaining butter and brush a baking dish with it. Transfer chicken pieces to baking dish, leaving a little space between them if possible. Mound ham and then cheese on top of each piece. Set aside.
6. Deglaze the skillet by pouring in wine and cooking over high heat for 1 minute, scraping up the brown bits.
7. Make sauce by stirring in Brown Sauce and tomato paste and bringing to a boil.
8. Pour sauce around chicken in baking dish. Place in a preheated 325° oven to bake until chicken is tender, about 10 to 15 minutes.

• To test for doneness, press chicken breasts with a fork: if the flesh is still soft, the breasts are not done; if the flesh springs back when touched, they are.
• Serve with Sautéed Mushroom Caps and Pine Nuts (see p. 176). **Makes 8 servings.**

## Chicken Pajorsky

| | |
|---|---|
| 3 whole chicken breasts | ½ teaspoon freshly cracked white pepper |
| 1 cup unsalted butter | ¼ teaspoon freshly grated nutmeg |
| 2 egg whites | |
| 2 slices bread | |
| ½ cup heavy cream | ¾ cup flour |
| 1½ teaspoons salt | 2 beaten eggs |

1 tablespoon vegetable oil,     ¼ cup cognac
optional     1 bunch watercress
¾ cup fine dry bread crumbs
(see p.7)

1. Bone and skin chicken breasts (see directions, p. 125). Work the flesh through a meat grinder, using the finest blade, or chop it finely with a knife.

2. Put ground chicken into mixer bowl and (with the flat whip if the mixer is a heavy-duty one) beat in ¼ cup of softened butter. Add egg whites and beat until mixture is well blended, about 5 to 10 minutes.

3. Trim crusts from bread, then cut in cubes, and soak in heavy cream until soft.

4. Mash cubes with a fork to make a paste, add to chicken mixture, and beat well. Season with salt, pepper, and nutmeg. If mixture is too soft to shape, refrigerate until it stiffens, or about ½ hour.

5. Sprinkle board with flour. Drop 2 heaping tablespoonfuls of the chicken mixture on the board and with your hands form it into a kidney-shaped cutlet. Coat the cutlet completely with flour, shaking off excess.

6. Shape and flour the remaining mixture—mixture should yield 6 to 8 cutlets—then dip the floured cutlets first in beaten egg (add 1 tablespoon oil to the beaten eggs if you wish; it will help to make the coating adhere), then in bread crumbs.

7. Melt the remaining ¼ cup of butter in a skillet, and when foaming subsides, add cutlets (do not let them touch). Sauté over high heat for 3 minutes on each side. Then warm cognac in a small long-handled pan, ignite it, and pour it, flaming, over the cutlets.

8. Arrange cutlets on a round serving platter with watercress in the center. Pour pan juices over.

• If you want a sauce with these cutlets, Hollandaise Sauce (see p. 246) and Béarnaise Sauce (see p. 248) are excellent. Or make a Velouté Sauce (see p. 246) with chicken stock and fold in 2 tablespoons Duxelles (see p. 130). **Makes 6 servings.**

## CHICKEN À LA KIEV WITH PAPRIKA SAUCE

4 whole chicken breasts     ¾ cup flour, about
2 tablespoons cognac     2 beaten eggs
¾ cup frozen unsalted butter     ¾ cup bread crumbs (see
4 teaspoons fresh chopped     p. 7)
    chives     2 cups vegetable shortening
2 teaspoons dried tarragon     1 bunch watercress
1 teaspoon salt     Paprika Sauce (recipe fol-
½ teaspoon freshly cracked     lows), optional
    white pepper

1. Bone and skin the chicken breasts (see directions, p. 125).

2. Lay the 8 pieces of chicken on waxed paper, with what was the skin side facing down. Cover them with another sheet of waxed paper and pound them thin with the flat side of a cleaver. Remove top piece of waxed paper.

3. Brush each piece of chicken with cognac.

4. Cut frozen butter into fingers and lay a finger of butter on each piece of chicken, along one side.

• When butter is frozen, it's much easier to handle and roll up in the chicken.

5. Sprinkle each piece of chicken with ½ teaspoon chopped chives, ¼ teaspoon tarragon, and salt and pepper.

• Classic Chicken Kiev has no herbs, only butter. But I think it's rather too bland. Instead of tarragon, you can use an equal amount of thyme or any other herb you prefer.

6. Roll edge of each piece of chicken over butter, tuck ends in to encase butter, and continue to roll like a jelly roll.

• The rolls don't have to be tied up or fastened with toothpicks; chicken is gelatinous and will adhere to itself.

7. One by one, dip chicken rolls in flour, shake off excess, dip in beaten egg, and roll in bread crumbs. Be sure to flour, egg, and crumb the ends.

8. Place rolls on a baking sheet or on a flat dish or pan, seam side down, and put them in a freezer for at least ½ hour or in a refrigerator for at least 1 hour.

• The rolls can be made ahead to this point and frozen for future use. Wrap them in plastic wrap or foil for storage.

9. Heat vegetable shortening to 375° in a deep-fat fryer or heavy saucepan.

• Use a fat thermometer to check temperature. Or test with a bread cube: if it browns nicely in 1 minute, the fat is about the right temperature. A thermometer is surer.

10. Fry rolls 2 at a time (if too many are put into fat at once, the temperature of the fat drops too low to cook the rolls properly), turning to brown both sides. It will take a total of about 5 minutes to cook 2 rolls. When they are deep golden brown, remove them from fat with a slotted spoon and drain on paper towels. Be sure fat is back to 375° before frying more rolls.

11. Arrange rolls on a serving platter, garnish with a bunch of watercress, and either serve as is or with Paprika Sauce, strained and poured over the rolls.

*Paprika Sauce*

½ cup finely chopped onion
2 tablespoons butter
½ cup dry white wine
2 tablespoons sweet Hungarian paprika
2 cups Velouté Sauce made with chicken stock (see p. 246)

Bouquet garni (see p. 7)
½ teaspoon salt
¼ teaspoon freshly cracked white pepper

1. Cook onion in butter over high heat until transparent. Stir with a wooden spatula, and don't let the onion brown.
2. Add wine and cook over medium heat until wine is reduced by half.
3. Remove from heat. Stir in paprika and Velouté Sauce. Add bouquet garni, salt and pepper, and simmer for at least ½ hour. *Makes 8 servings.*

## COLD CHICKEN MOUSSE

3 whole chicken breasts
2 cups chicken stock (see p. 241)
½ cup chopped carrot
¾ cup chopped onion
½ cup chopped celery
1 cup butter
¼ cup flour
1½ cups milk
1 teaspoon salt
½ teaspoon freshly cracked white pepper

2 tablespoons chopped parsley
2 teaspoons dried tarragon
3 tablespoons dairy sour cream
Vegetable oil to grease mold
1 bunch watercress
1 cup cherry tomatoes and/ or black olives

1. Put chicken breasts in a saucepan and cover with chicken stock. Add carrot, onion, and celery and bring to a boil. Reduce heat to simmer, cover, and cook for 20 minutes. Cool breasts in the stock.
2. Meanwhile, make a *panade*, or thickening agent, by melting ¼ cup of butter in a small saucepan, stirring in flour with a wooden spatula, and cooking over high heat, stirring, for 2 minutes (do not let the mixture brown), then removing from heat and adding milk, whisking vigorously, returning to high heat and cooking 3 minutes, stirring, until very thick. Pour the panade into a baking dish and chill in a refrigerator about ½ hour or until set.
3. When chicken is cool enough to handle, remove skin and bones and

work the meat through a meat grinder, using the finest blade, or chop finely with a knife.

4. Put the ground chicken into a bowl and beat in ¾ cup of softened butter either with a mixer (use the flat whip, if it's a heavy-duty mixer) or, over ice, with a wooden spatula.

• If you are beating the mixture by hand, chilling it causes the natural gelatin in the chicken to react to thicken it and thus helps compensate for the lack of the forcefulness of the mixer beating.

5. Beat in the chilled panade and add salt, pepper, parsley, tarragon, and sour cream. Mix thoroughly.

6. Pour the mixture into an oiled 1-quart mold or soufflé dish, cover with waxed paper, and put it in refrigerator to chill at least 3 hours.

• This can be done the day before the mousse is to be served.
• To unmold, run a little knife around the edge of the mold, using an up-and-down motion, put a serving plate over the mold, invert, give a shake, and lift off mold.

7. Garnish with watercress and with cherry tomatoes and/or black olives.

• If a ring mold was used, fill center with cherry tomatoes, or if you like with Cucumber Salad with Yoghurt (see p. 193). *Makes 6 servings.*

### POACHED CHICKEN CUTLETS

This is an exquisite dish, made by packing a chicken mousse mixture into cutlet molds and poaching in chicken stock. As the mousse cooks, it floats out of the molds in light and lovely cutlet shapes. The molds, which are about 4 inches long and ½ inch deep, are available in most gourmet shops. For this recipe, 8 to 10 are needed.

| | |
|---|---|
| 2 *whole chicken breasts* | ½ *cup flour* |
| 3 *egg whites* | 1 *egg* |
| 1 *cup light cream* | 2 *tablespoons dairy sour* |
| 1 *tablespoon chopped shal-* | *cream* |
| *lot* | 2 *tablespoons cognac* |
| 1 *medium clove chopped* | 2 *quarts chicken stock (see* |
| *garlic* | *p. 241)* |
| 3 *tablespoons butter, plus* | 1½ *cups Velouté Sauce made* |
| *butter to grease molds* | *with chicken stock (see* |
| 1½ *teaspoons salt* | *p. 246)* |
| ½ *teaspoon freshly cracked* | ⅓ *cup heavy cream* |
| *white pepper* | 8 *to 10 slices truffle* |
| 2 *teaspoons dried tarragon* | 1 *bunch watercress* |

1. Bone and skin chicken breasts (see directions, p. 125), then work the flesh through a meat grinder, using the finest blade, or chop finely with a knife.

• The discarded bones and skin can be used in making the chicken stock.

2. Put ground chicken into a bowl, add 2 egg whites, and beat—either with a mixer (use the flat whip if it's a heavy-duty mixer) or, over ice, with a wooden spatula—until smooth and fluffy.

3. Add light cream, 1 tablespoonful at a time, and beat it in.

4. Cook shallot and garlic at high heat in 2 tablespoons of butter until transparent. Do not let it brown. Beat it into chicken mixture along with 1 teaspoon salt, pepper, and tarragon.

5. Make the panade, or thickening agent, by putting ½ cup of water, ½ teaspoon of salt, and 1 tablespoon of butter into a small saucepan, bringing to a rolling boil, and immediately, all at once, dumping in ½ cup of flour, then beating over high heat with a wooden spatula until the mixture is smooth and leaves the side of the pan, then removing from heat and thoroughly beating in the whole egg and the 1 remaining egg white.

6. Add panade, a spoonful at a time, to chicken mixture, beating it in. Beat in sour cream and cognac.

7. Butter 8 to 10 cutlet molds and fill them with the chicken mixture, smoothing off tops with a wet spatula. Bang the molds on a table to settle the mixture.

• The cutlets can be made ahead to this point and poached at the last minute. Cover the filled molds with waxed paper and store in a refrigerator. Let the molds come to room temperature before poaching.

8. Fill a 4-quart saucepan half full of chicken stock and bring to a boil. Then reduce heat to simmer, drop in the molds, bottoms down (stock should cover the molds), and poach gently for about 15 minutes, or until the mousse floats out of the molds and to the surface of the stock.

9. Gently lift the mousse cutlets out of the stock with a slotted spoon and arrange them in a circle on a warm round platter.

10. Pour a ribbon of Velouté Sauce over each cutlet, first thinning the Velouté with a little heavy cream. Garnish each cutlet with a slice of truffle. Place a bunch of watercress in the center of the platter.

• If dinner is delayed, the cutlets will hold for a short while, about 15 minutes, in a warm oven. *Makes 4 to 5 servings of 2 cutlets each.*

## HUNGARIAN CHICKEN PAPRIKA

1 3½-lb. chicken
1½ teaspoons salt
¾ teaspoon freshly cracked
   white pepper
6 tablespoons butter
½ cup sliced carrot
1 cup sliced celery
1 cup chopped yellow onion
¼ cup medium sweet Hun-
   garian paprika

¼ cup flour
2 tablespoons tomato paste
2 cups strong chicken stock
   (see p. 241)
1 cup dairy sour cream
2 green and/or red peppers
   cut into rings

1. Wash and dry chicken and cut into 6 serving pieces, leaving wings attached to breast meat. Season with 1 teaspoon salt and ½ teaspoon pepper.

2. Melt ¼ cup of butter in a heavy casserole. When foaming subsides, add chicken pieces and brown all over, over high heat, turning with wooden spatulas. Don't let pieces touch. Remove chicken from casserole and set aside.

3. Add the remaining 2 tablespoons of butter to casserole. When hot, stir in carrot, celery, and onion and cook over high heat 5 to 7 minutes, or until onion is transparent but not brown.

4. Add paprika, blending it in with a spatula. Stir in flour and cook at high heat for a couple of minutes until completely blended, stirring constantly. Add tomato paste, remaining ½ teaspoon of salt, remaining ¼ teaspoon of pepper and pour in chicken stock, stirring vigorously. Bring to a boil, reduce to a simmer, and cook, covered, about 20 minutes, or until vegetables are tender but not mushy.

5. Pour into a blender jar (to avoid overflows, never fill a blender more than half full of a hot mixture) and purée.

6. Return mixture to casserole, add browned chicken pieces—slit the legs to the bone so they'll cook in the same length of time as the breast meat—cover, and simmer until chicken is tender, about 20 minutes (to test for tenderness, prick flesh with fork; juice should run clear).

7. Arrange chicken pieces on a platter and keep warm. Whisk sour cream, 1 tablespoon at a time, into sauce in the casserole and heat through.

• You can even boil this sauce; it won't curdle—the flour in it does the trick.

8. Pour sauce over chicken. Garnish with blanched pepper rings overlapped on top of chicken.

• Serve with rice, Italian Gnocchi (see p. 180), noodles, or Spaetzle (see p. 181). *Makes 4 to 6 servings.*

## CHICKEN DAUPHINOISE

I adapted this from a recipe made popular by Jean Noel Escudier, an authority on Provençale cooking, better known as Monsieur Provence. The original recipe calls for 40 to 50 cloves of garlic! But garlic in Provence is not as strong as that in the United States. Blanching the garlic first removes some of the pungency.

| | |
|---|---|
| 30 *medium cloves garlic* | 1 *teaspoon salt* |
| 3 *to 4 lbs. chicken pieces, breasts, thighs, legs, or a combination* | ½ *teaspoon freshly cracked white pepper* |
| 2 *tablespoons olive oil* | ½ *cup chicken stock (see p. 241)* |
| 3 *tablespoons butter* | 2 *tablespoons chopped parsley* |
| 1 *small bay leaf* | |
| ½ *teaspoon thyme* | ¼ *cup dry white wine* |

1. Peel the garlic cloves (30 cloves is correct) and put them into a saucepan. Blanch them by covering with cold water, bringing to a boil, and cooking 2 minutes at a rapid boil. Drain the cloves in a sieve and pat them dry with paper towels.

2. Wash and dry the chicken pieces. Then heat oil and 2 tablespoons of butter in a heavy skillet (or a casserole) and sauté the pieces over high heat for about 15 minutes, or until brown. Do not let chicken pieces touch: do only as many at one time as the pan (or casserole) will accommodate. Turn them with wooden spatulas to brown evenly.

3. When chicken is golden brown, remove from skillet and set aside.

4. Add the remaining 1 tablespoon of butter to the skillet. Add blanched garlic and sauté, over medium heat, stirring the cloves around until they're well coated with butter; do not let them brown.

5. Return the chicken pieces to the skillet. (If you have included legs, slit them to the bone so they'll cook in the same length of time as the breasts.) Add bay leaf and thyme, sprinkle with salt and pepper, and add chicken stock. Bring to a boil, reduce heat to simmer, then cover the skillet and cook very gently for about ½ hour, or until chicken is tender.

6. Remove the chicken to a platter. Scoop up the garlic cloves with a slotted spoon and scatter them over the chicken. Sprinkle with chopped parsley.

7. Deglaze the skillet by adding wine and bringing it to a boil. Scrape up the brown bits and boil to reduce the mixture a little. Check seasoning, and pour over chicken. *Makes 6 servings.*

## CHICKEN IN A SEALED POT

*3 to 4 lbs. chicken pieces, breasts, thighs, legs, or a combination*
*6 tablespoons butter*
*¼ cup cognac*
*18 small white onions*
*2 large fluted sautéed mushroom caps (see p. 11)*
*1 medium clove finely chopped garlic*
*2 teaspoons potato starch*
*½ teaspoon meat glaze (see p. 244)*

*1 bay leaf*
*¼ teaspoon thyme*
*¾ cup chicken stock (see p. 241)*
*½ teaspoon salt*
*½ teaspoon freshly cracked white pepper*
*1 cup dry red Burgundy*
*2 cups flour*
*1 egg yolk*
*2 tablespoons chopped parsley*

1. Wash and dry the chicken pieces. Then melt ¼ cup of butter in a heavy 3- to 4-quart casserole, and when foaming subsides, brown chicken, over high heat, a few pieces at a time. Do not let the pieces touch. Turn them with wooden spatulas to brown evenly, and don't prick them with a fork. It takes about 15 minutes to brown chicken nicely.

2. Put all the browned pieces in the casserole and flame with 2 tablespoons cognac—that is, warm the cognac in a small long-handled pan, ignite it, and pour it, flaming, over the chicken.

3. Peel the onions (the smaller they are, the better), then, in a frying pan, melt 2 tablespoons butter and brown them, over high heat, shaking the pan so they roll around and brown evenly. Add to chicken in casserole.

• If you can't get small onions, cut larger ones in half or boil them 15 minutes before browning.
• To peel onions the easy way, drop them into boiling water for 30 seconds before removing the skins.

4. Add sautéed mushroom caps to chicken in casserole.

5. Make sauce by stirring the potato starch and meat glaze into the butter and juices remaining in the pan, then adding garlic, bay leaf, thyme, chicken stock, salt, pepper, and wine and bringing to a boil, stirring constantly.

6. Pour sauce over chicken in casserole, add the remaining 2 table-spoons of cognac, and seal the casserole with a lute (sealing paste) made by mixing flour with 1 cup of water to form a paste, laying it on a board and rolling it into a long rope. Place the rope around the rim of the casserole and press the lid on top, tightly. Press the lute with fork tines, and brush it with egg yolk mixed with 1 tablespoon water so it will shine.

7. Put the sealed casserole into a preheated 350° oven and bake for 45 minutes.

8. Bring the sealed casserole to the table and break the seal (you may need a chisel and a small hammer) there—the fragrance is glorious! Sprinkle with chopped parsley before serving. *Makes 6 servings.*

## ROAST CHICKEN BALLOTINE

A ballottine is a fowl or piece of meat that is boned, stuffed, and pressed back into shape, usually served hot. This one is stuffed—ever so de-liciously—with chicken mousse, tongue (or ham), and pistachio nuts, and it's excellent served hot or cold.

| | |
|---|---|
| 1 3½-lb. chicken | 1 tablespoon chopped truffle |
| 2 whole chicken breasts | 8 slices bacon |
| 2 egg whites | ¼ cup melted butter, plus |
| 1½ cups light cream | butter to brush on arti- |
| 6 tablespoons cognac | choke bottoms |
| 1 teaspoon salt | 8 fluted and sautéed mush- |
| ½ teaspoon freshly cracked | room caps (see p. 11) |
| white pepper | 1 bunch watercress |
| ½ cup natural pistachio nuts | 8 canned artichoke bottoms |
| ¼ lb. tongue or ham | |

1. Wash and dry chicken and bone it (see directions, p. 126). Cut off the wing tips and the knobby ends of the leg bones. This is done so the bird will look more shapely when it's re-formed.

• The carcass can be used to make chicken stock.

2. Prepare chicken mousse as follows. Bone and skin chicken breasts (see directions, p. 125) and work the flesh through a meat grinder, using the finest blade, or chop finely with a knife. Put the flesh in a bowl and beat in egg whites either with a mixer (use the flat whip if it's a heavy-

duty mixer) or, over ice, with a wooden spatula. Then beat in cream gradually, 1 tablespoonful at a time.

• If you are beating the mixture by hand, chilling it causes the natural gelatin in the chicken to react to thicken it and thus helps compensate for the lack of the forcefulness of the mixer beating.

3. Lay the boned chicken, with what was the skin side facing down, on a cutting board and spread it open. Brush the flesh with cognac—use 2 tablespoons of it—and sprinkle with salt and pepper.

4. Spread chicken mousse over boned chicken, leaving a ½-inch margin all around. Sprinkle with pistachio nuts. Then cut pieces of tongue or ham the shape and size of your index finger, lay them on top of the nuts, and scatter chopped truffle over all.

5. Form the chicken into a compact roll and sew it up with needle and thread.

6. Cover the rolled chicken with overlapping slices of blanched bacon —that is, bacon that has been put in a saucepan, covered with cold water, brought to a boil, and boiled 1 minute. Drain the bacon in a sieve before using it.

7. Tie the bacon on with string every inch or so, but don't tie it too tightly, for if there's no give, the expansion of the mousse inside the chicken will cause string marks on the roasted bird.

8. Place chicken on a rack in a roasting pan and put it into a pre-heated 375° oven to roast for 1 hour. Every 15 minutes baste it, twice with 2 tablespoons melted butter and 2 tablespoons of cognac; the third time use a bulb baster to draw up the liquid in the pan and squirt it over chicken.

9. Before serving, remove strings, bacon, and threads holding roast together; cut into neat slices and overlap them on a platter. Garnish platter with mushroom caps, watercress, and artichoke bottoms that have been rinsed and dried, brushed with butter, and heated through in a 325° oven.

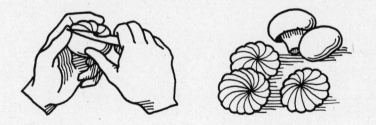

• Pass Basic Brown Sauce (see p. 248) if you wish, but this chicken is good plain. *Makes 8 servings.*

## Truffled Chicken or Turkey Flambé

This is a fast method for roasting a bird. The skin gets beautifully crisp, and the meat is unbelievably moist. I've tried roasting birds both slowly and quickly. This is the method I prefer. Note that to allow time for the perfume of the truffle to permeate the bird, truffle slices should be placed under the skin and the bird should be trussed (steps 1 to 5, below) 24 hours before it is to be roasted.

| | |
|---|---|
| 8 ⅛-inch slices truffle | 2 tablespoons lemon juice |
| 7 tablespoons armagnac, or more | 2 tablespoons finely chopped shallots |
| 1 4-lb. roasting chicken or 1 5-lb. turkey | ½ cup dry red wine |
| 1 tablespoon salt | ½ teaspoon meat glaze (see p. 244) |
| 1 teaspoon freshly cracked white pepper | ½ teaspoon tomato paste |
| 10 tablespoons unsalted butter | ¾ cup chicken stock (see p. 241) |
| | 1 bunch watercress |

1. Marinate truffle slices in ¼ cup of armagnac for 1 hour. When finished, reserve the armagnac to use for basting the bird.

• Armagnac is a brandy made southeast of Bordeaux, in what was ancient Gascony. It has a drier taste than most brandies.

2. Remove giblets and neck from the bird's cavity, trim wing tips, and wash the bird, drying it thoroughly. Season the cavity with 1 teaspoon of salt and ½ teaspoon pepper and put a lump of unsalted butter—¼ cup —in it.

3. Loosen the skin on breast and legs: start at the neck, lifting the skin over the breast—don't use a knife, just push the skin away from the flesh with thumb and fingers, taking care not to tear the skin; when the breast skin is loosened, go to work on the skin over the thighs.

4. Insert 1 truffle slice under the skin on each thigh. Place the remaining 6 slices under the breast skin, 3 on each side, making a design.

5. Rub the outside of the bird with lemon juice, 2 tablespoons softened butter, remaining 2 teaspoons salt, and remaining ½ teaspoon pepper. Truss the bird (see directions, p. 127), wrap it in foil and refrigerate it for 24 hours.

6. The next day take the bird from the refrigerator, bring it to room temperature, and place it on its side, on a rack in a shallow roasting pan. Roast in a preheated 475° oven for 15 minutes; meanwhile make a basting mixture of ¼ cup of melted butter and ¼ cup of reserved armagnac,

baste the bird, turn it onto its other side, baste it, and roast it for another 15 minutes.

7. Turn the bird breast side up. Reduce oven to 425°, baste again and every 15 minutes until roast is done.

• Use a bulb baster to draw up the liquid in the pan and squirt it over the bird.

• A 4-lb. chicken takes about 45 minutes, a 5-lb. turkey takes about 1½ hours.

8. Remove bird to an ovenproof platter and keep warm.

9. Pour out all but 2 tablespoons of fat from the roasting pan. Place pan over high heat, add shallots and cook for 1 to 2 minutes, without browning them.

10. Add red wine, meat glaze, tomato paste, and chicken stock. Bring to a boil over moderate heat and boil 15 minutes to reduce mixture until it is syrupy. Taste for and, if desired, adjust seasoning, then pour into a bowl to serve as sauce.

11. Garnish bird with watercress. Heat remaining 3 tablespoons of armagnac in a small long-handled pan until just warm to the touch. Ignite the armagnac, pour it over the bird, and take the bird, flaming, to the table.

12. When carving bird, take off first one side of the breast (including wing), then the other; cut the 2 breast sections across into 3 pieces each —this way there will be 6 servings of breast meat with skin and truffle, then remove legs and thighs. *Makes 6 servings.*

### ROAST GOOSE

To many people, Christmas wouldn't be Christmas without a succulent goose. For any occasion, try to get a fresh goose; a nice, plump one.

| | |
|---|---|
| 1 10-to-12-lb. goose | 1 teaspoon freshly cracked |
| 1 tablespoon coarse salt | black pepper |

1. Wash the goose inside and out and dry it carefully with paper towels. Remove as much fat as possible (you'll find large chunks of fat under the neck skin and in the cavity).

• Stuff the goose if you wish, with 2½ lbs. of sauerkraut, or with 2½ lbs. of sausage meat, or with 4 cups of chopped onions sautéed in goose fat until they're lightly browned.

2. Rub the goose all over with coarse salt and pepper. Truss it (see directions, p. 127), and put it on a rack in a roasting pan, breast up, and

place in a preheated 375° oven. Roast for a total of 20 minutes per pound but before the last ½ hour remove goose, prick it all over with a fork (this will release a lot of the fat), and before returning goose to finish roasting, reduce oven heat to 325°.

• To test for doneness, prick a leg with a fork; if the juices run clear, the goose is done.

3. Serve goose with all the traditional holiday vegetables: glazed turnips, onions, mashed parsnips, glazed carrots, sweet potatoes, chestnuts, Brussels sprouts. *Makes 8 to 10 servings.*

## NORMANDY DUCK

Heavy cream, apples, and Calvados are all products of Normandy. Hence the name for this delicious duck.

2 *4- to 5-lb. Long Island ducklings*
8 *slices firm home-style white bread, plus heels of the loaf*
6 *cups roughly chopped peeled-and-cored apples*
2 *teaspoons cinnamon*
1 *tablespoon salt*
1 *teaspoon freshly cracked black pepper*

4 *beaten eggs*
¾ *cup Calvados, or apple brandy, about*
½ *cup chicken stock (see p. 241), about*
1 *cup melted apple jelly*
1 *cup heavy cream*

1. Wash and dry ducks; stuff paper towels into the cavities to dry them thoroughly.
2. Cut the bread slices into cubes (trim off crusts or not, as you prefer), put the cubes in a large bowl and make stuffing by tossing them with apples, cinnamon, 2 teaspoons salt, and ½ teaspoon pepper, then adding eggs and enough Calvados—about 3 to 4 tablespoonfuls—to moisten the mixture.
3. Stuff ducks *loosely.* (Stuffing expands as ducks roast.) Close the cavity of each duck with heel of a loaf of bread, then truss ducks (see directions, p. 127), rub them all over with the remaining salt and pepper, place them on a rack in roasting pan, and put them in a preheated 325° oven to roast for a total of 20 minutes per pound. During all but the last 20 minutes of roasting, baste ducks every ¼ hour with Calvados mixed with chicken stock, using about ¼ cup of each in all. (Use a bulb baster to draw up the liquid in the pan and squirt it over the ducks.)

4. About 20 minutes before ducks are done, take them out of the oven and glaze them with apple jelly. Apply it with a pastry brush.

5. Return the ducks to oven, and when they are done, remove them to a carving board and keep warm.

• To test for doneness, prick a thigh with a fork; when juices are no longer pink, the duck is done.

6. Pour off all but 1 tablespoon of fat from the roasting pan and deglaze the pan with the remaining ¼ cup Calvados, like this: pour the Calvados into the pan, give it a few seconds to warm, then ignite it.

7. Scrape up the brown bits, add the remaining ¼ cup chicken stock and the heavy cream, and make sauce by bringing to a boil, then cooking to reduce sauce and thicken slightly. Strain sauce and serve it separately, in a bowl. *Makes 4 to 6 servings.*

### DUCK WITH PEACHES

*1 4- to 5-lb. Long Island duckling*
*1 tablespoon coarse salt*
*1 teaspoon freshly cracked black pepper*
*2 1-lb. cans white peach halves, or 6 peeled, pitted, and halved fresh white peaches*
*8 to 10 tablespoons dry white wine*

*¼ to ½ cup sugar*
*¼ cup wine (or cider) vinegar*
*2 cups Basic Brown Sauce (see p. 248)*
*1 tablespoon dry Madeira*
*1 tablespoon cognac*
*⅓ cup melted apricot jam*
*2 teaspoons potato starch, optional*
*1 bunch watercress*

1. Wash duck and dry thoroughly. Remove giblets, neck, and wing tips, then truss the duck (see directions, p. 127), rub it all over with salt and pepper, and place it, breast up, on a rack in a roasting pan along with giblets and trimmings. Roast in a preheated 350° oven for 1 hour.

2. Put canned peach halves, with their juice, into a saucepan, add ¼ cup wine, and simmer slowly for 3 to 5 minutes until heated through. Or bring a mixture of ¼ cup wine, ¼ cup sugar, and ¾ cup water to a boil, add fresh peach halves, and simmer for 10 minutes. Drain and set aside the peaches—and save the liquid in which they cooked for possible addition to sauce (see step 9, below).

3. Make caramel by dissolving ¼ cup of sugar in vinegar over low heat in a heavy pan. After sugar dissolves, do not stir, just tip the pan back and forth over the heat until the contents turn a clear caramel color.

4. Add Brown Sauce very slowly to caramel. Stir over low heat adding Madeira and cognac. Taste for seasoning and add salt and pepper if desired. Set aside.

5. After duck has roasted 1 hour, remove it from the oven and brush it with apricot jam, using a pastry brush. Return duck to oven for another 15 minutes, or until done.

• To test for doneness, tip the duck so juice runs out of its cavity; when juices run yellow, duck is done. Or prick a thigh with a fork; when juices are no longer pink, duck is done.

• The duck and the sauce (see steps 7 to 9, below) can be made several hours ahead of when the duck is to be served if the duck is under-cooked—that is, cooked 15 minutes less than called for—refrigerated, then brought to room temperature and reheated for 10 minutes in a 350° oven.

6. When duck is done, remove it to a carving board or a serving platter and keep warm.

7. Pour off all but 1 tablespoon fat from the roasting pan and deglaze the pan by pouring in ¼ cup wine, and bringing the wine to a boil.

8. Scrape up the brown bits and strain contents of pan into the caramel mixture to make sauce.

9. Thicken the sauce, if necessary, by adding potato starch that has been stirred into 2 tablespoons of dry white wine and cooking over high heat, stirring constantly, for 1 or 2 minutes. If sauce is too thick, thin it with some of the liquid in which the peaches cooked.

10. Place peach halves around the duck, spoon a little sauce on each half and serve the remaining sauce in a bowl. Garnish the carving board or serving platter with watercress and carve duck (see directions, p. 127) at table. *Makes 2 to 3 servings.*

### SQUABS WITH CUMBERLAND SAUCE

Squabs are in season in the wintertime. They are domestically raised little birds, with all dark meat, and they tend to be dry if not faithfully basted. Plan on 1 whole squab per person. And serve squabs with finger bowls: it's not only proper but quite necessary to nibble on the little bones.

| | |
|---|---|
| *1 cup wild rice* | *¾ cup butter, plus butter to* |
| *¾ cup very finely chopped* | *brush on squabs* |
| *onion* | *4 teaspoons salt* |
| *1 medium clove finely* | *1 teaspoon freshly cracked* |
| *chopped garlic* | *black pepper* |

2 tablespoons chopped pars-    1 teaspoon potato starch, op-
ley    tional
2 cups seedless white grapes,    1 tablespoon port wine, op-
washed and stemmed    tional
8 1¼- to 1½-lb. squabs    1 bunch watercress, optional
Cumberland Sauce (recipe    Frosted White Grapes (see
follows)    p. 95), optional

1. Soak rice in 1½ cups of cold water for 1 hour. Drain, then put in a saucepan with 2 cups cold water and bring to a boil, lower heat, and simmer, covered, for 30 minutes, or until done.

• To test for doneness, pinch a grain between your fingers: it should have a little hardness but not be mushy.

2. When rice is done, drain it and put it in a bowl.

3. Sauté onion and garlic over high heat, in 1 tablespoon of butter, stirring with a wooden spatula until transparent.

4. Add onion-garlic mixture, 1 teaspoon salt, ½ teaspoon pepper, 3 tablespoons melted butter, and the chopped parsley to rice. Mix together with fork, adding 1 cup of grapes. Set aside.

5. Wash the squabs and dry them thoroughly. Trim off wing tips and cut off necks. Stuff squabs with rice-grape mixture.

6. Truss squabs (see directions, p. 127), then brush them with melted butter—use 2 tablespoonfuls—and sprinkle with the remaining salt and pepper.

7. Put squabs in a roasting pan and roast them, uncovered, in a preheated 375° oven for 45 minutes. Baste them often—at least 3 times while roasting—with melted butter, using about ½ cup.

• If tender squab is preferred, roast an extra 10 to 15 minutes, but keep in mind that squab tends to become dry as it's cooked.

8. When squabs are done, remove them to a warm platter and keep warm.

9. Make sauce by pouring off all but about 2 tablespoons of fat from the roasting pan, then pouring in Cumberland Sauce and bringing to a boil, scraping up brown bits. Thicken the sauce, if you wish, by adding potato starch that has been stirred into port wine and boiling 1 minute, stirring constantly.

10. Add the remaining cup of grapes to sauce and heat through. Remove trussing cords from squabs and arrange them on the platter. If desired, decorate the platter either with a watercress garnish or with Frosted White Grapes. Serve sauce separately, in a sauce boat.

### Cumberland Sauce

Cumberland Sauce can be served hot or cold. It is excellent with poultry, ham, or tongue. Try it with Pâté Maison (see p. 28), too.

| | |
|---|---|
| *1 cup red currant jelly* | *Grated peel of 1 orange* |
| *½ cup fresh orange juice* | *Grated peel of 1 lemon* |
| *½ teaspoon dry mustard* | *1 cup port wine* |
| *¼ teaspoon powdered ginger* | |

Put all ingredients in a saucepan and cook over low heat, stirring constantly, until jelly melts. **Makes 8 servings.**

## SQUABS WITH PINEAPPLE

| | |
|---|---|
| *1 large ripe pineapple* | *1 cup unsweetened canned* |
| *8 1¼- to 1½-lb. squabs* | *pineapple juice* |
| *½ cup pâté de fois gras* | *1 cup Basic Brown Sauce* |
| *1 tablespoon salt* | *(see p. 248)* |
| *1 teaspoon freshly cracked* | *1 teaspoon potato starch,* |
| *black pepper* | *optional* |
| *1 cup butter* | *1 recipe Chestnut Purée (see* |
| *2 tablespoons cognac* | *p. 173)* |
| *1½ cups port wine* | |

1. Remove plumage from pineapple and save for garnish. Peel the pineapple (the easiest way is by standing it on a cutting board and slicing down, all around, with a large sharp knife), dig out the eyes, and cut the pineapple in half, then cut the halves into slices ½ inch thick. Cut out and discard the core, and after reserving 8 of the most attractive slices as garnishes for the squabs, cut the remaining pineapple slices in half.

2. Wash and dry the squabs. Trim off wing tips and cut off necks. Reserve giblets and trimmings.

3. Into the cavity of each squab put 1 tablespoon of pâté and a piece of pineapple. Truss squabs (see directions, p. 127), then rub them with salt and pepper.

4. Melt ¼ cup of butter in a large heavy casserole and when no longer foaming, brown squabs, giblets, and trimmings thoroughly, over high heat, turning them with wooden spatulas. Don't prick the skins with a fork; don't let the pieces touch each other—that is, brown at once only as many as can fit into the casserole without crowding, and allow plenty of time—about 15 minutes for each batch.

• If the birds touch, they will braise instead of browning.

5. Put all the squabs, giblets, and trimmings into the casserole and flame them with cognac—that is, warm the cognac in a small long-handled pan, ignite it, and pour it, flaming, into the casserole.

6. Scrape up the brown bits in the casserole. Then pour in ¾ cup of melted butter and roast, uncovered, in a preheated 375° oven for 45 minutes. Baste often—at least 3 times during roasting—with pan juices, using a bulb baster to take them up and squirt them over squabs.

7. While squabs roast, poach reserved pineapple slices in wine and pineapple juice for 10 minutes. Remove slices and keep them warm. Boil liquid to reduce it by half, then add Basic Brown Sauce, bring to a boil again, and remove from heat. Taste for seasoning and add salt and pepper if desired. Thicken slightly, if desired, by adding potato starch that has been mixed with 1 tablespoon of cold water and cooking over high heat, stirring constantly.

8. When birds are done, arrange them on a platter and keep warm.

• If you want crisp brown skin on them, put squabs under a broiler for about 5 minutes before arranging them on the platter.

9. Pour off all but 2 tablespoons of the fat in the casserole, add the wine-brown-sauce mixture and the giblets—chop them first—and bring to a boil, scraping up the brown bits. Strain into a serving bowl.

10. Arrange a pineapple slice over each squab and garnish with a rosette of Chestnut Purée made by putting the purée into a pastry bag fitted with a star tube and piping the rosette on each pineapple slice. Decorate the platter with reserved pineapple plumage. *Makes 8 servings.*

# EGGS AND CRÊPES

## Eggs

Eggs are one of the best buys on the food market today. They are high in protein yet low in price. And eggs will keep well in a refrigerator for up to two weeks.

I always prefer to use large eggs; this is especially important if you plan to serve eggs whole—they just look so much better when they're large. But please note that there is no difference in the nutritional value or taste of brown eggs compared with white ones, and brown eggs are often less expensive.

Eggs are the most versatile food imaginable. They can be served for breakfast, lunch, or supper, and they can be baked, boiled, fried, or poached, or turned into omelettes and soufflés. Eggs can also be combined with almost any ingredient you have on hand to provide an endless variety of new dishes.

You'll find that it's a good idea always to have some eggs on hand; with just a few eggs, and only a few minutes' time in the kitchen, you can create a quick yet elegant brunch, luncheon, or light supper.

## FRENCH OMELETTES

A French omelette should be a perfect oval, pointed at both ends and plump in the center; the outside should be pale yellow (if it's brown, the pan was too hot); and inside, the omelette should be mellow and creamy (what the French call *baveuse*).

Learn to make a perfect French omelette and you'll have one of the most useful skills in a cook's repertoire. With 3 eggs in the house, you can always offer an unexpected guest a plain omelette, a flaming jam omelette, or an omelette filled with vegetables, ham, herbs, cheese—whatever happens to be handy. And giving an omelette party for large groups—I've had as many as sixty people at once—can be great fun. In my family room is an antique stove I've had electrified; I use it to make omelettes to order. First I serve a good hearty potage, then the omelettes with green salad and French bread; the dessert is fruit and cheese.

For making omelettes it's wise although not absolutely necessary to have a pan with some weight, and one that's not too large, since individual omelettes are easier to make than are large ones. The pan I like best is of cast aluminum, with a comfortable wooden handle; the pan measures 10 inches across the top and 8 inches across the bottom and is the perfect size for a 3-egg omelette—for 1 serving, that is.

To season an omelette pan, fill it ¾ full of vegetable oil (don't use olive oil), set it over low heat, and when the oil reaches the point of smoking—this takes about 20 minutes—turn off heat and let the pan stand at room temperature overnight. In the morning pour off the oil and discard it. Wipe out the pan with paper towels, and from this point on, *never, never* wash it—just wipe it out with paper towels. If the pan should inadvertently be washed, season it again before using. Use this pan only for omelettes. And if you've never made omelettes before, use it first for practice—making omelettes requires it. Buy yourself a couple of dozen eggs and make one omelette right after the other; feed them to the dog, or throw them away if you have to—it's worth the slight investment in eggs and time.

But if an omelette made for a guest isn't quite perfect, don't panic—just cover the top more generously than usual with chopped parsley. No one will know.

| | |
|---|---|
| 3 *eggs, at room temperature* | *Generous 1 tablespoon butter,* |
| *Scant ½ teaspoon salt* | *plus butter to brush on top* |
| ¼ *teaspoon freshly cracked* | *of omelette* |
| *white pepper* | 1 *tablespoon chopped parsley* |

1. Break eggs into a bowl, add salt and pepper, and beat with a fork just enough to mix—about 30 strokes.

2. Put a seasoned omelette pan on low heat and heat slowly—the slower, the better—until a tiny bit of butter if put in the pan sizzles briskly without browning.

• If the butter browns, swing the pan through the air a couple of times to cool it; then try again.

3. When the pan is the right temperature, put 1 generous tablespoon butter into it. The butter will sizzle and foam as it melts. Be ready to add the eggs the instant the butter stops foaming (before it browns, that is).

• At the moment the eggs go into the pan, increase heat to medium high.

4. As soon as the eggs hit the pan, stir them quickly with a fork held in one hand while shaking the pan back and forth over the heat with the other. Keep the tines of the fork flat on the pan and stir vigorously, first clockwise, then counterclockwise. Stir and shake with enthusiasm. It takes only 30 seconds to cook the omelette, so really bend over the pan and move.

• The shaking and stirring motion takes practice and coordination. It's rather like patting your head and rubbing your stomach at the same time. But once you get the hang of it, it's easy.

5. The omelette is now ready to fold and turn out. As soon as the egg mixture *starts* to set but while it is still quite moist and creamy-looking, pat it out evenly over the bottom of the pan with the fork.

•If the omelette is to be filled, the filling goes in now.

6. Rotate the pan about ¼ turn (to the left if you're right-handed so you can change the position of your hand on the handle and grip it with palm underneath). Tip up the pan, and keeping it tipped with one hand, use the fork with the other to loosen the omelette around the edge near the handle, then to fold it over and roll it—guiding it with the fork and tucking in the edges as you go—until it is in the curve of the pan opposite the handle.

7. Bring the edge of a warm plate to the edge of the pan and, literally turning the pan upside down over the plate, tip the omelette out onto the plate.

• The omelette won't stick if the pan was well seasoned, if it was the right temperature, and if a generous tablespoon of butter was used. If

it does stick, put butter at the sticking points and let the melting butter help your fork loosen the omelette.

• Sometimes fillings get under the eggs and into the pan and cause sticking. Loosen the omelette with butter, and before making another omelette, rub the pan out with paper toweling, and if necessary, a little coarse salt.

8. Before serving the omelette, brush the top with melted butter and sprinkle with chopped parsley. *Makes 1 serving.*

### Cheese Omelette

Proceed as above, but before folding the omelette, drop about 2 table-spoons of grated cheese—use Cheddar, Swiss, Gruyère, or any other well-flavored kind—in the center of the egg mixture.

### Mincemeat Omelette Flambé

Put 2 tablespoons of hot mincemeat in the omelette before folding it. Tip the omelette out onto a stainless steel or other flameproof serving dish, sift confectioners' sugar over it, and flame it by warming 2 tablespoons of rum in a small long-handled pan, igniting the rum, then pouring it, flaming, over the omelette.

### Jam Omelette Flambé

Before folding the omelette, fill it with 2 tablespoons of raspberry, strawberry, or apricot jam, or 2 tablespoons of orange marmalade. Tip the omelette out onto a stainless steel or other flameproof serving dish. Sift confectioners' sugar over it. Decorate the top with crisscross lines burned into the sugar with a red-hot skewer. Flame the omelette by pouring over it 2 tablespoons of rum, cognac, framboise, or kirsch that has been warmed in a small long-handled pan, then ignited.

### Truffle Omelette Flambé

When the egg mixture goes into the pan add to it as many truffle slices as the budget allows. Tip the omelette out onto a stainless steel or other flameproof serving dish, decorate with a slice of truffle, and flame by warming 2 tablespoons of cognac in a small long-handled pan, igniting the cognac, and pouring it, flaming, over the omelette.

### Ham or Bacon Omelette

When the egg mixture goes into the pan add to it, stirring, ½ cup of diced cooked ham or ½ cup of bacon that has been cut in tiny pieces, fried until crisp, and drained on paper towels.

### Mushroom Omelette

Before cooking omelette, slice 4 or 5 mushrooms, sprinkle them with 2 teaspoons of lemon juice, ½ teaspoon of salt, and ¼ teaspoon of freshly cracked white pepper, and sauté them (in another pan) in 2 tablespoons of foaming butter, tossing them over high heat for 3 minutes only. Add mushrooms to the omelette just before folding it. Decorate omelette with a fluted sautéed mushroom cap (see p. 11) and chopped parsley.

### Caviar Omelette

After omelette has been tipped from the pan to a plate, slit it from end to end and fill it with red or black caviar. Put a big spoonful of sour cream on the side and garnish with chopped fresh dill.

## Watercress Omelette

Before cooking omelette, trim stems off and wash and dry enough watercress (or baby spinach, or sorrel leaves) to have a handful (about ½ cup) of the leaves. Add them, stirring, to the egg mixture at the time it goes into the pan and cook the omelette just a bit longer than usual. Because of water in the leaves, it needs a few extra seconds over heat. Spoon a little sour cream over the omelette.

## Herb Omelette

Before cooking omelette, chop 2 tablespoons of any fresh herb or combination of herbs, and when the egg mixture goes into the pan, add them to it, stirring; or stir 1 teaspoon of dry herbs into 2 tablespoons of sour cream and add to omelette just before folding it. Garnish omelette with 1 tablespoon of the fresh herbs or with chopped parsley.

## COLD POACHED EGGS

This is an inexpensive, handsome-looking luncheon dish.

6 eggs
¾ cup red wine vinegar
3 peeled, stemmed tomatoes
2 tablespoons tarragon or red wine vinegar
5 tablespoons olive oil
½ teaspoon salt
¼ teaspoon freshly cracked black pepper

1 recipe Seven-Minute Green Beans (see p. 164)
6 large lettuce leaves
1 cup mayonnaise (see p. 251)
2 tablespoons chopped parsley

1. Poach eggs as follows. Fill 8-inch skillet ¾ full of water, add ¾ cup wine vinegar, and heat to simmering. Break 3 eggs close to the surface of the water and drop them in one after the other. With a skimmer in one hand gently smooth the top of the water just enough to keep it moving on the surface, and at the same time, use the other hand to tip the pan a just a bit, also to keep the water moving. Smoothing the water and keeping the pan tipped, poach eggs for 2 to 2½ minutes. Remove eggs from water with a slotted spoon and plunge immediately into cold water to stop the cooking. Set aside, and follow the above procedure for the 3 remaining eggs.

2. Place eggs in refrigerator, still in the cold water, to chill about ½ hour.

3. Cut the tomatoes in half. Hollow out the halves just enough to make beds for the eggs.

4. In a mixture of the remaining 2 tablespoons of vinegar, oil, salt, and pepper marinate the cooked green beans in a refrigerator ½ hour.

5. Before serving, arrange a lettuce leaf on each of 6 plates, put a tomato half in the lettuce, an egg in the tomato half, mask with mayonnaise, and sprinkle with parsley. Arrange the marinated beans alongside. **Makes 6 servings.**

## EGGS IN GELATIN

| | |
|---|---|
| 6 eggs | 6 small slices truffle |
| 2 tablespoons (2 envelopes) unflavored gelatin | 12 leaves fresh tarragon |
| | 6 small pieces of thin-sliced |
| 1 quart chicken stock (see p. 241) | ham (about 1 inch square) |
| | 6 large lettuce leaves |

1. Poach the eggs, following directions in step 1 of the recipe for Cold Poached Eggs (see p. 155). Place eggs in refrigerator to chill.

2. Soften gelatin by sprinkling it in ½ cup of cold chicken stock. Set the container of gelatin and stock in a pan of hot water, and stirring occasionally, heat until gelatin is dissolved.

3. Heat the remaining chicken stock in a saucepan, then stir the dissolved gelatin into it and remove from heat.

4. Stir mixture over ice until it reaches the syrupy stage and is about ready to set, then put a spoonful of it—reserve the rest—in the bottom of each of 6 oval dariole molds—oval molds 3 inches wide and 1½ inches deep—and refrigerate for about 15 minutes or until set.

5. Dip slices of truffle into the reserved gelatin mixture, then put the slices in the middle of the molds on top of the gelatin. Return to refrigerator for about 5 minutes to set.

6. Cover the truffle layers with a bit more of the gelatin mixture and crisscross two tarragon leaves over the top. Refrigerate again for about 15 minutes or until set.

• If you don't have fresh tarragon, cut long thin leaf shapes from scallion tops or sprinkle the molds with chopped parsley to get the green color.

7. When the tarragon layers have set, coat the pieces of ham with gelatin mixture and lay them on top.

• The ham should be a little bigger than the truffle, so the pink will later (after unmolding) show around the black.

8. Coat the ham layers with more gelatin and put the molds back in refrigerator to set.

9. Carefully lay a chilled poached egg in each mold, and cover with remaining gelatin mixture, this time to the top of each mold. Return to refrigerator and chill thoroughly, about 1 hour.

• The molds in this recipe can be prepared and refrigerated the day before they are to be served.

10. To unmold, run the tip of a small knife around each mold with an up-and-down motion. Place lettuce on a serving plate, invert mold over serving plate with a bang, then lift off mold.

• If a mold sticks set the bottom of it in warm water for 1 or 2 seconds, then try again.

11. Serve with cold cooked vegetables or Rice Salad (see p. 197). Pass mayonnaise (see p. 251) if you wish. *Makes 6 servings.*

### EGG MOUSSE WITH CUCUMBER

This is good for luncheon, as an hors d'oeuvre, or as a first course.

*1 tablespoon (1 envelope) unflavored gelatin*
*⅓ cup dry white wine*
*¾ cup mayonnaise (see p. 251)*
*1 tablespoon anchovy paste*
*½ cup grated onion*
*3 tablespoons chopped parsley*
*12 coarsely chopped hard-cooked eggs*
*1 cup medium Béchamel Sauce (see p. 245) at room temperature*
*1 cup heavy cream*
*3 to 4 drops Tabasco sauce*
*Vegetable oil to grease soufflé dish*
*1 cucumber*

1. Soften gelatin by sprinkling it in wine. Set the container of gelatin and wine in a pan of hot water, and heat, stirring occasionally, over high heat, until gelatin is dissolved.

2. In a large bowl, mix together mayonnaise, anchovy paste, onion, and 2 tablespoons of the parsley. Add chopped eggs and fold together.

3. Mix dissolved gelatin into Béchamel Sauce and fold sauce into egg mixture.

4. Whip cream lightly, season it with Tabasco, then fold it into egg-sauce mixture. Taste for seasoning and add salt, if desired.

5. Pour mixture into a lightly oiled 6-cup soufflé dish and chill in refrigerator at least 2 hours.

• I usually do this much the day before I want to serve the mousse so that flavors have a chance to blend.

6. When set, unmold on a serving plate.

• To unmold, run a little knife around the edge of the mold with an up-and-down motion. Place serving dish over mold, invert, give a shake, and lift off mold.

7. Garnish the edge of the mold with cucumber ruffles made by slicing the cucumbers (with the skins on) into thin rounds, slitting each round from an outside edge to just beyond the center, then grasping the cut ends and twisting in opposite direction. Garnish the center of the mold with the remaining chopped parsley. *Makes 12 to 16 servings.*

# Crêpes

No matter what goes inside of a crêpe, the result is an elegant one. The simplest dishes become party fare when they are wrapped in a crêpe and covered with a sauce. Crêpes can be made ahead and kept in a refrigerator or freezer, and with prepared crêpes on hand you are always ready for last-minute entertaining or for a lovely treat for the family.

Crêpes can be served at almost any time of the day and can be an appetizer, a main dish, or a dessert (for dessert crêpes, see pp. 204–207). And crêpes can be served flaming for an extra festive touch.

Try some of your favorite dishes wrapped in crêpes for new and exciting variations.

## CRÊPES

This is the recipe to use when plain unsweetened crêpes are needed.

*½ cup flour*
*¼ teaspoon salt*
*2 eggs*
*2 egg yolks*

*¼ cup vegetable oil, plus oil*
*to grease crêpe pan*
*½ cup milk*

1. Make batter by putting all ingredients (except the oil to grease pan) into a blender jar or a bowl and either blending at top speed or whisking until smooth.

• If lumps or flour specks remain in the batter, strain it.

2. Put the batter into a refrigerator for at least 1 hour to give the flour granules time to swell and thus to make the resulting crêpes tenderer than they would otherwise be.

• When it is removed from the refrigerator the batter should be the consistency of heavy cream. If it is too thick, thin it with a little milk or water.

3. Fry crêpes 1 at a time in a seasoned 5- or 7-inch iron crêpe pan. Brush the pan lightly with a little oil (or film the pan with oil by wiping it with a folded paper towel dipped in oil), and place pan over high heat. When the oil is very hot (at the point of smoking), pour in a scant ¼ cup of batter, then quickly tilt the pan in all directions to coat the bottom with it. (The crêpe should be very thin. If there's too much batter —more than enough to coat the bottom of the pan—pour the excess back into the jar or bowl. The first crêpe will help you judge the amount of batter to use for subsequent ones.) Fry the crêpe about 1 minute, or until the edges brown and pull away from the sides of the pan, then turn the crêpe (use a spatula for the whole turn, or lift a corner of the crêpe with a spatula and use your fingers to flip over the rest) and fry the other side, which will not brown evenly (so this is the side to always roll or fold inward), for about 30 seconds. Brush the pan lightly with oil (or film it) again before frying the next crêpe.

• Crêpes can be frozen if they're stacked with plastic wrap or waxed paper between them, then either overwrapped tightly with plastic wrap or foil or sealed in a plastic bag. Defrost in a refrigerator, or in a 250° oven.

• To season a crêpe pan, fill it ¾ full of vegetable oil, heat the oil to the point of smoking, let it stand overnight in the pan, and in the morning, discard the oil and wipe out the pan with paper towels. Never wash the pan—just wipe it out with paper towels after each use. *Makes 8 7-inch or 12 5-inch crêpes.*

## CRÊPES STUFFED WITH CHEESE SOUFFLÉ

6 tablespoons butter, plus
    butter to grease pan
3 tablespoons flour
¾ cup milk
3 to 4 drops Tabasco sauce
1½ cups grated Parmesan,
    Swiss, or Cheddar cheese

5 egg yolks
7 egg whites
¼ teaspoon cream of tartar
8 7-inch crêpes (see p. 158)

1. Make a roux by melting 3 tablespoons butter in saucepan, stirring in flour with a wooden spatula, and cooking over high heat, stirring, for about 2 minutes. Do not let it brown.

2. Remove pan from heat and add milk, whisking vigorously. Return pan to heat and bring to a boil, whisking constantly. Mixture will be very thick.

3. Remove from heat and stir in Tabasco sauce and 1 cup of the cheese.

• Any well-flavored cheese may be used. I prefer freshly grated imported Parmesan.

4. Beat in egg yolks. Mixture will be fairly stiff.

5. Beat egg whites until very stiff, adding the cream of tartar just after egg whites begin to foam.

• Egg whites are stiff if most of the mixture can be scooped onto the whisk or beater at one time or if, when the bowl is turned over, the mixture doesn't fall out.

6. Make soufflé mixture by stirring a spoonful of the beaten whites into the cheese mixture to lighten it, then, with a rubber spatula, lightly folding in the remaining whites.

7. Lay the 8 crêpes out on 2 generously buttered baking sheets or in buttered ramekins. Put a big spoonful of soufflé mixture on one half of each crêpe, then fold the other half over, but do not line up the edges— leave about ½ inch margin.

8. Sprinkle the top of each crêpe with 1 teaspoon of melted butter and 1 tablespoon of grated cheese.

9. Put baking sheets or ramekins into a preheated 375° oven and bake for 8 to 10 minutes, or until soufflés puff. Serve immediately, plain or with Hollandaise Sauce (see p. 246) or Mornay Sauce (see p. 245). *Makes 8 servings.*

## SPINACH CRÊPES

2 (10 oz.) packages frozen chopped spinach
1 recipe basic crêpe batter (see p. 158)
1 cup dairy sour cream
¼ teaspoon freshly grated nutmeg
½ teaspoon salt
¼ teaspoon freshly cracked black pepper

1½ cups finely diced prosciutto
2 tablespoons melted butter
2 cups Mornay Sauce (see p. 245)
3 beaten egg yolks, optional
¼ cup freshly grated Parmesan cheese

1. Cook spinach in a covered pan over high heat just until thawed; do not add water. Drain and squeeze dry—press it in a sieve to release all moisture.

2. Add 2 tablespoons of the spinach to crêpe batter and fry crêpes as recipe directs, using a 7-inch pan. Stack crêpes on a plate until ready to fill.

3. To make filling: return remaining spinach to saucepan; add sour cream, nutmeg, salt, pepper, and prosciutto. Combine and cook over high heat 5 to 7 minutes or until heated through.

4. Butter an ovenproof serving dish. Put 2 tablespoons of spinach-prosciutto filling on the edge of each crêpe (on the undercooked, or second side), roll up and place seam side down in serving dish.

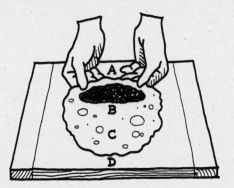

5. Make Mornay Sauce, enriching it if desired with 3 egg yolks. Spoon the sauce over the crêpes, sprinkle with cheese, and bake in a preheated 375° oven for 15 minutes or until bubbly. *Makes 8 servings.*

# VEGETABLES
# AND OTHER
# ACCOMPANIMENTS

It's much easier to cook vegetables right than to ruin them. The key word is *simplicity,* for vegetables are at a peak of deliciousness when simply steamed or cooked in very little liquid, seasoned with salt and pepper, and dressed with melted butter. And there are other easy ways with vegetables. Try, for example, Sautéed Cherry Tomatoes (see p. 189), Minted Cucumbers (see p. 174), Seven-Minute Green Beans (see p. 164), Whipped Carrots (see p. 170), or Pea Purée (see p. 182). All are perfect!

While admittedly a convenience, frozen vegetables never have the exquisite flavor of those just gathered from the earth. Americans are fortunate to be living in a land that supplies such a bountiful variety the whole year around. But few Americans seem to know that for the best flavor, vegetables should be picked just after ripening when they are as small as possible. Prizes are often awarded gardeners for gargantuan green beans or peas the size of cannonballs; my prizes go to the growers of matchstick green beans and minuscule peas.

A well-balanced meal should include at least one vegetable or a green leafy salad. Certain vegetables—artichokes and asparagus, for example, and all vegetable soufflés—deserve to be served as a separate course. Individual serving plates designed for these elite vegetables are very nice to own.

Many other vegetables go hand in hand with some particular main dish: imagine poached fish without its parslied potato or a fine steak or roast without a perfectly baked potato. Vegetables can be wonderful!

## Artichokes with Vinaigrette Sauce

6 large artichokes            Vinaigrette Sauce (see p. 252)
2 tablespoons salt

1. Break off stems and trim bases—remove the few short outer leaves around them—so that artichokes stand evenly. With scissors, cut the tips off the leaves, and with a knife, cut ½ inch off the very top of each artichoke.

2. Put the artichokes in a large kettle and cover them with boiling water—enough so they swim around. Add salt, boil, uncovered, 25 to 35 minutes, or until done.

• The time will depend on the size of the artichokes. To test, pull out a leaf: if it comes easily, the artichoke is done.

3. Turn artichokes upside down to drain. When they are cool enough to handle, spread the leaves apart so that the little center cone of leaves can be pulled out with your fingers. Below this cone is the fuzzy choke. Use a spoon to scrape out all the fuzz, exposing the meaty artichoke bottom.

4. If desired, Vinaigrette Sauce can be poured into the hollowed-out centers, or the sauce can be served in little cups alongside the artichokes.

• Instead of Vinaigrette, Hollandaise Sauce (see p. 246) can be served.
*Makes 6 servings.*

## Asparagus Hollandaise

For this recipe, try to choose a bunch of asparagus with all spears about the same thickness.

1 2- to 2½-lb. bunch asparagus    Hollandaise Sauce (see p. 246)
1 teaspoon salt

1. Cut off ½ inch from the hard white end of each asparagus spear. Peel the spears with a vegetable peeler, ¾ of the way up to the tip.

• This helps the spears to cook in about the same time as the tender tips; it also removes any dirt hiding under the scales.

2. Lay the spears in a large skillet of boiling salted water to ⅔ its depth. Do not cover. Bring to a boil and boil 10 to 20 minutes until bases of stalks are tender when tested with a fork. (The time will depend on the thickness of the spears.) Drain well.

3. Serve asparagus as a separate course, putting 4 to 5 spears on each plate. Sprinkle with salt and pepper to taste and serve with Hollandaise Sauce.

• Or serve asparagus spears cool, but not cold, with Vinaigrette Sauce (see p. 252). *Makes 4 to 6 servings.*

## SEVEN-MINUTE GREEN BEANS

| | |
|---|---|
| 1½ lbs. green beans | ½ teaspoon freshly cracked |
| 4 teaspoons salt | black pepper |
| 2 tablespoons lemon juice | ¼ cup melted butter |

1. Top and tail the beans, wash them, and put them into a large saucepan with 2 quarts of boiling water and 1 tablespoon of salt.
2. Reduce heat to simmer, and cook for 7 minutes only, uncovered. (The beans lose their bright color when covered during cooking.)
3. Drain beans and plunge them immediately into cold water to refresh and set their color.

• This can be done in the morning and the beans refrigerated until dinner.

4. Return beans to the saucepan, add lemon juice, the remaining 1 teaspoon of salt, pepper, and melted butter, and shake over high heat until the beans are warmed—about 5 minutes. *Makes 6 servings.*

## MOLDED GREEN BEANS

| | |
|---|---|
| 1 lb. very finely minced mushrooms | 2 lbs. whole green beans or 3 10-oz. pkgs. frozen whole green beans |
| 1 cup minced yellow onion | |
| ¼ cup butter | 4 beaten eggs |

1 cup grated Gruyère cheese
¼ cup bread crumbs (see p. 7)
1 teaspoon salt
½ teaspoon freshly cracked
    black pepper
¼ teaspoon freshly grated
    nutmeg
1 cup Lemon Butter (see
    p. 253)

1. Sauté mushrooms and onion in foaming butter over high heat until mushrooms are dry. Set aside.

• Before sautéing the mushrooms, put them, a handful at a time, in the corner of a tea towel and wring them out. Not absolutely necessary, but it helps get rid of excess moisture.

2. Cook fresh beans in a small amount of boiling water for 7 minutes, or cook frozen beans according to the package directions, but for just half the recommended time.

3. Drain beans and mix with onion and mushrooms in a big bowl.

4. Add beaten eggs, cheese, bread crumbs, salt, pepper, and nutmeg, then pack the mixture into an oiled 10-inch ring mold or a kugelhof mold.

5. Stand the mold in a pan of boiling water, put it in a preheated 350° oven, and bake for ½ hour.

• If dinner is delayed, the mold can remain in the water bath, in a 200° oven, for about ½ hour longer.

• The mold can be baked ahead, refrigerated overnight, then brought to room temperature and reheated in the water bath in a preheated 350° oven. Reheating will take 10 minutes.

6. Remove mold from water bath, let it stand 5 minutes, then run a knife around the edge to loosen it, invert it on a platter, and shake to unmold.

7. Serve with hot Lemon Butter. *Makes 12 to 16 servings.*

## FLAGEOLETS

Flageolets are green kidney beans from France. Since they are quite bland, the little beans, which are especially good with Rack of Lamb (see p. 104), need the chopped garlic for flavor.

1 box (about 2 cups) dried or
    1 large can flageolets
1 quart chicken stock (see
    p. 241)
2 tablespoons lamb drippings
    or melted butter
1 medium clove chopped
    garlic
½ teaspoon salt
¼ teaspoon freshly cracked
    black or white pepper
1 tablespoon chopped parsley

1. Soak dried beans overnight in enough cold water to cover.
2. Drain beans and put them in a saucepan with chicken stock.
3. Bring to a boil, cover pan, reduce heat to simmer, and cook until beans are tender, about 1 hour.
4. Drain beans and toss them in lamb drippings, or butter, flavored with the chopped garlic. Season with salt and pepper and garnish with chopped parsley.

• If canned beans are used, drain and rinse them, place in saucepan with drippings or butter and garlic and cook over medium heat 5 to 10 minutes or until heated through. *Makes 6 servings.*

## STEWED DRIED BEANS

Almost any kind of dried bean can be used in this recipe, but I prefer the small dried pea bean. I like to serve this with Braised Boned Leg of Lamb (see p. 107).

| | |
|---|---|
| *1 lb. dried pea beans* | *¼ cup braising liquid from* |
| *1 to 1½ quarts light chicken* | *lamb or other meat, op-* |
| *stock (p. 241)* | *tional* |
| *1 teaspoon salt* | *2 tablespoons chopped* |
| *½ teaspoon freshly cracked* | *parsley* |
| *black pepper* | |

1. Put beans in enough cold water to cover and either soak them overnight or bring the water to a boil, boil 2 minutes, cover the pan, and let the beans soak 1 hour; but, first, read the package directions, since these days some dried beans are presoaked, hence quicker to prepare.
2. Drain beans, cover with chicken stock, and bring to a boil. Cover the pan and turn heat down to simmer. Cook until the beans are tender and all the stock is absorbed. This should take about 1 hour, but it's difficult to give an exact cooking time for beans: sometimes they'll take only 20 minutes, but in hard water, they may never get tender—unless a pinch of baking soda is added. Start testing the beans, by pressing one between your thumb and forefinger, after 20 minutes of cooking, and watch them closely if soda has been added.
3. Before serving, season the beans with salt and pepper and moisten them with a little braising liquid if available. Garnish with chopped parsley.

• Stewed dried beans may be cooked the day before or in the morning. Undercook them if they're to be reheated.
• To keep beans warm without additional cooking, stand them in a pan of warm water. *Makes 8 servings.*

## BRAISED BRUSSELS SPROUTS

*1 quart Brussels sprouts, the*      *½ cup butter*
*smallest available*      *½ teaspoon freshly cracked*
*1 teaspoon salt, plus salt to*      *black pepper*
*clean sprouts*      *¼ cup lemon juice*

1. Trim wilted leaves from the Brussels sprouts and trim around the bases—but not too deeply, or the sprouts will fall apart.
2. Let the sprouts soak for a few minutes in a bowl of salted water.

• Sometimes there are tiny bugs in Brussels sprouts. Salted water draws them out.

3. Drain the sprouts and put them in a heavy casserole—one with a tight-fitting lid. Lay butter on the sprouts, sprinkle with 1 teaspoon salt, pepper, and lemon juice, cover, and place in a preheated 350° oven to braise for 25 to 35 minutes, or until barely tender. Every 10 minutes remove cover and stir the sprouts to be sure they don't stick.

• They will cook in the butter juice, and the small amount of moisture clinging to them. Neither water nor broth is needed. But do keep an eye on them, lest they scorch.
• Baby onions and turnips can be cooked the same way; sprinkle them with 1 teaspoon of sugar when adding the salt, pepper, and lemon juice. **Makes 6 servings.**

## BROCCOLI SOUFFLÉ

*2 10-oz. pkgs. frozen broccoli*      *¼ teaspoon cayenne pepper*
*¼ cup butter*      *¼ teaspoon freshly grated*
*¼ cup flour*      *nutmeg*
*2 cups milk*      *6 beaten egg yolks*
*½ cup grated Parmesan cheese*      *8 egg whites*
*½ teaspoon salt*      *¼ teaspoon cream of tartar*

1. Cook broccoli according to package directions. Drain and purée in a blender or through a food mill, using the medium disk.
2. Melt butter in a saucepan, stir in flour, and cook over high heat, stirring with a wooden spatula, for 2 minutes.
3. Remove from heat, add milk and whisk vigorously.
4. Return to high heat and cook until thick and smooth, stirring with a whisk.

5. Stir in cheese, salt, cayenne pepper, and nutmeg; then remove from heat.

6. Stir a little of the hot mixture into the egg yolks to warm them, then stir the warmed yolks into the saucepan, return pan to heat, and cook 1 minute more, but do not boil (or mixture will curdle).

7. Stir in broccoli purée and set aside.

• The soufflé may be made ahead up to this point and stored in a refrigerator several hours.

8. Beat egg whites and cream of tartar until very stiff.

• Egg whites are stiff when most of them can be scooped onto the beater at one time.

9. Put the broccoli mixture in a large bowl, add about ⅓ of the egg whites and fold in well to lighten the mixture, then lightly and quickly fold in the rest of the egg whites.

• Don't overmix when folding in egg whites. It's better to leave little fluffs of white showing than to risk the soufflé's not rising properly.

10. Pour the mixture into an unbuttered 8-cup soufflé dish and bake 45 minutes in a preheated 350° oven. Serve at once—soufflés wait for no one. *Makes 6 to 8 servings.*

## CABBAGE STUFFED WITH CABBAGE

Green, white, or red cabbage can be used. The red is especially good with game or pork. As a change, add meat—about ¾ cup of chopped ham or sausage meat, or ground beef—to the stuffing. Little new potatoes boiled in the water with the cabbage are delicious.

1 medium-size (1½- to 2-lb.) cabbage
¾ cup butter
½ cup finely chopped onion
¼ cup fine bread crumbs (see p. 7)
4 teaspoons salt
½ teaspoon freshly cracked white pepper
¼ teaspoon freshly grated nutmeg
3 tablespoons chopped parsley
2 lightly beaten eggs
2 tablespoons lemon juice

1. Remove and discard damaged leaves from cabbage; then peel off 5 or 6 leaves, keeping them as perfect as possible.

• The trick here is to cut the leaves loose at the base to release them. If the cabbage head is firm, run it under warm water to loosen the leaves.

2. Line a 2-quart bowl with a cloth at least 12 inches square and place the 5 or 6 leaves, stem ends up, in it, overlapping them to form a cup or nest.

3. Remove the core from the remaining cabbage and chop the cabbage very fine.

4. Melt ¼ cup of butter in a large skillet and sauté cabbage with chopped onion over high heat for about 15 minutes, or until cabbage is limp. Do not let it brown.

5. Put the sautéed cabbage and onion into a bowl and add bread crumbs, 1 teaspoon salt, pepper, nutmeg, 2 tablespoons of parsley, and the beaten eggs.

• The cabbage will be hot, so stir the eggs in quickly to avoid curdling.

6. Stuff the mixture into the cloth lined with cabbage leaves and twist the cloth very tight. Tie with a string, leaving a long end with which to pull the cabbage out of the water.

7. Drop the tied cloth into a large kettle of boiling salted—about 1 tablespoon of salt—water, reduce heat, and simmer, uncovered, for 1 hour. Turn once during cooking.

• The cabbage can be prepared ahead by tying it and cooking it for 45 minutes, then setting it aside, for up to 3 hours, then reheating it by simmering for the remaining 15 minutes in water that has been first brought to a boil.

8. Drain the cloth in a large strainer. Untie it and turn the cabbage out on a serving dish.

9. Make sauce by melting the remaining ½ cup of butter and adding the remaining 1 tablespoon of parsley and the lemon juice.

10. Pour sauce over cabbage. Cut in pie-shaped wedges to serve. *Makes 6 servings.*

## CARROTS VICHY

10 peeled carrots
½ cup melted butter
2 teaspoons sugar
1 teaspoon salt
½ teaspoon freshly cracked
   white pepper

2 tablespoons finely chopped
   parsley
1 tablespoon finely chopped
   mint, optional

1. Cut carrots into very thin slices, using a vegetable cutter or *mandoline.*

2. Put the slices into a pan with ¼ cup of the butter, 2 tablespoons of cold water, sugar, salt, and pepper. Cover with foil, pressing it right down on the carrots, and put the lid on the pan.

3. Place the pan over moderately high heat, and shaking it occasionally, cook about 20 minutes, or until carrots (which will cook in their own juices) are tender.

4. Place carrots in a serving bowl, add the remaining ¼ cup of butter, and sprinkle with parsley, and if desired, with mint. *Makes 6 to 8 servings.*

## WHIPPED CARROTS

12 peeled carrots
1 teaspoon salt
3 tablespoons butter
1 teaspoon lemon juice
¼ teaspoon freshly grated
   nutmeg

¼ teaspoon freshly cracked
   white pepper
2 tablespoons chopped parsley

1. Cut carrots in half crosswise and put them in a saucepan with enough water to cover generously.

2. Add salt, bring to a boil, cover, reduce heat, and simmer about 10 minutes, or until carrots are tender.

3. Drain carrots and purée them through a ricer or food mill or beat them in an electric mixer.

4. Beat in butter, lemon juice, nutmeg, and pepper.

5. Taste for seasoning and add more salt if desired. Garnish with chopped parsley. *Makes 8 servings.*

## CARROT RING

This carrot custard can be prepared ahead of time to the point of baking. Or it can be underbaked prior to dinner, left to stand in warm water for 1 hour and then reheated. Or it can be baked, unmolded, and reheated in a 250° oven—if you do this, I'd recommend serving the ring with piping hot Lemon Butter (see p. 253).

*5 cups peeled and grated raw carrots*
*2 teaspoons salt*
*4 well-beaten eggs*
*1½ cups light cream*
*½ teaspoon freshly cracked white pepper*
*1 teaspoon sugar*

*1 tablespoon lemon juice*
*½ cup blanched shredded almonds*
*¼ cup bread crumbs (see p. 7)*
*Vegetable oil to grease mold*
*1 lb. fluted and sautéed mushrooms (see p. 11)*

1. Boil carrots in water with 1 teaspoon of salt added for 5 minutes. Drain and put in a bowl.
2. Add the remaining ingredients, except mushrooms (and oil), and mix together.
3. Pour mixture into an oiled 9-inch ring mold, set in a pan of hot water and bake in a preheated 350° oven for 1 hour, or until mixture starts to shrink from the sides of the mold.
4. Let stand for 5 minutes. Turn out on a serving platter. Fill the center of the ring with mushrooms. *Makes 8 to 10 servings.*

## CAULIFLOWER MOUSSE

This is good to serve with any kind of roast.

*2 lbs. (2 average-size heads) cauliflower*
*1 tablespoon salt*
*⅛ teaspoon cayenne pepper*
*¼ teaspoon freshly grated nutmeg*
*1 cup medium Béchamel Sauce (see p. 245)*

*6 eggs*
*Butter to grease soufflé dish*
*2 tablespoons bread crumbs (see p. 7)*
*2 tablespoons chopped parsley*

1. Trim leafy stalks from cauliflower and cut heads into large pieces.
2. Put cauliflower in a saucepan with 1 tablespoon of salt and enough water to cover, and cook over high heat until tender. Drain.

3. Add cayenne pepper and nutmeg to cauliflower and purée through a food mill, using the finest disk. Do not put it in a blender.

• Catch the purée in a large bowl. By the time sauce and egg are mixed in, you will see why.

4. Mix the sauce into the cauliflower purée.

5. Beat eggs just enough to mix them (they should not be frothy), then fold them into the cauliflower mixture.

6. Taste for salt, and if desired, add some.

• For a flavor change, add ½ cup of grated Parmesan cheese or 2 table-spoons of chopped chives.

7. Pour mixture into a buttered 6- to 8-cup soufflé dish that has been dusted with bread crumbs.

8. Set the dish in a pan of hot water and bake it in a preheated 350° oven for 45 to 55 minutes, or until the mousse begins to pull away from the edge of the dish (or until a knife inserted in the mousse comes out clean).

• The water bath keeps the mousse creamy and smooth in texture. It is the equivalent of a double boiler that is used to cook a sauce over hot water.

• The mousse will continue to cook after it's taken out of the oven. If overcooked, it will tend to separate and become watery.

9. Bring the soufflé dish to the table to serve or unmold the mousse onto a platter. Garnish with parsley sprinkled around the edge and in the center.

• Serve plain or with Mornay Sauce (see p. 245) or Beurre Noir (see p. 253). *Makes 8 to 10 servings.*

## CELERY STICKS

| | |
|---|---|
| *1 large bunch celery* | *½ teaspoon salt* |
| *2 cups chicken stock (see* | *¼ teaspoon freshly cracked* |
| *p. 241)* | *white pepper* |
| *1 medium cored green pepper* | *1 tablespoon chopped parsley* |
| *½ cup butter* | |

1. Remove leaves from celery and cut the ribs into sticks 2½ inches long and ¼ inch wide. Tie the sticks into bundles—about 10 to a bundle —with string.

2. Put bundles into a saucepan, add stock, and bring to a boil, then cover, reduce heat, and simmer 12 to 15 minutes, or until celery is tender-crisp.

3. Remove from heat and drain.

4. Circle the bundles with ¼-inch-thick pepper rings—or top the bundles with half circles of pepper—that have been put in a saucepan of cold water, brought to a boil, boiled 1 minute, then drained and plunged immediately into cold water to set their color. Then arrange the bundles in a serving dish and remove the strings.

5. Heat butter in a small skillet until brown but not burned.

6. Season celery with salt and pepper, pour the Beurre Noir on top, and sprinkle with chopped parsley.

• If the celery sticks are prepared in advance, arrange them in an oven-proof serving dish, and before serving, pour the hot butter over them and put them in a preheated 350° oven for 5 minutes to heat through. *Makes 8 servings.*

## CHESTNUT PURÉE

| | |
|---|---|
| 2 lbs. fresh chestnuts | ½ teaspoon freshly cracked |
| 2½ cups beef stock (see p. 240) | black pepper |
| 1 teaspoon salt | 3 tablespoons butter |

1. Put the chestnuts in a saucepan, cover them with water, and bring to a boil. Remove the chestnuts from the pan 2 or 3 at a time, peel with a small sharp knife, and remove the inner brown skins.

• If the peel on any nut is especially stubborn, return the nut to boiling water for a few seconds—no chestnut is easy to peel, but warm ones seem a bit easier. A special chestnut knife helps cut through the shell.

2. Simmer nuts in beef stock about ½ hour, or until tender. When nuts are tender a knife blade should go in easily.

3. Purée the nuts through a ricer or through a food mill, using the medium disk.

4. Add salt, pepper, and butter and beat until smooth. The consistency should be suitable for piping through a pastry bag, to make rosettes.

• Use purée to garnish ducks or squabs. *Makes 6 to 8 servings.*

## CHESTNUT CROQUETTES

| | |
|---|---|
| 1 16-oz. can unsweetened chestnut purée or 1 recipe chestnut purée (see above) | ½ teaspoon salt |
| | ¼ teaspoon freshly cracked black pepper |
| 2 tablespoons chopped shallots | 1 tablespoon dry Madeira or dry sherry |
| 2 tablespoons butter | 3 beaten eggs |

¾ *cup ground almonds, about*     ¾ *cup bread crumbs (see*
½ *cup flour*                                      *p. 7)*
1 *tablespoon vegetable oil*        2 *cups vegetable shortening*

1. Put chestnut purée in a mixer bowl and beat until creamy.
2. Sauté shallots in butter until transparent; do not let them take on color.
3. Add sautéed shallots, salt, pepper, Madeira, and 1 beaten egg to the chestnut purée.
4. Taste and add more salt if desired.
5. Beat in ¾ cup of ground almonds and chill for ½ hour. If mixture seems too thin to shape, add more ground almonds.
6. Form mixture into cork-shaped croquettes about 2 inches long and roll in flour, shaking off the excess.
7. Dip the croquettes into a mixture of 2 beaten eggs and oil, then roll them in bread crumbs. Chill ½ hour.
8. Heat vegetable shortening to 375° in a heavy saucepan or an electric skillet and fry croquettes, 2 at a time, until brown and crisp. Drain on paper towels.

• Chestnut Croquettes may be fried in the morning, refrigerated and reheated. To reheat: set cake racks on a baking sheet, cover with two layers of brown paper, and lay the croquettes on the paper, and place in a preheated 350° oven for a few minutes. *Makes 8 servings.*

## MINTED CUCUMBERS

6 *large peeled cucumbers*        1 *tablespoon chopped fresh*
¼ *cup butter*                              *mint, or 1 teaspoon dried*
1 *teaspoon salt*                         *mint*
½ *teaspoon freshly cracked*
  *white pepper*

1. Cut ends off cucumbers, cut them in half lengthwise, and scoop out the seeds with the tip of a spoon. Cut the halves crosswise into pieces 1 inch long.
2. Put the pieces in a pan, cover with water, bring to a rolling boil, and boil for 1 minute. (This parboiling takes away any bitterness.)
3. Drain the cucumber pieces, run cold water on them, and return them to the pan. Add butter, salt, pepper, and mint.
4. Cover with foil, pressing it down on the cucumber pieces, then put the lid on the pan and cook the cucumber pieces in their own juice over moderately high heat for 8 minutes. Shake the pan frequently.

• Instead of mint, 1 tablespoon of chopped parsley or chopped fresh dill can be used. The dill is especially good when cucumbers are served with fish. *Makes 6 to 8 servings.*

## BRAISED BELGIAN ENDIVE

| | |
|---|---|
| 12 *heads Belgian endive* | 1 *teaspoon sugar* |
| 1 *tablespoon salt* | ½ *teaspoon freshly cracked* |
| 1 *slice bread* | *white pepper* |
| ½ *cup butter* | |

1. Wash endive. Trim around the root of each head, but do not detach the leaves. Remove any brown or wilted leaves.
2. Put the endive in a saucepan and add 3 to 4 cups of water. Add 2 teaspoons of salt, bring to a boil, and lay the slice of bread, crust and all, in the water. (The bread will take away some of the bitter flavor of the endive.) Boil for 7 minutes.
3. Melt ¼ cup of butter in a sauté pan—one with a tight-fitting lid.
4. Drain the heads of endive and put them into the butter with the water that clings to them.
5. Top with the remaining ¼ cup of butter and sprinkle with sugar, pepper, and the remaining 1 teaspoon of salt.
6. Cover the pan and shake it back and forth over high heat until the endive is golden on all sides. This will take about 20 minutes. Endive should be barely tender. *Makes 6 servings.*

## BRAISED BOSTON LETTUCE

| | |
|---|---|
| 5 *heads Boston lettuce* | 1 *teaspoon salt* |
| 2 *tablespoons butter, about* | ½ *teaspoon freshly cracked* |
| ¼ *lb. thickly sliced bacon* | *white pepper* |
| ¾ *cup finely chopped onion* | 2 *tablespoons chopped pars-* |
| ½ *cup chicken stock (see* | *ley* |
| *p. 241)* | |

1. Remove any damaged or loose outer leaves from the lettuce, then cut the heads in half, wash them, and shake off excess moisture.
2. Butter a large oval ovenproof dish—use about 2 tablespoons of butter—and arrange the lettuce in the dish, cut sides down.
3. Dice the bacon and sprinkle it over the dish, pushing some pieces underneath the lettuce halves.
4. Sprinkle with onion, pour on chicken stock, and season with salt and

pepper, then cover the dish with a piece of foil and set it in a preheated 350° oven for 1 hour.

5. Remove the dish from the oven and if there is too much liquid in the dish, pour it into a saucepan and boil rapidly to reduce it, then pour it back over the lettuce.

6. Before serving, sprinkle with chopped parsley. *Makes 10 servings.*

## SAUTÉED MUSHROOM CAPS AND PINE NUTS

*1½ lbs. mushrooms*
*2 teaspoons lemon juice, plus lemon juice to clean mushrooms*
*¼ cup butter*
*½ cup pine nuts*
*½ teaspoon salt*
*¼ teaspoon freshly cracked white pepper*

1. Wipe mushrooms with a paper towel dipped in acidulated water (1 quart of water with 1 tablespoon lemon juice) to clean them. Wipe them dry and trim off stems.

2. Heat butter in a large skillet, and when foaming subsides, add pine nuts and sauté them over high heat until lightly browned.

3. Add mushrooms, salt, pepper, and 2 teaspoons lemon juice. Shake the pan, tossing the mushrooms over high heat, for 3 minutes. Serve immediately. *Makes 8 servings.*

## MUSHROOM ROLL

Serve this hot, with Hollandaise Sauce (see p. 246) or hot melted butter; or serve it cold, without a sauce.

*Vegetable oil to grease pan and baking paper*
*1½ lbs. very finely chopped mushrooms*
*6 separated eggs*
*½ cup melted butter*
*½ teaspoon salt*
*¼ teaspoon freshly cracked white pepper*
*2 tablespoons lemon juice*
*4 or 5 fluted and sautéed mushrooms (see p. 11)*
*2 tablespoons chopped parsley*

1. Brush a jelly-roll pan with vegetable oil, then line it with waxed paper, letting the paper extend 4 inches on each end. Brush the paper with vegetable oil and set aside.

2. Put the chopped mushrooms in the corner of a tea towel, a handful at a time, wring them out to remove excess moisture, and put them in a bowl.

3. Beat egg yolks until fluffy. Add them, the melted butter, salt, pepper, and lemon juice to the mushrooms.

• Good flavor change: add 1 tablespoon chopped fresh tarragon, rosemary, or parsley to the mushroom mixture.

4. Beat egg whites until they form soft peaks and fold them into the mushroom mixture.

5. Pour the mixture into the prepared pan, spread it evenly, and bake in a preheated 350° oven for 15 minutes, or until the mixture starts to pull away from the sides of the pan.

6. Turn the mixture out of the pan onto 2 overlapping sheets of waxed paper, and with the paper to help, roll it up like a jelly roll.

• For a cool summer luncheon, roll it up with a crab-meat-and-sour-cream mixture inside (1 lb. crab meat mixed with 1 cup sour cream).
• The roll can be made in advance, then reheated, but it's better when it's fresh. If it's made ahead, place it in a preheated 300° oven for 10 minutes to warm it, and before serving, pour ½ cup of sizzling hot melted butter over the top.

7. Place the roll on a long narrow platter or board, garnish it with mushroom caps placed down the center, and sprinkle it with parsley. *Makes 8 to 10 servings.*

## Mushroom Soufflé

Should you butter a soufflé dish or not? We have found in our Creative Cooking classes that the soufflé climbs higher when the dish is not buttered. If you like a soufflé that's a bit crusty around the edges, bake this one as directed. If you prefer one that's tender, set the soufflé dish—use a 6-cup one or a 4-cup one with a paper collar tied around it—in a pan of hot water during baking.

1 lb. finely chopped mush-   ½ teaspoon salt
   rooms                    ¼ teaspoon freshly cracked
6 tablespoons butter         black pepper
1 cup finely chopped onion  ¼ teaspoon freshly grated
2 tablespoons flour        nutmeg
½ cup chicken stock (see   4 beaten egg yolks
   p. 241)                 6 egg whites
½ cup light cream

1. When mushrooms are chopped as finely as possible, squeeze out the excess juice by wringing them, a handful at a time, in the corner of a tea towel.

• There's a lot of moisture in mushrooms, and for this recipe it should be removed so the soufflé doesn't take too long to bake.

2. Melt ¼ cup of butter in a skillet, and when it is hot and foaming, add mushrooms and onion. Cook over high heat, stirring constantly with a wooden spatula, for about 15 minutes, or until mixture looks dry. Set aside.

3. Melt the remaining 2 tablespoons of butter in a small saucepan, stir in flour with a wooden spatula, and after it is blended in, continue stirring over high heat for 2 minutes.

4. Remove pan from heat and whisk in chicken stock and cream.

5. Return to high heat and cook, whisking constantly, until mixture begins to thicken.

6. Season with salt, pepper, and nutmeg.

7. Stir some of the hot mixture into the beaten egg yolks to warm them gradually, then stir the warmed yolks into the pan, cook over medium heat 1 minute more—but do not boil, or egg yolks will curdle—and set aside to cool slightly.

8. Beat egg whites until very stiff.

• Egg whites are stiff when most of them can be scooped onto the beater or whisk at one time.

9. Combine mushroom-onion mixture and contents of the saucepan in a large bowl and add about ⅓ of the egg whites. Fold whites in well to lighten the mixture, then lightly and quickly fold in the rest of the egg whites.

• It's better to leave little fluffs of egg white showing than to overmix and risk the soufflé not rising properly. It is the air bubbles beaten into the egg whites that make the soufflé rise.

10. Pour mixture into a soufflé dish (6-cup size or 4-cup size with a paper collar attached), put in a preheated 375° oven and bake 25 minutes

for a moist soufflé, 30 to 35 minutes for a drier one. As soon as the soufflé is taken from the oven, serve it—soufflés won't wait. *Makes 4 to 6 servings.*

## STUFFED MUSHROOMS

Serve these as appetizers or as an accompaniment to meat. Either way, they're very good.

| | |
|---|---|
| 1 lb. large white mushrooms | ½ teaspoon salt |
| Lemon juice to clean mushrooms | ¼ teaspoon freshly cracked black pepper |
| ¼ cup bread crumbs (see p. 7) | 1 to 2 tablespoons cognac |
| 1 tablespoon chopped shallots | ¼ lb. sliced bacon |
| | 1 tablespoon melted butter |

1. Wipe mushrooms with a damp cloth or paper towel wrung out in acidulated water (water with a little lemon juice in it), then remove and chop the stems and set the caps aside.

2. Put the chopped stems in a bowl with an equal amount of freshly made bread crumbs, then add shallots, salt, pepper, and enough cognac to moisten.

3. Partly cook the bacon, drain it on paper towels, chop it into little pieces. Combine bacon with the crumb mixture, and pack this stuffing into the cavities of the mushroom caps.

4. Sprinkle the caps with melted butter, place them on a baking sheet, and put in a preheated 350° oven to bake for about 15 minutes, or until stuffing is nicely browned. *Makes 6 servings.*

## NOODLE NESTS

To make noodle nests, which can be filled with peas (or any other vegetable) and served as the accompaniment for a roast, a wire "bird's nest" basket is necessary. It's a French utensil (imported by gourmet shops and mail order houses) that consists of two bowllike baskets, one larger than the other, with long handles. The baskets clamp together, and the noodles are held between them for deep frying.

| | |
|---|---|
| 1 8-oz. pkg. very fine noodles | 4 cups vegetable shortening |

1. Cook the noodles in 3 quarts of boiling water for 3 minutes only (they should be undercooked for frying), then drain them in a colander, rinse them with cold water, and spread them on paper towels to dry thoroughly.

2. In a deep saucepan, heat shortening to 375°.

• Check the temperature either with a fat thermometer or by dropping a bread cube into the fat: if the cube browns nicely in 1 minute, the fat is the right temperature.

3. Heat a "bird's nest" basket in the fat. Put about ⅙ of the noodles into the bottom part—be careful, for the basket will be very hot when removed from the fat—clamp on the top to shape the nest, and put the basket back into hot fat for 5 minutes, or until the noodles turn brown; then unclamp the top part of the basket, let the noodle nest cool for a few seconds, and turn it out.

4. Proceed as above with the remaining noodles. *Makes 6 servings.*

### ITALIAN GNOCCHI

| | |
|---|---|
| 2 cups milk | 2 teaspoons Dijon mustard |
| 2 teaspoons salt | ¾ cup grated Parmesan cheese |
| ¾ cup semolina | 6 tablespoons butter |
| ½ teaspoon freshly cracked white pepper | |

1. Put milk, salt, and 2 cups of water into a saucepan and bring to a boil. Slowly add semolina, stirring all the while with a wooden spatula (to prevent lumping). Continue stirring and cooking over high heat until the mixture pulls away from the sides of the pan.

2. Stir in pepper, mustard, ½ cup of grated cheese, and ¼ cup of butter.

3. Rinse a baking sheet with water and spread the mixture—it should form a layer about ½ inch thick—on the wet sheet. Chill it in a refrigerator ½ hour.

4. With a knife or a cookie cutter, cut the chilled mixture into diamonds, crescents—whatever shape or shapes you wish.

5. Overlap the cut pieces in an au gratin dish or an ovenproof baking dish, drizzle them with 2 tablespoons of melted butter and sprinkle with the remaining ¼ cup of cheese.

• This much can be done ahead, and the mixture stored in a refrigerator, ready for heating.

6. Before serving, put the dish under a broiler until the pieces are brown and bubbly—5 to 10 minutes—or set it in a preheated 250° oven for 10 to 15 minutes (the gnocchi can be held in a low oven for a little while longer if dinner is delayed), then brown the pieces under a broiler. *Makes 6 servings.*

## SPAETZLE

Spaetzle are little dumplings that go perfectly with Hungarian Chicken Paprika (see p. 137) and Hungarian Goulash (see p. 91). They can be shaped in a spaetzle machine which looks like a food mill with holes the size of half a dime, or the dough can be pressed through a colander or cut into tiny pieces with a knife.

|  |  |
|---|---|
| 2 *eggs* | ½ *cup melted butter* |
| 4 *teaspoons salt* | ¼ *teaspoon freshly cracked* |
| 2¼ *cups flour* | *black pepper* |
| ⅔ *cup milk* | |

1. Beat eggs in a bowl with a fork. Add ½ teaspoon salt, flour, a little at a time, and mix together.
2. Add milk, beating it in with a wooden spatula or an electric mixer.
3. The dough will be soft. Let it rest for about ½ hour.
4. Bring 2 quarts of water and 1 tablespoon of salt to a boil in a saucepan.
5. Put the dough into a spaetzle machine or press it through a colander with large holes, hold it over the boiling water, and tipping or shaking the pan just enough to keep the water moving (this helps to keep the spaetzle from sticking together), drop little bits of dough into the water by turning the handle of the machine or by pressing the dough through the colander with a wooden spatula, or cut the dough in tiny pieces with a knife and drop the pieces into the boiling water.
6. Boil spaetzle until they rise to the surface. This will take 3 to 4 minutes.
7. Before serving, drain spaetzle in a colander, put them in a warm serving dish, and toss with melted butter, pepper, and ½ teaspoon salt.

• Another serving idea: sauté the cooked spaetzle in butter and sprinkle with bread crumbs (see p. 7) before serving. *Makes 6 servings.*

## ONIONS À LA GRECQUE

These can be served as a relish with ham or tongue. Or they are delicious as appetizers, served either hot or at room temperature. Don't serve them cold.

| | |
|---|---|
| 36 *small white onions* | ½ *teaspoon dried thyme* |
| ¼ *cup olive oil* | 1 *bay leaf* |
| ⅔ *cup dry white wine* | ½ *teaspoon saffron* |
| 1 *teaspoon sugar* | 1 *cup white raisins or cur-* |
| 1 *teaspoon salt* | *rants* |
| 1 *sprig fennel, if available* | |

1. Peel the onions, then with the point of a knife, cut a little cross in the root end of each (this will help keep the onion in shape).

• The easiest way to peel small onions is by dropping them into boiling water for 30 seconds, draining them, then slipping off the skins.

2. Put the onions into a sauté pan along with the olive oil and wine, ½ cup of water, and the sugar, salt, fennel, thyme, and bay leaf. Bring to a boil, cover, then reduce heat and simmer until the onions are barely tender—the time, depending on the size of the onions, can be as little as 10 minutes or up to ½ hour.

3. Remove lid and discard bay leaf and fennel, add saffron and white raisins or currants, and toss onions around in the pan. If there is a surfeit of pan sauce, remove the onions, boil the sauce to reduce it, then return the onions. *Makes 6 servings.*


## PEA PURÉE

Most lovely light, delicate pea purées one gets in fine restaurants are made in commercial blenders. This recipe comes as close as is possible.

| | |
|---|---|
| 2 *10-oz. pkgs. frozen peas* | 1 *tablespoon melted butter* |
| 1 *teaspoon salt* | 2 *tablespoons heavy cream or* |
| 1 *teaspoon sugar* | *dairy sour cream, optional* |

1. Put peas in a saucepan with ¼ cup of water, salt, and sugar. Cover and bring to a boil. Boil for 3 to 4 minutes.

2. Drain peas well, and either purée them through a food mill, using the medium disk, then whip in melted butter, or for additional flavor, put them in a blender with the melted butter and heavy or sour cream and blend until smooth.

• Another way to give the peas more flavor is by puréeing them, then adding, instead of the melted butter, ½ teaspoon of salt, 1 tablespoon of sour or whipped cream, and a brown roux made by melting 3 tablespoons of butter in a small saucepan, stirring in 3 tablespoons of flour, and cooking over high heat, stirring constantly with a wooden spatula, until the mixture is brown (this takes at least 5 minutes).

• Still another way: purée peas, then, instead of adding melted butter, beat in ½ teaspoon of salt, ¼ teaspoon of freshly cracked black pepper, 2 tablespoons of heavy cream, and 1 tablespoon of bacon fat. *Makes 4 servings.*

## POTATOES ANNA

6 large baking potatoes  
¾ cup butter, about  
2 teaspoons salt

½ teaspoon freshly cracked  
white pepper

1. Peel the potatoes, wash and dry them well, then slice them ⅛ inch thick with a cutter or *mandoline*.

2. Butter a shallow ovenproof baking dish (or a 9- to 10-inch pie plate) generously—use about 2 tablespoons of butter.

3. Lay the potato slices, overlapping them, in concentric circles on the bottom of the dish (or pie plate). Build up layers of slices, sprinkling each layer with salt and pepper and dotting generously with butter. Potatoes should fill the container.

4. Lay a flat lid on the potatoes and weight it down with a 3-lb. weight. Bake in a preheated 375° oven for 1 hour.

5. Remove weight and lid from potatoes. Turn oven heat to 450° and bake potatoes about 15 minutes or until they brown on top. Turn out on a warm platter before serving. *Makes 6 to 8 servings.*

## POTATOES DAUPHINOISE

Serve this potato casserole with Truffled Chicken (see p. 142), Rack of Lamb (see p. 104) or Rib Roast (see p. 81).

6 large baking potatoes  
2 cups milk  
6 tablespoons butter  
1 clove chopped garlic  
¼ teaspoon freshly grated  
   nutmeg

1 teaspoon freshly cracked  
white pepper  
1¼ cups grated Swiss cheese  
1 egg

1. Peel the potatoes, wash and dry them well, and slice them ⅛ inch thick with a cutter or *mandoline*.

2. Put the slices into a saucepan, cover with milk, bring to a boil, and simmer, uncovered, for 10 minutes.

3. Drain the potatoes—reserve the milk—and dry them on paper towels.

4. Cream ¼ cup of butter, beat in the chopped garlic, and set aside.

5. Melt the remaining 2 tablespoons of butter and brush a large au gratin dish or an ovenproof baking dish with it.

6. Arrange ½ the potato slices in the dish and sprinkle with nutmeg, pepper, and ¾ cup of the cheese (no need for salt, since the cheese is salty). Put the remaining potato slices on top.

7. Beat egg with a fork and mix it into the reserved milk. Pour over the potatoes, dot the tops with the garlic-butter mixture, and sprinkle with the remaining ½ cup of cheese.

8. Set the dish in a pan of boiling water and bake in a preheated 375° oven for 45 to 60 minutes, or until potatoes are tender.

• This casserole can be made ahead if it's reheated (in the water bath) in a 375° oven.

• If dinner is delayed, an extra 30 minutes in a 250° oven won't hurt the potatoes a bit. *Makes 6 to 8 servings.*

## POTATOES SAVOYARD

| | |
|---|---|
| *6 large baking potatoes* | *6 tablespoons butter* |
| *2 cups chicken stock (see* | *1 teaspoon freshly cracked* |
| *p. 241) or beef stock (see* | *white pepper* |
| *p. 240)* | *1¼ cups grated Swiss cheese* |

1. Peel potatoes and slice them ⅛ inch thick with a vegetable cutter or *mandoline.*

2. Put the slices into a saucepan with the stock, bring to a boil, and simmer, uncovered, for 10 minutes.

3. Drain the potatoes—reserve the stock—and dry them on paper towels.

4. Melt 2 tablespoons of butter and brush an au gratin dish or an ovenproof baking dish with it.

5. Arrange ½ the potato slices in the dish and sprinkle with pepper and ¼ cup of the cheese (no salt is needed, because cheese is salty). Put the remaining potato slices on top.

6. Pour enough of the reserved stock over potatoes to come ¾ of the way up the dish. Dot the top of the potatoes with the remaining butter and sprinkle with the remaining ½ cup of cheese.

7. Put the dish in a preheated 375° oven to bake 45 to 60 minutes, or until the potatoes are tender. *Makes 6 to 8 servings.*

## POTATOES SARLADAISE

These are truffled potatoes served in one large cake, crisp and brown on the outside, moist and tender inside.

6 *large baking potatoes*              1½ *cups vegetable shortening*
1 *large truffle*
4 *large canned artichoke*
  *bottoms*

1. Peel the potatoes and slice them ⅛ inch thick with a vegetable cutter or *mandoline*.
2. Cut the slices into sticks the size of thin French fries. (Stack two or three slices together and cut them with a large knife—it's easy this way), and as the sticks are cut, put them in a bowl of cold water.
3. Soak the sticks for about ½ hour.
4. Cut the truffle into slivers and cut the artichoke bottoms into sticks the size of kitchen matches.
5. Drain the potato sticks, dry them thoroughly with paper towels, then combine them with the truffle slivers and cut artichoke bottoms.
6. Heat shortening in a heavy 8- to 10-inch iron skillet, and when the shortening is very hot—almost smoking—drop in the potato mixture and pat it into a flat cake with a spatula.
7. Cover the skillet and cook over high heat for about ½ hour, or until the potato cake is brown and crisp on the bottom. Then turn the potato cake over and cook until the other side is brown and crisp.

• A good way to turn the cake is by lifting it out onto a flat lid with a broad spatula, then turning the lid and the cake over together.

8. Drain the cake and cut it in wedges to serve. *Makes 8 to 10 servings.*

### Pommes Pailles

Follow the recipe for Potatoes Sarladaise (see above), but omit the truffle and artichoke bottoms and cut the potatoes like straws. (*Paille* means straw.)

### German Potatoes

Follow the recipe for Potatoes Sarladaise (see above) but do not cut the ⅛-inch potato slices into sticks, omit the truffle and artichoke bottoms, and put ½ the potatoes into the hot shortening, then sprinkle them with ½ a grated onion before adding the remaining potatoes and forming into a cake.

### WAFFLED POTATOES

| | |
|---|---|
| *4 large baking potatoes* | *2 teaspoons salt* |
| *2 cups vegetable shortening* | |

1. Peel the potatoes, wash and dry them, and using the serrated cutting edge of a *mandoline* or a vegetable slicer, cut them as thin as possible, in a waffle pattern.

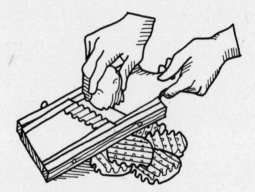

2. Soak the slices in iced water for 1 hour.

• A lot of the starch is removed from potatoes when they're soaked. The potatoes can be sliced in the morning and kept in water, in a refrigerator, until cooking time. Don't add salt to the water, for potatoes that stand in salted water turn dark.

3. When ready to fry the potatoes, drain the slices and dry them on paper towels, then heat shortening to 375° in an electric skillet, a deep fat fryer, or a heavy saucepan and fry a few slices at a time, until golden brown. Remove with a slotted spoon and drain on paper towels.

• Waffled potatoes can be fried ahead of time and reheated. To reheat: set cake racks on a baking sheet, cover with brown paper, lay the potatoes on the paper, and place in a preheated 350° oven for a few minutes.

4. Sprinkle with salt just before serving. *Makes 8 servings.*


### RICE PILAF

Rice Pilaf, which can be made with any stock or with water, can be served in the casserole in which it cooked, or it can be turned out onto an au gratin dish, the top first smoothed with a spatula, then indented to make a design. However you present it, give the rice a border of chopped parsley.

½ cup butter
1 finely chopped medium-size yellow onion
1 cup long-grain rice
2 cups chicken stock (see p. 241) or beef stock (see p. 240)

1 teaspoon salt
½ teaspoon freshly cracked black pepper
2 tablespoons chopped parsley

1. Melt ¼ cup of butter in a heavy casserole—one with a tight-fitting lid—and sauté the onion over high heat until it is translucent, about 2 minutes. Do not brown it.

2. Add the rice, stirring it around to coat the grains with butter.

3. Pour in the stock, add salt and pepper, bring to a full boil over high heat, then immediately put the lid on the casserole and turn the heat down to simmer.

4. Cook for 23 minutes (use a timer if you have one), without lifting the lid, then remove the lid, fluff the rice with 2 forks, sprinkle it with the remaining ¼ cup melted butter, and add a border of chopped parsley.

• Rice Pilaf can be cooked a day in advance, refrigerated, and reheated. To reheat: place the casserole, uncovered, over low heat and stir in ½ cup of melted butter. *Makes 6 to 8 servings.*

### Rice Timbales

1 recipe of Rice Pilaf (see p. 186)
2 tablespoons finely chopped celery

1 clove chopped garlic
¼ teaspoon freshly grated nutmeg
Oil to grease molds

1. Follow recipe for Rice Pilaf adding celery, garlic, and nutmeg to cooking liquid. Bring liquid to boil and proceed with recipe as directed.

2. When rice is cooked, pack it, hot, into 8 small oval molds greased with oil. Pack firmly, then let molds set for 1 minute before tipping them out. *Makes 8 servings.*

## SAFFRON RICE

Saffron Rice is made like Rice Pilaf (see p. 186). The only difference is in the flavorings.

2 tablespoons butter
2 tablespoons olive oil
1 finely chopped medium-
   size onion
½ teaspoon chopped garlic
1½ cups long-grain rice
1 teaspoon saffron filaments

3 cups shrimp stock, if available (see p. 72, step 2) or
3 cups chicken stock (see
   p. 241)
1 teaspoon salt
½ teaspoon freshly cracked
   white pepper

1. Heat butter and oil in a heavy casserole—one with a tight-fitting lid—and sauté onion and garlic in the mixture for about 3 minutes. Do not let it brown.

2. Add the rice, stirring it around to coat the grains with butter and oil.

3. Dissolve saffron in 1 tablespoon of stock, pour the remaining stock into the casserole, add the dissolved saffron, season with salt and pepper, and bring to a full boil over high heat, then immediately cover tightly and reduce heat to simmer.

4. Cook for 23 minutes, without lifting the lid, then remove the lid and fluff the rice with 2 forks.

• If dinner is delayed, keep the casserole warm in a 250° oven, without the lid (if it's left on, the rice will continue to steam), but covered with cheesecloth or a tea towel. To hold the rice even longer, pour ½ cup melted butter over it, stand the casserole in a pan of warm water, and half cover the pan with a lid. *Makes 6 to 8 servings.*


## RICE RING

2 cups long-grain rice
14 tablespoons butter
1 teaspoon salt
½ teaspoon freshly cracked
   black pepper

1 cup finely chopped parsley,
   optional

1. Put rice and 1 quart of water into a heavy saucepan or a casserole with a tight-fitting lid. Bring the water to a boil, put on the lid, reduce heat to simmer, and cook for 20 minutes, after which the water should be absorbed. If some is left, drain it off.

2. Stir in ¾ cup of melted butter, salt, and pepper. If you want a green rice ring, add the parsley.

3. Use 2 tablespoons of butter to grease a 9-inch ring mold. Pack the rice into the mold, place the mold on a baking sheet, and put into a preheated 350° oven to bake for 10 minutes.

4. Let stand at room temperature for 5 minutes before unmolding onto a serving plate. *Makes 8 servings.*

## SAUTÉED CHERRY TOMATOES

Here's a quick vegetable garnish that looks beautiful on a meat platter.

2 boxes (1 quart) cherry tomatoes
¼ cup butter
½ teaspoon sugar
½ teaspoon salt

¼ teaspoon freshly cracked
black pepper
1 heaping tablespoon
chopped parsley

1. Remove stems, then wash and dry the cherry tomatoes.
2. Heat butter in a large sauté pan. When it is foaming, add the tomatoes. Toss them over high heat, shaking the pan back and forth and sprinkling the tomatoes with sugar (this gives them a shiny glaze), for about 3 minutes. Don't overcook, or the skins will split, and the tomatoes will be too soft.
3. Season with salt and pepper and garnish with chopped parsley. *Makes 6 to 8 servings.*

## STUFFED TOMATOES

4 large tomatoes
6 tablespoons butter
¾ cup finely chopped onion
1 clove finely chopped garlic
½ cup soft bread crumbs (see
p. 7)

2 tablespoons ehopped parsley
½ teaspoon salt
¼ teaspoon freshly cracked
black pepper
½ cup grated Parmesan cheese

1. Cut tomatoes in half, crosswise, and cut off stem ends. Trim enough off the bottom of each half so that the tomatoes will stand without tiping.
2. Scoop out the tomatoes and reserve the pulp. Place the shells in a baking dish and set aside.
3. Melt 2 tablespoons of butter in a small pan, stir in onion and garlic, and cook over high heat, stirring, until transparent. Do not let the onions and garlic brown.
4. Stir in tomato pulp and cook over high heat 10 minutes.
5. Add bread crumbs, parsley, salt, and pepper, mix, then fill the set-aside tomato shells with the mixture. Dot the tomato halves generously with the remaining butter, sprinkle with grated cheese, and bake in a preheated 350° oven for 25 minutes. *Makes 8 servings.*

## ROMAN TOMATOES

Tomato cups filled with Rice Salad—the perfect chilled vegetable to serve with Vitello Tonnato (see p. 115).

| | |
|---|---|
| 8 *large tomatoes* | 8 *sprigs parsley* |
| 1 *recipe Rice Salad (see* | |
| *p. 197)* | |

1. Cut slices off the stem ends of tomatoes thick enough to serve as lids; reserve them. Then hollow out the tomatoes and turn them upside down on paper towels to drain.
2. Fill tomato shells with Rice Salad, mounding it slightly, and use the remaining Rice Salad to make a bed on a long narrow platter.
3. Stand the stuffed tomatoes on the rice bed, slit the reserved lids to the center, thread a sprig of parsley through each slit, and put the lids with their parsley plumes on top of the stuffed tomatoes. *Makes 8 servings.*


## ZUCCHINI PROVENÇAL

This zucchini can be made in advance and reheated. In fact, it's even better the next day.

| | |
|---|---|
| 6 *zucchini* | ¼ *teaspoon freshly cracked* |
| ½ *cup olive oil* | *black pepper* |
| 2 *large or 3 small cloves* | 2 *tablespoons chopped pars-* |
| *minced garlic* | *ley* |
| ½ *teaspoon salt* | |

1. Scrub the zucchini, cut them in half lengthwise, then cut the halves in very thin slices.

• Use a vegetable cutter or a *mandoline* to get even slices.

2. Heat olive oil in a large skillet and cook garlic over high heat in the oil until transparent. Do not let it brown.
3. Add zucchini slices and toss over high heat for about 3 minutes. Season with salt and pepper, and just before serving, sprinkle with chopped parsley. *Makes 6 to 8 servings.*

# SALADS

Mutiny threatens in my kitchen whenever I make a salad, for I refuse to honor all the rules set down by the classicists. In particular, I use glass, pottery, stainless steel, aluminum, or plastic salad bowls—any kind but wooden, for the very idea of a wooden bowl that has been rubbed with oil and garlic time and time again is repugnant to me. (If, however, you are loyal to a wooden bowl, scrub it with warm soapy water and rinse and dry it well after every use.) And though classicists may consider it heresy, I cut greens with a knife or scissors, for I find that less damage is done to greens by cutting than by tearing. And, also, cutting is faster.

For formal dinners, I serve salad as a separate course after the main course. For informal meals, I like the idea of serving salad as a first course. Some salads, such as Salade Niçoise (see p. 196), *are* the main course for luncheon or supper.

Any of the salad greens—romaine, Bibb, or Boston, for example—may be used alone as the basis of a salad or mixed with other greens, such as watercress, endive, chicory, celery, dandelion leaves, or young spinach leaves. However they're used, greens should first be washed thoroughly in cold water, then shaken to remove excess water, and placed on paper towels, rolled up loosely in the paper towels, wrapped in a tea towel, and placed in a refrigerator for at least ½ hour to crisp and become completely dry.

The simplest and best dressing for most salads is made with oil (4 parts) and vinegar (1 part) and seasoned with salt and pepper. This is a true French dressing. To vary the flavor, try different vinegars—tarragon, cider, red- or white-wine vinegar—or substitute fresh lemon juice for the vinegar. The best oil is olive oil, but it's interesting to experiment with vegetable oils and peanut oils. Use coarse salt (kosher salt or sea salt) and freshly cracked pepper from a mill. A little crushed garlic can be added, as can mustard or herbs.

Salads should be served immediately after they're dressed; otherwise the greens wilt and become sodden. When sturdy greens, such as romaine, spinach, or Belgian endive are used, the dressing can be made in advance in the salad bowl and the greens placed on top; then the bowl can be covered with plastic wrap and refrigerated until serving time, when the salad can be tossed and served on chilled plates.

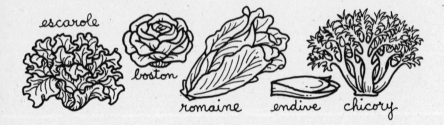

### Celeriac Rémoulade

The common name for celeriac is celery root, but do not confuse it with ordinary celery. Celeriac looks like a knobby turnip. It is a winter vegetable, and in the winter, when beautiful lettuce isn't around, it makes an excellent salad. Celeriac Rémoulade can also be served as a first course.

| | |
|---|---|
| *4 celeriac* | *½ teaspoon freshly cracked* |
| *⅔ cup mayonnaise (see p. 251)* | *white pepper* |
| *1 tablespoon Dijon mustard* | *2 tablespoons chopped pars-* |
| *1 teaspoon coarse salt* | *ley* |

1. Peel the celeriac and cut into matchstick-size pieces.

• The easy way to do this is to cut the celeriac in half, place the halves, cut sides down, on a chopping board, and slice, then to stack 3 or 4 slices and cut them into matchsticks.

2. Put the matchstick slices into a saucepan, add 2 cups of cold water, and bring to a rolling boil. Boil for 5 minutes.

• Not everyone parboils celeriac, but I prefer to do so. Parboiling seems to remove the bitter taste, and it makes celeriac more tender than it would otherwise be.

3. Drain the slices in a colander, rinse them with cold water, and dry them on paper towels or tea towels, then put them into a salad bowl, and add a mixture of mayonnaise, mustard, salt, pepper, and parsley, and toss with forks to mix.

4. Chill for at least 15 to 20 minutes in a refrigerator before serving.

• Celeriac Rémoulade can be made 2 to 3 hours in advance and kept in a refrigerator until ready to serve. *Makes 6 servings.*

## CUCUMBER SALAD WITH YOGHURT

| | |
|---|---|
| 6 cucumbers | 1 tablespoon freshly chopped |
| 2 teaspoons coarse salt | dill |
| 1 clove minced garlic | 2 tablespoons freshly chopped |
| 2 tablespoons vinegar | mint leaves |
| 1 cup yoghurt | |

1. Peel cucumbers, cut off the ends, and cut them in half lengthwise. Scoop out the seeds with the tip of a spoon, then cut the cucumber pieces in half crosswise and cut the resulting quarters into very thin julienne slices.

2. Put the slices in a salad bowl and sprinkle with salt and garlic.

3. Mix vinegar, yoghurt, and dill together, fold into cucumbers, and marinate them in a refrigerator.

4. Before serving, sprinkle with chopped mint leaves. Serve *very* cold.

• This salad is especially good with lamb. *Makes 6 to 8 servings.*

## BELGIAN ENDIVE SALAD

This is a good buffet salad because Belgian endive holds up well after tossing. The dressing, a mustardy vinaigrette, can be mixed in the bottom of the salad bowl, the endive placed on top, and the bowl covered with plastic wrap and refrigerated until serving time, when the salad can then be tossed.

| | |
|---|---|
| 12 heads Belgian endive | ½ cup tarragon vinegar |
| 1 teaspoon coarse salt | ½ cup French olive oil |
| ½ teaspoon freshly cracked white pepper | 2 tablespoons chopped parsley |
| 1 tablespoon Dijon mustard | |

1. Trim root ends of endive and wash and dry the heads well. Cut them into long thin strips with a chef's knife.

2. To make dressing, mix salt, pepper, mustard, vinegar, and oil together with a fork.

• Taste the dressing for seasoning and add more salt if desired.

3. Put the strips of endive into a salad bowl with the chopped parsley and toss the endive, parsley, and dressing together before serving. *Makes 12 servings.*

## BELGIAN ENDIVE AND CITRUS SALAD

12 *heads Belgian endive*
8 *scallions*
2 *large navel oranges*
1 *medium grapefruit*
½ *cup lemon juice*

½ *cup olive oil*
1 *teaspoon coarse salt*
½ *teaspoon dried rosemary*
2 *tablespoons chopped parsley*

1. Trim root ends of endive, wash and dry the heads thoroughly, then slice them crosswise, into rings, and put the rings into a salad bowl.

2. Trim roots and green tops from scallions, then cut the scallions into thin rings and scatter the rings over the endive rings.

3. Peel oranges and grapefruit, trim off all the bitter white inner covering, and section by cutting as close to membrane of each section as possible. Add to salad bowl.

• If desired, all oranges, or all grapefruit, can be used.

4. Make dressing by shaking lemon juice, oil, salt, and rosemary in a small jar or by stirring them together in a small bowl.

• The salad can be made to this point the day before it is to be served. Store the dressing and the salad bowl separately in a refrigerator, and toss contents together at the last minute.

5. Sprinkle chopped parsley over salad, pour on dressing, and toss. Serve on chilled plates. *Makes 6 to 8 servings.*

## FRENCH GREEN SALAD

2 *or 3 heads of tender lettuce*
2 *tablespoons chopped parsley*
1 *teaspoon coarse salt*
½ *teaspoon freshly cracked black pepper*

2 *tablespoons tarragon vinegar*
½ *cup French olive oil*

1. Separate the lettuce leaves, discarding any damaged ones, and wash in cold water. Dry the leaves in single layers on a double thickness of paper towels, roll the leaves loosely in the paper towels, then wrap in a tea towel, and put in a refrigerator to crisp.

• This can be done the day before the salad is to be served.

2. Cut the leaves into pieces with a large chef's knife or with kitchen shears, then put the pieces into a chilled salad bowl and sprinkle with chopped parsley.

• Instead of, or in addition to, chopped parsley, other chopped fresh herbs—1 tablespoon of chopped chives, for instance, or of tarragon, or basil—can be used.

3. To make dressing, combine salt, pepper, vinegar, and oil in a small bowl (or a small jar) and stir or shake until mixed.

• The dressing can be varied to taste by using 5 parts rather than 4 parts oil to 1 part of vinegar; by using red- or white-wine or cider vinegar instead of tarragon vinegar, or vegetable oil or imported French peanut oil instead of olive oil; or by adding 1 clove of crushed garlic to it or if you want it to coat the lettuce more heavily, 1 beaten egg.

4. Pour dressing on lettuce, toss lightly, and serve at once, on chilled plates.

• Overdressing the salad causes the lettuce to wilt. It is proper to use just enough dressing to coat the greens. *Makes 4 to 6 servings.*

### RAW MUSHROOM SALAD

*1 lb. fresh large white mush-*
*rooms*
*½ cup lemon juice, plus lemon*
*juice to clean mushrooms*
*½ cup French olive oil*
*1 teaspoon coarse salt*

*½ teaspoon freshly cracked*
*white pepper*
*¼ teaspoon oregano*
*2 tablespoons chopped pars-*
*ley*

1. Clean mushrooms either by dipping them in acidulated water—water with a little lemon juice (about 1 tablespoon to 1 quart of water) in it—or by wiping them with towels that have been dipped in acidulated water.

2. Dry the mushrooms with paper towels, then trim the stems even with the base of the caps and slice the caps paper thin.

3. Put the slices in a bowl, add lemon juice, olive oil, salt, pepper, and oregano, mix together, and marinate for 1 hour at room temperature.

4. Sprinkle with parsley and serve on chilled plates. ***Makes 4 servings.***

## SALADE NIÇOISE

This is my own variation on the classic recipe.

*1 medium clove garlic*
*1 head romaine or other sturdy green*
*1 cooked chicken breast, cut in julienne strips*
*¼ lb. baked ham, or smoked tongue, cut in julienne strips*
*3 peeled and quartered hard-cooked eggs*
*2 peeled, seeded, and quartered tomatoes*
*1 can flat anchovy fillets*
*6 canned beets, cut in julienne strips*
*6 small boiled and sliced potatoes*
*2 sliced ribs celery*

*1 green or red pepper, sliced in rings*
*1 medium peeled red onion, sliced in rings*
*1 7-oz. can tuna*
*24 black olives*
*1 teaspoon coarse salt*
*1 teaspoon freshly cracked black pepper*
*1 teaspoon Dijon mustard*
*½ cup French olive oil*
*2 tablespoons red-wine vinegar*
*2 tablespoons chopped parsley*
*6 lemon slices*

1. Cut garlic clove in half and use the halves to rub the inside of a large salad bowl.

2. Wash romaine, roll up in paper towels and then in a tea towel, and put in a refrigerator for ½ hour to crisp.

3. Cut the leaves into shreds with a large chef's knife, line the salad bowl with them, then arrange the chicken, ham or tongue, eggs, tomatoes, anchovies, beets, potatoes, celery, pepper, onion, tuna, and olives in layers on top.

4. Cover bowl with plastic wrap and place it in a refrigerator until serving time.

• This can be done in the morning.

5. Make dressing by shaking salt, pepper, mustard, olive oil, and vinegar in a small jar or stirring them in a small bowl.

6. When ready to serve, pour dressing over salad and toss. Sprinkle with chopped parsley and garnish with thin slices of lemon. ***Makes 4 servings.***

## French Potato Salad

8 to 10 medium-size potatoes
1 teaspoon salt
¼ cup tarragon vinegar
½ cup French olive oil
2 tablespoons chopped fresh chives
1 teaspoon Dijon mustard
½ teaspoon freshly cracked black pepper
1 teaspoon coarse salt
2 tablespoons mayonnaise (see p. 251)
2 tablespoons freshly chopped parsley

1. Put unpeeled potatoes into a saucepan of boiling water with 1 teaspoon salt added, and cook over medium high heat 15 to 25 minutes or until tender. Drain and cool slightly.

2. When the potatoes are comfortable to handle, peel them and slice them—¼ inch thick—into a bowl.

3. Mix together the vinegar, olive oil, chives, mustard, pepper, and 1 teaspoon coarse salt; while the potato slices are still warm, pour the mixture over them and toss with a fork.

4. Let the potato slices marinate at room temperature until cool, about 1 hour, turning them over in the bowl occasionally, then put them in a refrigerator to chill.

5. Serve cold, garnished with mayonnaise and chopped parsley. *Makes 6 servings.*

## Rice Salad

1 cup long-grain rice
1 teaspoon salt
½ teaspoon freshly cracked black pepper
¼ cup olive oil
2 tablespoons wine vinegar
2 teaspoons Dijon mustard
2 cups mixed cooked vegetables—carrots, green beans, peas, corn kernels, or other vegetables
½ finely diced green pepper
½ peeled and diced cucumber

1. Put rice, salt, pepper, and 2 cups of water in a small heavy pan or a casserole—one with a tight-fitting lid. Bring to a boil, cover, then reduce heat and simmer, covered, for 20 minutes.

2. Put cooked rice in a bowl, add oil, vinegar, and mustard, and toss with a fork to mix.

3. Gently mix in cooked vegetables (these can be leftovers, and in any combination you wish), green pepper, and cucumber.

4. Taste for, and if necessary, adjust seasoning. Serve cold.

• Foods to be served cold usually require more seasoning than do other foods.

• If desired, Rice Salad can be packed into an oiled ring or melon mold, an oiled loaf pan—even a mixing bowl—chilled, then unmolded (by inverting the container) on a serving platter. *Makes 8 servings.*

## ROMAINE SALAD

2 heads romaine
½ lb. sliced bacon
1½ cups bread cubes
2 teaspoons coarse salt
1 teaspoon freshly cracked black pepper
1 teaspoon Dijon mustard
1 teaspoon finely chopped garlic
2 tablespoons lemon juice

2 tablespoons red-wine vinegar
½ cup vegetable oil
2 tablespoons French olive oil
1 egg
2 tablespoons chopped parsley
2 hard-cooked eggs
8 flat anchovy fillets

1. Wash the romaine in cold water, then cut the leaves crosswise. Shake off all water, and wrap the cut leaves in paper towels and then, together, in a tea towel, and put them in a refrigerator to crisp for at least ½ hour.

2. Cut the bacon into small bits, fry slowly until crisp, then remove the bacon bits with a slotted spoon and pour off all but 2 tablespoons of the fat in the frying pan. Dry the bacon bits and set them aside.

3. Fry bread cubes in the bacon fat until brown and crisp. Set aside.

4. In the bottom of a big salad bowl, mix together salt, pepper, mustard, garlic, lemon juice, vinegar, vegetable oil, olive oil, and egg. Stir with a fork to mix thoroughly, then pile the romaine on top and sprinkle with bacon bits and bread cubes.

5. Sprinkle chopped parsley over all and either toss and serve immediately, or cover the bowl with plastic wrap, and refrigerate until time to serve, and toss then.

6. After tossing salad, shell, then quarter hard-cooked eggs. Arrange the quarters around the edge of the salad and lay an anchovy fillet on each quarter. *Makes 8 servings.*

## RAW SPINACH SALAD

1½ lbs. fresh young spinach
1 tablespoon grated onion
2 teaspoons Dijon mustard
⅛ teaspoon freshly cracked black pepper
½ teaspoon coarse salt

2 tablespoons white-wine vinegar
½ cup walnut oil (available in gourmet shops)
4½ teaspoons lemon juice

1. Pick over spinach, eliminating damaged leaves, remove stems, and wash thoroughly, first in warm water, then in cold. Dry the leaves thoroughly by rolling them up in paper towels, wrapping them all in a tea towel, and putting in a refrigerator to crisp for at least ½ hour.

2. Mix remaining ingredients together in a small bowl. Pour over spinach, and toss.

• Taste the salad for seasoning before serving it. More salt may be necessary; nine times out of ten, it is. *Makes 6 servings.*

## BEEFSTEAK TOMATO AND RED ONION SALAD

| | |
|---|---|
| 6 *beefsteak tomatoes* | ¼ *cup red-wine vinegar* |
| 2 *red onions* | ¾ *cup oil* |
| 1 *teaspoon coarse salt* | 2 *tablespoons fresh chopped* |
| ½ *teaspoon freshly cracked* | *chives* |
| *black pepper* | 2 *cloves finely chopped garlic* |

1. Do not peel tomatoes. Cut off tops and bottoms, then cut the tomatoes into ½-inch-thick slices.

2. Peel the onions and cut them into thin (⅛-inch) slices.

3. Arrange the tomato slices alternately with the onion slices, overlapping them, on a long narrow platter.

4. To make dressing, put salt, pepper, vinegar, and oil in a small bowl (or a small jar) and stir (or shake) until mixed.

5. Pour dressing over tomato and onion slices, sprinkle with chives and garlic, and let marinate for ½ hour at room temperature before serving. *Makes 6 to 8 servings.*

## SPANISH SALAD

| | |
|---|---|
| 2 *large navel oranges* | 2 *tablespoons dry sherry* |
| 1 *small red onion* | 1 *teaspoon coarse salt* |
| 2 *heads romaine* | ½ *teaspoon freshly cracked* |
| ½ *cup Spanish olive oil (avail-* | *black pepper* |
| *able in gourmet shops)* | ½ *cup chopped black olives* |
| 2 *tablespoons red-wine vine-* | 1 *4-oz. jar drained and* |
| *gar* | *slivered pimientos* |

1. Peel oranges, trim off all the bitter white inner covering, and section by cutting as close to the membrane of each section as possible.

2. Peel the onion, cut it into thin slices, and press the slices to make onion rings.

3. Wash the romaine, cut the leaves crosswise. Shake off all water, dry

the cut leaves by rolling in paper towels, then wrapping in a tea towel, and put them in a refrigerator to crisp.

4. Make dressing by shaking olive oil, vinegar, sherry, salt, and pepper in a small jar or by stirring them together in a small bowl.

5. When ready to serve, put orange sections, onion rings, and romaine in a salad bowl, sprinkle with chopped olives and pimiento slivers, pour on dressing, and toss. Serve on chilled plates. *Makes 8 servings.*

## COLD VEGETABLE SALAD VINAIGRETTE

2 cups cooked peas
2 cups diced cooked green beans
1 cup diced cooked potato
½ cup diced cooked carrot
1 cup diced canned beets
1 cup diced cooked ham
1½ teaspoons coarse salt

½ teaspoon freshly cracked white pepper
¾ cup oil
¼ cup red-wine vinegar
½ teaspoon freshly cracked black pepper
1 cup mayonnaise (see p. 251)
Lettuce, optional

1. Put peas, beans, potato, carrot, beets, ham, 1 teaspoon salt, and white pepper into a salad bowl.

2. Make a vinaigrette dressing by beating oil, vinegar, black pepper, and the remaining ½ teaspoon of salt together with a fork.

3. Pour dressing over vegetables, toss to coat, and let marinate in refrigerator for 2 hours.

4. Drain off the dressing, add mayonnaise, and toss to mix.

5. Spoon the salad onto individual beds of lettuce, or pack it into a mold and turn it out on a chilled serving platter. *Makes 6 servings.*

## WATERCRESS AND MUSHROOM SALAD

3 bunches watercress
½ lb. fresh large white mushrooms
¼ cup walnut or other oil (walnut oil is available in gourmet shops)

4½ teaspoons lemon juice, plus lemon juice to clean mushrooms
1 teaspoon coarse salt
½ teaspoon freshly cracked black pepper

1. Wash watercress. Shake off excess water and trim heavy stems, then roll the watercress in paper towels and place it in a plastic bag. Put in refrigerator at least ½ hour.

• Instead of watercress, 3 heads of Bibb lettuce can be used. Wash the lettuce—separate the leaves to do this—and dry carefully. Wrap leaves in paper towels, then in a tea towel, and put in a refrigerator to crisp.

2. Clean mushrooms either by dipping them in acidulated water—water with a little lemon juice (about 1 tablespoon to 1 quart) in it—or by wiping them clean with towels dipped in acidulated water.

3. Wipe the mushrooms dry with paper towels, then trim the stems even with the base of the caps and slice the caps paper thin.

4. Mix dressing in a salad bowl by beating oil, lemon juice, salt, and pepper together with a fork.

5. Add mushrooms and watercress. Toss and serve immediately. *Makes 4 to 6 servings.*

## Zucchini Salad

| | |
|---|---|
| 6 *small- to medium-size zucchini* | 2 *tablespoons chopped fresh chives* |
| 1 *cup dairy sour cream* | 1 *tablespoon chopped fresh tarragon or 1 teaspoon dried* |
| 1 *teaspoon coarse salt* | |
| ½ *teaspoon freshly cracked white pepper* | 2 *tablespoons chopped parsley* |

1. Scrub, but do not peel, the zucchini, then slice them paper thin, using a vegetable cutter or *mandoline*.

2. Put the slices in a salad bowl and fold in sour cream, salt, pepper, chives, and tarragon. Chill thoroughly.

3. Before serving, toss, then sprinkle with chopped parsley. Serve icy-cold on chilled plates. *Makes 6 servings.*

# DESSERTS

To many people, dessert is the most important part of the meal. These are the people you see in restaurants reading the menu from bottom to top, choosing an entrée to go with the sweet. If they're to be your guests, why not indulge them? After a rich dinner a light dessert is generally called for, but after a simple one, why not pull out all the stops and serve an extravagant, absolutely luscious concoction?

Both kinds of dessert—simple and extravagant—are in this chapter, in generous variety. Here, too, a reminder: fruit and cheese are still the perfect ending to many a meal, and with an abundance of fresh fruit the year around, and America's growing interest in cheese, dessert need never be a problem.

Many desserts—cold soufflés, mousses, and tarts, to name a few—can or must be prepared in advance. Meringue Shells (see p. 232), made days or even weeks ahead, then filled with ice cream, and covered with Chocolate Fudge Sauce (see p. 233) or fruit can make any dinner seem like a party.

A Sponge Cake (see p. 215) that has been baked and frozen is quickly ready to be turned into Italian Rum Cake (see p. 213) and layers of Yellow Butter Cake (see p. 212) are the beginnings of an elegant Charlotte Portugaise (see p. 211). The fruit syrup for Oranges Orientale (see

p. 225) kept in the refrigerator in a jar, will last almost indefinitely; pour it over any cut-up fresh fruit, and the sweet course is ready.

More than almost any other foods, desserts have shape and style. Specific equipment is needed for preparing and serving them. Soufflé dishes, flan rings, cake pans and tart pans, *barquette* molds, and mousse cups are all available in department stores and gourmet shops. Nice serving extras to have are special dessert plates, a nest of glass or crystal bowls, pot-de-crème pots, parfait glasses, and a chocolate-roll board.

For final flourishes, depend on the pastry bag and star tube (see p. 11). With these and a little whipped cream, the simplest dessert can be turned into a creation—one that can be accented with candied violets, a sprinkling of praline powder (see p. 209), grated nuts, or chocolate curls.

### BEIGNETS WITH RASPBERRY SAUCE

| | |
|---|---|
| ½ cup unsalted butter | 2 cups vegetable shortening |
| 1 cup flour | ½ cup confectioners' sugar |
| 3 to 4 eggs | Raspberry Sauce (recipe fol- |
| 1 tablespoon framboise | lows) |

1. Put butter and 1 cup of cold water into a saucepan and bring to a boil.

2. As soon as the butter has melted, and with mixture still boiling, dump in the flour—all at once—and stir vigorously over high heat until mixture leaves the sides of the pan.

3. Remove from heat, and beat in 3 eggs, one at a time, beating each in thoroughly before adding the next, and the framboise. If the mixture does not fall lightly from the spoon when it is lifted, add another egg, ½ of it at a time, beaten enough to mix.

4. Heat shortening to 375° in a heavy saucepan—one about 3 inches deep. Check temperature with a fat thermometer, or test it with a bread cube, which will brown nicely in 1 minute if the temperature is right.

5. Drop the batter from a teaspoon directly into the hot fat. Fry about 6 teaspoonfuls, 6 beignets, for 1 to 1½ minutes on each side, or until both sides are browned.

• Allow fat to return to 375° before frying more beignets.
• Mixture makes about 24 beignets.

6. Remove beignets from fat with a slotted spoon, drain them on brown paper or paper towels; and to keep them warm while you fry the remaining beignets, put them on a cake rack lined with brown paper, set the rack on a baking sheet, and place it in a low (250°) oven.

7. When all the beignets are fried, heap them on a serving platter and sift confectioners' sugar over them. Serve immediately, with Raspberry Sauce.

• Beignets may be made ahead and left at room temperature for up to 6 hours and reheated by placing them on a baking sheet in a 250° oven for about 10 minutes or until heated through.

### Raspberry Sauce

2 10-oz. pkgs. frozen raspberries
½ cup confectioners' sugar
2 tablespoons framboise

1 teaspoon arrowroot
½ cup red currant jelly
3 tablespoons lime juice

1. Thaw raspberries—reserve 1 tablespoon of the juice—and place berries and remaining juice in a blender, and purée them. Strain into a saucepan.
2. Stir in confectioners' sugar and framboise.
3. Mix arrowroot with a little cold raspberry juice and stir it into saucepan.
4. Add currant jelly and lime juice and heat, stirring constantly, about 5 minutes or until slightly thickened. *Makes 6 to 8 servings.*

### CRÊPES À LA JULIE

For this unusual dessert, stuff plain crêpes with Pastry Cream mixed with candied pineapple, roll the crêpes, coat them with cooky crumbs, and fry in deep fat.

½ cup chopped candied pineapple
½ cup rum
1 recipe Pastry Cream (recipe
follows) made without additional egg whites or heavy
cream

8 5-inch crêpes (see p. 158)
made a little thicker than
usual
2 lightly beaten egg whites
¾ cup crumbed vanilla wafers
2 cups vegetable shortening

1. Marinate the candied pineapple in rum for 1 hour.

• Instead of rum, cognac or Madeira can be used. Instead of candied pineapple, orange peel, marinated in Grand Marnier.

2. Drain the pineapple and fold it into the Pastry Cream.
3. Lay out the crêpes, light side up, and spoon pineapple and Pastry Cream onto each one.

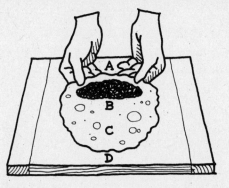

4. Roll the crêpes, folding in the edges to enclose the filling—work fast, for the cooled Pastry Cream will be close to setting—and place them, seam side down, on a baking sheet.

• For a lighter version of this dessert use warm crêpes and after filling them, flame and serve.

5. Dip the rolled crêpes in lightly beaten egg whites, then coat with cooky crumbs.

• The crêpes can be prepared a day ahead up to this point, then refrigerated. They're really better if they stay in the refrigerator overnight. Don't freeze them.

6. Heat fat to 375° in a heavy saucepan or a deep-fat fryer. Check temperature with a fat thermometer, or test it with a bread cube, which will brown nicely in 1 minute if the temperature is right.

7. Fry crêpes, 2 at a time, in the hot fat. Fry just until brown and crispy—about 3 minutes.

• Allow fat to return to 375° before frying each pair of crêpes.

8. Drain on paper towels and serve immediately. *Makes 8 servings.*


## Pastry Cream

Pastry Cream is a delicious filling for cakes and hollow pastries. The classic recipe is thickened with eggs and flour, but I've found that the addition of gelatin makes success more certain. For an extra-luscious filling, Pastry Cream can be enriched with egg whites or heavy cream, or both.

| | |
|---|---|
| 2 *eggs* | 2 *cups milk* |
| 2 *egg yolks* | 2 *egg whites, optional* |
| ½ *cup flour* | 1½ *cups heavy cream, op-* |
| ½ *cup sugar* | *tional* |
| 2 *tablespoons (2 envelopes)* | |
| *unflavored gelatin* | |

1. Put eggs, egg yolks, flour, and sugar in a heavy saucepan—not an aluminum one—and beat with a whisk until well mixed.
2. Stir in gelatin, straight from the envelopes.

• The eggs serve as the cold liquid necessary to soften gelatin before dissolving it.

3. Add milk, place the pan over high heat, and constantly moving the whisk all over the pan (this prevents lumping), cook until the mixture is thick and creamy.
4. Remove from heat and allow to cool.
5. For enriched Pastry Cream, fold stiffly beaten egg whites or heavy cream whipped to the same consistency as the Pastry Cream, or both, into the cooled Pastry Cream.

• Pastry Cream can be made ahead and refrigerated. Cover it tightly with plastic wrap until ready to use it. It should not be frozen, but it will keep in a refrigerator for 2 to 3 days. ***Makes enough to fill 1 cake or 8 crêpes or tartlets.***


## Dessert Crêpes Flambées

With prepared crêpes in your freezer, you always have the makings of a glamorous dessert. Here are some suggestions for elegant flaming desserts that call for only last-minute preparation. Each of the recipes below calls for 1 recipe basic crêpes (see p. 158) and makes 8 7-inch or 12 5-inch crêpes. The crêpes should be warmed before filling.

### Apricot Crêpes Flambées

Fold ½ cup of chopped walnuts or almonds into 1 cup of apricot jam or jelly. Fill and roll crêpes and put them seam-side down in a flame-proof serving dish. Sprinkle with ¼ cup melted butter and 3 tablespoons sugar and heat for about 10 minutes in a preheated 350° oven. Flame the crêpes with 2 tablespoons of rum and bring them to the table flaming.

### Jam Crêpes Flambées

Fill crêpes with 1 cup of strawberry or raspberry jam. Sprinkle them with ¼ cup melted butter and 3 tablespoons sugar and heat in a pre-heated 350° oven for 10 minutes. Flame with 2 tablespoons framboise.

### Banana Crêpes Flambées

Slice 3 bananas. Melt 2 tablespoons of butter in a skillet, stir in 2 tablespoons of brown sugar and ¼ teaspoon of cinnamon. Heat bananas in mixture over high heat for about 5 minutes or until they are caramelized. Roll bananas in crêpes, sprinkle with ¼ cup melted butter and 3 tablespoons sugar, and flame with rum. *Makes 8 to 12 servings.*

## CHOCOLATE CRÊPES

| | |
|---|---|
| 6 *tablespoons flour* | ⅓ *cup milk* |
| 2 *tablespoons cocoa* | 2 *cups heavy cream* |
| ¼ *teaspoon salt* | ¼ *cup confectioners' sugar* |
| 2 *eggs* | 3 *tablespoons instant coffee* |
| 2 *egg yolks* | 1 *recipe Chocolate Fudge* |
| 1 *tablespoon sugar* | *Sauce (see p. 233)* |
| ¼ *cup vegetable oil* | |

1. Make batter by putting flour, cocoa, salt, eggs, egg yolks, sugar, oil, and milk into a blender jar and blending at medium speed until smooth.

2. Refrigerate the batter for 1 hour to allow flavor to blend.

• The batter should have a consistency between that of light and that of heavy cream. If it comes out too thick, thin it with a little milk.

3. Fry the batter, following the directions for crêpes (see p. 158) and using a 5-inch crêpe pan. Makes 12 crêpes.

4. Whisk heavy cream in a large bowl over ice. When cream mounds softly, add confectioners' sugar and instant coffee. Continue whisking until cream will stand in peaks when the whisk is lifted.

5. Put a big spoonful of the cream mixture on each crêpe and roll it up. Arrange 2 rolled crêpes on each of 6 individual serving dishes and top with Chocolate Fudge Sauce. *Makes 6 servings.*

## LEMON CURD

Lemon Curd is an English lemon butter, which can be stored, in covered jars, in a refrigerator for about 1 week. Its uses are legion. It can be spread on toast at teatime; it is a delectable filling for pâte brisée shells (see p. 36), cakes, and sponge cake roll (see recipe for Marron Roll, p. 217); or it can be served, as here, in individual soufflé cups, dressed up with whipped cream and candied violets.

*4 large lemons*
*2 cups sugar*
*2 cups unsalted butter*
*6 beaten eggs*
*⅛ teaspoon salt*
*1 cup heavy cream*

*2 tablespoons confectioners'*
*sugar*
*12 to 14 candied violets*
*(available in gourmet*
*shops)*

1. Grate the peel from all 4 lemons, squeeze out the juice, and put peel and juice, sugar, butter, beaten eggs, and salt into the top part of a large double boiler.

2. Cook the mixture over boiling water—do not let the water touch the bottom of the inset pan—stirring constantly with a wooden spatula for about ½ hour, or until the mixture has the consistency of thick cream sauce.

3. Pour the mixture into individual soufflé cups and put them into a refrigerator for several hours, until they are firm and cold.

4. Whip the cream with the confectioners' sugar over ice until it stands in peaks, then spoon it into a pastry bag fitted with a star tube and pipe a fat rosette on each soufflé cup. Decorate each with a candied violet. *Makes 12 to 14 servings.*

## PRALINE FLAN

*1 cup blanched or un-*
*blanched almonds*
*¼ teaspoon cream of tartar*
*1½ cups sugar*
*Butter to grease baking sheet*
*2 tablespoons vegetable oil*
*5 egg yolks whisked with 5*
*tablespoons sugar*

*2 tablespoons (2 envelopes)*
*unflavored gelatin*
*1½ cups light cream*
*5 egg whites*
*1½ cups heavy cream*
*2 tablespoons confectioners'*
*sugar*
*2 tablespoons rum*

1. Put almonds, cream of tartar, and 1½ cups sugar in a heavy saucepan or skillet and stir constantly, with a wooden spatula, over medium heat until the sugar melts and the mixture turns a dark caramel color. This will take about 15 minutes, and when the mixture is ready, it will give off a slight puff of smoke and boil up with lots of bubbles. Remove from heat immediately.

2. Immediately pour the caramel mixture onto a buttered baking sheet. Let it get hard, then break it into pieces and either put it into a blender and blend it to a powder or roll it to a powder with a rolling pin (or pound it with a mallet). Set aside.

• This powder—called praline powder—can be kept on a pantry shelf in a covered jar, for a month.

3. Lightly oil a 9-inch round cake pan, one with a removable bottom, and set it on a baking sheet.

4. Soften the gelatin by sprinkling it in the egg-yolk mixture.

5. In a saucepan, not an aluminum one, scald the light cream—that is, heat the cream until little bubbles form around the edges of the pan.

6. Pour the scalded cream into the bowl with the egg-yolk mixture in a thin stream, stirring constantly. Then pour the contents of the bowl back into the saucepan, return it to low heat, and cook, stirring constantly, for 10 to 15 minutes, or until the mixture will coat the back of a spoon.

7. Remove from heat, cover the saucepan with plastic wrap or foil, and put in a refrigerator to chill 10 minutes or until syrupy, on the verge of setting.

• Instead of refrigerating the mixture can be stirred over ice to hasten the cooling.

8. Whisk the egg whites until they form stiff peaks, then—very gently —fold them into the cooled yolk mixture.

9. Whip ¼ cup of the heavy cream with 1 tablespoon of the confectioners' sugar, and when this mixture is the same consistency as the egg mixture, add the rum and ¼ cup of the set-aside powder to it, gently fold it into the egg mixture, and pour into the oiled pan.

10. Put the pan in a refrigerator for at least 2 hours, or until the mixture sets.

• This can be done the day before the flan is to be served.

11. Whip the remaining ¼ cup of heavy cream with the remaining 1 tablespoon of confectioners' sugar, and when mixture is fairly stiff put it into a pastry bag fitted with a star tube.

12. Remove mixture from refrigerator, run a knife around the edge of the pan to loosen the flan, then turn the pan over on a serving dish and lift off, first, the rim, then the removable bottom.

13. Decorate the top of the flan with rosettes of whipped cream and sprinkle it with the remaining praline powder. *Makes 8 servings.*

## Coffee Pot de Crème

| | |
|---|---|
| 4 cups heavy cream | 1 teaspoon powdered chicory |
| 1 cup strong black coffee | 2 tablespoons instant coffee |
| 5 tablespoons sugar | or ¼ cup candied coffee |
| 10 egg yolks | beans, optional |
| ¼ cup coffee essence | |

1. Put the cream in a heavy saucepan, scald it—that is, heat it until little bubbles appear around the edges of the pan—then stir in coffee and sugar and stir over high heat until sugar is dissolved.

2. Beat egg yolks at medium speed in the large bowl of an electric mixer, and when they are light and fluffy, pour coffee mixture over them in a thin stream, stirring to keep the yolks from curdling.

3. Stir in coffee essence and chicory.

• Look in gourmet food stores for coffee essence, a concentrated coffee flavoring, for powdered chicory, which is ground from the root of the chicory plant and sometimes used to flavor coffee, and for candied coffee beans.

4. Pour the cream mixture into 10 small pot-de-crème pots, set them in a pan of boiling water, and bake in a preheated 350° oven for about 25 minutes, or until mixture is barely set.

5. Remove from oven and chill 1 to 2 hours in a refrigerator.

6. Before serving, garnish, if desired, either with instant coffee or with candied coffee beans. *Makes 10 servings.*

## Biscuit Tortoni

| | |
|---|---|
| ¾ cup sugar | 2 cups heavy cream |
| 5 egg yolks | 2 tablespoons ground |
| ¼ cup dry or cream sherry | blanched almonds |

1. Put sugar and ¼ cup of water in a small saucepan, bring to a boil, stirring to dissolve the sugar, then cook, uncovered, over high heat for 5 minutes to make syrup.

2. In the large bowl of an electric mixer, beat egg yolks at medium speed until they are fluffy.

3. Continue beating while adding syrup in a thin steady stream.

4. Transfer the mixture to the top of a double boiler and stir it over hot—not boiling—water until it is very thick.

5. Remove from heat and add sherry.

• Instead of sherry, sweet Marsala can be used.

6. Strain mixture through a fine sieve into a bowl. Cool completely.

7. Whip the cream until stiff and fold into the cooled custard.

8. Pour into 12 small paper soufflé cases, sprinkle top of each with about ½ teaspoon of ground almonds, and set in a freezer for at least 3 hours.

• Tortoni can be poured into parfait glasses instead of paper cups if desired.
• Instead of sprinkling almonds on top, the ground almonds can be folded into the custard after step 7.

9. Before serving, let stand at room temperature about 1 minute (Tortoni starts to soften almost immediately). *Makes 12 servings.*

### CHARLOTTE PORTUGAISE

This is a meringue-frosted cake that is steeped in liqueur and crème anglaise. Make it in the morning of the day it is to be served, or make it the day before, or bake and fill the cake the day before and pipe on the meringue just before serving.

| | |
|---|---|
| 2 9-inch layers Yellow Butter Cake (recipe follows) | 1½ cups sugar |
| 10 tablespoons Grand Marnier or other orange liqueur | 2 cups half-and-half |
| | Grated peel of 1 orange |
| | 6 egg whites |
| 4 egg yolks | ¾ cup sliced or slivered blanched almonds |

1. Prick top of cake layers lightly in many places with a fork, then sprinkle each layer with liqueur, using about 3 tablespoons for each.

2. Make crème anglaise by whisking the egg yolks in a bowl, adding ½ cup of sugar, and whisking until thick and lemony in color.

3. Heat the half-and-half to the boiling point in a stainless-steel-lined or an enamel-on-iron pan.

• An egg mixture—one is to be added here—tends to discolor when cooked in aluminum.

4. Gradually pour hot half-and-half into egg mixture, whisking constantly. Then pour the egg–half-and-half mixture into the saucepan and cook over high heat, stirring with whisk, until it thickens slightly.

• The mixture will be thin, but it should coat the back of a spoon—that is, it should film the back of the spoon enough so that a line can be drawn in the film with your finger.

5. Stir orange peel and the remaining ¼ cup of liqueur into the mixture.

6. Put a layer of cake on a stainless-steel tray or an ovenproof platter or serving dish and spoon warm crème anglaise over it. Let the crème anglaise soak in.

7. Stack the second layer on top and soak it with the crème anglaise. Prick the cake with a fork so that the crème will soak in.

8. Make the meringue by beating the egg whites until foamy in an electric mixer, adding the remaining 1 cup of sugar, 1 tablespoon at a time (if the sugar is added too fast, the meringue will get watery), and beating until the mixture looks like marshmallow. This will take a lot of beating. Rub a bit of the mixture between your fingers, and if it feels granular, beat it longer. When it is smooth, it's ready to use.

9. Put meringue in a large pastry bag fitted with a star tube and pipe meringue up and down to cover the sides of the cake, extending it over the top edge. Cover the top with rosettes. The cake should be completely covered.

10. Throw almonds against top and sides of cake so they stick to the meringue.

11. Bake in a preheated 400° oven for 5 to 6 minutes, or until meringue is set, then place cake in refrigerator to chill. *Makes 12 servings.*

## YELLOW BUTTER CAKE

Before starting to make this cake have all ingredients at room temperature.

| | |
|---|---|
| *1 cup unsalted butter, plus butter to grease cake pan or pans* | *2 cups superfine sugar* |
| | *4 separated eggs* |
| | *1 tablespoon vanilla extract* |
| *3 cups sifted cake flour, plus flour to shake into pan or pans* | *1 tablespoon baking powder* |
| | *1 cup milk* |

1. Prepare 2 9-inch layer-cake pans or 1 deep 10-inch pan by buttering generously, then shaking in flour and tapping out the excess flour.

2. In an electric mixer bowl, cream remaining 1 cup of butter and gradually add sugar. Beat until very light and fluffy.

3. Beat in egg yolks, one at a time, and continue beating until well mixed.

4. Beat in vanilla.

5. Sift baking powder and 3 cups of flour together, then make batter by adding them to the butter-egg-yolk mixture alternately with milk. Begin and end with flour and beat well after each addition.

6. In another bowl, beat egg whites until they stand in stiff peaks.

• Be certain beaters are completely clean.

7. Stir a spoonful of the whites into the batter to lighten it, then fold in the remaining whites.

8. Pour mixture into the prepared cake pan or pans—divide it evenly if 2 pans are used—and put in a preheated 350° oven for 25 to 30 minutes, or until a cake tester is clean when inserted and removed.

• An oven rack should be placed so the top of the cake pan (or the tops of the 2 pans) will be in the middle of the oven, with the pan sides not touching the oven walls, and if 2 pans are used, not touching each other. This will allow heat to circulate freely around the pan or pans and help the batter to bake evenly.

9. Set the pan or pans on a cake rack to cool for about 10 minutes, then run a knife around the edges to loosen the cake, and turn it out to cool completely.

• This cake can be frozen if it's wrapped well in plastic wrap or foil. *Makes 2 9-inch layers.*

## ITALIAN RUM CAKE

A wildly magnificent rococo cake, elaborately decorated. Although it takes some time, little real skill is needed to make it.

| | |
|---|---|
| 1 cup mixed candied fruits | 3 cups heavy cream |
| ½ cup rum, about | 8 candied cherries |
| 1 10-inch Sponge Cake (recipe follows) | 16 tiny pieces candied angelica (available in gourmet shops) |
| 3 lbs. ricotta cheese | ¼ cup chopped green pistachios |
| 1½ cups confectioners' sugar | |
| 2 tablespoons crème de cacao | |
| 1 cup shaved dark sweet chocolate | |

1. Soak the mixed candied fruits in 6 tablespoons of rum for 1 hour, then drain and reserve the rum. Set fruits aside.

2. Cut the sponge cake—not while it's warm—into 3 layers either with a serrated knife or by sawing it through with a thread.

• To make the layers even, mark the cuts all around the cake with toothpicks.

3. Sprinkle the layers with rum, using the reserved rum plus enough additional rum (6 tablespoons in all) to get 2 tablespoons on each layer. Let it soak in.

4. In the big bowl of an electric mixer, beat ricotta cheese at medium speed until fluffy. Beat in 1 cup of confectioners' sugar and continue beating until very fluffy. Beat in crème de cacao.

5. Transfer ⅓ of the cheese mixture to another bowl and fold ½ cup of the shaved chocolate into it.

6. Fold the set-aside candied fruits into the remaining cheese mixture.

7. Place the bottom layer of the cake, cut side up, on a serving platter and cover the top of this layer with ½ the candied-fruit-cheese mixture. Then put the next layer in place and cover the top of it with the chocolate-cheese mixture. Finally, put the top layer in place and cover it and the sides of the cake with remaining candied-fruit–cheese mixture.

8. Whip the cream at medium speed in a large bowl of an electric mixer, adding the remaining ½ cup of confectioners' sugar gradually and beating until stiff.

• For best results, bowl, beaters, and cream should all be chilled. Watch carefully when the cream starts to get stiff. There's a very fine line between stiffly whipped cream and butter. Cream should be stiff enough to stand in peaks when beater blades are lifted.

9. Stir in the remaining 2 tablespoons of rum.

10. Use about ¼ of whipped cream and frost the cake all over, smoothing it with a spatula. Try to get the top very smooth.

11. Fill a large pastry bag, fitted with a star tube, with the remaining whipped cream and pipe it up and down to cover the sides and the top edge of the cake. Leave the top smooth.

12. Soak angelica for about 20 minutes in warm water to soften it, then cut it into 8 leaf shapes.

13. Decorate the top of the cake by spacing candied cherries around the edge, placing the angelica leaves beside the cherries, then sprinkling on chopped pistachios and the remaining shaved chocolate.

14. Put cake in a refrigerator to allow the flavors to blend for 24 hours before serving. *Makes 12 servings.*

### SPONGE CAKE

| | |
|---|---|
| 6 *separated eggs* | 1½ *cups sugar* |
| 1 *tablespoon grated orange* | ¼ *teaspoon salt* |
| *peel* | 1⅓ *cups sifted cake flour* |
| ½ *cup orange juice* | 1 *teaspoon cream of tartar* |

1. In an electric-mixer bowl, beat egg yolks at high speed for 5 minutes.

2. Add orange peel and juice and continue beating.

3. Beat in 1 cup of sugar and salt, 1 tablespoon at a time, and continue beating until the mixture will "form the ribbon"—that is, until some will fall from the beaters and look like a ribbon on the surface of the rest.

4. Fold flour into mixture and set aside.

• To sift and measure cake flour, place measuring cups on waxed paper, sift flour directly into cups, and level off the tops with a spatula.

5. In another bowl, and with clean beaters, beat egg whites until they begin to foam, then add cream of tartar, beat until the mixture forms soft peaks, add the remaining ½ cup of sugar, 1 tablespoon at a time, and beat until the mixture forms stiff peaks.

• It is important that bowl and beaters be absolutely clean—with no fat or grease and not the tiniest trace of egg yolk; otherwise the egg whites will not beat properly.

6. Gently, with a rubber spatula, fold the egg-white mixture into the egg-yolk mixture.

7. Pour folded mixture into an ungreased 10-inch tube pan with a removable bottom and place in a preheated 325° oven for 55 minutes, or until a cake tester, inserted in cake, comes out clean.

8. Place cake upside down on a bottle (if cake pan hasn't legs) to cool for about 1 hour.

9. When cake is completely cooled, loosen it from the sides of the pan with a knife, using an up-and-down motion, and turn it out.

• Sponge cake can be frozen for up to 1 month. *Makes 1 10-inch cake.*

## Hazelnut Roll with Whipped-Cream Filling

Ground nuts replace flour in this unusual cake roll.

*Oil to grease baking pan and
paper*
*7 separated eggs*
*1 cup sugar*
*2 teaspoons baking powder*
*1¼ cup ground hazelnuts*

*2 tablespoons confectioners'
sugar, plus confectioners'
sugar to dust on cake*
*1½ cups heavy cream*
*1 tablespoon rum*

1. Oil an 11-by-17-inch jelly-roll pan or baking tray, line it with waxed paper, letting the paper extend about 3 inches over the ends, and oil again. Set aside.

2. In an electric mixer bowl, beat egg yolks at medium speed. Gradually add sugar and beat 5 to 7 minutes until the mixture is thick and will "form the ribbon"—that is, until part of it will fall from the beaters and look like a ribbon on the surface of the rest.

3. Mix baking powder with ground hazelnuts and add to egg mixture. Beat at low speed just enough to mix.

• Hazelnuts can be bought ground. If you grind your own in a blender, spread them out on a baking sheet overnight to dry.

4. In another bowl, with clean beaters, beat egg whites until they form soft peaks. Egg whites should not be dry.

5. Stir ¼ of the egg whites into the nut mixture to lighten it, then gently fold in the remaining whites.

• To fold, cut down through the center of the bowl with a big rubber spatula, then cut across the bottom, up a side, over to the center, down again, and so on. Keep turning the bowl as you fold. And do not overfold: flecks of white should still be visible when the mixture is turned into the baking pan.

6. Spread mixture in the prepared baking pan and bake in a preheated 350° oven for 15 minutes.

7. Let cake cool for a few minutes with paper towels spread over it to prevent crust from forming. Remove towels, loosen cake from edge of pan, and dust generously with confectioners' sugar.

8. Lay 2 strips of waxed paper, overlapping lengthwise, on a table or counter, dust the waxed paper with confectioners' sugar, turn the baking pan over onto the paper, then lift the pan off the cake and peel away the paper lining.

9. In a bowl set over ice, whip heavy cream, with a whisk, sweetening it with 2 tablespoons of confectioners' sugar. Stir in rum.

10. Spread whipped cream on the cake, then roll up the cake like a jelly roll, starting on the long side. Use waxed paper strips to help you roll the cake and transfer it to a long serving board. Remove all waxed paper.

• The roll can be put in a plastic bag or wrapped in plastic wrap or foil and frozen. Defrost it in a refrigerator.

11. Sift confectioners' sugar over the cake before serving. **Makes 8 to 10 servings.**

### MARRON ROLL

One of my favorite desserts—maybe because it's indestructible. The sponge roll can be filled with jelly or with strawberries mixed with sour cream, or with Lemon Curd (see p. 207). This version, filled with preserved marrons (chestnuts packed in syrup) and whipped cream, can be completely finished, including the decorations, and frozen for use later on.

*5 separated eggs*
*¼ cup sugar*
*¼ cup flour*
*2 tablespoons vanilla extract*
*or rum*
*Vegetable oil to grease baking*
*pan and paper*

*2 cups heavy cream*
*¼ cup confectioners' sugar*
*¾ cup preserved chopped*
*chestnuts, drained*
*4 whole preserved chestnuts*

1. Beat egg yolks with an electric mixer at medium speed until light and fluffy.

2. Add sugar and continue beating until the mixture is thick and lemon-colored.

3. Stir in flour and 1 tablespoon of vanilla (or rum) and set aside.

4. In another bowl, with clean, dry beaters, beat egg whites until stiff but not dry. They should make soft peaks.

5. Fold whites into egg-yolk mixture to make sponge-roll batter.

6. Oil an 11-by-17-inch jelly-roll pan, line it with waxed paper, oil the waxed paper, and pour batter on the paper. Spread evenly.

7. Bake in a preheated 400° oven for 12 minutes, when cake should be golden.

8. Loosen the edges of the cake, turn it out on 2 overlapping sheets of waxed paper or on a tea towel, roll it up lengthwise in the waxed paper or the towel, and chill 20 minutes.

9. Whip cream by beating it in a bowl set over ice. Beat in 2 tablespoons of confectioners' sugar and 1 tablespoon of vanilla (or rum). Cream should be firm enough to hold a definite shape, but take care not to overbeat it, for it can turn to butter very quickly.

• Cream whipped over ice (and sweetened with confectioners' sugar instead of granulated sugar) is less likely than other cream to get watery or separate later.

10. Into ¾ of the whipped cream—reserve the rest for decoration—fold chopped chestnuts. Unroll the cake, spread filling on it, then roll it up again and place it on a long wooden board (this is called a chocolate-roll board) or a narrow silver platter.

11. Decorate the top of the roll with 4 rosettes of whipped cream made with a pastry bag and a large star tube.

12. Place a whole preserved chestnut on each rosette, sift confectioners' sugar over the decorated roll, and refrigerate until serving time.

• If the roll is to be frozen, wrap it loosely in plastic wrap or foil. Defrost in refrigerator. *Makes 10 servings.*

# Rehrücken

## *(Mock Saddle of Venison Cake)*

This Viennese almond cake is baked in a rectangular ribbed mold that supposedly resembles the back of a deer.

| | |
|---|---|
| 1 tablespoon butter | 6 tablespoons sugar |
| ½ cup bread crumbs (see p. 7) | ½ cup ground blanched almonds |
| 3 egg yolks | ¼ teaspoon ground cinnamon |

3 tablespoons very finely
  chopped citron (available
  in gourmet shops)
⅓ cup grated bittersweet
  chocolate
4 egg whites
¼ teaspoon cream of tartar

Chocolate Glaze (recipe follows)
½ cup halved or slivered
  blanched almonds
1 cup heavy cream
2 tablespoons confectioners'
  sugar

1. Butter—use 1 tablespoon of butter—a 1-quart Rehrücken mold measuring approximately 4 inches by 12 inches. Dust it with ¼ cup of bread crumbs and turn it upside down to knock out the excess crumbs.

2. In the large bowl of the electric mixer, beat egg yolks at medium speed until thick and light in color.

3. Gradually beat in ¼ cup of sugar at high speed and beat until the mixture will "form the ribbon"—that is, until part of it will fall from the lifted beaters and look like a ribbon on the surface of the rest. This will take about 5 minutes of beating.

4. Slow the mixer to medium speed and add ground almonds, cinnamon, citron, chocolate, and the remaining ¼ cup of bread crumbs. Beat to form a dense, moist mass. Set aside.

5. In another bowl, with clean beaters, beat egg whites and cream of tartar at medium speed until foamy.

6. Add the remaining 2 tablespoons of sugar, 1 tablespoon at a time, and beat until egg whites form soft peaks.

7. Fold ¼ of the egg-white mixture into the egg-yolk mixture to lighten it, then gently fold the lightened egg-yolk mixture into the remaining egg-white mixture, folding just until all trace of egg white disappears.

8. Pour mixture into the prepared mold and put it in a preheated 375° oven for 40 minutes, or until the cake is golden brown and springs back when touched lightly.

9. Cool the cake in the mold for 2 to 3 minutes, then turn it out on a cake rack to cool completely, about 30 minutes.

10. When the cake is cool, set the rack on waxed paper (which will catch any drippings) and spoon slightly cooled Chocolate Glaze evenly over it.

11. Toast the almond halves or slivers by spreading them on a shallow pan and putting them in a preheated 300° oven for about 15 minutes, or until they're lightly browned. Toss them around a couple of times as they brown.

12. Stick the toasted almonds, like porcupine quills, into the glaze in even rows along the ribs of the cake (see illustration, p. 220).

13. Whip the heavy cream with confectioners' sugar until it will hold a definite shape. Serve separately with the cake.

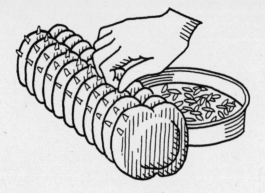

### Chocolate Glaze

⅓ cup heavy cream      ¾ cup sugar
3 tablespoons butter      ½ teaspoon vanilla
½ cup cocoa

1. Put all ingredients except vanilla into a saucepan, set over medium heat, and cook, stirring constantly, for 3 to 4 minutes.
2. Remove pan from heat and stir in vanilla.

• Glaze should be smooth, thick, and shiny. *Makes 8 servings.*

### VIENNESE ALMOND BALLS

1 cup butter      1½ cups flour, about, plus
½ cup confectioners' sugar,      flour to dust on baking
about      sheet
¼ teaspoon salt      ¼ cup rum
1 cup ground blanched al-
monds

1. Beat butter with an electric mixer at medium speed until light and fluffy, then add 6 tablespoons confectioners' sugar, 1 tablespoon at a time, add salt, and continue beating until well mixed. Scrape sides and bottom of mixing bowl when necessary, using a rubber spatula.
2. Add ground almonds and beat well.
3. Gradually add flour—a little more than 1½ cups if necessary—to make a stiff batter.
4. Mix in rum. Chill the batter 20 minutes.

5. Roll the batter into balls the size of marbles, place the balls on a lightly floured baking sheet, and bake in a preheated 350° oven for about 15 minutes, or until the balls are light brown in color.

6. Cool the balls slightly, then roll them in about 2 tablespoons confectioners' sugar—twice if necessary—to coat generously. *Makes about 24 balls.*

## Oeufs à la Neige

This is a spectacular dessert—a pyramid of poached meringue "eggs" floating in custard and decorated (if desired) with spun caramel.

| | |
|---|---|
| 1 quart milk | 6 separated eggs |
| ¾ cup sugar, plus ½ cup sugar, optional (for caramel) | ¼ teaspoon salt |
| | ⅛ teaspoon cream of tartar |
| 1 2-inch piece of vanilla bean or 2 teaspoons vanilla extract | 1 teaspoon cornstarch |
| | 1 tablespoon rum |

1. Prepare poaching mixture by bringing milk to a boil in a skillet, then stirring in 6 tablespoons of sugar and vanilla bean or extract, and reducing heat to simmer.

• To flavor milk with vanilla bean: split the pod, scrape out the seeds, and drop both seeds and pod into the sugar-milk mixture.

2. While the milk simmers, make meringue mixture in a mixer bowl by beating egg whites at high speed until foamy, and adding salt and cream of tartar. Continue beating, adding 6 tablespoons of sugar, 1 tablespoon at a time, then adding cornstarch. Beat until the mixture looks like marshmallow.

• It's almost impossible to overbeat. The mixture must be very, very stiff. The classic recipe does not call for the addition of starch, but this holds up the egg whites during poaching.

3. To shape the meringue mixture dip 2 serving spoons in a bowl of hot water, scoop up a mound of the mixture in one spoon, and round it off—it should be egg-shaped—with the other spoon.

4. Slide the shaped mixture from the spoon into the simmering milk, repeat step 3 once or twice more (depending on the size of the skillet), slide the 1 or 2 more "eggs" into the milk, and poach about 30 seconds on each side (turn the "eggs" over with 2 forks).

5. Drain the poached "eggs" on paper towels.

6. Keep repeating steps 3, 4, and 5 until the rest of the meringue mixture has been used up, then strain the milk.

7. Make custard, by beating the egg yolks until foamy, then gradually pouring on the strained milk, stirring with a whisk. Pour the mixture into a saucepan (not an aluminum one) and cook at medium high heat, stirring constantly, until it is the consistency of heavy cream and will coat the back of a spoon so that a line can be drawn on the film with your finger. Flavor with rum and strain into a shallow glass serving dish.

8. Pile the meringue "eggs" in a pyramid on the custard and then, if desired, make caramel to be spun over them.

9. Make caramel by putting ½ cup of sugar and ¼ cup of water into a small heavy saucepan and cooking over high heat, stirring, until the sugar is dissolved. Do not stir any more, but keep tilting the pan back and forth over heat to keep the syrup moving, for about 15 minutes.

• Caramelizing sugar is touchy but it is interesting to do. It is imperative to watch it closely, as it turns from white to butterscotch to dark amber. I like it almost burned. If you don't, take it off the heat before it gets too dark.

• Just before the syrup is ready it gives off a little puff of smoke and boils up with lots of big bubbles.

• Another test, if you have tough fingers and are careful (the hot syrup can burn badly): pinch a drop of syrup between thumb and forefinger and pull apart; if there is a thread, the caramel is ready.

10. Take caramel off heat. Stop the cooking by setting the saucepan in cold water or over ice. Dip into the caramel with a fork, lift the fork,

and use it to spin threads of caramel round and round the pyramid of "eggs."

• Instead of spun caramel, the "eggs" can be garnished with shaved chocolate, or Raspberry Sauce (see p. 204) can be poured over them.

• Refrigerate the "eggs" uncovered if you're not ready to serve. But they won't hold for more than 2 or 3 hours; then the meringue "eggs" begin to weep—that is, they begin to give off liquid. *Makes 6 servings.*

### GERMAN APPLE PANCAKE

¼ cup flour
7 teaspoons sugar, plus sugar
   to sprinkle on pancake
¼ teaspoon salt
2 eggs
⅔ cup milk
¼ cup butter

2½ cups peeled, cored, and
   thinly sliced apples
1 teaspoon cinnamon, plus
   cinnamon to sprinkle on
   pancake
½ cup dairy sour cream

1. Make batter by putting flour, 1 teaspoon of sugar, salt, eggs, and milk in a blender jar and blending until smooth.

2. Refrigerate the batter for 1 hour.

3. Melt 2 tablespoons of butter and sauté the apple slices in it, stirring, until they begin to look transparent.

4. Add 2 tablespoons sugar and 1 teaspoon of cinnamon and cook over high heat until the apple slices are soft and caramelized. This will take about 10 minutes. Set aside.

5. When ready to bake the pancake, melt the remaining 2 tablespoons of butter in a 10-inch skillet.

• A good pan to use for this is one lined with Teflon.

6. When the butter is sizzling, pour on ¾ of the batter. Let it set for 2 seconds, then spread the apple mixture over it, patting the apple mixture out to cover the batter.

7. Pour the remaining batter over the apple mixture, then tip the pan back and forth over high heat to allow the uncooked batter to run underneath the pancake. If the pan is hot enough, this will take only about 5 minutes.

8. Shake the pan smartly to loosen the pancake. Tip the pan to aid in rolling the pancake like an omelette and turn it out on a warm serving platter.

9. Sprinkle it generously with a mixture of sugar and cinnamon, and serve with sour cream on the side. *Makes 2 servings.*

## BANANAS VIEUX CARRÉ

This is a New Orleans specialty that's simple to make and nice to do for company. The bananas can be readied for baking before dinner, baked while you eat, then flamed at the table.

*½ cup butter*
*6 bananas*
*Grated peel of 2 oranges*
*½ cup orange juice*
*3 tablespoons lime juice*

*½ teaspoon cinnamon*
*¼ cup honey*
*⅓ cup light rum*
*Crème Fraîche, optional*
*(recipe follows)*

1. Melt ¼ cup of the butter in an ovenproof dish that can be taken to the table (an oval au gratin dish is ideal).
2. Peel the bananas, split them lengthwise, and roll the halves in the melted butter. Coat well.
3. Dot the remaining ¼ cup of butter on the banana halves, sprinkle them with grated orange peel, orange and lime juice, cinnamon, and honey, and bake them for 15 minutes in a preheated 375° oven.
4. Flame with rum by warming rum in a small pan and igniting and spooning the flaming sauce over the bananas until the flames die down and serve with the rum sauce and also, if desired, with Crème Fraîche.

### Crème Fraîche

There is nothing in the United States like the French Crème Fraîche, a naturally thick cream with a flavor all its own, usually served in a crock with a wooden spoon. This is how I make a pseudo Crème Fraîche to serve either with Bananas Vieux Carré or over berries.

*3 oz. cream cheese*
*½ cup dairy sour cream*

*1 cup heavy cream*

1. Bring all ingredients to room temperature.
2. Soften the cream cheese and beat it with sour cream, using a whisk or an electric mixer.
3. Combine with heavy cream, barely whipped.
4. Let the mixture stand at room temperature for an hour before serving (don't refrigerate it, or the cheese will set), preferably in a tall crock with a wooden spoon. ***Makes 6 servings.***

## CHERRY FRITTERS

| | |
|---|---|
| *1 lb. Bing cherries, with stems* | *1 tablespoon melted butter* |
| *2 separated eggs* | *½ teaspoon baking powder* |
| *⅔ cup milk* | *1 tablespoon kirsch* |
| *1 tablespoon sugar* | *2 cups vegetable shortening* |
| *1 cup flour* | *½ cup confectioners' sugar* |
| *¼ teaspoon salt* | |

1. Wash and dry cherries. Leave the stems on and the pits in (pits help the fritters stay warm).

2. Beat egg yolks and stir in milk, sugar, flour, salt, butter, baking powder, and kirsch. Beat until smooth.

3. Beat egg whites until they form soft peaks, then fold them into the yolk mixture.

4. Heat the shortening to 375° in a heavy saucepan. Check the temperature with a fat thermometer, or test it with a bread cube, which will brown nicely in 1 minute if the temperature of the fat is right.

5. Hold a cherry by the stem, dip it into fritter batter, then drop it into the hot shortening. Dip and drop in about 5 more cherries (fry no more than 6 fritters at a time, or the fat will cool too much for the fritters to brown properly), fry for about 2 minutes or until the fritters are golden brown and crusty, then remove the fritters with a slotted spoon and drain them on brown paper or paper towels.

6. Return the shortening to 375° (check the temperature again), then repeat step 5; repeat as many times as necessary to use up all the cherries.

7. Heap the fritters in a pyramid on a serving plate and sift confectioners' sugar over them.

• The most efficient way to do this is to put the sugar in a sieve and stir it with a spoon. *Makes 4 to 6 servings.*

## ORANGES ORIENTALE

| | |
|---|---|
| *8 large navel oranges* | *1 tablespoon grenadine or a* |
| *2 cups sugar* | *few drops of red food color-* |
| *¼ teaspoon cream of tartar* | *ing* |
| *½ cup Cointreau or any other* | *8 candied violets (available in* |
| *orange liqueur* | *gourmet shops)* |

1. Make orange-peel syrup by peeling the oranges as thinly as possible with a potato peeler, removing the orange-colored covering but

not the bitter white part. Setting the oranges aside, lay the peel on a chopping board, and with a chef's knife, cut it into the finest shreds or slivers possible.

2. Put the slivers into a saucepan with 2 cups of water, sugar, and cream of tartar (cream of tartar keeps syrups from crystallizing), bring to a boil, then reduce heat to simmer, and cook until thick and syrupy—about 25 to 30 minutes.

3. Remove from heat, stir in liqueur, then add grenadine or enough red food coloring to tint the syrup a pretty orange color. Chill.

4. Finish peeling the oranges, cutting off all the white part. Leave the oranges whole and pile them in a pyramid in a glass bowl. Refrigerate them for 2 hours.

5. Before serving, spoon chilled syrup over the oranges, spooning as much as possible of the shredded peel over the top of the oranges, and garnish each orange with a candied violet. *Makes 8 servings.*

## Pears in Red Wine

The pears used for this recipe should be either green winter pears or brown Boscs, and they should be firm but not hard. If they're not ripe enough when you buy them, leave them overnight in a closed brown paper bag at room temperature.

| | |
|---|---|
| *8 pears* | *1 cup red currant jelly* |
| *1 tablespoon lemon juice* | *½ teaspoon red food coloring* |
| *1 cup sugar* | *1 cinnamon stick, optional* |
| *2 cups port wine* | *8 fresh mint leaves* |

1. Leaving the stems on, peel the pears with a vegetable peeler, cut a little slice off the bottom of each pear so it will stand upright, and immediately drop each into a bowl containing 1 quart of water mixed with 1 tablespoon of lemon juice. (This will keep the pears from turning dark.)

2. In a saucepan big enough to hold all the pears, boil together the sugar, wine, jelly, red food coloring, and if you like cinnamon, the cinnamon stick, for 5 minutes.

3. Put pears into the mixture, return to a boil and then lower heat to a simmer. Poach the pears in this mixture, spooning it over them or turning them in it to get them an even red color. After 15 minutes begin to test with a fork for tenderness.

4. When the pears are tender, remove them from syrup with a slotted spoon and place them upright on a cake rack set on a tray and put them in a refrigerator to chill for 1 hour.

5. Boil the liquid in which the pears cooked until it thickens slightly; and when the pears are chilled, take them out of the refrigerator, spoon some of the hot liquid over each, collect the drippings in the tray, and return them to the saucepan. Put the pears in the refrigerator for 1 hour to chill again. Repeat this glazing-chilling process 2 more times, or until the pears are very shiny and a deep red color.

• The liquid clings best when it's hot and the pears are cold.

6. Before serving, decorate the stem of each pear with a mint leaf.

• Serve plain or with sour cream. *Makes 8 servings.*

## PEARS HÉLÈNE

6 *Bartlett pears*
1 *cup sugar*
1 *tablespoon vanilla extract*
6 *slices Sponge Cake (see p. 215)*
1 *pint vanilla ice cream*
2 *cups Chocolate Fudge Sauce (see p. 233)*

1 *cup heavy cream*
2 *tablespoons confectioners' sugar*
6 *candied violets (available in gourmet shops)*

1. Peel and core the pears, leaving them whole.
2. Combine sugar and 1 quart of water in a saucepan, bring to a boil, then add the pears, reduce heat, and simmer, uncovered, for 10 minutes, or until the pears are tender. Turn the pears occasionally so they cook evenly.

• The cooking time will depend on the ripeness of the pears. Test them with the tip of a paring knife; if it goes in easily the pears are done.

3. Remove pan from heat, add vanilla, and let the pears cool in the liquid, spooning it over them a couple of times while they're cooling.
4. Cut the cake slices in rounds, place them on individual serving dishes, and top each round with a slice of ice cream.
5. Stand a drained pear on each slice of ice cream and coat with chocolate fudge sauce.
6. Whip cream with confectioners' sugar until stiff, put it into a pastry bag fitted with a star tube, and pipe a rosette of whipped cream on each chocolate-covered pear.
7. Decorate each rosette with a candied violet. *Makes 6 servings.*

## Apricot Mousse with Chocolate Cornets

*Vegetable oil to grease collar of soufflé dish*
*1½ 12-oz. pkgs. dried apricots*
*2 tablespoons (2 envelopes) unflavored gelatin*
*⅓ cup cognac*
*7 egg whites*
*¼ teaspoon salt*

*18 tablespoons (1 cup plus 2 tablespoons) sugar*
*3 tablespoons Grand Marnier*
*2 cups heavy cream*
*2 tablespoons confectioners' sugar*
*2 Chocolate Cornets (recipe follows)*

1. Prepare a 4-cup soufflé dish with a paper collar: fold a strip of waxed paper about 2 feet long in half lengthwise to make a strip about 7 inches wide, oil the collar, place it around the outside of the dish and extending 4 to 5 inches above it, then tie a string around it.

2. Soak the apricots in cold water to cover for 2 hours.

3. Drain the apricots, put them in a saucepan, cover with fresh water, and bring to a boil. Cover, reduce heat, and simmer for 20 to 25 minutes or until soft.

4. Drain off all but ¼ cup of liquid from the apricots and purée them in a blender. There must be 2 cups of purée.

5. Put cognac in a glass measuring cup, sprinkle gelatin over it, let it stand about 5 minutes while the gelatin softens, then set it in a pan of boiling water and stir until the gelatin dissolves.

6. Stir the dissolved gelatin mixture into the apricot purée. Mix well.

7. In large mixer bowl, beat egg whites, adding salt when they begin to foam.

8. Add sugar, 1 tablespoon at a time, and continue beating until the mixture looks like marshmallow. Pinch a bit of it between your fingers; if it feels smooth, it's ready.

9. Beat in the apricot purée and 2 tablespoons of Grand Marnier.

10. In another bowl, whip 1 cup of cream to the same consistency as the apricot mixture.

11. Fold the cream into the apricot mixture, pile into the prepared soufflé dish, and put in a refrigerator for several hours to set.

• This can be done the day before the mousse is to be served.

12. Whip the remaining 1 cup of cream with confectioners' sugar until stiff and mix in the remaining 1 tablespoon of Grand Marnier.

13. Put the cream into a pastry bag with a star tube, and after carefully removing the waxed-paper collar from the soufflé dish, pipe whipped-cream rosettes around the top of the mousse.

14. Pipe cream into 2 chocolate cornets and place them in the center of the mousse, facing in opposite directions. *Makes 12 generous servings.*

## Chocolate Cornets

To get 2 cornets, it's wise to make 4, allowing for breakage.

*¼ lb. dark sweet chocolate*

1. Melt the chocolate—just enough to make it spreadable—in a heat-proof glass dish set over a saucepan of simmering water in such a way that steam won't rise around the dish and touch the chocolate.

• Melting chocolate directly over heat or getting a drop of water in it will cause it to separate.

2. Make 4 waxed-paper cones by cutting triangles of waxed paper 6 by 6 by 8½ inches, twisting them into cone shapes and fastening them with bits of tape.

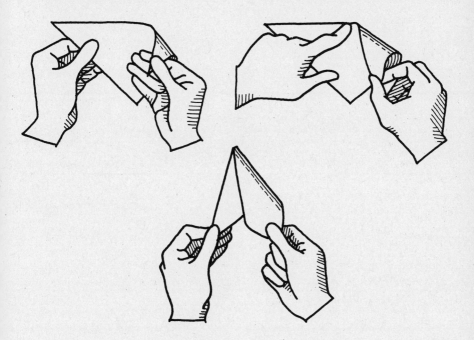

3. Place the waxed-paper cones inside 4 cornucopia molds or 4 cone-shaped paper drinking cups, then coat them *inside* with chocolate, using a tiny spatula or demitasse spoon.

4. Stand the molds in flat-bottomed paper cups and put in a refrigerator for about 1 hour, or until set.

• Don't put the molds in a freezer, or the chocolate will turn gray.

5. Remove the waxed-paper cones from the molds or cups and very carefully peel the waxed paper from the chocolate. *Makes 4 cones.*


## BUTTERSCOTCH-RUM PARFAIT

The true parfait has a boiled sugar syrup added to an egg-yolk base, and it is sinfully rich. If butterscotch isn't your favorite, use this same technique to make chocolate or fresh fruit parfaits.

| | |
|---|---|
| *¾ cup brown sugar* | *⅛ teaspoon salt* |
| *¼ cup butter* | *2 cups whipped heavy cream* |
| *3 egg yolks* | *3 tablespoons crushed* |
| *1 tablespoon rum* | *blanched almonds* |

1. In a small saucepan, make syrup by bringing brown sugar, butter, and ¾ cup of water to a boil, stirring to dissolve the sugar, then boiling hard for 3 minutes. Set aside.

• For flavor changes, make the syrup with granulated sugar instead of brown sugar, flavor the egg yolks (step 4) with 1 tablespoon of vanilla extract instead of with rum, and fold in ½ cup of melted chocolate, or chocolate and coffee-flavored liqueur, or fresh berries, or peaches along with the whipped cream (step 6). Or invent your own parfait.

2. In a small electric mixer bowl, beat egg yolks at medium speed until light and fluffy.

3. Gradually pour in the set-aside syrup, in a thin stream, beating all the while.

4. Beat in rum and salt, then place the mixture in a saucepan and whisk over high heat until it is as thick as heavy cream.

5. Set mixing bowl over ice, and whisk about 10 minutes or until cool.

6. Fold in whipped cream, pour into parfait glasses, and set in a freezer for at least 1 hour.

• The cream should be whipped to the same consistency as the parfait base but not as thick as cream whipped for decorating.
• The longer the parfait stays in the freezer, the more solid it becomes. I like to make it the day before I plan to serve it.

7. Three hours before serving, remove parfaits from freezer and place in refrigerator.

• When served, parfaits should be the consistency of frozen custard.

8. Sprinkle tops with crushed almonds. **Makes 6 servings.**

## PEACH TART

1 wholly baked 9-inch pastry
  shell (see p. 36)
2 tablespoons bread crumbs
  (see p. 7)
1½ cups heavy cream
2 tablespoons framboise

5 tablespoons confectioners
  sugar
1 to 2 1-pound cans snow
  peach halves
½ cup apricot jam or jelly
¼ cup natural pistachio nuts

1. Sprinkle the bottom of the pastry shell with bread crumbs to prevent filling from soaking into the shell.

2. Whip the cream by hand in a large bowl set over ice until it will stand in stiff peaks. Beat in framboise and 3 tablespoons of the confectioners' sugar.

• Cream whipped over ice and sweetened with confectioners' sugar doesn't tend to separate on standing. This allows you to assemble the tart in the morning, for dinner that night.

3. Spread cream into the pastry shell.

4. Drain and dry 1 can of peach halves and arrange them, rounded sides up, over the cream. If more peaches are needed to fill the tart (the number of peaches in a can varies), open the other can.

5. Make glaze by putting the jam or jelly into a small pan with 1 tablespoon of cold water, stirring over high heat until the jam or jelly melts, bringing it to a boil, then straining.

• Apricot glaze, which can be kept in a small jar in the refrigerator, can be used on any light-colored fruit.

6. With a pastry brush, paint the peach halves with glaze. Take care that none drips onto the whipped cream.

• For other fruit tarts: white grapes, cherries, large strawberries, or other berries can be substituted. Arrange over cream and follow directions for glazing, except that for red fruits or berries—cherries, strawberries, raspberries—make glaze with red currant jelly rather than with apricot jam or jelly. If using berries, omit nuts (step 7); if using grapes, substitute blanched almonds for pistachios.

• For fruit tartlets, an assortment of which makes an excellent dessert, bake pastry in individual tart shells or barquette molds.

7. Put the pistachios between 2 sheets of waxed paper, crush them with a rolling pin or mallet, then sprinkle them over the peach halves.

8. Before serving, sift the remaining 2 tablespoons of confectioners' sugar around the edge of the tart. *Makes 6 servings.*

## CASSIS SHERBET

| | |
|---|---|
| *4 cups light cream* | *1 cup sugar* |
| *⅔ cup black currant jam* | *⅔ cup cassis liqueur* |
| *6 egg yolks* | *3 cups heavy cream* |

1. Scald the light cream in a saucepan—that is, heat the cream in the pan until bubbles appear around the edges.

2. Add jam to the scalded cream and stir over high heat until the jam dissolves.

3. Beat egg yolks until light and fluffy.

4. Gradually beat in sugar and continue beating until the mixture will "form the ribbon"—that is, until some will fall from the lifted beaters and look like a ribbon on the surface of the rest.

5. Slowly pour the cream mixture into the egg-yolk mixture, stirring with a whisk.

6. Whisk well, pour into the saucepan used for the cream, place over heat, and cook over high heat, stirring constantly, until the mixture will coat the back of a spoon enough so that a line can be drawn in the film with your finger.

7. Chill in a freezer about 10 minutes, then stir in cassis and refrigerate until cold.

8. Whip the heavy cream and fold it into the cassis mixture.

9. Pour into the can of an ice-cream freezer and freeze according to manufacturer's directions, or pour into ice-cube trays, freeze about 1 hour or until mushy, remove from trays, beat with an electric mixer, return to the trays, and freeze about 2 hours or until firm. *Makes 8 to 10 servings.*

## MERINGUE SHELLS

Filled with fruit and whipped cream or filled with ice cream and topped with a favorite sauce these shells make delicious desserts. They can be kept in a plastic bag or air-tight container on your pantry shelf for 1 month.

| | |
|---|---|
| 6 egg whites | 1 teaspoon white vinegar |
| 2 cups sugar | 1 teaspoon vanilla |

1. Put egg whites in a large electric mixer bowl and beat until foamy; then, beating all the while, add 1 cup of sugar, 1 tablespoon at a time, add vinegar and vanilla, and add the remaining 1 cup of sugar, 1 tablespoon at a time.

2. Continue beating for 5 to 10 minutes, or until the mixture looks like marshmallow and is smooth, not granular, when you pinch a bit of it between thumb and forefinger.

3. Put mixture into a large pastry bag fitted with a plain round tube

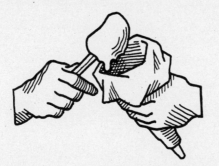

and pipe out solid circles—there should be 10 to 12 of them—from 3 to 4 inches in diameter by starting in the center of each circle and spiraling out; then build up the sides of each shell to the desired depth by piping the mixture around the edge of each circle, 1 ring on top of another.

4. Set the formed shells aside for several hours to dry out; then place them either on baking sheets lined with baking parchment or brown paper or on Teflon-coated baking sheets and bake them in a preheated 250° oven for about 45 minutes, or until they are hard to the touch. They should be white or creamy white; never brown.

5. Turn off the oven and let the shells stand in it with the door closed until they're cool. *Makes 10 to 12 shells.*

## CHOCOLATE FUDGE SAUCE

This is the best fudge sauce I know. Serve it hot or cold, on cakes, ice cream brownies, puddings—you name it.

| | |
|---|---|
| ½ cup cocoa | 3 tablespoons butter |
| 1 cup sugar | ¼ teaspoon salt |
| 1 cup light corn syrup | 1 teaspoon vanilla |
| ½ cup light cream | |

1. Put all ingredients except vanilla into a small saucepan, bring to a boil, and boil 5 minutes.

2. Remove from heat and stir in vanilla. *Makes almost 2 cups.*

## Notes on Soufflés

The reputation hot soufflés have for being tricky dates back to the days of ovens without heat controls. Today fabulous high-rising soufflés can be produced every time. But one word of caution: guests must wait for soufflés; soufflés will not wait for guests.

To serve a soufflé, open it with a serving spoon and fork held back to back; don't plunge into it with a spoon, or it will deflate immediately. For each serving, lift out some of the crusty part first, then some from the center, which should be moist, almost like a sauce.

Egg whites make soufflés rise. The recipes in this book say to beat them (sometimes with cream of tartar, which helps to stabilize them) in an unlined copper bowl, using a piano-wire balloon whisk, for egg whites beaten this way mound higher—and thus make higher soufflés —than do those beaten in an electric mixer.

Before using the bowl, clean it with 1 tablespoon of coarse salt and 1 tablespoon of vinegar, rub it out with paper towels, and rinse it with *hot* water; dry it thoroughly. Before using the whisk, make sure it, too, is clean—completely free of grease, that is, and without a speck of egg yolk, which is fatty, which will keep the whites from mounding properly. If you don't own an unlined copper bowl or a piano-wire balloon whisk, use an electric mixer or a rotary beater, making sure the beaters and whatever bowl is used are thoroughly clean.

Eggs are easiest to separate when they're cold from a refrigerator, but eggs whites that are to be beaten should be at room temperature. For the best results, don't try to beat more than 8 whites at a time; and, keeping the tip of the whisk always in the bowl, swing the whisk round and round—use wrist muscles, not shoulder muscles—to beat as much air as is possible into the whites.

Stirring a big spoonful of egg whites into the base mixture lightens it, making it easier to blend the mixture completely.

When adding the remaining egg whites to the mixture—folding them in, that is—work quickly and lightly. Use a big rubber spatula and cut down through the center of the mixture and to the bottom of the bowl, then move across the bottom and up a side, over to the center, down again, and so on. Keep turning the bowl as you fold. And do not overmix: it's better to leave a few fluffs of white showing than to risk deflating the egg whites.

For a crustier-than-usual outside, bake the soufflé on the bottom shelf of the oven; for a softer outside, stand the soufflé in a pan of hot water and bake it 15 minutes longer than recipes state.

Some experts say you can prepare a soufflé ahead and keep it under an inverted bowl for ½ hour before baking it, but I don't recommend you try this. Soufflés can't be prepared in advance; I don't care what anyone says. Do the base mixture far ahead; then excuse yourself from your guests, beat the egg whites, fold the soufflé together, and put it in the oven—it doesn't take long, and the results are well worth the wait.

## Vanilla Soufflé

For this recipe use either a 6-cup soufflé dish or a 4-cup soufflé dish fitted with a paper collar made by folding a 2-foot strip of waxed paper in half lengthwise, wrapping it around the top of the dish so it extends 4 to 5 inches above the dish, and tying it around the dish with string; it is not necessary to butter the dish, but if a collar is used, butter the inside of it. Or use 6 or 8 individual soufflé cups, ¾- or 1-cup size.

| | |
|---|---|
| *3 tablespoons butter* | *5 egg yolks* |
| *3 tablespoons flour* | *2 tablespoons vanilla* |
| *1 cup milk* | *7 egg whites* |
| *⅓ cup sugar* | *¼ teaspoon cream of tartar* |

1. Melt butter in a non-aluminum saucepan over high heat and stir in flour with a wooden spatula.

• For a hot lemon soufflé, use ¼ cup of butter and ¼ cup of flour here, and in step 5, eliminate the vanilla and use ½ cup of lemon juice and 1 tablespoon of grated lemon rind instead.

2. Cook the flour, stirring constantly, for a few minutes. Do not let it brown.

3. Remove from heat and add milk, whisking vigorously, then return to high heat, add sugar, and cook, stirring constantly, until the mixture comes to a boil and is thick and smooth. Set aside to cool slightly before adding egg yolks.

4. Beat in egg yolks 1 at a time, or beat the yolks together enough to mix them and then beat them into the mixture with a whisk.

5. Add vanilla. Mixture should be the consistency of mayonnaise. If it's too thin, set the pan over low heat and cook, whisking vigorously, until thickened. Cool slightly.

• Soufflé can be made ahead to this point and refrigerated for several hours.

• For a Grand Marnier soufflé, substitute 2 tablespoons of Grand Marnier for the vanilla and add 1 tablespoon of grated orange peel.

6. Beat egg whites in an unlined copper bowl, using a piano-wire balloon whisk. When whites foam slightly, add cream of tartar. Continue beating until the mixture is stiff but not dry.

• Egg whites are ready when most of them can be scooped onto the whisk.

7. Stir about ⅛ of the egg whites into the egg-yolk mixture to lighten it, then fold in the remaining egg white.

8. Either pour the mixture into a single soufflé dish and place it on the bottom shelf of a preheated 375° oven and bake for 30 minutes, or pour it into individual cups, rounding it a little (but don't make the cups too full), and bake for 15 minutes. Serve immediately.

• For a vanilla soufflé with macaroons: soak 12 macaroons for 10 minutes in ½ cup of Grand Marnier; pour ½ the soufflé mixture into a single dish and sprinkle on ½ the soaked macaroon crumbs; pour in the remaining soufflé mixture and sprinkle the remaining crumbs around the edge; then bake. For a soufflé with ladyfingers: dip 6 ladyfingers in liqueur, place them in half-filled soufflé dish; fill the dish with mixture; and bake. *Makes 6 to 8 servings.*

### Frozen Lemon Soufflé

For this recipe use an 8-cup soufflé dish with a paper collar made from a length of waxed paper long enough to go around the dish with some overlap. Fold the paper in half lengthwise and brush the inside edge with vegetable oil, then tie it around the top of the dish, extending 4 to 5 inches above it.

10 *separated eggs*
2 *cups sugar*
*Grated peel of 4 lemons*
1 *cup lemon juice*
¼ *teaspoon salt*
2 *tablespoons (2 envelopes)*
  *unflavored gelatin*

½ *cup light or dark rum*
3 *cups heavy cream*
2 *tablespoons confectioners'*
  *sugar*
½ *cup ground almonds*
*Candied violets (available in*
  *gourmet shops)*

1. In an electric mixer bowl, beat egg yolks until light and fluffy.

2. Gradually add 1 cup of sugar and continue beating until the mixture will "form the ribbon"—that is, until some of it will fall from the beaters and look like a ribbon on the surface of the rest.

3. Add grated lemon peel, lemon juice, and salt.

• Use a small hand grater on the lemons. Grate off just the thin yellow layer of peel; don't dig into the bitter white part.
• Lemons keep best when they are wrapped in plastic bags and stored in the vegetable drawer of a refrigerator.
• For a Frozen Daiquiri Soufflé, use the grated peel of 2 lemons and 2 limes with ½ cup of lemon juice and ½ cup of lime juice here; use ground pistachios in step 12; and if desired, decorate the center of the soufflé with a slice of lime dipped in crystallized sugar.

4. Blend thoroughly, then transfer the mixture to a heavy pan (not aluminum) and stir it over low heat, constantly, until it thickens enough to coat the back of a spoon—to film the spoon, that is, enough so that a line can be drawn in the film with your finger. The mixture must not curdle; if it seems to be getting too hot, take the pan off heat for 1 or 2 seconds.

5. Sprinkle the gelatin over rum to soften it, then stir the rum-gelatin mixture into the egg-and-lemon mixture. Stir until the gelatin is completely dissolved, then remove mixture from heat, pour it into a large bowl, and let it cool, stirring occasionally.

6. In another bowl and with clean beaters, beat egg whites until foamy. Gradually add the remaining 1 cup of sugar, 1 tablespoon at a time, and beat until the mixture looks like marshmallow. Feel it between thumb and forefinger; if it feels smooth, it's ready.

7. In a chilled bowl, beat 2 cups of the heavy cream until it mounds nicely but isn't too stiff.

8. Fold egg-white mixture into the egg-and-lemon mixture thoroughly. Then fold in the whipped cream.

9. Pour the mixture into the prepared soufflé dish and put it in a refrigerator to set for at least 3 hours. It's better to refrigerate the mixture longer so that flavors have time to blend.

10. Before serving, whip the remaining 1 cup of cream with confec-

tioners' sugar until stiff, then put it into a pastry bag fitted with a star tube.

11. Carefully remove collar from soufflé.

• When the collar is put on with the fold at the bottom (and the open edges at the top), a warmed table knife can be run between the pieces of waxed paper to loosen it.

12. Decorate the sides of the soufflé extending above the dish with ground nuts by holding the dish with one hand (hold it over a pan or a piece of waxed paper), and scooping up nuts and pressing them against the soufflé with the other hand.

13. Pipe rosettes of whipped cream around the top of the soufflé and put a candied violet on each.

• If desired, put some candied lemon peel dipped in crystallized sugar in the center. *Makes 12 to 14 servings.*

# STOCK AND SAUCES

## STOCK

There are three basic types of stock: beef (see p. 240), chicken (see p. 241), and fish (see p. 242). The technique used for each is the same, and it is easy. Although preparing stock takes several hours, the flavor that homemade stock adds to recipes makes the time spent simmering meat (or poultry or fish), bones, vegetables, herbs, and water together in a large kettle well worth it.

It isn't necessary to watch stock closely while it cooks, and it is virtually impossible to ruin it. Stock can be stored in wide-mouth jars or plastic containers in a refrigerator for up to a week if it is brought to a boil each day to destroy any foreign organisms, or it can be frozen (I like to freeze it in measured amounts) for up to 2 months. Many cooks store bones and scraps of meat, poultry, or fish in their freezers until they've collected enough for a large quantity of stock; then they make enough at one time to serve their cooking needs for 1 or 2 months.

Stock is often called the building block of the kitchen, for the uses for it are almost endless. It serves as the liquid for braising meats or for poaching poultry or fish. It is also used to cook hearty vegetables, to flavor rice dishes, and to provide the traditional base for classic sauces

—from light Brown Sauce (see p. 248) to rich Velouté (see p. 246)—and for homemade soups. Moreover, when clarified, stock is an instantly elegant consommé (see p. 243); jellied, it becomes a tasty and decorative aspic (see p. 243); and concentrated, it is meat glaze (see p. 244), which provides a wonderful lift for the sauce or gravy that is missing "something."

Stock should certainly be in the repertoire of any aspiring cook. Take the time to learn about it, and the recipes will remain among the most frequently used in your collection.

## BEEF STOCK

2 lbs. cubed lean beef brisket or shin
2 lbs. raw beef bones
1 veal knuckle
1 cup sliced carrots
2 medium peeled onions
4 whole cloves
1 cup sliced celery ribs, with leaves
1 cup dry white wine
1 medium clove mashed garlic
½ teaspoon dried thyme
1 bay leaf
3 sprigs parsley
2 tablespoons tomato paste
1 tablespoon salt
½ teaspoon freshly cracked black pepper

1. Put beef, beef bones, veal knuckle, carrots, celery, and onions stuck with cloves all together into a roasting pan and place in a preheated 450° oven for about 30 minutes, or until the beef is thoroughly browned. To make sure the vegetables do not scorch, take the pan from the oven occasionally and stir them with a wooden spatula; remove them as soon as they are brown.

2. Put the browned vegetables and meat and the bones in a deep kettle or stock pot. Then pour 1 cup of cold water into the roasting pan and scrape up the brown bits. Pour the water and brown bits into the kettle or stock pot, add enough cold water to make 4 quarts in all, add wine, garlic, thyme, bay leaf, parsley, tomato paste, salt, and pepper, and bring to a boil very slowly. Skim off all scum that rises to the top.

3. Reduce heat, partially cover the kettle or pot, and simmer gently for 4 hours. Skim occasionally.

4. Strain through a sieve lined with a double thickness of cheesecloth wrung out in cold water.

• Taste for seasoning, if desired. But note, stock should be underseasoned, for many times it is used in reduced or concentrated sauces, which too highly seasoned stock may ruin.

• If recipe calls for extra-strength stock, boil ordinary stock, uncovered, over moderately high heat until it is reduced by one third. *Makes 2 to 3 quarts.*

## CHICKEN STOCK

Do not confuse chicken stock with chicken soup, which contains many more ingredients, but for sublime chicken soup, first make chicken stock, then use the stock to cook chicken for the soup.

4 lbs. chicken backs, wings, necks, and giblets or a 4-lb. whole chicken
1 cup sliced carrots
1 cup sliced celery ribs, with leaves
2 medium peeled onions
4 whole cloves
1 cup dry white wine

1 medium clove mashed garlic
½ teaspoon dried thyme
1 bay leaf
3 sprigs parsley
2 tablespoons tomato paste
1 tablespoon salt
½ teaspoon freshly cracked black pepper

1. Place all ingredients and 4 quarts of cold water in a deep kettle or stock pot, sticking 2 whole cloves into each onion, and bring to a boil slowly. Skim off any scum that rises to the top.

• Chicken parts to be used for stock can be stored in a freezer as you collect them and stock made when the collection is large enough.

2. Reduce heat, partially cover the kettle or pot, and simmer gently for 1½ hours.

3. Remove the chicken, strip the meat from the bones, return the bones to the kettle or pot, and simmer for another 2½ hours.

• The stripped meat can be used in salads or sandwiches, or in any recipe calling for cooked chicken.

4. Strain through a sieve lined with a double thickness of cheesecloth wrung out in cold water.

• Taste for seasoning if desired. But note, stock is often used in reduced or concentrated sauces, and if it's already seasoned to taste, intensification may ruin the sauce.

• If recipe calls for extra-strength stock, boil ordinary stock, uncovered, over moderately high heat until it is reduced by one third. *Makes 2 to 3 quarts.*

*Veal Stock*

Follow the recipe for chicken stock, substituting veal and veal bones for the chicken.

## FISH STOCK

*1 cup sliced onion*
*½ cup sliced celery rib*
*½ cup sliced carrot*
*2 lbs. fish bones and trim-*
*mings, all from lean fish*

*1 cup dry white wine*
*Bouquet garni (see p. 7)*
*1 teaspoon salt*
*½ teaspoon freshly cracked*
*white pepper*

1. Put all ingredients and 1 quart of cold water into a kettle or stock pot and bring to a boil. Skim off any scum that rises to the top.
2. Reduce heat, partially cover the kettle or pot, and simmer ½ hour. Skim if necessary.
3. Strain through a fine sieve.

• For stronger stock, boil to reduce.
• Fish stock can be frozen in plastic containers or wide-mouth jars. **Makes 3 to 4 cups.**

## COURT BOUILLON

Court bouillon, unlike fish stock, contains no fish trimmings and takes only about 10 minutes to prepare. It can be used for poaching or boiling any fish or shellfish, but never, never drop fish or shellfish into boiling Court Bouillon—it will toughen the fish.

*2 cups dry vermouth or other*
*dry white wine or 2 cups*
*cider vinegar*
*½ cup roughly chopped onion*
*½ cup roughly chopped carrot*
*½ cup roughly chopped celery*
*rib*

*2 teaspoons salt*
*8 peppercorns*
*3 sprigs parsley*
*1 bay leaf*
*1 clove*
*¼ teaspoon dried thyme*

1. Put all ingredients and 2 quarts of cold water into a large sauce-pan or kettle, bring to a boil, and boil rapidly for ½ hour.
2. Strain bouillon and cool. **Makes 9 to 10 cups.**

## Beef and Chicken Consommés

 3 quarts beef stock (see
   p. 240) or chicken stock (see
   p. 241)
½ cup sliced carrot
 2 tablespoons sliced leek,
   white part only

½ cup small sliced onion
½ cup sliced celery rib
 1 tablespoon tomato paste
 3 egg whites

1. Degrease stock—thoroughly—by putting it in a refrigerator to chill, then lifting off the fat that comes to the top and solidifies.

2. Put cold stock in a kettle, add remaining ingredients, and bring to a boil, whisking constantly to make the egg whites foamy. The whites will then attract floating particles in the stock, thus clarifying it.

• The flavor of beef consommé can be intensified by adding small pieces of raw beef.

3. Reduce heat and simmer gently for ½ hour. As the stock simmers, the egg whites and particles attracted to them will coagulate and form an island; don't disturb this island.

4. Strain through a sieve lined with a double thickness of cheesecloth wrung out in cold water, pouring carefully so as not to disturb the island, which should not be squeezed or pushed through the cheesecloth. Do not let the sieve touch the clear broth that has dripped through it, or the consommé will be cloudy. *Makes 2½ quarts.*

## Aspic

 2 cups strong chicken stock
   (see p. 241), fish stock (see
   p. 242), or veal stock (see
   p. 242)
½ cup tomato juice
 2 envelopes unflavored gelatin

 1 crushed eggshell
 2 lightly beaten egg whites
 2 tablespoons cognac, brandy,
   Madeira, or white wine
 1 teaspoon salt
½ teaspoon freshly cracked
   black pepper

1. Combine all ingredients in a saucepan and bring slowly to a boil, whisking constantly.

2. Remove from heat and let stand 5 minutes.

3. Strain into a bowl through a strainer lined with a double thickness cf wet cheesecloth. Do not force it through, just let it drip through by itself. Keep the strainer well above level of the aspic. If not clear, pour it through the strainer again.

4. Place in a refrigerator for 1 hour to set.

• Aspic can be made a day ahead and kept refrigerated but it should not be frozen. *Makes about 2 cups.*

## MEAT GLAZE
### *(Glace de Viande)*

Meat glaze, which is nothing more than strained beef stock reduced to a syrup, can be bought, but it's easy to make and store—in a covered jar in the refrigerator. Use it whenever a concentrated beef flavor is desired (particularly good for seasoning sauces).

> *3 quarts beef stock (see*
> *p. 240)*

1. Boil stock, in a large kettle for ½ hour, or until it's reduced to about 1 quart.
2. Strain the reduced stock into a small saucepan and boil ½ hour, or until it is further reduced, to about 1½ cups.

• Watch it carefully near the end, so it doesn't burn.

3. Cool about 1 hour.

• Always use a clean spoon to dip into meat glaze. *Makes about 1½ cups.*

# *Sauces*

It would take an entire cookbook to describe the hundreds of different sauces that can be used to complete or to enhance meat dishes, fish, poultry, eggs, vegetables, and salads. This section is not designed as a definitive sauce-book, but rather as a basic primer of sauces. Every one of the classic sauces, no matter how complicated, is just a variation of one of the basic or mother sauces. After you have mastered the preparation of the sauces in this section, no other sauce recipe will be difficult for you—it will only be a variation of a technique with which you are already familiar.

There are five basic warm sauces: three of them, Béchamel (see p. 245), Velouté (see p. 246), and Hollandaise (see p. 246) are light-colored; two,

Demiglace (see p. 248) and Tomato (see p. 250), are dark. Cold sauces stem from two basic roots, Mayonnaise (see p. 251) and Vinaigrette (see p. 252), both of which are light-colored. Finally there are all of the butter-based sauces, which may be served hot or cold and are either light or dark in color.

I've included recipes for some of my own favorite variations of the basic sauce groups, but I do hope that you will experiment with your own favorite herbs and additions to develop personal variations.

## BÉCHAMEL SAUCE

This white sauce can be made thin, medium, or thick. It is used as a base for soufflés and I make it when I want a cream sauce for vegetables.

| | |
|---|---|
| 2 cups milk | ⅛ teaspoon freshly grated |
| ¾ cup chopped onion | nutmeg |
| 1 small bay leaf | 1 to 3 tablespoons butter |
| ½ teaspoon salt | 1 to 3 tablespoons flour |
| ¼ teaspoon freshly cracked white pepper | |

1. Put milk, onion, bay leaf, salt, pepper, and nutmeg into a saucepan and simmer, uncovered, for 15 minutes.
2. Strain. There should be 1 cup of seasoned milk.
3. Melt butter in a saucepan—for thin Béchamel use 1 tablespoon, for medium use 2 tablespoons, and for thick use 3. Then make a roux by stirring in flour—1 tablespoon for thin Béchamel, 2 tablespoons for medium, and 3 tablespoons for thick—with a wooden spatula and cooking, over high heat, stirring, for at least 2 minutes.
4. Remove from heat and add the seasoned milk, beating vigorously with a wire whisk for 5 minutes.
5. Return to heat and cook, stirring constantly, until smooth and thick. **Makes 2 cups.**

### Mornay Sauce

Stir ½ cup grated Parmesan or Swiss cheese into 2 cups hot Béchamel Sauce in step 5. Use over cauliflower or crêpes.

### Duxelles Sauce

Stir 1 recipe Duxelles (see p. 130) into 2 cups hot Béchamel Sauce. Great over poached poultry or sautéed veal.

### Aurore Sauce

Stir ½ cup tomato paste or puree and 2 tablespoons sherry into 2 cups hot Béchamel Sauce. Serve over vegetables or eggs.

## VELOUTÉ SAUCE

Velouté is a white sauce made with stock. For chicken dishes, use chicken stock; for fish, fish stock; for veal, veal stock.

> ¼ cup butter
> ¼ cup flour
> 2½ cups chicken stock (see
>
> p. 241), fish stock (see
> p. 242) or veal stock (see
> p. 242)

1. Melt butter in a saucepan and stir in flour with a wooden spatula. Cook over high heat, stirring constantly, for at least 2 minutes. Do not let the flour brown.

• The quick way to save any mixture that's suddenly getting too hot is to lift the pan off the heat. It's as simple as that. Don't waste time turning a knob or pushing a button.

2. Take the pan off heat and add stock all at once, beating vigorously with a wire whisk for 3 minutes.

3. Return the pan to high heat and cook, stirring, until the mixture thickens and comes to a boil. Boil 1 minute. *Makes 2 cups.*

### Sauce Bonne Femme

Add ¼ cup heavy cream and 2 tablespoons lemon juice to 2 cups Velouté. Use on broiled or sautéed foods.

### Sauce Suprême

Fold ¼ cup whipped cream and 2 tablespoons butter into 2 cups Velouté. Serve with green vegetables or poached chicken.

### Sauce Bercy

Simmer 1 cup finely minced onions in ¾ cups dry white wine until all of the liquid is absorbed. Then stir onions into 2 cups hot Velouté Sauce. Serve over sautéed liver, poached chicken, or seafood casseroles.

## HOLLANDAISE SAUCE

Hollandaise is an easy sauce to make. I prefer to use the direct heat method, which is faster and yields slightly more sauce than do the other methods.

½ cup butter
3 egg yolks
2 tablespoons lemon juice

¼ teaspoon salt
¼ teaspoon freshly cracked
white pepper

1. Melt butter, which should be very hot when you are ready for it.
2. Put egg yolks and 3 tablespoons of cold water in a small non-aluminum pan and whisk them together over high heat, raising and lowering the pan over heat as you whisk. The outside of the pan must not get too hot to touch or the sauce will curdle. If it starts to get hot, take the pan completely off the heat for a moment, but don't stop whisking. Whisk about 10 minutes, or until the mixture starts to mound and is the consistency of heavy cream.

• For blender Hollandaise, blend egg yolks, lemon juice, salt, and pepper 1 minute, then with the blender on high speed, pour in very hot melted butter (use the opening in the top of the blender) in a thin stream. Sauce will thicken by itself.

3. Take the pan off heat, whisk in ¼ cup of the hot melted butter, 1 tablespoon at a time, then return the pan to high heat, and still whisking, add the remaining butter in a thin stream. Whisk about 5 minutes until the mixture is thick and creamy, and snatch the pan off the heat for a moment—but don't stop whisking—if it starts to get too hot.
4. Add lemon juice, salt, and pepper, and if necessary to hold the sauce until serving time, stand the pan in warm water (Hollandaise should not be served hot, just warm, on hot food) and whisk occasionally.

• If the sauce isn't thick enough, put it back on heat and whisk until it thickens.
• If it curdles because of overcooking, it can be brought back by whisking in 1 tablespoon of cold water or 1 tablespoon of boiling water or by first whisking a fresh egg yolk, then very slowly whisking the sauce into it.

### Minted Hollandaise

Add 1 tablespoon of fresh chopped mint leaves to Hollandaise sauce before serving. Serve with lamb.

### Sauce Maltaise

Omit lemon juice and before serving season Hollandaise with the juice of ½ orange and 2 teaspoons of freshly grated orange rind.

• Maltaise is especially good on vegetables.

## BÉARNAISE SAUCE

This sauce is part of the Hollandaise family and is especially good with steak. I also like it with lamb and over green vegetables.

½ cup butter
1 tablespoon chopped shallot
½ cup tarragon vinegar
1 tablespoon dried tarragon
or 3 tablespoons finely
chopped fresh tarragon

3 egg yolks
¼ teaspoon salt
¼ teaspoon freshly cracked
white pepper
2 tablespoons chopped parsley, optional

1. Melt butter, which should be very hot when you are ready for it.
2. Put shallot, vinegar, and tarragon in a small heavy pan and cook, stirring with a wooden spatula, over moderately high heat about 5 minutes, or until all liquid evaporates. Do not let the mixture burn.
3. Take the pan off the heat, add egg yolks and 2 tablespoons of cold water and whisk together until well blended.
4. Return the pan to heat and whisk the egg-yolk mixture, raising and lowering the pan over heat (to keep it from getting too hot), until the mixture is the consistency of heavy cream.
5. Take the pan off heat, whisk in ¼ cup of the hot butter, 1 tablespoon at a time, then return the pan to heat, and still whisking, add the remaining butter in a thin stream. Whisk, raising and lowering the pan over heat, until the mixture is thick.

• Strain sauce, if desired, before adding parsley.

6. Season with salt and pepper.

• Stir in parsley if desired. *Makes ¾ to 1 cup.*

## BASIC BROWN SAUCE

### (Demiglace)

Purists insist that Brown Sauce must cook for several days, but I doubt that many people have palates sensitive enough to tell the difference between a purist's Brown Sauce and mine, which is a quick one.

3 tablespoons butter
¾ cup finely minced onion
½ cup diced carrot
4½ teaspoons flour

2 cups beef stock (see p. 240)
1 tablespoon minced shallot
2 medium cloves minced
garlic

*Bouquet garni (see p. 7)*  *½ teaspoon meat glaze (see*
*2 teaspoons tomato paste*  *p. 244)*
*¼ teaspoon freshly cracked*
    *black pepper*

1. Melt butter in a small pan, and when it is hot and foaming, add onion and carrot and cook over high heat for 5 minutes, stirring with a wooden spatula.

2. Blend in flour, stirring with the wooden spatula, to make a roux.

3. Cook the roux, stirring constantly, about 10 minutes, or until it turns brown.

• The browned roux gives the sauce its characteristic flavor.

4. Remove pan from heat and add beef stock, beating vigorously with a wire whisk.

5. Add shallot, garlic, bouquet garni, tomato paste, pepper, and meat glaze, then return pan to heat, bring mixture to a boil, reduce heat, cover the pan, and cook mixture *very* slowly for ½ hour, or if there is time, longer (I prefer to cook about 2 hours in all) to intensify flavor.

6. Strain through a fine sieve, then taste for, and if necessary, adjust seasoning.

• Brown sauce freezes well (I like to store measured cupfuls in the freezer); in a refrigerator it will keep for 1 week. **Makes 1 cup.**


## Sauce Robert

A hearty, spicy sauce—very good with pork.

*2 tablespoons butter*  *¼ cup chopped gherkins*
*¾ cup very finely chopped*  *1 teaspoon Dijon mustard*
    *onion*  *1 tablespoon chopped parsley*
*¼ cup wine vinegar*
*1 cup Basic Brown Sauce (see*
    *p. 248)*

1. Melt butter in a small saucepan, add onion, and cook, stirring, until mixture is transparent. Do not let it brown.

2. Add vinegar and cook over moderately high heat until vinegar is reduced by one half.

3. Add Basic Brown Sauce, bring to a boil, and reduce heat.

4. Simmer for 15 minutes, then stir in gherkins, mustard, and parsley, and bring to a boil again.

*Sauce Périgourdine*

A truly elegant sauce to serve with good beef.

| | |
|---|---|
| *1 cup Basic Brown Sauce (see p. 248)* | *2 tablespoons chopped truffle* |
| *½ cup dry Madeira* | *Reserved pan drippings* |

1. Strain Basic Brown Sauce, then boil it until it is reduced by one third.

2. Stir in Madeira and chopped truffle and add the pan drippings reserved from the beef. Taste for seasoning and, if desired, add salt and pepper. Serve warm.

*Madeira Sauce*

Good on beef, excellent on sweetbreads.

| | |
|---|---|
| *1 recipe of Basic Brown Sauce (see p. 248)* | *9 tablespoons Madeira* |
| *2 tablespoons minced shallots* | *1 tablespoon cognac* |

1. Cook shallots and ½ cup of the Madeira in a saucepan over medium heat until mixture is reduced to 1 tablespoon. Take care that it doesn't burn.

2. Strain Brown Sauce and whisk it into the pan. Mix well. Return pan to heat. Heat contents, but do not let them boil.

3. Remove pan from heat, stir in cognac, and the remaining 1 tablespoon of Madeira.

## TOMATO SAUCE

| | |
|---|---|
| *1 cup chopped onion* | *4 cups diced fresh tomatoes or 4 cups canned Italian plum tomatoes, squeezed through your fingers* |
| *½ cup chopped carrot* | |
| *½ cup chopped celery* | |
| *2 medium cloves chopped garlic* | |
| | *2 teaspoons salt* |
| *¼ cup butter* | *¼ teaspoon freshly cracked black pepper* |
| *3 tablespoons flour* | |
| *1 cup strong beef stock (see p. 240) or chicken stock (see p. 241)* | *Bouquet garni (see p. 7)* |

1. Simmer the onion, carrot, celery, and garlic in butter for 20 minutes, in a covered skillet.

2. Stir in the flour and cook without browning for 3 minutes.

3. Add remaining ingredients and cook for 3 hours to develop flavor and reduce some of the liquid. Half-cover the kettle. Stir the mixture frequently. If it gets too thick, add more stock.

4. Remove bouquet garni, and puree the mixture through a food mill, using the finest blade. Taste the sauce and adjust seasoning. Use, or freeze for later use. *Makes about 4 cups.*

### Sauce Italienne

Add ½ teaspoon oregano and ½ teaspoon basil in step 3. Wonderful on pasta.

### Sauce Portugaise

Combine an equal amount of Tomato Sauce and Brown Sauce and serve over fish, poultry, or meat.

### Sauce Provençale

Add 1 medium clove chopped garlic to 4 cups Tomato Sauce. Serve with fish, poultry, or eggs.

### MAYONNAISE

*½ teaspoon salt*
*1 tablespoon tarragon, red- or white-wine, or cider vinegar or 1 tablespoon lemon juice*
*1 egg yolk*

*¼ teaspoon freshly cracked black or white pepper*
*1 cup olive or vegetable oil or a mixture of the two*

1. Put salt, vinegar (or lemon juice), pepper, and egg yolk into a small (about 1-quart) bowl and whisk well.

• For blender mayonnaise, blend salt, vinegar (or lemon juice), pepper, 2 egg yolks, and 2 tablespoons of oil for a few seconds to mix, then with the blender on high speed, pour in the remaining oil in a thin stream.

2. Whisk in ¼ cup of oil, 1 tablespoon at a time (whisk thoroughly after the addition of each spoonful), then pour in the remaining oil in a thin stream (use a measuring cup with a pouring lip), whisking constantly about 5 minutes, or until mixture is thick and smooth.

• If the oil is added too quickly, the mixture will curdle. If it does, whisk a fresh egg yolk in another bowl, and whisking constantly, add the curdled mixture to it, 1 teaspoon at a time.

• I like to season mayonnaise by adding either 1 teaspoon of Dijon mustard or 1 tablespoon of chopped fresh herbs. *Makes 1 cup.*

### Green Mayonnaise

Cover 4 or 5 spinach leaves with boiling water, boil 1 minute, then drain, squeeze out excess water, chop as fine as possible, and stir into 1 cup mayonnaise. Use on cold fish.

### Tartar Sauce

Add 1 small dill pickle, finely chopped, 2 tablespoons of drained capers, and 2 tablespoons of finely chopped parsley to mayonnaise. Serve with fish.

### Aioli

Stir 4 or more finely mashed cloves garlic into 1 cup mayonnaise. Wonderful as a dip with raw vegetables.

## VINAIGRETTE SAUCE

True French vinaigrette is made with salt, pepper, vinegar, and oil in varying proportions, depending on what it's to be used for. To Americanize the vinaigrette, try the following, which is particularly good with artichokes (see p. 163) and asparagus (see p. 163) and in the hollows of pitted ripe avocado halves.

| | |
|---|---|
| 1 tablespoon vinegar | 1 teaspoon dried tarragon or |
| ½ teaspoon salt | 1 tablespoon fresh |
| ¼ teaspoon freshly cracked | 2 tablespoons washed and |
| black pepper | dried capers |
| 2 tablespoons lemon juice | 1 tablespoon chopped scallion, white part only |
| 6 tablespoons olive oil | |
| ½ teaspoon dry mustard | ½ teaspoon chopped shallot |
| 1 chopped hard-cooked egg | 1 tablespoon chopped fresh |
| 1 tablespoon chopped parsley | chives, if available |

Put all ingredients into a bowl and stir with a fork to mix. *Makes ¾ cup.*

### Maître d'Hôtel Butter

Pack this butter in little containers and store them in a refrigerator or freezer. Brush this butter over hot steak or chops at the table.

½ cup butter
1 tablespoon lemon juice
½ teaspoon salt
¼ teaspoon freshly cracked
  black pepper
1 tablespoon finely chopped
  parsley

1 teaspoon finely chopped
  shallot, optional
¼ teaspoon finely chopped
  garlic, optional

1. Cream butter in an electric mixer (use the flat whip if the mixer is a heavy-duty one).
2. Beat in lemon juice, salt, pepper, parsley, and if you like (I do, since otherwise I find Maître d'Hôtel Butter a little bland), shallot and garlic. **Makes ½ cup.**

#### Lemon Butter

Stir 2 tablespoons lemon juice and 1 tablespoon chopped parsley into ½ cup hot melted butter. Serve over vegetables or fish.

#### Beurre Noir

Melt ¼ lb. of butter over *very* low heat; take about 15 minutes to do this so that the butter toasts but does not burn. This sauce is especially good on cauliflower or any green vegetable, fried eggs, or sautéed fish.

#### Truffle Butter

Add 1 tablespoon finely chopped truffle to ½ cup hot melted butter. This very elegant sauce is served with beef or poached chicken.

# CREATIVE COOKING SCHOOL MENUS

## Brunch, Lunch, or Light Supper

Assorted Hors d'Oeuvre
French Omelettes
Hot French bread, pot of unsalted
    butter
Peach Tart

Quiche
Country Soup
Beefsteak Tomato and Onion Salad
Pears in Red Wine

Shrimp Pâté
Crêpes Stuffed with Cheese Soufflé
Watercress and Mushroom Salad
Coffee Pot de Crème

Pâté Maison
Minestrone alla Milanese

Italian bread
French Green Salad
Gorgonzola cheese and fresh fruit

Salmon Roll
Raw Mushroom Salad
Fresh fruit and cheese

Garlic Soup
Salad Niçoise
Pears in Red Wine

Mushroom Soup Royale
Parmesan Sticks
Egg Mousse with Cucumber or
    Cold Lobster Mousse
Oranges Orientale

Ring Mold of Flounder Stuffed with
Salmon Mousse
Minted Cucumbers
Lemon sherbet served with half
fresh lemon

Senegalese
Flounder in Parchment
Lemon Curd

Poached Striped Bass with Sauce
Gribiche

Broccoli Soufflé
Pears Hélène

Whitebait with Caper Mayonnaise
Minted Cucumbers
Lemon Curd

Cold Curried Avocado Soup
Lamb Chops in Mint Aspic
French Potato Salad
Meringue Shells filled with Cassis
Sherbet

## DINNER

Pyramid of Cheese Balls
Chicken Breasts Duxelles with
White Wine Sauce
Rice Pilaf
French Green Salad
Cassis Sherbet (pass bottle of
cassis)
Viennese Almond Balls

Mushroom Soup Royale
Flounder with Champagne Sauce
Filet of Beef in Crust with
Sauce Périgourdine
French Green Salad
Roquefort Mousse with toasted
crackers
Oranges Orientale

Manhattan Clam Chowder
Baked Lobster Nicholas
Waffled Potatoes
Romaine Salad
Frozen Lemon Soufflé

Mussel Soup
Roast Filet of Beef
Braised Belgian Endive

Potatoes Anna
Oeufs à la Neige

Pumpkin Soup
Truffled Turkey Flambé
Braised Brussels Sprouts
Chestnut Croquettes
Belgian Endive Salad
Fresh Fruit

Oysters Bienville
Roast Goose
Celery Sticks
Carrot Ring
Marron Roll

Lobster Bisque
Roast Veal
Potatoes Savoyard
Raw Spinach Salad
Beignets with Raspberry Sauce

Chestnut Soup
Duck with Peaches
Seven-Minute Green Beans
Crêpes Flambées

Hungarian Chicken Paprika
Spaetzle
French Green Salad or Raw Spinach Salad
Vanilla Soufflé (Fudge Sauce, optional)

Mussels Marinara
Petti di Pollo
Sautéed Mushroom Caps and Pine Nuts
Romaine Salad or Zucchini Salad
Italian Rum Cake

Crudités with Skordalia
Ham in Crust
Molded Green Beans
Charlotte Portugaise

Stuffed Ham with Champagne Sauce and Frosted White Grapes
Mushroom Roll
Belgian Endive Salad
Frozen Daiquiri Soufflé

Piroshki
Shrimp à la Kiev
Onions à la Grecque
Butterscotch-Rum Parfait

Braised Boned Leg of Lamb
Stewed Dried Beans
French Green Salad
Marron Roll or Apricot Mousse

Blanquette de Veau or Veal Casserole
Rice Timbales or Rice Ring
Romaine Salad
Chocolate Crêpes

Carrot Soup
Leg of Lamb with Parsley Dressing

Cauliflower Mousse
Fresh pears

Saddle of Lamb
Potatoes Sarladaise
Sautéed Cherry Tomatoes
Praline Flan

Rib Roast of Beef
Potatoes Dauphinoise
Carrots Vichy
Hazelnut Roll with Whipped-Cream Filling

Liptauer Cheese
Hungarian Goulash
Spaetzle
German Apple Pancake

Pâté
Vitello Tonnato
Roman Tomatoes
Cherry Fritters

Mushrooms à la Grecque
Curried Shrimp with Condiments
Saffron Rice
Cucumber Salad with Yoghurt
Frozen Lemon Soufflé

Ham Slice with Madeira
Cabbage Stuffed with Cabbage
Cherry Fritters

Melon and Prosciutto
Veal Piccata
Italian Gnocchi
Zucchini Provençal or Raw Mushroom Salad
Biscuit Tortoni

Pork with Pistachios
Braised Boston Lettuce

Whipped Carrots
Crêpes à la Julie

Crudités with Skordalia—Pâté
  Maison
Cioppino
French Green Salad
Italian bread
Italian Rum Cake

French Pot Roast
Molded Green Beans
Potatoes Dauphinoise
French Green Salad
Bananas Vieux Carré with Crème
  Fraîche

Steak au Poivre or Noisettes of
  Lamb
Noodle Nests filled with Pea Puree
Belgian Endive and Citrus Salad
Apricot Mousse with Chocolate
  Cornets

Parsley Soup
Barbecued Spareribs
Potatoes Savoyard
Beefsteak Tomato and Red Onion
  Salad
Fresh fruit or vanilla ice cream
  with Fudge Sauce

Trout Meunière
Rack of Lamb
Pommes Pailles
Flageolets
Oranges Orientale

Lobster Flambé or Steak Diane
Pommes Pailles
Artichokes Vinaigrette
Charlotte Portugaise

Pot Roast in Beer
Whipped Carrots
French Green Salad
Fruit and cheese

# *MEASURES*

## COMMONLY USED MEASURES

3 teaspoons = 1 tablespoon
4 tablespoons = ¼ cup
5⅓ tablespoons = ⅓ cup
8 tablespoons = ½ cup
10⅔ tablespoons = ⅔ cup
12 tablespoons = ¾ cup
16 tablespoons = 1 cup
2 cups liquid = 1 pint
4 cups liquid = 1 quart

## *Miscellaneous Equivalents*

Bread: 1 slice = ½ cup cubes or crumbs
Butter: 1 pound = 2 cups or 32 tablespoons
    ¼ pound stick = ½ cup or 8 tablespoons
Carrots: 1 medium = ½ cup chopped
Celery: 1 medium rib = ½ cup chopped

Cheese: ¼ pound = 1 cup grated
Garlic: 1 medium clove = 1 teaspoon chopped
Gelatin: 1 envelope = 1 tablespoon
Herbs: 1 teaspoon dried = 1 tablespoon fresh
Lemon juice: Juice of 1 medium lemon = 3 tablespoons
Mushrooms: ¼ pound = 1 cup sliced
Onions: 1 medium = ¾ cup chopped
Potatoes: 1 medium = 1 cup chopped
Shallots: 1 medium = 1 tablespoon chopped
Tomatoes: 1 medium = ¾ cup chopped
Yeast: 1 package dry = ¼ ounce

# Index

Aioli, 252
Almond Viennese balls, 220–221
Anchovy appetizer rolls, 23
Appetizers, 16–41
  anchovy rolls, 23
  blini with caviar, 34
  bourekakia, 27–28
  cheese balls, pyramid of, 19
  crudités with skordalia, 25
  Edam cheese, stuffed, 40–41
  eggs mimosa, 23–24
  general data on, 16–17
  ginger sausage rounds, 24
  Gouda cheese, stuffed, 40–41
  Grace Zia Chu's shrimp toast, 26–27
  hors d'oeuvres, assorted, 20
  Liptauer cheese, 29–30
  mushrooms à la Grecque, 25–26
  oysters Bienville, 21–22
  Parmesan sticks, 30
  pâté, 17–18
    maison, 28–29
    shrimp, 20–21
  piroshki, 33–34
  puff pastry, all-purpose, 30–33
  quiche
    crab, 38–39
    Lorraine, 35
    onion, 37–38
    smoked salmon, 39
    spinach, 38
  reheating French-fried, 12
  Roquefort mousse, 40
  tart shell, 36–37
Apple
  German pancake, 223
  and mushroom stuffing for flounder, 62–63
Apricot
  crêpes flambées, 206
  mousse with chocolate cornets, 228–230
Artichokes with vinaigrette sauce, 163
Asparagus Hollandaise, 163–164
Aspic, 243–244
  mint, lamb chops in, 104–105
Aurore sauce, 246
Avocado soup, curried, 51–52

Bacon omelette, 154
Ballotine of roast chicken, 140–141
Banana(s)
  crêpes flambées, 207
  Vieux Carré, 224
Barbecued spareribs, 102
Bass, striped, poached with sauce gribiche, 64–66
Beans
  dried, stewed, 166
    flageolets, 165–166
  green, molded, 164–165
    seven-minute, 164
Béarnaise sauce, 248       rerts, 164–165
Béchamel sauce, 245
Beef, 81–93
  braised oxtails, 93
  consommé, 243
  filet of beef in crust with sauce Péri-
    gourdine, 84–87

  general data on, 80–81
  hamburgers
    with caper butter, 92–93
    with ice water, 92
  Hélène's sweet and sour, 88–89
  Hungarian goulash, 91–92
  piroshki, 33–34
  ragoût de boeuf, 89–91
  roast
    fillet of, 82
    French pot, 87–88
    pot, in beer, 89
    rib of, 81–82
  steak
    Diane, 83–84
    au poivre, 82–83
  stock, 240–241
    consommé, 243
Beer, pot roast in, 89
Beignets with raspberry sauce, 203–204
Belgian endive
  braised, 175
  salad, 193–194
    and citrus, 194
Bercy sauce, 246
Beurre noir, 253
Biscuit tortoni, 210–211
Bisque, lobster, 46–47
Blanching, 7
Blini with caviar, 34
Bonne femme sauce, 246
Bouillon, court, 242
Bouquet garni, 7
Bourekakia, 27–28
Bread crumbs, 7
Broccoli soufflé, 167–168
Broth, short, 242
Brown sauce, basic, 248–249
Brunch menus, 254–255
Brussels sprouts, braised, 167
Butter, 7
  caper, hamburgers with, 92–93
  sauces, 253
    beurre noir, 253
    lemon, 253
    maître d'hôtel, 253
    truffle, 253
Butterscotch-rum parfait, 230–231

Cabbage stuffed with cabbage, 168–170
Cakes
  hazelnut roll with whipped-cream filling,
    216–217
  Italian rum, 213–215
  marron roll, 217–218
  mock saddle of venison, 218–220
  rehrücken, 218–220
  rolling up, 12–13
  sponge, 215
  yellow butter, 212–213
Calves' liver
  with onion-and-sour-cream sauce, 93–94
  pâté maison, 28–29
Calves' sweetbreads with Madeira sauce,
  123–124

Caper
  butter, hamburgers with, 92–93
  mayonnaise, whitebait with, 68
Carrot(s)
  ring, 171
  soup, 50–51
  Vichy, 170
  whipped, 170
Casserole(s)
  cooking in, 8
  seafood, 76–78
  veal, 120–121
Cassis sherbet, 232
Cauliflower mousse, 171–172
Caviar
  blini with, 34
  omelette, 154
Celeriac rémoulade, 192–193
Celery sticks, 172–173
Champagne sauce
  flounder with, 59–61
  stuffed ham with frosted white grapes and,
    94–96
Charlotte Portugaise, 211–212
Cheese
  balls, pyramid of, 19
  Edam, stuffed, 40–41
  Gouda, stuffed, 40–41
  Liptauer, 29–30
  omelette, 153
  Parmesan sticks, 30
  quiche Lorraine, 35
  Roquefort mousse, 40
  soufflé, crêpes stuffed with, 159–160
Cherry fritters, 225
Chestnut
  croquettes, 173–174
  purée, 173
  soup, 45–46
Chicken, 125–143
  boning, 125–127
  breasts
    boning, 125–126
    with duxelles and white wine sauce, 128–
      130
    à la Kiev, with paprika sauce, 132–134
    mousse, cold, 134–135
    Pajorsky, 131–132
    petti di pollo, 131
    poached cutlets, 135–136
    skinning, 125–126
  consommé, 243
  Dauphinoise, 138–139
  Hungarian paprika, 137–138
  roast
    ballotine, 140–141
    truffled, 142–143
    in a sealed pot, 139–140
  skinning, 125–126
  stock, 241
    consommé, 243
  trussing, 127
Chicken liver pâté, 17–18
Chocolate
  cornets, apricot mousse with, 228–230
  crêpes, 207
  fudge sauce, 233–234
  glaze for rehrücken, 218–220
Chowder, Manhattan clam, 49–50
Cioppino, 78–79
Clam chowder, Manhattan, 49–50
Coffee pot de crème, 210
Consommé
  beef, 243

chicken, 243
country soup, 43–44
Court bouillon, 242
Crab meat quiche, 38–39
Crème de Crécy, 50–51
Crème fraîche, 224
Crêpes, 158–161
  basic, 158–159
  blini with caviar, 34
  dessert
    apricot flambées, 206
    banana flambées, 207
    chocolate, 207
    jam flambées, 207
    à la Julie, 204–205
  general data on, 158
  spinach, 160–161
  stuffed with cheese soufflé, 159–160
Croquettes, chestnut, 173–174
Crudités with skordalia, 25
Cucumber(s)
  egg mousse with, 157–158
  minted, 174–175
  salad, with yoghurt, 193
  soup, cold cream of, 55–56
Cumberland sauce, squabs with, 146–148
Curried
  avocado soup, 51–52
  shrimp with condiments, 71–73
Custard(s), 8
  royale, for mushroom soup, 47–48

Deep frying, 8
Deglazing pans, 8
Demiglace, 248–249
Desserts, 202–238
  apricot mousse with chocolate cornets,
    228–230
  bananas Vieux Carré, 224
  beignets with raspberry sauce, 203–204
  biscuit tortoni, 210–211
  butterscotch-rum parfait, 230–231
  cakes
    hazelnut roll with whipped-cream filling,
      216–217
    Italian rum, 213–215
    marron roll, 217–218
    mock saddle of venison, 218–220
    rehrücken, 218–220
    rolling up, 12–13
    sponge, 215
    yellow butter, 212–213
  cassis sherbet, 232
  Charlotte Portugaise, 211–212
  cherry fritters, 225
  chocolate fudge sauce, 233–234
  coffee pot de crème, 210
  crêpes
    apricot flambées, 206
    banana flambées, 207
    chocolate, 207
    jam flambées, 207
    à la Julie, 204–205
  general data on, 202–203
  German apple pancake, 223
  lemon curd, 207–208
  meringue shells, 232–233
  oeufs à la neige, 221–223
  oranges Orientale, 225–226
  pastry cream, 205–206
  peach tart, 231–232
  pears in red
    wine, 226–227

pears Hélène, 227
praline flan, 208–209
soufflés, 234–238
  frozen lemon, 236–238
  general data on, 234–235
  vanilla, 235–236
  Viennese almond balls, 220–221
Dinner menus, 255–257
Discoloring, 9
Dried beans
  flageolets, 165–166
  soissons, 166
Duckling, 144–146
  carving, 127
  Normand, 144–145
  with peaches, 145–146
Duxelles
  chicken breasts with wine sauce and, 128–130
  sauce, 245
  uses for, 130

Edam cheese, stuffed, 40–41
Eggs, 150–158
  beating whites of, 9
  blending in whites of, 9
  cold poached, 155–158
    basic, 155–156
    in gelatin, 156–157
    mousse, with cucumber, 157–158
  enriching sauces with yolks of, 10
  French omelettes, 151–155
    bacon, 154
    basic, 151–153
    caviar, 154
    cheese, 153
    ham, 154
    herb, 155
    jam flambé, 154
    mincemeat flambé, 154
    mushroom, 154
    truffle flambé, 154
    watercress, 155
  general data on, 9–10, 150
  hard-cooking, 9
  mimosa, 23–24

Fish, *see* Seafood
Flageolets, 165–166
Flaming, 10
Flan, praline, 208–209
Flounder
  with champagne sauce, 59–61
  in parchment, 61–63
  ring mold of, stuffed with salmon mousse, 63–64
Folding, 10
Freezing foods, 10
Fritters, cherry, 225
Fudge sauce, chocolate, 233–234

Garlic soup, 54–55
German
  apple pancake, 223
  potatoes, 185
Ginger sausage rounds, 24
Glace de viande, 244
Glaze
  chocolate, for rehrücken, 218–220
  meat, 244
Gnocchi, 180
Goose, roast, 143–144
Gouda cheese, stuffed, 40–41

Goulash, Hungarian, 91–92
Grace Zia Chu's shrimp toast, 26–27
Grapefruit in Belgian endive salad, 194
Grapes, frosted white, stuffed ham with, 94–96
Green beans
  molded, 164–165
  seven-minute, 164
Green mayonnaise, 252
Green salad, French, 194–195
Gribiche sauce, poached striped bass with, 64–66

Ham, 94–100
  braised, 98
  in crust, 96–98
  mousse, hot, 99
  omelette, 154
  slice, with Madeira, 99–100
  stuffed, with champagne sauce and frosted white grapes, 94–96
Hamburgers, 92–93
Hazelnut roll with whipped-cream filling, 216–217
Hélène's sweet and sour beef, 88–89
Herb(s)
  general data on, 11
  omelette, 155
  toast fingers for soup, 56
High heat, cooking over, 8
Hollandaise sauce, 246–247
  asparagus with, 163–164
  minted, 247
Hors d'oeuvres
  assorted, 20
  *See also* Appetizers
Hungarian
  chicken paprika, 137–138
  goulash, 91–92

Italian
  gnocchi, 180
  rum cake, 213–215
Italienne sauce, 251

Jam
  crêpes flambées, 207
  omelette flambé, 154

Kidneys, veal, 123

Lamb, 102–110
  chops, in mint aspic, 104–105
  general data on, 80–81
  leg of, braised boned, 107–108
  with parsley dressing, 106–107
  noisettes of, 105–106
  rack of, 104
  ragoût of, 109–110
  saddle of, 102–104
  shanks, braised, 108–109
Lemon
  butter, 253
  curd, 207–208
  soufflé, frozen, 236–238
Lettuce
  braised, 175–176
  French green salad, 194–195
  romaine salad, 198
Liptauer cheese, 29–30
Liver
  calves'
    with onion-and-sour-cream sauce, 93–94

pâté maison, 28–29
chicken pâté, 17–18
Lobster
  baked, Nicholas, 69–70
  bisque, 46–47
  cold mousse, 70–71
  flambé, 68–69
Lunch menus, 254–255

Madeira sauce, 250
  calves' sweetbreads with, 123–124
  ham slice with, 99–100
Maître d'hôtel butter, 253
Maltaise sauce, 247
Manhattan clam chowder, 49–50
Marron roll, 217–218
Mayonnaise, 251–252
  aioli, 252
  caper, whitebait with, 68
  crudités with skordalia, 25
  green, 252
  mustard, 20
  tartar, 252
Measures, 258–259
Meat(s), 80–124
  general data on, 80–81
  glaze, 244
  *See also* Beef; Lamb; Pork; Veal
Menus, 254–257
Meringue
  general data on, 9–10
  shells, 232–233
Mincemeat omelette flambé, 154
Minestrone alla Milanese, 44–45
Minted
  aspic, lamb chops in, 104–105
  cucumbers, 174–175
  Hollandaise sauce, 247
Mock saddle of venison cake, 218–220
Molded Green Beans, 164–165
Mornay sauce, 245
Mousse
  apricot, with chocolate cornets, 228–230
  cauliflower, 171–172
  chicken, cold, 134–135
  egg, with cucumber, 157–158
  ham, hot, 99
  lobster, cold, 70–71
  Roquefort, 40
  salmon, ring mold of flounder stuffed with, 63–64
  shrimp, hot, 74–75
Mushroom(s)
  and apple stuffing for flounder, 62–63
  blanquette de veau with velouté sauce and, 121–123
  cleaning, 11
  duxelles
    chicken breasts with wine sauce and, 128–130
    sauce, 245
    uses for, 130
  fluting, 11
  à la Grecque, 25–26
  omelette, 154
  roll, 176–177
  salad
    raw, 195–196
    and watercress, 200–201
  sauce for seafood casserole, 76–78
  sautéed, and pine nuts, 176
  sautéing, 11
  slicing, 11

soufflé, 177–179
soup royale, 47–48
stuffed, 179
Mussels
  marinara, 75–76
  soup, cream of, 53–54
Mustard
  cream, pork chops in, 101–102
  mayonnaise, 20

Niçoise, salade, 196
Noisettes of lamb, 105–106
Noodle nests, 179–180

Oeufs à la neige, 221–223
Omelettes, French, 151–155
  bacon, 154
  basic, 151–153
  caviar, 154
  cheese, 153
  ham, 154
  herb, 155
  jam flambé, 154
  mincemeat flambé, 154
  mushroom, 154
  truffle flambé, 154
  watercress, 155
Onion(s)
  à la Grecque, 181–182
  quiche, 37–38
  red, and beefsteak tomato salad, 199
  -and-sour-cream sauce, liver with, 93–94
Oranges
  in Belgian endive salad, 194
  Orientale, 225–226
Oxtails, braised, 93
Oysters Bienville, 21–22

Pajorsky, chicken, 131–132
Pancakes, German apple, 223
Paprika, Hungarian chicken, 137–138
Paprika sauce, chicken à la Kiev with, 132–134
Parfait, butterscotch-rum, 230–231
Parmesan sticks, 30
Parsley soup, 53
Pastry
  bags and tubes, 11–12
  puff
    all-purpose, 30–33
    rough, 85–87
  sour cream, for ham en croûte, 96–98
Pastry cream, 205–206
Pâté, 17–18
  maison, 28–29
  shrimp, 20–21
Pâte brisée shell, 36–37
Pea purée, 182–183
Peach(es)
  duck with, 145–146
  tart, 231–232
Pears
  Hélène, 227
  in red wine, 226–227
Périgourdine sauce, 250
  filet de boeuf en croûte with, 84–87
Petti di pollo, 131
Piccata, veal, 119–120
Pilaf, rice, 186–187
Pine nuts, sautéed mushrooms and, 176
Pineapple, squabs with, 148–149
Piroshki, 33–34

Pistachios, pork with, 100–101
Poaching, 12
Pommes pailles, 185
Pork, 94–102
  bacon omelette, 154
  barbecued spareribs, 102
  chops, 101–102
  general data on, 80–81
  ham, 94–100
    braised, 98
    en croûte, 96–98
    mousse, hot, 99
    omelette, 154
    slice, with Madeira, 99–100
    stuffed, with champagne sauce and frosted white grapes, 94–96
    with pistachios, 100–101
    sausage ginger rounds, 24
Portugaise sauce, 251
Potage paysanne, 43–44
Potato(es)
  Anna, 183
  Dauphinoise, 183–184
  German, 185
  pommes pailles, 185
  salad, French, 197
  sarlandaise, 185
  savoyard, 184
  truffled, 185
  waffled, 186
Poultry, 125–149
  boning, 125–127
  general data on, 125–127
  skinning, 125–126
  trussing, 127
  *See also* Chicken; Duckling; Goose; Squab; Turkey
Praline flan, 208–209
Provençale sauce, 251
Puff pastry
  all-purpose, 30–33
  rough, 85–87
Pumpkin soup, 48–49

Quiche
  crab, 38–39
  Lorraine, 35
  onion, 37–38
  smoked salmon, 39
  spinach, 38

Raspberry sauce, beignets with, 203–204
Rehrücken, 218–220
Rice
  pilaf, 186–187
  ring, 188
  saffron, 187–188
  salad, 197–198
  timbales, 187
    blanquette de veau with, 121–123
Ris de veau with Madeira sauce, 123–124
Robert sauce, 249
  pork chops with, 101
Romaine salad, 198
Roman tomatoes, 190
Roquefort cheese mousse, 40
Rum
  -butterscotch parfait, 230–231
  cake, Italian, 213–215

Saffron rice, 187–188
Salads, 191–201
  beefsteak tomato and red onion, 199

Belgian endive, 193–194
  and citrus, 194
celeriac rémoulade, 192–193
cold vegetable, vinaigrette, 200
cucumber, with yoghurt, 193
ensalada Valenciana, 199–200
general data on, 191–192
green, French, 194–195
mushroom
  raw, 195–196
  and watercress, 200–201
Niçoise, 196
potato, French, 197
rice, 197–198
romaine, 198
Spanish, 199–200
spinach, raw, 198–199
watercress and mushroom, 200–201
zucchini, 201
Salmon
  mousse, ring mold of flounder stuffed with, 63–64
  roll of, 66–67
  smoked, quiche, 39
Salt, 13
Saltimbocca, 116–117
Sauces, 244–253
  aurore, 246
  basic brown, 248–249
  Béarnaise, 248
  béchamel, 245
  Bercy, 246
  bonne femme, 246
  butter, 253
    beurre noir, 253
    lemon, 253
    maître d'hôtel, 253
    truffle, 253
  champagne
    flounder with, 59–61
    stuffed ham with, 94–96
  chocolate fudge, 233–234
  Cumberland, squabs with, 146–148
  demiglace, 248–249
  duxelles, 245
  enriching with egg yolks, 10
  general data on, 244–245
  gribiche, poached striped bass with, 64–65
  Hollandaise, 246–247
    asparagus with, 163–164
    minted, 247
  Madeira, 250
    calves' sweetbreads with, 123–124
    ham slice with, 99–100
  Maltaise, 247
  mayonnaise, 251–252
    aioli, 252
    caper, whitebait with, 68
    crudités with skordalia, 25
    green, 252
    mustard, 20
    tartar, 252
  Mornay, 245
  mushroom, for seafood casserole, 76–78
  onion-and-sour-cream, liver with, 93–94
  paprika, chicken à la Kiev with, 132–134
  Périgourdine, 250
    filet of beef in crust with, 84–87
  raspberry, beignets with, 203–204
  Robert, 249
    pork chops with, 101
  skimming fat from, 13

suprême, 246
tomato, 250–251
  Italienne, 251
  Portugaise, 251
  Provençale, 251
velouté, 246
  blanquette de veau with mushrooms and,
    121–123
vinaigrette, 252
  artichokes with, 163
  cold vegetable salad with, 200
wine, chicken breasts with duxelles and,
  128–130
Sausage ginger rounds, 24
Seafood, 57–59
cioppino, 78–79
clam chowder, Manhattan, 49–50
crab meat quiche, 38–39
fish stock, 242
flounder
  with champagne sauce, 59–61
  en papillote, 61–63
  ring mold of, stuffed with salmon
    mousse, 63–64
frozen, 58–59
general data on, 57–59
lobster
  baked, Nicholas, 69–70
  bisque, 46–47
  cold mousse, 70–71
  flambé, 68–69
mussel(s)
  marinara, 75–76
  soup, cream of, 53–54
oysters Bienville, 21–22
salmon
  mousse, ring mold of flounder stuffed
    with, 63–64
  roll of, 66–67
  smoked, quiche, 39
  seafood casserole, 76–78
shrimp
  curried, with condiments, 71–73
  deveining, 8
  Grace Zia Chu's toast, 26–27
  hot mousse, 74–75
  à la Kiev, 73–74
  pâté, 20–21
striped bass poached with sauce gribiche,
  64–66
trout meunière, 67–68
whitebait with caper mayonnaise, 68
Seasoning cold food, 13
Saddle of lamb, 102–104
Senegalese soup, 52
Sherbet cassis, 232
Shrimp
curried, with condiments, 71–73
deveining, 8
Grace Zia Chu's toast, 26–27
hot mousse, 74–75
à la Kiev, 73–74
pâté, 20–21
Skordalia, crudités with, 25
Soissons, 166
Soufflés
broccoli, 167–168
cheese crêpes stuffed with, 159–160
dessert, 234–238
  frozen lemon, 236–238
  general data on, 234–235
  vanilla, 235–236
general data on, 13–14

mushroom, 177–179
Soup(s), 42–56
avocado, curried, 51–52
carrot, 50–51
chestnut, 45–46
country soup, 43–44
cucumber, cold cream of, 55–56
garlic, 54–55
garnishes for, 42–43
general data on, 42–43
herb toast fingers for, 56
lobster bisque, 46–47
Manhattan clam chowder, 49–50
minestrone alla Milanese, 44–45
mushroom royale, 47–48
mussel, cream of, 53–54
parsley, 53
pumpkin, 48–49
Senegalese, 52
turtle, cream of, 50
Sour cream
-and-onion sauce, liver with, 93–94
pastry, for ham in crust, 96–98
Spaetzle, 181
spanish salad 199–200
Spareribs, barbecued, 102
Spinach
crêpes, 160–161
quiche, 38
salad, raw, 198–199
Sponge cake, 215
Squabs, 146–149
with Cumberland sauce, 146–148
with pineapple, 148–149
Steak
Diane, 83–84
au poivre, 82–83
Stew
of beef, 89–91
of lamb, 109–110
Stock, 239–244
aspic, 243–244
  mint, lamb chops in, 104–105
beef, 240–241
  consommé, 243
chicken, 241
  consommé, 243
court bouillon, 242
fish, 242
general data on, 239–240
glace de viande, 244
meat glaze, 244
skimming fat from, 13
veal, 242
stuffed shoulder of veal, 112–113
Supper menus, 254–255
Suprême sauce, 246
Sweet and sour beef, Hélène's, 88–89
Sweetbreads with Madeira sauce, 123–124

Tart shell, 36–37
Tartar sauce, 252
Tart, peach 231–232
Timbales, rice, 187
blanquette de veau with, 121–123
Toast
Grace Zia Chu's shrimp, 26–27
herb fingers, for soup, 56
Tomato(es)
beefsteak, and red onion salad, 199
cherry, sautéed, 189
peeling, 14

Roman, 190
sauce, 250–251
  Italienne, 251
  Portugaise, 251
  Provençale, 251
seeding, 14
slicing, 14
stuffed, 189
Trout meunière, 67–68
Truffle
  butter, 253
  omelette flambé, 154
Truffled
  chicken, 142–143
  potatoes, 185
Turkey
  boning, 125–127
  flambé, 142–143
  trussing, 127
Turtle soup, cream of, 50

Unmolding, 14

Vanilla soufflé, 235–236
Veal, 110–124
  blanquette de veau with rice timbales, 121–123
  calves' liver
    with onion-and-sour-cream sauce, 93–94
    pâté maison, 28–29
  calves' sweetbreads with Madeira sauce, 123–124
  casserole, 120–121
  Decameron, 117–118
  general data on, 80–81
  kidneys, 123
  piccata, 119–120
  ris de veau with Madeira sauce, 123–124
  roast, 110–112
  saltimbocca, 116–117

stock, 242
stuffed, 113–115
  shoulder of, 112–113
  viennoise, 118–119
  vitello tonnato, 115
Vegetable(s), 162–190
  cold salad vinaigrette, 200
  general data on, 162–163
  refreshing, 14
  slicing, 15
  *See also* names of vegetables
Velouté sauce, 246
  with mushrooms, blanquette de veau with, 121–123
Venison cake, mock saddle of, 218–220
Viennese almond balls, 220–221
Vinaigrette sauce, 252
  artichokes with, 163
  cold vegetable salad with, 200
Vitello tonnato, 115

Waffled potatoes, 186
Watercress
  and mushroom salad, 200–201
  omelette, 155
Whipped cream
  general data on, 15
  hazelnut roll with filling of, 216–217
Whitebait with caper mayonnaise, 68
Wine sauce, chicken breasts with duxelles and 128–130

Yellow butter cake, 212–213
Yoghurt, cucumber salad with, 193

Zucchini
  Provençal, 190
  salad, 201

*Volume Two*

✳

# MENUS FOR
# ALL OCCASIONS

✳

*Drawings by Regina Shekerjian*

For H.M.D., Jr.

The author wishes to thank her past and present assistants, namely Fritzie Grabosky, Claire Felix, Mary Hopkins, Jo Klein, Maxine Rogers, and especially Sandy Ainsworth who assisted me for five years. A special thanks to Kathryn Larson who assisted me in preparing this book.

# CONTENTS
## for Volume Two

Introduction                          1

Methods and Techniques                5

Breakfasts and Brunches               9

Luncheons                            39

Dinners                              91

Buffets                             181

Suppers                             215

Cocktail Parties                    227

Teas                                243

Outdoor Entertaining                251

Basic Recipes                       277

Index                               291

*Volume Two*

\*

# MENUS FOR
# ALL OCCASIONS

# *Introduction*

Let me tell you about entertaining as a way of life. I count my years in menus rather than days.

During the months that my cooking school is open, I "entertain" three, four, and sometimes five times during the week, preparing food each day to be served to from twenty-five to thirty-five students. (How fast my students learn to be critical, and how they keep me on my toes!) At home I invite guests over at least once a week, so I constantly put my teaching to practical tests. Or is it my social experience that makes my teaching more practical? Each side of my cooking life fuels the other. This is a collection of the best menus from both worlds, those special combinations I have found, from experience, to please. Sometimes you will wish to duplicate the menus exactly; at other times you may decide to substitute a salad, a plain vegetable, or fresh fruit

*1*

for the richer counterparts I've suggested. And you may wish to vary menus because of your guests' known preferences. Always keep your options open in this way. My menu suggestions are just that—suggestions, ideas, starting points.

I've tried to steer clear of menus that are either tricky or cute. Every one of the recipes in this book, first and foremost, is *doable*. And because I never assume that a dish will *look* good just because it tastes good, I've emphasized throughout the garnishing and presentation of each dish. Many of the menus are introduced with notes on the preparation, timing, background, or special delights of the dishes represented, and in all I've aimed for the kind of step-by-step directions that instruct without either wearying or intimidating.

While it may sound dull, I can't overemphasize the importance of planning. Successful entertaining is part cooking, part list-making, and I recommend writing down on paper each stage of your party, from your marketing list and cooking schedule to your table appointments and seating arrangement. If possible, start planning three days ahead of serving time. With list in hand, you will be able to pace yourself through even a complicated party. Believe me, there is nothing more steadying when you're under stress than this reassurance that you have not forgotten anything. If you have help in the kitchen, be sure to leave them an equally explicit list before you join your guests.

The most important part of planning relates directly to the preparation of the food. With this in mind, I have included as many make-ahead dishes as possible, leaving only as many last-minute saucing, reheating, and unmolding steps as can be reasonably managed. A good number can be prepared several days ahead or even frozen. If you do this, remember to bring the dish to room temperature before either reheating it or continuing with the recipe.

The other best advice I can give you is to tell your butcher everything—take him into your confidence, and listen to his suggestions, too. Be suspicious of a butcher who only wants to sell you fillet of beef for a party. Almost everyone appreciates a simple meal, superbly cooked, so have the courage to produce one. Once when Dione Lucas was a guest, I was anxious to serve my most elegant recipes. She would have none of it; she informed me ahead of time that she was hungry for sauerkraut. What would you have done? I fixed choucroute garni, lentil salad, and steamed potatoes with caraway and melted butter. The recipes are in this book, along with one for the dessert I served on that most successful evening, a caramelized apple dish called Tart Tatin, which Dione loved. Dione, by the way, as well as other experts with whom I have studied—among them James Beard, Richard Olney, Ann Roe Robbins, Michael Field, and Simone Beck—have all greatly influenced my cooking and helped me to develop a style of my own.

My entertaining has changed since we sold our suburban house, patio and all, and moved into a large, five-story town house in center-city Philadelphia. It's a beautiful house, and the only structural work we did was in ripping out the kitchen—a dismal basement workroom—and redesigning it as a warm, low-ceilinged country-French-style kitchen. The overhead pipes were covered in weathered oak to create a beamed effect, and the rough white plaster walls set off the natural terra-cotta tile floor and the blue and gold Portuguese tiles framing the work counters, shelves, range, and cooktop. All the counter tops are chopping blocks, with a marble slab built in for pastry-making. I have no wall cabinets; instead there are floor-to-ceiling storage shelves at one end of the room. We eat and entertain at the other end, where I can seat eight at two round slate-topped tables. Guests love to eat in the kitchen, and I sometimes even throw black-tie dinners here.

In my dining room upstairs, which I use for more formal occasions, I finally have the table I've always wanted—a long walnut one perfectly sized for the room and seating twelve comfortably. It also unhooks to make three individual square tables, which I cover with pleated tablecloths to the floor—and suddenly the room has a more relaxed character. Guests remember a formal meal when you add a few flourishes. When I use the dining room, I write out the menus on white cards edged in gold. Wines are listed too, and I like to serve two or maybe three at a very formal dinner. On these evenings, we have cocktails in the library on the second floor and coffee in the drawing room on the first floor, for I have discovered that guests like to move around from one room or area to another, enjoying the contrast in settings.

It's certainly not necessary to have an excuse for a party, but I do think it heightens the mood if there's an occasion to celebrate, a person to recognize. I put my house to the test recently when Mme Simone Beck visited. Her new book, *Simca's Cuisine*, had just been published, and the list of Philadelphia food and press people that I wanted to meet her grew to 140! James Beard came in from New York, pleased to honor our friend, and the party was a glorious, milling, moving feast.

From simple to elegant, informal to formal, readers will, I hope, find a menu here for every occasion—from breakfast to lunch or dinner to midnight supper—for every season of the year. Many of the menus feature recipes from Alsace, the home of my maternal grandmother and a source of inspiration, in turn, for my mother's cooking. Alsace, lying on France's German border, is rich farming country, and its cuisine draws on the traditions of both countries to make full and delectable use of the variety of foods available—pork, goose, game, trout, goose livers for pâté, chestnuts for delicious purees, cabbage for sauerkraut, fresh berries and fruits for tarts and pies. I have also included a goodly number of American regional dishes, particularly those of the mid-Atlantic states. Perhaps the most dominant influence on my cooking, however, has been the various great cuisines of Europe. I travel twice a year to Europe searching for new ideas and new recipes for my school and party files. I visit food shops, hardware stores, flea markets, coffeehouses, and tea shops, as well as fine restaurants and country inns. Whenever I taste something I like, I pull out my notebook and write a description of it, together with an educated guess about what the actual recipe is. These notes are my starting points for experiments when I return to Philadelphia—inspiration for another series of lessons at my school, another round of dinner parties at home.

# *Methods and Techniques*

Here are a few hints and pieces of information that I think you will find helpful—these techniques are used over and over in the recipes that follow.

All baking ingredients should be at room temperature unless "chilled" is specified.

Except in a few cake recipes that call for sifted flour, all flour in my recipes is measured as follows: before measuring, I stir or aerate the flour (which is stored in a canister) with a scoop or spoon, to loosen it; then I lightly scoop it into the measuring cup and level it off with a straight-edged knife. I'm careful not to pack it or shake it down into the cup. You'll see that flour is described in many recipes as "lightly spooned." When mixing dry ingredients (such as salt or baking powder) into the flour, it's usually sufficient just to stir them in. The recipe states when sifting is required.

When stirring flour and fat together (as when making a sauce), I always use a wooden spatula; then I switch to a whisk when liquid is added, to avoid lumps.

Some recipes call for a thickening agent such as cornstarch or potato starch. If you don't happen to have the one listed at hand, remember that potato starch (potato flour), cornstarch, and arrowroot are virtually interchangeable. Just substitute an equal amount of the thickener you do have.

Many herbs, such as tarragon and thyme, are sometimes available fresh but much more readily available, year-round, in their dried form. The measurements are therefore for dried herbs. If you have fresh, just remember that 1 tablespoon fresh equals 1 teaspoon dried. Of course, parsley, garlic, and dill in my recipes are *always* fresh.

I like to cook on high heat, in heavy pans, for many steps in my recipes—such as cooking onions or stirring flour into butter for a sauce base. This saves time. If, however, you have lightweight pans, or are nervous using high heat, use a lower flame or burner setting.

Reheating instructions may be varied to suit the needs of the menu. If you make up your own menu and find that a dish to be reheated at 350° is now paired with one to be baked at 375°, don't hesitate to change the directions. By the way, I nearly always bring food to room temperature before reheating, so do this unless the instructions tell you to put a refrigerated dish straight in the oven. Food at room temperature generally takes about 15 to 20 minutes in a 350° oven to reheat. It's a good idea, too, when cooking a recipe ahead, to undercook it slightly, allowing for the reheating.

Your freezer makes it possible to space out preparations for a dinner party or weekend guests, but I hope you'll use it like a checking account, not a long-term savings bank! I'm constantly putting food in and drawing it out; I believe in a fast turnover, nothing stored overlong. A 1-month limit is a good rule for all prepared items such as sauced main dishes, desserts, and breads. Quality goes only one way: down. Enjoy the good things you fix before they get tired.

If you wish to assemble ahead of time—and store in the refrigerator—a dessert decorated with whipped cream, be sure to whip the cream in a metal bowl, over ice, with a piano-wire balloon whisk. Cream beaten in the usual way with electric or rotary beaters, weeps. Confectioners' sugar (preferable to granulated) for sweetening should be added when the cream is mounding softly.

# Breakfasts
## and Brunches

My favorite food memories from childhood begin at sunrise, when I would walk into my mother's kitchen, irresistibly drawn to the black coal stove where there'd always be a pot of soup simmering and, in wintertime, a heavy pan with the creamiest oatmeal ever. When my mother spooned it out, she pushed a lump of butter into it and sprinkled it with brown sugar; at the table, we poured on our own thick cream.

We always had fruit, fresh when it was ripe in the garden, but more often cooked. Whole baked pears, or sautéed cinnamon apples, or spicy-thick apple butter—the perfect complement to crisp-fried scrapple. A Sunday treat was double-dipped French toast with ginger sauce or maple syrup, and special breakfast bacon cut one inch thick and sautéed for half an hour until it was beautifully crisp.

Our cellar cold room was lined with jars of jelly and jam, the fruit and year of each identified by hand-lettered labels. We used it lavishly: rolled up in crêpes, or packed in crocks for everyone to help himself. Thanks to my mother's Alsatian background, we had plenty of breads and rolls to spread it on—and coffee cakes of all kinds and shapes besides.

When I think of inviting friends for early or late breakfast—or brunch, as the latter is almost always called nowadays—it's this yeasty-smelling, buttered-and-jellied cooked breakfast from my childhood that I remember: homey, heartwarming, hospitable, a wonderful way to entertain. It's a relaxed time of day: guests don't expect—or want!—elaborate, multicourse meals. You can devote yourself to one mainstay dish—and to bread-making. Service is usually informal; I often cook in front of my guests. Still, there's room for surprise in even a short menu, and many ways to depart from the bacon-and-eggs routine. Consider Onion Soup, Polenta Croquettes, Chicken Livers en Brochette, Ham Roulade, Roast Beef Hash. The menus in this chapter will suggest the range of dishes open to you at this most appealing hour.

Keep the drink service casual too. I usually have a pitcher of bloody Marys, bullshots, or screwdrivers ready to pour, as well as icy-cold fruit juices for nonimbibers. At late brunches I sometimes serve black velvets—that incomparably smooth mixture of stout and champagne. Wines, too, are always welcome, and of course there is nothing more festive and more refreshing than champagne when you have an occasion to celebrate—or even when you don't.

On chilly winter mornings you might consider leading off with steaming mugs of soup—my mother would have approved—and always, whatever the season, have plenty of freshly brewed coffee on hand, as well as tea, if anyone prefers it. It's fun to experiment with different kinds of coffee: espresso, cappuccino, Viennese coffee, or, for a very warm glow, Irish coffee, to name only a few.

And, whatever else is on your menu, add the indulgent extras: an assortment of home-baked rolls, breadsticks, coffee cakes, and doughnuts, plus pots of sweet butter and a generous selection of jams.

## A Classic Continental Breakfast
## for Any Number

Brioche and croissants
Assortment of jams, jellies, and conserves
Pot of unsalted butter
Café au lait

### BRIOCHE

2 packages active dry yeast
½ cup warm water (105° to 115°)
4 cups lightly spooned flour

1½ cups butter
6 eggs
1 tablespoon sugar
1 teaspoon salt

Sprinkle yeast into warm water; stir until dissolved. Measure 1 cup of flour into a small bowl, add yeast mixture, stir to make a stiff dough, and knead until smooth. Form into a ball, cut a cross or X in the top with a knife (to help the dough rise), and drop the ball into a bowl of lukewarm water. The ball of yeast sponge should rise to the top of the water in about 7 minutes; if it doesn't, the yeast isn't working; throw it out and start over.

While yeast sponge is rising, whip butter until smooth and creamy (use the flat beater throughout recipe if you have a heavy-duty mixer) and set aside. In another bowl, beat together eggs, remaining 3 cups of flour, sugar, and salt. Use electric mixer and flat beater or beat by hand with a wooden spoon. Dough should become shiny, sticky, wet-looking, and very elastic. If it's very sticky and hard to get off the sides of the bowl, beat in another egg. (You'll develop a feel for brioche; don't expect to make it perfectly the first time.)

Remove yeast sponge from water, letting water run off. Add sponge and creamed butter to egg dough and beat until thoroughly mixed, using the flat beater or wooden spoon. Grease and lightly flour a large bowl. Place dough in bowl, cover with plastic wrap, and let rise in a warm place, free from drafts, for about 1 hour. The dough does not have to double in bulk, but indentations should remain when you press fingertip into dough. When it's risen, stir it down; re-cover with plastic wrap and refrigerate overnight. The next day, shape brioche according to the following directions, or as directed in other recipes in this book, and bake.

*Note:* You can freeze brioche dough for up to a month. When you are ready to use it, remove the freezer wrapping, place in a bowl, cover with plastic wrap, and refrigerate it overnight to defrost.

### INDIVIDUAL BRIOCHE

Butter 30 individual 2-inch brioche molds (or use muffin pans or ovenproof custard cups). Turn refrigerated dough, which will be sticky, onto a lightly floured board and shape into a roll. Cut off small pieces of dough and shape to fill molds about ¾ full. To make the typical brioche knob or crown, cut a cross in the center of dough in each mold and open it up like flower petals. Brush opening with egg wash (1 egg yolk mixed with 1 tablespoon water). Form a smaller piece of dough with a pointy bottom and fit it into the opening. Cover brioche loosely with a cloth towel or plastic wrap and let rise away from drafts until doubled and puffing above the edge of the mold, about 1 hour. Brush with egg wash and bake in a preheated 375° oven for 15 to 20 minutes, or until nicely browned.

### GIANT BRIOCHE

Butter a 2-quart charlotte mold (or you can use a round casserole). Turn refrigerated dough onto a lightly floured board. Shape ¾ of the dough into a ball and place it in the buttered mold. Cut a cross in the center of the dough and open it up like flower petals. Brush opening with egg wash. Shape remaining ¼ of dough with a pointy bottom and rounded top; fit the point into the opening. Cover brioche loosely with plastic wrap or a cloth towel and let rise away from drafts until doubled, about 1 hour. Brush with egg wash and bake in a preheated 375° oven for about 50 to 55 minutes, or until nicely browned and brioche begins to pull away from the sides of the mold. If it browns too fast, cover loosely with foil during baking

## CROISSANTS

¾ cup butter
3 cups lightly spooned flour
¾ cup milk
¼ cup warm water (105° to 115°)

1 package active dry yeast
3 tablespoons sugar
1 teaspoon salt
2 eggs
1 tablespoon cream

Work butter into ¼ cup of the flour until mixture is a smooth paste. Place between 2 sheets of waxed paper and roll out to small rectangle. Chill for 1 hour.

When butter mixture is chilled, scald milk and cool to luke-warm. Measure warm water into a large, warmed mixing bowl, sprinkle with yeast, and stir until dissolved. Add sugar, salt, 1 beaten egg, milk, and 1 cup flour, and beat until smooth with an electric mixer or wooden spoon. Stir in remaining flour and mix until completely blended.

Turn out dough onto a well-floured board and roll out to a 12-inch square. Carefully peel waxed paper from chilled butter mixture and place it over the center third of rolled dough. Fold both ends of dough over butter mixture into thirds (like a business letter). Give dough a quarter turn (folds will be on right and left), roll out again to a 12-inch square, and fold in thirds as before. Turn, roll, and fold dough 3 more times. (Rechill the dough if it softens while you are working with it. After 20 to 30 minutes in the refrigerator, it will be ready for you to continue with the recipe.) Wrap in waxed paper and refrigerate for 3 hours. (*Recipe can be prepared ahead to this point and held in refrigerator overnight or up to 12 hours.*)

To shape croissants, divide chilled dough into thirds. Take each third in turn, refrigerating remainder, and roll out to a 12-inch circle. Cut into 8 pie-shaped wedges. Brush point of each wedge with a mixture of 1 egg beaten with cream. Beginning at the wide end, roll up each wedge tightly and pinch point to seal. Place on a greased baking sheet with the point underneath and curve to form a crescent. Cover with plastic wrap or towel and let rise in a warm place free from drafts until almost doubled, about 30 to 45 minutes. Brush each croissant with egg-cream mixture and bake in a preheated 375° oven for about 12 to 15 minutes or until lightly browned. Makes 24 croissants. *Baked croissants may be frozen for up to one month. Bring to room temperature; warm if desired.*

## CAFÉ AU LAIT

Make strong coffee. Heat (but do not boil) an equal amount of half-and-half. Pour them simultaneously into large breakfast cups and sweeten to taste.

## A Country Breakfast
### for 6 to 8

---

Baked cinnamon apples
Breakfast bacon
Roesti potatoes
Easy coffee cake or Kugelhopf

## BAKED CINNAMON APPLES

6 cups green apples, peeled, cored, and cut in eighths
1 cup sugar
2 teaspoons cinnamon
½ teaspoon freshly grated nutmeg

2 tablespoons apple brandy
Juice of 1 lemon
4 tablespoons melted butter
Sour cream, optional

Mix thoroughly apples, sugar, cinnamon, and nutmeg, using your hands. Put into a casserole dish and sprinkle with brandy, lemon juice, and melted butter. Cover and bake in a preheated 375° oven for 35 to 45 minutes, or until apples are soft. (*Apples can be cooked ahead and reheated.*) Serve hot or warm, with sour cream if you wish.

## BREAKFAST BACON

Trim the rind from a 1-pound slab of bacon and cut it into slices 1 inch thick. Cook in an iron skillet over medium heat for about 30 minutes, turning occasionally. Do not pour off fat. Bacon will cook crisp all the way through. Drain on paper towels before serving.


## ROESTI POTATOES

The trick is to keep the potatoes from sticking to the pan while they cook. You want to keep the potato cake "afloat" so you can turn it out, brown and crusty, on your serving plate. A non-stick pan helps.

| | |
|---|---|
| 6 large baking potatoes | 2 teaspoons salt |
| ½ cup butter | ½ teaspoon freshly cracked |
| 2 tablespoons vegetable oil | white pepper |
|    or bacon fat | 6 tablespoons melted butter |

Put potatoes in a saucepan, cover with cold water, and bring to a boil; boil hard, uncovered, for about 10 minutes. Peel potatoes while still warm and grate them. Heat the ½ cup butter with the oil in a large skillet over high heat until foaming subsides, being careful not to let butter brown. Put about half of the grated potatoes into the skillet, pressing them down firmly with a spatula. Sprinkle with half the salt and pepper and drizzle with 4 tablespoons melted butter. Add remaining potatoes; press firmly with spatula. Shake the pan to make sure the potato cake moves freely; if it is sticking, use the spatula to push potatoes in from the edge of the pan. Drizzle with remaining 2 tablespoons butter and sprinkle with remaining salt and pepper. Cook over high heat for 5 minutes. Then press down hard on potatoes, using a flat lid just a bit smaller than skillet. Reduce heat to medium and cook, keeping the lid on, about 20 minutes or until potatoes are crusty on the bottom. Shake the skillet every few minutes to ensure that the potatoes stay afloat. Unmold on a round serving plate, crusty side up.


## EASY COFFEE CAKE

This recipe makes enough yeast dough for 2 coffee cakes. You can fill and bake one cake, and store the dough for a second in the refrigerator for 5 to 6 days. Or you can freeze the dough, for up to one month, thawing it overnight in the refrigerator before using it. Or you can form the extra dough into small dinner rolls.

½ cup light cream  
2 packages active dry yeast  
1 cup butter  
½ cup sugar  
¼ cup sour cream  
3 well-beaten eggs  

1½ teaspoons salt  
4 cups lightly spooned flour  
   Filling (recipe follows)  
1 egg white, slightly beaten  
¼ cup slivered almonds  

Heat cream to lukewarm; sprinkle with yeast and stir to dissolve. In a large bowl, cream butter and sugar together until fluffy. Add sour cream, eggs, and yeast mixture and beat very well until thoroughly blended (using an electric mixer if you wish). Mix salt with 1 cup of the flour and beat into yeast mixture. Add remaining flour gradually, mixing thoroughly. Shape the dough into a ball and put into a greased bowl, turning the ball to grease lightly all over; then cover dough with waxed paper and a towel and refrigerate overnight. The next day, divide dough in half. Refrigerate (or freeze) half for another occasion.

Place dough for 1 coffee cake on floured waxed paper. Sprinkle it lightly with flour and cover with a second sheet of waxed paper. Roll dough between sheets of waxed paper to make a 9 x 15-inch rectangle, ½ inch thick. If the paper begins sticking to the dough (lift the paper to check this), dust on a bit more flour. Peel off top sheet of waxed paper and, turning the dough upside down, carefully fit dough into a 9 x 5 x 3-inch bread pan, allowing it to drape over the sides of pan. Peel off second sheet of waxed paper. Spoon filling over dough in pan and fold dough over filling, pinching it to seal securely. Brush the top of the loaf with slightly beaten egg white and sprinkle with almonds. Place *at once* into a preheated 350° oven and bake for 1 hour. This loaf does not need to rise before going into the oven.

## FILLING FOR 1 COFFEE CAKE

1½ cups cottage cheese  
2 tablespoons flour  
2 tablespoons light cream  
3 egg yolks  
¼ cup sugar  

1 tablespoon melted butter  
1 teaspoon vanilla extract  
¼ cup raisins  
2 egg whites  
¼ teaspoon salt  

Press the cottage cheese through a sieve. Add flour and cream and mix well. Beat egg yolks, beat in sugar and butter, and add to the cheese, along with vanilla and raisins. Beat egg whites with salt until stiff and fold into cheese mixture.

## KUGELHOPF

½ cup milk
½ cup granulated sugar
1 teaspoon salt
¼ cup butter
¼ cup warm water (105° to 115°)
1 package active dry yeast
2 beaten eggs
2 cups lightly spooned flour

2 tablespoons fine bread crumbs
16 whole blanched almonds
½ cup raisins
½ teaspoon grated lemon peel
½ teaspoon freshly grated nutmeg
Confectioners' sugar

Scald the milk. Stir in sugar, salt, and butter and cool to lukewarm. Measure warm water into electric mixer bowl and sprinkle with yeast; stir until dissolved. Stir in the lukewarm milk mixture; add the beaten eggs and the flour and beat vigorously with electric mixer for about 5 minutes. Cover the bowl and let the dough rise in a warm place, free from drafts, until double in bulk, about 1 to 1½ hours.

Butter generously a 1½-quart Kugelhopf mold and sprinkle sides and bottom with bread crumbs. Arrange the almonds decoratively in bottom of mold. When dough has risen, stir it down, beating thoroughly. Beat in raisins, lemon peel, and nutmeg, and pour into the prepared mold. Let rise again in a warm place until double in bulk, about 1 hour. Bake in a preheated 350° oven for 50 to 60 minutes. Turn out to cool on a cake rack. To serve, sprinkle Kugelhopf with confectioners' sugar and poke a pleated paper doily, like a flag, into the hole in the center of the cake. *Baked Kugelhopf also freezes well.*

## *A Hearty Winter Breakfast for 6 to 8*

Poached apples with meringue
Pennsylvania scrapple
Polenta croquettes
Popovers

If your family or guests enjoy appetite-building hikes on frosty mornings, here's the breakfast to welcome them home and warm them up. It's a mixture of things I like: poached apples, Pennsylvania Dutch scrapple—good with polenta, the Italian cornmeal—and crusty popovers with lots of butter. Some guests choose what they want; hungry ones eat it all!

To manage this menu with one oven, do half of it ahead of time. The apples can be fully prepared, scorched meringue and all, and held at room temperature ready to serve. You can also bake popovers ahead and reheat them; you can even freeze them and reheat them. Just be sure they're completely baked, so the shell is strong; they deflate if underbaked. Keep croquettes warm and reheat popovers while you fry the scrapple.

## POACHED APPLES WITH MERINGUE

8 baking apples, Rome Beauty,    3 cups sugar
    Winesap, or Stayman    2 cups water
⅓ cup Calvados    6 egg whites
½ cup mincemeat    ¼ teaspoon cream of tartar

Peel and core the apples, but do not pierce through the bottom. Place them in a baking pan; do not let them touch each other. Put 1 teaspoon Calvados and 1 tablespoon mincemeat into each apple. In a saucepan, heat 2 cups sugar, the water, and remaining Calvados, stirring until sugar is dissolved and mixture boils. Pour around apples and cover the baking pan with aluminum foil. Place in a preheated 350° oven and poach apples until barely tender but not mushy, about 30 to 45 minutes. The time depends on the size and kind of apples. Remove apples to an ovenproof serving dish.

Boil down the syrup until thick enough to coat a spoon and ladle it over the apples. Beat egg whites and cream of tartar with electric mixer until foamy. Gradually beat in remaining 1 cup sugar, 1 tablespoon at a time. Continue beating until meringue looks thick and glossy, like marshmallow, and no longer feels grainy when you pinch it. Put meringue into a large pastry bag fitted with a star tube and pipe onto apples. You can cover the top only, or the entire apple, or make designs up and down the sides of the apple. Run apples under the broiler to set and scorch the meringue. *May be cooked ahead of time and served at room temperature.*

## PENNSYLVANIA SCRAPPLE

Scrapple is the tasty product of German and Pennsylvania Dutch thriftiness. Wasting nothing at butchering time, we grind pork scraps and livers to mix with cornmeal and buckwheat flour, seasoning it well. The thinner you slice it the better, I think.

Cut 1 pound of scrapple into slices about ¼ inch thick, allowing 2 slices for each guest. Heat 2 tablespoons vegetable oil in a heavy skillet and sauté scrapple over fairly high heat for 3 to 5 minutes on each side. Do not let pieces touch each other. Scrapple should be crusty-brown, with a soft interior.

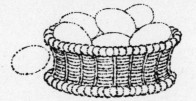

## POLENTA

8 cups water
2 cups quick-cooking polenta
½ cup butter
¾ cup grated Parmesan cheese
2 tablespoons chopped
   parsley
1 finely chopped clove garlic

2 teaspoons salt
½ teaspoon freshly cracked
   white pepper
¼ teaspoon freshly grated
   nutmeg
3 eggs

In a saucepan, bring water to a boil; add polenta gradually, in a thin stream, stirring. Stir continuously and cook over medium heat until it becomes so thick the spoon will stand upright—this will take about 5 minutes. Pour mixture into a big bowl and add butter, Parmesan cheese, parsley, garlic, salt, pepper, and nutmeg; blend them in. Beat the eggs and warm them with a bit of the polenta mixture; then stir eggs into polenta. Taste for seasoning.

*Note:* Yellow cornmeal is a substitute for polenta. If you can't find the quick-cooking variety, use the same amounts of regular polenta and water. It will take longer to cook it, however. When it thickens, set saucepan into a pan of boiling water and cook for another 30 to 35 minutes, over low heat, stirring occasionally.

## POLENTA CROQUETTES

1 recipe Polenta (preceding        2 cups bread crumbs
  recipe)                         Fat for deep frying
1 cup flour                        ½ recipe Tomato Sauce (see
2 beaten eggs                        p. 64)

Spread polenta mixture in a baking tray or jelly-roll pan rinsed with cold water; smooth with a spatula and chill for at least ½ hour, or cover with plastic wrap and chill overnight. To form croquettes, take a good tablespoonful of the chilled mixture and, using the heel of your hand, very lightly shape it into a cork shape. Or cut mixture with a knife or with cutters to make squares, diamonds, or other shapes. Coat the shapes with flour, patting off excess; then dip in beaten egg and roll in crumbs. Chill again for at least ½ hour. Heat fat in saucepan or deep-fat fryer to 375° and fry croquettes, 2 or 3 at a time, for about 2 minutes or until nicely browned. Drain on paper towels and hold them in a 350° oven to keep warm while you fry remaining croquettes. Serve hot with Tomato Sauce.

*Variation:* Cut chilled mixture into squares or fancy shapes, then simply flour and sauté in butter, instead of deep-frying. Or place thinly sliced cheese (you can use any firm cheese, such as Cheddar or Swiss) and/or ham between 2 squares and bake in a preheated 350° oven for 15 to 20 minutes.

## POPOVERS

Have all ingredients at room temperature before proceeding. Served with jam, popovers make an excellent dessertlike finale to this menu.

2 eggs                             1 cup lightly spooned flour
1 cup milk                         1 teaspoon salt

Beat the eggs with an egg beater for about 1 minute. Add milk and beat just until blended. Stir the flour and salt together in a mixing bowl. Make a well in the center and pour in the egg mixture, stirring with a wooden spoon until flour is dampened. Then beat (with egg beater) 1 minute longer. Place 8 ovenproof glass custard cups with narrow bottoms on a baking tray and grease them lightly. Half-fill each cup with batter. Place in a preheated 425° oven and bake for 30 minutes, or until puffed and brown. Turn heat down to 350° and continue baking for 15 to 20 minutes more, to dry out. (*Popovers may be baked ahead, removed from cups, and cooled or frozen. Reheat in a 350° oven for about 5 minutes; if frozen, bring to room temperature before reheating.*) Split popovers while hot and serve with unsalted butter and your favorite jam.

## *Breakfast for 4 for Weekend Guests*

Baked pears with heavy cream
Double-dipped French toast with ginger sauce
Baked Canadian bacon
Panettone
Espresso coffee

### BAKED PEARS WITH HEAVY CREAM

4 pears, half-ripe
½ cup sugar
2 teaspoons cinnamon
1 tablespoon butter
4 tablespoons light corn syrup

4 tablespoons melted butter
½ cup heavy cream, plus
   additional heavy cream,
   optional

Peel pears with a potato peeler and cut a slice off bottoms so they will stand upright. Do not core. Mix sugar and cinnamon and roll pears in mixture to coat well. Butter a baking dish and stand pears upright. Pour on any sugar mixture remaining. Drizzle each pear with 1 tablespoon corn syrup and 1 tablespoon melted butter. Cover pears with a tent of aluminum foil and bake them in a preheated 375° oven for 25 minutes, basting occasionally with pan juices. Remove foil, turn oven down to 350°, and continue baking until pears are tender-firm—test with point of knife at base of pear. Remove pears to serving dishes. Stir heavy cream into the juices in the baking dish and pour over pears. Serve warm, with additional heavy cream if you wish.

## DOUBLE-DIPPED FRENCH TOAST

4 eggs
⅛ teaspoon salt
¼ cup sugar
1 cup milk
1 cup light cream
¼ teaspoon freshly grated
    nutmeg

4 slices day-old French bread,
    2½ inches thick
½ cup butter
Confectioners' sugar
Ginger Sauce (recipe follows)

Beat eggs, salt, sugar, milk, cream, and nutmeg together with a whisk or rotary beater. Dip bread into mixture, quickly, on both sides, and remove to a platter; let stand for 10 minutes. Dip again in egg mixture, turning bread so that it soaks up liquid all the way through. (*Recipe can be made ahead to this point.*)

Heat butter in a heavy skillet until foamy. Brown the bread for 3 to 5 minutes on each side, over medium heat. Shake confectioners' sugar over each piece before serving. Serve with Ginger Sauce.

## GINGER SAUCE

1 cup light corn syrup
1 tablespoon grated lemon peel
3 tablespoons lemon juice

½ cup drained and finely
    chopped preserved ginger
    in syrup
½ cup finely chopped crystal-
    lized ginger, optional

Heat syrup with lemon peel and lemon juice over low heat 1 minute, just to blend. Add chopped preserved ginger and serve warm with French toast. Pass chopped crystallized ginger in a small bowl, if you wish.

## BAKED CANADIAN BACON

Remove the casing from a piece of Canadian bacon weighing about 1½ pounds. Lay it on a rack in a baking pan and brush with 2 tablespoons melted butter. Pour hot water into pan to a depth of ¼ inch and place in a preheated 325° oven. Bake for about 30 minutes. To serve, slice it very, very thin.

## PANETTONE

Panettone is a traditional Italian fruitcake—and a delicious, dessertlike finale to this menu.

1 package active dry yeast
¼ cup lukewarm milk
4 cups lightly spooned flour, about
¾ cup butter
½ cup sugar
3 beaten eggs
2 beaten egg yolks
1 teaspoon anise extract
1 teaspoon salt

½ cup raisins
¼ cup chopped candied orange peel
½ cup chopped citron
¼ cup chopped blanched almonds
Whole almonds or pine nuts, optional
Sugar, optional

Sprinkle yeast into lukewarm milk and stir to dissolve. Stir in ½ cup of the flour and let stand in a warm place until bubbly, about 1 hour. In electric mixer bowl, cream butter and sugar together. Add beaten eggs and egg yolks and the yeast mixture. Beat in anise, salt, and enough of remaining flour to make a dough that is soft but not too sticky. Turn dough out on a floured board and knead in fruits and chopped almonds; knead until dough is smooth and elastic, about 10 to 15 minutes. Place in a greased bowl, turning to grease top; cover and set in a warm place to rise until double in bulk, about 1 hour.

While dough rises, butter a 2-pound coffee can or Kugelhopf mold. Arrange whole almonds or pine nuts in bottom of mold, if you wish, and sprinkle with sugar. When dough has risen, punch it down and turn out on board; knead again for 3 to 5 minutes. Shape it into a ball and put it into coffee can, or shape it like a doughnut and place in Kugelhopf mold. Cover and let rise in a warm place until double in bulk, about 1 hour. Bake in a preheated 400° oven for 10 minutes; reduce oven temperature to 350° and bake 50 minutes longer. If top browns too fast, lay a piece of aluminum foil over it. Remove from pan and cool on cake rack.

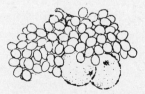

## Brunch by the Fireplace
### for 6

Glazed pineapple in kirsch
Roast beef hash
Danish pastry
Viennese coffee

When you expect guests to eat off their knees, serve fork food—
hash is perfect. In front of the fire, this breakfast would be a
leisurely one—fruit first, then hash, then pastry and coffee. Set it
up buffet-style and let guests help themselves.

### GLAZED PINEAPPLE IN KIRSCH

1 fresh pineapple
2 cups water
2 cups sugar
6 tablespoons light corn syrup
½ cup kirsch
2 tablespoons crystallized
angelica, about, optional

Cut the top off the pineapple, trim it of damaged leaves, wash
it, and set it aside, to garnish serving dish. Peel pineapple: stand
it upright and with a serrated knife cut off the peel in strips from
top to bottom. Remove eyes. (There's an easy way to do this:
observe that the eyes are arranged in diagonal rows. With a sharp
knife, cut diagonal grooves all around the pineapple and lift out
the eyes in rows.) Slice the pineapple across, making thin slices
(about ⅜ inch thick), and cut out the tough centers with a 1- to 1½-
inch round cutter and reserve.

In a large skillet, bring water, sugar, and corn syrup to a
boil, stirring until sugar dissolves. Add pineapple centers to syrup
to help flavor it. Poach pineapple slices in boiling syrup over
medium-high heat, a few at a time, until barely tender and a little
translucent, about 7 minutes. Remove slices to serving dish. Keep
syrup on high heat; when it is just shading to a pale caramel color,
add kirsch and let it bubble for a minute. Pour syrup over pineapple slices, garnish with pineapple top placed at one end of
serving dish and chopped crystallized angelica if you wish. Serve
warm, cold, or at room temperature.

## ROAST BEEF HASH

4 tablespoons butter
1 cup finely chopped onion
1 minced clove garlic
½ cup finely chopped green
   pepper
4 cups leftover roast beef,
   chopped
1 tablespoon Worcestershire
   sauce

2 teaspoons salt
½ teaspoon freshly cracked
   black pepper
1 cup finely diced raw potato
1 cup beef gravy *or* 1 cup beef
   stock (see p. 277) or
   chicken stock (see p. 278)
6 slices toast, optional

Heat butter in a heavy skillet and sauté onion, garlic, and green pepper over high heat until onion is transparent—do not let it brown. Add roast beef, Worcestershire sauce, salt, pepper, and potato. Pour on gravy or stock, cover, and cook over low heat until potatoes are tender, about 20 to 25 minutes. (*Recipe can be made ahead to this point; it can be frozen for up to one month if you wish. Bring to room temperature before reheating.*) Remove lid and cook for another 10 minutes to evaporate some of the liquid. (Consistency of hash will still be quite soft.) Serve with toast on the side if desired.

## DANISH PASTRY

2 packages active dry yeast
½ cup warm water (105° to
   115°)
4 tablespoons butter, melted
   and cooled to lukewarm
5 tablespoons sugar
3 beaten eggs
½ cup lukewarm milk
1 teaspoon salt
1 teaspoon grated lemon peel
1 teaspoon vanilla extract

4½ cups lightly spooned flour
1 cup softened butter
1 egg yolk
1 tablespoon water
⅔ cup raisins
1 tablespoon cinnamon
   Flaked toasted almonds
   Apricot Glaze (recipe
   follows)
   Vanilla Water Icing (recipe
   follows)

In a large warm mixing bowl, sprinkle yeast over warm water and stir to dissolve. Let rest 5 minutes. Then, with a wire whisk or electric mixer, beat in melted butter, sugar, eggs, milk, salt, lemon peel, and vanilla. Mix well. Beat in flour (use electric mixer or change from whisk to wooden spoon), to make a soft dough. Mix thoroughly—this dough is not kneaded. Cover the bowl with a towel and let dough rest in a warm place, free from drafts, to rise, for about 30 minutes.

Turn dough out onto a lightly floured board and roll it into a 10 x 20-inch rectangle. Mark dough lightly into 4 sections, each 10 x 5 inches. Dot the 2 center sections with ⅔ of softened butter. Fold 2 end sections over center sections and roll out with rolling pin. Dot half of dough with remaining butter and fold the other half over; roll out again with rolling pin. (*Note:* In these and subsequent foldings and rollings, turn dough so that you are rolling from open end to open end, not from fold to fold. Each "turn" consists of 2 foldings and rollings.)

Wrap dough in a damp towel and refrigerate for 30 minutes. Roll dough again into a 10 x 20-inch rectangle, fold end sections over center, roll out, fold in half, roll out again, wrap in towel, and refrigerate for another 30 minutes. Repeat rolling and folding once or twice more, letting dough rest 30 minutes in refrigerator after each "turn." After last turn, let dough rest overnight if possible.

To shape into twists, roll dough out ¼ inch thick into a 12 x 24-inch rectangle. Brush dough with egg wash (1 egg yolk mixed with 1 tablespoon water) and sprinkle half of it with raisins and cinnamon. Fold other half over and flatten very lightly with rolling pin. With a sharp knife, cut dough into strips about ¾ inch wide and 6 inches long. Twist ends of each strip in opposite directions and place 3 inches apart on baking sheets lined with baking parchment. Cover with a towel and let rise in a warm place, free from drafts, until almost double, about 20 to 30 minutes. Brush twists with additional egg wash and sprinkle with flaked toasted almonds. Bake in a preheated 400° oven for about 15 to 20 minutes, or until lightly browned. Remove and brush first with hot Apricot Glaze and then with Vanilla Water Icing.

## APRICOT GLAZE

Heat ½ cup apricot jam with 1 tablespoon of water to boiling and push through a strainer. Any glaze left over may be stored in refrigerator.

## VANILLA WATER ICING

Sift 2 cups confectioners' sugar into a bowl. Add 1 teaspoon vanilla extract and just enough boiling water to make a mixture of spreading consistency—it doesn't take much water, so be careful.

## VIENNESE COFFEE

Coffee turns Viennese when it's topped with a big spoonful of *schlagobers*—whipped cream. Real Viennese whipped cream tastes sweet and fresh; to approximate it, add 1 tablespoon confectioners' sugar to 1 cup heavy cream when it's partly whipped; then whip fairly stiff. Coffee should be strong, and sweetened or not, as your guests prefer.

## A Light Summer Brunch
### for 4

Strawberries in fresh orange juice
Chicken livers en brochette
Sautéed mushrooms ( see p. 284)
Brioche slices with mustard butter

Serve breakfast strawberries as they do in Spain: pour fresh orange juice over them. The colors are good together and so is the taste. The berries will not need sugar. One pound of sautéed mushrooms will make generous servings for four.

## CHICKEN LIVERS EN BROCHETTE

| | |
|---|---|
| 6 slices bacon | ½ teaspoon freshly cracked |
| 24 whole chicken livers | black pepper |
| ¼ cup flour | ½ cup melted butter |
| 1 teaspoon salt | |

Cut each piece of bacon into 5 pieces. Dry the chicken livers and roll them in flour. On 4 skewers, alternate chicken livers—

skewering them through fleshy lobes—with bacon pieces. Sprinkle with salt and pepper and place on a rack about 4 inches from broiler. Baste with the melted butter and turn frequently. Broil for a total of 6 minutes. Livers should be crisp and brown on the outside, still pink inside.

### BRIOCHE SLICES WITH MUSTARD BUTTER

Cut very thin slices from giant brioche (see p. 12) and serve with mustard butter, made by beating 2 teaspoons Dijon mustard into ½ cup softened butter. The brioche will be easier to slice if you've chilled it in the refrigerator.

## *Breakfast for 8, the Morning after a Late Party*

Bowl of fresh fruit
French onion soup, gratiné
Toasted French bread
Ice-cold beer or ale
Steaming cups of black coffee

French people don't eat onion soup before dinner—they eat it for breakfast or as an early-morning snack. You can trust their taste. It's a splendid way to revitalize your guests, and easy for you, too—the soup can be made ahead, ready for last-minute reheating and broiling. Offer both beer or ale and coffee.

### BOWL OF FRESH FRUIT

Whenever fresh fruit is on your menu, make it your center-piece too. Arrange fruits in season in a beautiful bowl, striving for contrasts in colors and shapes: oranges, perfect pears, a few bananas, a bunch of black grapes, tangerines. Always provide fruit knives, as well as scissors to snip off bunchlets of grapes.

## FRENCH ONION SOUP, GRATINÉ

Onion soup is only as good as the stock that goes into it. The stock simmers for 4 hours, but the onions for only ½ hour. Have extra toasted French bread for hungry guests and pass more Parmesan cheese separately, if you wish.

½ cup butter
8 cups sliced onions
1 tablespoon flour
2 quarts beef stock (see p. 277)
2 tablespoons brandy
   Meat glaze, optional (see
   p. 280)

Day-old French bread, at
   least ½ loaf
1 cup shredded Gruyère
   cheese
½ cup grated Parmesan cheese,
   plus more, optional

Melt butter in a large saucepan or kettle. Add onions and cook until golden, about 10 minutes—do not brown. Stir in flour. Pour on beef stock and brandy. Bring to a boil, reduce heat to simmer, half-cover the pan, and simmer for ½ hour. Taste for seasoning; add meat glaze if soup doesn't have the deep dark flavor you like.

Meanwhile, cut French bread in slices 1 inch thick and toast in a 300° oven for about 30 minutes. It should be completely dry and hard all the way through, like Melba toast.

To serve, fill broiler-resistant soup bowls half-full, sprinkle about 1 tablespoon of the shredded Gruyère on each, and broil for 2 to 3 minutes to melt cheese. This cheese layer will keep toast from sinking. Place 1 slice of toast in each bowl, cover with grated Parmesan and remaining Gruyère, and broil again until cheese melts, about 2 to 3 minutes.

## *Breakfast in Bed*
## *for 2*

Melon with port wine
Jelly crêpes
Sautéed Canadian bacon slices

Here's a happy way to keep house guests out of the kitchen while you're getting the luncheon menu under way. If the crêpes are prepared ahead, a child could also treat his or her parents to breakfast in bed with the Sunday paper.

## MELON WITH PORT WINE

Serve ½ melon each (or 1 whole melon if cantaloupes are small). Cut in half (or cut off top, to make a lid) and scoop out seeds. In each melon half (or whole melon) put 2 teaspoons honey and fill to top with port wine. Cover with aluminum foil (or lid) and chill overnight. Serve *very cold*.

## JELLY CRÊPES

½ recipe basic crêpes (see p. 285)
6 tablespoons melted butter

6 tablespoons jelly or jam
2 tablespoons confectioners' sugar

Count 2 large or 3 small crêpes for each serving. Brush the "wrong" (30-second) side of each crêpe generously with melted butter and spread with jelly or jam. Roll up and place in a buttered au gratin dish. Sprinkle with remaining butter. (*Recipe can be prepared ahead to this point.*) Place in a preheated 350° oven for about 15 minutes, or until heated through. Sift confectioners' sugar over crêpes just before serving.

## SAUTÉED CANADIAN BACON SLICES

Cut 4 slices of Canadian bacon, ¼ inch thick, and remove casing. Heat 1 tablespoon butter in a skillet until hot and foamy; cook bacon over high heat about 2 minutes on each side.

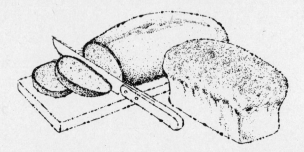

## *Holiday Brunch Buffet*
## *for 16*

Glazed fruit
Giant brioche stuffed with scrambled eggs
Individual ham rolls
Grilled tomatoes
Mushroom fritters
Assorted breads: croissants (see p. 13),
brioche (see p. 11), English muffins,
toasted French bread
Assorted jams

### GLAZED FRUIT

Choose a cool time of the year to prepare and serve glazed fruit. The recipe doesn't work if it's hot and humid, and the fruit holds its hard, crackly glaze for only about 3 hours on the best of days. You cannot make it ahead and it should not be refrigerated. But it *is* good and worth trying—it looks spectacular!

48 pieces of fruit: tangerine sections, black and white grapes with stems left on
4½ cups (2 pounds) sugar
1 cup water
2 tablespoons light corn syrup
¼ teaspoon cream of tartar

Section tangerines and separate grapes, leaving stem on each grape and using care not to pierce skin of fruit. Mix sugar, water, corn syrup, and cream of tartar together in a saucepan and bring to a boil over high heat, stirring until sugar dissolves. Turn heat to medium and cook syrup to the hard-crack stage (300° to 320° on a candy thermometer). Remove pan from heat and immediately put it in a pan of warm water to stop the cooking. Using small tongs or tweezer, dip fruit in syrup and place on a greased platter or marble slab to set (this takes only a few minutes). Syrup is *hot,* so watch your fingers!

## GIANT BRIOCHE STUFFED
## WITH SCRAMBLED EGGS

2 giant brioche (see p. 12)   1½ teaspoons salt
1 cup butter   ¾ teaspoon freshly cracked
32 eggs   white pepper
¾ cup light cream

Cut tops off brioche, about a quarter of the way down. Scoop out interiors, leaving shells. (Save or freeze crumbs for another use—in place of bread crumbs.) Melt butter in a *big* saucepan; reserve ¼ cup of melted butter to brush insides of brioche shells. Beat eggs with cream, salt, and pepper and stir into hot butter in saucepan; set saucepan in a skillet filled with hot water. Cook the eggs, stirring constantly, over low heat, until they begin to set—this will take about 15 minutes. Eggs should be very creamy. Brush insides of brioche shells with reserved butter and divide the eggs between the 2 shells. Put brioche tops in place and serve immediately (or hold filled brioche in a 250° oven for 5 to 10 minutes if necessary).

## INDIVIDUAL HAM ROLLS

1 pound ground ham   2 tablespoons finely chopped
6 beaten eggs   parsley
1 cup bread crumbs   16 square pieces of boiled
2 teaspoons tarragon   ham, approximately
¼ cup chopped capers   6 inches square and
1 teaspoon salt   ⅛ inch thick
½ teaspoon freshly cracked   ½ cup Madeira
black pepper   ¼ cup melted butter
1 tablespoon Dijon mustard

Mix together ground ham, eggs, bread crumbs, tarragon, capers, salt, pepper, Dijon mustard, and parsley. Brush ham squares with ¼ cup Madeira and spoon ground ham mixture along one edge. Roll up and lay seam side down in a buttered baking dish. (*Recipe can be made ahead to this point.*) Place in a preheated 350° oven and bake for 30 minutes. Baste 3 times during baking with remaining Madeira and melted butter. Then turn oven to 250° and hold ham rolls, along with other foods, until serving time.

## GRILLED TOMATOES

8 tomatoes
2 teaspoons salt
1 teaspoon freshly cracked
   black pepper
1 finely chopped clove garlic

1 tablespoon finely chopped
   shallots
1 tablespoon chopped parsley
8 teaspoons olive oil

Cut tomatoes in half. Put them on a broiler tray and sprinkle with salt, pepper, garlic, shallots, and parsley. Drizzle 1 teaspoon olive oil on each half. (*Recipe can be prepared ahead to this point.*) Broil for 6 to 8 minutes, or until bubbly. Keep warm in a low (250°) oven until ready to serve. *If you don't have a separate broiler, you can bake the tomatoes instead of broiling them—allow about 15 minutes in the 350° oven. Then hold in the 250° oven until serving time.*

## MUSHROOM FRITTERS

32 large mushrooms
 1 recipe beer batter (see
    p. 285)

Fat for deep frying
¼ cup chopped parsley
2 lemons cut in 8 wedges each

Clean mushrooms with paper towels dipped in acidulated water (1 quart water with 1 tablespoon lemon juice added) and wipe dry. Trim the stems but do not cut them off. Dip in beer batter, coating mushrooms completely. Fry them, a few at a time, in deep hot fat (375°) until golden, about 4 to 5 minutes. Remove with slotted spoon and drain on paper towels. (*Recipe may be made ahead to this point. To reheat, set cake racks on a baking sheet, cover with brown paper, lay mushrooms on the paper, and place in a 350° oven for several minutes.*) Keep warm in a 250° oven until ready to serve. Sprinkle with chopped parsley and serve with lemon wedges.

## *A Hunt Breakfast*
## *for 10*

Sliced oranges and grapefruit
Sautéed crab meat on Virginia ham
Hominy soufflé
Grilled tomatoes
Croissants (see p. 13) and carrot bread

Even if you don't have occasion to gallop through Eastern hunt country, this breakfast is a good ending for a morning ride, or after any strenuous early exercise. Fresh crab meat is easiest to obtain in the Chesapeake Bay region, but frozen or canned crab meat is widely available. If you're not familiar with hominy grits, try the soufflé. Hominy is the kernels of hulled dried white corn; when coarsely ground, it's called hominy grits, or grits for short. You cook it like other cooked cereals or grains, in boiling water, to make the base for the soufflé. In contrast with the somewhat heavy texture of the soufflé, the carrot bread is very light and delicate, almost cakelike—and marvelous served with soft butter.

### SAUTÉED CRAB MEAT ON VIRGINIA HAM

½ cup butter
20 slices Virginia ham, cut
     very thin
3 pounds crab meat
     (preferably lump crab
     meat)

3 tablespoons lemon juice
1½ teaspoons salt
½ teaspoon freshly cracked
     white pepper
1 tablespoon freshly chopped
     parsley

Heat 2 tablespoons of the butter in a big skillet until hot and foaming. Sauté ham slices on both sides and line a large baking dish or 2 smaller au gratin dishes with the slices. Keep warm. Add remaining butter to skillet and heat to foaming. Add crab meat, lemon juice, salt, and pepper and toss over high heat until heated through, about 5 minutes. Pile in ham-lined baking dish and sprinkle with chopped parsley.

## HOMINY SOUFFLÉ

| | |
|---|---|
| 4 cups water | 2 cups milk |
| 2 teaspoons salt | 6 tablespoons butter |
| ¾ cup hominy grits | 8 eggs, separated |

Bring water to a boil, add salt, and pour in hominy grits slowly, in a thin stream, stirring with a wooden spatula. Stir until water returns to a boil; then cook uncovered over very low heat for about 25 minutes, stirring occasionally. (Mixture will be very thick.) Let it cool. Meanwhile, heat milk and butter until butter melts and let cool. Combine cooled hominy and milk in a big mixing bowl and beat with a whisk until blended. Beat the egg yolks and blend them into the hominy mixture. (*May be prepared ahead to this point.*) Beat the egg whites stiff and fold them in. Pour into a buttered 8-cup soufflé dish and place in a pan with one inch of boiling water. Bake in a preheated 375° oven until very brown on top, about 45 minutes. This soufflé doesn't rise much, but it holds up quite well, and it has a heavier texture than other soufflés. Serve immediately.

## GRILLED TOMATOES

See p. 33, but use 5 tomatoes (1 tomato half per serving) and adjust oil and seasonings.

## CARROT BREAD

| | |
|---|---|
| 2 tablespoons vegetable oil | 1 egg |
| ¼ cup soft butter | 1 cup lightly packed brown |
| ¾ cup vegetable shortening | sugar |
| 1¼ cups sifted flour | 1 cup grated raw carrots |
| 1 teaspoon baking soda | (about 2 large) |
| 1 teaspoon baking powder | 2 tablespoons orange juice |
| ½ teaspoon salt | |

Brush an 8-cup ring mold with oil and dust it with flour; set aside. Cream butter and shortening together in electric mixer bowl. Sift flour with baking soda, baking powder, and salt, add it and remaining ingredients to shortening mixture, and beat to mix well. Pour batter into prepared mold and bake in a preheated 350° oven for 45 to 60 minutes, or until bread tests done with a cake tester. Cool bread in mold on a cake rack for about 5 minutes. Then loosen edges with a small knife and turn it out on a serving plate.

## A Champagne Breakfast
### for 6

Fresh peaches with champagne
Ham roulade with mustard sour cream
Individual brioche (see p. 12)
Espresso coffee

## FRESH PEACHES WITH CHAMPAGNE

6 ripe peaches
Juice of ½ lemon

½ cup sugar
1 split champagne, chilled

Scald peaches in boiling water for about 10 seconds, peel, and leave whole. Sprinkle with lemon juice and sugar and put in the refrigerator to chill thoroughly. To serve, place 1 whole peach in each of 6 saucer champagne glasses and pour on champagne.

## HAM ROULADE WITH MUSTARD SOUR CREAM

2 tablespoons vegetable oil
1 pound finely ground ham
6 eggs, separated
½ cup butter, melted and cooled
½ cup flour
½ teaspoon salt
½ teaspoon freshly cracked black pepper
2 tablespoons chopped parsley

2 teaspoons dried or 2 tablespoons chopped fresh tarragon
¼ cup dry Madeira

SAUCE:
1 cup sour cream
1 tablespoon Dijon mustard
1 teaspoon dried or 1 tablespoon chopped fresh tarragon

Brush a jelly-roll pan with vegetable oil, then line it with waxed paper, letting the paper extend 4 inches on each end. Brush the paper with vegetable oil and set aside. In a mixing bowl, mix together ham, egg yolks, melted butter, flour, salt, pepper, parsley, tarragon, and Madeira. Fold in egg whites, stiffly beaten. Spread in prepared pan and bake in a preheated 375° oven for 20 minutes. Turn out onto 2 overlapping sheets of waxed paper, peel off lining paper, and with the waxed paper to help, roll it up like a jelly roll and place on a serving platter. (*If made ahead to this point, reheat it in a 300° oven for 10 minutes. Just before serving, pour ½ cup sizzling hot butter over it.*) Serve with sour cream flavored with Dijon mustard and tarragon.

# *Luncheons*

Since few men live close enough to their work to make it home for lunch, I think mainly of women when planning luncheon menus. I especially welcome more formal luncheons as a chance to show off. Why not use the arrival of a friend from out of town as an excuse for a party? Bring out your best china and embroidered placemats, have plenty of fresh flowers around, and serve something truly elegant—Chaudfroid Chicken followed by a dessert of Strawberry Barquettes, for instance. Another dazzler is Avocado with Crab Meat, which, when ready to be served to each guest, looks like a decorated Easter egg.

You'll have many an occasion, also, to entertain mixed groups—guests visiting for the weekend, for example, or maybe a crowd invited over on a Saturday to view network football. Depending on the degree of informality you wish, your choice of an entrée might range from Shrimp en Brochette or an unusual Polenta Ring filled with grilled mushrooms—an original of mine— to Hamburgers with Green Peppercorns, a selection of Danish open-face sandwiches, or a hearty kielbasa sausage baked in brioche.

Luncheons are an excellent time to practice new cooking techniques. The menus are simpler, with fewer courses, and thus fewer items to organize in the kitchen. If you've never prepared anything *en gelée,* by all means do so the next time it's your turn for the bridge foursome. Then you'll feel secure when you tackle a glamorous aspic for a large buffet.

Consider the occasion and try to make the food complement it if you can do this without being coy. It amuses me to make Butterfish en Papillote to honor a new bride, but it's a private joke since I'm the only one who knows I cut the baking parchment in heart shapes to wrap up the fish for baking. You could pay tribute to a bride more openly with Coeur à la Crème for dessert.

Almost never do I offer cocktails at lunch. A glass of sherry or Lillet seems just right at one o'clock, and we usually sit down for lunch at one-thirty.

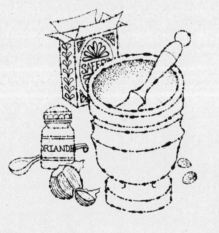

# A Ladies' Luncheon
## for 8

Eggs à la Princesse Caramon
Watercress and Belgian endive salad
Toasted Melba rounds
Apricot marzipan tart

### EGGS À LA PRINCESSE CARAMON

12 hard-cooked eggs
12 tablespoons butter
4 tablespoons flour
1½ cups light cream
1 teaspoon salt
½ teaspoon freshly cracked white pepper
½ teaspoon finely chopped garlic
2 tablespoons finely chopped shallots
1½ cups finely chopped mushrooms
2 tablespoons chopped parsley
1 teaspoon dried or 1 tablespoon fresh tarragon
1 teaspoon dry mustard
1 cup heavy cream
½ cup shredded Gruyère cheese
4 tablespoons grated Parmesan cheese
2 tablespoons bread crumbs

Cut the eggs in half lengthwise, rub yolks through a very fine sieve into a mixing bowl, and set aside. Melt 3 tablespoons of the butter in a saucepan, stir in flour, and cook for 2 minutes over high heat, stirring with a wooden spatula; do not let it brown. Remove from heat, change to a whisk, and gradually add light cream, whisking vigorously. Return to heat and cook, stirring, until sauce thickens and comes to a boil. Lower heat and cook about 5 minutes. Season with salt and pepper.

Remove from heat and stir 4 tablespoons of the white sauce into sieved egg yolks. In a skillet, over high heat, melt 3 tablespoons butter and add garlic, shallots, and chopped mushrooms. Toss over high heat until mixture looks dry, about 5 to 10 minutes. Add to sieved egg yolks along with parsley, tarragon, and dry mustard. Beat in 4 tablespoons softened butter, and add more salt and pepper if needed. Stuff mixture into egg whites.

Thin out remaining white sauce with heavy cream, bring to

a boil, and stir in shredded Gruyère. Taste for seasoning. Spoon some of the sauce into an ovenproof serving dish. Arrange stuffed eggs on sauce and spoon more sauce over eggs, masking completely. Sprinkle with grated Parmesan and bread crumbs and drizzle with 2 tablespoons melted butter. (*Can be prepared to this point the day before, covered with plastic wrap, and refrigerated.*) When ready to serve, place in a preheated 350° oven and bake for 20 minutes.

## WATERCRESS AND BELGIAN ENDIVE SALAD

| | |
|---|---|
| 2 bunches watercress | 1 teaspoon salt |
| 6 heads Belgian endive | ½ teaspoon freshly cracked |
| 2 tablespoons lemon juice | white pepper |
| 5 tablespoons olive oil | |

Trim stems from watercress. Trim root end of Belgian endive heads and remove any discolored leaves. With a chef's knife cut heads lengthwise into matchsticks. Dry thoroughly. (*May be prepared to this point the day before, wrapped in plastic wrap, and refrigerated.*) Just before serving, toss in a chilled salad bowl with a vinaigrette dressing made by beating together lemon juice, olive oil, salt, and pepper.

## TOASTED MELBA ROUNDS

With a 2-inch cookie cutter, cut 24 rounds of very thinly sliced white bread. Put on a baking sheet and brush with ½ cup melted butter. Place in a preheated 350° oven for 15 minutes; turn oven down to 250° and bake 15 to 20 minutes longer, or until rounds are crispy and beautifully browned. You can bake these ahead of time and freeze them for up to 3 months—or freeze leftovers. Or make the day before and put in airtight container or plastic bag. Serve at room temperature, or reheat if desired.

## APRICOT MARZIPAN TART

PASTRY:
2 cups lightly spooned flour
2 tablespoons sugar
¾ cup soft butter
2 egg yolks
1½ tablespoons ice water

FILLING:
½ cup unsalted butter
8 ounces almond paste
2 eggs
1 tablespoon flour
4 tablespoons brandy
1 28-ounce can apricot halves
¾ cup apricot preserves

Put flour in a bowl and stir in sugar. Blend in butter with your fingertips. Add egg yolks and water and mix with a pastry fork—dough will be sticky. Turn it out on a floured board and knead lightly. Wrap it in waxed paper and chill until firm enough to roll, about ½ hour. Roll between 2 sheets of waxed paper to make a round about ⅛ inch thick. Fit into a 10-inch flan ring or springform pan. Prick bottom and sides of pastry with a fork. Bake in a preheated 350° oven for 10 minutes.

While crust is baking, prepare filling. Cream butter and almond paste together, add eggs, and beat well with electric mixer, wire whisk, or wooden spatula. Blend in flour and 2 table-spoons brandy. Spread the almond mixture in the partly baked crust and return to oven, setting it on the lowest rack, to bake for another 45 minutes.

When tart comes out of the oven, drain apricot halves and arrange over almond filling. Heat apricot preserves with remaining 2 tablespoons brandy over medium heat until syrupy, about 5 minutes, stirring with wooden spatula; push through a sieve and brush generously over apricots and filling. Allow to cool and serve at room temperature.

## An Elegant Luncheon
## for 8

Cheese roll, four ways
Fish en croûte
Chinese carrots
Peaches in port

Both the cheese roll and the fish en croûte recipes are my own creations, and the carrots provide a delicious taste contrast to the fish.

### CHEESE ROLL, FOUR WAYS

2  tablespoons butter
2  tablespoons flour
1  cup milk
5  eggs, separated

1 cup freshly grated Parmesan cheese
Filling or sauce
Parsley or watercress for garnish

Brush an 11 x 17-inch jelly-roll pan with vegetable oil, line it with waxed paper, brush the paper with oil, and set aside. Melt the butter in a saucepan over medium-high heat and stir in flour. Cook, stirring with wooden spatula, for 2 minutes—do not let it brown. Remove from heat, change to a whisk, and add milk, whisking vigorously. Return to heat and cook, stirring, until mixture thickens and boils. Remove from heat and set aside to cool for 5 to 10 minutes. Beat egg yolks and beat them into the white sauce, to mix thoroughly. Beat egg whites until they form soft peaks. Stir one third of them into sauce; then fold in remainder. Lightly fold in grated Parmesan. Spread mixture in prepared jelly-roll pan and bake in a preheated 350° oven for 15 minutes.

Remove from oven and turn out onto 2 sheets of waxed paper, overlapping lengthwise. Serve either warm or cold, rolled up with 1 of these 4 fillings or sauces: (1) ¼ cup freshly grated Parmesan cheese sprinkled on rolled-up roll; (2) 1 recipe Mushroom Duxelles (see p. 283), as filling; (3) ¾ cup creamed butter mixed with ¾ cup chopped walnuts, as filling; (4) ½ recipe Tomato

Sauce (see p. 64), poured over rolled-up roll. Garnish with chopped parsley sprinkled over roll, if desired, or with a large bunch of watercress at one end of the platter.

### FISH EN CROÛTE

1 recipe sour cream pastry (see p. 288)

8 brook trout, about ¾ to 1 pound each (or other small whole fish, such as butterfish, porgies, or small rockfish)

½ cup lemon juice, plus lemon juice to wash fish

1 tablespoon salt

1 teaspoon freshly cracked white pepper

½ cup butter

3 tablespoons melted butter

Lemon wedges for garnish

Prepare pastry and chill in the refrigerator for at least 1½ hours, or overnight. Scale and clean trout, or ask your fish seller to do it, being careful to leave heads and tails intact. Wash the fish in water acidulated with lemon juice (1 tablespoon to 1 quart), and dry them carefully. Remove the backbone of each fish by slitting the fish along the belly from head to tail and running a small sharp knife tight against the bone on each side. Use kitchen shears to snip through bone at head and tail and pull it out. Do not cut through the top (the back) of the fish. Sprinkle insides of fish with half the salt and pepper and inside each one put 1 tablespoon lemon juice and 1 tablespoon butter. Pinch the slit together—fish is gelatinous and it will hold without tying. Brush outside of fish with melted butter and sprinkle with remaining salt and pepper.

On a lightly floured board, roll chilled pastry into a rectangle about 15 by 12 inches and ⅛ inch thick. Cut it into 8 strips, 15 inches long and 1½ inches wide. Starting at the tail, on the underside, wind one strip of pastry around each fish. Do not overlap the pastry—the fish should show through the pastry spiral. Try to end near the head, on the underside. (*Recipe may be prepared to this point 1 or 2 hours before baking and held in refrigerator.*) Place fish on a buttered baking sheet and put into a preheated 375° oven to bake until pastry is golden brown and fish are done, about 15 to 20 minutes. Garnish with wedges of lemon.

## CHINESE CARROTS

| | |
|---|---|
| 12 carrots | 1 tablespoon soy sauce |
| 2 tablespoons vegetable oil | 1 tablespoon vinegar |
| 3 slices fresh ginger | ½ teaspoon sugar |
| 1 teaspoon salt | 2 tablespoons chopped parsley |
| ½ cup chicken stock (see p. 278) | |

Peel carrots and cut them in diagonal slices about 1 inch thick. Or roll-cut carrots the way the Chinese do: lay carrot on a chopping board and make a diagonal cut, straight down, at wide end. Roll carrot a quarter turn (diagonal surface facing up) and make another diagonal cut straight down. Repeat until carrot is cut up. Each diagonal cut bisects the diagonal surface of previous cut.

Put carrots into saucepan, cover with cold water, and bring to a boil; boil 5 minutes; drain and set aside. In a skillet or wok, heat oil almost to smoking over high heat. Add ginger and stir for 1 minute; add carrots and stir-fry for about 3 minutes longer. Sprinkle with salt and pour on chicken stock mixed with soy sauce, vinegar, and sugar. Cover and cook, still over high heat, for about 10 minutes or until very tender. Garnish with chopped parsley.

## PEACHES IN PORT

| | |
|---|---|
| 8 fresh peaches | ½ teaspoon freshly grated nutmeg |
| 2 cups sugar | |
| Grated peel and juice of 2 lemons | 2 cups port wine |
| | 1½ cups sour cream *or* 1 cup heavy cream, whipped |

Scald peaches in boiling water for 10 seconds to loosen skins. Peel and put them whole in a baking dish. In a saucepan, mix together sugar, lemon peel and lemon juice, nutmeg, and port wine; bring to a boil, and pour over peaches. Cover peaches with aluminum foil and bake in a preheated 400° oven for 20 to 30 minutes, or until tender, basting 3 times during cooking. Serve warm or chilled, with sour cream or whipped cream.

# *Formal Summer Luncheon for 12*

Melon and prosciutto
Chaudfroid chicken
Salad of Bibb lettuce and cucumber
Strawberry barquettes

The French words "hot" and "cold" not only name but describe the method of preparation for this platter of cold chicken that looks as glamorous as Paris under lights. It's a three-step recipe, all done the day before your party: poach the chicken breasts; coat them with the chaudfroid white sauce; glaze them with aspic.

## MELON AND PROSCIUTTO

Cut 3 large ripe cantaloupes (or other melon, such as Persian, Spanish, honeydew, or casaba) into thin slices, removing rind. Arrange 3 or 4 slices of melon on plates with 3 or 4 paper-thin slices of prosciutto ham (you will need about 1 pound). Season generously with freshly cracked black pepper and garnish with lime wedges, or lemon wedges.

## CHAUDFROID CHICKEN

6 whole chicken breasts
2 teaspoons salt
½ cup chopped celery
¾ cup chopped onion
½ cup chopped carrot
7 cups chicken stock (use poaching liquid)
9 tablespoons (9 envelopes) plus 1 teaspoon unflavored gelatine
1 cup dry white wine
2 tablespoons tomato paste
Pinch of salt

3 egg whites
6 tablespoons vegetable oil
6 tablespoons flour
1 cup milk
½ teaspoon salt
3 or 4 drops Tabasco sauce
3 tablespoons light cream
Truffle or mushrooms, for garnish
1 can (400 grams) pâté de fois gras, chilled
Watercress, for garnish

Put chicken breasts in a deep kettle, cover with cold water, and add 2 teaspoons salt, celery, onion, and carrot. Bring to a boil over high heat, turn heat to simmer, and simmer 20 minutes only—do not overcook. Let chicken breasts cool in stock; this keeps them firm. When cool, peel off skin and, using a small knife and your fingers, carefully remove each side of the breast meat in one piece. Trim pieces so they look neat and lay them on cake racks set on a baking tray—the pieces should not touch. Refrigerate.

To make aspic, strain 6 cups of poaching liquid into saucepan; set over medium heat. Sprinkle 8 tablespoons of the gelatine into stock and stir to dissolve. Add wine, tomato paste, and pinch of salt. Beat egg whites to a froth and whisk them into the stock along with 3 eggshells. Bring to a boil, whisking constantly. Take off heat and let stand for 10 minutes. Line a strainer with 2 thicknesses of cheesecloth wrung out in cold water and pour aspic through it into a bowl. Let the liquid drain through without stirring or forcing it in any way. Pour the strained aspic into a baking tray and place it in the refrigerator to set (this takes about 1 to 2 hours).

To make the chaudfroid coating, heat vegetable oil in a saucepan. Stir in flour and cook, stirring with a wooden spatula, for 2 minutes—do not let it brown. Stir remaining gelatine into this *roux* and cook for 1 minute, to dissolve gelatine. Remove from heat, change to a whisk, and add 1 cup chicken stock and the milk all at once, whisking vigorously. Return to heat and cook, stirring, until sauce begins to thicken. Add salt and Tabasco. Set saucepan over ice and stir sauce until it is just to the point of setting; take it off ice. If necessary, thin it with a little of the light cream; it should be just fluid enough to coat or nap the chicken when spooned on. Remove chicken breasts—still on racks set on baking tray—from the refrigerator. Using a large spoon, coat each breast half with the chaudfroid sauce—one swoop of the spoon makes a smooth coat. Work fast, letting excess sauce run off chicken into tray. If the sauce in the pan sets while you're working, warm it; then stir it again over ice until it is of napping consistency. You can also warm and reuse the runover in the tray if you need it. Refrigerate the coated chicken breasts until set, about ½ to 1 hour.

Remove aspic from refrigerator. Scrape one third of it into a saucepan and set it over heat to melt. Turn out remaining aspic on a sheet of waxed paper on a chopping board and chop it into small cubes with a big chef's knife. Transfer the shimmery chopped aspic to a serving platter. Spread it out, making a bed of chopped aspic, and put the platter in the refrigerator.

When the chaudfroid is set, bring chicken from the refrigerator to decorate with a black truffle thinly sliced and cut in fancy shapes with tiny aspic cutters, or with a couple of mushrooms sliced thin from top to stem. Set the melted aspic over ice and stir until it's cool, thick, and syrupy, about 5 minutes. Dip truffle or mushroom slices in the aspic and place them on chicken breasts— the aspic "glue" sets immediately. Do not overdecorate! One large mushroom slice or 3 tiny truffle cutouts in a row will be ample. Finally, coat each decorated chicken breast with a spoonful of aspic—this gives the chicken a shine and also keeps the chaudfroid coating from drying out. Return chicken to refrigerator. Slice pâté de fois gras in pieces about the size of the chicken breasts. Arrange pâté on the platter of chopped aspic and place a chicken breast on top of each slice. Keep refrigerated until ready to serve. Garnish platter with watercress.

## SALAD OF BIBB LETTUCE AND CUCUMBER

| | |
|---|---|
| 8 heads Bibb lettuce | 2 tablespoons red wine vinegar |
| 1 cucumber | 1 teaspoon Dijon mustard |
| 1 small onion, grated | 1 teaspoon salt |
| 6 tablespoons vegetable or olive oil | ½ teaspoon freshly cracked black pepper |

Wash, dry, and chill the lettuce, separating the leaves; place in a chilled salad bowl. Peel the cucumber and shave it lengthwise with a potato peeler; shave just the flesh—discard seeds. Add to salad bowl along with grated onion. Beat oil, vinegar, mustard, salt, and pepper together and pour over greens. Toss and serve immediately.

## STRAWBERRY BARQUETTES

Barquettes are small boat-shaped tin molds, about 3½ inches long. You'll need a stack of them for baking the pastry boats— about 44 if you bake them all together, fewer if you bake in shifts.

2  cups lightly spooned flour
1  teaspoon salt
¾  cup chilled unsalted butter
¼  cup ice water
1  8-ounce jar currant jelly

2  tablespoons framboise or
   kirsch
1  quart sliced strawberries,
   about
   Confectioners' sugar

Measure flour into a bowl and stir in salt. Cut chilled butter in chips and work it into the flour with pastry blender or fingertips until mixture resembles coarse cornmeal. Add ice water, only 2 tablespoons at first, more if needed, but no more than ¼ cup, and mix with a fork until you can press dough together to form a ball. Turn dough out on a lightly floured board. Using the heel of your hand, push the dough, bit by bit, against the board and away from you in short, quick smears. Work fast; you just want to smooth the dough a bit. Then form it into a ball, dust with flour, wrap in waxed paper, and refrigerate for at least 30 minutes.

On a lightly floured surface, roll out dough about ⅛ inch thick and fill barquette molds. (If you wish, you can work with half the dough at a time.) Line up the molds in 2 or 3 rows, fairly close together. Lay rolled-out pastry over the molds, gently push pastry down into each mold with your finger, and then roll over tops of molds with rolling pin to cut edges. Pinch pastry firmly into each mold. Stack one filled mold on top of another, 3 to a stack, place an empty mold on top, and press them all tightly together. Arrange the stacked molds on a baking sheet, lay a second baking sheet on top, and weight it with a brick. Bake in a preheated 375° oven until light brown, about 25 minutes. Remove from oven and let cool for a few minutes. Remove weight and carefully remove barquettes from molds. Cool. They'll keep for a week on the shelf, or you may wrap and freeze them. To store on shelf, package them in plastic bags or an airtight container. Crisp them in the oven when you take them out of storage. Makes 32 barquettes.

To fill barquettes, melt currant jelly with framboise or kirsch. Brush this glaze on the shells, fill with sliced fresh strawberries, carefully arranged, and brush berries with more glaze. (*Barquettes can be filled and glazed 2 hours ahead. Any remaining glaze can be kept in a jar in the refrigerator.*) Just before serving, sift confectioners' sugar over barquettes. Count 1 or 2 barquettes per serving.

### A Light and Delicate
### Luncheon for 6

Mushroom broth garnished with mushroom rounds
Cold spinach mousse, filled
with crab-meat salad
Green mayonnaise
Hot French finger rolls
Peaches with champagne (see p. 36)

## MUSHROOM BROTH GARNISHED
## WITH MUSHROOM ROUNDS

10  cups strong chicken stock
    (see p. 278)
1½ cups finely chopped mush-
    rooms, plus 4 whole
    mushrooms for garnish

1  teaspoon salt
½  teaspoon freshly cracked
    black pepper
2  egg whites

In a large saucepan, over high heat, bring chicken stock and mushrooms to a boil; reduce heat to simmer, cover, and cook ½ hour. Strain and return broth to saucepan. Season with salt and pepper. Beat egg whites until foamy, add to broth, to clarify it, and whisk while you bring broth to a boil over high heat. Remove from heat and let stand for 15 minutes. Strain through a sieve lined with a double thickness of cheesecloth wrung out in cold water, pouring carefully so as not to disturb coagulated egg whites. Let consommé drip through by itself—do not push or squeeze it. Taste for seasoning. (*Recipe can be made ahead to this point.*) To serve, reheat it and garnish with very thin rounds cut from fresh mushrooms.

## COLD SPINACH MOUSSE

The various elements of this dish—spinach mousse, aspic-coated eggs, crab-meat salad, and green mayonnaise—may all be made the day before and unmolded and assembled an hour or so before serving. The effect of the eggs nestled along the top of the spinach ring is truly beautiful. Incidentally, this is an original recipe, which I adapted from something like it that I had one time in Vienna.

2 tablespoons vegetable oil
3 10-ounce packages frozen
  chopped spinach
1 teaspoon salt
½ teaspoon freshly cracked
  black pepper
½ teaspoon freshly grated
  nutmeg
1 small onion
1 cup mayonnaise (see p. 283)

2 tablespoons (2 envelopes)
  unflavored gelatine
½ cup lemon juice
1 cup heavy cream
6 hard-cooked eggs
1½ cups aspic (see p. 280)
  Crab-meat Salad (recipe
  follows)
  Green Mayonnaise (recipe
  follows)

Oil a 6-cup ring mold and set aside. Cook spinach according to package directions. Drain well and squeeze out excess moisture. Chop with chef's knife as fine as possible. You should have about 1½ to 2 cups. Put it in a large bowl and season with salt, pepper, and nutmeg. Grate onion and add it to spinach along with mayonnaise. Soften gelatine in lemon juice; set mixture in a pan of hot water and stir to dissolve; add to spinach. Whip heavy cream until stiff and fold into spinach mixture; pour into prepared mold. Chill 2 hours.

To serve, unmold spinach ring on a serving plate. With the back of a spoon, make 6 depressions, equally spaced, on spinach ring. Place a hard-cooked egg, shelled and coated with aspic, in each. Fill center of ring with Crab-meat Salad. Serve with Green Mayonnaise.

### CRAB-MEAT SALAD

1 pound lump crab meat,
  preferably fresh
1½ tablespoons drained capers
½ teaspoon salt

3 drops Tabasco sauce
2 tablespoons fresh chopped
  chives
½ cup mayonnaise (see p. 283)

Pick over crab meat to remove any bits of shell or filament. Mix all ingredients in a bowl, tossing with a fork to blend—do not mash.

## GREEN MAYONNAISE

Drop 12 watercress leaves, 6 sprigs of parsley, and 12 spinach leaves into boiling water; blanch 1 minute. Drain and refresh with cold water. Drain well, squeeze dry, and chop with chef's knife until pureed. Stir into 1 recipe mayonnaise (see p. 283).

## *Formal Luncheon for 8*

---

Mushroom flan
Butterfish en papillote with tartar sauce
Pea roulade
Raspberry ice with cassis

A formal luncheon is accomplished with greater ease if you have an extra pair of hands in the kitchen, moving things in and out of the oven—a teen-age daughter, perhaps, or hired help. But everything is prepared ahead, and you can manage this yourself if necessary. Glaze the flan just before you invite guests to the table, and put the fish in to bake while you eat the flan. When you take the fish out of the oven, put the pea roulade in to reheat; it will be ready by the time you've arranged the parchment packets of fish on your serving dish, ready for the dining room. Guests are ecstatic when you present food en papillote.

## MUSHROOM FLAN

2 pounds mushrooms
½ cup butter
2 tablespoons chopped shallots
  Juice of ½ lemon
¼ cup dry Madeira or dry
  sherry
1 tablespoon flour
1 teaspoon salt
½ teaspoon freshly cracked
  white pepper
2 cups heavy cream
1 wholly baked 9-inch pâte
  brisée shell (see p. 288)
2 tablespoons chopped parsley
¼ cup freshly grated Parmesan
  cheese

Roughly chop the mushrooms. Heat butter in a heavy skillet over high heat and cook shallots for 3 minutes, stirring—do not let them brown. Add chopped mushrooms and lemon juice. Cook, stirring, until mixture looks dry. Add Madeira and cook until it evaporates. Sprinkle flour, salt, and pepper over mushrooms and stir in. Add heavy cream and continue cooking until sauce is reduced and of napping consistency. Pour into baked tart shell and sprinkle with chopped parsley and Parmesan cheese. (*Tart may be made ahead to this point. It freezes well, too. Thaw in refrigerator before heating.*) Heat under a broiler until bubbly, about 3 to 5 minutes, or place in a preheated 350° oven for 15 minutes.

## BUTTERFISH EN PAPILLOTE WITH TARTAR SAUCE

| | |
|---|---|
| 8 butterfish, about ½ to ¾ pound each | 2 tablespoons grated onion |
| Lemon juice to wash fish | 2 teaspoons salt |
| 8 pieces baking parchment | 1 teaspoon freshly cracked black pepper |
| 2 tablespoons melted butter | 8 teaspoons tomato puree |
| 8 thin slices ham | 2 tablespoons finely chopped parsley |
| 1 cup soft butter | Tartar Sauce (recipe follows) |
| 2 tablespoons anchovy paste | |

Clean fish—or ask your fish seller to do it—leaving head and tails intact. Wash them in acidulated water (1 tablespoon lemon juice to 1 quart water) and dry them. From baking parchment cut 8 wide hearts with a very slight dip in the center, large enough to enclose fish. Brush parchment with melted butter. Place 1 slice ham on right-hand half of each heart. Mix ½ cup of soft butter with anchovy paste and grated onion; spread on ham. Place fish on buttered ham and top with remaining butter (1 tablespoon per fish), salt and pepper, tomato puree (1 teaspoon per fish), and chopped parsley. Fold left half of parchment heart over fish, match edges, and fold them over together in 2 or 3 narrow folds, to lock fish inside. (*Recipe may be made ahead to this point and refrigerated, or frozen for up to 1 month. Bring to room temperature before baking.*) Place on baking tray and bake in a preheated 425° oven for 10 minutes or until parchment puffs.

## TARTAR SAUCE

To 1 cup homemade mayonnaise (see p. 283), add 1 finely chopped small dill pickle, 2 tablespoons drained capers, and 2 tablespoons finely chopped parsley.

## PEA ROULADE

| | |
|---|---|
| 2 10-ounce packages frozen peas | ¼ teaspoon freshly cracked white pepper |
| 2 tablespoons butter | ½ teaspoon freshly grated nutmeg |
| 6 tablespoons flour | |
| 1 cup milk | 1 cup sour cream |
| 3 eggs, separated | ½ cup melted butter |
| ½ teaspoon salt | 2 tablespoons chopped parsley |

Oil a 10 x 15-inch jelly-roll pan. Line it with waxed paper, leaving 3 inches overhanging each end. Oil the waxed paper. Flour it and bang out excess flour. Cook frozen peas according to package directions. Puree the drained cooked peas through a food mill, using the finest disk. Do not puree in blender. You should have a heaping cup of pea puree.

Melt 2 tablespoons butter over high heat and stir in flour with wooden spatula. This is a higher proportion of flour to butter than you generally use in making a *roux,* and it will lump. Keep stirring it and cook for 3 to 5 minutes to brown the flour. Mixture will look like brown sugar. Remove pan from heat and add milk a little at a time, stirring constantly. Lower heat to medium-high, return pan to heat, change to a whisk, and cook, whisking vigorously. Mixture will be very thick and perhaps still a little lumpy—don't worry about this. Remove sauce from heat; stir in pea puree, egg yolks, salt, pepper, and nutmeg. Beat egg whites until stiff peaks form; fold into pea mixture and spread in jelly-roll pan. Bake in a preheated 375° oven for 18 minutes.

Remove roll from oven and loosen it around the edges. Lay two strips of waxed paper on the counter, overlapping lengthwise. Turn roll out upside down on waxed paper; peel off the waxed paper liner. Let roll cool slightly. Spread it with sour cream, roll it up, and transfer it to serving platter with the aid of the waxed paper. Reheat it if necessary in a preheated 300° oven for a few minutes. Just before serving, pour sizzling hot melted butter over the roll and sprinkle with chopped parsley.

*Note:* 1 cup of mushroom duxelles (see p. 283) is an excellent filling that you might wish to try with other recipe combinations.


## RASPBERRY ICE WITH CASSIS

1 quart fresh raspberries *or*
  2 10-ounce packages
  frozen raspberries
1 cup water
1 cup orange juice
  Juice of 1 lime or ½ lemon,
  for frozen berries only
1 teaspoon unflavored gelatine

3 tablespoons cold water
½ cup light corn syrup
¼ cup water
1 cup firmly packed light
  brown sugar
½ cup honey
1 to 2 tablespoons crème de
  cassis

Wash and drain fresh raspberries; put them in a saucepan with 1 cup water and the orange juice, bring to a boil, and simmer for 10 minutes. (If using frozen berries, no cooking is necessary. Instead thaw berries, drain, reserving juice, measure juice and add water to make 1 cup. Add orange juice and the lime or lemon juice.) Soak gelatine in 3 tablespoons cold water. Bring to a boil the corn syrup and remaining ¼ cup water and boil for 5 minutes; stir in gelatine mixture to dissolve. Add brown sugar and honey. Puree berries in electric blender and press them through a sieve to remove seeds. Combine with sugar-honey mixture and pour into refrigerator trays. When partly frozen, remove from trays and beat with rotary beater; return to freezer. Serve in parfait glasses with crème de cassis poured over.


## *An Elegant but Easy Lunch for 8*

Shrimp en brochette
Risotto
Romaine salad
Coeur à la crème

The risotto in this menu is so delicious that it can stand on its own as a meal in itself. Here it is an excellent accompaniment to broiled shrimp. As served in Italy, the rice should remain slightly "hard to the bite."

## SHRIMP EN BROCHETTE

2 pounds medium-size fresh or frozen raw shrimp
⅓ cup soy sauce
½ cup dry white wine

1 teaspoon freshly cracked black pepper
½ teaspoon ground ginger
1 cup sesame seeds

Peel, devein, and wash the shrimp. Mix together soy sauce, wine, pepper, and ginger; pour over shrimp and marinate for 2 to 3 hours in the refrigerator, turning shrimp about every half hour. Remove shrimp from marinade, roll in sesame seeds, and thread on skewers (not too tightly—leave a little space in between so that they cook properly). Broil 2 inches from heat, turning shrimp and basting with marinade, for a total of about 4 to 5 minutes. Serve at once.

## RISOTTO

5 cups or more chicken stock (see p. 278) or veal stock (see p. 279)
6 tablespoons butter
1½ cups chopped onion
1 teaspoon chopped garlic
2 cups Italian rice
6 tablespoons dry white wine

1 teaspoon salt
½ teaspoon freshly cracked white pepper
½ teaspoon saffron shreds, optional
½ cup melted butter
2 tablespoons freshly grated Parmesan cheese

Bring stock to a boil and hold at a simmer. In another saucepan melt the butter and stir in onion and garlic; cook over high heat for a few minutes until onion is transparent; then reduce heat to simmer. Add the rice, stirring to coat well with butter. Add wine, stir, and cook over medium-high heat until wine is absorbed; add salt and pepper. Stir saffron (if desired) into 1 cup of hot stock, add to rice, stir, and cook over medium-high heat, stirring occasionally. As liquid is absorbed add more stock, 1 cup at a time, stirring only occasionally to keep rice from sticking, until rice is done and liquid very nearly absorbed (this will take about a half hour). Do not cover the pan. To test for doneness, taste a kernel of rice; it should be, like spaghetti, *al dente*—tender, but with a bite to it. And it should be a little wet—not the dry, separate kernels you want with steamed rice. To serve, mound the rice in a serving dish, pour melted butter over it, and sprinkle with grated Parmesan cheese.

## ROMAINE SALAD

2 large heads romaine
2 cloves garlic
¼ cup olive oil

¾ cup ¼-inch bread cubes
French vinaigrette dressing
  (see p. 282)
2 hard-cooked egg yolks,
  sieved

Wash romaine, shake off water, break into bite-size pieces, roll in towels, and crisp in refrigerator. Crush garlic cloves and heat with olive oil in a small skillet; add bread cubes and fry over medium heat until croutons are crisp, tossing or stirring with wooden spatula to ensure they crisp evenly. Cool slightly. When ready to serve, pour dressing over greens in a chilled salad bowl, add croutons and sieved egg yolks, and toss.

## COEUR À LA CRÈME

For this recipe you will need about 10 individual coeur à la crème molds, approximately 3 inches long, 3 inches wide, and 1½ inches deep.

1 8-ounce package cream
  cheese
½ cup cottage cheese
½ cup confectioners' sugar
1½ teaspoons vanilla extract *or*
  seeds from ½-inch piece
  of vanilla bean

2 cups heavy cream
6 tablespoons currant jelly
1 tablespoon framboise
1 pint whole fresh straw-
  berries

Beat cream cheese with electric mixer until soft and fluffy. Add cottage cheese and continue to beat. Add sugar and vanilla and beat until smooth. In another bowl, whip cream until stiff. Fold whipped cream into the cream cheese mixture. Cut a strip of cheesecloth into 6-inch squares or pieces big enough to line heart-shaped coeur à la crème molds. Wring out cheesecloth in salted cold water and press into molds, letting edges hang over. Spoon the cream-cheese mixture into the molds and fold the cheesecloth over the top of the cream. Give molds a tap to allow mixture to settle. Set molds on cake racks set over baking sheets and put them in the refrigerator to drain overnight. A few hours before serving, prepare strawberries. Melt the currant jelly over high heat, stir in framboise, and pour over strawberries; let macerate. To serve, unmold coeur à la crème, remove cheesecloth, and place on dessert dishes. Spoon on berries and sauce.

## A Celebration Luncheon
## for 12

Chicory salad
Chicken Périgourdine
Noodle ring
Macédoine of fruit
Sand tarts

Plan a celebration luncheon as a tribute to a retiring garden club president or to praise the chairman of a fund drive that went over the top. Maybe someone you know has published a book. Or you want to honor your best friend's out-of-town guest. All such occasions call for elegant food. Chicken Périgourdine, with two sauces, and garnished with truffles, couldn't be more exquisite. Lead up to this rich main course by serving a crisp salad first, California style.

### CHICORY SALAD

Wash 4 heads of chicory (curly endive), shake off water, break into bite-size pieces, roll in towels, and crisp in refrigerator. Serve from a chilled salad bowl, tossed with French vinaigrette dressing (see p. 282).

## CHICKEN PÉRIGOURDINE

8 whole chicken breasts
8 tablespoons butter
¼ cup brandy
3 tablespoons flour
1½ cups chicken stock (see p. 278)
½ cup light cream
½ teaspoon salt
¼ teaspoon freshly cracked white pepper
¼ cup dry sherry
1 pound fresh mushrooms

2 teaspoons lemon juice, plus 1 tablespoon to wash mushrooms
½ teaspoon salt
¼ teaspoon freshly cracked white pepper
1 teaspoon potato starch or arrowroot, optional
1 recipe Hollandaise Sauce (see p. 281)
2 tablespoons chopped truffles

Skin and bone chicken breasts carefully and trim them into neat ovals. These are called suprêmes; you will have 16 of them, 2 from each whole breast. Heat 4 tablespoons butter in a large skillet and sauté chicken breasts a few at a time, over high heat, for 2 minutes on each side—just enough to stiffen them. Remove from skillet.

Heat brandy in a small pan just until warm, ignite it, and pour it flaming into the skillet. When flames die down, scrape up the brown bits. Add 2 tablespoons butter to skillet and stir in the flour with a wooden spatula. Cook, stirring, over high heat for 2 minutes to eliminate the raw flour taste. Take pan off heat, change to a whisk, and add chicken stock all at once, whisking vigorously. Return to heat and bring to a boil, whisking. Add cream, ½ teaspoon salt, ¼ teaspoon pepper, and the sherry. Return chicken breasts to skillet along with their juices, cover, and simmer chicken for 15 minutes.

Wipe mushrooms clean with a paper towel dipped in acidulated water (1 quart water mixed with 1 tablespoon lemon juice). Wipe dry and trim stems. Reserve 6 perfect mushrooms for fluting and slice remaining mushrooms. Heat remaining 2 tablespoons butter in another large skillet; when foaming subsides, add mushrooms (both sliced and whole fluted), sprinkling them with 2 teaspoons lemon juice, ½ teaspoon salt, and ¼ teaspoon pepper. Toss over high heat for about 3 minutes and set aside.

To serve, lift out chicken from sauce and arrange in a large au gratin dish. Add sliced mushrooms and their liquid to the sauce. Thicken sauce if you wish with 1 teaspoon potato starch or arrowroot dissolved in 1 tablespoon water. Spoon sauce over chicken;

be sure each piece of chicken has some sliced mushrooms on it. (*May be prepared ahead to this point, covered with plastic wrap, and refrigerated. Let stand 1 hour at room temperature and then reheat in a 375° oven for 15 minutes.*) With a large spoon, shake a ribbon of Hollandaise Sauce over the chicken, down the center of the platter. Sprinkle this ribbon with chopped truffles, and decorate the platter with the fluted mushrooms.

## NOODLE RING

1 pound noodles, ¼ inch wide
1 tablespoon vegetable oil
3 cups milk
2 cups soft bread crumbs
½ cup plus 4 tablespoons softened butter, plus butter for mold

1 pound grated Cheddar cheese
6 eggs, beaten lightly
2 teaspoons salt
1 teaspoon freshly cracked white pepper

Cook noodles in 4 quarts of boiling salted water according to package directions, adding a little oil to the water so noodles won't stick together. While noodles cook, prepare cheese sauce. Bring milk to a boil, lower heat, add bread crumbs, and stir with a whisk. Beat in ½ cup softened butter and the cheese, and whisk over low heat until smooth. Pour a little of the hot sauce into the eggs, to warm them; then stir eggs into sauce. Heat through over medium heat, but do not boil. Stir in salt and pepper. When noodles are done (they should be tender, but firm to the bite), drain thoroughly and toss in a large bowl with remaining 4 tablespoons softened butter to keep them from sticking. Stir in cheese sauce and pour mixture into a heavily buttered 12-cup ring mold or soufflé dish. Set it in a *bain marie* (a water bath—water should be 1 inch deep and hot) and put it in a preheated 375° oven. Bake for 45 minutes. Remove from oven and let the mold stand in the hot water for 5 minutes, before turning it out onto a serving platter.

## MACÉDOINE OF FRUIT

Fresh fruit macerated in a liqueur or liquor—kirsch, framboise, Scotch, bourbon, gin, Cognac, Grand Marnier, Cointreau, anything you want—will not taste raw if you sugar the fruit.

That's the trick. If fruit served to you in a restaurant has too strong a taste of liquor, sprinkle a bit of sugar on it and wait a few minutes. You'll enjoy it more.

3 red apples
2 Golden Delicious apples
2 pears
2 bananas
½ cantaloupe
　Grapes, both green and
　　purple, 1 small bunch of
　　each

1 quart jar fresh citrus fruit
½ cup sugar
¾ cup liqueur or liquor
Juice of 1 lemon
Fresh berries for garnish

Peel, core, and slice the apples and pears. Peel and slice bananas. Cut cantaloupe with melon baller. Seed grapes. Drain the jar of citrus fruit, removing the maraschino cherries. Place fruit in a large glass bowl, sprinkle with sugar, liqueur, and lemon juice, turning the fruit over in the liquid with big spoons. Cover bowl with plastic wrap and refrigerate for at least 2 hours. Decorate with fresh berries just before serving.

## SAND TARTS

¾ cup unsalted butter
1¼ cups plus 1 tablespoon
　sugar
1 egg
1 egg yolk
1½ teaspoons vanilla extract

¼ teaspoon salt
2½ cups lightly spooned flour
1 egg white, lightly beaten
½ cup slivered or shaved
　blanched almonds
1 tablespoon cinnamon

Beat butter and 1¼ cups sugar in electric mixer bowl until light and fluffy. Beat in egg and egg yolk; add vanilla. Stir salt into flour and add to butter mixture, mixing well. Shape dough into a roll and refrigerate overnight in plastic wrap.

When ready to bake, divide dough in 4 pieces and roll out each piece ⅛ inch thick. (Keep remaining dough refrigerated until ready to roll.) Cut into crescent shapes with cookie cutter and place on buttered baking sheets. Or, if you don't want to roll dough, cut thin slices from roll, to make round cookies. Brush cookies with egg white and sprinkle with almonds and a mixture of cinnamon and 1 tablespoon sugar. Bake in a preheated 375° oven for 10 minutes or until lightly browned. Cool cookies on cake racks. Serve together with Macédoine of Fruit. Makes 3 dozen. Cookies will freeze.

## A Pleasant and Inexpensive Luncheon for a Crowd of 12 to 16

Salami cornucopias on pumpernickel
Cheese croquettes with tomato sauce
Green pepper salad
Ginger roll

The next time it's your turn to entertain members of your pet committee, try this menu.

### SALAMI CORNUCOPIAS ON PUMPERNICKEL

1 pound Italian salami, or any round, hard luncheon meat about 3 inches in diameter, thinly sliced
½ cup unsalted butter for filling, plus butter to form cornucopias
1 8-ounce can liver pâté
2 tablespoons brandy
½ teaspoon salt
½ teaspoon freshly cracked white pepper
Black olives or parsley, for garnish
Pumpernickel bread, thinly sliced

Remove rind from salami slices. Cut a slit from the edge of each slice to the center. Overlap cut edges to form a cone, pinching them together with a dab of butter. To make filling, cream butter with electric mixer; beat in pâté, brandy, and seasonings. Put mixture into a pastry bag fitted with a star tube and pipe into cornucopias. Decorate each with a bit of diced black olive or a small tuft of parsley, pressed into the filling, and place on small squares or rounds of pumpernickel.

## CHEESE CROQUETTES WITH TOMATO SAUCE

¾ cup butter
2 cups lightly spooned flour
1 quart milk
1 pound grated cheese,
   Cheddar, Swiss, or
   Gruyère
1 teaspoon salt, about
½ teaspoon freshly cracked
   white pepper

2 teaspoons Dijon mustard
4 egg yolks, lightly beaten
2 tablespoons chopped chives
3 beaten eggs
2 cups bread crumbs
   Fat for deep frying
   Tomato Sauce (recipe
   follows)

Melt the butter in a large saucepan over high heat and stir in 1 cup flour with wooden spatula. Cook, stirring, for 2 minutes; do not let it brown. Remove pan from heat, switch to a whisk, and add milk all at once, whisking vigorously. Return to heat and cook, still over high heat, whisking, until mixture comes to a boil; it will be very thick. Stir in cheese and whisk over heat until cheese melts and mixture is smooth. Add salt (but taste cheese mixture first—the cheese may be extra salty), pepper, and mustard and stir well. Stir a little of the sauce into the egg yolks, to warm them; then stir them into sauce. Stir in chives. Spread the mixture on a baking tray, cover with plastic wrap, and put in the refrigerator to chill for several hours, preferably overnight.

To form croquettes, pick up a good tablespoonful of the chilled mixture and, using the heel of your hand, very lightly shape it into a cork shape. Or cut shapes with cutters, if you wish. Coat the shapes with remaining 1 cup flour, patting off excess, then dip in beaten egg and roll in crumbs. Chill again for at least ½ hour. Heat 2 inches fat in saucepan or deep-fat fryer to 375° and fry croquettes, 2 or 3 at a time, for about 2 minutes or until nicely browned. Drain on paper towels and hold them in a 350° oven to keep warm while you fry remaining croquettes. Serve hot with Tomato Sauce.

### *TOMATO SAUCE*

½ cup olive oil
   ıps chopped onions
   ıely chopped cloves garlic
   -ounce cans Italian-style
   tomatoes

2 teaspoons salt
1 teaspoon freshly cracked
   black pepper

Heat the olive oil in a large saucepan. Stir in onions and garlic and cook over high heat, stirring, until golden. Do not let burn. Add tomatoes, mashing them, and cook until mixture thickens, about 30 minutes. Stir frequently to prevent sauce from sticking.

## GREEN PEPPER SALAD

5 cups very finely diced celery
3 green peppers, seeded and
   very finely diced
1 large, very finely diced,
   red onion
2 teaspoons salt

1 teaspoon freshly cracked
   black pepper
1 tablespoon Dijon mustard
2 tablespoons red wine vinegar
6 tablespoons vegetable oil
2 tablespoons chopped parsley

Combine diced vegetables in a serving bowl. Mix together salt, pepper, mustard, vinegar, and vegetable oil and pour over salad. Sprinkle with parsley and toss. Prepare ahead and marinate in refrigerator for at least 3 hours.

## GINGER ROLL

2 tablespoons vegetable oil
3 eggs
½ cup sugar
¼ teaspoon salt
⅔ cup lightly spooned cake
   flour
2 teaspoons baking powder
1 teaspoon cinnamon
1 teaspoon ground ginger

1 teaspoon ground allspice
¼ cup dark molasses

FILLING:
1½ cups apple sauce
½ cup apricot jam
1 teaspoon grated lemon peel
2 tablespoons brandy

Brush a jelly-roll pan with vegetable oil, then line it with waxed paper, letting the paper extend 4 inches on each end. Brush the paper with vegetable oil and set aside. Beat eggs in mixing bowl with sugar and salt until mixture is very thick and holds its shape (this will take about 5 minutes). Sift together flour, baking powder, and spices; add to egg mixture and fold in very gently. Fold in molasses. Spread mixture in prepared jelly-roll pan and bake in a preheated 375° oven for 12 to 14 minutes. Remove from oven, dust surface of mixture with granulated sugar, and turn out upside down onto 2 overlapping sheets of waxed paper. Peel off lining paper and roll up like a jelly roll. Chill for at least 1 hour. Unroll carefully. Mix filling ingredients together and spread over roll; roll it up again and chill before serving. *Recipe may be fully prepared ahead; it also freezes well, for up to 1 month.*

## Informal Lunch
### for 8

Hamburgers with green peppercorns
Red onion and black olive salad
Toasted French bread
Pears stuffed with Roquefort cheese

## HAMBURGERS WITH GREEN PEPPERCORNS

Here is a new way of preparing hamburgers that elevates them to company food. Green peppercorns are unripe peppercorns and come mainly from Madagascar. I like the ones packed in water rather than in strong-tasting brine or vinegar.

⅓ cup green peppercorns
2 chopped cloves garlic
3 pounds ground beef
   Salt, to taste
6 tablespoons butter

¼ cup red wine *or* 2 tablespoons brandy
2 tablespoons chopped shallots
1 teaspoon Dijon mustard
1 cup heavy cream

Drain the peppercorns and, if packed in vinegar, rinse them. Put into a mortar with the garlic and crush lightly. Shape ground beef into 8 patties ¾ to 1 inch thick; use a light touch—don't compress the beef. Salt the patties and press the pepper-garlic mixture on both sides. Heat 4 tablespoons butter in a heavy skillet and for rare meat sauté patties over high heat 3 minutes on each side—don't let them touch. Warning: the pepper may spatter. Remove patties to serving platter, scraping up any peppercorns that have fallen off. Deglaze the pan with red wine, or with flaming brandy. Add remaining 2 tablespoons butter; stir in shallots, mustard, and heavy cream. Bring to a boil and shake pan over heat until sauce thickens slightly. Taste for seasoning, and pour over patties.

## RED ONION AND BLACK OLIVE SALAD

5 red onions
1 cup finely chopped black
 olives
½ cup vegetable oil
2 tablespoons soy sauce
1 tablespoon dry sherry

1 tablespoon vinegar
½ teaspoon freshly cracked
 black pepper
2 tablespoons finely chopped
 parsley

Peel onions and slice very thin; put slices in a bowl and cover with ice water for 1 hour, until crisp. Drain and pat dry with paper towels. Place in salad bowl and sprinkle on chopped black olives. Combine oil, soy sauce, sherry, vinegar, and pepper. Pour over onions, sprinkle with chopped parsley, and refrigerate for about 3 hours; flavor improves as it marinates. Toss before serving.

## PEARS STUFFED WITH ROQUEFORT CHEESE

8 ripe but firm pears
1 pound Roquefort cheese

1 cup unsalted butter

Wash pears; do not peel. Remove cores with apple corer from blossom end, leaving stems on. Cut a slice from bottoms, so pears will stand upright on dessert plates. Beat Roquefort cheese and butter together until very creamy. Put mixture in a pastry bag fitted with a small rose tube and fill cavities of pears. Decorate pears with a ribbon of the cheese-butter mixture, up one side and down the other. Refrigerate if not serving immediately, but remove from refrigerator 1 hour before serving.

## A Robust Lunch
### for 8 after Tennis or Golf

Olive butter, radishes
Kielbasa in brioche with assorted mustards
Onions stuffed with onions
Mostarda (mustard fruit from Cremona, Italy)
Assorted cheeses and crackers

This menu offers your palate some good contrasts—sweetness, tartness, and blandness—and a variety of textures. The dishes are by no means as strong-tasting as they may sound. Butter smooths out the flavors in the olive butter, making it lovely and subtle in combination with crisp radishes. Onions lose their bite when they're baked. Mostarda is a mixture of fruits—apricots, pineapple, pears, peaches, cherries—preserved in a very sweet, beautifully clear syrup. It contains mustard, but you won't detect it. It comes from Cremona and Italians serve it as a classic accompaniment to ham and tongue. Cheese stores today urge shoppers to sample; you can try their recommendations, or collect some Muenster, Cheddar, and Port Salut to serve with unsalted crackers for dessert.

### OLIVE BUTTER

1 cup butter
1 1-pound can black olives, finely chopped
2 finely chopped cloves garlic
6 anchovy fillets, drained and chopped
½ teaspoon freshly cracked black pepper
1 teaspoon anisette, or any licorice-flavored liqueur
Salt, optional
Radishes
Pumpernickel bread

Cream butter with electric mixer. Add olives, garlic, anchovies, pepper, and anisette. Mix thoroughly, taste to see if it needs salt, and pack into a crock. Serve with plenty of whole radishes and small rounds of pumpernickel.

## KIELBASA IN BRIOCHE
## WITH ASSORTED MUSTARDS

2 pounds kielbasa
1 recipe brioche (see p. 11)
1 tablespoon Dijon mustard

1 egg yolk
Assorted mustards: Dijon,
Düsseldorf, Creole

Put sausage in saucepan and cover with cold water; bring to a boil and boil quite rapidly for 10 minutes, to remove grease. Drain sausage, and when cool enough to handle, remove and discard the casing. Roll out brioche dough a little longer and wider than sausage. Spread with mustard. Wrap sausage in dough, pinching to seal seam and tucking in ends. Place seam side down on a baking tray and brush dough all over with egg yolk beaten with a tablespoon of cold water. Cut 3 gashes in top to let out steam. (*Recipe can be made ahead to this point, covered with plastic wrap, and refrigerated overnight.*) When ready to proceed, let sausage and brioche stand at room temperature for about 40 minutes to rise—brioche does not have to double. Place in a preheated 375° oven for 35 to 40 minutes or until crust is nicely browned. Serve warm, cut in 1-inch slices, with an assortment of mustards.

## ONIONS STUFFED WITH ONIONS

8 medium-size onions, each
  about 2 inches in diameter
4 tablespoons butter or bacon
  fat
6 slices bacon, cooked and
  crumbled
2 tablespoons bread crumbs

2 tablespoons finely chopped
  parsley
½ teaspoon freshly cracked
  white pepper
½ cup chicken stock (see
  p. 278)

With a knife, cut out centers of onions, leaving a wall about ¼ inch thick. (Cut centers into 4 quarters and dig them out with a spoon.) Chop centers very finely. Heat butter or bacon fat in a skillet and cook chopped onion over high heat until transparent— do not brown. Stir in bacon; remove from heat and add bread crumbs, parsley, and pepper. Mix thoroughly. Stuff onion shells with mixture and place them in a buttered baking dish. (*Recipe can be prepared ahead to this point, or you can partially bake stuffed onions, undercooking them slightly and finishing them when you reheat.*) Pour on chicken stock, cover dish with foil, and place in a preheated 375° oven to bake until onions are barely tender, about 30 minutes.

## Summer Lunch for 4 Ladies and 8 Children

Deviled eggs
Cold barbecued chicken wings
Relishes, carrots, radishes, cucumbers,
pickles, and olives
Breadsticks
Alice Peterson's chocolate cheesecake

### DEVILED EGGS

12 hard-cooked eggs
¾ cup unsalted butter
1 tablespoon Dijon mustard
  *or* 3 tablespoons tomato
  paste

1½ teaspoons salt
5 or 6 drops Tabasco sauce
  Parsley, for garnish

Peel hard-cooked eggs and split them lengthwise. Remove yolks and rub them through a fine sieve into a mixer bowl. Beat until creamy and smooth. Beat in butter, 1 tablespoonful at a time, and continue beating until extremely light and fluffy. Season with mustard or tomato paste, salt, and Tabasco. Put the egg yolk mixture into a pastry bag fitted with a star tube and pipe it into the reserved egg whites—there's enough filling to pile it high. Decorate with tiny sprigs of parsley.

### COLD BARBECUED CHICKEN WINGS

Children adore chicken wings, and they are fairly inexpensive. When meaty (and they can be) they are fun to eat with one's fingers. They are also great for a picnic.

48 meaty chicken wings
1 12-ounce jar chili sauce
2 tablespoons Worcestershire
   sauce
½ cup cider vinegar
½ cup vegetable oil
½ cup firmly packed brown
   sugar
1 medium-size onion, grated
2 chopped cloves garlic
2 teaspoons salt
1 teaspoon freshly cracked
   black pepper

Lay chicken wings in a large roasting pan. Mix remaining ingredients together to make barbecue sauce and spread half of it over chicken. Bake in a preheated 375° oven for 30 minutes. Turn chicken wings over and spread with remaining barbecue sauce. Return to oven and bake for 30 minutes more, or until brown and tender. Run them under the broiler, if necessary, to brown. (*Recipe may be made ahead to this point.*) Cover and store in refrigerator, but bring to room temperature before serving.

## ALICE PETERSON'S CHOCOLATE CHEESECAKE

This is the best chocolate cheesecake I have ever tasted. Alice Peterson was the food editor of the New York *Daily News* for years and was always expert at developing recipes. This one is a gem.

18 graham crackers
½ cup butter, plus butter to
   grease pan
¼ cup plus ⅔ cup sugar
2 8-ounce packages cream
   cheese
2 6-ounce packages semi-
   sweet chocolate bits
½ cup strong black coffee
4 eggs, separated
2 tablespoons dark rum
⅛ teaspoon salt
1 cup heavy cream
   Shaved chocolate or cocoa,
   for garnish

Crush graham crackers to make coarse crumbs (packaged crumbs are too fine). Melt ½ cup butter and stir it and ¼ cup sugar into crumbs; mixture should look like wet sand. Butter the sides of a 9-inch springform pan and press graham cracker mixture against bottom and sides of pan. Set aside.

Bring cream cheese to room temperature. Melt chocolate in coffee over low heat. In electric mixer bowl, beat egg yolks until sticky; add ⅓ cup sugar and beat until pale yellow and thickened. Gradually beat in cream cheese, a bit at a time, and beat until it looks like whipped butter. This takes 5 to 10 minutes, depending on your mixer; but you can't overbeat this cheese mixture. Beat in rum and salt.

In another bowl, beat egg whites until foamy; add remaining ⅓ cup sugar gradually, a tablespoonful at a time, and beat until glossy, but not stiff. Set aside. With mixer on low speed, beat the hot coffee-chocolate mixture into cheese mixture—batter will be thin. Then fold in egg whites and pour into prepared pan. Place on the middle shelf of a preheated 350° oven and bake 1 hour. Turn off oven and leave cake in the oven, door closed, until oven is cold. The cake will crack as it bakes, and sink as it cools—this is normal.

To serve, loosen cake from pan with a small knife; invert on serving plate and remove springform. Whip the heavy cream over ice; do not sweeten it. Pack into a pastry bag fitted with a star tube, and pipe rosettes of whipped cream all over the top. Decorate with shaved chocolate curls or with cocoa, sieved and sifted over cake with a teaspoon. Serve at room temperature. If there is any cake left over, store it in refrigerator.

## A Refreshing Summer Lunch
### for 6

---

Avocado with crab meat

Tomatoes with chives

Hot baking powder biscuits

Meringue cake with peaches

When you can serve something that everyone likes in a dramatic new way, your luncheon will be talked about. Here's a familiar dish—avocado stuffed with crab meat—that looks like a large, beautifully decorated Easter egg when it is assembled and ready to be served. Scoop the avocado halves out in one piece, pile the crab meat into the shells, and place the avocado meat over the salad, rounded side up; then decorate.

## AVOCADO WITH CRAB MEAT

1 recipe crab-meat salad (see p. 52)
3 ripe avocados
3 tablespoons lime juice
2 hard-cooked eggs
2 tablespoons chopped parsley
¾ cup mayonnaise (see p. 283)
Watercress, for garnish

Make crab-meat salad and refrigerate. Split the avocados (unpeeled) lengthwise, remove pits, and carefully pry the flesh out in one piece. To do this, ease the tip of a tablespoon between flesh and skin until you can lift the flesh out. Take care not to split the shells, and set them aside. As you remove each avocado half, sprinkle it immediately with lime juice to help keep it from darkening. Spoon crab-meat salad into the *shells;* place avocado halves over the crab meat, rounded side up—it will look like a whole avocado again. Peel hard-cooked eggs and chop the whites and sieve the yolks. Sprinkle avocados with whites first, then yolks, then chopped parsley. Put mayonnaise in a pastry bag fitted with a small star tube and pipe a ribbon of mayonnaise around the seam of each avocado, where flesh and shell meet. Add a mayonnaise rosette on top. Store avocados in refrigerator until ready to serve; they'll hold well for up to 2 hours. Garnish plates with watercress.

## TOMATOES WITH CHIVES

3 large tomatoes
¼ cup finely chopped chives
1 teaspoon salt
½ teaspoon freshly cracked black pepper
3 tablespoons tarragon vinegar
2 teaspoons sugar

Scald tomatoes for 10 seconds in boiling water (or hold them, on a fork, in a gas flame until the skin splits). Peel and slice vertically, from stem to bottom. Arrange them, overlapping, on a long narrow platter. Sprinkle with chives, salt, pepper, vinegar, and sugar.

## HOT BAKING POWDER BISCUITS

2 cups lightly spooned flour  
2 teaspoons baking powder  
1 teaspoon salt  

1 teaspoon sugar  
4 tablespoons butter  
¾ cup milk  

Put flour, baking powder, salt, and sugar in a bowl; stir to mix. Rub in the butter, using your fingers or a pastry blender, until the mixture looks like coarse cornmeal. Add milk and mix well to make a soft dough. Turn out on a lightly floured board and pat out ¾ inch thick. Cut biscuits with a 2-inch round cutter or cut in 2-inch squares with a sharp knife. Place on well-buttered baking tray and bake in a preheated 450° oven for about 12 minutes, or until biscuits are golden brown. Serve with a crock of butter. Makes 12 2-inch biscuits.

## MERINGUE CAKE WITH PEACHES

½ cup butter  
1½ cups sugar  
4 eggs, separated  
¼ cup milk  
½ teaspoon vanilla extract  
1 cup lightly spooned flour  
1¼ teaspoons baking powder  
⅛ teaspoon salt  

¼ cup chopped nuts, walnuts  
   or pecans  
1 cup heavy cream  
2 tablespoons confectioners'  
   sugar  
2 fresh peaches, peeled and  
   diced, or 4 canned peach  
   halves, diced  

Grease 2 8-inch cake pans and line bottoms with waxed paper. Preheat oven to 350°. In electric mixer bowl, cream the butter, slowly add ½ cup of the sugar, and beat until light and fluffy. Beat in egg yolks, one at a time, then add milk and vanilla. Sift the flour and baking powder together and add to egg yolk mixture, beating slowly until mixed. Mixture will be thick. Stop the beater, scrape the sides of the bowl, and continue beating at least 2 minutes. Divide the batter between the 2 pans, smoothing the tops with a spatula.

In another bowl, beat the egg whites with salt until stiff. Add remaining 1 cup sugar, 1 tablespoon at a time, beating constantly. Continue to beat until mixture is like marshmallow and feels smooth when you pinch it. Spread meringue over cake batter in pans, and sprinkle *one* layer only with chopped nuts. Bake for 30 minutes. To assemble the cake, whip the heavy cream, sweeten it with confectioners' sugar, and fold in peaches. Place the un-nutted layer, meringue side down, on a serving plate. Spread with whipped cream and peaches. Place second layer, nut side up, on top. Chill in refrigerator before serving.

## A Late Lunch
## on a Wintry Day for 8

Hot oyster stew
Gougère
Black radish slices vinaigrette
Chocolate mousse

### HOT OYSTER STEW

1 quart oysters
½ cup butter
2 quarts half-and-half, scalded
2 teaspoons salt

1 teaspoon freshly cracked
    white pepper
Paprika
2 tablespoons finely chopped
    parsley

Heat oysters in their liquid over high heat until edges begin to curl, about 2 to 3 minutes. Add butter, cut in pieces, and scalded half-and-half, still piping hot. Season with salt and pepper and pour into heated tureen. Dust with paprika and sprinkle with chopped parsley. Don't boil or overcook this stew; if you do, the oysters will get rubbery.

### GOUGÈRE

Imagine cream puff pastry, sharply flavored with cheese and baked in a ring until it's puffed, crusty, and golden brown. That's gougère, popular in Burgundy. It's good hot or cold, with a glass of Burgundy wine.

4 tablespoons butter
1 cup water
1 cup lightly spooned flour
4 eggs
1 tablespoon Dijon mustard
1 teaspoon salt

½ teaspoon freshly cracked
   white pepper
1½ cups grated Parmesan
   cheese
1 egg yolk
8 thin triangular slices of
   Gruyère cheese

To make *pâte à choux,* or cream puff paste, place the butter, cut in pieces, and the water in a saucepan and bring to a boil. As soon as butter melts, dump in flour all at once and stir vigorously. Beat the mixture over high heat until it leaves sides of pan and starts to film bottom, about 2 minutes. Remove pan from heat and beat in eggs, one at a time. Beat in each egg thoroughly before adding the next, and beat about 5 minutes more, until mixture is shiny, using the flat whip of an electric mixer if you have one. Beat in mustard, salt, pepper, and 1 cup of the grated Parmesan cheese. (*Recipe can be made ahead to this point.*)

Put mixture into a pastry bag fitted with a large (dime-size) round tube. Grease baking sheets or line with baking parchment and draw 2 8-inch rings (if you can use an 8-inch cake pan as a guide). Pipe *pâte à choux* mixture in a circle just inside these rings. Brush tops but not sides of rings with egg wash (egg yolk beaten with 1 tablespoon cold water), balance 4 cheese triangles along the tops of each ring, and sprinkle with remaining Parmesan cheese. Bake in a preheated 450° oven for 15 minutes. Turn heat to 350° and bake 10 minutes, then to 325° and bake for another 20 minutes. Serve warm, cut in wedges.

## BLACK RADISH SLICES VINAIGRETTE

Black radishes look like large black turnips—about the size of a fist; you can find them during the late fall and winter in gourmet or middle European markets. They're snowy white inside, with a fairly sharp taste. When you slice them paper-thin and put them into cold water, they ruffle. The black edges outline the ruffles and they really look fantastic—no one knows what they are.

Scrub 4 or 5 black radishes and slice them paper-thin on a vegetable cutter or mandoline. Soak them in cold water for about ½ hour. Put them in a chilled salad bowl, pour on French vinaigrette dressing (see p. 282), and toss. Let marinate 2 hours. Sprinkle with 2 tablespoons chopped parsley.

## CHOCOLATE MOUSSE

½ pound dark sweet chocolate
5 tablespoons water *or* strong
   black coffee
5 eggs, separated
2 tablespoons orange liqueur,
   optional

Sweetened whipped cream,
   optional
Chocolate for garnish,
   optional

Cut chocolate into little pieces and melt in a saucepan, with water or coffee, over very low heat. Stir while melting, and don't let it get too hot. Beat egg whites until stiff but not dry. In another bowl, beat egg yolks to mix, then whisk chocolate into them. Beat in orange liqueur, if desired. Stir a spoonful of egg whites into chocolate mixture, to lighten it, then fold in remaining egg whites. Pour mousse into a crystal serving bowl, or into individual small white pots, and place in the refrigerator to chill, at least 2 hours, or overnight. Serve plain, or decorated with rosettes of sweetened whipped cream and garnished with a grating of chocolate.

## *A Holiday-Season Luncheon for 6*

Passatelli soup
Ham roulade
Raw mushroom salad with a dressing of
sour cream, caraway, and chives
Steamed chocolate pudding with hard sauce

If you're looking for a new and unusual way to use up leftovers from a holiday ham, try this delicious ham roulade, which can be found on p. 36. Instead of the mustard sour cream, serve it with a lemon butter sauce (made by melting ½ cup butter, then adding the juice of ½ lemon and 1 tablespoon chopped parsley) or plain with Dijon mustard. The steamed pudding adds a further traditional holiday touch. The passatelli soup is adapted from a soup I had in Rome, and the ham roulade is one of my own original recipes.

## PASSATELLI SOUP

2 eggs
4 to 6 tablespoons bread
   crumbs
1 tablespoon plus 1 teaspoon
   flour
6 tablespoons grated Parmesan
   cheese
6 tablespoons soft butter

2 tablespoons finely chopped
   parsley
½ teaspoon salt
½ teaspoon freshly cracked
   white pepper
¼ teaspoon freshly grated
   nutmeg
9 cups strong chicken stock
   (see p. 278)

Mix together in a bowl eggs, 3 tablespoons bread crumbs, flour, cheese, butter, parsley, salt, pepper, and nutmeg, working the mixture with a wooden spatula to form a stiff dough. Add more bread crumbs if necessary. (*Recipe may be made ahead to this point and refrigerated in covered container.*) Bring chicken stock to a boil. Put the cheese dough into a spaetzle machine or colander with large holes, hold it over boiling stock, and press dough through machine or colander so that it drops, in small bits, into stock. In 1 to 2 minutes, the tiny dumplings will rise to the surface; turn off heat and let stand for about 5 minutes before serving.

## RAW MUSHROOM SALAD WITH A DRESSING OF SOUR CREAM, CARAWAY, AND CHIVES

1½ pounds very thinly sliced
    mushrooms
¾ cup sour cream
1 tablespoon caraway seeds

4 tablespoons chopped fresh
   chives
½ teaspoon salt
¼ teaspoon freshly cracked
   white pepper

Put sliced mushrooms in a bowl; mix together remaining ingredients and pour over mushrooms. Toss to coat mushrooms well and marinate for about 2 hours in the refrigerator. Taste for seasoning, and stir again just before serving.

## STEAMED CHOCOLATE PUDDING
## WITH HARD SAUCE

2 tablespoons butter to grease
  mold
6 ounces dark sweet chocolate
3 eggs
1½ cups sugar
3 tablespoons soft butter

3 tablespoons orange
  marmalade
3 cups lightly spooned flour
2 teaspoons baking powder
½ teaspoon salt
1½ cups heavy cream
Hard Sauce (recipe follows)

Heavily butter an 8-cup steamed pudding mold or 2-quart bowl. Melt chocolate over very low heat, stirring constantly with a wooden spatula, and set aside. Beat eggs in electric mixer bowl; add sugar gradually, beating until light and fluffy. Beat in cooled (but not set) chocolate, soft butter, and orange marmalade. Sift flour with baking powder and salt and beat into egg-sugar mixture alternately with cream, about one third at a time. Pour batter into mold; it should be about ¾ inch from top of mold. (If you have extra batter, put in custard cup, cover, and steam like the big pudding.) Fasten lid tightly (or cover the 2-quart bowl with cloth and then aluminum foil, tied tightly with string) and stand mold on a rack in a large pot filled halfway up sides of mold with boiling water. Cover pot and steam the pudding in boiling water on top of the stove for 2 hours. Replenish boiling water as necessary. (*Recipe may be made ahead to this point. Leave the pudding in the mold and reheat in boiling water. Or steam it for 1½ hours and reheat for ½ hour.*) Turn pudding out onto a platter and serve with hard sauce.

### HARD SAUCE

Cream ½ cup butter in mixing bowl and gradually add 1 cup confectioners' sugar. Beat in 1 teaspoon lemon juice and 2 tablespoons rum, brandy, sherry, or more lemon juice. Beat until fluffy.

## *Danish Open-face Sandwich*
## *Luncheon for 12*

Assorted Danish open-face sandwiches
Ice-cold beer
Brandy curls

### ASSORTED DANISH OPEN-FACE SANDWICHES

Danish open-face sandwiches are a delicious and eye-pleasing departure from the usual. Really try to stretch your imagination in decorating them! They always taste best if assembled just before serving.

No matter what combination of ingredients you select, first butter the bread thoroughly with a thin layer of softened butter. This will prevent the bread from getting soggy. Be sure to have on hand ample mayonnaise (see p. 283), mustard mayonnaise (mayonnaise flavored to taste with Dijon mustard), and whipped cream cheese to spread or pipe (from pastry bags fitted with small star tubes) onto sandwiches. For garnish, make tomato and cucumber "riders": cut the vegetables into thin slices, make a cut from the edge to the center of each slice, grasp the resulting ends, and pull them apart, twisting the slice as you pull. Make orange or lemon riders in the same way.

Several sandwich suggestions follow the ingredients list. Count 2 sandwiches per person.

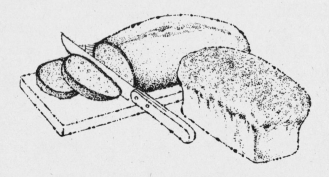

1 loaf Danish rye bread, thinly sliced
1 loaf pumpernickel, thinly sliced
Butter
Mayonnaise
Dijon mustard
Cream cheese
Danish liver pâté
Bacon strips, crisply fried
Hard-cooked egg, sliced
Scrambled egg
Cooked chicken, sliced
Rare roast beef, sliced
Steak Tartare (see p. 221)
Boiled ham, sliced
Danish salami, sliced
Tiny canned shrimp
Pickled herring
Smoked salmon
Danish blue cheese
Coleslaw
Potato salad
Tomatoes, sliced
Cucumbers, sliced
Raw mushrooms, sliced
Onion rings
Lettuce leaves
Watercress sprigs
Gherkins
Sweet pickles
Capers
Orange slices
Lemon slices
Cooked prunes
Black olives, sliced
Parsley, chopped and in sprigs
Black caviar
Chives, chopped

## SANDWICH SUGGESTIONS

1. Lettuce, liver pâté, a few slices of raw mushroom, a sweet pickle, and a piece of crisply fried bacon, all topped with a tomato rider.

2. Lettuce, 4 overlapping slices hard-cooked egg on 1 side of the bread, overlapping tomato slices on the other side, mayonnaise piped down the center, and a dab of black caviar for garnish.

3. Three slices of ham, rolled up, topped with mustard mayonnaise, an orange rider, 2 cooked prunes, and a small sprig of parsley.

4. Ham slices topped with a rider made by sandwiching a slice of cucumber between 2 slices of tomato. Stand the rider on a ribbon of cream cheese sprinkled with chopped chives.

5. Lettuce and sliced chicken, topped with a rosette of mayonnaise, 2 cucumber riders, and a sprig of watercress.

6. Two slices roast beef topped with coleslaw nested in a bit of lettuce. Decorate with tomato rider and a gherkin thinly sliced at one end and spread to look like a fan.

7. Lettuce, overlapping slices of salami, onion rings, and a sprig of parsley.

8. Tiny shrimp, lined up in rows, with mayonnaise piped down the center, garnished with a bit of lettuce, a lemon rider, and chopped parsley.

9. Lettuce, pickled herring, and overlapping onion rings, garnished on one corner with tomato sliver and sprig of parsley.

10. Lettuce and overlapping thin slices of Danish blue cheese, garnished with a row of sliced black olives.

11. Steak tartare, decorated in a crisscross pattern with back of knife, garnished with pickles and/or capers.

12. Smoked salmon, plain with freshly cracked black pepper or topped with a diagonal stripe of scrambled egg.

13. Two slices roast beef topped with potato salad, garnished with watercress and tomato rider.

## BRANDY CURLS

1¼ cups lightly spooned flour
⅔ cup sugar
1 tablespoon ground ginger
¼ teaspoon salt
½ cup molasses
½ cup butter

4 tablespoons brandy
1 cup heavy cream
2 tablespoons confectioners' sugar
3 tablespoons chopped crystallized ginger

Sift flour, sugar, ginger, and salt together. In a saucepan, bring molasses and butter to a boil over medium-high heat. Remove from heat and gradually stir in dry ingredients. Return to medium-high heat, stirring until blended. Remove from heat and stir in 3 tablespoons brandy. Drop batter by half teaspoonfuls on a greased baking sheet, 3 inches apart. Bake only 6 cookies at one time, in a preheated 300° oven, for 8 minutes, or until they stop bubbling. Cool 1 minute. Quickly remove each cookie with a spatula and drape it over a wood dowel or small rolling pin so that it will harden in a curl. Or roll it at once around the handle of a wooden spoon to make a scroll. When cool, store curls in an airtight container or plastic bags. When ready to serve, whip cream, adding confectioners' sugar, chopped ginger, and remaining 1 tablespoon brandy. Put cream in a pastry bag fitted with a star tube and pipe it into cookie curls. Or fill with vanilla ice cream. Recipe makes 50 curls.

## A Country-Kitchen Luncheon
## for 6

Polenta ring mold with
sautéed fluted mushroom caps
Braised celery
Oranges Grand Marnier

### POLENTA RING MOLD WITH
### SAUTÉED FLUTED MUSHROOM CAPS

½ pound thinly sliced
  prosciutto ham
1 recipe polenta (see p. 19)
8 ounces mozzarella cheese,
  diced

½ recipe Tomato Sauce (see
  p. 64) or 1 recipe Pesto
  (see p. 202)
1 pound Sautéed Fluted Mushroom Caps (see p. 284)

Brush an 8-cup ring mold with vegetable oil and line it with
overlapping slices of prosciutto ham, letting slices overhang rim
of mold. Spoon half the polenta mixture into the prepared mold
and bang the mold to settle it. Spread with diced mozzarella.
Spoon on remaining polenta and bang the mold again. Fold ham
ends over top. (*Recipe can be made ahead to this point.*) Set
mold in a pan of hot water, with the water three-quarters of the
way up the mold, and bake in a preheated 350° oven for 25 minutes. You can hold this dish in the water bath (oven turned off)
for up to 2 hours, or let it cool and reheat it in the water bath.
Before unmolding, take mold out of the water bath and let stand
for 5 minutes. Then run a knife around the edge to loosen it and
turn it out on a serving dish. Serve with Tomato Sauce or Pesto.
Fill center or ring with Sautéed Fluted Mushrooms.

### BRAISED CELERY

3 heads celery
2 teaspoons salt
3 tablespoons chopped shallots
1 cup beef stock (see p. 277)
3 tablespoons butter

½ teaspoon freshly cracked
  black pepper
2 tablespoons freshly chopped
  parsley

Cut off tops and trim roots of celery to make from each head a heart about 6 to 8 inches long; cut them in half lengthwise and put them in a saucepan. Cover with cold water, add 1 teaspoon salt, and parboil 10 minutes. Drain and place in an ovenproof serving dish. Scatter shallots over celery, pour on beef stock, dot with butter, and sprinkle with remaining 1 teaspoon salt and the pepper. Lay a piece of buttered waxed paper or aluminum foil over the celery and bake in a preheated 350° oven until celery is barely tender, from 30 to 45 minutes. (*Recipe can be made ahead and reheated.*) Sprinkle with chopped parsley before serving.

## ORANGES GRAND MARNIER

Peel 6 oranges, removing all the white membrane. Slice them crosswise in very thin slices, sprinkle with about 2 tablespoons sugar and ½ cup Grand Marnier (or other orange liqueur), and let macerate for 30 minutes or so.

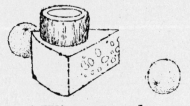

## A Winter Lunch
### for 12

Radishes with olive butter
Black bean soup with garnishes
Onion pie
Fruit and cheese

## RADISHES WITH OLIVE BUTTER

Scrub 3 or 4 black radishes—available in the fall and winter from gourmet and middle European markets—and slice them paper-thin on a vegetable cutter or mandoline. Soak them in cold water for about ½ hour. Scrub and trim 2 bunches of red and white radishes, but leave stems on. Serve with olive butter (see p. 68).

## BLACK BEAN SOUP WITH GARNISHES

1½ pounds dry black beans
2 quarts chicken stock
　(see p. 278)
1 2-pound smoked pork
　shoulder butt *or* leftover
　ham bone with meat
　clinging to it
1½ cups diced onions
1 cup diced carrots
1 cup diced celery
2 teaspoons finely chopped
　garlic
1 tablespoon salt, more if
　needed

1 teaspoon freshly cracked
　black pepper
½ cup dry sherry or Madeira

GARNISHES:
1 cup finely diced green
　pepper
1 cup finely diced onion
1 cup cooked rice
2 thinly sliced lemons
1 cup sour cream
1 cup chopped ham

Rinse beans well, cover with cold water, and let stand overnight. Drain beans, put them in a kettle, and cover with chicken stock. Add pork butt or ham bone, onions, carrots, celery, garlic, salt, and pepper. Bring to a boil over high heat, cover kettle, turn heat to simmer, and cook until beans are tender, about 3 to 4 hours. Remove half the beans from the soup and puree them in blender or food mill, using the fine disk; return to soup. Add sherry or Madeira, taste for seasoning, and serve hot. Pass garnishes in individual bowls. This soup is better if made the day before, and it will freeze for up to 1 month.

## ONION PIE

1 pound yellow onions, plus 1
　large yellow onion
2 tablespoons bacon fat
2 eggs
2 egg yolks
2 teaspoons Dijon mustard
½ cup grated Parmesan cheese

1¼ cups light cream, scalded
1 10-inch partly baked pâte
　brisée shell (see p. 288)
Flour
1 recipe beer batter (see
　p. 285)
Fat for deep frying

Slice 1 pound onions and cook them slowly in bacon fat, stirring, until they are limp, about 5 minutes. Drain on paper towels. Beat together lightly eggs, egg yolks, mustard, and Parmesan cheese. Stir in onions and add hot scalded cream slowly, stirring, so as not to curdle eggs. Pour into partly baked pâte brisée shell and bake in a preheated 350° oven for 25 minutes, or until custard tests done. (*Recipe can be made ahead to this point and reheated; it will also freeze.*)

While pie is baking, prepare garnish: Slice remaining large onion ¼ inch thick, separate into rings, and dust with flour. Dip rings into beer batter and deep-fry in 2 inches of hot fat (375°). Overlap them around edge of pie.

## A Light, Easy-to-Prepare Lunch for 4

Sautéed bay scallops
Mixed yellow and green beans,
with shallots and butter
Tomato salad
Dessert omelette

### SAUTÉED BAY SCALLOPS

1½ pounds bay scallops
½ cup flour
½ cup butter
Juice of ½ lemon

1 teaspoon salt
½ teaspoon freshly cracked
    white pepper
2 tablespoons chopped parsley

Dry scallops well and roll in flour. Heat butter in a skillet; when it's foaming, add scallops and shake them over heat for 3 to 4 minutes—do not overcook. Sprinkle with lemon juice, salt, pepper, and parsley and give them another shake. Serve at once.

### MIXED YELLOW AND GREEN BEANS, WITH SHALLOTS AND BUTTER

¾ pound yellow wax beans
¾ pound green beans
1 tablespoon salt
4 tablespoons butter

3 tablespoons finely chopped
    shallots
1 teaspoon salt
½ teaspoon freshly cracked
    black pepper

Tip and tail the beans and put them in boiling salted water. Boil uncovered for 7 minutes. Drain; then refresh them in cold water. (*May be cooked in advance to this point and refrigerated*.) When ready to serve, heat butter in a small pan and sauté the shallots over high heat for a minute or two. Set aside. Put the beans in a skillet and shake them over high heat until they are completely dry. Dress them with butter and shallots and season with 1 teaspoon salt and the pepper.

## TOMATO SALAD

4 medium-size tomatoes
1 large red onion
1 recipe French vinaigrette
dressing (see p. 282)

2 tablespoons finely chopped
capers
2 tablespoons finely chopped
parsley

Peel tomatoes, first dropping them in boiling water for 10 seconds to loosen skins, and slice. Peel and slice onion very thinly. Layer tomato and onion in a salad bowl, sprinkling each layer with vinaigrette. Sprinkle capers and parsley over salad and let stand in a cool place (not the refrigerator) until ready to serve.

## DESSERT OMELETTE

4 tablespoons sugar
4 egg yolks
1 tablespoon vanilla extract *or*
liqueur such as Cointreau
or Grand Marnier

5 egg whites
2 tablespoons confectioners'
sugar

In electric mixer bowl, beat together sugar and egg yolks until very thick, about 5 minutes. Beat in flavoring. (*May be prepared ahead to this point.*) In another bowl, beat egg whites until very stiff. Fold ⅓ of the egg whites into egg yolk mixture to lighten it. Then lightly and quickly fold in remaining egg whites. Mound ⅓ of omelette mixture in an ovenproof serving dish. Put remaining mixture into a large pastry bag fitted with a large star tube, and pipe it in swirls up and down and around the sides of the base mound. Sift confectioners' sugar over the omelette and place it in a preheated 375° oven to bake until set, about 7 minutes.

## A *Low-Calorie Lunch*
## *for 4*

Consommé Normande (see p. 119)
Sautéed crab meat
Lemon-dressed lettuce
Fruit and champagne

An elegant lunch for those watching their weight. The Consommé Normande is an extremely delicate and successful light soup, and the crunchiness of the lettuce is just right with the crab.

### SAUTÉED CRAB MEAT

If you cannot find fresh crab meat, use frozen; canned crab meat is the third choice.

| | |
|---|---|
| 1 pound lump crab meat, preferably fresh | ½ teaspoon salt |
| 2 tablespoons butter | ¼ teaspoon freshly cracked white pepper |
| 1 tablespoon lemon juice | 1 tablespoon chopped parsley |

Pick over crab meat to remove any bits of shell or filament. Heat butter in a skillet; when it's foaming, add crab meat and sprinkle with lemon juice, salt, and pepper. Toss over high heat about 5 minutes or until heated through. Serve immediately, sprinkled with chopped parsley.

### LEMON-DRESSED LETTUCE

Wash leaves from 2 small heads of tender lettuce, roll in towels, and chill. When ready to serve, toss with the juice of 1 lemon, ½ teaspoon salt, and ¼ teaspoon freshly cracked black pepper.

## FRUIT AND CHAMPAGNE

3 or 4 ripe peaches or
   nectarines
1 pint raspberries or strawberries
2 tablespoons Curaçao or
   Cointreau

2 tablespoons honey
1 pint orange, lemon, or
   raspberry ice
1 large bottle champagne

Peel and slice the peaches or nectarines; wash and drain the berries and place all in a bowl. Drizzle with liqueur and honey. When ready to serve, spoon fruit ice into goblets, fill with fruit, and flood with champagne. You'll have enough champagne left for 4 glasses, too.

## *Summer Lunch at Tables under a Shade Tree for 8*

Chaudfroid chicken on cold capered rice
Fava beans with coarse salt
Raspberries with chilled framboise

Because it's spectacular—and completely do-ahead—chaudfroid chicken is always worth a repeat. In this version, skip the pâté and arrange the decorated chicken breasts on a bed of cold capered rice instead of chopped aspic. Fava beans are crisp and different; eat them with your fingers, like radishes. Dip the raspberries with your fingers, too. Under a shade tree, this meal is like a picnic.

## CHAUDFROID CHICKEN
## ON COLD CAPERED RICE

Follow directions for Chaudfroid Chicken (see p. 47), allowing ½ chicken breast per person (4 whole breasts). You'll need only enough aspic to coat the chicken breasts, so make aspic from 2 cups chicken stock, 4 teaspoons unflavored gelatine, 2 teaspoons tomato paste, and a tiny pinch of salt; clarify with 1 egg white.

### COLD CAPERED RICE

| | |
|---|---|
| 1 cup long-grain rice | 2 tablespoons wine vinegar |
| 1 teaspoon salt | 2 teaspoons Dijon mustard |
| ½ teaspoon freshly cracked | ¼ cup drained capers |
| black pepper | 2 tablespoons chopped parsley |
| ¼ cup olive oil | |

Put rice, salt, pepper, and 2 cups of water in a small heavy pan with a tight-fitting lid. Bring to a boil, cover, reduce heat, and simmer, covered, for 20 minutes. Put cooked rice in a bowl and add oil, vinegar, mustard, capers, and parsley. Toss to mix, and chill. Spread on serving platter and arrange chaudfroid chicken breasts on top.

### FAVA BEANS WITH COARSE SALT

Shell fresh young fava beans (sometimes called broad beans), allowing 6 to 8 beans per person, and serve them raw, with a dish of coarse salt on the side to dip them in.

### RASPBERRIES WITH CHILLED FRAMBOISE

Heap fresh raspberries—¾ cup for each serving—on individual plates garnished with leaves. (Use any beautiful green leaves you can find, such as maple, magnolia, or grape; if you have none in your yard, get some from the florist.) Serve with icy-cold framboise and confectioners' sugar on the side; guests dip the berries into the framboise and then the sugar.

# Dinners

If you wish to give a successful dinner party, build the guest list with as much care as you plan the menu. The invitation "come to dinner" means "come for the evening." If you spend hours ahead of time perfecting the food, you deserve a reward: hours of good conversation. Make sure you get it by mixing in new friends with old. Always the same group means always the same talk, and that can be as boring as always serving roast beef. A surprisingly good conversation starter—or "picker-upper"—for people meeting each other for the first time is the food they are eating. With this in mind, I plan food guests can talk about—at least one dish in the menu that's unfamiliar or unusual.

A cardinal rule in planning any dinner party, whether it is an informal or formal occasion, is to be realistic about what you can do given the time you have at your disposal, the work space in your kitchen, the refrigerator and freezer storage available, whether or not you have two ovens, whether you will be hiring help for the evening, and—not least—your talent as a cook. Always plan a menu you can manage, so that you will be relaxed and at ease when your guests arrive.

Three or possibly four courses for dinner are ample, as is a one-vegetable accompaniment to the meat if you are also serving a salad. Add formality to your dinner by serving the salad as a separate course after the main course. Never follow a rich first or main course with a too rich dessert. Be serene about cutting down on food, knowing that most hostesses tend to serve too much. A shorter menu, with each dish perfectly prepared, is the better showcase for your talents. Knowledgeable guests with chic palates appreciate this.

Think your menu through to be certain that a good part of it is truly make-ahead and that there are only as many last-minute saucing, reheating, or unmolding steps as you can handle. Read the recipes in advance from beginning to end, check your cupboards for supplies, and complete your shopping list.

The season of the year is usually my starting point for menu-thinking. Strawberries ripened in Pennsylvania's warm June sun just taste better to me than California's December crop airlifted east, miracle though that may be. You'll see I've indulged this personal prejudice by labeling many of the menus in this chapter as particularly suited to either summer or winter. Others I have designated as formal or informal in the kinds of dishes offered and their manner of presentation.

No matter what the season or occasion, though, I hope you will approach the menus here in a spirit of openness. They are not intended to be rigid fiats, but suggestions inviting your active participation. If a given menu seems too rich for the guests you have in mind, make a substitution: a green salad for a creamed vegetable, a fruit compote for a chocolate mousse. Relax—and experiment. It's half the fun!

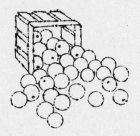

## A Potluck Dinner
### for 4

Chicken pie
Leeks vinaigrette
Hot chocolate mint soufflé

### CHICKEN PIE

1 recipe sour cream pastry
(see p. 288)
3 pounds chicken pieces
2 cups chicken stock (see
p. 278)
⅓ cup chopped carrot
¾ cup chopped onion
½ cup chopped celery
6 hard-cooked eggs
½ pound thickly sliced mushrooms

4 tablespoons butter
4 tablespoons flour
1 cup light cream
¼ cup heavy cream
2 tablespoons chopped parsley
1 teaspoon salt
½ teaspoon freshly cracked
white pepper
1 egg, lightly beaten

Make pastry and put it in the refrigerator to chill for at least 1½ hours. In a saucepan, cover chicken pieces with chicken stock, add carrot, onion, and celery, and bring to a boil over high heat. Reduce heat to simmer and simmer, covered, for 25 minutes. Cool chicken in stock. When chicken is cool enough to handle, remove skin and bones, reserving stock to make sauce. Cut chicken in large pieces and put it in a bowl with hard-cooked eggs, cut in half lengthwise, and mushrooms. Set aside.

Boil reserved chicken stock to reduce it to 1 cup, and make sauce: melt butter in a saucepan, stir in flour with a wooden spatula, and cook, stirring, over high heat for 2 minutes; do not let it brown. Take pan off heat, change to a whisk, and add strained chicken stock and light cream all at once, whisking vigorously. Return pan to high heat and cook, stirring with whisk, until sauce comes to a boil and thickens. Thin it with heavy cream as necessary—the sauce should be of coating consistency. Add chopped parsley, salt, and pepper and carefully fold sauce into the chicken-egg-mushroom mixture. Pour into a 9-inch pie pan and set it in the refrigerator to chill, for at least ½ hour.

When chicken has chilled, roll out pastry on a lightly floured board, about ½ inch thick. Brush the rim of the pie pan with beaten egg and lay crust over chicken, pressing edge to rim. Trim neatly. Cut 2 slits in center of crust. Cut pastry trimmings into leaves or flower shapes to decorate top. Brush the crust with egg, add decorations and brush them with egg, too. (*Recipe may be prepared ahead to this point. Omit hard-cooked eggs if you plan to freeze it—it can be frozen for up to 1 month.*) Put the pie pan on a baking sheet and bake in a preheated 375° oven for 40 minutes. Be sure that the crust, which is thick, is baked through.

## LEEKS VINAIGRETTE

12 leeks
 2 cups water
 1 tablespoon salt

1 recipe French vinaigrette dressing (see p. 282)
2 tablespoons chopped chives, for garnish

Cut the roots and tops off the leeks, leaving about 1 inch of green, split lengthwise, and hold under running water, separating the layers, to wash thoroughly. Put them in a saucepan, cover with salted water, and cook, uncovered, over medium heat until barely tender, about 15 minutes. Drain them in a sieve and rinse under cold water. Leave them in the sieve to dry and put in refrigerator to chill slightly, about 15 minutes. Make vinaigrette, arrange leeks in a serving dish, cover with vinaigrette, sprinkle with chopped chives, and chill until ready to serve.

## HOT CHOCOLATE MINT SOUFFLÉ

Butter and sugar to coat soufflé dish
6 ounces dark sweet chocolate
1¼ cups light cream
3 tablespoons butter
4 tablespoons flour
1 tablespoon vanilla extract *or* seeds scraped from 1 inch of vanilla bean

¼ cup white crème de menthe
4 egg yolks
4 tablespoons sugar, plus sugar to sprinkle on top
6 egg whites
Pinch of salt
Confectioners' sugar

Butter a 6-cup soufflé dish and sprinkle with sugar on bottom and sides, knocking out excess. Melt chocolate in cream over medium-high heat, stirring occasionally. In another pan, melt butter, stir in flour, and cook, stirring, for 2 minutes—do not let it brown. Remove from heat and add chocolate-cream mixture. Return to medium-high heat and stir until smooth and thick. Remove from heat and let cool slightly. Add vanilla and crème de menthe. In a large bowl, beat egg yolks with sugar until light and fluffy. Add chocolate mixture and blend thoroughly. (*Recipe can be made ahead to this point.*) Beat egg whites with a pinch of salt until stiff. Fold into chocolate mixture. Pour into prepared soufflé dish and sprinkle top with sugar. Bake in a preheated 375° oven until firm, about 20 minutes. Sift confectioners' sugar over soufflé and serve at once.

## An Autumn Dinner for 6, with an Alsatian Touch

Rack of pork
Red cabbage
Mashed potatoes and celeriac
Apple chausson with sour cream

When fall shades into winter, I get hungry for the hearty Alsatian cooking I grew up with. This menu borrows from both the German and French traditions of the border province of Alsace—pork and red cabbage, fruit turnover. The celeriac and potatoes make a wonderful companion to pork.

### RACK OF PORK

Notice that the pork roast is carved as a saddle—that means that, instead of cutting between the bones, you carve the meat in long strips. An interesting twist to serving pork.

1 center-cut pork loin roast containing 8 rib chops, about 6 to 7 pounds
1 tablespoon salt
1 teaspoon freshly cracked black pepper
2 slivered cloves garlic
1 piece bacon rind, 5 x 8 inches

Trim gristle and fat from roast to expose about 2 inches of the rib bones. Rub·meat all over with salt and pepper. Poke slivers of garlic into the meat by inserting the point of a small knife in the fatty side and using the knife blade as a slide to push slivers into holes. Cut bacon rind into strips ½ inch wide and 5 inches long, tie each in a loop, and arrange them in the pan around the roast (which should be spine side down). Roast for 25 minutes per pound in a preheated 325° oven, or until meat thermometer registers 170°. Remove roast to carving board and keep warm; let rest 15 minutes before carving. Drain the bacon loops on paper towels and ring them over the bones. Carve the meat parallel to the spine in long thin slices, using a ham slicer if you have one. Turn it to cut loose the tenderloin (fillet section) and carve it in long thin slices, too.

## RED CABBAGE

| | |
|---|---|
| 1 large red cabbage | 1 teaspoon salt |
| 3 tablespoons butter | ½ teaspoon freshly cracked |
| 1 cup finely chopped onions |    black pepper |
| ½ cup dry red wine | 1 teaspoon cornstarch |
| 2 tablespoons brown sugar | |

Trim cabbage of any bruised leaves and shred it very thin, using a large chef's knife (do not grate it). Soak cabbage in cold water for 5 minutes. Heat butter in a large saucepan and cook onions over high heat until limp, about 5 minutes. Drain cabbage and add to onions. Mix wine, brown sugar, salt, and pepper and pour over cabbage. Cover pan tightly and cook slowly over low heat until cabbage is tender, 30 to 45 minutes. (Young cabbage will take less time.) Drain cabbage and place in serving dish, reserving ½ cup liquid. Dissolve cornstarch in 1 tablespoon cold water, stir into cabbage liquid, and cook until it thickens. Pour over cabbage and mix lightly together. *This recipe can be made entirely ahead and reheated.*

## MASHED POTATOES AND CELERIAC

1 pound celeriac
4 medium-size potatoes
3 teaspoons salt
¾ cup heated heavy cream,
   plus more if needed

6 tablespoons soft butter
1 teaspoon freshly cracked
   white pepper
2 tablespoons chopped parsley

Peel and cube celeriac and potatoes and put them into 2 saucepans to cook separately. Cover each with cold water seasoned with 1 teaspoon salt, and bring to a boil. Reduce heat, cover pans, and simmer until tender, about 20 minutes. Drain. Put both through a potato ricer or food mill—mixing them together if you wish—and beat in cream, butter, pepper, and remaining teaspoon salt. Beat until fluffy, adding more cream if necessary. Keep warm by placing serving dish in a pan of simmering water. Sprinkle with parsley just before serving.

## APPLE CHAUSSON

CRUST:
3½ cups lightly spooned flour
2 tablespoons sugar
1 teaspoon salt
1 cup chilled butter
3 lightly beaten egg yolks
   Ice water, if necessary

½ cup butter
¼ cup Calvados, brandy, or
   rum
1 teaspoon cinnamon, optional
¼ teaspoon grated nutmeg,
   optional

FILLING:
8 large, or 10 small, Winesap
   (or Greenings, Cortland,
   or McIntosh) apples,
   peeled, cored, and cut in
   eighths
¾ to 1 cup sugar
   Grated peel of 1 orange
   Juice of 1 orange

1 egg yolk
1 tablespoon water
   Confectioners' sugar
   Sour cream or whipped
   cream, optional
2 tablespoons Calvados,
   brandy, or rum, optional

To make crust, stir flour with sugar and salt, cut the 1 cup chilled butter in chips, and toss with flour. Add 3 lightly beaten egg yolks and work with pastry blender or fingertips until mixture is granular. Press together; if mixture remains granular, add just enough ice water to make it hold. Turn dough out onto a lightly floured board and, using the heel of your hand, push the dough, bit by bit, against the board and away from you in short, quick smears. Work fast. Scrape up the dough, shape it into a ball, dust with flour, wrap in waxed paper, and refrigerate for at least 30 minutes.

Cook apple slices, sugar, orange peel, orange juice, and the ½ cup butter in a saucepan over high heat, covered, for 10 minutes, stirring mixture often to be sure it doesn't burn. Uncover and cook 10 minutes more, or until juice evaporates and mixture looks like a thick puree. Stir in Calvados and cinnamon or nutmeg if desired; chill for at least ½ hour, or overnight, in refrigerator.

Roll out pastry ⅛ inch thick and place on baking tray. Pile chilled apple mixture on one half of the circle of pastry and turn the other half over the filling. Roll edges back on themselves and press with a fork to seal. Cut 3 long 3-inch gashes across the top of the turnover. Brush dough with egg yolk mixed with water. Chill 20 minutes or longer. (*Recipe can be made ahead to this point; it may be frozen for up to 1 month; defrost for 24 hours in refrigerator.*) Bake in a preheated 375° oven until pastry is nicely browned, about 30 minutes. Serve warm, dusted with confectioners' sugar and topped with sour cream or with whipped cream, sweetened and flavored with Calvados.

## A Relaxed Sunday Night Dinner for 6

Cream of mushroom soup
Roast chicken with tarragon butter
Cauliflower and black olive salad
Swedish almond cake

Here is a pleasant way to end an active weekend, or redeem an uninspired one.

## CREAM OF MUSHROOM SOUP

1 pound mushrooms
4 cups chicken stock (see
   p. 278)
¾ cup finely chopped onion
7 tablespoons butter
6 tablespoons flour
3 cups light cream
1 cup heavy cream

1 teaspoon salt
½ teaspoon freshly cracked
   white pepper
2 tablespoons dry sherry or dry
   Madeira
1 tablespoon lemon juice
1 tablespoon chopped parsley

Reserve 6 mushroom caps, and chop the rest, including stems. Put the chopped mushrooms into a saucepan with chicken stock and chopped onion, bring to a boil, lower to simmer, cover, and cook for 30 minutes. In another pan, melt 6 tablespoons of the butter and stir in flour. Cook, stirring with a wooden spatula, over high heat for 2 minutes—do not let it brown. Remove from heat, change to a whisk, and add the light cream, whisking vigorously. Return to high heat and cook, stirring, until mixture is thick. Stir in heavy cream and the mushroom mixture. Season with salt and pepper. (*Recipe can be made ahead to this point.*) When ready to serve, reheat soup, adding dry sherry. Slice the reserved mushroom caps and sauté quickly in remaining 1 tablespoon butter, adding the lemon juice. Garnish soup bowls with sliced mushrooms and sprinkle with chopped parsley.

## ROAST CHICKEN WITH TARRAGON BUTTER

Follow directions for Roast Capon or Turkey (see p. 147) substituting a 4- to 5-pound roasting chicken for the capon, and decreasing butter to ½ cup, tarragon and parsley to 2 teaspoons each. Omit truffle. Figure 20 minutes per pound total roasting time, or 1 hour 40 minutes for a 5-pound bird. Preheat oven to 475° and roast for 30 minutes, basting every 15 minutes with red wine and pan juices. Reduce heat to 425° and roast 50 to 70 minutes longer; continue basting. Garnish the serving platter with a bunch of watercress.

## CAULIFLOWER AND BLACK OLIVE SALAD

1 head cauliflower
12 large or 24 small black
   olives, pitted
2 tablespoons chopped
   shallots
1 2-ounce can flat anchovy
   fillets, drained and
   chopped

2 tablespoons capers, drained
2 tablespoons chopped parsley
2 tablespoons red wine vinegar
4 to 5 tablespoons olive oil
Freshly grated white pepper

Trim cauliflower and cut into flowerets. Put into a saucepan, cover with cold water, and bring to a boil. Reduce heat to simmer and simmer 15 minutes. Drain flowerets and drop them into cold water to stop the cooking. Drain again and place in a salad bowl. Add olives, shallots, anchovies, capers, parsley, vinegar, olive oil, and pepper and mix gently. Cover with plastic wrap and refrigerate overnight. Serve at room temperature.

## SWEDISH ALMOND CAKE

½ cup butter, plus butter to
   grease cake pan
1 cup plus 1 tablespoon
   lightly spooned flour
1½ teaspoons baking powder
⅛ teaspoon salt
2 eggs
1 cup sugar

1 teaspoon vanilla extract
¼ cup cream, light or heavy

TOPPING:

4 tablespoons butter
⅓ cup slivered almonds
3 tablespoons sugar
2 tablespoons flour
1 tablespoon cream

Melt butter and set aside to cool. Butter an 8-inch round pan heavily and set aside. Sift flour after measuring with the baking powder and salt; set aside. Beat eggs with electric mixer; add sugar gradually and beat until thick and lemony. Add vanilla; then add flour alternately with cream and beat just to mix. Do not overbeat. Pour in the cooled melted butter and blend with a spatula. Pour into cake pan and place on the middle shelf of a preheated 350° oven to bake for 30 minutes (or 5 minutes longer if cake moves slightly in the center when you give it a little push). While cake bakes, prepare topping. Mix topping ingredients in a small saucepan and cook over high heat until sugar dissolves.

Remove cake from oven, raise oven temperature to 375°, spread topping over cake, and return to oven for about 10 minutes, or until it sizzles and browns—look at it after 5 minutes. The cake sinks when you add topping. *Cake may be prepared ahead, and it may also be frozen.*

## An Informal Dinner
### for 8

Asparagus soup
London broil
Roesti potatoes (see p. 15)
Braised fennel
Lemon tart

### ASPARAGUS SOUP

¾ cup butter
4 cups finely chopped onions
6 medium-size potatoes, diced
3 pounds asparagus, cut up in 2-inch pieces
4 cups chicken stock (see p. 278)

2 teaspoons salt
1 teaspoon freshly cracked white pepper
2 cups light cream
¼ teaspoon freshly grated nutmeg

Heat ½ cup butter in a large saucepan and cook onions over high heat until they are wilted, about 5 minutes. Stir in potatoes and asparagus, reserving tips. Pour on chicken stock and water, if needed, to cover vegetables. Season with salt and pepper, bring to a boil, cover, reduce heat to simmer, and cook until vegetables are tender, about 20 minutes. Put mixture through a food mill, using the finest disk. (*Soup can be prepared ahead to this point.*) Add light cream, nutmeg, and reserved asparagus tips and bring to a boil. Pour into heated tureen and float remaining ¼ cup butter, cut in chips, on the top.

## LONDON BROIL

The cut of beef I use as "London broil" is the top 2 inches cut from the top of the round. It weighs up to 4½ pounds. It should be at least 1½ inches thick, and it must be prime quality.

| | |
|---|---|
| 1 London broil, 3½ to 4 pounds | 1 teaspoon thyme |
| 1 cup olive oil | ¼ cup brown sugar |
| ½ cup red wine vinegar | 2 tablespoons chili sauce |
| Juice of 2 limes | 2 mashed cloves garlic |
| 1 teaspoon oregano | 3 tablespoons soy sauce |

Marinate the London broil for 24 hours in a marinade made from the remaining ingredients, turning it frequently. Heat the broiler or prepare a bed of coals. Adjust broiler rack to place meat 2 inches from heat in an oven broiler, or 2 to 3 inches from coals. For rare beef—and London broil should always be served rare—count 10 minutes total broiling time per inch thickness of meat. Thus, if your meat is 1½ inches thick, broil 7½ minutes on each side; if it's 2 inches thick, broil 10 minutes on each side. Carve the meat into *thin* slices, cutting across the grain and on a diagonal.

## BRAISED FENNEL

| | |
|---|---|
| 4 heads fennel | 1 teaspoon salt |
| 1 tablespoon salt | ½ teaspoon freshly cracked |
| 4 tablespoons butter | white pepper |
| 2 cups chicken stock (see | 1 teaspoon potato starch, |
| p. 278) | optional |
| 1 tablespoon sugar | 1 tablespoon water, optional |
| Juice of 1 lemon | |

Cut tops from fennel, pull off the feathery leaves, and chop and set them aside. Cut fennel heads or bulbs in half, discard hard outside pieces, put the heads in a saucepan, cover with cold water, add 1 tablespoon salt, and bring to a boil. Boil, uncovered, over high heat, for 15 minutes. Drain. Place fennel in a big skillet and add butter, chicken stock, sugar, lemon juice, 1 teaspoon salt, and pepper. Bring to a boil, then reduce heat and simmer, covered, for 20 to 45 minutes, or until fennel is tender—test it with the point of a small knife. Shake the pan a time or two, so fennel doesn't glaze. When fennel is done, remove to serving dish.

Thicken broth in pan by boiling to reduce it, or stir in potato starch dissolved in cold water. Pour sauce over fennel and sprinkle with chopped fennel leaves. *Recipe can be made ahead and reheated in the oven.*

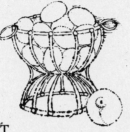

## LEMON TART

PASTRY:
2½ cups lightly spooned flour
½ cup sugar
¼ teaspoon salt
10 tablespoons butter
1 egg
1 tablespoon water

FILLING:
4 lemons
1½ cups sugar
5 lightly beaten eggs

½ cup plus 1 tablespoon
    softened butter
2 tablespoons light rum

MERINGUE:
2 egg whites
¼ teaspoon cream of tartar
¼ teaspoon salt
2 tablespoons sugar
1 tablespoon confectioners'
    sugar

To make pastry, combine flour, sugar, and salt in a bowl. Cut in butter until mixture looks like coarse crumbs. Beat egg with water, add to flour mixture, and toss to blend. Gather dough into a ball, dust with flour, wrap in waxed paper, and chill for 30 minutes. Roll it out and fit it into a 9-inch flan ring or pie pan.

To prepare filling, grind the lemons, including rinds, in a food chopper or grinder. Combine with sugar, eggs, butter, and rum, and blend well. Pour into the pastry shell and bake in a preheated 375° oven for about 30 to 35 minutes or until set. Cool on a rack before adding meringue.

To make meringue, beat egg whites until foamy; add cream of tartar and salt and beat until they hold soft peaks. Beat in sugar and confectioners' sugar a spoonful at a time and continue beating until meringue is very glossy and smooth, not grainy, when you pinch it. Spread over lemon filling and bake in a 350° oven about 10 minutes or until meringue peaks are lightly browned. Serve warm or cooled, as desired.

## A Duckling Dinner
### for 6

Broiled duckling
Brown rice pilaf with pine nuts
Braised onions and carrots
Salzburger Nockerln

For a different approach to duck, try broiling small 3-pound ducklings. They're tender and not so fatty when done this way. I don't recommend broiling larger ducks, though—it takes too long.

### BROILED DUCKLING

3 3-pound ducklings
3 tablespoons salt
3 teaspoons freshly cracked
black pepper
1 cup apricot jam
¼ cup lemon juice
2 tablespoons butter
2 tablespoons brandy
2 cups basic brown sauce
(see p. 281)

1 tablespoon vinegar
½ teaspoon meat glaze (see
p. 280)
1 20-ounce can whole water-
packed marrons, drained
1 20-ounce can apricot halves,
drained
2 tablespoons chopped parsley

With poultry shears cut the necks off and the backbones out of the ducklings. Spread them flat for broiling, skin side down, with wings tucked under, or cut each duckling into 4 to 6 pieces, separating legs from breast and cutting breast pieces in half. Place ducklings on broiler rack, skin side down. Broil 3 inches from heat for 20 minutes. Turn, sprinkle with salt and pepper, and brush with apricot jam thinned with lemon juice. Broil 10 minutes longer or until done—test duckling for doneness by pricking it; juices should run clear.

To make sauce, melt butter in skillet and quickly sauté duckling livers until they are browned on the outside but still pink inside. Warm brandy in a little pan, ignite it, and pour it over livers. Remove livers, scrape up brown bits in pan, and stir in brown sauce. Chop livers and return to sauce along with their juices. Stir in vinegar and meat glaze. Add marrons and the apricot halves, dried on paper towels, reduce heat, and heat through. Taste for seasoning. (*The sauce can be made ahead, but do not broil duckling until ready to serve.*) Arrange duckling on serving platter and pour sauce over it. Sprinkle with chopped parsley.

## BROWN RICE PILAF WITH PINE NUTS

4 tablespoons butter
¾ cup finely chopped onion
½ cup pine nuts
1½ cups brown rice
4½ cups chicken stock (see p. 278)

1½ teaspoons salt
½ teaspoon freshly cracked black pepper
2 tablespoons chopped parsley

In a heavy flameproof casserole with a tight-fitting lid, melt butter and stir in onion, cooking over high heat until it is wilted, about 3 minutes. Stir in pine nuts and cook until they take on a little color, about 2 minutes. Add brown rice and stir to coat well with butter. Pour on chicken stock, add salt and pepper, and bring to a boil. Turn heat to simmer, cover casserole, and set timer for 30 to 35 minutes. Do not lift lid until timer sounds. Fluff rice with 2 forks; if liquid is not absorbed and the rice tender, cover and cook for 5 to 10 minutes longer. (*Rice can be cooked ahead and reheated—to reheat, pour 2 tablespoons melted butter over it, cover, and set over low heat.*) To serve, fluff with forks and sprinkle with chopped parsley.

## BRAISED ONIONS AND CARROTS

24 small white onions
24 diagonally cut carrot pieces (see p. 46)
4 tablespoons butter
4 tablespoons lard, melted pork fat, or oil

1 teaspoon salt
½ teaspoon freshly cracked black pepper
1 tablespoon chopped parsley

Peel onions—cutting a cross in the root end of each—and parboil for 10 minutes. Parboil carrots for 5 minutes. Melt butter and lard in a shallow baking dish and add drained vegetables, rolling them around to coat well with fat. Season with salt and pepper and bake, uncovered, on the bottom shelf of a preheated 375° oven until browned and tender-crisp, about 1 hour. Baste occasionally or stir with spoon. (*Recipe can be cooked ahead to this point and reheated.*) Sprinkle with parsley to serve.

## SALZBURGER NOCKERLN

Butter and sugar to coat
  baking dish
6 eggs, separated
1 tablespoon flour
1 teaspoon freshly grated
  lemon peel *or* 1 teaspoon
  vanilla extract *or* 1 tablespoon rum

½ teaspoon cream of tartar
4 tablespoons sugar
Strawberry Sauce (recipe
  follows)

Heavily butter an oval baking or au gratin dish and sprinkle with sugar; knock out excess sugar and set aside. In a bowl, beat egg yolks lightly, add flour and lemon peel or flavoring, and set aside. Beat egg whites in mixer bowl until they start to foam. Add cream of tartar and, while continuing to beat, gradually add sugar, 1 tablespoon at a time. Beat until stiff and shiny, almost like meringue. Pour yolk mixture over whites and fold in very lightly. Heap in baking dish, making 3 mounds—this is the traditional way to shape a Salzburg soufflé. Bake in a preheated 425° oven for 10 to 12 minutes, or until puffed and lightly brown. Serve at once—it deflates as fast as any soufflé. Pass Strawberry Sauce.

## *STRAWBERRY SAUCE*

6 tablespoons butter
½ cup sugar
¼ cup framboise or kirsch

1 quart strawberries, washed,
  dried, and hulled, or about
  3 8-ounce packages frozen
  strawberries

Melt butter in a skillet. Add sugar, liqueur, and strawberries and shake over high heat for about 5 minutes. Berries do not cook—they just get heated through.

## An Informal Dinner
## for 6

Turkey-breast and ham paupiettes
Cauliflower covered with broccoli puree
Marinated cucumber balls
Meringue bananas

You can get a whole turkey breast where poultry parts are sold, but you may have to order it in advance. (Sometimes I slice one *very* thin and use it like veal to fool guests.) Cauliflower, masked by a pale-green broccoli puree, is an unusual and interesting accompaniment, and the crunchy marinated cucumber balls provide a good texture contrast.

### TURKEY-BREAST AND HAM PAUPIETTES

6  thin slices raw turkey breast meat
4  tablespoons melted butter
1  teaspoon salt
½  teaspoon freshly cracked white pepper
6  slices prosciutto ham
½  cup flour
2  beaten eggs
1  cup fine bread crumbs
Fat for deep frying
1½  cups Velouté Sauce, optional (see p. 280)
3  tablespoons Mushroom Duxelles, optional (see p. 283)

Place turkey slices between 2 sheets of waxed paper, pound flat, then trim each slice to approximately equal size. Brush with melted butter and season with salt and pepper. Lay a slice of ham on each and roll up loosely, fastening ends with toothpicks. Roll in flour, dip into beaten egg, and roll in bread crumbs; chill paupiettes for at least 5 minutes. (*May be prepared ahead to this point or deep-fried in advance and reheated. Reheat paupiettes, in an au gratin dish and brushed with butter, in a 350° oven for 10 to 15 minutes.*) In a deep saucepan, heat 3 inches of fat—I prefer solid vegetable shortening—to 375° and fry paupiettes, 3 at a time, for about 8 minutes. Drain on paper towels and keep warm in low oven. Serve plain or with Velouté Sauce into which you've stirred Mushroom Duxelles.

*Variation:* If you do not wish to deep-fry the paupiettes, place them in a buttered au gratin dish, brush generously with melted butter, sprinkle with 2 to 3 tablespoons grated Parmesan cheese, and bake in a preheated 350° oven for about 15 minutes, basting frequently with melted butter.

## CAULIFLOWER COVERED WITH BROCCOLI PUREE

| | |
|---|---|
| 1 head cauliflower | Salt |
| ¼ cup milk | Freshly cracked white |
| 1 slice bread | pepper |
| ½ cup melted butter | Broccoli Puree (recipe |
| ¼ cup freshly grated Parmesan | follows) |
| cheese | 2 tablespoons chopped parsley |

Trim cauliflower, leaving head whole. Place in a saucepan and add water almost to cover, milk (to keep cauliflower white), and bread (to mask odor). Boil, uncovered, over high heat until almost done, then cover and simmer until cauliflower is tender, about 30 to 45 minutes total. Drain cauliflower and place on a serving platter. Pour melted butter over cauliflower and sprinkle with cheese, salt, and pepper. Nap with Broccoli Puree and reheat, if necessary, in a 350° oven. Just before serving, sprinkle with chopped parsley.

### *BROCCOLI PUREE*

| | |
|---|---|
| 2 10-ounce packages frozen broccoli | ¼ teaspoon freshly grated nutmeg |
| 2 tablespoons butter | 6 tablespoons heavy cream or |
| 2 tablespoons flour | sour cream |
| 1 teaspoon salt | 3 tablespoons melted butter |
| ½ teaspoon freshly cracked white pepper | |

Cook broccoli according to package directions. Drain and puree through a food mill, using the finest disk. Melt butter in a saucepan, stir in flour, and cook, stirring, over high heat until the *roux* is nicely browned. Add pureed broccoli and beat over high heat with a wooden spatula. Add salt, pepper, and nutmeg. Thin the mixture with enough heavy cream or sour cream to make a smooth puree that will mask the cauliflower. (*Recipe may be made ahead to this point and held over hot water for up to ½ hour.*) Stir in melted butter and pour over cauliflower.

## MARINATED CUCUMBER BALLS

Peel 6 medium-size cucumbers with a potato peeler and cut into balls with a melon baller. Marinate in 1 recipe French vinaigrette dressing (see p. 282) for an hour or so. Sprinkle with 2 tablespoons chopped parsley.

## MERINGUE BANANAS

| | |
|---|---|
| 8 bananas, ripe but firm | 2 tablespoons melted butter |
| 3 tablespoons butter | 5 egg whites |
| 12 tablespoons sugar | ¼ teaspoon cream of tartar |
| 2 tablespoons rum | |

Peel bananas and cut them in half lengthwise. Melt 3 tablespoons butter in a large skillet, add bananas, sprinkle with 2 tablespoons sugar, and sauté gently over high heat for 2 minutes, turning once. Remove pan from heat. Warm rum in a little pan, ignite it, and pour it over bananas, shaking pan until flames die. Arrange bananas in a buttered ovenproof serving dish—each 2 halves close together, cut side up. Score the surface of the bananas with a table knife, making crosswise cuts about 1 inch apart.

Make meringue as follows: beat egg whites in large bowl of electric mixer. When they start to foam, add cream of tartar, and continue beating until soft peaks form. Add remaining 10 tablespoons sugar, 1 tablespoon at a time, beating constantly, and continue beating until meringue looks like marshmallow. Pinch it; it's ready when it no longer feels grainy. Fit a large pastry bag with a star tube and fill it with the meringue. Pipe meringue over bananas, covering each pair of halves completely. (*Recipe may be made 1 hour ahead to this point.*) Place bananas in a preheated 400° oven and bake until meringue is set and lightly browned, about 10 minutes. Serve hot or cold.

# A Formal Dinner for 8 on a Winter's Evening

Caviar barquettes
Crown of lamb, Béarnaise
Brown rice pilaf with almond slivers
Celeriac sticks
Bibb lettuce salad
Cold Grand Marnier soufflé

## CAVIAR BARQUETTES

1 recipe barquettes (see p. 49)   ½ cup sour cream
8 ounces red and/or black         Parsley sprigs, for garnish
  caviar

Prepare barquettes or unfreeze and crisp them in the oven. Fill with caviar and top with a dot of sour cream, with a little parsley sprig placed on the sour cream. Allow 4 per person with drinks—if cocktail hour is prolonged—or 2 per person as a first course.

## CROWN OF LAMB, BÉARNAISE

Crown of lamb is most elegant when served to pink perfection. Too often it is cooked to death and has no lamb taste. Europeans generally eat lamb rare or pink, and I suspect that many Americans who think they don't like lamb would like it better if they tried it this way.

Ask your butcher to prepare a crown of lamb for you by tying or sewing 2 rib roasts or racks together in a crown shape. Rub the meat all over with 1 tablespoon coarse salt and 1 teaspoon freshly cracked black pepper. If you like a garlic seasoning, cut 2 cloves into slivers and insert by sticking a knife point into meat here and there and, using knife blade as a slide, poking sliver into meat. Put ball of aluminum foil in center of meat so it will keep its shape while roasting, cover ends of rib bones with foil, stand crown upright in pan, and roast in a preheated 425° oven for 45 minutes.

no more. This will yield a pink piece of meat. Fill center of crown with brown rice pilaf (recipe follows). Remove foil from bone ends and cover with paper frills. Serve with Béarnaise Sauce (see p. 282).

## BROWN RICE PILAF WITH ALMOND SLIVERS

Following recipe for Brown Rice Pilaf with Pine Nuts on page 105, substituting ½ cup slivered almonds for pine nuts. If desired, add ½ cup light raisins soaked in ¼ cup dry sherry along with the almonds.

## CELERIAC STICKS

| | |
|---|---|
| 4 large celeriac | ½ teaspoon freshly cracked |
| 4 teaspoons salt | white pepper |
| Juice of ½ lemon | ½ cup melted butter |
| | 2 tablespoons chopped parsley |

Peel the celeriac and cut them into julienne strips about the size of kitchen matches. Drop them into a saucepan of cold water to cover. Add 3 teaspoons of the salt and the lemon juice and bring to a boil on high heat. Turn heat to medium, cover pan, and cook until barely tender, about 20 minutes. Drain. Return celeriac to pan, add the remaining teaspoon of salt, the pepper, and melted butter. Shake over high heat for 2 minutes. Sprinkle with chopped parsley.

## BIBB LETTUCE SALAD

| | |
|---|---|
| 4 heads Bibb lettuce | French vinaigrette dressing |
| 1 large tomato, peeled and seeded | (see p. 282) |
| | 1 tablespoon chopped parsley |

Wash lettuce, trim, and roll in towels to chill thoroughly. Cut tomato into slivers, place in a chilled salad bowl with lettuce and parsley, and toss with vinaigrette dressing to taste just before serving. Serve as a separate course.

## COLD GRAND MARNIER SOUFFLÉ

An original recipe, and an unbelievably elegant dessert. To facilitate its preparation, assemble and ready all ingredients ahead of time. While the soufflé may be prepared the night before, the garnishing is better done nearer the serving time. Put orange slices on no more than 2 hours ahead, or sugar will dissolve. The whipped cream rosettes may be piped on the night before only if cream is beaten over ice—otherwise it will weep.

Grated peel of 2 oranges and
  1 lemon
¾ cup orange juice
¼ cup lemon juice
2 tablespoons (2 envelopes)
  unflavored gelatine
¼ cup Grand Marnier

6 eggs, separated
2 cups sugar
½ teaspoon salt
2½ cups heavy cream
1 orange, for garnish
1 egg white
¼ cup crystallized sugar

Make a waxed paper collar for a 6-cup soufflé dish by folding paper in half, lengthwise, brushing inside edge with vegetable oil, and tying it around the top of the dish so that it extends 4 to 5 inches above it. Set aside. Grate oranges and lemon and squeeze juice. Sprinkle gelatine into ½ cup of the orange juice and set aside. In a saucepan, put the grated peel, remaining ¼ cup orange juice, lemon juice, Grand Marnier, 6 egg yolks, 1¼ cups of the sugar, and the salt. Beat until fluffy; then stir over low heat until the mixture coats the back of a spoon. Remove from heat and stir in the softened gelatine–orange juice mixture, stirring until gelatine dissolves. Place in the refrigerator to cool until the mixture mounds slightly when dropped from a spoon, about 20 minutes.

Meanwhile, beat egg whites to soft peaks. Beat in remaining ¾ cup sugar, 1 tablespoon at a time, and beat until stiff and glossy. Beat 2 cups of the heavy cream until it mounds nicely, but isn't too stiff. Fold egg whites and then whipped cream into egg yolk custard and pour into prepared dish—work quickly, the cold whipped cream makes it set up quickly. Place in refrigerator to chill. Mixture sets quickly, but the flavor is better if you chill it overnight.

Prepare garnish: Use a lemon stripper to cut grooves in orange, ¼ inch apart. Slice orange crosswise; edges will look fluted. Dip slices in beaten egg white and then in crystallized sugar. Whip remaining ½ cup heavy cream and put it into a pastry bag fitted with a rose tube. Pipe rosettes around edge of soufflé, and overlap the sugared orange slices in a ring just inside the whipped cream. Remove the collar carefully just before serving.

### A Rich and Delicious
### Formal Dinner for 8

Poached trout with Hollandaise sauce
Roast sirloin strip with maître d'hôtel butter
Endive à la crème
Chinese carrots (see p. 46)
White asparagus vinaigrette
Riz à l'impératrice

### POACHED TROUT WITH HOLLANDAISE SAUCE

The secret of this really delicate recipe lies in undercooking rather than overcooking the trout. To keep the fish you cook first warm while simmering the rest, hold them in an oven at low heat. Or cook the fish ahead, keep them in the cooled court bouillon, and then reheat slightly. In this case, be very careful to undercook the fish in the beginning.

8 small trout, less than 1
  pound each
1 recipe court bouillon (see
  p. 279)
¼ cup melted butter

1 lemon
1 bunch watercress
1 recipe Hollandaise Sauce
  (see p. 281)

Buy trout cleaned and degutted but not split, and with heads and tails intact. Handle them as little as possible as they are very fragile. Do not wash them: the slime with which they're covered gives them a blue color when you cook them—like European blue trout. Tie fish in crescent shape: push a trussing needle threaded with string through the body just above the tail and through the eye sockets; pull tight and knot. Leave the string end long enough to help you later to remove trout from the pot. (*Fish may be prepared ahead to this point and refrigerated.*)

Drop fish 2 at a time into simmering (not boiling) court bouillon. Set timer. For each inch thickness of fish (measured through the middle), poach 7 minutes. For example, for trout ¾ inch thick, poach 5 minutes only. Remove fish from poaching liquid and arrange on serving dish. Keep warm while you poach remaining fish. Remove strings—fish will stay in crescent shape. Brush with melted butter. With a small knife make zigzag cuts around center of lemon, pull halves apart, and nest them in the watercress. Serve with Hollandaise Sauce, passed separately.

## ROAST SIRLOIN STRIP

This is an excellent roast, very expensive, but you have no waste. A 10-pound sirloin strip will leave you with leftovers, and it's good cold. Bring meat to room temperature. Rub all over with 1 tablespoon coarse salt and 1 teaspoon freshly cracked black pepper. Put it on a rack in a shallow pan and roast it in a preheated 350° oven for 10 minutes per pound, or until it registers 125° on a meat thermometer. (This timing is for rare meat; for medium-rare, roast for 12 minutes per pound, and for medium, 15 minutes per pound.) Remove from oven and let it stand for 15 to 20 minutes to set the juices. Carve into thin slices and serve with a ball of Maître d'Hôtel Butter on top of each slice.

## MAÎTRE D'HÔTEL BUTTER

In electric mixer bowl, cream ½ cup butter. Beat in 1 tablespoon lemon juice, ½ teaspoon salt, ¼ teaspoon freshly cracked black pepper, 1 tablespoon chopped parsley, and—if you wish— 1 teaspoon finely chopped shallot and ¼ teaspoon finely chopped garlic. *Prepare butter ahead and store in refrigerator.*

## ENDIVE À LA CRÈME

| | |
|---|---|
| 12  heads Belgian endive | 1  tablespoon sugar |
| 2  quarts boiling water | ¾  cup chicken stock (see |
| ½  teaspoon salt | p. 278) |
| 1  slice bread | 6  tablespoons heavy cream |
| 6  tablespoons butter | 2  tablespoons chopped parsley |

Count on 1 or 2 heads of endive per person. Trim stem ends. Drop into boiling salted water, along with the bread, and boil 7 minutes. (The bread helps draw out the bitter taste of endive.) Melt butter in a large skillet over high heat; add sugar and chicken stock. Place parboiled endive heads in skillet, side by side, cover, and cook over high heat for 10 minutes. Reduce heat to simmer, turn endive heads over, re-cover, and cook for 20 minutes longer, or until endive heads are tender and a glaze forms in the bottom of the pan. Watch them carefully; do not let them burn. Arrange endive heads in a serving dish. Pour cream into pan juices and bring to a boil, stirring and scraping up brown bits. Boil 1 minute. Pour sauce over endive and sprinkle with chopped parsley. *Recipe can be done ahead and reheated.*

## WHITE ASPARAGUS VINAIGRETTE

Use only the very best canned white asparagus available. Rinse and dry stalks, dress with French vinaigrette dressing (see p. 282), and sprinkle with chopped parsley. Count 3 stalks for each person.

## RIZ À L'IMPÉRATRICE

1 cup long-grain rice
4½ cups light cream, plus more if necessary
2 inches vanilla bean, or 1 tablespoon vanilla extract
8 egg yolks
1 cup sugar
2 tablespoons (2 envelopes) unflavored gelatine

½ cup water
2 tablespoons lemon juice
2 cups heavy cream
4 tablespoons confectioners' sugar
½ cup finely chopped mixed candied fruits soaked in rum or fresh strawberries, or fresh raspberries

In a saucepan, stir rice into 3 cups light cream, add a 1-inch piece of vanilla bean, slit and scraped, or 1½ teaspoons vanilla extract, and cook very slowly over low heat until rice is soft, about 20 to 30 minutes. Stir constantly with a wooden spatula—don't rush it. Add more cream if necessary. In a bowl, beat egg yolks, add sugar gradually, and beat until light and fluffy. Blend into mixture the remaining 1½ cups light cream and a 1-inch piece of vanilla bean, slit and scraped, or remaining 1½ teaspoons vanilla. Transfer the mixture to a nonaluminum pan—or place bowl in a pan of simmering water—and stir over low heat until custard thickens. In a cup, soften gelatine in water and lemon juice, set cup in a pan of hot water, and stir until gelatine dissolves. Stir dissolved gelatine into custard and strain the mixture. Stir. rice into strained custard—first removing vanilla beans; place bowl over a bowl of ice, and stir until it thickens, or chill in refrigerator, stirring occasionally. Whip the heavy cream over ice until it thickens, then sweeten with confectioners' sugar. Fold it slowly, a spoonful at a time, into the custard-rice mixture, stir in candied fruits or berries, and pile high in a crystal bowl. *Recipe can be prepared a day ahead, covered with plastic wrap, and refrigerated.*

## A Formal Dinner
### for 6

Oysters Rockefeller
Lamb noisettes with veal mousse
Soufflé potatoes
Watercress and Belgian endive salad
Glazed pineapple with kirsch

Ideally, formal service means extra hands in the kitchen, and certainly this dinner party will go more smoothly if the hostess has help. But if you intend to manage it alone, here are some do-ahead changes to make in the recipes . . . or in the menu.

Both oysters and potatoes are best if prepared no more than 2 hours ahead, so you may want to substitute Pommes Parisienne (see p. 255) for the Soufflé Potatoes. In fact, Soufflé Potatoes are rather tricky and only accomplished cooks should try them. The potatoes can be deep-fried 2 hours ahead and held in the kitchen near the oven; they should not be held *in* the oven. Better to serve them at room temperature, if necessary. The Lamb Noisettes with Veal Mousse may be completely done ahead as follows: cut baking time from 20 to 15 minutes; refrigerate; then bring to room temperature before reheating in a 350° oven for 5 to 10 minutes, while you eat oysters. You will find the recipe for Watercress and Belgian Endive Salad on p. 42 and for Glazed Pineapple with Kirsch on p. 24.

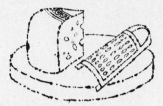

## OYSTERS ROCKEFELLER

3 dozen oysters on half shell
½ package (10 ounces) frozen chopped spinach
½ cup chopped parsley
½ cup chopped scallions
½ cup chopped Boston lettuce
1 clove garlic
  Clam juice, if necessary
½ cup butter
1 cup bread crumbs

1 tablespoon Worcestershire sauce
1 teaspoon anchovy paste
4 drops Tabasco sauce
1½ tablespoons Pernod
½ teaspoon salt
¼ cup freshly grated Parmesan cheese
  Melted butter
  Rock salt

Open oysters or have them opened for you—open them as close to serving time as possible and never more than 2 hours before serving—and reserve oyster juice. Put thawed spinach, parsley, scallions, lettuce, and garlic in a blender with about 2 tablespoons oyster juice, or clam juice, if there is not enough oyster juice, and blend thoroughly. Cream butter in a bowl, blend in ¾ cup of the bread crumbs, and combine it with spinach puree. Add Worcestershire sauce, anchovy paste, Tabasco, Pernod, and salt. Mix thoroughly. Drain any excess liquid still remaining from oysters, add it to sauce, and cover each oyster with a spoonful of the sauce. Sprinkle with Parmesan cheese and remaining ¼ cup of bread crumbs and drizzle with melted butter. (*Recipe may be prepared ahead to this point and refrigerated. Bring to room temperature before baking.*)

Twenty minutes before you are ready to bake oysters, spread an ovenproof serving dish with a layer of rock salt and place it in a preheated 450° oven to heat the salt. Place oysters in their half shells on the hot rock salt and return pan to oven to bake for about 20 minutes, or until oysters are lightly browned. Do not overcook.

## LAMB NOISETTES WITH VEAL MOUSSE

4 slices bacon
8 loin lamb chops, 1½ inches
   thick
2 teaspoons salt
1 teaspoon freshly cracked
   black pepper
2 tablespoons butter
½ pound veal, ground twice
2 egg whites
½ cup light cream
1 teaspoon salt

½ teaspoon freshly cracked
   black pepper
½ teaspoon chopped garlic
6 tablespoons brandy
½ cup melted butter
1 cup basic brown sauce
   (see p. 281)
Black truffle cutouts or
   sautéed fluted mushroom
   caps (see p. 284), for
   garnish
Watercress, for garnish

Blanch the bacon slices: put them in a saucepan, cover with cold water, bring to a boil, and boil 1 minute. Drain. Bone the lamb chops, sprinkle them generously with 2 teaspoons salt and 1 teaspoon pepper, and wrap a piece of blanched bacon around the edge of each, tying it on with string. Melt 2 tablespoons butter in a heavy skillet and sauté noisettes over high heat on one side only, for 2 minutes only, just to brown them. Place noisettes, browned side down, in a baking pan.

Make veal mousse as follows. Put veal into electric mixer bowl—using the flat whip if you have a heavy-duty mixer—gradually add egg whites, and beat thoroughly, or place bowl over ice and beat with a wooden spatula. Gradually beat in cream. Add 1 teaspoon salt, ½ teaspoon pepper, garlic, and 2 tablespoons brandy, and beat thoroughly. Mound or "dome up" veal mixture on each lamb noisette. If veal mixture is too soft to dome up, put it in the refrigerator to stiffen. Drizzle veal-topped noisettes with 4 tablespoons melted butter. Add remaining butter and brandy to baking pan, to use for basting. (*May be prepared ahead to this point.*) Place noisettes in preheated 350° oven and bake for 20 minutes, basting frequently with the butter-brandy mixture. Remove from baking pan and arrange on a warm platter. Pour off excess fat from pan, leaving 1 tablespoonful. Add basic brown sauce to pan and bring to a boil, scraping up brown bits. Spoon sauce over platter. Garnish each chop with a truffle cutout (see p. 49 for instructions) or sautéed fluted mushroom cap. *Can be made ahead to this point, but bake for only 15 minutes to allow for reheating. May be refrigerated; then bring to room tempera-*

*ture and reheat in a 350° oven for 5 to 10 minutes.* Garnish platter with watercress.

### SOUFFLÉ POTATOES

Count 9 Idaho potatoes for 6 people—some of them won't puff in the hot fat, so you need some reserves. Peel potatoes and slice them lengthwise or diagonally on a vegetable cutter or mandoline, so that they are elongated oval in shape and the thickness of a fifty-cent piece. Cover with cold water and soak for 15 minutes. Drain and dry well. Heat vegetable shortening in 2 saucepans (2 inches deep in each), one pan to 300° and the second to 450°. Drop 2 to 3 potato slices at a time into the 300° fat and fry for 2½ minutes. Remove with slotted spoon and drop into 450° fat. They should puff up—the centers will be hollow. This takes about 2 to 3 minutes. Remove when puffed and crisp, drain on paper towels, and salt and serve immediately.

*Note:* You can do the initial 300° frying of the potato slices earlier in the day, draining them on paper towels and refrigerating. Bring to room temperature before second frying. Give them the 450° plunge just before serving. Keep checking temperature of fat and don't overload the pans. Hold slices at room temperature or near (but not in) oven when they are fried.

## *A Winter Dinner for 6*

---

Consommé Normande
Chicken suprêmes with champagne sauce
Spinach timbales
Watercress salad
Coffee praline ice cream

### CONSOMMÉ NORMANDE

6 cups strong chicken stock
   (see p. 278)
1 egg white

6 tablespoons Calvados
2 tablespoons freshly grated
   apple

Heat chicken stock. Beat egg white until foamy and add to stock, to clarify it, whisking while you bring the stock to a boil. Remove from heat and let stand for 15 minutes. Strain broth through a sieve lined with a double thickness of cheesecloth wrung out in cold water, pouring carefully so as not to disturb the coagulated egg white. Let consommé drip through by itself. Taste for seasoning. (*Recipe may be made ahead to this point.*) When ready to serve, reheat consommé, stir in Calvados, and garnish each bowl with 1 teaspoon grated apple.

## CHICKEN SUPRÊMES
## WITH CHAMPAGNE SAUCE

6 whole chicken breasts
6 tablespoons brandy
   Mushroom-ham stuffing
   (recipe follows)
5 to 6 tablespoons butter
1 teaspoon finely chopped
   garlic
2 tablespoons finely chopped
   shallots
3 tablespoons flour
½ teaspoon meat glaze (see
   p. 280)
2 tablespoons chopped truffle

2 teaspoons tarragon
1 cup champagne *or* dry white
   wine *or* dry vermouth
½ cup chicken stock (see
   p. 278)
½ cup heavy cream
¼ teaspoon freshly cracked
   white pepper
2 tablespoons freshly grated
   Parmesan cheese
   Chopped parsley
1 bunch watercress

Bone and skin chicken breasts carefully and trim into neat ovals. You will have 12 suprêmes, 2 from each breast. Cut a pocket in each suprême from the thicker side. Brush pockets with 4 tablespoons of brandy and put about 1 tablespoon stuffing in each pocket. Pinch to seal. Heat 3 to 4 tablespoons butter in a heavy skillet and sauté chicken over high heat—to stiffen it, the meat should not brown—3 minutes on each side. Cook it under a flat lid, pressed down with a 2- to 3-pound weight to help keep stuffing from coming out. Remove chicken and set aside.

Deglaze skillet over medium-high heat with remaining 2 tablespoons brandy and scrape up any brown bits. Add remaining 2 tablespoons butter and stir in garlic and shallots. Cook for a minute or two over high heat. Stir in flour and cook for 2 minutes. Add meat glaze, chopped truffle, tarragon, champagne, chicken stock, and heavy cream. Whisk and cook over medium-high heat until sauce thickens and is smooth. Season with pepper and Parmesan cheese. Return chicken and chicken juices to skillet and baste with sauce. (*May be prepared ahead to this point, covered with plastic wrap, and refrigerated or frozen. Bring to room temperature before final cooking.*) Cover and simmer chicken for 10 to 15 minutes—do not overcook. Arrange chicken on serving platter, pour sauce over it, and sprinkle with chopped parsley. Arrange a bunch of watercress at one end of platter.

### MUSHROOM-HAM STUFFING

Sauté ½ pound sliced mushrooms and 4 thin slices of boiled ham, cut in dice, in 2 tablespoons butter. Sprinkle with 2 tablespoons lemon juice and season with ½ teaspoon salt and ¼ teaspoon freshly cracked black pepper.

### SPINACH TIMBALES

Vegetable oil to oil molds
2 10-ounce packages frozen chopped spinach
3 eggs
1 egg yolk
¼ cup grated onion
½ chopped clove garlic
2 teaspoons salt
½ teaspoon freshly cracked black pepper
½ teaspoon freshly grated nutmeg
2 cups milk
4 tablespoons grated Parmesan cheese, optional

Brush 10 *oeuf en gelée* molds, or one 6-cup ring mold, with vegetable oil. Cook spinach according to package directions. Drain it in a sieve and, when cooled, squeeze it in your hands to press out all excess moisture. Lay it on a chopping board and chop very fine, even though it has been previously chopped. Put it in a bowl and stir in eggs, egg yolk, onion, garlic, salt, pepper, nutmeg, and milk. Add grated Parmesan cheese if desired. Fill molds almost to the top with spinach mixture and set them in a pan of very hot water. Place in a preheated 350° oven and bake about 35 minutes or until custard tests done. It will begin to pull away from sides of mold, and a knife inserted in custard will come out clean. (*Timbales may be baked ahead to this point and reheated in the water bath—but cut original cooking time by 5 minutes.*) Remove molds from hot water bath and let stand for a few minutes. Then run a knife around the edges and unmold. Serve immediately.


### WATERCRESS SALAD

Wash 3 bunches of watercress, remove stems, roll in towels, and chill. When ready to serve, toss with 1 tablespoon chopped shallots and French vinaigrette dressing (see p. 282).


### COFFEE PRALINE ICE CREAM

Churned ice cream is always a treat. When I was a child, my father and uncles took turns cranking our hand-operated freezer; now people who value ice cream own an electric freezer. Of course, you can still-freeze ice cream in refrigerator trays if you whip the cream lightly, but the texture of churned ice cream is better. This is definitely a make-ahead recipe; after churning, the ice cream should be ripened for a few hours before you serve it. For a 1-gallon ice-cream freezer, you'll need about 20 pounds of ice and about 6 cups of rock salt.

If you do not wish to make your own ice cream, buy rich vanilla ice cream, serve in individual dishes, and sprinkle the powdered praline over.

¾ cup sugar
¼ teaspoon cream of
   tartar
⅓ cup cold water
3 egg yolks
1½ cups heavy cream

2 tablespoons coffee essence,
   or 2 tablespoons instant
   coffee dissolved in 1 tablespoon boiling water
1 cup praline powder (recipe
   follows)

Combine sugar, cream of tartar, and water in a small saucepan. Stir over heat until sugar dissolves, then cook until syrup spins a thread (230° on candy thermometer). When syrup is almost ready, beat egg yolks well with electric mixer. Slowly add the hot syrup, in a thin stream, beating constantly. Continue beating until mixture is cold and thick. Blend in heavy cream and flavor with coffee essence.

Chill the ice-cream mixture and pour it in the freezer can—from two-thirds to three-quarters full, to leave room for expansion. Put the can in the freezer and adjust the dasher and cover; follow manufacturer's directions if using an electric freezer. Pack the freezer with ice mixed with rock salt—3 parts ice to 1 part salt. If using a hand-operated freezer, turn the dasher slowly until enough ice melts to form a brine; then turn the handle fast and steadily, adding more ice and salt to maintain the ice level. When ice cream is partly frozen, add praline powder (or other fruits or flavorings)—clear ice and salt away from the cover before you open the can! Continue freezing until the machine begins to labor. Again clear away ice below cover line and open the can to remove the dasher. To ripen ice cream, pack it down into the can, cover can with foil, plug the opening in the cover, and put it back on. Pack more ice and salt as needed around the can to fill freezer, and cover entire freezer with heavy cloth or newspapers.

*Note:* Melting ice will drain from the freezer—the whole process of making ice cream is an outdoor or in-the-sink job.

### PRALINE POWDER

In a heavy skillet over medium heat, stir and melt 1½ cups sugar with 1 cup almonds (blanched or unblanched) and ¼ teaspoon cream of tartar. Stir continuously with wooden spatula until mixture turns a dark caramel color, about 15 minutes. Remove from heat, immediately pour onto a buttered baking sheet, and let it harden. When hard, break it into pieces and pulverize it in a blender or pound it to powder with a mallet. *It may be made ahead and stored on the shelf in an airtight jar, for up to a month.*

## An Elegant Summer Dinner
## for 6

Glazed poached trout on aspic
Rack of veal, Béarnaise
Sautéed fluted mushroom caps
Green salad with Roquefort cheese
Peaches in port

This menu presents fine ingredients in a simple classic style. The sauces and garnishes lend distinction, yet the dinner remains light and perfect for summertime. Allow about 4 mushrooms per person (the basic recipe is on p. 284) and, if you wish, pass fresh French bread for guests to nibble on. The recipe for Peaches in Port is on p. 46.

## GLAZED POACHED TROUT ON ASPIC

You can, if you wish, poach the trout, decorate it, and arrange it on aspic the day before serving it. Cover it with plastic wrap and refrigerate until you're ready to bring it to the table. When you prepare the aspic, use the court bouillon from poaching trout instead of chicken broth.

6 small trout, poached in
   crescent shape (see
   p. 113)

1 recipe aspic (see p. 279)
   Sprigs of fresh dill
1 sliced truffle
1 hard-cooked egg

Remove skin and strings from poached trout and place fish on cake racks set on a tray or shallow pan. Put in refrigerator to chill for at least ½ hour. Melt aspic and then stir it over a bowl of ice. It should be syrupy, on the point of setting, when you work with it; if it begins to set, remelt it and stir it again over ice. Use a pastry brush to brush the first coat of aspic on chilled trout; return to refrigerator until aspic sets, about ½ hour. Spoon on a second, thicker coat of aspic and chill until set.

Decorate each fish by dipping decorations in aspic and placing them on fish. Put a dill sprig on the head. Use hors d'oeuvre cutters to cut fancy shapes from thin slices of truffle and place 1 cutout on back of each fish. Cut eyes from hard-cooked egg white. Mix egg yolk with a bit of mustard or cream and put in a tiny paper cone or pastry bag to pipe on eyebrows. Spoon a third coat of aspic over fish to set decorations. Chill extra, runover aspic until it sets, chop it on waxed paper with a chef's knife, and spread it on a serving platter. Arrange glazed trout on bed of aspic and refrigerate until serving time.

## RACK OF VEAL, BÉARNAISE

Fat adds both tenderness and flavor to meat. Since veal is a very dry meat, it is often enhanced, as here, when barded, or covered with a thin sheet of fat that serves to baste meat as it roasts. Barding fat is available from most butchers.

| | |
|---|---|
| 1  rack of veal, about 8 chops | 1  teaspoon freshly cracked |
|      Fresh pork fat for barding |        white pepper |
| 2  teaspoons coarse salt | Béarnaise Sauce (see p. 282) |

Have the butcher trim the rack, or trim it yourself, so that about 2 inches of bone are exposed on each chop. The chine bone, or backbone, should be removed, to make rack easier to carve into chops. Tie the barding fat onto the back of the rack. (*Veal may be prepared ahead to this point.*) Stand fat side up in roasting pan and roast in a preheated 350° oven 25 minutes per pound or until meat thermometer registers 170°. (Veal should not be pink.) Remove barding fat, sprinkle meat with salt and pepper, and let it rest for 10 to 15 minutes before carving between the bones. Serve with Béarnaise Sauce, passed separately.

## GREEN SALAD WITH ROQUEFORT CHEESE

Serve this unusual salad-and-cheese as a separate course after the veal—it's well worth such formal attention! I first encountered it at the home of a friend, returned from Europe after eleven years, and I've served it many times myself. Guests are invariably enchanted.

| | |
|---|---|
| ¾  pound Roquefort cheese | 1  recipe French vinaigrette |
| ¼  cup unsalted butter |        dressing (see p. 282) |
| 3  or 4 heads Bibb lettuce, | 2  tablespoons chopped parsley |
|      yielding 36 to 42 leaves | |

Beat Roquefort cheese and butter together until very creamy. Pack into a medium-size pastry bag fitted with a star tube and pipe a pointy mound of cheese into the center of each individual salad plate. Poke the stems of 6 or 7 Bibb lettuce leaves into each cheese mound—it should look like a small head of lettuce. Spoon 2 tablespoons vinaigrette over each salad and sprinkle with chopped parsley.

## Formal Summer Dinner
## for 8

Cold tomato and dill soup
Glazed Cornish hens or squabs
Straw potatoes
Celery Victor
Raspberry tart

Each course in this joyful menu has its own assertive taste. First the dill, quite subtle. Then the sweet glaze on the birds, contrasted with salty straw potatoes and crisp-cooked celery garnished with anchovy and pimento. The sweet ending is a glorious fresh raspberry tart.

### COLD TOMATO AND DILL SOUP

½ cup butter
1 tablespoon chopped garlic
1½ cups chopped onions
8 tomatoes, plus 4 for garnish
¼ cup flour
1 teaspoon salt
½ teaspoon freshly cracked white pepper

4 cups chicken stock (see p. 278)
1 tablespoon tomato paste
1 cup light cream
½ cup heavy cream
3 tablespoons chopped fresh dill

Melt butter in a large saucepan, add garlic and onions, and stir over high heat until onions are transparent. Do not let them brown. Slice (but do not peel) 8 tomatoes and add to onion mixture. Continue stirring over high heat and smooth in the flour. Add salt, pepper, and chicken stock, and bring it to a boil. Stir in tomato paste, then cover and simmer for about 30 minutes. Peel remaining tomatoes for garnish: quarter them, remove seeds and pulp and add to soup kettle, and cut tomato flesh in shreds; set aside. Puree the soup through a food mill, using the fine disk, or in the blender; then push the puree through a sieve to strain out all the seeds. Taste for seasoning and chill thoroughly. (*Recipe can be made to this point and refrigerated or frozen.*) When ready to serve, stir in light cream. Lightly whip the heavy cream, just past the foaming stage, and fold it into the soup. Garnish each serving with tomato shreds and sprinkle with fresh chopped dill.

## GLAZED CORNISH HENS OR SQUABS

8 12- to 15-ounce Cornish hens or small squabs
4 tablespoons butter, more if needed
2 teaspoons salt
1 teaspoon freshly cracked black pepper
1 8-ounce jar currant jelly, melted

Wash birds, dry thoroughly, and truss. Heat butter in a large skillet and thoroughly brown the birds all over, not letting them touch each other; take plenty of time to do this, at least 20 minutes. If necessary, brown birds a few at a time, adding more butter if needed. Put in roasting pan and season with salt and pepper. Roast in preheated 375° oven, uncovered, for about 30 minutes, basting every 5 minutes with melted currant jelly. Birds should be brown and shiny at the end of cooking time. If not, boost oven temperature to 450° for the last 5 to 10 minutes. They're good served hot, warm, or cold, and they can be frozen without losing their glaze. *May be fully prepared ahead and put in oven to warm through.*

## STRAW POTATOES

4 large Idaho potatoes
Fat for deep frying
1 tablespoon salt

Peel potatoes and slice as thin as possible with a vegetable slicer or mandoline. Stack 3 or 4 slices at a time on cutting board and cut them, thinner than matchsticks, hair-thin if possible, with your chef's knife. Put in cold water immediately and let them soak for 15 minutes. Drain them and dry thoroughly. In a saucepan, heat 3 inches vegetable shortening to 375° and fry potatoes a handful at a time, until they turn straw color. Remove with a slotted spoon and drain on paper towels. Spread them on a baking sheet. (*Can be done ahead to this point, and they freeze well. Bring to room temperature before reheating.*) Just before serving, run potato sticks into a moderate oven to warm through and crisp (may be reheated in oven with Cornish hens). Sprinkle with salt and serve hot.

## CELERY VICTOR

1 bunch celery
2 cups chicken stock (see
  p. 278)
1 teaspoon coarse salt
½ teaspoon freshly cracked
  white pepper

2 tablespoons red wine vinegar
½ cup olive oil
1 2-ounce can flat anchovy
  fillets, drained
1 pimento, sliced
2 tablespoons chopped parsley

Slice or dice the celery, put it in a saucepan, and cover with chicken stock. Cook over high heat until barely tender, about 15 to 20 minutes. Don't overcook. Drain celery, put in a bowl, cover and refrigerate. (*Can be made the day before.*) Strain the stock and save it for consommé—it's quite flavorful. When ready to serve, make vinaigrette dressing: Beat salt, pepper, vinegar, and oil together in a small bowl with a fork, or shake in a small jar, pour over celery, decorate with anchovy fillets and sliced pimento, and sprinkle with parsley.

## RASPBERRY TART

2 to 4 large, or 4 to 8 small,
  macaroons
⅓ cup flour
¾ cup sugar
  Pinch of salt
2 eggs
2 egg yolks
2 cups scalded milk
1 tablespoon kirsch

1 wholly baked 9-inch pâte
  brisée shell (see p. 288)
2 tablespoons dry bread
  crumbs, if needed
1 quart fresh raspberries, or
  2 10-ounce packages frozen
  whole raspberries
½ cup currant jelly
1 tablespoon cassis syrup
  Confectioners' sugar

Unwrap macaroons to let dry overnight and chop them up; you should have about 2 cups. Set aside. To make pastry cream, put flour, sugar, and salt into a nonaluminum saucepan. Mix in 1 egg and 1 egg yolk with a wooden spatula, then add remaining egg and egg yolk, mixing well. Change to a whisk and pour scalded milk into egg mixture, whisking constantly. Set over medium-high heat and stir with whisk until custard thickens to consistency of thick mayonnaise. This mixture burns easily, so watch it carefully. Remove from heat, stir in kirsch, and let cool. Stir it now and then as it cools, or cool it quickly by stirring over ice. (*Pastry cream may be made 1 day ahead, covered closely with plastic wrap, and refrigerated.*) If you want to assemble whole tart in advance—but not more than 2 hours in advance—sprinkle shell with bread crumbs to help prevent pastry from getting soggy. (Bread crumbs are not necessary if tart is not prepared in advance.) Stir macaroon crumbs into cooled pastry cream, and fill pastry shell. Arrange raspberries on filling, around the edge in neat rows, stem side down, and piled up in the middle of the tart. Melt currant jelly, stir in cassis, and dab over berries with a pastry brush to glaze. Just before serving, sift confectioners' sugar around. the edge of the tart.

### *Formal Dinner for 6 on the Terrace*

Cold truffled lobster halves, vinaigrette
Roast lamb with soubise
Roman asparagus
Platter of crisp raw vegetables (cherry tomatoes,
fava beans, celery sticks, carrot curls, etc.)
Fresh pear tart

### COLD TRUFFLED LOBSTER HALVES, VINAIGRETTE

3 live lobsters, about 1¼
  pounds each
1 recipe court bouillon (see
  p. 279)

18 slices truffle
1 recipe French vinaigrette
  dressing (see p. 282)

Drop live lobsters into boiling court bouillon and boil until they turn red, about 6 to 10 minutes. Let lobsters cool in the broth to room temperature, about 1 hour. Remove and split them down the center back, discarding the sac between the eyes and the intestinal vein. Carefully remove the one large piece of meat from each half—keeping it whole—turn it over, and put it back into the half shell so the red, rounded side is now up. Make 3 slits in the meat of each half lobster and insert a slice of truffle in each slit. Spoon vinaigrette over the lobster halves and let marinate for at least 1 hour before serving. (*Recipe may be done ahead to this point, covered with plastic wrap, and refrigerated. Bring to room temperature before serving.*) Serve lobster halves accompanied by the claws and individual bowls of extra vinaigrette on the side, for dipping claw meat into. The claws should be already cracked for easy handling.

## ROAST LAMB WITH SOUBISE

If you've never made soubise, you should know that it is quite bland despite being an onion-based sauce—it's just enough to give lamb or veal a lift. This version is thickened with potatoes; sometimes rice, or rice-and-potato is the thickener.

| | |
|---|---|
| 1 7-pound leg of lamb, boned | 1 thinly sliced medium-size |
| 2 cloves garlic | baking potato |
| Coarse salt | 2 tablespoons flour |
| Freshly cracked black pepper | ½ cup light cream |
| ½ cup plus 2 tablespoons butter | 2 egg yolks |
| 1 teaspoon salt | ¼ cup chopped parsley |
| ½ teaspoon freshly cracked | ¼ cup dry red wine |
| white pepper | ¼ cup dry bread crumbs |
| 3 thinly sliced onions | ¼ cup melted butter |

Trim excess fat from lamb—leave no more than ¼ inch on it. Cut garlic cloves into slivers. With a small sharp knife, make little slits all over the meat and, using the knife blade as a slide, push the garlic slivers into the meat. Tie the leg at intervals with butcher's cord to re-form it; it should look like a roll of lamb. Rub it with coarse salt and pepper, set on rack in roasting pan, and roast in a preheated 350° oven 12 to 15 minutes per pound for pink lamb.

To make soubise, melt ½ cup butter in a heavy saucepan; stir in salt and pepper, onions, and potato, and cover and cook over medium-high heat for 20 to 30 minutes or until vegetables are soft. Stir occasionally during cooking, so onions won't burn. When vegetables are soft, puree the mixture in a blender or put it through a food mill, using the fine blade. In another saucepan, melt 2 tablespoons butter, stir in the flour, and cook it, stirring with a wooden spatula, over high heat for 2 minutes. Remove from heat, change to a whisk, and add light cream, whisking vigorously. Return to high heat, and cook, stirring, until mixture is really thick. Beat egg yolks with a fork. Stir a little of the sauce into the yolks to warm them; then stir yolks, onion-potato puree, and chopped parsley into the sauce and taste for seasoning.

When lamb is done, let it rest on a carving board while you deglaze roasting pan. Pour off all but 1 tablespoon fat; pour in wine and set pan over heat for a minute while you scrape up the brown bits. Pour this liquid into a large au gratin serving dish. Carve the lamb into slices about ¼ inch thick and pour its juices into serving dish. Spread lamb slices with the soubise and arrange them, overlapping, in the serving dish. Sprinkle with bread crumbs and drizzle with melted butter. (*Recipe can be made ahead to this point. Cool in refrigerator, uncovered, for ½ hour or longer; then cover with plastic wrap and refrigerate. Bring to room temperature before reheating.*) When ready to serve, preheat oven to 400° and heat lamb. If you overcooked lamb when you roasted it, reheat it for 10 to 15 minutes. If lamb was too pink when you carved it, reheat it for 20 to 25 minutes.

### ROMAN ASPARAGUS

2 pounds very thin fresh asparagus
½ cup melted butter
Juice of 1 lemon

½ cup freshly grated Parmesan cheese, plus more if needed
Freshly cracked white pepper
Salt, if necessary

It's not necessary to peel thin asparagus, but check to see if there's sand under scales, and trim the ends. Place asparagus in a large skillet containing boiling water almost to cover. Reduce heat, and simmer until asparagus is tender-crisp, only a few minutes. Do not cover pan; do not add salt to water. Drain cooked asparagus and spread on a towel to dry. Brush a serving dish with butter; arrange asparagus in a thin layer; pour on melted butter and lemon juice and sprinkle with Parmesan cheese. You may need more than ½ cup cheese to cover asparagus. Sprinkle with pepper and a tiny bit of salt if cheese is not salty. (*Can be made ahead to this point.*) Bake in a preheated 400° oven for 10 minutes.

### FRESH PEAR TART

6 fresh pears
2 cups sugar
2 cups water
1 8-ounce jar currant jelly
1 wholly baked 9-inch pâte
   brisée shell (see p. 288)
1½ cups heavy cream

2 tablespoons confectioners'
   sugar, plus more for
   sifting
2 tablespoons kirsch
12 strawberries
¼ cup chopped almonds

Peel, cut in half, and core pears and poach them in a syrup of sugar and water until barely tender, about 15 to 20 minutes. Melt the currant jelly and spread half of it over the bottom of the tart shell. Whip the cream, sweetening it with confectioners' sugar and kirsch, and spread over the currant glaze. Drain pear halves and arrange them, cored side up, on the whipped cream. Glaze the strawberries with remaining currant jelly and place a strawberry on each pear half. Sprinkle entire tart with chopped almonds. (*May be assembled 2 hours ahead.*) Just before serving, sift a little confectioners' sugar around the rim of the tart.

## A Summer Dinner
### for 8

Seafood mélange
Veal birds with brown sauce
French-fried zucchini
Berries with cold zabaglione

### SEAFOOD MÉLANGE

1 pound shrimp, fresh or
   frozen
1 pound crab meat, fresh,
   frozen, or canned
5 tablespoons butter
¼ cup dry sherry or Madeira
3 tablespoons flour
1½ cups milk
1 cup light cream

1 egg yolk
½ teaspoon salt
¼ teaspoon freshly cracked
   white pepper
4 tablespoons freshly grated
   Parmesan cheese
½ cup bread crumbs
½ cup softened butter

If shrimp are frozen, put them in water to cover, bring to a boil and turn off heat. Let cool. Shell and devein shrimp and chop in large pieces. Pick over crab meat. Melt 2 tablespoons butter in a heavy skillet, add shrimp and crab meat, and toss over high heat to mix, trying to avoid shredding crab meat. Add sherry and cook until wine evaporates, about 3 to 5 minutes. Set aside. In a sauce-pan, melt remaining 3 tablespoons butter, stir in flour, and cook, stirring with a wooden spatula, over high heat for 2 minutes. Do not let it brown. Remove from heat, change to a whisk, and add milk, whisking vigorously. Add cream. Return to medium-high heat and cook, stirring, until sauce thickens. Stir a little of the hot sauce into the egg yolk, to warm it; then stir yolk into sauce. Bring it to the boiling point (but do not boil) and remove from heat. Add seafood, season with salt and pepper, and pour into an au gratin dish, or into individual scallop shells or ramekins. Sprinkle with cheese and bread crumbs and dot with butter. (*Can be made ahead to this point, covered with plastic wrap, and refrigerated. Bring to room temperature before heating.*) Bake in a preheated 350° oven, 15 to 20 minutes for au gratin dish, about 10 minutes for scallop shells, or until bubbly and lightly browned.

## VEAL BIRDS WITH BROWN SAUCE

| | |
|---|---|
| 8 slices veal, cut from leg, each about ½ inch thick | ½ pound veal, ground twice |
| 4 tablespoons brandy | 2 tablespoons chopped parsley |
| 1 teaspoon salt | 1 teaspoon dried tarragon |
| ½ teaspoon freshly cracked white pepper | 1 beaten egg |
| ¾ cup finely chopped onion | ¼ pound smoked cooked tongue, all in 1 piece |
| 1 finely chopped clove garlic | Black truffle |
| 5 tablespoons butter | 1 recipe basic brown sauce (see p. 281) |

Place veal slices between 2 sheets of waxed paper and pound thin. Brush them with 2 tablespoons brandy and sprinkle with ½ teaspoon salt and ¼ teaspoon pepper. Cook onion and garlic over high heat in 2 tablespoons butter, stirring with a wooden spatula, until onion is transparent—do not let it brown. In a bowl, mix together ground veal, onion, garlic, chopped parsley, tarragon, beaten egg, and remaining salt and pepper. Spread ground veal mixture over veal slices. Cut tongue into fingers and lay 1 finger down the center of each piece of veal. Put a wedge of black truffle in the center. Roll up the veal around the tongue and tie ends loosely with string. Heat remaining 3 tablespoons butter in a heavy skillet and sauté veal birds in butter, over high heat, turning them to brown on all sides. Flame with remaining 2 tablespoons brandy and remove from pan. Add basic brown sauce to pan and bring it to a boil over high heat, scraping up the brown bits. Return veal birds to pan. (*Recipe may be done ahead to this point and refrigerated, or frozen for up to 1 month.*) Cook veal, covered, over low heat, for about 20 minutes. Arrange on serving platter, remove strings, and pour on sauce.

## FRENCH-FRIED ZUCCHINI

8 small zucchini
½ cup flour
2 cups vegetable shortening

1 teaspoon salt
½ teaspoon freshly cracked white pepper

Peel the zucchini with a vegetable peeler and cut into matchsticks. Dredge the sticks with flour, put them in a coarse sieve, and bang it to shake off excess flour. In a heavy saucepan, electric skillet, or deep-fat fryer, heat vegetable shortening to 375°. Fry zucchini sticks, a handful at a time, until light brown, about 3 minutes. Remove them with a slotted spoon and drain on brown paper or paper towels. Keep warm in a low oven while you fry remaining sticks. (*Or prepare ahead to this point. To reheat, spread sticks on brown paper set over cake racks on a baking sheet, and warm in a 350° oven for several minutes.*) Salt and pepper the zucchini and heap in a serving dish.

## BERRIES WITH COLD ZABAGLIONE

Follow the directions for Zabaglione on page 203, but reduce ingredients to 1 egg, 2 egg yolks, 3 tablespoons sugar, and 3 tablespoons Marsala. When zabaglione is thick and creamy, remove from heat, set the pot or bowl in a bowl of ice, and continue beating over ice until mixture is cold. Whip 1 cup heavy cream to the same consistency as zabaglione and fold in. Cover and store in refrigerator until serving time. Spoon over raspberries or strawberries in dessert bowls.

## *An Informal Alsatian Dinner*
### *for 6*

---

Lentil salad
Choucroute garni
Steamed potatoes with caraway
and melted butter
Tart Tatin

### LENTIL SALAD

½ pound lentils
3 slices bacon
1 finely minced onion
  Juice of ½ lemon
1 teaspoon salt
½ teaspoon freshly cracked
  white pepper
2 teaspoons mustard

2 tablespoons red wine vinegar,
  or tarragon vinegar
4 tablespoons olive oil
1 chopped clove garlic
1 2-ounce can flat anchovy
  fillets
6 black olives
2 tablespoons chopped parsley

Put lentils in a saucepan, cover with cold water, and bring to a boil. Turn heat to simmer, cook lentils for about 35 minutes, and test for doneness: if a lentil gives between your fingers when you pinch it, it is done. Drain and set aside. Cut bacon into large dice and partly fry it, over high heat—it should remain limp. Stir in onion and wilt it; this takes about 2 minutes. Add lentils, mix, and heat through. Pour into a large bowl and sprinkle with lemon juice. Make a dressing by beating or shaking together salt, pepper, mustard, vinegar, olive oil, and garlic; pour over warm lentils and toss to mix. (*Recipe can be made a day ahead to this point.*) Serve at room temperature, garnished with anchovies, black olives, and chopped parsley.

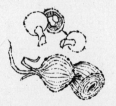

## CHOUCROUTE GARNI

A marvelous traditional dish with a gala presentation.

½ pound salt pork, about
2 pounds sauerkraut
2 apples, peeled, cored, and
   sliced
2 medium-size onions, cut in
   eighths
4 juniper berries
1 bay leaf
¼ teaspoon ground coriander
   seed
2 whole cloves
2 mashed cloves garlic
½ teaspoon freshly cracked
   white pepper
1 pound bacon, uncut

6 smoked pork chops
3 pounds pork tenderloin,
   optional
1 2-pound smoked pork butt,
   cut in ¾-inch slices,
   optional
1 rack spareribs, optional
1 garlic sausage
6 knackwurst, optional
1 cup Riesling dry white wine
1 cup chicken stock (see
   p. 278)
1 potato
1 split champagne, optional

Cut a few strips of salt pork and lay them in the bottom of a large flameproof casserole. Rinse and drain the sauerkraut and put it in the casserole along with apple slices, onions, juniper berries, bay leaf, coriander, cloves, garlic, and pepper. Dice the bacon and spread it over sauerkraut. Add meats, except sausage and knackwurst, and pour in wine and chicken stock. (*Recipe can be prepared ahead to this point.*) Cover, bring to a boil over high heat, and place casserole in a preheated 350° oven to cook for 1½ to 2 hours, or longer if you wish—sauerkraut must be thoroughly cooked. About 45 minutes before serving time, add sausage and knackwurst and grate the raw potato into the casserole to absorb any sour taste and excess salt. (*May be made ahead and reheated in oven or on top of stove.*)

To serve, arrange smoked meats at ends of platter. Remove bay leaf, toss the sauerkraut, salt pork, and bacon dice together, and spoon into the center of the platter. Bring platter to the table, uncork the champagne, and pour it over the sauerkraut. Put the platter over a spirit lamp and flame the champagne. Cover with another platter and let it simmer for 15 minutes to absorb the champagne.

## STEAMED POTATOES WITH CARAWAY AND MELTED BUTTER

24 peeled small new potatoes
2 cups water
1 chopped celery rib
½ chopped onion
1 tablespoon salt

½ teaspoon freshly cracked black pepper
2 tablespoons caraway seeds
6 tablespoons hot melted butter

"Turn" or shape the potatoes with a paring knife so that they are all the same size, or cut larger ones into smaller pieces and trim. Put them in a steamer basket over water flavored with celery, onion, salt, and pepper. Cover and steam until potatoes are tender—test with the point of a knife after 10 minutes. Just before serving, sprinkle with caraway seeds and pour on butter; roll potatoes around in the pan to coat them well. *You can peel potatoes ahead; keep them covered with cold water to prevent darkening. Measure ingredients into steamer bottom ahead, too— but do not cook potatoes until ready to serve.*

## TART TATIN

2 tablespoons softened butter
2 cups sugar
8 medium-size apples, greenings, if available
2 tablespoons Calvados, apple brandy, or brandy
½ teaspoon freshly grated nutmeg
½ cup butter

1 recipe pâte brisée (see p. 288)
2 tablespoons confectioners' sugar
Whipped cream or vanilla ice cream, optional
3 tablespoons confectioners' sugar, optional
3 tablespoons Calvados or apple brandy, optional

Spread butter over bottom and sides of a 9-inch ovenproof glass pie pan. Add 1 cup sugar and shake the pan to distribute sugar evenly. Peel, core, and slice apples ⅛ inch thick; heap them in the pan, making a dome in the center—the pan will look overflowing, but the apples cook down. Sprinkle apples with Calvados, nutmeg, and remaining 1 cup sugar. Dot all over with ½ cup butter. Roll a pastry circle ¼ inch thick and place over apples, turning back the edge of the pastry all around so that it does not touch the rim of the pan—leave about ¼ inch gap. Place pan on the bottom shelf of a preheated 375° oven and bake for 30 minutes. Turn oven to 325° and bake 2 hours longer (time is correct). Do not put foil around the dish to catch drippings and do not set pan on a baking sheet. (These directions are necessary to caramelize the tart; it helps to have a self-cleaning oven.) If crust begins to get too brown, lay aluminum foil loosely over the top.

Remove from oven and cool 5 minutes. Run a knife around the edge of the tart, lifting up as you go, and invert onto an oven-proof serving plate. If you find, when you turn it out, that the bottom of the tart isn't caramelized, run it under the broiler for a minute or two. (*May be baked ahead and served at room temperature or reheated in a 350° oven for 15 minutes.*) Sift confectioners' sugar around edge of tart just before serving (stir it through a small sieve with a teaspoon). If desired, whip 1½ cups heavy cream; leave unsweetened, or flavor it with 3 tablespoons confectioners' sugar and 3 tablespoons Calvados or apple brandy. Or serve tart with ice cream.

## A Game Dinner
## for 6

Trout amandine
Venison Bourguignonne
Red cabbage
Kartoffelklösse
Chestnut tart

### TROUT AMANDINE

6 trout, about 1 pound each
1 tablespoon lemon juice
1 quart water
1 cup milk
1 cup flour
1 teaspoon salt
½ teaspoon freshly cracked white pepper
½ cup vegetable oil
½ cup butter
¾ cup sliced blanched almonds

Scale, clean, and split (but do not halve) trout—or ask your fish seller to do it—leaving heads and tails intact. Wash trout in a mixture of water and lemon juice and dry them. Dip in milk, roll in flour, pat off excess flour, and season with salt and pepper. Heat oil in large skillet and sauté trout for 6 minutes over medium-high heat, without moving them. Turn them over carefully with 2 spatulas and cook 6 minutes on the other side. Remove to serving platter and keep warm. Pour oil out of pan and add butter; when it's hot, add almonds. Sauté almonds for 3 to 4 minutes over medium-high heat, shaking the pan, and pour almonds and butter over fish.

## VENISON BOURGUIGNONNE

3 pounds venison, rump or loin, cut into 1½-inch cubes
4 tablespoons butter
½ cup brandy
24 small white onions, peeled
½ pound mushrooms
2 teaspoons tomato paste
1 teaspoon meat glaze (see p. 280)
3 teaspoons potato flour
½ cup dry red wine
½ cup dry sherry

2 cups chicken stock (see p. 278)
1 teaspoon freshly cracked black pepper
1 teaspoon red currant jelly
1 bouquet garni (see p. 283) but substitute 1 table-spoon fresh tarragon or 1 teaspoon dry tarragon for the thyme
½ pound finely diced salt pork
2 tablespoons finely chopped parsley

In a heavy casserole, over high heat, brown the venison cubes in 3 tablespoons hot butter, a few pieces at a time—do not let them touch. When all cubes are brown, put them all back in the pan and flame with ¼ cup brandy. Remove meat and set aside. Add remaining 1 tablespoon butter to pan and stir in the peeled onions; cook, stirring, for about 3 minutes. Stir in mushrooms—cut any large mushrooms in half—to coat well with butter. Remove from heat, stir in tomato paste, meat glaze, and potato flour; mix until smooth. Add red wine, sherry, and chicken stock and mix until smooth. Return to medium-high heat and bring to a boil. Add black pepper, currant jelly, and the bouquet garni. Return venison to casserole. (*Can be made ahead to this point or fully cooked the day before and reheated.*) Cover with foil and a heavy lid and place in a preheated 350° oven to cook for 1½ to 2 hours or until tender. Baste it 4 times during cooking, adding a tablespoonful of brandy each time. Remove the bouquet garni after 45 minutes.

When venison is nearly done, blanch, drain, and sauté the diced salt pork until crisp, and add to casserole. When ready, sprinkle with parsley and serve from the casserole.

## RED CABBAGE

Follow recipe on p. 96, but while cabbage is cooking, prepare 4 green apples: peel, core, and slice the apples and sauté in 3 tablespoons butter. Add 2 tablespoons lemon juice and 1 tablespoon cinnamon and cook until tender. Add apples to cabbage in serving dish, pour on the cornstarch-thickened liquid, and mix lightly together.

## KARTOFFELKLÖSSE

| | |
|---|---|
| 6 medium-size all-purpose potatoes | ¼ teaspoon freshly grated nutmeg |
| 2 beaten eggs | 1 teaspoon salt |
| ½ cup flour | ½ teaspoon freshly cracked black pepper |
| ½ cup grated onion | |
| 1 tablespoon finely chopped parsley | 2 quarts chicken stock (see p. 278) |

Peel potatoes, cover with cold water, and boil until tender. Put them through a potato ricer or food mill. Add eggs, flour, onion, parsley, nutmeg, salt, and pepper. Beat with a fork until fluffy. Roll the mixture into balls the size of walnuts. (*Can be done ahead to this point.*) When ready to cook, bring chicken stock to a boil; drop potato balls into stock and cook them at a low boil, covered, for 15 minutes. If you have a large pot, cook the potato balls all at once—they can be crowded together. Or cook them in relays, keeping those already cooked warm in a low oven (first removing the venison casserole, which can be held on top of the stove over a low flame, or in a hot water bath).

## CHESTNUT TART

1 15-ounce can sweetened
 chestnut puree
1 cup unsalted butter
 Confectioners' sugar,
 optional
2 tablespoons kirsch
½ cup chopped toasted almonds

1 wholly baked 9-inch pâte
 brisée shell (see p. 288)
1 cup heavy cream, whipped
2 tablespoons confectioners'
 sugar
12 whole marrons

Beat chestnut puree and butter together with an electric mixer or wooden spatula until smooth and creamy. Taste for sweetness and add confectioners' sugar to taste. Stir in kirsch and toasted almonds. Spread mixture into baked pastry shell, smooth the top, and garnish with rosettes of whipped cream sweetened with 2 tablespoons confectioners' sugar and piped from a large pastry bag fitted with a star tube. Place whole marrons around edge of tart. Serve cold. *Tart may be fully assembled 3 to 4 hours before serving.*

## A Chinese Dinner
## for 6 to 8

Puffed shrimp
Paper-wrapped chicken
Barbecued spareribs
Stir-fried beef
Fried rice
Glacéed apples and bananas

If you don't like to cook in front of your guests, don't attempt Chinese food. All of these dishes should be cooked at the last minute to retain flavor, texture, and crispness. You can do the chopping, measuring, and preparing ahead of time, but then it's cook-and-serve—fast! I recommend that you serve the shrimp, chicken, and spareribs together. Then let your guests take a break —they won't mind!—while you prepare a second course of beef and rice. The apple and banana dessert, a real treat, makes up the third course.

### PUFFED SHRIMP

30 to 35 medium-size shrimp
    Vegetable shortening for
      deep frying
    Flour for coating shrimp

1 recipe beer batter (see p. 285)
Soy Dipping Sauce (recipe follows)

Clean the shrimp but leave the tails on. Heat 2 inches of vegetable shortening in a wok, electric skillet, deep-fat fryer, or heavy saucepan to 375°. Flour shrimp, patting off excess flour, dip in beer batter, and drop them, 2 or 3 at a time, into hot fat. Cook until nicely browned—do not overcook. Drain on paper towels. (*May be prepared ahead and reheated. To reheat: set cake racks on a baking sheet, cover with brown paper, lay shrimp on paper, and heat for a few minutes in a 350° oven.*) Serve hot with Soy Dipping Sauce.

### SOY DIPPING SAUCE

Mix together ¾ cup soy sauce, ¾ cup red wine vinegar, ¼ cup vegetable oil, and 2 very finely chopped cloves of garlic.

### PAPER-WRAPPED CHICKEN

3 whole chicken breasts
1 teaspoon salt
2 tablespoons plus 1 pint
    peanut oil
2 tablespoons chopped
    scallions
¼ cup soy sauce

1 teaspoon ground ginger
3 tablespoons sherry
30 pieces of baking parch-
    ment, waxed paper or
    aluminum foil, about
    5 inches square

Skin and bone chicken breasts and cut meat into pieces about 1 inch square. Put them into a bowl, cover with salt, 2 tablespoons peanut oil, chopped scallions, soy sauce, ground ginger, and sherry. Stir to mix well and marinate for 2 hours. Lay 1 or 2 chicken pieces on each paper or foil square. Fold 1 corner over chicken, fold in both side corners (like an envelope); then fold this squared end once more and tuck remaining free corner into resulting pocket to make a tight, secure package. (*May be made ahead to this point.*) Heat 1 pint peanut oil in wok or skillet to the point of smoking. Add chicken parcels, 3 or 4 at a time, and fry 5 minutes only. Hold cooked chicken parcels in a 350° oven to keep warm. Serve chicken pieces directly from their paper packages. Use chopsticks or forks to open packages and eat chicken.

## BARBECUED SPARERIBS

Chinese 5-spice powder is a strong and pungent mixture of star anise, peppercorns, fennel, cloves, and cinnamon and is readily available in Chinese and gourmet shops. Very little is used, as too much will overpower any dish.

3 pounds spareribs
5 tablespoons soy sauce
2 tablespoons sherry
½ teaspoon Chinese 5-spice
   powder
1 tablespoon sugar
2 teaspoons ground ginger
1 tablespoon finely chopped
   garlic
¼ cup honey

Trim excess fat and gristle from ribs and cut between every 2 ribs, but do not separate completely. Mix together soy sauce, sherry, 5-spice powder, sugar, ginger, and garlic, and marinate ribs for 2 hours, turning frequently. Place ribs on a rack in a roasting pan, pour 1 inch hot water into bottom of pan (to help keep ribs moist), and bake in a preheated 350° oven for 1 hour, turning ribs frequently. After 30 minutes, glaze ribs with honey and continue baking. *Ribs can be baked ahead and reheated in a 350° oven for 15 minutes.*

*Note:* Another way to bake the ribs is to hang them in the oven over the pan of hot water. Bend wire or strong paper clips into S-hooks, hook one end into meat, and hang the other end over rung of oven rack.

### STIR-FRIED BEEF

2½  pounds beef, sliced ¼ inch
thick
4  tablespoons soy sauce
2  tablespoons sherry
½  teaspoon salt
½  teaspoon sugar
1  teaspoon Chinese 5-spice
powder
1  pound vegetables (choose
any 5 or 6 from the fol-
lowing: celery, mush-
rooms, scallions, red
onion, green pepper,
snow peas, fresh or
frozen, Chinese cabbage,
bean sprouts, canned
water chestnuts, drained,
or canned bamboo
shoots, drained)
4  tablespoons peanut oil
1  chopped clove garlic
2  chopped slices fresh ginger
root
2  teaspoons cornstarch
1½  cups chicken stock (see
p. 278)
¼  cup walnuts or almonds,
optional

Cut slices of meat into 1-inch squares. Mix together soy
sauce, sherry, salt, sugar, and 5-spice powder, stir into meat, and
let marinate for 1 hour. Slice all vegetables except bean sprouts
and snow peas into 1-inch pieces; cut celery, Chinese cabbage, and
scallions on the diagonal. Set aside. Heat 2 tablespoons oil in the
wok, or large skillet. Add chopped garlic and gingerroot and
stir-fry over high heat for 1 minute. Add beef and stir-fry for 2
minutes. Remove beef and set aside. Add remaining 2 tablespoons
oil, stir in vegetables (except snow peas), and return meat to wok.
Stir cornstarch into chicken stock and add. Cook, stirring, until
sauce thickens, about 5 minutes. Put lid on wok and cook over
high heat until all vegetables are tender-crisp, about 5 minutes.
Add snow peas the last minute of cooking, and the nuts last, just
to heat through.

*Note:* Ingredients may be collected, measured, and chopped
ahead of time, but stir-fry cooking is always done at the last
minute.

### FRIED RICE

5  cups cooked cold rice (about
1¾ cups uncooked)
5  eggs
3  tablespoons water
¼  cup peanut oil
1  teaspoon salt
½  teaspoon freshly cracked
black pepper
¼  cup chopped scallions or
Chinese parsley

Dampen hands and separate rice grains so fried rice won't be lumpy. Beat eggs with water and set aside. Heat peanut oil in wok or large skillet almost to smoking. Add rice and stir-fry over high heat until rice is heated through. Season with salt and pepper. Pour in beaten eggs and quickly fold eggs and rice together with a spatula or large spoon. Sprinkle with chopped scallions or Chinese parsley and serve hot. Stir-frying time is no more than 5 minutes—can be done while beef (previous recipe) simmers.

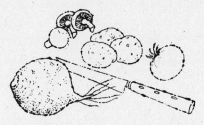

## GLACÉED APPLES AND BANANAS

This dessert creates a spectacular effect when served using chopsticks; each guest dips pieces of glazed fruit into a bowl of ice-cold water. As the fruit comes in contact with the water, the glaze hardens instantly, surrounding the soft fruit with a crackly, crunchy syrup shell.

| | |
|---|---|
| 6 to 8 apples (1 per person) | ¼ teaspoon cream of tartar |
| 3 or 4 bananas (½ per person) | ¾ cup flour |
| 4½ cups (2 pounds) sugar | 4 beaten eggs |
| 1 cup water | Peanut oil |
| 2 tablespoons light corn syrup | 6 to 8 bowls of iced water |

Peel and core apples and cut in eighths. Peel bananas and cut in chunks about ½ inch thick. Mix sugar, water, corn syrup, and cream of tartar together in a saucepan and bring to a boil over high heat, stirring until sugar dissolves. Turn heat to medium and cook syrup to the hard-crack stage (300° to 320° on a candy thermometer). Remove pan from heat and immediately put it in a pan of warm water to stop the cooking. Roll fruit pieces in flour and shake off excess. Dip in beaten egg. Heat 2 inches of peanut oil in wok or skillet. Deep-fry fruit a few pieces at a time in hot fat until golden, about 1 minute. Remove and drain on paper towels. While still hot, dip fruit into sugar syrup (use tongs or chopsticks—syrup is hot) and place dipped fruit on a buttered platter. Serve hot with bowls of iced water into which the glazed fruit is dipped.

# A Thanksgiving Dinner
## for 8

Jerusalem artichoke soup
Roast capon or turkey with tarragon butter
Wild rice ring
Bibb lettuce salad (see p. 111)
Chestnut tart (see p. 141)

## JERUSALEM ARTICHOKE SOUP

The Jerusalem artichoke does not look anything like the globe artichoke and resembles it only slightly in flavor. It doesn't come from Palestine either. Actually, it's a species of North American sunflower, cultivated by Indians at the time of the Pilgrims and introduced to France at the beginning of the seventeenth century. The tuber is the edible part. You'll find Jerusalem artichokes on the market in winter; they're knobby-looking but should be very firm, with no wrinkles.

| | |
|---|---|
| 2 pounds Jerusalem artichokes | 2 teaspoons salt |
| 4 cups chicken stock (see p. 278) | 1 teaspoon freshly cracked white pepper |
| 3 cups milk | ¼ teaspoon freshly grated nutmeg |
| 4 tablespoons butter | |
| 1 cup chopped onion | 4 egg yolks, optional |
| 2 cups chopped celery | 1 cup heavy cream |
| 2 tablespoons chopped shallots | 2 tablespoons chopped parsley |

Scrub and slice (but do not peel) Jerusalem artichokes. Put them in a large soup kettle and cover with chicken stock and milk. Melt butter in a skillet, add onion, celery, and shallots, and toss over high heat for about 5 minutes. Add to soup kettle along with salt, pepper, and nutmeg. Bring to a boil, cover, and simmer until vegetables are tender, 20 to 30 minutes. Puree the soup through a food mill, using the medium disk. Taste for seasoning. (*Recipe can be made ahead to this point.*) Beat egg yolks into heavy cream and whisk into soup. Bring to the boiling point, but do not boil. Serve from a tureen, sprinkled with chopped parsley.

## ROAST CAPON OR TURKEY
## WITH TARRAGON BUTTER

1 6- to 7-pound capon or small
   turkey
¾ cup butter
1 tablespoon fresh or 1 teaspoon dried tarragon
1 tablespoon chopped parsley
½ roughly chopped black
   truffle
   Salt and pepper

1 finely chopped carrot
1 finely chopped celery rib
1 finely chopped onion
1 cup dry red wine
1 bunch watercress
1 lemon
1 truffle
2 Sautéed Fluted Mushroom
   Caps (see p. 284)

Loosen the skin on the breast of the bird—and, if possible, the legs, too—by working your hands under the skin, next to the flesh. Try not to tear it. Cream butter with tarragon, parsley, chopped truffle, ½ teaspoon salt, and a few grinds of pepper. With a wooden spatula, place tarragon butter, a dollop at a time, under the skin; press down on skin with your hand while you withdraw spatula, leaving butter under skin. Then pat and press the bird to spread the butter around. Truss bird. (*May be prepared ahead to this point, wrapped in foil, and refrigerated.*)

Place bird on its side on rack in roasting pan. Spread a *mirepoix*—chopped carrot, celery, and onion—together with giblets, the neck from the bird, and ½ cup red wine in the bottom of the roasting pan. Salt and pepper the bird and put it into a preheated 475° oven for 15 minutes. Baste and turn bird to its other side for another 15 minutes. Baste again. Turn bird breast up, reduce oven heat to 425°, and roast until done, basting every 15 minutes. Each time you baste, add 2 tablespoons red wine to pan juices, draw juices up with bulb baster, and squirt over bird. To calculate roasting time, count 20 minutes per pound, including the first half hour at high heat. Remove bird from oven and let rest for 15 minutes before bringing to the table.

To make a sauce strain pan juices and cook to reduce by half, skimming off fat. Prepare a garnish for bird: make zigzag cuts around center of lemon with a small knife and pull lemon halves apart. Thread lemon halves on an *attelet*—skewer-shaped utensil with an ornamental top—along with 1 whole black truffle and 2 fluted mushroom caps, and spear into breast of bird. Stuff cavity entrance with a bunch of watercress. To carve a small bird: cut off legs and cut thigh from drumstick through the joint. Cut down center of breast and take off each side of breast meat in 1 piece.

Cut each breast piece in two across the middle. Pass sauce separately in a sauceboat.

## WILD RICE RING

1 cup wild rice
3 teaspoons salt
½ cup pine nuts
4 tablespoons butter
1 cup finely chopped onion

½ teaspoon freshly cracked
  black pepper
½ cup melted butter
1 bunch watercress

Soak rice overnight in cold water. Next day, drain it, put it in a saucepan, add water to cover, stir in 2 teaspoons of the salt, and bring to a boil. Reduce heat to simmer, cover pan, and cook 45 minutes or until barely tender. Drain. Spread pine nuts on a baking sheet and brown in a 350° oven for 10 to 15 minutes. Melt butter in a small skillet and stir in chopped onion; cook over high heat until limp, about 5 minutes. Combine cooked rice, browned pine nuts, and onions, and season with remaining 1 teaspoon salt and the pepper. Add melted butter and mix well. Taste for seasoning. Oil heavily a 4-cup ring mold and pack rice *firmly* into mold. (*Can be made ahead to this point. Cooked rice also freezes well. Bring to room temperature before reheating.*) Set mold in a pan of hot water and place in a preheated 350° oven for 30 minutes. Remove from oven and let stand for 5 minutes. Unmold rice onto a serving plate and fill center of ring with a bunch of watercress.

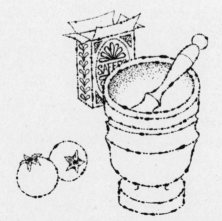

## *A Hearty Christmas Dinner for 8*

Smoked salmon with caviar
Mushroom broth garnished with
mushroom rounds (see p. 51)
Roast goose with giblet sauce
Braised turnips
Relish dish: radishes, black and green olives,
celery, scallions, cherry tomatoes
Mincemeat roll with hard sauce

Roast goose is rich, but for many families, it's not Christmas without it. The relish dish—raw vegetables and olives, unadorned—offers the necessary something crisp and crunchy. Incidentally, don't plan to serve the apple stuffing—you'll find it much too greasy. The apples give flavor to the goose.

### SMOKED SALMON WITH CAVIAR

On individual plates arrange very thinly sliced smoked salmon—top quality—2 slices on each plate. In the center of each, put a small demitasse spoonful of black caviar, also the best. Serve with a lemon wedge and garnish each plate with watercress. Pass the black pepper mill.

### ROAST GOOSE WITH GIBLET SAUCE

1 goose, 10 to 12 pounds
8 apples
1 tablespoon salt
1 tablespoon butter
1 cup boiling water
1 bunch watercress
Giblet Sauce (recipe
  follows)

Wash and dry goose. Peel, core, and quarter apples, stuff them into cavity, and truss legs with string. Secure neck skin onto the back with a skewer, and twist wings behind back. Rub the bird with salt and prick all over with a fork. Spread butter over breast and place the bird on a rack in a roasting pan. Add boiling water to pan and put the goose in a preheated 375° oven. Count 20 minutes per pound. Turn the goose so that it browns lightly on all sides, and baste frequently during roasting with the simmering giblet stock. When goose is done, remove trussing strings and skewers, place on a serving platter, and keep warm while you complete the giblet sauce. Decorate platter with a bunch of watercress and place paper frills on drumsticks.

### GIBLET SAUCE

While goose is roasting, simmer neck, heart, and gizzard in chicken stock to cover, adding 1 onion, salt to taste, a pinch of thyme, ½ carrot, and ½ celery rib. After 2 hours, strain the stock and set aside. Chop the heart and gizzard. Sauté the liver in butter and chop it. When goose is done, pour off all but ¼ cup fat from the roasting pan and stir into it 2 teaspoons potato starch. Cook, stirring, over high heat for about 5 minutes. Gradually add 1½ cups of strained giblet stock to the pan and cook, stirring, for another 5 minutes. Add the chopped giblets and serve sauce separately.

### BRAISED TURNIPS

| | |
|---|---|
| 32  small white turnips | 2  teaspoons salt |
| ½  cup butter | 1  teaspoon freshly cracked |
| 2  teaspoons sugar |    white pepper |

Peel turnips, cutting off root and stem ends, parboil 5 minutes, and drain. Put into a heavy pan with butter and seasonings and place in preheated 350° oven or over high heat and bake or cook until tender—about 30 to 35 minutes. Shake the pan frequently to avoid scorching turnips. *Can be cooked ahead and reheated.*

### MINCEMEAT ROLL WITH HARD SAUCE

| | |
|---|---|
| 1  recipe Sandy's piecrust | 1  egg yolk |
|    (see p. 287) | 1  tablespoon water |
| 1  1-pound jar mincemeat | Hard Sauce (see p. 79) |
| 4  tablespoons brandy | |

Roll out piecrust pastry on a lightly floured board to a rectangle 17 by 10 inches and ⅛ inch thick. Trim edges. Spread with mincemeat ½ inch thick, sprinkle with brandy, and roll up, like a jelly roll, from the long side. Tuck in edges and place on baking sheet, seam side down. Beat egg yolk with 1 tablespoon water to make egg wash and brush on pastry. Cut 4 gashes to let out steam. (*Can be prepared ahead to this point. Baked roll will freeze, for up to 1 month. Thaw overnight in refrigerator before baking.*) Bake in a preheated 350° oven for 35 to 40 minutes, or until crust is brown and crisp. Slice and serve warm with Hard Sauce, flavored with brandy.

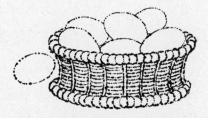

## *An Unusual Easter Dinner for 8*

Eggs Andalouse
Roast fresh ham
Tyropita
Mustard ring
Paskha

This Easter dinner menu upholds tradition by beginning with eggs, which are stuffed and re-formed to look like whole eggs, then coated with sauce. The mustard ring with fresh roast ham is bity but smooth. Tyropita will introduce you to Greek feta cheese and filo pastry, and for dessert you'll learn how to make paskha, an Easter tradition in Russia. If you happen to have a paskha mold, you can shape it, as they do, into a four-sided pyramid. But it will taste as good formed in a sieve, as the recipe directs. Allow 4 hours to roast the ham; everything else is prepared ahead.

### EGGS ANDALOUSE

10 hard-cooked eggs
. 1 cup unsalted butter
1½ tablespoons tomato paste
2 teaspoons salt
½ teaspoon freshly cracked
   white pepper

SAUCE:
1 cup mayonnaise (see p. 283)
½ cup sour cream
3 tablespoons tomato paste

Parsley, for garnish
Tomato roses, for garnish
(see p. 284)

Cut eggs in half; remove yolks and press them through a sieve. Beat butter with an electric mixer or by hand with wooden spatula until creamy; beat in sieved yolks, tomato paste, salt, and pepper. Fill egg whites with mixture and press 2 halves together to re-form whole eggs. Cover with plastic wrap and refrigerate. Prepare mayonnaise, seasoning it well; add sour cream and tomato paste; store in a jar in the refrigerator. (*Recipe can be made ahead to this point.*) When ready to serve, arrange eggs on platter, spoon sauce over each egg, and garnish with chopped parsley. Place 2 tomato roses on parsley bed in center of platter.

### ROAST FRESH HAM

Do not remove skin from meat; it becomes beautifully crisp when roasted.

1 8-pound fresh ham (pork
   leg roast)
2 teaspoons coarse salt
1 teaspoon freshly cracked
   black pepper

1½ cups Madeira, about
1 bunch watercress, for
   garnish
Spiced crab apples, for
   garnish

Score pork skin in diamond shapes and rub all over with salt and pepper. Lay fat side up in a roasting pan and roast in a preheated 325° oven for 30 minutes per pound, or about 4 hours, raising temperature to 350° for last half hour, while baking Tyropita. (Temperature on meat thermometer should read 170°, and never mind the listing on the thermometer for pork. This new lower temperature has general approval; pork will be thoroughly cooked but not dry and overdone.) Baste every 30 minutes while roasting with 2 tablespoons Madeira. When done, remove pork to a carving board and keep warm. Add ½ cup Madeira to pan juices and boil, scraping up brown bits. Reduce by half. Skim off fat, rectify seasoning, and pass in sauceboat. Garnish meat platter with a bunch of watercress and spiced crab apples.

## TYROPITA

The best feta cheese—or Greek goat cheese—is packed in brine. Rinse off brine and taste the cheese; if it is overpoweringly salty, soak it in milk for 1 hour. Filo dough, a pastry thin as an onion skin, comes in sheets and is available in Greek or Armenian grocery stores. Because it is fragile and dries out rapidly, work with only 1 filo sheet at a time, keeping the remaining sheets covered with a damp, not wet, towel.

| | |
|---|---|
| 1 pound feta cheese | 1 cup grated Parmesan cheese |
| 3 tablespoons butter | 4 beaten eggs |
| 4 tablespoons flour | 8 sheets filo dough, each |
| 2 cups milk | about 11 inches by 15 |
| ½ teaspoon freshly cracked | inches |
| white pepper | ½ cup melted butter |
| ¼ teaspoon freshly grated | |
| nutmeg | |

Drain cheese, mash it, and set it aside. Melt butter in a saucepan and stir in flour. Cook, stirring constantly, over high heat for 2 minutes; do not let it brown. Remove from heat, change to a whisk, and add milk, whisking vigorously. Return to high heat and cook, stirring with whisk, until sauce comes to a boil and thickens. Add pepper, nutmeg, and Parmesan cheese; whisk until cheese melts. Stir some of the hot sauce into the eggs, to warm them; then stir the warmed eggs into the sauce. Mix sauce with cheese and set aside. Brush an oven-to-table baking dish (about 7 by 11 or 8 by 10 inches) with melted butter. Line dish with 4 filo sheets, brushing each sheet with melted butter as you lay it in. Let edges hang over dish. Pour in cheese mixture. Cover with remaining 4 filo sheets, again brushing each sheet with melted butter. Fold the overhang back over the top and brush with butter. (*Recipe can be made ahead to this point, and refrigerated or frozen.*) Bake in a preheated 350° oven for 30 minutes or until brown; the crust will puff up nicely. Serve immediately.

*Note:* If making recipe ahead, brush top well with melted butter and cover with plastic wrap. Refrigerate it if holding for more than 1 hour; let it come back to room temperature, still covered with wrap, before you bake it. It can be frozen, ready to bake, too. Defrost in refrigerator and then bring to room temperature. If you bake this and reheat it, it will not puff.

## MUSTARD RING

| | |
|---|---|
| 2 tablespoons oil, to oil ring mold | 2 tablespoons Dijon mustard |
| 1 tablespoon (1 envelope) unflavored gelatine | ½ teaspoon salt |
| | ½ cup cider vinegar |
| ¼ cup lemon juice | ½ cup water |
| 4 beaten eggs | 1 cup heavy cream |
| ¾ cup sugar | 2 tablespoons chopped parsley |

Oil 4-cup ring mold and set aside. Soften gelatine in lemon juice and place over hot water, stirring to dissolve. In a non-aluminum saucepan combine eggs, sugar, mustard, salt, vinegar, and water, and beat well. Add gelatine mixture and place over low heat; stir with a whisk and cook until mixture thickens to custard consistency. Cool in refrigerator until mixture is on the point of setting. Whip heavy cream and fold into mixture along with parsley; pour into prepared mold and chill in the refrigerator until firm, at least 2 hours, or overnight.

## PASKHA

| | |
|---|---|
| 1 cup unsalted butter | 8 ounces candied fruits *or* 8 ounces citron *or* 8 ounces mixed dark and light raisins |
| 2 pounds cream cheese | |
| 3 egg yolks | |
| 2 cups confectioners' sugar | |
| 1 pint large-curd cottage cheese, optional | Fresh strawberries, for garnish |
| 2 teaspoons vanilla extract | Angelica, for garnish |
| ¾ cup toasted slivered almonds | |

Bring butter, cheese, and egg yolks to room temperature. Put butter in large mixer bowl and beat, using the flat whip if you have a heavy-duty mixer, or beat by hand with wooden spatula. Beat in cream cheese and egg yolks, and add sugar a little at a time, lowering mixer speed as you do so. Drain cottage cheese (if adding it), press it through a sieve, and beat into mixture on low speed. Add vanilla, almonds, and candied fruits or raisins. Line a large sieve (or other container with drainage) with a double thickness of cheesecloth wrung out in cold water. Spoon in cheese mixture, smooth the top, and fold the cheesecloth over. Rest the sieve on the rim of a large bowl, so it can drain, and place in refrigerator overnight. When ready to serve, unmold dessert on a serving plate and decorate with 4 strawberry halves at center top and whole berries around base. Cut angelica into leaf shapes and add to berry decoration.

### *A Dinner for 6*
### *Special Friends*

Mussels en brochette, Béarnaise
Veal Orloff
Grilled tomatoes
Watercress salad
Macédoine of fruit
Sand tarts

Veal Orloff is a marvelous main course on two counts: it's rich and satisfying, so accompaniments can be simple and light. And it can be *completely* prepared a day ahead, ready for reheating. The mussels on skewers are deep-fried but exceedingly light. To serve 6, you'll want to halve the recipes for grilled tomatoes (p. 33) and macédoine of fruit (p. 61); and add an extra bunch of watercress to stretch the salad (p. 122). Any leftover sand tarts (see p. 62) can be frozen for later use.

### MUSSELS EN BROCHETTE, BÉARNAISE

36 mussels
¼ cup dry white wine
Flour
1 recipe beer batter (see
p. 285)

Fat for deep frying
1 recipe Béarnaise Sauce (see
p. 282)

Scrub mussels well, remove beards, and wash in several changes of cold water. Put them in a pan with wine, cover, and shake over high heat until mussels open. Remove mussels from shells (the broth in the pan belongs to the cook), dip in flour, and thread on skewers—6 mussels to a skewer. (*Can be prepared ahead to this point.*) Dip the whole skewer in beer batter and deep-fry, 1 skewer at a time, in 3 inches of hot vegetable shortening (370° on frying thermometer), until brown and crisp, about 3 to 5 minutes. Drain on paper towels and keep warm in a low oven while you fry remaining mussels. Serve with Béarnaise Sauce.

*Note:* Mussels can be fully prepared ahead and reheated. To reheat: set cake racks on a baking sheet, cover with brown paper, lay skewers on the paper, and place in a 350° oven for several minutes.

## VEAL ORLOFF

You can use almost any cut of veal—rump, shoulder, sirloin, or loin; loin is the most expensive. Have it boned and tied every inch to make a cylinder about 4 inches in diameter.

1 3-pound roast of veal, boned and tied (reserve bones)
3 tablespoons butter
1 tablespoon coarse salt
1 teaspoon freshly cracked black pepper
1 tablespoon vegetable oil
1 cup sliced onions
1 cup sliced carrots
1½ cups sliced celery

Bouquet garni (see p. 283)
½ cup (more if needed) chicken stock (see p. 278) or dry white wine
Soubise filling (recipe follows)
Mornay sauce (recipe follows)
¼ cup bread crumbs
1 tablespoon softened butter

Rub veal with 2 tablespoons butter, coarse salt, and pepper. Heat 1 tablespoon butter and the oil in a heavy casserole and brown the meat on all sides over high heat. Remove from casserole and brown the bones (this helps flavor the juices, which you'll use later to make the sauce). Stir in onions, carrots, and celery and cook over high heat until wilted. Return veal to casserole and add a bouquet garni and chicken stock or dry white wine. Cover pan with aluminum foil and casserole lid, and place in a preheated 325° oven to braise for about 1 hour. Veal is done when juices run clear when you prick it, or when meat thermometer reaches 170°. While the veal braises, prepare soubise filling.

When veal is done, remove it from the casserole and strain

the drippings into a 2-cup measure. Deglaze the casserole by pouring in a little chicken stock or white wine, letting it boil for 1 minute, and scraping up the brown bits. Add this liquid to drippings, along with enough chicken stock to make 1½ cups; prepare Mornay sauce, using this liquid. Carve the veal into slices about ¼ inch thick. Spoon about ½ cup of the Mornay sauce into a buttered ovenproof serving platter or au gratin dish. Spread each slice of veal with soubise filling and arrange the slices, overlapping, in the serving dish. Spread any remaining soubise over top of meat. Cover with Mornay sauce, sprinkle with bread crumbs, and dot with softened butter. (*Recipe can be made the day before to this point, covered with plastic wrap, and refrigerated; or it can be frozen for up to 1 month—thaw in refrigerator before reheating.*) Reheat before serving in a 400° oven until sauce bubbles; or run it under broiler to glaze.

### SOUBISE FILLING

| | |
|---|---|
| 4 tablespoons butter | ¼ cup heavy cream |
| 4 cups chopped onions | 2 egg yolks |
| 6 tablespoons raw rice | 1 tablespoon lemon juice |
| ⅔ cup (more if needed) chicken stock (see p. 278) | 1 teaspoon salt |
| | ½ teaspoon pepper |

Melt butter in a heavy ovenproof saucepan. Stir in onions and rice and cook for a minute, stirring, over high heat, to coat well with butter. Add chicken stock and bring to a boil. Cover tightly and set in preheated 325° oven. Look at it in 20 minutes; if dry, add a little more hot chicken stock. Continue cooking until onions and rice are tender, about 40 minutes total time. Puree through a food mill and stir in heavy cream, egg yolks, and lemon juice. Add more cream if necessary—the sauce should fall lazily from a spoon. Season with salt and pepper.

### MORNAY SAUCE

| | |
|---|---|
| 3 tablespoons butter | ½ cup heavy cream |
| 4 tablespoons flour | ¼ cup grated Swiss cheese |
| 1½ cups liquid (drippings from veal plus chicken stock) | Salt |
| | Freshly cracked white pepper |

Melt butter in a saucepan and stir in flour with a wooden spatula. Cook, stirring constantly, over high heat for at least 2 minutes. Do not let the flour brown. Take the pan off heat and add liquid all at once, beating vigorously with a whisk. Return pan to high heat and cook, stirring, until mixture thickens and comes to a boil. Stir in heavy cream and grated cheese; cook until cheese melts. Season to taste.

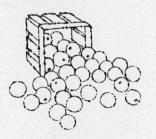

## *Dinner for 8,*
## *with an American Flavor*

---

Cherry tomatoes stuffed with guacamole
Sautéed crab meat on Virginia ham
Cornish hens with tangerines
Whipped sweet potatoes
Pecan pie

American foodstuffs and specialties highlight this unusual and satisfying menu. Serve the stuffed cherry tomatoes with drinks; they make a colorful, one-bite appetizer. Tangerines and juniper berries give the sauce for the Cornish hens a light, bright flavor, not at all sweet, and buttered and seasoned sweet potatoes are perfect with the birds. You'll find the recipe for Sautéed Crab Meat on Virginia Ham on page 34—but cut it back to serve 8. Use 8 slices of ham and 2 pounds of crab meat. The all-American ending is pecan pie.

## CHERRY TOMATOES STUFFED WITH GUACAMOLE

These are excellent served with drinks. Guacamole also makes a good dip. Keep the avocado pit buried in the mixture until serving time, to help keep it from discoloring, and serve with deep-fried pappadoms.

32 cherry tomatoes
1 large ripe avocado
1 tablespoon lime juice
2 tablespoons grated onion
1 tablespoon canned green
   chili sauce

1 teaspoon salt
2 teaspoons olive oil
¼ teaspoon ground coriander
   seed

Hollow out cherry tomatoes with a grapefruit knife. Peel and mash the avocado, add lime juice, grated onion, green chili sauce, salt, olive oil, and coriander seed, and whip with a whisk until smooth. Fill cherry tomatoes with mixture. *May be prepared ahead and refrigerated.*

## CORNISH HENS WITH TANGERINES

4 tangerines
8 12- to 14-ounce Cornish hens
6 tablespoons butter
2 tablespoons vegetable oil
¼ cup brandy
¼ cup chopped shallots
½ pound sliced mushrooms
1 tablespoon lemon juice
1 teaspoon salt
½ teaspoon freshly cracked
   white pepper

1 cup dry Marsala
1 teaspoon potato starch or
   cornstarch
1 tablespoon cold water
20 crushed juniper berries or
   2 tablespoons gin
½ teaspoon meat glaze,
   optional (see p. 280)
1 bunch watercress

Peel the tangerines and separate them into segments; stuff into hens and truss. Heat 4 tablespoons butter and the oil in a heavy skillet and, over high heat, brown the hens all over. Place them in a large heavy casserole. Pour off fat from skillet and deglaze the pan with brandy; pour brandy over hens. Heat remaining 2 tablespoons butter in the skillet, add shallots, and cook for a minute or two, then add mushrooms, lemon juice, salt, and pepper. Toss over high heat for 3 minutes. Add Marsala and heat to boiling. Remove from heat; stir in potato starch dissolved in cold water. Return to heat and cook over high heat until sauce thickens. Pour mushroom sauce over hens in casserole. Sprinkle crushed juniper berries over (or substitute 2 tablespoons gin). Cover casserole with foil and heavy lid. (*May be prepared ahead to this point.*) Place casserole in a preheated 400° oven for about 30 minutes, or until birds test done (juices run clear when you prick the thick part of leg with a fork). Remove trussing strings, arrange birds on a serving platter, and keep warm. Taste the sauce, adding salt if necessary. If sauce is too thin, cook it down over high heat to reduce. Add ½ teaspoon meat glaze, if desired, to intensify flavor. Spoon sauce with mushrooms over each bird and decorate platter with watercress garnish. *If you wish to make dish completely ahead, undercook the birds by 15 minutes; cool to room temperature and refrigerate. Bring to room temperature before reheating; cook until birds test done, about 15 minutes.*

## WHIPPED SWEET POTATOES

10  medium-size sweet  
    potatoes  
¾  cup butter  
2  teaspoons salt  

1  teaspoon freshly cracked  
    white pepper  
½  cup heavy cream  

Scrub potatoes and put in a saucepan; cover with cold water. Bring to a boil, cover pan, reduce heat to maintain a low boil, and cook until potatoes are tender. Drain and peel while warm. Put through a potato ricer or food mill (medium disk). Put riced potatoes in mixer bowl and beat in ½ cup butter, salt, pepper, and heavy cream. Beat until fluffy. (*Recipe can be made ahead to this point. Reheat in pan over simmering water. Before serving, beat again with wooden spatula.*) Pile in serving dish and bury remaining ¼ cup butter in the middle.

## PECAN PIE

½  recipe Sandy's piecrust  
    (see p. 287)  
1  cup dark corn syrup  
1  cup sugar  

4  beaten eggs  
2  teaspoons vanilla extract  
½  teaspoon salt  
1  cup pecan halves  

Roll out piecrust and fit into 9-inch pie pan. Mix together dark corn syrup and sugar. Stir in beaten eggs, vanilla, salt, and pecan halves. Pour into shell and bake in a preheated 350° oven for 50 to 60 minutes, or until knife inserted in center of pie comes out clean. *The pie can be completely baked ahead, and also frozen. Thaw it, in wrappings, at room temperature. Just before serving, reheat it for 5 minutes in a 350° oven.*

### *Early Dinner for 8*
### *Before a Gala*

---

Chicken with almonds
Gnocchi à la Parisienne
Watercress salad with cherry tomatoes
and chives
Poached pears in cassis

## CHICKEN WITH ALMONDS

5 to 6 pounds chicken pieces,
mixed breasts, thighs,
and legs
2 teaspoons salt
1 teaspoon freshly cracked
white pepper
8 tablespoons butter
1½ cups finely chopped onion
3 finely chopped cloves garlic

1½ cups (more if needed)
chicken stock (see p. 278)
½ cup dry Madeira
1 cup blanched almonds,
finely ground
12 drops Tabasco sauce
2 tablespoons chopped
parsley

Wash and dry the chicken pieces and sprinkle with salt and pepper. Melt 6 tablespoons butter in a heavy casserole and brown chicken pieces. Remove from pan and keep warm. Add remaining 2 tablespoons butter to casserole, stir in onion and garlic, and cook, stirring, until onion is transparent—do not let it brown. Pour on chicken stock and Madeira and bring to a boil. Return chicken to casserole, turn heat to simmer, and cook, covered, for about 30 minutes, or until chicken is tender. Remove chicken from casserole and keep warm. Add ground almonds and Tabasco to casserole (12 drops is correct—this dish should have a hot taste), mix together, and puree in a blender. Return sauce—if it's too thick, thin it with a little chicken stock—and chicken to casserole. (*Recipe can be made ahead to this point.*) Before serving, heat through and sprinkle with chopped parsley.

### GNOCCHI À LA PARISIENNE

| | |
|---|---|
| 1¾ cups water | 2 teaspoons salt |
| 4 tablespoons butter | 1 teaspoon freshly cracked |
| 1¾ cups lightly spooned flour | white pepper |
| 3 eggs | ¾ cup grated Parmesan cheese |
| 1 teaspoon Dijon mustard | 4 tablespoons melted butter |

Put water and 4 tablespoons butter, cut in pieces, into a saucepan and bring to a boil. As soon as butter melts, dump in the flour all at once and mix vigorously with a wooden spatula until mixture forms a smooth ball. Add eggs, 1 at a time, beating well. Beat in mustard, salt, pepper, and ½ cup grated Parmesan cheese. Pack mixture into a pastry bag fitted with a dime-size plain round tube and pipe it into a large pan three-quarters full of simmering water. Rest the bag on the side of the pan and press out the dough steadily, cutting it off in 1-inch pieces with a small knife. Simmer 15 minutes. With a slotted spoon, remove gnocchi to a buttered serving dish. (*May be made ahead to this point and reheated.*) Dress with 4 tablespoons melted butter and sprinkle with remaining ¼ cup grated cheese.

### WATERCRESS SALAD WITH CHERRY TOMATOES AND CHIVES

Wash 4 bunches of watercress, remove stems, roll in towels, and chill. When ready to serve, toss with 16 cherry tomatoes, 2 tablespoons finely chopped fresh chives, and French vinaigrette dressing (see p. 282).

### POACHED PEARS IN CASSIS

| | |
|---|---|
| 8 firm but ripe pears | SAUCE: |
| 2 cups sugar | ½ cup butter |
| 3 cups water | 1 cup sugar |
| 2 inches of vanilla bean, | ¾ cup cassis syrup or crème |
| or 1 teaspoon vanilla | de cassis |
| extract | ¼ cup kirsch |

Peel but do not core pears and leave stems on. Cut a thin slice from bottoms so pears will stand upright. Heat sugar and water in saucepan, stirring until sugar dissolves. Cut vanilla bean lengthwise and scrape seeds into sugar water. Add the pod, too. Stand pears in syrup, cover pan with lid or aluminum foil, and simmer until pears are tender, basting occasionally. This may take from 5 to 25 minutes—it depends on ripeness of pears. Do not overcook; pears should not be mushy. (*Recipe may be prepared ahead to this point. Hold pears in poaching liquid.*)

To make sauce, melt butter and sugar in skillet, stirring constantly. When mixture is thick and white, like taffy—this takes about 5 minutes—add cassis and cook until sugar is completely dissolved. Remove pears from poaching liquid, put in sauce in skillet, and baste with sauce to warm them through. Warm kirsch in a small long-handled pan, ignite, and pour over pears. Serve pears with sauce.

## A Dinner for 6
### Frogs' Legs Lovers

Mushroom, onion, and sausage flan
Frogs' legs Provençale
Watercress and Belgian endive salad
Pears poached in white wine

Frogs' legs may be fried ahead of time, but don't try to keep them warm. Put them in a heatproof serving dish and let stand; when it's time to serve them, cover them with Provençale sauce and reheat on top of the stove. The flan may be made ahead and reheated. To adjust the Watercress and Belgian Endive Salad recipe (p. 42) for 6, use 4 instead of 6 heads of endive.

### MUSHROOM, ONION, AND SAUSAGE FLAN

1 partly baked pâte brisée shell (see p. 288); use an 8-inch pan, 2 inches deep
1 recipe onion pie filling (see p. 85)
½ pound bulk sausage
½ pound sliced mushrooms
2 tablespoons butter
1 tablespoon lemon juice
½ teaspoon salt
¼ teaspoon freshly cracked black pepper

Prepare pâte brisée shell and onion pie filling. Cook sausage in a dry skillet over high heat, crumbling and stirring it until done. Drain on paper towels and cool. Sauté sliced mushrooms in butter, sprinkling with lemon juice, salt, and pepper, over high heat for 2 or 3 minutes; let cool. Stir drained sausage and mushrooms into onion pie filling and pour into the partly baked pastry shell. Bake in a preheated 350° oven for 20 to 25 minutes, or until custard tests done (when knife inserted in center comes out clean). *Flan may be reheated and it can be frozen.*

### FROGS' LEGS PROVENÇALE

30 small frogs' legs
¾ cup flour
2 beaten eggs
¾ cup bread crumbs

Fat for deep frying
Provençale Sauce (recipe
follows)

Dip frogs' legs in flour and then in beaten egg and roll in crumbs. Chill for about 15 minutes. Deep-fry a few at a time in 3 inches of hot vegetable shortening (365° to 370°) until brown and crisp, about 7 minutes. Drain on paper towels and place in heatproof serving dish. (*May be prepared ahead to this point.*) When ready to serve, pour Provençale Sauce over frogs' legs and simmer 10 minutes.

### *PROVENÇALE SAUCE*

½ cup butter
2 teaspoons finely chopped
garlic
2 tablespoons chopped
shallots
½ cup chopped onion

½ pound sliced mushrooms
1 cup chopped green pepper
2 tablespoons chopped parsley
2 cups chopped fresh or
canned tomatoes

Heat butter in saucepan. Cook garlic, shallots, and onion over high heat until onion is transparent, about 5 minutes—do not let them burn. Add mushrooms and green pepper and cook 5 minutes longer. Stir in chopped parsley and tomatoes and simmer for 15 to 20 minutes. *Sauce may be prepared ahead.*

## PEARS POACHED IN WHITE WINE

8 firm but ripe pears
2 cups sugar

3 cups white wine, preferably dry
2 inches of vanilla bean

Peel pears, cut in half, and remove cores. Boil sugar and wine together, stirring until sugar dissolves. Cut vanilla bean length-

dinner with style.
wise, scraping seeds into syrup; drop the pod in, too. Add pears and cook over medium heat, basting them with the syrup, until they're tender but not mushy, about 10 to 15 minutes. Remove pears to a serving dish and boil syrup rapidly to reduce by one half. Pour syrup over pears. Serve warm or chilled.

## A Chic Spring Dinner
### for 8

Poached shad roe, Hollandaise
Squabs or Cornish hens, à l'orange
Brown rice pilaf
White asparagus vinaigrette (see p. 115)
Almond torte

Ask me how to celebrate spring, and the first food I think of is shad roe. Rather than sautéing it, my mother always poached it; this is a twist you may like, too. Shad roe introduces a poultry

## POACHED SHAD ROE, HOLLANDAISE

4 pairs shad roe
4 cups dry white wine
2 tablespoons chopped parsley

Hollandaise Sauce (see p. 281), substituting cooled cooking wine for lemon juice

Put roe in a shallow pan and cover with white wine. Bring to a boil, reduce heat, and simmer for 5 minutes. Carefully remove roe to a platter and keep warm. Sprinkle with chopped parsley, and serve with Hollandaise Sauce on the side.

## SQUABS OR CORNISH HENS, À L'ORANGE

8 squabs, 1¼ to 1½ pounds, or
   8 Cornish hens, 12 to
   15 ounces
2 tablespoons coarse salt
2 teaspoons freshly cracked
   black pepper
4 oranges
½ cup sugar
½ cup red wine vinegar or
   cider vinegar
4 cups basic brown sauce
   (see p. 281)

¾ cup dry red wine
¼ cup Grand Marnier
1¼ cups bitter orange
   (Seville) marmalade
2 teaspoons potato starch or
   cornstarch, optional
3 tablespoons dry red wine,
   optional
1 bunch watercress, for
   garnish

Wash and dry birds thoroughly. Remove giblets, necks, and wing tips. Truss birds and rub them all over with salt and pepper. Place on racks in a roasting pan, add giblets and trimmings, and roast in a preheated 350° oven—1 hour and 15 minutes for squabs, 1 hour for Cornish hens, or until juices run clear when you prick leg.

While birds roast, prepare blanched orange peel for sauce: with a potato peeler, thinly peel 2 of the oranges. Cut peelings into slivers, that is, julienne them, with a chef's knife. Put the slivers into a saucepan, cover with cold water, bring to a rolling boil, drain, and rinse in cold water to set the color. Set aside. Reserve peeled oranges for garnish. Prepare a caramel for sauce: in a heavy pan dissolve sugar in vinegar, stirring, over low heat. When sugar is dissolved, tip the pan back and forth (without stirring) over medium-high heat until it turns to caramel, about 15 minutes. (Caramel will look like thin molasses and be very sticky.) Slowly add brown sauce to caramel, then ½ cup dry red wine and the Grand Marnier. Add the blanched orange peel, along with ¼ cup bitter orange marmalade. Taste for seasoning. Thicken sauce if you wish with potato starch, dissolved in 3 tablespoons dry red wine, or boil to reduce and thicken. You should have about 1½ cups sauce. (*Sauce may be made ahead to this point.*)

Fifteen minutes before birds are done, remove them from the oven and, with a pastry brush, spread over them the remaining 1 cup bitter orange marmalade. Return to oven to glaze. When birds are done, remove them to serving platter and keep warm. Pour off fat from roasting pan and deglaze pan with the remaining ¼ cup wine. Boil wine to loosen the brown bits, scraping at them if necessary, and strain into sauce. Decorate the serving platter with a bunch of watercress, orange sections from peeled and reserved oranges or serrated orange slices: with a lemon stripper, cut longitudinal grooves into the skin of the 2 remaining oranges, slice, then cut slices in half. Spoon a little sauce over each bird and pass the remainder.

## BROWN RICE PILAF

Follow recipe for Brown Rice Pilaf with Pine Nuts (see p. 105), but omit pine nuts.

## ALMOND TORTE

The flavor of torte layers is enhanced if they are baked 2 or 3 days in advance. Store at room temperature, covered with plastic wrap.

¾ pound blanched almonds, about—to make 3 cups ground
Oil for baking pans
6 eggs, separated
1½ cups plus 1 tablespoon sugar
2 teaspoons vanilla extract
1 teaspoon almond extract
2 tablespoons flour
2 teaspoons baking powder
⅛ teaspoon salt
2 cups heavy cream
4 tablespoons confectioners' sugar, plus more for sifting

The day before baking torte layers, grind almonds in a blender and spread on a baking sheet to dry overnight. (Do not buy ground almonds—they're too fine.) Oil 2 8-inch round cake pans with vegetable oil, line with waxed paper, and oil paper; or line with baking parchment. Set aside. Beat egg yolks in an electric mixer bowl; add 1½ cups sugar gradually and continue beating until very thick and mixture forms ribbons. Beat in 1 teaspoon vanilla and ½ teaspoon almond extract. Mix flour and baking powder with nuts and fold into egg yolk mixture—batter will be stiff. Beat egg whites, adding 1 tablespoon sugar and the salt after they foam, and beat to stiff but not dry peaks. Fold into egg yolk–nut mixture. Spread in pans and bake in a preheated 375° oven for 25 to 30 minutes. Test with toothpick—if it comes out clean, torte is done. Cool on racks before removing torte from pans.

To serve, whip heavy cream, flavoring it with 4 tablespoons confectioners' sugar, 1 teaspoon vanilla, and ½ teaspoon almond extract. Spread half of whipped cream on bottom layer; top with second layer. Lay 2 strips of waxed paper across cake to make a cross and sift confectioners' sugar over exposed part of cake. Remove waxed paper. Pack remaining whipped cream into a pastry bag fitted with a star tube and pipe a rosette onto each quarter of cake. Pipe 8 ribbons of whipped cream up the sides of cake.

## *Cooking Lesson Show-off*
## *Dinner for 8*

Quenelles de brochet
Orange leg of lamb en croûte
Hearts of palm salad
Cold chocolate almond soufflé

When checking out a new restaurant, a knowledgeable gourmet frequently will order quenelles—an exacting test of a chef's skill. Undoubtedly this is why students in cooking school always want to learn how to make them; prepared correctly, nothing is more "show-off." The Orange Leg of Lamb en Croûte is an original recipe and a specialty of my school. Serve the salad with the lamb in this menu (although hearts of palm are usually served as a separate course).

### QUENELLES DE BROCHET

1 pound boneless pike or
    haddock
4 tablespoons butter
1 cup water
1 cup lightly spooned flour
2 eggs
2 egg whites
¾ cup butter, at room
    temperature

⅓ cup heavy cream
3 teaspoons salt
½ teaspoon freshly grated
    nutmeg
Sauce (recipe follows)
¼ cup freshly grated
    Parmesan cheese
Butter to dot top of serving
    dish

Using the fine blade of a meat grinder, grind fish twice and set aside. To make a *panade,* or thickener, add 4 tablespoons butter, cut in chips, to water in saucepan and heat slowly until butter melts and water begins to boil. Dump in flour all at once and beat until the mixture clears the sides of the pan. Remove from heat and beat in eggs, one at a time. Add egg whites little by little and beat them in. Put *panade* in a bowl and, if you have a heavy-duty mixer, use the flat whip to beat in the ground fish 1 teaspoonful at a time. Otherwise, beat by hand, using a wooden spoon—mixture will clog a regular electric mixer attachment.

In another bowl, again using the flat whip, beat ¾ cup butter until light. Gradually beat in the fish mixture, 1 tablespoon at a time. Then beat in heavy cream, salt, and nutmeg. Cover and chill in refrigerator at least 30 minutes or overnight. While mixture chills, prepare sauce.

On a lightly floured board, shape quenelles into sausagelike pieces about 3 inches long. (*Quenelles can be prepared ahead to this point.*) Poach quenelles in simmering water for about 20 minutes. Drain well and arrange in a shallow ovenproof serving dish. Spoon hot sauce over them, sprinkle with grated Parmesan, and dot with butter. Run the dish under the broiler to brown lightly—about 5 minutes, but watch closely. *May also be fully prepared, including browning under broiler, and reheated in oven with the lamb (following recipe).*

## SAUCE FOR QUENELLES DE BROCHET

**FISH STOCK:**
Skin, head, and bones of pike
　or a small piece of fish
1 cup dry white wine
3 cups water
½ cup chopped celery
½ cup chopped carrot
½ cup chopped onion
3 sprigs parsley
2 teaspoons salt

**SAUCE:**
6 tablespoons butter
4 tablespoons flour
1½ cups strained fish stock
½ cup light cream
¼ cup freshly grated
　Parmesan cheese
2 egg yolks
2 tablespoons dry sherry

Put skin, head, and bones of pike into a saucepan, or cut up small piece of fish. Add dry white wine and water and bring to a boil. Skim. Add celery, carrot, onion, parsley, and salt. Simmer about 1 hour, strain, and reserve.

To make sauce, melt butter in saucepan, stir in flour, and cook over high heat, stirring with wooden spatula, for 2 minutes—do not let it brown. Remove from heat, change to a whisk, and add strained fish stock, whisking vigorously. Return to medium-high heat and cook, stirring, until sauce comes to a boil and thickens. Stir in ⅓ cup of the light cream and the grated Parmesan cheese. Beat egg yolks lightly with a fork. Beat in sherry and remaining light cream. Stir in some of the hot sauce to warm egg yolks, then stir egg yolk mixture into the sauce. Return to heat and cook until sauce thickens—do not let it boil. Taste for seasoning. *Sauce may be prepared ahead and reheated.*

## ORANGE LEG OF LAMB EN CROÛTE

1  6- to 7-pound leg of lamb, partly boned
Peel of 1 orange
½ cup butter
2  teaspoons rosemary
1  chopped clove garlic
2  tablespoons vegetable oil
2  teaspoons coarse salt
½  teaspoon freshly cracked black pepper
Pastry (recipe follows)
1  egg yolk
1  bunch watercress, for garnish
1  orange, for garnish

Remove center (thigh) bone from lamb, leaving the end bone. Cut a thin peel about 5 inches long from the orange and cut into slivers. Poke slivers into the meat by inserting the point of a small knife in the fatty side and using the knife blade as a slide to push slivers down into the meat. Grate the remaining orange peel; you should have 1 tablespoonful. Cream butter with grated orange peel, 1 teaspoon rosemary, and the chopped garlic. Pack this butter into the cavity where thigh bone was removed. Brush lamb all over with oil and rub with salt, pepper, and remaining 1 teaspoon rosemary. Place lamb on a baking tray and roast in a preheated 500° oven for 15 minutes to sear meat. Remove from oven and cool to room temperature.

On a floured board roll out pastry ¼ inch thick, in a rectangular shape to cover lamb. Trim off irregular edges (save trimmings for decoration), roll pastry over pin, and unroll over lamb, pressing around meat but not covering meat on bottom side. Paint crust with egg yolk mixed with 1 tablespoon cold water. Cut trimmings into petal and leaf shapes, apply to crust, and paint with egg wash. Prick crust all over with tip of knife. (*Can be done*

*ahead to this point and refrigerated or frozen. If frozen, defrost
in refrigerator and bring to room temperature before baking.*)
Place the wrapped lamb on a baking tray and bake in a preheated
375° oven 12 minutes per pound for very rare lamb, 15 minutes
for medium, and 18 for well done. Garnish platter with a bunch
of watercress and an orange cut in half with a zigzag, serrated cut.

### PASTRY

2 teaspoons salt
3 cups lightly spooned flour
1¾ *sticks* butter (¾ cup plus
 2 tablespoons)

4 tablespoons solid vegetable
 shortening
½ cup iced water

Stir salt into flour and cut in butter and shortening until mixture looks like coarse meal. Add just enough ice water (no more
than ½ cup) so you can gather the mixture into a ball. Wrap the
ball in waxed paper or plastic wrap and refrigerate at least ½ hour
or overnight.

### HEARTS OF PALM SALAD

3 1-pound cans hearts of
 palm
8 lettuce leaves

1 recipe French vinaigrette
 dressing (see p. 282)
3 tablespoons chopped parsley

Rinse and dry hearts of palm. Cut in rounds or leave in strips;
count 2 strips per person. Arrange on lettuce leaves on individual
salad plates. Spoon 2 tablespoons vinaigrette over each salad and
sprinkle with chopped parsley.

### COLD CHOCOLATE ALMOND SOUFFLÉ

2 tablespoons (2 envelopes)
 unflavored gelatine
½ cup rum
8 ounces dark sweet chocolate
2 cups light cream
1 cup confectioners' sugar

½ teaspoon salt
5 cups heavy cream
½ cup slivered toasted salted
 almonds
¾ cup shaved chocolate

Make a waxed paper collar for a 2-quart soufflé dish by folding paper in half, lengthwise, brushing inside edge with vegetable oil, and tying it around the top of the dish so that it extends 4 to 5 inches above it. Set aside. Sprinkle gelatine into rum in a cup, let stand a few minutes, then set the cup in a pan of boiling water and stir to dissolve gelatine. In a saucepan, over medium-high heat, melt chocolate in light cream and beat with a whisk until smooth. Beat in dissolved gelatine, confectioners' sugar, and salt. Remove from heat and let cool until the mixture is almost at the point of setting. Whip 4 cups of the heavy cream and gradually beat in the chocolate mixture a little at a time, whisking until smooth after each addition. Fold in almonds. Pour into prepared dish and refrigerate for at least 3 to 4 hours. (*Recipe can be done to this point the day before.*) Whip remaining 1 cup heavy cream. Remove paper collar and decorate soufflé with rosettes of whipped cream. Sprinkle with shaved chocolate.

## *A Dinner for 6*
## *Sweetbread Lovers*

Ris de veau, velouté sauce
Broccoli timbales
Cherry tomatoes vinaigrette
Oranges Grand Marnier (see p. 84)

### RIS DE VEAU, VELOUTÉ SAUCE

| | |
|---|---|
| 6 pairs calves' sweetbreads | 1 teaspoon tomato paste |
| ½ cup flour | 2 cups chicken stock (see p. 278) |
| 1¼ cups heavy cream | |
| 6 tablespoons butter | 1 teaspoon salt |
| 4 tablespoons Calvados | ½ teaspoon freshly cracked white pepper |
| 1 finely chopped truffle | |
| 1 teaspoon finely chopped garlic | 2 tablespoons chopped parsley |

Put sweetbreads in a pan and cover them with cold water. Slowly bring them to a boil, reduce heat, and simmer, uncovered, for 5 to 7 minutes. Turn over once during cooking. Drain and plunge immediately into ice water. Carefully remove the skin, sinews, and tubes. Cut them in half lengthwise and lay them on a plate. Cover with another plate and weight; place in the refrigerator for at least 1 hour.

When ready to cook, dry sweetbreads with paper towels and dust lightly with ¼ cup flour. Barely whip the heavy cream—just past the foaming stage—and set aside. Heat 4 tablespoons butter in a large skillet, over high heat. When butter is foaming, add sweetbreads—do not let them touch each other—and cover them with a flat lid and weight, to keep them flat. Brown 1 minute on each side. Flame them with Calvados; when flames die, remove sweetbreads and set aside. Scrape up brown bits. Stir in truffle and garlic and cook 1 minute. Add tomato paste and remaining 2 tablespoons butter. Stir in remaining ¼ cup flour with a wooden spatula and cook, stirring, for 2 minutes—do not let it brown. Remove from heat, change to a whisk, and add chicken stock, whisking vigorously. Return to high heat and cook sauce until it thickens and comes to a boil, stirring. Beat heavy cream into the sauce. Season with salt and pepper. Return sweetbreads to skillet, basting them with the sauce. (*Recipe can be made ahead to this point, covered, and refrigerated.*) Cover skillet with aluminum foil and a heavy lid and simmer over low heat for 15 minutes. Arrange on a serving platter and spoon sauce over; sprinkle with chopped parsley.

### BROCCOLI TIMBALES

Follow recipe for Spinach Timbales, on page 121, but substitute frozen chopped broccoli for the spinach, omit the nutmeg, and add 1 tablespoon lemon juice.

### CHERRY TOMATOES VINAIGRETTE

Count 8 cherry tomatoes per person; put them in a salad bowl with French vinaigrette dressing (see p. 282) and 2 tablespoons chopped parsley. Mix well and marinate for 2 hours at room temperature, turning occasionally, before serving.

## *An Old-Fashioned Shore Dinner for 8*

---

Clams on the half shell ( see p. 266)
Baked stuffed fish
Corn on the cob
Beefsteak tomatoes and chives
marinated in sour cream dressing
Strawberries over homemade
vanilla ice cream

### BAKED STUFFED FISH

1 whole striped bass, 4 to 6
   pounds, or other whole
   fish such as bluefish or
   mackerel
1 tablespoon salt
1 teaspoon freshly cracked
   black pepper
   Juice of ½ lemon
3 tablespoons butter
3 tablespoons chopped
   shallots
1½ to 2 cups chopped mushrooms

Salt and pepper
2 tablespoons chopped parsley
½ cup bread crumbs
½ cup plus 2 tablespoons dry
   white wine
4 tablespoons melted butter
   Mushroom Sauce (recipe
   follows)
1 thinly sliced lemon, for
   garnish
2 tablespoons chopped parsley,
   for garnish

Scale and clean the fish—or ask fish seller to do it—with the
head and tail left intact. Wash the fish well in cold water and
trim the tail neatly. To make more room for the stuffing, cut 2
pockets in the fish, one each side of the backbone, by slitting from
the belly, with the knife blade parallel—and close—to the backbone. Be careful not to cut through the back of the fish. Salt and
pepper the 2 cavities you've made and sprinkle with lemon juice.
To make stuffing, melt butter in a skillet and add the shallots.
Cook for a minute or two over high heat, then add the chopped
mushrooms and toss over high heat. Add salt and pepper to taste,
parsley, and bread crumbs. Moisten with 2 tablespoons dry white
wine. Pack the stuffing into the fish along the bone and skewer

the opening crosswise. Butter an ovenproof serving dish and curl the fish into it, belly down—the skewers will form a platform to hold the fish in position. Cover fish's head and tail with aluminum foil. Sprinkle fish with salt and pepper and brush with one third each of the melted butter and ½ cup dry white wine. Place in a preheated 400° oven and bake for about 30 minutes (figure about 8 minutes per pound), but test for doneness after 25 minutes— touch fish with a toothpick to see if it flakes. Baste fish with butter and wine 2 times while baking. When done, use a bulb baster to take up the juice in the serving dish and add it to the Mushroom Sauce. Decorate the back of the fish with lemon slices dipped in parsley and serve fish at once from cooking dish. Pass sauce separately.

## MUSHROOM SAUCE

4　tablespoons butter  
4　tablespoons flour  
2　cups fish stock, if available (see p. 279) or clam juice  
1　cup sliced mushrooms  
¼　cup dry white wine  
1　teaspoon salt  
½　teaspoon freshly cracked black pepper  
1　tablespoon chopped parsley  
3　egg yolks, optional  
3　tablespoons heavy cream, optional  

Melt butter in a saucepan and stir in flour with a wooden spatula. Cook over high heat, stirring constantly, for 2 minutes to cook flour, but do not let it brown. Remove from heat, change to a whisk, and add the fish stock all at once, whisking vigorously. Return to heat and bring to a boil, whisking. In another pan, cook mushrooms in white wine over high heat until all liquid is absorbed. Do not let the mushrooms burn—shake the pan as they cook. Pour the sauce into the mushrooms, add salt, pepper, and parsley. (*May be prepared ahead to this point.*) When ready to proceed, add juices from pan in which fish has cooked, and enrich the sauce if you wish: beat together egg yolks and heavy cream, stir a little hot sauce into the egg yolk—cream mixture to warm it, and stir this mixture back into the sauce. Heat sauce through, but do not let it boil.

## CORN ON THE COB

Count 1 or 2 ears per person. Buy it on the same day you plan to serve it, store in refrigerator, and husk just before cooking. Drop ears into a big kettle of unsalted boiling water. (Add 1 teaspoon sugar if you think your corn is a bit mature.) Boil from 3 to 6 minutes after water returns to boil—do not overcook. Serve hot with plenty of melted butter, salt, and pepper in a mill.

## BEEFSTEAK TOMATOES AND CHIVES MARINATED IN SOUR CREAM DRESSING

5 or 6 beefsteak tomatoes
¼ cup chopped chives
¾ cup dairy sour cream
2 tablespoons tarragon vinegar

1 teaspoon salt
½ teaspoon freshly cracked
    pepper

Peel tomatoes if you wish and slice ½ inch thick. Allow 3 slices per person. Overlap in a flat serving dish and sprinkle with chopped chives. Mix sour cream with vinegar, salt, and pepper and pour over tomatoes. Let marinate for 1 hour in refrigerator before serving.

## STRAWBERRIES OVER HOMEMADE VANILLA ICE CREAM

3 cups light cream
4 eggs, separated
1½ cups sugar
2 tablespoons cornstarch

1 tablespoon vanilla extract
½ teaspoon salt
2 cups heavy cream
3 pints strawberries

In a nonaluminum pan, scald the light cream. Beat egg yolks and beat in 1 cup sugar and the cornstarch. Slowly pour scalded cream onto egg yolk mixture, stirring, and place over low heat. Cook until custard coats the back of a spoon, about 10 minutes, stirring constantly. Let cool. When cool, stir in vanilla. Beat egg whites with salt until stiff and fold them into custard. Pour into freezer trays and chill until the mixture is a heavy mush. Put it into a bowl and beat it until fluffy. Whip the heavy cream—not too stiff—and fold it into the mixture. Return to freezer trays.

Make ice cream a few hours ahead to be sure it chills thoroughly and becomes really firm.

If you have an ice-cream freezer, do not whip the heavy cream. Instead, add it, unwhipped, to the egg yolk custard along with the beaten egg whites. Pour the mixture into freezer can and freeze following directions for your freezer.

Prepare strawberries about 1 hour before serving. Hull the berries, dip them quickly in and out of water, and leave them whole or slice them in half. Sprinkle with ½ cup sugar and let stand. Mash them slightly before serving if you wish.

## An Adult Birthday Dinner
### for 4 to 6

Beef Burgundy
Barley pilaf
Carrot salad
Gâteau Saint-Honoré

St. Honoré is the patron saint of pastrycooks and bakers and the "cake" that is named in his honor is a *tour de force* of the pastry chef's artistry. It's not an American-style layer cake. The base is rolled-out pastry baked with a ring of cream puff paste. The center that results from this construction is filled with pastry cream, and the cake is further embellished with tiny cream puffs around the rim and a lacy network of caramel threads over the top. It is chilled before serving, so you can do it all ahead.

## BEEF BURGUNDY

3 pounds beef round, sirloin, or
   chuck, cut in 2-inch cubes
6 tablespoons butter
1 teaspoon salt
½ teaspoon freshly cracked
   black pepper
½ cup brandy, about
2 teaspoons chopped garlic
3 tablespoons chopped shallots
2 teaspoons dried or 2 tablespoons fresh tarragon

1 teaspoon tomato paste
4 teaspoons potato starch or
   cornstarch
2½ cups chicken stock (see
   p. 278)
1 cup dry red wine
1 bouquet garni (see p. 283)
12 small white onions
12 mushroom caps
2 tablespoons finely chopped
   parsley

Dry beef cubes with paper towels. Heat 4 tablespoons butter in a heavy casserole and brown the beef cubes on all sides over high heat—do not let pieces touch. Sprinkle with salt and pepper and flame with 3 tablespoons of the brandy. (Warm brandy in a small pan, ignite, and pour it, flaming, over beef.) Remove beef from pan, add the remaining 2 tablespoons butter, and stir to loosen brown bits. Stir in garlic and shallots and cook for a minute. Then stir in tarragon, tomato paste, and potato starch and let cook 2 minutes more. Add chicken stock, wine, and bouquet garni. Return beef to casserole. (*May be prepared ahead to this point.*) Bring sauce to a boil, cover the casserole with aluminum foil and a heavy lid, and place in a preheated 350° oven to simmer for about 1½ hours or until beef is tender. Baste 3 times during cooking with 2 tablespoons brandy each time. While beef simmers, peel onions and parboil for 15 minutes, and clean and trim mushroom caps. Add them to casserole the last 30 minutes of cooking. When ready to serve, sprinkle with chopped parsley. *May be completely made ahead and reheated. If you plan to do this, undercook the dish slightly and wait until the reheating to add onions and mushrooms.*

## BARLEY PILAF

4 tablespoons butter
1½ cups chopped onions
1¾ cups pearl barley
3½ to 4 cups chicken stock
   (see p. 278)

1 teaspoon salt
½ teaspoon freshly cracked
   black pepper

Melt butter in a heavy casserole, stir in onions and cook, stirring, over high heat until onions are transparent. Add barley and continue cooking and stirring until golden brown. Pour on 1¾ cups of the chicken stock, add salt and pepper, and bring to a boil. Cover and place in a preheated 350° oven. Bake for 30 minutes; add 1¾ cups more chicken stock and continue baking for 30 minutes longer. If barley looks dry, add another ½ cup chicken stock. Bake 20 minutes longer or until barley is tender but not mushy.

## CARROT SALAD

1 pound carrots
½ cup French vinaigrette
   dressing ( see p. 282 )
¼ cup grated orange peel

2 tablespoons mayonnaise
Salt and pepper, optional

Marinate the grated orange peel in vinaigrette dressing for 1 hour. Shred the carrots—you should have about 2½ to 3 cups. Mix dressing with mayonnaise and toss with carrots. Taste for seasoning and add salt and pepper if desired.

## GÂTEAU SAINT-HONORÉ

½ recipe for pâte brisée pastry
   ( see p. 288 )
1 recipe pâte à choux ( cream
   puff paste, see p. 286 )
1 egg yolk

1 tablespoon water
Pastry cream ( recipe fol-
   lows )
Caramel ( recipe follows )

Prepare pâte brisée pastry, wrap it in waxed paper, and put it in the refrigerator to chill. Prepare pâte à choux paste and pack it into a large pastry bag fitted with a round tube. Roll out the pâte brisée pastry ⅛ inch thick and trim it to make an 8-inch circle. Place the pastry circle on a baking tray lined with baking parchment (if you do not have baking parchment, grease the baking tray) and prick it all over with a fork. Beat egg yolk with water and brush it around the edge of the pastry circle. Pipe a ring of pâte à choux paste around the edge of the pastry circle, ¼ inch inside. Pipe a second ring on top of the first. Pipe out remaining paste onto the baking parchment to make 8 to 10 individual small puffs. With the back of a spoon, flatten any points on the puffs and brush the *tops only* of ring and puffs with egg yolk mixture; don't let it dribble down the sides, or the puffs won't rise. Place in a preheated 425° oven and bake for 15 minutes. Quickly poke the tip of a knife into the sides of both the puffs and the rings in 4 places; return to oven and bake for 20 minutes more at 375°. While pastry circle is baking, prepare pastry cream.

When both pastry ring and pastry cream filling are cool, fill the shell with the pastry cream. Also, split the individual puffs and fill them with pastry cream. Prepare the caramel, dip the bottoms of the filled puffs in the hot caramel, and stick them to the top of the ring. When caramel spins a thread, dip a fork into it and wave it over the cake, round and round; continue until the cake is laced with caramel threads. *May be fully prepared ahead; serve chilled.*

## PASTRY CREAM

| | |
|---|---|
| 1 egg | 1 cup scalded milk |
| 1 egg yolk | 1 teaspoon vanilla extract |
| 3 tablespoons sugar | 1 cup heavy cream |
| 3 tablespoons flour | 2 tablespoons confectioners' |
| 2 teaspoons unflavored gelatine | sugar |

Combine egg, egg yolk, sugar, and flour in a bowl and beat well with a whisk. Stir in gelatine. Slowly pour scalded milk into egg mixture, whisking constantly. Return mixture to saucepan (nonaluminum) and stir it over low heat until it thickens. Mixture scorches easily, so move the whisk all around the pan; let it bubble just once and remove from heat. Add vanilla. Set the pan in a bowl of ice to chill, and stir constantly for about 5 minutes; or chill it in the refrigerator, stirring frequently, for about 20 minutes. When cool, whip the heavy cream, sweetening it with confectioners' sugar, and fold whipped cream into pastry cream.

## CARAMEL

Put ⅔ cup sugar, ½ cup water, and ¼ teaspoon cream of tartar into a small skillet and cook over medium heat, stirring until sugar dissolves. Then tip the pan over heat, swirling the mixture, until it turns quite brown. This takes about 15 minutes. Remove from heat immediately.

# Buffets

Buffets are the dinners (or lunches or breakfasts) you plan when your guest list grows beyond the capacity of your dining table, or when you expect to manage things yourself without help. Your guests serve themselves—and save you a good deal of work.

Not only the ease of buffets but the help-yourself fun of them have made them increasingly popular. Many of the dinners in the preceding chapter can be served as buffets, although you may want to make a change or two in the menus. Successful buffet food must be a little more durable than food served directly from the kitchen to already seated guests. Electric hot trays and carts are invaluable for maintaining food at the proper temperature without further cooking. Chafing dishes, sectioned serving dishes set over hot water, even a spirit lamp or Sterno are other alternatives. There's no reason to rule out a three-course menu. You can serve a first course with drinks and later offer desserts at a separate buffet table, which you might set up in another room, with coffee.

If possible, I like to seat my guests at tables even when I serve buffet-style, particularly if they will need to use both a fork *and* knife. If this means setting up card tables, or even individual tables, fine—any surface is better than your lap. When guests don't have to carry their own silver and napkins, I count it a plus.

When you're in the planning stages for your party, bring out your serving dishes and decide early on what goes in what. Compose a logical and interesting arrangement, playing off round, square, oblong, and oval shapes for contrast. An effective buffet also has an up-and-down dimension, and a tiered server can help you out in this. Remind yourself of food colors as you read recipes. Guests should get hungry just approaching your table.

## A Lap Buffet
## for 12

Salami cornucopias on pumpernickel (see p. 63)
Coulibiac of beef with mustard Hollandaise
Baked tomatoes with Soubise
Endive, mushroom, and cucumber salad
Pistachio Bavarian cream

### COULIBIAC OF BEEF
### WITH MUSTARD HOLLANDAISE

1 recipe brioche (see p. 11)

PANADE:

2 cups water
1 teaspoon salt
6 tablespoons farina
2 eggs
3 tablespoons butter
¼ cup freshly grated Parmesan cheese
1 teaspoon dry mustard
1 teaspoon Dijon mustard

FILLING:

2 thinly sliced mushrooms
2 teaspoons butter
Few drops of lemon juice
¼ teaspoon salt
⅛ teaspoon freshly ground black pepper

2 tablespoons fresh chopped dill
1 teaspoon finely chopped garlic
1 tablespoon finely chopped shallots
1 cup sour cream
1½ pounds fillet of beef, cut in finger-size pieces
3 finely chopped hard-cooked eggs

¼ cup melted butter
1 egg yolk
1 tablespoon water
2 teaspoons Dijon mustard
1 recipe Hollandaise Sauce (see p. 281)

Make brioche dough the day before and refrigerate it overnight. Prepare the *panade,* or thickener: heat water in a saucepan to boiling, add salt, and slowly pour in farina, stirring constantly. Cook, stirring, over high heat, until thick. Remove from heat and beat in eggs—do this quickly, so eggs won't scramble. Beat in butter, grated cheese, and mustards and place in refrigerator to chill, at least ½ hour. Sauté the mushrooms for the filling in butter for 2 minutes, sprinkling them with lemon juice, salt, and pepper; set aside. Stir dill, garlic, and shallots into sour cream and set aside. (*May be prepared ahead to this point.*)

To assemble coulibiac: brush a 6 x 10 x 3-inch loaf pan with oil. Turn the refrigerated brioche dough out onto a lightly floured board; dough will be sticky. Cut off about one quarter of the dough and put it back in the refrigerator. Roll out remaining dough to make a rectangle about 12 x 16 inches, and line the pan with it, tucking dough into corners and pinching it over the edge of the pan. Brush dough with ¼ cup melted butter. Spread about a third of the farina *panade* into the mold and then add, in layers, half of each of the sour cream, beef, mushrooms, and hard-cooked eggs. Repeat layers, ending with a final layer of farina. Roll out reserved brioche dough to make a lid. Beat the egg yolk with the 1 tablespoon water (to make egg wash) and brush top edges of brioche in pan with it; press lid in place, pinching edges together. Cover with a towel and let stand about 20 minutes. Cut slits in lid and brush dough all over with more egg wash. (*Recipe can be made ahead to this point and refrigerated.*) Place pan on a baking sheet and bake in a preheated 425° oven for 40 minutes. If crust browns too fast, cover it loosely with aluminum foil.

To unmold coulibiac, loosen it around the edges with a knife and ease it out with a wide spatula. Or serve it in the pan, dressed up in a pleated paper ruffle around outside of pan. If you bake coulibiac in a throwaway aluminum pan, you can cut the pan away to unmold it. Serve with Mustard Hollandaise, made by adding—after sauce is made—2 teaspoons Dijon mustard to 1 recipe Hollandaise Sauce.

## BAKED TOMATOES WITH SOUBISE

6 to 8 tomatoes
1 teaspoon salt
½ teaspoon freshly cracked
   black pepper

1 recipe soubise filling (see
   p. 157)
¼ cup freshly grated Parmesan
   cheese

Slice tomatoes ½ inch thick; allow 2 slices per person. Sprinkle with salt and pepper and lay on a baking tray. Put 1 tablespoonful of soubise filling on each tomato piece and top with 1 teaspoon Parmesan cheese. (*May be prepared ahead to this point.*) Bake in a preheated 350° oven until tops are bubbly, about 15 to 20 minutes, or at 425° for about 10 minutes.

## ENDIVE, MUSHROOM, AND CUCUMBER SALAD

6 heads Belgian endive
1 pound white mushrooms
2 cucumbers
2 tablespoons finely chopped
  parsley

2 tablespoons finely chopped
  shallots
French vinaigrette dressing
  (see p. 282)

Trim root ends of endive, removing any discolored leaves, and wash and drain. With a chef's knife, cut into julienne pieces. Clean mushrooms in acidulated water (1 tablespoon lemon juice to 1 quart water), trim stems, and slice thinly. Peel cucumbers with potato peeler and slice thinly. Put in a chilled bowl and sprinkle with chopped parsley. Add chopped shallots to vinaigrette and, just before serving, pour over vegetables and toss to mix.

## PISTACHIO BAVARIAN CREAM

5 eggs, separated
5 rounded tablespoons sugar
2 tablespoons (2 envelopes)
  unflavored gelatine
1½ cups scalded milk
2 to 3 tablespoons dark rum
3 or 4 drops green food
  coloring

1½ cups heavy cream
½ cup plus 2 tablespoons
  chopped natural pistachio
  nuts
1 tablespoon confectioners'
  sugar

Oil a 9 x 1½-inch pan with loose bottom and set aside. W a whisk, beat egg yolks, sugar, and gelatine until thick and sticky. Scald milk (do not use aluminum pan) and slowly pour into egg yolk mixture in a thin stream, whisking. Return mixture to pan and cook over low heat, stirring constantly, until it coats the back of a spoon. Remove from heat and cool—stir it over ice, or place in refrigerator, stirring a few times, until cooked base is syrupy, on the point of setting. Flavor with rum and tint with food coloring. Beat egg whites to soft peaks and fold into base. Whip ¾ cup of heavy cream—not too stiff—and fold it into base, along with ½ cup chopped pistachios. Pour into prepared pan and place in refrigerator to set for at least 2 hours, preferably overnight. (*Recipe can be made ahead to this point; it will freeze.*) Unmold on serving plate and decorate with rosettes of remaining ¾ cup heavy cream,

sweetened with 1 tablespoon confectioners' sugar. Sprinkle with
remaining 2 tablespoons chopped pistachios.

## A Sit-down Buffet
## for 12

Mussels marinière
Beef à la mode
Garniture bourgeoise
Russian gnocchi
Beet salad
Mont Blanc

### MUSSELS MARINIÈRE

10 quarts mussels
1½ cups chopped celery
1½ cups chopped onions
 3 tablespoons chopped
   shallots
  tablespoons chopped
   parsley, plus ½ cup for
   garnish

6 thin slices lemon
1 teaspoon freshly cracked
   black pepper
1 teaspoon salt
½ teaspoon thyme
3 cups dry vermouth

Scrub mussels, using several changes of cold water, and remove beards with a stiff brush or knife. This is a difficult job and
will take time; discard any mussels that are open. Put the scrubbed
mussels into a *very* large pot with remaining ingredients (except
parsley for garnish), cover, bring to a boil, turn down to simmer,
and cook, shaking the pot often, for about 12 minutes, or until
all mussels open. Discard any mussels that do not open during
cooking. When ready to serve, remove mussels with a slotted
spoon to soup plates. Divide the broth among the plates and
sprinkle with chopped parsley.

## BEEF À LA MODE

| | |
|---|---|
| 1 8-pound beef roast, eye of the round or boned rump, cut in a long narrow shape | 2½ cups dry red wine |
| | 1 teaspoon salt |
| | ½ teaspoon freshly cracked black pepper |
| 1 cup chopped onions | ⅓ cup plus 2 tablespoons brandy |
| 1 cup chopped carrots | |
| 1 cup chopped celery, including leaves | 2 tablespoons butter |
| | 2 tablespoons oil |
| 1 chopped clove garlic | 1 veal knuckle or calf's foot |
| 1 bay leaf | 1 teaspoon potato starch or cornstarch, optional |
| ½ teaspoon thyme | |
| 5 or 6 sprigs of parsley | 1 bunch watercress |

Tie, or have the butcher tie, the meat every 2 inches so that it will retain its round shape. In a nonaluminum casserole large enough to hold beef, mix together the onions, carrots, celery, garlic, bay leaf, thyme, parsley, wine, salt, pepper, and ⅓ cup brandy, and marinate meat, in the refrigerator, for at least 12 hours or overnight, turning it over with wooden spatulas every 2 hours or so. Remove meat—reserving marinade—and pat dry with paper towels. Heat the butter and oil in a heavy skillet and brown the meat thoroughly, over high heat—take at least 20 minutes for this. Pour off excess fat from pan, warm 2 tablespoons brandy in a small long-handled pan, ignite it, and pour it over meat. When flames die, return meat to casserole. Scrape up brown bits in skillet and add them to the marinade in the casserole. Add the veal knuckle or calf's foot. Cover casserole with aluminum foil and a heavy lid and braise in a preheated 350° oven for 2½ to 3 hours. Turn the meat at least twice during cooking. Beef is done when a fork can be easily inserted into meat. (*Recipe can be made ahead to this point the day before and reheated gently on the top of the stove—in flameproof casserole—or in 350° oven.*)

Remove beef to carving board and keep warm. Skim fat from liquid in casserole. If meat has rendered a lot of juice, cook it over high heat to reduce and concentrate the sauce to 3 cups. Taste for seasoning. Serve it as is, or puree it through a food mill, using fine disk, or in the blender. Thicken it, if you wish, with potato starch dissolved in a little cold water or wine. Let beef rest 15 minutes before carving into thin slices. Arrange slices, overlapping, on a serving platter, spoon sauce over beef, and decorate platter with a bunch of watercress.

### GARNITURE BOURGEOISE

| | |
|---|---|
| 24  small white onions | ½  teaspoon freshly cracked |
| 5  or 6 carrots | black pepper |
| Suet | 2  tablespoons melted butter |
| ½  teaspoon salt | 1  teaspoon sugar |

Peel onions and parboil about 15 minutes. Cut carrots diagonally into 24 pieces and parboil 15 minutes. Fry suet over high heat to render beef fat—you need about ¼ cup. Arrange vegetables 1 layer deep in an ovenproof serving dish, sprinkle with salt and pepper, and spoon melted butter and beef fat over them, being sure to coat each piece. Sprinkle with sugar to give them a glaze. Place on bottom shelf of a preheated 350° oven and bake until brown and crisp, about 1 hour, basting occasionally. Serve in separate dish to accompany Beef à la Mode. *May be made ahead and reheated.*

### RUSSIAN GNOCCHI

Very delicate, Russian gnocchi are also an excellent accompaniment to Beef Stroganoff or any kind of beef stew.

| | |
|---|---|
| 1  pound cottage cheese | ½  teaspoon freshly cracked |
| ½  pound cream cheese | white pepper |
| 2  beaten eggs | ¾  cup freshly grated |
| ¼  to ½ cup lightly spooned flour | Parmesan cheese |
| 1  teaspoon plus 1 tablespoon salt | 10  tablespoons melted unsalted butter |

Push the cottage cheese and cream cheese through a fine sieve into a mixing bowl. Add the beaten eggs and beat well with a wooden spatula. Stir in flour, 2 tablespoons at a time, adding just enough to bind the mixture. Season with 1 teaspoon salt and the pepper, cover, and refrigerate for at least 30 minutes. Bring about 3 inches of water to boil in a large pan or deep skillet. Add 1 tablespoon salt to water. Reduce heat to simmer and drop cheese mixture by the teaspoonful into simmering water. (It helps to dip the spoon in cold water and to use a second spoon as a pusher.) Simmer gnocchi—do not let boil—for about 20 minutes. When cooked, they'll rise to the surface and be firm to your touch. (*Recipe may be made ahead to this point, cooled in water, and gently reheated at serving time.*) Drain gnocchi and sprinkle with Parmesan cheese and melted butter.

## BEET SALAD

8 medium-size beets
6 hard-cooked eggs
1 red onion
1 teaspoon salt
½ teaspoon freshly cracked
    black pepper

½ cup tarragon vinegar
¾ cup oil
Romaine lettuce leaves to
    line salad bowl
2 tablespoons chopped parsley

Scrub fresh beets with a brush. Cut stems 2 inches above beet crowns but do not trim roots. Cover with salted water and cook, covered, over high heat, until tender, 30 minutes to 1 hour, longer for older beets. Drain and rub off skins under cold water. Cut off stems and roots, and slice beets into a bowl. Chop the hard-cooked eggs—setting aside about ¼ of them—and onion and combine with beet slices. Mix salt, pepper, vinegar, and oil and pour over beets. Mix thoroughly. Line salad bowl with romaine. When ready to serve, spoon beet mixture into bowl, and sprinkle with reserved chopped egg and parsley.

## MONT BLANC

Make this rich, sweet dessert fantasy by filling a ring of egg-shaped meringues with chestnut butter cream and decorating it with meringue mushrooms and whipped cream.

MERINGUE:
9 egg whites
½ teaspoon cream of tartar
1¾ cups sugar
1 ounce finely grated dark
    sweet chocolate

4 egg yolks
1½ cups unsalted butter,
    chilled
1 15-ounce can unsweetened
    chestnut puree
2 tablespoons kirsch

CHESTNUT BUTTERCREAM:
1½ cups sugar
¾ cup water
½ teaspoon cream of tartar

GARNISH:
1 cup heavy cream
1 tablespoon kirsch

To make meringues, beat egg whites and cream of tartar with an electric mixer until soft peaks form. Gradually beat in sugar, a tablespoonful at a time, and continue beating until mixture is thick and glossy, like marshmallow, and feels smooth when you pinch it. Put three quarters of mixture into a pastry bag fitted with a plain round tube. Line a baking tray with baking parchment or brown paper and pipe out 12 large egg shapes, 12 rounded domes in several sizes to resemble mushroom caps, and an equal number of pointed cones to make mushroom stems. Put remaining meringue mixture into another pastry bag fitted with a star tube and pipe a ring of stars or dots around a large, round oven-proof serving plate, inside the rim. Place meringues (including ring of stars) in a preheated 250° oven and bake for about 45 minutes or until they are hard to the touch and creamy white, not brown. When "eggs" are baked, glue them together in a ring inside the ring of stars on the serving plate using a bit of meringue saved for this purpose. Dip the bottoms of the mushroom caps into grated chocolate and push the pointed ends of stems into caps.

To make chestnut buttercream, boil together sugar, water, and cream of tartar, stirring until sugar dissolves. Boil until mixture spins a thread (230° on candy thermometer). Beat egg yolks with an electric mixer until light and fluffy. Pour sugar syrup onto beaten egg yolks in a thin stream, beating constantly until mixture cools. Beat in butter, 1 tablespoonful at a time, then chestnut puree. Flavor with kirsch. When ready to pipe cream—meringue should be cooled—put mixture into a pastry bag fitted with very small plain round tube and pipe it, like vermicelli, crisscrossing in a long, thin, continuous stream, into the center of the meringue ring. Decorate the chestnut "mountain" with meringue mushrooms. Garnish with rosettes made from whipped cream flavored with kirsch and piped out from a pastry bag fitted with a star tube. Serve cold. *The meringues and chestnut buttercream can be made a day ahead and the Mont Blanc assembled a few hours before serving.*

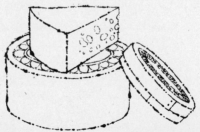

## A Make-Your-Own Salad Buffet
## for 24

Hot or cold watercress soup
Salad assortment, with French, Roquefort,
and Russian dressings
Assorted breads and breadsticks with butter
Assorted cheeses, with crackers and fruits

This is a simple and pleasing way to entertain a number of people for luncheon or perhaps an early supper—and fun for your guests as well. They literally put together their own meals. As hostess, you can, of course, prepare this buffet for as few or as many people as you choose by varying the kinds and quantities of ingredients you offer.

### WATERCRESS SOUP

8 large, roughly chopped potatoes
8 roughly chopped onions
2 roughly chopped carrots
4 roughly chopped ribs celery, including leaves
4 cups chicken stock (see p. 278), more if needed
2 peeled cloves garlic

2 tablespoons salt
2 teaspoons freshly cracked white pepper
1 cup butter
4 large bunches watercress
2 cups light cream, more if needed
2 cups heavy cream
2 tablespoons chopped parsley

Put the potatoes, onions, carrots, and celery in a large kettle and cover with chicken stock. Add garlic and 1 inch water. Add salt and pepper and lay the butter on top. Bring to a boil, reduce heat to simmer, cover, and cook until vegetables are mushy. Trim heavy stems from watercress if you plan to puree the soup in a food mill (leave them on if you're going to puree it in a blender) and add cress to soup; cook, stirring, for not more than 5 minutes. Puree soup, using electric blender or medium disk of food mill. (*May be prepared ahead to this point.*)

If serving soup hot, return puree to kettle, stir in light and heavy cream, bring just to the boiling point, and taste for seasoning. If pureed in a blender, it may need to be thinned with up to 2 cups more of light cream, milk, or chicken stock. If serving cold, chill the puree. At serving time, stir in chilled light cream and heavy cream and taste for seasoning. Chilled foods usually need more salt. Ladle from a tureen, garnishing with chopped parsley, into mugs for easy handling.

## SALAD ASSORTMENT

| | |
|---|---|
| Romaine | Carrot curls |
| Bibb lettuce | Sliced radishes |
| Watercress | Cucumber rings |
| Chinese cabbage | Black olives |
| Chicory | Tomato wedges |
| Avocado slices | Scallions or chives |
| Red onion rings | Green pepper rings |

## SALAD DRESSINGS

### FRENCH

Beat together 2 teaspoons coarse salt, 1 teaspoon freshly cracked black pepper, ¼ cup tarragon vinegar, and 1 cup French olive oil.

### ROQUEFORT

Mash ½ pound Roquefort cheese and add it and 1 teaspoon Worcestershire sauce to basic French dressing.

### RUSSIAN

Beat ¼ cup chili sauce into 2 cups mayonnaise (see p. 283).

## ASSORTED CHEESES

For a crowd of 24, plan on between ¼ and ½ pound of cheese apiece, depending on anticipated appetites. A good selection would include different flavors—strong to mild—and textures—soft, semisoft, and hard. You might care to feature an international medley: for example, the French Pont l'Evêque, Brie or Camembert, Port du Salut, Chevret (made from goats' milk), and Muenster (an Alsatian specialty), the Swiss Gruyère, Italian Bel Paese, Dutch Gouda, and English or American Cheddar. Serve at room temperature with unsalted water biscuits and a selection of apples and pears.

*Note:* Make a cheese crock from any cheese left over. Add to it one half its weight in butter and 1 to 2 shots of brandy, mix well, pack into a crock, and refrigerate. It will keep for months.

## A New Year's Eve Sit-down Buffet for 16

---

Gigot Provençale
Onion crêpes
Tossed green salad
Meringue torte with chocolate buttercream

### GIGOT PROVENÇALE

Prepare 2 legs of lamb for 16 guests. Have your husband or a male guest carve the legs of lamb in front of the guests. If this does not seem practical to you, carve them in the kitchen but arrange the slices on the platter as prettily as possible, with the bone ends of the lamb at one end of the platter for a better effect.

| | |
|---|---|
| 2 2-ounce cans flat anchovy fillets | ½ cup olive oil |
| 10 slices bacon | 1½ cups white wine |
| 2 legs of lamb, 6 to 7 pounds each | 1 cup water |
| 2 tablespoons coarse salt | ½ cup brandy |
| 2 teaspoons freshly cracked black pepper | 40 cloves garlic |
| | 2 bunches watercress, for garnish |

Cut up the anchovies and dice 4 strips of the bacon. With the point of a small knife, cut slits over the entire surface of the lamb and poke bits of anchovy and bacon into the slits, using the tip of the knife as a slide. Rub the lamb all over with coarse salt and pepper. Heat olive oil in a heavy skillet and brown the legs thoroughly over high heat. Put legs of lamb on 2 racks, fatty side up, in a roasting pan. Pour excess fat from skillet, deglaze it with 4 tablespoons white wine, and pour juices into roasting pan, together with another cup white wine, the water, and 4 tablespoons of the brandy. Cut remaining 6 slices bacon into squares and add to pan. (*May be prepared ahead to this point.*) Cover lamb closely with heavy aluminum foil, pinching it around pan edges to seal tightly. Place in a preheated 325° oven and roast 18 minutes per pound or about 1¾ hours for each 6-pound leg of lamb. Lamb will be rare.

While lamb roasts, peel garlic cloves, place in a saucepan, cover with water, and boil over high heat until garlic is very soft, about 15 minutes. Drain and push through a sieve or food mill, using the fine disk, or puree in a blender. Set aside.

When legs of lamb are done, remove them to a carving board and keep warm. Remove bacon pieces from roasting pan. Add remaining 4 tablespoons white wine and 4 tablespoons brandy and set pan over high heat. Add pureed garlic; cook and stir 5 minutes over high heat until well blended and reduced slightly. Taste sauce for seasoning—it may need pepper.

When brought to the table, a leg of lamb should wear a frill over the bone end—it looks better and keeps the carver's hands clean. To make frill, cut white paper to a 10 x 15-inch rectangle. Fold it in half lengthwise, without creasing, and make cuts about 3 inches deep at ½-inch intervals along the folded edge. Unfold it and refold it, inside out, again without creasing, to make frill puffier. Coil it to a diameter of 1½ inches to fit over bone, and fasten it with staples or cellophane tape. Garnish platter with watercress and serve sauce separately in a warmed bowl.

## ONION CRÊPES

| | |
|---|---|
| 3 tablespoons butter | 1 recipe soubise filling (see p. 157) |
| 1½ cups very finely chopped onions | 1 cup melted butter |
| 2 recipes basic crêpes (see p. 285) | 1 cup freshly grated Parmesan cheese |

Heat 3 tablespoons butter in a skillet, stir in onions, and cook, stirring, until they are limp but not brown, about 15 minutes.

Drain and cool and add to crêpes batter. Fry crêpes—7-inch size. Fill each crêpe with 1 tablespoon soubise filling and roll up. Brush an au gratin dish with 2 tablespoons of the melted butter and arrange crêpes. Sprinkle them with remaining melted butter and Parmesan cheese. (*Recipe can be made ahead to this point.*) Place in a preheated 350° oven for about 15 to 20 minutes, or a 325° oven for 20 to 25 minutes, or until heated through.

### TOSSED GREEN SALAD

| | |
|---|---|
| 3 or 4 heads of tender lettuce | 2 tablespoons chopped parsley |
| 2 cucumbers | French vinaigrette dressing |
| 4 heads of Belgian endive | (see p. 282) |
| ½ pound mushrooms | |

Separate and wash lettuce leaves, roll up in towels, and refrigerate to crisp. Peel cucumbers and shave them into strips, the length of the cucumber, with a potato peeler. Wash Belgian endive heads, discarding discolored outer leaves, and cut into julienne pieces. Wipe mushrooms clean with acidulated water (1 tablespoon lemon juice to 1 quart of water), trim stems, and slice very thinly. When ready to serve, put all greens and vegetables into a chilled salad bowl, sprinkle with chopped parsley, and toss with vinaigrette dressing.

### MERINGUE TORTE
### WITH CHOCOLATE BUTTERCREAM

| | |
|---|---|
| 10 egg whites | 1 recipe chocolate butter- |
| ½ teaspoon cream of tartar | cream (recipe follows) |
| 2½ cups sugar | 1 cup heavy cream |
| ½ cup toasted flaked almonds | Confectioners' sugar |

In electric mixer bowl, beat egg whites until foamy. Add cream of tartar and continue beating while adding sugar, 1 tablespoon at a time. Beat until mixture looks like marshmallow and no longer feels grainy when you pinch it. Pack the meringue into a big pastry bag fitted with a star tube. Line 2 trays with baking parchment and draw a 9-inch circle on each (trace around a 9-inch cake pan). Following the outline, pipe out a ring of meringue and spiral into the center to make an entire layer of meringue. Decorate one of the layers (the top layer when you assemble torte) with some scallops. Also pipe out separately some shell shapes by humping the extrusion just a bit. (Lift or push up the pastry bag a little so that a rounded shell shape emerges.) Sprinkle layers and shells with toasted almonds and bake in a preheated 250° oven for about 1 hour or until firm. This will be a somewhat chewy meringue—not a dry, crisp one. Let cool.

Make buttercream and pack it into a pastry bag fitted with a star tube. Pipe over bottom layer of meringue in loose curlicues. Place top layer over filling and pipe remaining buttercream in a floral design on top. (*May be made to this point the day before.*) Whip the heavy cream, pack it in a pastry bag fitted with star tube, and decorate sides of torte. Push the meringue shell shapes into the whipped cream at intervals around edge of torte. Dust the entire torte with confectioners' sugar stirred through a sieve. Cut into wedges for guests to help themselves. *May be decorated a few hours ahead—whip heavy cream over ice with a piano-wire whisk so it will hold up.*

*Note:* Instead of a single torte, you can make individual meringue shells; fill each with buttercream and decorate with a rosette of whipped cream.

### CHOCOLATE BUTTERCREAM

6 ounces dark sweet
  chocolate
2 tablespoons water
2 tablespoons rum
1 cup sugar
⅔ cup water

¼ teaspoon cream of tartar
1 tablespoon lemon juice
3 egg yolks
1½ cups chilled unsalted butter
1 tablespoon vegetable
  shortening, if needed

Melt chocolate with 2 tablespoons water and the rum. In another pan combine sugar, ⅔ cup water, the cream of tartar, and the lemon juice. Stir over high heat until sugar dissolves; then cook until syrup spins a thread (230° on a candy thermometer). Meanwhile, beat egg yolks in an electric mixer bowl until thick and lemony. When syrup is ready, pour it in a *thin* stream into egg yolks, beating constantly at high speed. Continue beating until bowl feels cool to touch. When mixture is cool, beat in the unsalted butter, a bit at a time. Have vegetable shortening measured and ready in case the mixture curdles. If it does, beat in shortening—this will bring it back. Beat in cooled chocolate mixture.

## A "Cook-in" Buffet
### for 6 to 8

---

Sautéed blowfish
Rack of lamb with green peppercorns
Carrot soufflé
Leeks Mornay
Baked Alaska

A "cook-in" buffet is one of my favorite methods of entertaining. I invite a small group of people—no more than can move around my kitchen easily—and have *them* do the cooking, under my supervision. When the food is ready, we set it up on a table, admire it, then eat. We usually eat the first course standing up around the kitchen, then present the main course at the buffet table. Dessert is served separately.

### SAUTÉED BLOWFISH

| | |
|---|---|
| 24 blowfish (sea squabs) | 2 teaspoons finely chopped garlic |
| Flour for dredging | |
| ¾ cup butter | 2 tablespoons finely chopped parsley |
| 1 teaspoon salt | |
| ½ teaspoon freshly cracked white pepper | Juice of ½ lemon |

The edible part of blowfish—a saltwater fish usually available in eastern markets—is the white meat on both sides of the backbone—a delicacy. When it is trimmed out of the blowfish and sold commercially, it is called sea squab, and it looks something like a frog's leg. To prepare the fish, cut off the head about 1 inch behind the eyes, strip off the skin and cut away the entrails. Leave backbone in. Wash and dry meat and dredge with flour, patting off excess. Heat ½ cup butter in a heavy skillet; when it's foaming, sauté the blowfish over high heat for about 3 minutes on each side—do not overcook. Sauté a few at a time—just one layer in pan. Season with salt and pepper, remove to a serving plate, and keep warm. Wash the skillet and heat the remaining ¼ cup butter. Add garlic, parsley, and lemon juice; swirl the pan for 1 minute only over high heat and pour over the fish.

## RACK OF LAMB
## WITH GREEN PEPPERCORNS

Green peppercorns, grown mainly in Madagascar, are picked before they are ripe, and strong in taste.

| | |
|---|---|
| 2 racks of lamb | 1 cup basic brown sauce (see |
| 2 tablespoons coarse salt | p. 281) |
| 2 teaspoons freshly cracked | 2 tablespoons drained green |
| black pepper | peppercorns |
| 2 slivered cloves garlic | 1 tablespoon butter |

Have the butcher remove the chine bones, to make carving easier, and trim the racks so that 1½ to 2 inches of bone are exposed on each chop. Rub the lamb all over with salt and pepper. With the point of a small knife, cut slits in the fatty side of the meat and push garlic slivers into the slits, using the tip of the knife as a slide. Place lamb, fatty side up, on a rack in a baking pan and roast in a preheated 425° oven for 35 minutes. Lamb will be pink. For sauce, combine basic brown sauce and drained green peppercorns and bring to a boil. Add butter and swirl over heat just until butter melts.

## CARROT SOUFFLÉ

| | |
|---|---|
| 4 or 5 carrots | 5 beaten egg yolks |
| 1 tablespoon grated orange | 1 teaspoon salt |
| peel | ½ teaspoon freshly cracked |
| 4 tablespoons butter | white pepper |
| 4 tablespoons flour | 2 tablespoons chopped parsley |
| ¾ cup milk | 7 egg whites |
| ¼ cup orange juice | ½ teaspoon cream of tartar |

Use a 6-cup soufflé dish, or prepare a 4-cup soufflé dish with a paper collar: fold a strip of waxed paper lengthwise and tie it around the top of the soufflé dish so that it extends 4 to 5 inches

above the dish. Oil the inside of the collar and set dish aside. Peel
and slice carrots crosswise into 1-inch pieces; boil them in water
to cover over high heat until tender and puree them in a blender
or a food mill, using the fine disk—you should have 1 cup puree.
Stir in grated orange peel and set aside. Melt the butter in a
saucepan and stir in flour with a wooden spatula. Cook, stirring,
over high heat for 2 minutes—do not let it brown. Remove from
heat, change to a whisk, and add milk and orange juice, whisking
vigorously. Return to heat and cook, stirring, until mixture thickens. Remove from heat and add beaten egg yolks—beat them in
quickly so they won't scramble. Add salt, pepper, carrot puree,
and chopped parsley and blend thoroughly. (*May be prepared
ahead to this point.*) When ready to proceed, beat egg whites until
foamy, add cream of tartar, and beat until stiff but not dry. Fold
egg whites into soufflé base and pour into soufflé dish. Bake in a
preheated 425° oven for 25 minutes.

## LEEKS MORNAY

| | |
|---|---|
| 12 leeks | ⅛ teaspoon freshly grated nutmeg |
| 2 cups water | |
| 1 tablespoon salt | 6 tablespoons grated Gruyère cheese |
| 2 tablespoons butter | |
| 2 tablespoons flour | 2 tablespoons cream |
| 1½ cups milk | 1 egg yolk |
| ½ teaspoon salt | 2 tablespoons freshly grated Parmesan cheese |
| ¼ teaspoon freshly cracked white pepper | |

Clean leeks: cut off the roots; cut off tops, leaving about 4
inches of green, and split leeks lengthwise. Hold under running
water, separating the layers, to wash thoroughly. Put them in a
saucepan, cover with salted water, bring to a boil, and simmer,
uncovered, until barely tender, about 15 minutes. Drain and set
aside. In another pan, over high heat, melt butter and stir in
flour. Cook, stirring with a wooden spatula, for 2 minutes—do not
let flour brown. Remove from heat, change to a whisk, and add
milk, whisking vigorously. Return to heat and cook, stirring, until
sauce thickens. Season with salt, pepper, and nutmeg. Stir in
Gruyère cheese. Beat the cream into the egg yolk, warm it with
2 tablespoons of the sauce, and then stir it into the sauce. Heat
through over medium-high heat but do not boil. Arrange leeks

in an ovenproof baking dish. Spoon sauce over leeks and sprinkle with Parmesan cheese. (*May be prepared ahead to this point.*) Bake in a preheated 350° oven for about 15 minutes or until bubbly. Glaze under the broiler before serving.

## BAKED ALASKA

| | |
|---|---|
| 1  9-inch layer gold cake (recipe follows) | ¼  teaspoon salt |
| | ½  teaspoon cream of tartar |
| 3  tablespoons white crème de cacao | 1¾  cups finely granulated sugar |
| | 1  quart chocolate ice cream, softened |
| 6  egg whites | |

Cover a heavy wood board (such as a cutting board for bread or the back of a carving board) with baking parchment and place cake layer on paper in the center of the board. Sprinkle cake with crème de cacao, poking holes in top of cake with a fork so liqueur will soak in. Beat egg whites with an electric mixer until foamy. Add salt and cream of tartar. Continue beaing until soft peaks form. Add 1 cup sugar gradually, 1 tablespoon at a time, beating constantly. Continue beating until mixture looks glossy, like marshmallow, and no longer feels grainy when you pinch it. Quickly fold in ½ cup sugar and put meringue into a large pastry bag fitted with a star tube. Spread softened ice cream on the cake, leaving a 1-inch margin around the edge. Pipe the meringue all over the cake and ice cream, covering both completely. Dust the top with the remaining ¼ cup sugar and place the cake, on the board, into the freezer for 15 minutes to set. (*Can be made ahead to this point and stored in freezer.*) Preheat oven to 450°; move the cake, still on the board, from freezer directly to oven and bake for about 5 minutes, or until meringue is delicately brown. Serve immediately.

## *GOLD CAKE*

| | |
|---|---|
| 1  tablespoon solid vegetable shortening | ½  cup butter |
| | 1½  cups lightly spooned cake flour |
| 4  eggs, separated | |
| 1½  cups sugar | ½  cup cornstarch |
| ½  cup cold water | ½  teaspoon salt |
| 2  teaspoons vanilla extract | 4  teaspoons baking powder |

Grease 2 9-inch layer pans with solid shortening. Line with waxed paper. Beat egg whites until foamy; beat in ½ cup sugar, adding it 1 tablespoon at a time, until mixture looks like marsh-mallow. With an electric mixer this takes about 5 minutes; by hand, about 15 minutes. In a separate bowl, whisk together egg yolks with cold water for 3 to 4 minutes, or until foamy. Add vanilla. In a third bowl, cream butter with the remaining cup of sugar. Add egg yolk mixture to butter mixture and combine well. Don't worry if mixture looks curdled. Sift together flour (if using all-purpose flour use 3 tablespoons less), cornstarch, salt, and baking powder. Add to butter mixture. Beat well for 2 minutes and fold in egg white mixture. Bake in 375° oven for 35 minutes. *This cake freezes well for 1 month.*

### *Italian Buffet*
### *for 8*

Stuffed zucchini
Fettuccini with pesto sauce
Braised fennel (see p. 102)
Grissini
Zabaglione
Pignolia cookies (see p. 249)
Espresso coffee

## STUFFED ZUCCHINI

| | |
|---|---|
| 8 small zucchini | ½ teaspoon oregano |
| 1 pound ground beef | 2 slices of bread |
| 1 egg | ¼ cup olive oil |
| 2 finely chopped cloves garlic | 2 tablespoons chopped parsley |
| 2 teaspoons salt | |

Wash zucchini. Cut off ends and seed with an apple corer. In a bowl, mix ground beef, egg, garlic, salt, oregano, and bread—soak the bread in water first, and squeeze it dry. Put meat mixture into a pastry bag fitted with a plain tube and pipe it into the zucchini from both ends. Sauté zucchini in olive oil over high heat until lightly browned. Arrange in a baking pan and pour on oil remaining in skillet. Bake about 20 minutes in a preheated 350° oven, or until tender. (*Can be made the day before and reheated for 10 minutes in a 350° oven, or served at room temperature.*) To serve, sprinkle with chopped parsley.

## FETTUCCINI WITH PESTO SAUCE

1 recipe homemade pasta (see p. 286)
8 quarts boiling water

1 tablespoon salt
Pesto alla Genovese (recipe follows)

Prepare and roll pasta; cut into noodles (use the wide noodle setting if you have a pasta machine, or cut noodles ¼ to ⅜ inch wide with a sharp knife). Let them dry at least 2 hours before cooking. (*They can be made ahead, packaged in plastic bags, and stored in the refrigerator for a day or two; or frozen for up to 1 month.*)

To cook noodles, bring water to a rolling boil, add salt, and add noodles gradually. Cook, stirring and lifting noodles with a wooden fork, until done, about 7 minutes. Test them by biting them—they should be *al dente*, slightly resistant. Drain in a colander and pour into warmed serving bowl. Toss with Pesto sauce and serve at once.

## PESTO ALLA GENOVESE

You can keep this for weeks in the refrigerator—pack it into a small jar and float a little olive oil over the top to preserve it.

1½ cups fresh basil leaves
¾ cup olive oil
4 tablespoons soft butter
¼ cup pine nuts
¾ cup grated Parmesan cheese

2 tablespoons chopped parsley
2 teaspoons chopped garlic
1 teaspoon salt
½ teaspoon freshly cracked black pepper

Put all ingredients except salt and pepper in a blender. Blend on low, then higher speed until mixture looks like pea puree. (If you have no blender, puree with a pestle and mortar, but this takes some time.) Season with salt and pepper. To serve with pasta, thin pesto with 6 tablespoons water drained from cooking noodles. Spoon over noodles and toss.

## ZABAGLIONE

You can beat zabaglione the cautious way, over hot water. But you should learn to work with eggs on a direct flame or burner—and making zabaglione is a great way to learn. There's even a special pot for it of heavy copper, with a dome-shaped bottom so that your whisk can reach everywhere to whip the zabaglione to thick, sweet creaminess. But if you don't have a zabaglione pot, you could use a copper or stainless-steel mixing bowl.

| | |
|---|---|
| 3 eggs | ⅔ cup sugar |
| 6 egg yolks | ¼ cup sweet Marsala |

Put eggs, egg yolks, sugar, and Marsala into zabaglione pot or metal bowl and beat with a whisk until blended. Hold pot over high heat and beat continuously, raising and lowering the pot so that it never gets too hot. *Or* put ingredients into a large glass bowl, stand the bowl in a pan of hot water over high heat, and beat with whisk or electric beater. When zabaglione is thick and creamy—it takes about 10 minutes over direct heat, 5 to 10 minutes longer over hot water—serve immediately.

### *Just Desserts Buffet*
### *for 25*

Carlsbad Oblaten cake
Grape tart
Cold chocolate soufflé
La Tourinoise
Crème caramel
Savarin
Chestnut mousse
Trifle
Orange almond torte
Macédoine of fruits (see p. 61)

Everybody has friends who are "dessert freaks." These are people who read the list of desserts on a menu first, then build their dinner around their dessert choice. Why not invite them to a dessert orgy—perhaps after a community meeting or tryouts for an amateur play or just for the fun of it. If there are leftovers, either your guests can take extras home with them or you can freeze the leftovers. The Oblaten cake, soufflé, Tourinoise, savarin, mousse, and torte all freeze well. I always supply lots of coffee and sometimes champagne or a sweet dessert wine.

## CARLSBAD OBLATEN CAKE

Oblaten, usually available in German or gourmet stores, are plain, gaufrette-type wafers.

9 ounces dark sweet chocolate
2 tablespoons rum or brandy
2 tablespoons water
1 cup sugar
⅔ cup water
⅛ teaspoon cream of tartar
3 egg yolks
1½ cups chilled butter

1 tablespoon solid vegetable shortening, if needed
2 cups heavy cream
4 tablespoons confectioners' sugar
1 package round Oblaten (8-inch-diameter wafers)
1 8-ounce jar apricot jam

Melt 6 ounces of the chocolate in a small pan with the rum and 2 tablespoons water. Stir it over low heat and watch that it doesn't burn. Set aside to cool. Separately, melt remaining 3 ounces of chocolate over low heat. With a teaspoon, spread rounds of this chocolate, like coins, on waxed paper set on a pan or on cardboard, and refrigerate. Make sugar syrup by cooking sugar, ⅔ cup water, and cream of tartar together in a small saucepan, over high heat, until syrup spins a thread (230° to 234° on a candy thermometer). Beat egg yolks in mixer bowl until light and fluffy. When syrup is ready, pour it in a thin stream into the egg yolks, beating all the while. Continue beating until mixture is cool. Beat in the butter a bit at a time. (Don't worry if mixture gets thin; it will get thick again. If it curdles, beat in a tablespoon of vegetable shortening to bring it back.) Finally, beat in the cooled chocolate-rum mixture and place the bowl of chocolate pastry cream in the refrigerator to chill for a few minutes.

Line a serving plate with triangles of waxed paper. (When you've finished putting the cake together, you can pull out the waxed paper, leaving a clean plate.) Whip the heavy cream until stiff, sweetening it with confectioners' sugar. Put the whipped cream into a pastry bag fitted with a star tube. Spread one of the wafers with jam to within 1 inch of the edge. Lay it on the serving plate and pipe whipped cream rosettes around the edge—4 rosettes on each layer. Spread jam on a second wafer, stack it on the first, pipe with whipped cream rosettes. Continue until all wafers are used, but do not put jam on the top wafer. Pipe bands of whipped cream vertically, up the sides of the stacked cake, leaving about 1½ inches between each band. Bring cream up just over the top edge. Fill another pastry bag, also fitted with a star tube, with the chocolate pastry cream. Pipe bands of pastry cream between the bands of whipped cream on sides of cake. Cover top of cake with pastry cream rosettes and decorate with the chocolate coins. Chill cake overnight in the refrigerator before serving. Cut slices carefully with a sharp knife.

## GRAPE TART

2 tablespoons bread crumbs
1 wholly baked 9-inch pâte
   brisée shell (see p. 288)
1½ cups heavy cream
3 tablespoons confectioners'
   sugar, plus more for
   sifting

2 tablespoons rum
1 bunch black grapes
1 bunch seedless white grapes
1 cup apricot jam
¼ cup light rum

Sprinkle bread crumbs into pâte brisée shell. Whip the heavy cream, adding 3 tablespoons confectioners' sugar and the rum, until stiff. Spread into tart shell. Remove stems from grapes. Carefully seed black grapes, pressing halves back together so they look whole. Cover the tart with grapes arranged in alternating rings of black and white. Make glaze: mix apricot jam with rum and stir over high heat until it dissolves. Rub through a strainer and brush grapes with apricot glaze. (*May be made ahead and refrigerated.*) Just before serving, sift confectioners' sugar around edge of tart.

## COLD CHOCOLATE SOUFFLÉ

Follow recipe for Cold Chocolate Almond Soufflé (see p. 171) but omit toasted almonds.

## LA TOURINOISE

1 cup butter
1 15-ounce can unsweetened
    chestnut puree
1 cup sugar
½ pound unsweetened choco-
    late, melted and cooled

1 teaspoon vanilla extract
2 tablespoons brandy or rum
½ cup toasted slivered al-
    monds, optional
    Confectioners' sugar
1 cup heavy cream

Oil a 6-cup loaf mold. Put the butter into an electric mixer bowl and beat it until light and creamy. Add chestnut puree 1 tablespoonful at a time and continue beating; mixture should be very creamy. Gradually beat in sugar, then cooled chocolate. Add vanilla, brandy, and almonds. Pack into the oiled mold and bang the mold on the counter to settle the mixture. Refrigerate overnight. To serve, turn out onto a serving dish and sift with confectioners' sugar. Cut in very thin slices and serve with unsweetened whipped cream.

## CRÈME CARAMEL

1½ cups plus 6 tablespoons
    sugar
4 eggs
3 egg yolks

2 teaspoons vanilla extract
⅛ teaspoon salt
1 quart milk

Make the caramel first, to coat the inside of an 8-cup soufflé dish. Put 1½ cups sugar in a heavy pan—an iron skillet is ideal. Place over high heat and stir until sugar dissolves. Use a wooden spatula and be sure you get into the corners of the pan. The sugar will lump at first; then it will dissolve and come to a boil. Watch carefully when it turns a butterscotch color; remove from heat when you see it give off small puffs of smoke. After a minute or two, pour the caramel into the soufflé dish and rotate the dish to spread caramel all over bottom and sides. Be careful; melted sugar is very hot. Set aside.

To make custard, whisk eggs and egg yolks in a large bowl just until blended. Whisk in remaining 6 tablespoons sugar and stir in the vanilla, salt, and milk. Strain this mixture through a fine sieve 10 times. Then pour into the caramel-coated soufflé dish and set it in a baking pan filled with 1 inch of hot water. Place in a preheated 350° oven and bake for 45 to 50 minutes. Custard is done when a knife, inserted near the edge of the dish, comes out clean. Remove from oven, take out of water bath, and let cool to room temperature. Then place custard in the refrigerator to chill. (*May be made to this point the day before.*) When ready to serve, unmold the custard on a rimmed serving dish. Baking dissolves the caramel, and you'll find a delicious pool of caramel sauce around the custard.

### SAVARIN

Follow recipe for Rum Babas (see p. 247) but instead of putting dough in *baba au rhum* molds, form it into a roll and fit it into a 4-cup savarin or ring mold. Bake for 25 minutes in a preheated 375° oven. Make a syrup by stirring ½ cup light rum, 1¼ cups sugar, and ¼ cup water over high heat until sugar dissolves. Simmer 10 minutes and then soak the hot savarin in rum syrup. Mix 1 cup apricot jam with ¼ cup light rum and stir over high heat until jam dissolves. Rub apricot glaze through strainer and brush savarin with it. Decorate with candied cherry halves and leaves cut from angelica. (*May be made the day before to this point.*) When ready to serve, fill the center of the ring with 1 cup heavy cream, whipped and sweetened with 2 tablespoons confectioners' sugar.

### CHESTNUT MOUSSE

| | |
|---|---|
| 2 tablespoons (2 envelopes) unflavored gelatine | 4 tablespoons dark rum |
| 1½ cups light cream | 2 tablespoons confectioners' sugar |
| ½ cup sugar | 3 cups heavy cream |
| 4 eggs, separated | 1 8-ounce can whole marrons glacés |
| 1 15-ounce can unsweetened chestnut puree | |

Oil a 6-cup soufflé dish and set aside. Sprinkle gelatine over light cream in a saucepan; stir in sugar. Place over low heat and stir until gelatine and sugar dissolve—do not boil. Beat egg yolks very well. Stir a little of the hot cream into egg yolks, to warm them, then stir into cream and cook, stirring constantly, until mixture thickens enough to coat the back of a spoon, about 10 minutes. Cool in refrigerator. Put the chestnut puree in an electric mixer bowl and add the rum. Beat it until very fluffy. When gelatine mixture has cooled just to the point of setting, beat it into the chestnut puree, a little at a time, until well blended. Beat egg whites until foamy; add confectioners' sugar and beat until stiff. Fold into chestnut mixture. Whip 2 cups of the heavy cream and fold into mixture. Pour into prepared soufflé dish and chill for several hours.

When ready to serve, whip the remaining 1 cup heavy cream and pack it into a pastry bag fitted with a star tube. Unmold the mousse onto a chilled platter and decorate all over with whipped cream rosettes. Press whole marrons glacés into rosettes.


## TRIFLE

JELLY ROLL:
4 eggs
½ cup sugar
⅓ cup flour
⅓ cup potato flour
½ cup jelly or seedless jam
2 tablespoons sherry, or
    Madeira, Marsala,
    brandy, or rum

BAVARIAN CREAM:
3 eggs, separated
½ cup sugar
6 tablespoons sherry, or
    Madeira, Marsala,
    brandy, or rum

1 tablespoon (1 envelope)
    unflavored gelatine
1½ cups milk
1 cup heavy cream

¼ cup sherry, or Madeira,
    Marsala, brandy, or rum

¼ cup heavy cream
1 tablespoon confectioners'
    sugar

Candied violets, for
    garnish, optional

Oil the jelly-roll pan, line it with waxed paper, and oil the paper; set aside. Beat eggs with sugar until very light and fluffy; this will take several minutes using an electric mixer. Mix the two flours and fold gently into the egg mixture. Spread batter in the jelly-roll pan and bake 10 minutes in a preheated 375° oven. Remove cake from oven and loosen around edges. Lay 2 strips of waxed paper on the counter, overlapping lengthwise. Turn cake out on waxed paper, peel off lining paper. Let cool for a minute or two; then spread with jelly. Roll up and cut the roll in 1-inch slices. Line a glass serving bowl with about half of the jelly-roll slices, reserving the rest, and sprinkle them with 2 tablespoons sherry.

To make the Bavarian cream, whisk the 3 egg yolks in a bowl. Add ½ cup sugar and whisk until thick. Pour ¼ cup sherry into a measuring cup, sprinkle it with the gelatine, and let stand for about 5 minutes. Then set the cup in a pan of boiling water and stir until gelatine dissolves. Whisk the dissolved gelatine into the egg yolk mixture. Add milk all at once and transfer to a heavy nonaluminum saucepan. Set over high heat and cook, whisking constantly, until mixture coats the back of a spoon. It will not be thick. Set the pan over ice and continue whisking until mixture is cool. Flavor with 2 tablespoons sherry. Beat egg whites until stiff peaks form and whip 1 cup of the heavy cream. When the cooked mixture is cool, fold in egg whites and whipped cream; mixture will be thin.

Spoon about half of the Bavarian cream over the jelly roll in the glass bowl. Lay remaining jelly-roll slices on the cream, sprinkle with remaining ¼ cup sherry, and spoon on the rest of the Bavarian cream. Refrigerate. (*Can be made the day before.*) When ready to serve, whip remaining ½ cup heavy cream, sweetening it with the confectioners' sugar. Put it in a pastry bag fitted with a star tube and pipe rosettes of whipped cream around the edge of the dessert. Decorate with candied violets.

## ORANGE ALMOND TORTE

Follow the directions for torte layers given in the recipe for Almond Torte (see p. 167), but omit vanilla and almond extracts and flavor the torte with 2 tablespoons freshly grated orange peel and 2 tablespoons Grand Marnier or other orange liqueur. To serve, whip 1½ cups heavy cream and flavor it with 3 tablespoons confectioners' sugar, 1 tablespoon freshly grated orange peel, and ¼ cup fresh orange juice. Spread over bottom layer of torte, reserving about ½ cup for decorating top of torte; top with second layer and decorate with whipped cream rosettes.

# A Summertime Seafood Buffet for 8

Scallops and prosciutto
Poached flounder paupiettes stuffed
with fish mousse, shrimp sauce
Lima beans with black butter
Hot violet soufflé, crème Anglaise

## SCALLOPS AND PROSCIUTTO

1½ pounds sea scallops
1 tablespoon chopped garlic
Juice of 2 limes or 2 lemons
2 teaspoons salt
½ teaspoon freshly cracked
white pepper
½ teaspoon basil or oregano
or tarragon
½ pound thinly sliced
prosciutto ham
Melted butter, optional

Cut sea scallops in half. Marinate them in the refrigerator overnight in garlic and lime juice. When ready to serve, season them with salt, pepper, and basil. Wrap in ham and serve raw, on picks. Or brush with melted butter and bake in a preheated 450° oven for about 10 minutes or until they sizzle.

## POACHED FLOUNDER PAUPIETTES STUFFED WITH FISH MOUSSE

1½ pounds fresh salmon or
halibut
4 egg whites
2 tablespoons chopped fresh
dill
3 tablespoons finely chopped
shallots
¼ teaspoon very finely
chopped garlic
¾ cup light cream, about
2 teaspoons salt
½ teaspoon freshly cracked
white pepper
8 medium-size flounder fillets
1 cup dry white wine
½ cup water
1 bay leaf
6 peppercorns
Shrimp Sauce (recipe
follows)

Grind the salmon or halibut and put it into the bowl of an electric mixer. Beat it about 5 minutes. Add egg whites a little at a time, still beating, and add dill, shallots, and garlic. Beat in cream, 1 tablespoonful at a time, just enough so that mixture will drop easily from a spatula. Add salt and pepper. Set aside. Lay flounder fillets on waxed paper, skin side up. Sprinkle generously with white wine. Spread each fillet with fish mousse and roll up like a jelly roll; fasten with toothpick. Place paupiettes in a baking dish; they may touch. Pour on remaining wine and the water and add bay leaf and peppercorns. Cover fish with buttered waxed paper. (*May be made ahead to this point and refrigerated.*)

Bake in a preheated 350° oven for 15 to 20 minutes, or until fish flakes when you touch it with a toothpick. Remove from oven and arrange in serving dish; use the poaching liquid to make the shrimp sauce. Remove toothpicks from the paupiettes, spoon on shrimp sauce, and reheat briefly in the oven before serving, about 5 minutes. *May be completely prepared ahead, covered with plastic wrap, and refrigerated. To reheat, bring to room temperature, then place in a 350° oven for 15 minutes, or glaze under the broiler for 1 minute.*

## SHRIMP SAUCE

2 tablespoons butter
1 tablespoon chopped shallots
2 tablespoons flour
1 tablespoon tomato paste
1 cup liquid, from poaching
   fish

½ cup light cream
1 tablespoon brandy, optional
½ pound chopped cooked
   shrimp

Melt butter in a saucepan, stir in shallots, and cook over high heat for 2 minutes—do not let them burn. Stir in flour and tomato paste and cook for 2 minutes more, stirring constantly. Remove from heat, change to a whisk, and add poaching liquid all at once, whisking vigorously. Return to high heat and bring to a boil, stirring constantly. Add cream, and brandy if desired, and bring to a boil again. Season to taste, add shrimp, and heat through. Spoon sauce over paupiettes.

## LIMA BEANS WITH BLACK PEPPER

Fresh lima beans are available in the summer mostly. Although you can substitute frozen lima beans (4 cups—preparing them according to package directions), the fresh limas are far superior.

| | |
|---|---|
| 3 pounds lima beans (about 4 cups, shelled) | 2 tablespoons vinegar |
| 2 teaspoons salt | ½ teaspoon freshly cracked black pepper |
| ½ cup butter | |

Shell the lima beans and put them into a saucepan, add just enough cold water to cover, and 1 teaspoon salt. Bring to a boil, reduce heat, and simmer, uncovered, until barely tender, about 20 to 30 minutes. Heat butter very slowly in a small skillet until it turns dark brown, about 10 to 15 minutes. Set aside. Put vinegar, remaining 1 teaspoon salt, and the pepper in a very small pan and simmer until it reduces to 1 tablespoon. Stir vinegar reduction into cooled butter; reheat and pour over lima beans. Toss them well and add seasoning, if necessary.

## HOT VIOLET SOUFFLÉ

| | |
|---|---|
| 3 tablespoons butter | 1½ cups chopped crystallized violets |
| 3 tablespoons flour | |
| 1 cup milk | 7 egg whites |
| ⅓ cup sugar | ¼ teaspoon cream of tartar |
| 5 egg yolks | Crème Anglaise (recipe follows) |
| 1 teaspoon vanilla extract | |
| 2 tablespoons crème de violette liqueur | |

Melt butter in a nonaluminum pan. Stir in flour and cook over high heat, stirring constantly, for 2 minutes. Do not let it brown. Remove from heat, change to a whisk, and add milk, whisking vigorously. Return to high heat, add sugar, and cook, stirring constantly, until mixture comes to a boil and is thick and smooth. Set aside to cool slightly; then beat in egg yolks 1 at a time. Flavor with vanilla and violet liqueur. (*May be prepared ahead to this point and refrigerated. Warm the mixture slightly before folding in egg whites.*) When ready to bake, fold crystallized violets into base. Beat egg whites with cream of tartar until stiff, fold into base mixture, and pour into 6-cup soufflé dish (or use a 4-cup soufflé dish fitted with a paper collar). Bake on the bottom shelf of a preheated 375° oven for 30 minutes, or a 425° oven for 25 minutes. Serve immediately with Crème Anglaise.

## CRÈME ANGLAISE

2 cups light cream
4 egg yolks

½ cup sugar
¼ cup crème de violette liqueur

Scald the cream. Beat egg yolks with sugar until very thick and lemony. Add the hot cream slowly, stirring constantly. Return to high heat and cook until the mixture coats the back of a spoon, stirring constantly. Flavor with crème de violette. Serve warm.

# *Suppers*

I think of suppers as late night entertainment—light and un-elaborate meals offered around eleven or eleven-thirty. It's always fun, for instance, to say "Come home with us" after an art opening or an evening at the theater or ballet. When you're excited about a show, you want to talk about it with friends.

If my invitation is impromptu, we collect in the kitchen and I pull out my omelette pans. But if I've planned and cooked ahead, the menu may be more elegant and may well include champagne. Still, the first rule for late nights is keep it simple. The best foods are completely prepared ahead, ready to go into the oven or chafing dish for quick reheating. Curried Chicken Pancakes or Lobster Thermidor are excellent choices. You'll be ready with either before your guests have had a round of drinks!

## *Supper for 8 after the Theater, Ballet, or Opera*

Pea pod soup
Curried chicken pancakes
with chutney
Stuffed oranges

### PEA POD SOUP

If the peas in your market are not fresh, don't make this soup. If fresh pods are available, they make a deliciously unusual soup, totally different from dried pea soup.

2 quarts washed pea pods
  (not snow peas)
6 cups strong chicken stock
  (see p. 278)
1 cup shredded lettuce, well
  packed
1 cup chopped onion
1 quart light cream
1 bay leaf
4 sprigs parsley

2 teaspoons salt
½ teaspoon freshly cracked
  white pepper
¼ teaspoon freshly grated
  nutmeg
2 egg yolks
4 teaspoons butter
4 teaspoons finely chopped
  parsley

In a large saucepan, combine pea pods, chicken stock, lettuce, and onion. Bring to a boil, reduce heat, cover, and simmer until pea pods are barely tender, about 20 to 30 minutes. Puree this mixture through a food mill, using the fine disk, or in a blender. Return to high heat and stir in light cream, bay leaf, and parsley. Bring to a boil. Season with salt, pepper, and nutmeg. (*Can be made ahead to this point.*) Beat egg yolks, warm them with a little of the hot soup, and stir them into soup. Heat just to boiling, but do not boil. Serve in individual soup bowls, garnished with butter and finely chopped parsley.

## CURRIED CHICKEN PANCAKES
## WITH CHUTNEY

1 4-pound chicken
4 cups chicken stock (see
  p. 278)
½ rib celery
4 whole peppercorns
1 small onion
2 whole cloves
¾ cup butter
2 cups chopped onions
½ cup chopped carrots
½ cup chopped celery

1 medium-size apple, un-
  peeled, but cored and
  chopped
3 to 4 tablespoons curry
  powder
3 tablespoons flour
1 cup light cream
1 cup canned unsweetened
  coconut milk
¼ cup finely chopped mango
  chutney
16 7-inch crêpes (see p. 285)
¼ cup melted butter

Poach the chicken in chicken stock, adding celery, pepper-corns, and onion stuck with cloves. Cool in broth. Remove meat from bones and cut into cubes. Set aside. Strain stock and set aside. Melt butter in a heavy skillet and add chopped onions, carrots, celery, and apple and cook over high heat until onions are transparent. With wooden spatula, smooth curry powder and flour into the vegetable mixture, and cook, stirring, for 2 minutes. Stir in 2 cups of reserved chicken stock and cook about 15 minutes, or until vegetables are tender. Add cream and coconut milk and cook a few minutes longer. Puree the sauce through a food mill, using the medium disk, or in a blender. Taste for seasoning. Mix half the sauce with chicken, adding the chopped chutney. Lay out the crêpes, light side up, and put 2 heaping tablespoons of chicken mixture on each; roll up and lay, seam side down, in a buttered ovenproof serving dish. Spoon remaining sauce over rolled crêpes. Drizzle with melted butter. (*Dish may be prepared ahead, covered with plastic wrap, and refrigerated, or frozen for up to 1 month. Any leftover chicken mixture may be frozen.*) When ready to serve, heat through in a 350° oven until brown and bubbly, about 10 to 15 minutes.

## STUFFED ORANGES

| | |
|---|---|
| 8 large navel oranges | 3 egg whites |
| 2 tablespoons bitter orange marmalade | ⅛ teaspoon cream of tartar |
| | 1 cup sugar |
| 8 tablespoons orange liqueur | 8 candied violets |
| 1 pint orange sherbet | |

Remove tops from oranges—in a slice about 1 inch thick—and scoop out the pulp with a grapefruit knife. Separate fruit from membranes and put fruit into a bowl. Add marmalade and stir to mix. Set aside. Spoon 1 tablespoon orange liqueur into each orange shell and fill shells with orange-marmalade mixture, dividing it equally among the 8 shells. Top each with a scoop of orange sherbet and set into the freezer for at least 15 minutes. (*Oranges may be filled in advance and stored in the freezer.*)

Make meringue: beat egg whites until foamy, add cream of tartar, and beat until soft peaks form. Gradually beat in sugar, 1 tablespoon at a time; continue beating until mixture looks like marshmallow and feels smooth, not grainy, when you pinch it. Put meringue into a large pastry bag fitted with a large star tube and pipe the meringue onto the oranges, covering sherbet and cut edge of orange shells completely. Place on a baking sheet and set in a preheated 450° oven for about 5 minutes, or until meringue is set. (*Baked orange shells may be frozen for 1 month; when frozen, wrap them in plastic wrap or foil for longer storage. To serve, defrost at room temperature for a few minutes, until meringue softens.*) The oranges look particularly pretty served on glass plates each lined with a big green leaf; garnish each orange with a candied violet.

## A Late Night Champagne Supper
### for 6

---

Lobster thermidor
Watercress salad (see p. 122)
Raspberry ice with cassis (see p. 56)

Lobster and champagne are about as elegant an offering as a hostess can make—delicious and unexpected after a play, opera, dance, or art show. I like to serve champagne before and during supper. Invite only those friends who would appreciate it.

## LOBSTER THERMIDOR

3 live lobsters, about 1½ pounds each
8 tablespoons butter
2 tablespoons oil
2 tablespoons brandy
2 cups minced onion
1½ teaspoons salt
½ teaspoon freshly cracked white pepper
1 cup dry white wine
3 tablespoons flour
1 tablespoon plus 1 teaspoon Dijon mustard
4 or 5 drops Tabasco sauce
2 cups heavy cream
4 tablespoons freshly grated Parmesan cheese
1 tablespoon melted butter

To kill lobsters: place lobster on cutting board with claws to your left and shell side up. Insert a knife point into the center of cross on head (this is clearly marked); split lengthwise. Remove sac behind eyes and the intestinal vein (the little membrane running the length of the lobster). Cut off large claws with knife or scissors. Cut off little claws and remove any tomalley and red coral (the roe). Heat 2 tablespoons butter and the oil in a large skillet until hot, add all lobster pieces (including tomalley and red coral), cover, and cook over medium-high heat for 3 minutes. Remove cover. Heat brandy in a small pan just until warm; ignite it and pour it over the lobster. Shake pan until flames die. Cover pan again and cook lobster briskly over medium-high heat for 5 minutes. As soon as lobster is cool enough to handle, remove meat from shells, being careful to keep shells intact, and from large claws. Meat comes out of shells easily—just pull it out with your fingers. To get meat from large claws, crack them with nutcracker and pull meat out. Cut into good-size pieces, and set aside, with any tomalley and red coral. Reserve shells, little claws, and pan juices.

In a saucepan, melt 3 tablespoons butter and stir in minced onion, 1 teaspoon salt, and the pepper. Cook over high heat, stirring, until onion is transparent; do not let it brown. Add white wine to onion and cook over high heat until wine completely evaporates. Leave the pan uncovered and stir occasionally; do not let onion burn. Set aside. In another pan, melt remaining 3 tablespoons butter, stir in the flour with a wooden spatula, and cook, stirring constantly, over high heat for 2 minutes to eliminate

the raw flour taste; do not let it brown. Add ½ teaspoon salt, the
mustard, Tabasco, and pan juices from flaming lobster. Remove
pan from heat, change to a whisk, and add the heavy cream all
at once, whisking vigorously. Return pan to high heat and cook,
whisking, until sauce thickens. Add onion mixture to sauce and
simmer for 3 to 5 minutes. Stir in 2 rounded tablespoons grated
Parmesan cheese. Add lobster meat and any tomalley or coral to
sauce and spoon it into reserved shells. Sprinkle lobster halves
with remaining Parmesan cheese and drizzle with melted butter.
(*Recipe may be made ahead in morning to this point, covered
with plastic wrap, and refrigerated. Reheat in 350° oven for 10
to 15 minutes before glazing.*) Run under the broiler to glaze.
Garnish the top of each serving with the tiny claws.

## A Robust Supper
## for 12 Poker Players

Potage Saint-Germain
Steak tartare
Black radish salad
French and pumpernickel breads
Assorted pickles and olives
Crock of Stilton cheese
Coffeehouse mousse

This is a perfect menu for a group of men. Hearty pea soup can
be served in mugs while the poker game is still on. Later, spread
the tartare on thinly or thickly sliced bread and serve it with a
crisp radish salad—biting in flavor and texture—and pickles and
olives. After Stilton and crackers, the mousse adds a final filip.

## POTAGE SAINT-GERMAIN

1½ pounds dried peas
6 cups chicken stock, more if
  necessary (see p. 278)
4 whole cloves
2 peeled onions
½ cup thinly sliced carrots
1 ham bone, with ham
  clinging to it
3 leeks
1 tablespoon salt, about
½ teaspoon freshly cracked
  white pepper

¼ teaspoon sugar
½ cup butter
½ cup fresh peas, cooked
½ pound ham, cut into shreds
½ cup light cream, heated,
  about
1 cup small croutons sautéed
  in butter
Fresh mint, optional

Soak the peas overnight in water to cover. Drain and wash them well and put them into a large heavy saucepan. Add chicken stock to cover. Bring to a boil and skim. Stick 2 cloves into each onion and add to soup, along with carrots and ham bone. Split leeks lengthwise and hold them under running water, separating layers, to wash away grit. Slice the leeks—use the white part plus 1 inch of the green—and add to soup. Bring back to a boil, turn heat to simmer, and cook slowly, partially covered, for about 1½ hours.

Remove the ham bone and puree the mixture through a food mill, using the medium disk, or in blender. Thin the soup, if you wish, with a little more hot chicken stock, but this soup should be thick. Season to taste with salt and pepper—add the salt 1 teaspoon at a time. Add sugar and beat in the butter, a teaspoonful at a time, using a whisk or wooden spatula. Add freshly cooked peas and shredded ham (cut from ham bone, or from another piece of ham), along with enough heated cream to thin soup to the consistency you want. (*Recipe can be made the day before and reheated.*) Reheat before serving. Garnish each serving with croutons and a sprig of fresh mint if you have it.

## STEAK TARTARE

Use the very best prime-quality beef—sirloin or fillet—and grind the meat just before serving it, and never more than 1 hour ahead of time. If you have a respectable-looking meat grinder, it's fun to grind and prepare the meat in front of your guests.

3 pounds prime beef, very
   freshly ground
3 egg yolks
1 cup chopped onion
½ cup capers, drained
3 tablespoons coarse salt

2 teaspoons freshly cracked
   black pepper
6 finely chopped anchovy
   fillets
¾ cup finely chopped parsley
   or chives

Mix thoroughly all ingredients, except parsley or chives, with your hands or a wooden spatula. Taste for salt and pepper; it should be well seasoned. Form into a sausage shape and roll in finely chopped parsley or chives. Serve on a wooden plank or chopping board.

### BLACK RADISH SALAD

4 large black radishes, about
   3 inches diameter (see
   p. 76)
2 egg yolks
1 teaspoon dry mustard
4 tablespoons vinegar *or* 2
   tablespoons vinegar and 2
   tablespoons lemon juice

1 teaspoon salt
½ teaspoon freshly cracked
   white pepper
2 cups vegetable oil
2 tablespoons light cream
1 tablespoon Dijon mustard
2 tablespoons chopped parsley

Wash and peel the black radishes like potatoes, slice them about ⅛ inch thick, and cut slices into very fine julienne sticks. To make mayonnaise dressing, put egg yolks and dry mustard in a bowl and whisk. Add 2 tablespoons of vinegar and the salt and pepper and whisk. Continue whisking and begin to add oil, very slowly, 1 teaspoon at a time, until it starts to thicken. Pour in remaining oil in a thin stream, whisking constantly about 5 minutes, until mixture is thick and smooth. Beat in cream and flavor with remaining vinegar (or lemon juice) and Dijon mustard. Fold mayonnaise into julienne radish sticks, mound in a serving dish, and decorate with chopped parsley. *Can be made in the morning and refrigerated.*

## COFFEEHOUSE MOUSSE

18 ladyfingers, split (see
   p. 265)
½ pound cream cheese
3 eggs, separated
6 ounces dark sweet chocolate
1 tablespoon (1 envelope)
   unflavored gelatine
2 tablespoons cold strong
   coffee
⅛ teaspoon salt

1 cup dark brown sugar
2 teaspoons vanilla extract
2½ cups heavy cream
3 tablespoons coffee liqueur
1 tablespoon coffee essence
1 tablespoon confectioners'
   sugar
Chocolate candy coffee
   beans, optional, for
   garnish

Oil an 8-inch springform pan and line the sides with split ladyfingers. Let cream cheese and separated eggs come to room temperature. Melt chocolate and set aside. Soften gelatine in cold coffee. In electric mixer bowl, beat egg whites and salt until soft peaks form. Beat in ½ cup brown sugar, a spoonful at a time; add vanilla and continue beating until thick, smooth, and glossy. In a separate, chilled bowl, whip 1½ cups heavy cream until stiff. In a third bowl, beat cream cheese until fluffy; beat in remaining ½ cup brown sugar, a tablespoonful at a time. Flavor with 2 tablespoons coffee liqueur and the coffee essence. Beat in egg yolks, one at a time. Dissolve the softened gelatine by placing it over simmering water. Beat it into cream cheese mixture in a thin stream, along with melted chocolate. Fold in the beaten egg whites and whipped cream and pour into the prepared pan. Chill in the refrigerator for at least 2 hours or overnight. (*Recipe is better if made the day before.*) When ready to serve, whip remaining 1 cup heavy cream with confectioners' sugar and remaining 1 tablespoon coffee liqueur until stiff. Put the cream into a pastry bag fitted with a star tube, unmold mousse, and decorate around top edge with rosettes of whipped cream. Garnish with chocolate coffee beans or with shreds of grated chocolate.

# *An Election Night Supper*
## *for 10*

Stuffed artichokes
Fried oysters, shrimp, and mussels,
with tartar sauce
Broccoli with white wine
Romaine salad (see p. 58)
Cold caramel soufflé

A tasty meal for people staying up late for election results. If you wish to lighten the menu, serve either broccoli or salad, rather than both.

## STUFFED ARTICHOKES

10  artichokes
 2  tablespoons salt
 5  cups chopped onions
1¼  cups butter
 ⅓  cup bread crumbs
 1  cup freshly grated
     Parmesan cheese

 1  teaspoon salt
 ½  teaspoon freshly cracked
     black pepper
    Olive oil to film serving dish

Break off stems and trim bases of artichokes so that they stand evenly. With scissors, cut the tips off the leaves, and with a knife, cut ½ inch off the very top of each. Put in a large kettle, cover with water, add 2 tablespoons salt, and bring to a boil. Do not cover. Boil about 25 to 35 minutes or until done. Drain upside down and cool until they can be handled. Spread leaves open and pull out the center cone. With a spoon, scrape out the hairy choke. Sauté chopped onions over high heat in 2 tablespoons of the butter, just until wilted. Mix with bread crumbs and Parmesan cheese; season with 1 teaspoon salt and the pepper. Melt remaining butter and use about ¼ cup of it to moisten the onion-cheese mixture. Stuff artichokes. (*Recipe can be made ahead to this point.*) Film an ovenproof serving dish with olive oil and arrange artichokes in dish. Drizzle with remaining butter and bake in a preheated 400° oven for 10 minutes.

## FRIED OYSTERS, SHRIMP, AND MUSSELS, WITH TARTAR SAUCE

| | |
|---|---|
| 40 mussels | 2 recipes beer batter (see |
| ¼ cup dry white wine | p. 285) |
| 40 raw shrimp | Fat for deep frying |
| 40 oysters | 2 recipes Tartar Sauce (see |
| 1 cup flour | p. 55) |

Scrub mussels with a stiff brush and remove the beards with a knife. Rinse in several changes of cold water to remove sand. Discard any mussels that are open. Put mussels in a pan with white wine, cover, and shake over high heat just long enough to open mussels. Discard any that do not open. Remove mussels from shells (broth in pan belongs to the cook). Shell and devein the shrimp. Remove oysters from shells and drain (save juice for another use). Dry mussels, shrimp, and oysters on paper towels and roll in flour; pat off excess. Dip in beer batter. Heat 3 inches of fat in a heavy saucepan or deep-fat fryer to 375°. Fry seafood, a few pieces at a time, until puffed and brown, about 3 to 4 minutes. Place on brown paper on cake rack on baking sheet in 325° oven to keep warm as you fry them. (*Can be fried ahead of time and reheated in same way.*) Serve hot with Tartar Sauce.

## BROCCOLI WITH WHITE WINE

| | |
|---|---|
| 2 bunches broccoli | 1 teaspoon salt |
| ¼ cup olive oil | ½ teaspoon freshly cracked |
| 1½ cups dry white wine | black pepper |

Wash broccoli well and trim off stem ends. Put it in a saucepan with olive oil, wine, salt, and pepper. Bring to a boil, half-cover the saucepan, reduce heat, and simmer until broccoli is barely tender, about 15 to 20 minutes. Arrange broccoli on a serving dish and keep it warm. Boil liquid to reduce it to about 1 cup. Pour over broccoli.

*Note:* Broccoli cooked in wine is also good cold, as a salad. Reduce cooking liquid to 1 cup to use, chilled, as a dressing.

## COLD CARAMEL SOUFFLÉ

| | |
|---|---|
| 2 cups sugar | 6 eggs, separated |
| ⅔ cup boiling water | 2½ cups heavy cream |
| 2 tablespoons (2 envelopes) unflavored gelatine | 2 tablespoons melted currant jelly |
| ½ cup rum | |

Prepare a 6-cup soufflé dish with a paper collar. Cut a length of waxed paper long enough to go around the dish with some overlap. Fold it in half, lengthwise, and brush the inside edge with vegetable oil. Tie it around the soufflé dish so that it extends about 4 to 5 inches above it.

To make caramel, melt 1½ cups sugar in a heavy skillet over high heat. Stir the sugar with a wooden spatula until lumps disappear; then let it bubble until it turns a light caramel color. Remove from heat and let bubbles subside. Have boiling water ready and add it *carefully* to caramel—keep your hand behind the pan to avoid scalding steam. Stir the caramel-water mixture until well blended and let it cool for about 10 minutes. Soften gelatine in rum in a custard cup; then stand the cup in a pan of simmering water and stir to dissolve gelatine. With electric mixer, beat egg yolks until foamy; beat in remaining ½ cup sugar. Gradually add caramel mixture in a thin stream, beating constantly. Beat in gelatine mixture. Continue beating until mixture cools, about 10 minutes—set the bowl over ice to hasten cooling.

In another bowl, beat egg whites until soft peaks form. Fold them into the cooled caramel mixture, along with 2 cups heavy cream, softly whipped. Pour into prepared soufflé dish and chill for at least 3 hours, or overnight, in the refrigerator. To serve, remove collar. Whip remaining ½ cup heavy cream until stiff. Put it into a pastry bag fitted with a star tube and pipe rosettes of whipped cream around top of soufflé. Drizzle rosettes with melted currant jelly.

# *Cocktail Parties*

There are two ways to look at a cocktail party. Undeniably, it's a useful way to pay off an unmanageable accumulation of social debts. But I take a more positive view: I love to give cocktail parties!

I like big, bashy affairs given to honor a friend or pay tribute to accomplishment. I invite as large a group as I can shoehorn into the house and set the party hours from four to six or five to seven. All the food is finger food, available on tables or, more usually, passed on trays constantly replenished in the kitchen. You need good help, including a good bartender, for a party of this kind.

If you want to feed your cocktail guests dinner in an informal way, invite them for a later hour and change your menu to more substantial food. At a cocktail buffet you might, for example, offer

227

your guests a Pâté en Croûte, Raw Vegetables with Olive Butter, Scallops and Prosciutto, Cold Baked Ham, Cold Fillet of Beef, and Tyropita—all recipes available in this book. Include a dessert, too, if you wish—a choice of crêpes makes a fantastic ending for a large party.

Now for party logistics. You'll be safe if you count six hors d'oeuvre per guest. There are twelve suggestions in the large cocktail party menu; you may want to fix fewer of these, doubling or tripling some of the recipes. Think hard about what you can manage, how much you can store in your refrigerator, even how many trays or plates you'll need.

Count four drinks per person. In addition to the usual hard liquors, be sure to offer your guests a choice of lighter drinks— white wine, or apéritifs such as sweet vermouth, white wine and cassis, or Lillet. My favorite advice for hassle-free bartending is to settle on one size glass for everything—perhaps a plain all-purpose wineglass (10-ounce size). Incidentally, for a large gathering, I find it simplest to rent all the glasses—they don't have to be washed, just rinsed and sent back.

Do everything you can ahead of time. Anything wrapped in bacon or deep-fried should be cooked well in advance, so that your house will be free of cooking odors when guests arrive. Prepare garnishes—giant fluted mushrooms, turnip and tomato roses—for your serving plates. Instruct your help to use fresh paper doilies when they refill trays. Lay in plenty of ice. Set out twice as many ashtrays as you think you'll need, and be sure someone's assigned to empty them and to pick up paper napkins and empty glasses.

Have fun!

## A Large Cocktail Party
## *for 50*

Pâté en croûte
Assorted canapés
Platter of raw vegetables with olive butter
Cherry tomatoes stuffed
with crab meat and guacamole
Onion pie, cut into wedges
Brandade of trout
Steak tartare
Shrimp maison
Roasted peppers and anchovies
Salami cornucopias on pumpernickel
Alpine logs
Fried oysters

Here is a generous selection of hors d'oeuvre from which you can pick and choose according to your tastes and the appetites of your guests. Several of these recipes appear elsewhere in the book: Onion Pie on p. 85, Steak Tartare on p. 221, and Salami Cornucopias on p. 63.

### PÂTÉ EN CROÛTE

Pâté molds, imported from France, are made of tin and hinged so that you can take the pan away from the loaf after it's baked, without damaging the crust—like a springform pan. Molds may be oblong or oval; to make this recipe, you will need one with a capacity of 4 to 5 cups. First you line the mold with pastry, then line that with blanched bacon, and pack it with forcemeat and filling. You put on the top crust, decorate it, and bake the pâté. When cool, you finish it off with aspic, poured under the crust. This recipe can be prepared ahead in stages, and it can be frozen after baking, but *before* the aspic is added.

PASTRY:

2 cups lightly spooned flour
1 teaspoon salt
10 tablespoons butter
3 egg yolks
2 tablespoons olive oil
¼ cup ice water

½ pound sliced bacon,
    blanched

FORCEMEAT:

½ pound veal, ground twice
½ pound pork, ground twice
1 egg
1 egg white
½ cup finely chopped onion
1 finely chopped clove garlic
1 tablespoon chopped
    parsley
1 teaspoon freshly cracked
    black pepper

1 teaspoon salt
2 tablespoons brandy

FILLING:

¼ pound boiled ham or tongue,
    thinly sliced
1 truffle, sliced

EGG WASH:

2 egg yolks
1 tablespoon water

ASPIC:

2 cups chicken or veal stock
    (see p. 278 or p. 279)
2 teaspoons tomato paste
2 tablespoons (2 envelopes)
    unflavored gelatine
2 tablespoons dry Madeira
2 egg whites, beaten just to a
    froth

To make pastry, put flour in a bowl, stir in salt, and cut in butter with a pastry blender until mixture looks like coarse cornmeal. Make a well in the flour mixture and drop in egg yolks and olive oil. Work this up quickly with a pastry fork, adding just enough ice water so the mixture can be gathered together in a dough ball. Wrap the ball in plastic wrap and chill it for at least 1 hour.

To line pâté mold, roll pastry dough out on a floured board, ¼ inch thick. Rolled dough should be long enough to cover length plus ends of mold, and wide enough to cover bottom and both sides; reserve extra dough for top crust and decorations. Dust the surface of the rolled pastry with flour (so it won't stick to itself) and fold pastry in half, lengthwise. Pinch the ends together to make an envelope. Shape the envelope and fit it into the mold, pressing it against sides and into corners, but using care not to stretch the dough. Trim off excess pastry, leaving about ⅛ inch above rim of mold; this rim of dough will give you something to anchor the top crust to. Store pastry-lined mold in refrigerator until you're ready to fill it.

To fill mold, line the pastry-lined mold with overlapping strips of blanched bacon, letting the bacon hang over the sides of the mold. Put all ingredients for forcemeat in a bowl, flaming the brandy as you add it, and mix well. Pack about half the forcemeat into the bacon-lined mold. Arrange the filling of ham slices and truffle down the center and cover with remaining forcemeat. Fold the bacon ends over to cover forcemeat completely.

Roll out remaining pastry, also ¼ inch thick, and trim it to fit top of mold. Beat egg yolks with water to make egg wash and brush the top edges of the pastry in the mold with this mixture. Lay top crust in place and pinch edges together with a pastry pincer or the back of a knife. The egg wash acts as a glue. Cut a little hole in the center of the top crust and insert a paper funnel. With a small leaf cutter, cut leaf shapes from pastry scraps; mark veins on leaves with a knife and place the leaves decoratively around the paper funnel, using the egg wash to hold them. Brush egg wash all over the top of the crust; this will make the crust brown and shiny when it's baked. (*If not baking immediately, cover the mold with aluminum foil and set in the refrigerator for up to 1 week or in the freezer for up to 1 month.*)

To bake pâté, bring mold from refrigerator or freezer and let it come to room temperature. Place it on a baking tray (protection in case the hinged mold oozes) and bake it in a preheated 375° oven for 1 hour; reduce heat to 300° and bake 30 minutes more. If pastry is not brown, bake another 15 minutes. Remove from oven, replace the paper funnel with a new one, and let cool. (*Refrigerate to chill thoroughly or freeze.*)

To make aspic, combine all ingredients in a saucepan, set over heat, and beat with a whisk until liquid comes to a rolling boil. Remove from heat; let stand 15 minutes. Line a fine sieve with a double thickness of cheesecloth wrung out in cold water and pour aspic through strainer into a bowl. Let the liquid drain through without stirring or forcing it in any way. Cool aspic over ice. When it's thick and syrupy, pour it down the funnel, to put a layer of aspic under the crust and on top of the meat. The meat shrinks away from the top crust when the loaf bakes, so there is space to fill. Remove funnel and refrigerate mold again until aspic sets, about ½ hour. Pour any extra aspic into a shallow pan and chill. To serve pâté, remove hinged mold and place pâté on a platter. Chop the chilled aspic and arrange it around the loaf of pâté. Slice pâté and serve on individual plates with fork.

## CANAPÉS

To be at their best, canapés should be served as soon as possible after they're assembled and certainly within an hour. You'll need good kitchen help to manage this. Reserve a good-sized counter in the kitchen for the assembly line, and prepare all the makings in advance. To guide your help, make up samples ahead to be duplicated as needed.

I have included a number of specific suggestions for canapés, but use your imagination to create others. Decorate canapé platters with watercress, tomato roses (see p. 284), fluted mushrooms (see p. 284), and turnip roses. The following ingredients will make enough canapés for 50 people.

| | |
|---|---|
| 6 loaves white bread, firm-textured, sliced extra thin | 2 large jars green stuffed olives |
| | 6 tomatoes |
| | 6 lemons |
| 1½ cups egg salad | 2 bunches parsley |
| 1½ cups tuna salad | 2 8-ounce packages cream cheese |
| 3 dozen hard-cooked eggs | |
| 2 pounds smoked salmon, thinly sliced | 1 tablespoon light cream |
| | 2 cups mayonnaise (see p. 283) |
| 2 pounds boiled ham, thinly sliced | |
| | 2 tablespoons Dijon mustard, about |
| 8 ounces caviar, red and black | |
| 2 7-ounce cans baby shrimp | 1 pound butter, softened |
| 4 4-ounce cans sardines | Horseradish |
| 6 2-ounce cans flat anchovy fillets | Mustard |
| | Anchovy paste |
| 3 bunches radishes | Lemon juice |
| 3 cucumbers | |

Cut bread in a variety of shapes—rounds, squares, rectangles, teardrops, fingers, diamonds, half-moons—using a knife or canapé cutters. For canapés that will be spread with soft fillings, lightly toast bread in a 350° oven and let it cool before spreading it. Since butter is not absorbed by cold toast, this will help prevent soggy canapés. Prepare egg and tuna salads using your favorite recipe; refrigerate until needed. Cool hard-cooked eggs rapidly and refrigerate. Cut some eggs in half and prepare balance for use as garnishing by sieving egg yolk and chopping egg white. Ready fish and meat for assembly and refrigerate. Prepare vegetables and garnishes: hollow out radishes. Slice cucumbers thinly on a vegetable cutter or mandoline; sprinkle with salt and refrigerate. Slice stuffed olives. Peel and seed tomatoes and cut flesh into small pieces. Cut strips of lemon peel with a lemon stripper. Chop parsley (but reserve a few tufts unchopped). Cover and refrigerate all of these until needed. Soften cream cheese by bringing it to room temperature and thinning it with a bit of cream. Flavor mayonnaise with Dijon mustard, to taste (about 1 tablespoon mustard per cup of mayonnaise). Put cream cheese and mayonnaise into small pastry bags or paper cones fitted with cake decorating tubes, ready for piping out into rosettes or stripes. Blend softened butter with flavorings to taste—horseradish, mustard, anchovy paste, lemon juice—your choice. Pound solid food flavorers, such as shrimp or caviar, in a mortar; blend in butter and push it through a sieve.

## INDIVIDUAL CANAPÉS

1. Fill hollowed-out radishes with caviar; decorate with a stripe of cream cheese.

2. Garnish hard-cooked egg halves with caviar and a tuft of parsley; pipe on a circlet of cream cheese.

3. Spread bread fingers with mustard mayonnaise. Lay 1 anchovy fillet on each. Dip 1 buttered end in chopped parsley and the other end in sieved egg yolk. Decorate with mayonnaise rosette.

4. Spread bread squares (including edges) with butter. Dip edges in chopped parsley. Pile on tuna salad; decorate with rosette of mayonnaise and a small piece of tomato.

5. Spread bread rectangles with butter, cover with egg salad, and decorate with olive slices.

6. Spread rounds with mustard mayonnaise. Cut thin boiled ham to fit bread, and decorate with cream cheese piped on a daisy design with a speck of caviar in the middle.

7. Spread half-moons (including edges) with butter. Dip in chopped parsley. Top with 2 slices of cucumber.

8. Spread bread fingers with mustard mayonnaise or lemon butter. Lay on 1 sardine, pipe on a wiggle of mayonnaise, and sprinkle with sieved egg yolk.

9. Spread bread teardrops with lemon butter and cover with baby shrimp. Pipe a U-shaped bit of cream cheese around shrimp and lay a strip of lemon peel across the U.

10. Butter squares (including edges) and dip edges in

chopped parsley. Lay on smoked salmon, decorate with an X shape of cream cheese, and sprinkle with sieved egg yolk.

11. Butter triangles with mustard mayonnaise. Heap with red caviar and chopped egg white.

## PLATTER OF RAW VEGETABLES WITH OLIVE BUTTER

Prepare as indicated and chill a selection of the following raw vegetables: celery sticks, carrot curls or sticks, baby turnip slices, zucchini slices or cubes, cauliflower flowerets, eggplant cubes, green or red pepper strips, white and red radishes, black radish slices, black olives, cherry tomatoes, fennel slices, and snow peas. Serve with olive butter, the recipe for which can be found on p. 68.

## CHERRY TOMATOES STUFFED WITH CRAB MEAT AND GUACAMOLE

Follow the recipe for Cherry Tomatoes Stuffed with Guacamole on p. 158, but double the quantity of tomatoes and stuff the rest with Crab-Meat Salad, the recipe for which is on p. 52.

## BRANDADE OF TROUT

2 smoked trout
½ cup unsalted butter
½ cup heavy cream, about
Juice of ½ lemon
½ teaspoon salt

¼ teaspoon freshly cracked black pepper
Chopped black olives, for garnish
1 loaf white bread, firm-textured, sliced extra thin

Skin and bone trout; you should have 1 pound of meat. Beat butter in electric mixer bowl, using the flat whip if you have a heavy-duty mixer. As butter gets creamy, add bits of the trout, about 1 teaspoonful at a time. Beat until mixture is smooth and very, very creamy; this will take about 15 to 20 minutes. Beat in just enough heavy cream to give mixture the consistency of whipped butter. Add lemon juice, salt, and pepper, and mix well. Pack it into a crock and chill thoroughly, at least 1 to 2 hours.

(*Can be made ahead and refrigerated up to 3 to 4 days.*) Serve pâté from the crock, its top decorated with chopped black olives. Serve with Melba toast, prepared by cutting bread into triangles and baking in a preheated 350° oven about 15 to 20 minutes or until brown, turning bread once.

## SHRIMP MAISON

2 pounds small or medium-size raw shrimp
½ cup butter
6 finely chopped cloves garlic
Juice of 2 lemons
½ teaspoon salt
¼ teaspoon freshly cracked white pepper
¾ cup dry white wine
2 tablespoons chopped parsley

Shell and devein the shrimp. Melt butter in flameproof serving dish. When butter foams, add shrimp; sauté briefly over high heat, shaking the pan, but do not let them brown. Add chopped garlic (6 cloves is correct), lemon juice, salt, pepper, and wine. (*Can be made ahead to this point.*) Cook for about 7 minutes over high heat, uncovered, or until shrimp turn pink. Sprinkle with chopped parsley and keep warm on a hot tray or candle-warmer.

## ROASTED PEPPERS AND ANCHOVIES

2 2-ounce cans flat anchovy fillets
2 tablespoons lemon juice
2 tablespoons olive oil
1 tablespoon finely chopped shallots
½ teaspoon finely chopped garlic
¼ teaspoon freshly cracked black pepper
4 tablespoons chopped parsley
1 tablespoon chopped fresh dill, optional
1 teaspoon chopped fresh chives, optional
1 12-ounce jar whole roasted peppers
Black olives, for garnish
Melba toast fingers (recipe follows)

Drain oil from anchovies into a bowl. Add lemon juice, olive oil, shallots, garlic, pepper, 2 tablespoons chopped parsley, the dill, and the chives and stir with a fork to make a paste. Put anchovy fillets into a sieve and rinse under cold water. Cut peppers in strips. Arrange anchovies and pepper strips on a serving platter (do not use a silver platter) and spoon paste over all. Sprinkle with remaining 2 tablespoons chopped parsley and garnish platter with black olives. Serve with Melba toast fingers.

### MELBA TOAST FINGERS

Buy thin-sliced, firm-textured white bread of good quality and cut it into fingers. Paint fingers on both sides with melted butter, if you wish. Lay fingers on a baking sheet and bake in a preheated 350° oven until brown, about 15 to 20 minutes. Turn fingers over once while baking. *Can be baked ahead and stored in plastic bags.*

### ALPINE LOGS

½ pound grated Swiss Appen-
zeller cheese
½ pound finely chopped dried
beef
2 slightly beaten eggs

2 tablespoons chopped
parsley
2 tablespoons caraway seeds
2 to 3 sheets filo dough, each
about 11 x 5 inches
¾ cup melted butter

Mix together the cheese, dried beef, eggs, parsley, and caraway seeds. Work with 1 sheet of filo dough at a time, keeping remaining sheets covered with a damp, not wet, towel. (Filo dough, an extrathin pastry, is available in Greek or Armenian grocery stores.) Lay a sheet of filo dough on a slightly damp towel and brush it all over with melted butter. Spoon the cheese mixture along one long edge of the sheet and roll it up like a jelly roll, brushing with more melted butter as you turn the roll. Repeat with remaining sheets and cheese mixture. Place on a baking sheet and brush all over with remaining melted butter. (*Can be made ahead to this point and covered closely with plastic wrap. Refrigerate if holding longer than 2 to 3 hours. May be frozen for up to 1 month; be sure it is fully thawed before baking.*) Bake in a preheated 350° oven for 15 to 20 minutes or until golden brown. Cut into 1-inch pieces. Serve hot or cold.

## FRIED OYSTERS

60 oysters
1 cup flour
1½ recipes beer batter (see
   p. 285)

Fat for deep frying
1 recipe Soy Dipping Sauce
   (see p. 142)

Drain oysters and dry with paper towels. Roll in flour, patting off excess. Dip in beer batter and fry, a few at a time, in 3 inches of hot fat heated to 375°, until puffed and golden brown. Drain on paper towels. (*May be prepared ahead—to allow time for frying odor to dissipate—and reheated. Lay on sheets of brown paper on cake racks on baking tray and reheat in oven.*) Serve warm with Soy Dipping Sauce.

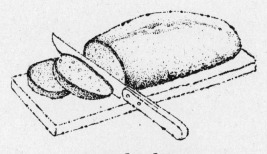

## *A Cocktail Party*
## *for 12*

Crostini, Salsa di alici
Seafood in strudel
Duck pâté
Meat balls
Platter of raw vegetables
with olive butter (see p. 234)

This menu provides a good variety without an enormous number of dishes—cheese-flavored crostini, seafood, poultry, meat, and the crispness of the raw vegetables. It's easy, too, to make up your own menu using this as a guide. For example, you could substitute Cheese Puffs (see p. 246) for the Crostini, or Scallops and Prosciutto (see p. 210) for Seafood in Strudel. Other good recipes for a party menu are Cold Fillet of Beef (p. 258), Baked Ham (p. 259), and Tyropita (p. 153).

## CROSTINI, SALSA DI ALICI

1 long loaf Italian bread, 1 day old
1 pound Swiss cheese
½ cup melted butter
½ teaspoon oregano

2 2-ounce cans flat anchovy fillets, drained and chopped
½ cup olive oil
2 finely chopped cloves garlic
2 tablespoons chopped parsley
¼ cup red wine vinegar

Cut ends off bread and cut into 2-inch squares, leaving crust on. Cut cheese into 1-inch cubes. Beginning and ending with bread, alternate bread and cheese cubes on 8-inch skewers; you'll fill 6 to 8 of them. Lay skewers in a buttered baking dish and brush generously with melted butter and oregano. (*Can be prepared the day before to this point.*) Bake in a preheated 350° oven until cheese begins to melt and bread browns a bit, about 10 to 15 minutes. Meanwhile, make sauce (*which also can be made ahead and reheated*). Mash the anchovies and combine with remaining ingredients. Heat to bubbling, stirring. To serve, bring Crostini to room on skewers; holding skewer in hand, with aid of fork, slip off contents onto platter. Pour sauce over and serve on plates with forks or toothpicks.

## SEAFOOD IN STRUDEL

½ cup fine bread crumbs
½ cup freshly grated Parmesan cheese
2 teaspoons dry mustard
1 very finely chopped onion
1 tablespoon butter
1½ cups mixed seafood, cut in pieces (halved bay or sea scallops, cooked lobster meat, cooked shrimp, poached salmon, raw crab meat)

1 cup sour cream
½ teaspoon salt
¼ teaspoon freshly cracked white pepper
2 tablespoons chopped fresh chives
2 tablespoons chopped parsley
4 sheets filo dough, about 11 x 13 inches
1¼ cups melted butter
Juice of 1 lemon

Put bread crumbs, grated Parmesan, and dry mustard into a small bowl and mix well. Set aside. Cook onion in butter over high heat until transparent, but do not let it brown. Mix seafood with sour cream; add onion, salt, pepper, chives, and parsley. Work with filo sheets—extrathin Greek or Armenian pastry—one at a time, keeping the remaining sheets covered with a damp, not wet, towel. On a sheet of waxed paper, stack the filo sheets, brushing each sheet with some of the ¼ cup melted butter before adding the next one. Brush the top sheet with melted butter, too, and sprinkle with the cheese–bread crumb mixture. Spoon seafood mixture 1 inch from one long edge of filo sheets, leaving a 1-inch margin at each end. Start rolling up the seafood in the pastry, folding in the ends as you roll, so that the seafood is wrapped securely inside the pastry package. Brush the filo as you roll it with melted butter. Use the waxed paper to help you roll it. Place roll on a baking sheet and brush it all over with melted butter. (*Can be made ahead to this point, and refrigerated, or frozen up to 1 month. Bring to room temperature before baking.*) Place in a preheated 375° oven on the middle rack, and bake for 30 minutes or until crisp and light brown. Slice 1½ inches thick and serve hot with lemon butter, made by mixing remaining 1 cup melted butter with the lemon juice.

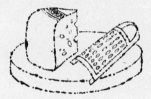

## DUCK PÂTÉ

Follow directions for Pâté en Croûte (see p. 229), making the following changes: instead of ham, use uncooked duck meat for the filling. Remove skin from duck and cut breast and leg meat from carcass. Cut meat into long thin strips and marinate them in brandy (preferably Cognac) for 1 hour. Use the duck carcass to make stock and substitute this stock for the chicken stock when you make the aspic. To make stock, put the carcass in a saucepan, cover with cold water. Add 1 small peeled onion, stuck with 2 whole cloves, 1 small sliced carrot, and a bouquet garni (see p. 283). Bring to a boil, skim, turn heat to simmer, cover, and simmer for 1½ hours. Strain stock before using and season to taste with salt and pepper.

## MEAT BALLS

| | |
|---|---|
| 1  pound veal, ground twice | SAUCE: |
| 1  pound pork, ground twice | 2  tablespoons brandy |
| 4  eggs | 2  tablespoons butter |
| 1½ cups finely chopped | 2  teaspoons chopped garlic |
|     onion | 2  tablespoons chopped shallots |
| 1  tablespoon finely chopped | 2  finely chopped mushrooms |
|     shallots | 1  tablespoon tomato paste |
| 1  teaspoon finely chopped | 1  teaspoon meat glaze |
|     garlic | 2  teaspoons potato starch, |
| 2  tablespoons chopped |     or cornstarch |
|     parsley | ½ cup dry Madeira, more if |
| 1  teaspoon salt |     necessary |
| ½ teaspoon freshly cracked | 2  cups chicken stock, more if |
|     black pepper |     necessary (see p. 278) |
| ¼ teaspoon freshly grated | 1  tablespoon currant jelly |
|     nutmeg | 2  tablespoons orange |
| ¼ teaspoon ground cardamom |     marmalade |
|     Heavy cream, if necessary |     Juice of ½ lemon |
| 4  tablespoons butter, more if | 2  tablespoons chopped celery |
|     necessary | 6  chopped anchovy fillets |

In a large bowl, mix together meat, eggs, onion, shallots, garlic, parsley, and seasonings. Mixture should be loose; if too stiff, thin it with heavy cream. Wet your hands and form meat balls. Do not compact the mixture; handle it lightly, moving the ball from palm to palm. Recipe makes about 70 small balls, 35 medium-size. (*Meat balls can be made ahead and frozen or refrigerated. Thaw frozen meat balls before cooking.*) Heat butter in a large skillet and brown the meat balls over high heat, a few at a time, first on one side, then the other. (Mixture is loose and balls will flatten, like patties.) As they brown, remove balls from skillet and set aside; they will cook through later, in the sauce.

To make sauce, pour off all but a thin film of fat from skillet, pour in brandy, and ignite it. When flames die, scrape up the brown bits. Add butter, melt it, and then add garlic and shallots; cook for a minute or two. Add mushrooms, tomato paste, meat glaze, and potato starch and stir to make a paste. Remove from heat, change to a whisk, and add Madeira and chicken stock, whisking vigorously. Return to heat and bring to a boil. Stir in currant jelly and orange marmalade. Add lemon juice, celery, and anchovies. If sauce is too thick, thin it with more Madeira or chicken stock. Return meat balls to skillet and baste with the sauce. (*Recipe can be made ahead to this point and refrigerated or frozen. Bring to room temperature before reheating.*) Cook for about 5 minutes. For buffet service, transfer to a chafing dish and keep warm.

# *Teas*

Invite neighbors, little girls, great-aunts, and grandmothers to tea—not to mention your best friends. It's a delightful way to entertain, a gentle way to encourage good manners, a pleasant meeting ground for the generations.

I remember my mother setting out her silver tea service a couple of times a week. When her friends stopped in, she'd bring out the thinnest sandwiches, the tiniest cookies. I was enchanted, and to this day I love the plain bread-and-butter sandwiches I first discovered then, their round edges dipped in parsley. It was one of my earliest experiences of being "grown up."

I hope our world never gets too busy for afternoon tea. Even if you drink it alone in a department store after a long day of shopping, it's a revitalizing and comforting ritual. When you dress up for it at home, it's truly civilizing.

Here is a chance to use your fine English bone china. Tea always seems to taste better in fragile cups. Everything on your table or tray or tea cart—the food included—should be dainty in appearance. For small parties, put your tea service and sandwiches on a large tray or low table and serve in the living room. You'll want to arrange a more elaborate tea in the dining room, inviting a friend to pour for you. For a very large group, serve the tea buffet-style and ask several friends to take turns pouring. And, if the weather is nice, don't forget the possibility of serving tea in the garden or on your terrace.

Everyone has his or her own ideas about making tea, and of course you'll want to accommodate individual preferences for lemon or milk. The British way to make tea is precise: water should be freshly drawn and brought to a full boil. Rinse the pot with some boiling water, to warm it. Pour this water out, measure in the tea (1 teaspoon per cup), and pour in fresh boiling water. Steep it for five minutes and stir. The tea is now ready to serve. For a large group, it's often best to make very strong tea and have a second pot of hot water on your tray, to dilute it to everyone's taste—and to refill the teapot for second cups.

Think of the coffee drinkers among your guests, too. There's no reason to offer *only* tea. And if you have very little girls at your party, pour their tea and milk into demitasse cups or doll's china— or make them a pot of cocoa.

## Substantial Tea
## for 12

Sandwiches of sliced cold roast turkey
on Sandy Ainsworth's white bread
Cheese puffs
Toasted English muffins and strawberry jam
Alice Peterson's chocolate cheesecake
(see p. 71)

### SANDY AINSWORTH'S WHITE BREAD

The cooking time for this delicious bread is shorter than usual. People always question it, but it is correct. Not only can this bread be put together very quickly, it will stay fresh for a long time.

1 cup warm water (105° to 115°)
1 teaspoon plus ½ cup sugar
2 packages active dry yeast
2 cups lukewarm water
1 tablespoon salt
½ cup vegetable oil
9 cups lightly spooned flour, about

Put warm water into a large warm bowl and dissolve 1 teaspoon sugar in it. Sprinkle with yeast; stir until blended and let stand 10 minutes. Stir in lukewarm water, ½ cup sugar, salt, and vegetable oil. Beat in flour, 1 cupful at a time, adding enough so that the mixture hangs together and is easy to handle, but still sticky. Scrape the dough out on a well-floured board and knead it for several minutes, until smooth and elastic; if too sticky to knead, add more flour. Form the kneaded dough into a ball, and put it into a lightly greased bowl, turning the ball over to grease the top lightly. Cover with a cloth and let dough rise in a warm place (about 85°), free from drafts, until doubled. This will take from 1 to 2 hours. Punch the dough down, turn it out on the board, and divide it into 3 equal parts. Shape the dough into loaves and place them in greased 8 x 4 x 2¾-inch loaf pans, cover with a towel, and let rise again, in a warm place, free from drafts, until doubled, about 1 hour. Put loaves into a preheated 400°

oven and bake for 20 minutes. Turn out at once and let cool on cake racks, away from draft. Bread will stay fresh for a week, and it freezes well, for up to 1 month.

## SANDWICHES OF SLICED COLD ROAST TURKEY ON SANDY AINSWORTH'S WHITE BREAD

Chill 1 loaf of Sandy Ainsworth's white bread so that you can slice it in very thin slices—use a serrated knife. Keep slices in order so that each pair will fit together neatly when you assemble sandwiches. Butter slices with softened butter. Arrange thin slices of freshly roasted turkey breast meat on half the slices; sprinkle with salt and pepper and top with a lettuce leaf, if you wish. Spread remaining slices with homemade mayonnaise (see p. 283) and lay over turkey. Cut each sandwich into 4 triangles. *Can be made up to 2 to 3 hours ahead and covered with a damp towel.*

## CHEESE PUFFS

| | |
|---|---|
| 4 ounces sharp cheese, grated coarsely | 1 teaspoon Dijon mustard |
| 1 generous teaspoon Worcestershire sauce | ¾ cup lightly spooned flour |
| | ¼ teaspoon salt |
| 3 or 4 drops Tabasco sauce | 4 tablespoons melted butter |
| | ¼ cup sesame seeds |

Mix all ingredients except sesame seeds together, adding the butter last, and shape dough into marble-size balls. Dip each ball into sesame seeds and place, seed side up, on baking sheets. Bake in a preheated 375° oven for 20 minutes or until lightly browned. Makes 30 puffs. Serve warm or at room temperature. *Can be made ahead and reheated if desired. Can be frozen for up to 1 month.*

## TOASTED ENGLISH MUFFINS AND STRAWBERRY JAM

Never slice English muffins. Jab them around the edge with a fork, then split them in half. Put them in a 300° oven for about 20 minutes to get hot and crisp, like Melba toast. Butter them and serve with a pot of strawberry jam.

## An Elegant Tea
### for 8

Sandy Ainsworth's bread-and-butter sandwiches
Rum babas
Strawberry roll
Florentines
Pignolia cookies
Chocolate leaves

### SANDY AINSWORTH'S
### BREAD-AND-BUTTER SANDWICHES

Chill 1 loaf of Sandy Ainsworth's white bread (see p. 245) so that you can slice it in very thin slices. Butter the slices with softened butter and press together to make sandwiches. With 1½-inch cookie cutter, cut 2 round sandwiches from each big sandwich. Dip edges of each round in mayonnaise and roll in finely chopped parsley. *Can be made 3 to 4 hours ahead and covered with a damp towel.*

### RUM BABAS

1 package active dry yeast
¼ cup lukewarm water
1¼ cups lightly spooned flour
3 large eggs at room
   temperature
1 tablespoon softened butter
1 tablespoon plus 1¼ cups
   sugar

½ teaspoon salt
2 tablespoons dried currants
½ cup light rum
¼ cup water
   Apricot glaze, optional

Brush 8 or 10 *baba au rhum* molds with oil and set aside. Sprinkle yeast into lukewarm water and stir to dissolve. Add yeast mixture to flour in a bowl and mix together with your hand. Beat eggs well and add to flour mixture, beating with your hand or a wooden spatula until the mixture is very light and shiny. Cover bowl with a cloth and set in a warm place, free from drafts, to rise until double, about 1 to 1½ hours. When risen, mix in softened butter, 1 tablespoon sugar, the salt, and currants. Half-fill the prepared baba molds; cover molds with a cloth and let rise again until dough almost reaches tops of molds. Place molds on a baking sheet and bake in a preheated 375° oven for about 25 minutes, or until nicely browned. Turn them out at once and soak them in rum syrup for ½ hour. To make syrup, put rum, 1¼ cups sugar, and ¼ cup water in a saucepan over high heat. Stir until sugar dissolves; then simmer 10 minutes.

After their soaking, babas may be brushed with apricot glaze: mix 1 cup apricot jam with ¼ cup light rum and stir over high heat until jam dissolves. Rub it through a strainer and brush on babas. *Babas may be completely prepared 2 to 3 days in advance.*

## STRAWBERRY ROLL

5 eggs, separated
¾ cup sugar
1 teaspoon vanilla extract
3 tablespoons flour
1½ cups heavy cream

2 tablespoons confectioners' sugar
1½ cups sliced strawberries
Whole strawberries, for garnish

Oil an 11 x 17-inch jelly-roll pan, line it with waxed paper, oil the waxed paper, and set aside. Beat egg yolks, add ¼ cup of the sugar, and beat until very thick and pale yellow. Beat egg whites until stiff peaks form. Add vanilla to egg yolks and carefully fold in flour and then egg whites. Spread batter in prepared pan and bake in a preheated 350° oven for 12 minutes. Loosen the edges of the cake, sprinkle it with ¼ cup of the sugar, and turn cake out, sugar side down, on 2 overlapping sheets of waxed paper. Carefully remove waxed paper liner from bottom of cake and sprinkle bottom with remaining ¼ cup sugar. Whip 1 cup of the heavy cream and sweeten it with confectioners' sugar. Fold in sliced strawberries. Spread on cake and roll up. (Cake should be rolled at room temperature.) Decorate cake roll with remaining ½ cup heavy cream, whipped and piped in rosettes down the length of the cake. Put a whole strawberry on each rosette. *May be made earlier the same day and refrigerated.*

## FLORENTINES

½ pound candied orange peel
1 cup blanched slivered
   almonds
½ cup heavy cream
3 tablespoons sugar

¼ cup flour
¼ teaspoon salt
2 ounces (2 squares) semisweet chocolate, optional

Finely chop the orange peel. Toast the almonds in a 350° oven for 15 to 20 minutes. Stir cream and sugar together; add orange peel, almonds, flour, and salt. Line 2 baking sheets with baking parchment. Drop batter by scant teaspoonfuls about 2 inches apart (batter will spread). Bake in a preheated 350° oven for about 35 minutes—but watch them closely, cookies burn easily. Remove from baking sheet with spatula and cool on racks. When cold, bottoms of cookies may be brushed with melted semisweet chocolate (this takes about 5 minutes to set). *May be made ahead and stored in tightly closed plastic bag or airtight tins for up to 1 month.* Makes 30 to 40 cookies.

## PIGNOLIA COOKIES

½ pound almond paste
1 cup sugar

2 lightly beaten egg whites
¼ pound pignolia (pine) nuts

Beat almond paste and sugar together to mix thoroughly. Add egg whites and beat until blended. With wet hands, form dough, 1 teaspoonful at a time, into crescents. Dip tops of cookies in pignolia nuts and place on a baking sheet lined with baking parchment or brown paper. Place in a preheated 350° oven and bake for 15 minutes. Cool completely before removing from baking sheet. *Can be made ahead and stored in an airtight tin for up to 1 month.* Makes about 2 dozen cookies.

## CHOCOLATE LEAVES

Wash and dry fresh-picked leaves of various sizes and shapes, such as grape ivy, small grape or magnolia leaves. Leaves must be absolutely dry. Melt 2 ounces semisweet or flavored sweet chocolate with 1 teaspoon vegetable shortening. With a brush (not nylon), brush chocolate on the backs of the leaves, just to the edges and about ⅛ inch thick. Chill until firm. Carefully peel leaves off chocolate—this takes patience—and keep the chocolate chilled until needed. *Make at least 1 week ahead and refrigerate.*

# *Outdoor Entertaining*

Where in all outdoors will you eat? The choices—and the food possibilities—are limitless. An outdoor menu can be anything from a snack packed in a cardboard box, to an elaborate picnic, to a black-tie dinner on the terrace next to your pool. When you do move your meal outdoors, count on heartier appetites. If you think the menus in this section look longer than those in the other chapters, you're correct. Fresh air is such a stimulant it even makes up for indifferent food.

If your husband enjoys cooking on an outdoor grill, support him with dishes prepared in the kitchen. His help, plus all the backyard to move around in, makes it possible to entertain more guests than you have room for inside. My husband has made a specialty of London broil, and it really is excellent cooked over coals. (You'll find a recipe on p. 102 for cooking it either way—in the oven or on the grill.) Most food, however, is better cooked indoors, on a heat-controlled stove. That's where I like to do it—ahead of time whenever possible. Thus, most of the recipes in this section are for food fixed in the kitchen and either carried out-doors or packed into picnic hampers. Besides these menus, there are many others among the luncheons and dinners—even the breakfasts—that you might want to carry out on a beautiful day. Don't feel that everything you eat outdoors has to sizzle on a backyard barbecue!

I love picnicking—whatever the excuse or season. There are only a few sensible things you need remember. Always bring along plenty of ice in a cooler, both for drinks and for keeping foods properly chilled. As for plates and glasses, be guided by the occa-sion and your own mood. Plastic and paper ware are always easy, but at least once consider a formal picnic in a natural setting. It's about as grand a way to eat as I can imagine. For this, pack linen, china, and stemware—and spread a tablecloth on the ground or on one or more card tables. The contrast between sophisticated food and service and a simple setting—a clearing in the woods or a meadow beside a stream—is worth savoring. Try it—and you may be hooked forever.

### *Formal Dinner*
### *on the Terrace for 6*

---

Cold sorrel soup
Beef birds
Pommes Parisienne
Salad of Bibb lettuce and cucumber
White chocolate roll

Sorrel, a wild plant with a slightly lemony flavor, goes by other names: sour grass or dock and, in Jewish cooking, *shav*. It's an easy-to-grow plant—in fact, much of what I use grows wild—and you'll also find its green, sometimes reddish leaves in many ethnic markets in big cities from spring through fall. If you see it, snap it up. The French cultivate sorrel and serve it as a vegetable, leaves cooked tender-crisp, or as a salad. Sorrel makes a marvelous sour-tasting soup, a sophisticated beginning for this menu. The salad of Bibb lettuce and cucumber on page 49 should be halved to serve 6.

### COLD SORREL SOUP

2  tablespoons butter
¾  cup chopped onion
2  tablespoons flour
5  cups chicken stock (see p. 278)

2  cups finely chopped sorrel leaves
1  cup sour cream
2  teaspoons salt
1  teaspoon freshly cracked white pepper

Melt the butter in a large saucepan and stir in onion. Cook over high heat for 3 to 5 minutes, or until onion is transparent. Stir in flour. Add chicken stock and sorrel leaves, bring to a boil, and simmer until sorrel is tender, about 10 minutes. Puree the soup through a food mill, using the fine disk, or in a blender, and chill. Just before serving, stir in sour cream and season with salt and pepper. *May be made the previous day and refrigerated.*

## BEEF BIRDS

| | |
|---|---|
| 8 slices beef, ¼ inch thick, about 3 by 5 inches | 1 teaspoon chopped garlic |
| 6 tablespoons brandy | 1½ cups dry red wine |
| 2 teaspoons salt | 1 cup basic brown sauce (see p. 281) |
| 1 teaspoon freshly cracked black pepper | 2 tablespoons chopped parsley |
| Stuffing (recipe follows) | 1 bunch watercress |
| 6 tablespoons butter | |
| 2 tablespoons chopped shallots | |

Put beef slices between 2 sheets of waxed paper and pound thin. Brush beef with 2 tablespoons brandy, sprinkle with the salt and pepper, and put a heaping tablespoonful of stuffing on each, dividing stuffing evenly among the 8 pieces of beef. Roll up loosely and tie with string at both ends. Heat 4 tablespoons of the butter in a heavy skillet and brown beef rolls over high heat. Remove from pan, pour off fat, and flame pan with remaining 4 tablespoons brandy. Add remaining 2 tablespoons butter to pan and cook chopped shallots and garlic for a minute or two. Add wine and boil to reduce by one third. Stir in basic brown sauce and simmer 5 minutes. Rectify seasoning. Return beef birds to skillet. (*Can be made ahead to this point the day before, covered with plastic wrap, and refrigerated.*) Cover skillet with aluminum foil and a heavy lid and simmer for 20 to 25 minutes. Turn birds once while cooking. When ready to serve, arrange birds in an au gratin dish, remove strings, pour sauce over, and sprinkle with chopped parsley. Garnish with watercress.

## *STUFFING*

| | |
|---|---|
| 4 tablespoons butter | ½ teaspoon thyme |
| 2 tablespoons chopped shallots | ½ cup bread crumbs |
| 1 teaspoon chopped garlic | ½ cup grated Gruyère cheese |
| ½ pound ground smoked tongue | 2 tablespoons chopped parsley |

Heat butter in a skillet and cook shallots and garlic over medium heat for 3 minutes—do not let them brown. Remove from heat and add remaining ingredients. Mix thoroughly.

## POMMES PARISIENNE

4 large baking potatoes
6 tablespoons butter
1 teaspoon salt

½ teaspoon freshly cracked
    white pepper
2 tablespoons chopped parsley

Peel the potatoes and dig out potato balls with a melon baller; drop them into cold water to keep them from turning dark. (*Can be made 2 hours ahead to this point and held in water at room temperature.*) When ready to cook, drop potato balls into boiling water and parboil for 5 minutes. Drain. Melt butter in a large skillet. Add potatoes, salt, and pepper, cover, and shake over high heat until potatoes are tender-crisp, about 15 minutes. Sprinkle with chopped parsley.

## WHITE CHOCOLATE ROLL

The use of white chocolate in this recipe produces a beautiful cake—the pale yellow color contrasting with the satiny brown filling.

½ pound white chocolate
5 tablespoons strong coffee
7 eggs, separated
1 cup sugar
2 tablespoons dark crème de
    cacao or Kahlúa

FILLING:
1½ cups heavy cream
½ cup unsweetened cocoa,
    less if desired
¼ cup confectioners' sugar,
    more if desired
2 tablespoons dark crème de
    cacao or Kahlúa

Melt white chocolate in coffee over low heat and set aside to cool. Oil an 11 x 17-inch jelly-roll pan, line with waxed paper, and oil the waxed paper. Set aside. Beat egg yolks in electric mixer bowl; gradually add sugar and beat until mixture is very light and creamy. Add chocolate mixture and blend well. Flavor with crème de cacao. In another bowl, beat egg whites until stiff. Fold into egg yolk mixture and spread in prepared jelly-roll pan. Place in a preheated 350° oven and bake for 15 minutes. Turn oven off and leave pan in oven 5 minutes longer. Remove from oven and turn cake out onto 2 overlapping strips of waxed paper; carefully remove lining paper and cover cake with a double thickness of paper towels wrung out in cold water. Let cool.

Prepare filling: whip the heavy cream, flavoring it with ¼

cup of the cocoa, the confectioners' sugar, and crème de cacao. Spread on cake and roll up. Just before serving, dust cake with remaining ¼ cup cocoa, or with an equivalent amount of confectioners' sugar. *May be made earlier the same day.*

## A Picnic in the Woods
### for 8

Antipasto
Pâté en croûte (see p. 229)
Oak-leaf lettuce with sour cream dressing
Melon wedges, crystallized ginger

### ANTIPASTO

Pack a picnic basket with an assortment of the following ingredients. The vegetables should be washed, trimmed, wrapped in individual plastic bags, and kept icy cold. When you reach your picnic site, spread everything out on a big platter or tray and serve with Italian olive oil, red wine vinegar, a basket of *grissini*—Italian breadsticks—and lots of fresh Italian bread. Don't forget salt and a pepper grinder.

Sardines

Tuna, garnished with mayonnaise and capers

Mortadella (Italian garlic sausage), sliced thin

Salami, sliced thin

Artichoke hearts

Pimento slices

Caponata (Italian-style eggplant salad, available canned)

Prosciutto, sliced thin

Provolone

Black and green olives

Fennel

Radishes

Celery

Tomatoes, sliced

Scallions

Small raw mushrooms

## OAK-LEAF LETTUCE
## WITH SOUR CREAM DRESSING

This is a very tender, buttery leaf lettuce with leaves shaped like those of an oak tree. Many gardeners grow it, but it's a rarity in markets. You can substitute the ruffly garden lettuce, or Bibb or Boston. To serve 8, you'll need about 2 quarts of the leaf or garden lettuce, or 2 large heads of Boston, or 6 heads of Bibb. The sour cream dressing on page 176 is light, just right for delicate greens. Rinse the lettuce at home, roll it in paper towels, put it in a plastic bag, and bring it to the picnic in a cooler to keep it crisp.

## MELON WEDGES, CRYSTALLIZED GINGER

Cut slices or wedges of ripe, juicy cantaloupe or honeydew melon and sprinkle them with finely chopped crystallized ginger. The ginger adds enough of a lively, piquant taste to point up the melon, but if you wish, you can squeeze a little lime or lemon juice over each serving, too.

## *A Tailgate Picnic*
## *for 8*

---

Fish chowder
Cold fillet of beef
on horseradish-buttered white bread
Jo Klein's baked ham in paper
on mustard-buttered French bread
Cornichons and watermelon rind pickles
Walnuts in the shell and dried fruits
*or* apples and Cheddar cheese

This is a perfect picnic feast to spread on the tailgate of a station wagon before a football game. Chowder, packed in Thermos bottles, will ward off the chills, and the cold meats with condiments are excellent in any weather. In fact, if it's sunny, picnicking on a brisk fall day is one of the pleasantest of experiences, not to be missed.

## FISH CHOWDER

| | |
|---|---|
| 3  pounds haddock or sea bass | 1  teaspoon salt |
| 2½  cups water | ½  teaspoon freshly cracked |
| ¼  pound diced bacon | white pepper |
| 1½  cups chopped onions | 1  quart light cream |
| 1  cup chopped celery | 2  tablespoons butter |
| 4  potatoes, peeled and diced | Dry sherry, optional |
| 1  bay leaf | 2  tablespoons chopped parsley |

Buy fish steaks with bone in, or have fishmonger bone them for you and save the bones. Cut fish into bite-size pieces and set aside. Put bones in a saucepan and cover with 2½ cups water, bring to a boil, and simmer, covered, for 15 minutes. Strain and reserve stock. Fry the bacon dice in a large saucepan over high heat. Add onions, celery, and potatoes; cook over high heat until the onions are transparent, stirring with a wooden spatula. Add fish and cook for another 2 minutes. Add strained fish stock. Crumble and add bay leaf, then add salt, pepper, cream, and butter. Bring the chowder almost to the boil, cover it, adjust heat to simmer, and simmer 30 minutes. (*Can be made a day ahead and reheated.*) Add 1 tablespoon sherry for each serving, if you wish. Stir parsley into chowder just before pouring it into Thermos bottles. (If serving fish chowder in bowls at the table, sprinkle each serving with chopped parsley.)

## COLD FILLET OF BEEF
## ON HORSERADISH-BUTTERED WHITE BREAD

Tie a well-trimmed 5- to 6-pound fillet of beef every 2 inches. Bring it to room temperature, rub it all over with 1 tablespoon coarse salt and 1 teaspoon freshly cracked black pepper, and place it on a rack in a shallow roasting pan. Roast in a preheated 425° oven for about 35 minutes, or until meat thermometer registers 125°. Remove from oven and let cool. Wrap and refrigerate, but bring to room temperature for serving. Slice thinly and serve with Sandy Ainsworth's white bread (see p. 245) and horseradish butter, made by adding 2 tablespoons prepared horseradish to ½ cup of butter.

### JO KLEIN'S BAKED HAM IN PAPER ON MUSTARD-BUTTERED FRENCH BREAD

Wrap a 5- to 6-pound half-ham, precooked and smoked, in white butcher paper. Paper should be long enough so that you can bring the ends together over the ham and fold them over two or three times—this is called a drugstore wrap, or lock-seal. Then fold or twist the open sides of your package to enclose the ham securely. Lay it on a baking sheet and put it in a preheated 325° oven to bake, for 25 minutes per pound, or 2 to 2½ hours. Remove from oven and let cool. Wrap and refrigerate, but bring to room temperature for serving. Serve with French bread and mustard butter, made by adding 2 tablespoons of Dijon mustard to ½ cup of butter.

## *Back Porch Supper*
## *for 8*

---

Gazpacho
Jellied chicken
Cold London broil ( see p. 102)
Apple and potato salad
Fresh garden lettuce, served plain
French bread with herb butter
Homemade vanilla ice cream, served
from the freezer ( see p. 176)
Pound cake

When I was a kid, supper on the back porch·meant a trestle table laden with food and a very informal mood. Serving dishes were passed, family-style; everyone helped himself, and second helpings were encouraged. (Many times the menu included leftovers, but my mother made the platters look so attractive we seldom realized it.) Your porch may be a patio, and you may want to serve the food buffet-style. But I think your guests will enjoy this generous country kind of meal with its choice of entrées as well as salads. Top it off with ice cream dipped from the freezer canister, and old-fashioned pound cake.

### GAZPACHO

¼ cup red wine vinegar
¼ cup olive oil
2 finely chopped cloves garlic
1 cucumber, peeled, seeded, and diced
1 green pepper, seeded and diced
¾ cup chopped onion
1 teaspoon salt
1 cup dry bread crumbs
2 pounds tomatoes
  Ice water

3 or 4 drops Tabasco sauce, optional

FOR GARNISH:
1 cucumber, peeled, seeded, and diced
1 green pepper, seeded and diced
1 tomato, peeled, seeded, and cut into fine shreds
1 cup garlic croutons
  Ice cubes

Put vinegar, olive oil, garlic, cucumber, green pepper, onion, salt, and bread crumbs into a blender and puree; mixture should be the consistency of heavy cream. Pour it into a serving bowl and taste it; add up to 2 tablespoons more vinegar if needed. Rub the tomatoes through a strainer and add them to the bread crumb mixture, along with enough ice water to thin the mixture to the consistency of light cream. It should look mushy but thin. Chill thoroughly. (*Gazpacho is best if made the day before. Taste for seasoning when soup is cold, adding Tabasco if desired.*) Prepare the garnish vegetables and chill. When ready to serve, add the garnish vegetables to the gazpacho in the serving bowl and sprinkle garlic croutons on top. Or place vegetables and croutons, as well as ice cubes (for thinning soup, if needed), in separate bowls for guests to serve themselves as desired.

### JELLIED CHICKEN

1 5-pound stewing chicken
½ cup chopped carrot
¾ cup chopped onion
½ cup chopped celery
2 cups chicken stock (see p. 278)
1½ cups dry white wine or dry vermouth
1 tablespoon dried tarragon
2 teaspoons salt

1 teaspoon freshly cracked black pepper
Juice of 1 lemon
1 egg white
2 tablespoons (2 envelopes) unflavored gelatine
8 deviled eggs (see p. 70)
Olives and lettuce, to garnish platter

Put the chicken in a pot or large saucepan with the carrot, onion, celery, chicken stock, and 1 cup of the dry white wine. Add tarragon, salt, pepper, and lemon juice. Bring to a boil, turn heat to simmer, half-cover the pot, and simmer until chicken is very tender, about 1 to 1½ hours. Cool chicken in broth. When cool, remove chicken and strip meat from the bones, keeping it in good-size (1-inch) pieces. Set aside. Strain the broth (do not mash the vegetables) and measure it; add water or additional chicken stock to make 3½ cups. Put it over low heat and beat in the egg white with a whisk. Whisk and simmer for 2 minutes. Remove from heat and set aside. Sprinkle gelatine over remaining ½ cup white wine, and set aside. Line a sieve with a double thickness of cheesecloth wrung out in cold water. Strain broth, letting it drain through the cheesecloth-lined sieve without stirring or forcing it in any way. Combine with gelatine mixture, stirring and reheating, if necessary, to dissolve gelatine. Cool. Arrange chicken pieces in an oiled mold (a bread pan is a good size and shape). Pour cooled gelatine over chicken. (Pour any extra gelatine into a shallow pan.) Chill mold until set. (*Recipe may be prepared ahead to this point and stored overnight.*) When ready to serve, unmold the chicken on a serving platter. Chop extra gelatine and sprinkle it around the mold. Decorate platter with lettuce leaves, olives, and deviled eggs.

## APPLE AND POTATO SALAD

4 cups sliced boiled potatoes
3 cups diced unpeeled apple
½ cup chopped onion
1 seeded, sliced cucumber
¼ cup red wine vinegar
1 teaspoon salt
½ teaspoon freshly cracked
    white pepper

1 to 2 tablespoons chopped
    fresh chives
2 cups sour cream *or* 1 cup sour
    cream and 1 cup mayon-
    naise
Romaine lettuce

Combine all ingredients except lettuce and chill. If the cucumber is heavily waxed, peel before slicing. When ready to serve, turn salad into a bowl lined with the lettuce leaves.

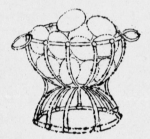

## POUND CAKE

4½ cups sifted flour
½ teaspoon salt
¼ teaspoon mace, optional
2 cups butter

2 cups sugar
10 eggs, separated
1 tablespoon vanilla extract

Sift the flour with salt and mace; set aside. Put the butter in electric mixer bowl and cream it. Gradually beat in sugar and beat until mixture is very light and fluffy. Beat egg yolks well and beat them into butter-sugar mixture, again beating until very light. Gradually beat in flour. When well mixed, flavor with vanilla. Beat egg whites until stiff and fold them into batter. Pour batter into 2 9 x 5 x 3-inch loaf pans that have been greased and lined with silicone paper (KVP baking parchment). Bake in a preheated 300° oven for 70 to 85 minutes, or until cake tester or toothpick comes out clean when pushed into center of cake. Cool on racks for 10 minutes; then remove cake from pans and cool completely. Wrap one of the cakes for the freezer—it freezes beautifully.

## *Formal Picnic*
## *for 8*

Vichyssoise
Breast of veal stuffed with pâté
Cherry tomatoes and fava beans
with coarse salt
Cold glazed squabs (see p. 127)
Hearts of palm salad (see p. 171)
Assorted cheeses, crackers, and breads
Ladyfingers and whole fresh peaches

When you move a feast into a perfect picnic setting, do what you can to make it even more memorable—a study in contrasts. Unpack white linen, stemmed wineglasses, and china to match the elegant food. Elegant as it is, the menu may be enjoyed picnic fashion, using fingers instead of forks. Every bite packs and travels well, but do choose the semisoft or harder cheeses, such as Muenster, Cheddar, Port Salut, Roquefort. Serve with whatever crackers and breads you like best: unsalted water biscuits, stone-ground thin crackers, breadsticks, homemade white bread, pumpernickel, or French bread.

### VICHYSSOISE

4 leeks
4 large baking potatoes,
    peeled and cubed
½ cup sliced celery
1½ cups sliced onions
1 tablespoon salt
1 teaspoon freshly cracked
    white pepper

1 cup strong chicken stock
    (see p. 278)
2 cups heavy cream
2 tablespoons chopped fresh
    chives

Clean leeks carefully by splitting them lengthwise and holding them under running water, separating the layers to rinse out all the sand and dirt. Slice them, using all the white part plus about 1 inch of the green. Put leeks, potatoes, celery, onions, salt, and pepper into a saucepan with just enough water to cover—use as little water as possible. Bring to a boil, turn heat to simmer, cover pan, and cook until vegetables are mushy. Add chicken stock and bring to a boil, stirring. Puree the mixture through a food mill, using the finest disk. Chill thoroughly. (*Can be made the day before to this point.*) Immediately before serving or packing in Thermoses for the picnic, whip cream just past the foaming stage and stir it into the soup. Serve icy cold in chilled cups with chopped chives sprinkled on.

## BREAST OF VEAL STUFFED WITH PÂTÉ

1  breast of veal, about
   4 pounds
¾  pound ground veal
¾  pound ground pork
2  tablespoons chopped
   shallots
1  teaspoon finely chopped
   garlic
2  eggs
2  teaspoons salt
1½ teaspoons freshly cracked
   black pepper

½  cup chopped natural
   pistachio nuts
½  truffle, chopped
2  tablespoons finely chopped
   parsley
6  tablespoons brandy
4  tablespoons melted butter
1  tablespoon coarse salt
2  tablespoons chicken stock
   (see p. 278) or veal stock
   (see p. 279)

Have the veal breast boned. Or bone breast yourself: place the meat on the counter, rib side up, with the breast bone hanging over the edge of the counter. Lean on it to break breast bone loose from rib bones, and cut around breast bone to separate it from the flesh. Then cut alongside each rib bone, and slide your knife under each rib, cutting against the bone to free the flesh. *Or*, after cutting alongside rib bones stand the breast up and lean on it—bones will pop out.

To make stuffing, mix together ground veal and pork (both ground twice—you can use all veal, if you wish), shallots garlic, eggs, salt, ½ teaspoon pepper, the pistachio nuts, truffle, and parsley. Warm ¼ cup of the brandy in a small, long handled pan, ignite, and pour, flaming, over stuffing mixture. To test stuffing for seasoning, sauté a bit of it in a small skillet until thoroughly cooked and taste. Cut a pocket in the meat, pack with stuffing, and sew up ends.

Brush stuffed veal with melted butter and sprinkle with 1 tablespoon coarse salt and 1 teaspoon pepper. Place in a roasting pan in a preheated 350° oven and roast for 2 to 2½ hours, or until well done. During roasting, baste after 15 minutes with remaining 2 tablespoons brandy, remaining melted butter, and chicken or veal stock, and then baste every 15 minutes with juices in pan. When done, cool and store in refrigerator. Bring to room temperature before carving in thin slices.

## CHERRY TOMATOES AND FAVA BEANS WITH COARSE SALT

Wash 1 quart cherry tomatoes, rinse 1 quart shelled fava beans, and pack each in a plastic freezer container, adding a few chips of ice to keep them damp. Serve with a bowl of coarse salt to dip them in. Another nice dip for cherry tomatoes is vodka.

## LADYFINGERS

3 eggs, separated  
⅓ cup plus 1 tablespoon sugar

1 teaspoon vanilla extract  
¾ cup sifted flour

Line baking sheets with baking parchment. In electric mixer bowl, beat egg yolks and sugar at high speed. Add vanilla and continue to beat until mixture is very thick, about 5 minutes. In a separate bowl and with clean beaters, beat egg whites until stiff. Fold one third of the flour and half of the egg whites alternately into egg yolk mixture, beginning and ending with the flour. Do this carefully, with a light touch. Put batter into a large pastry bag fitted with a plain round tube and pipe batter out onto lined baking sheets, making straight lines about 3 inches long. Space them 2 inches apart. Place baking sheets on the middle shelf of preheated 350° oven and bake until set, about 7 to 8 minutes. Do not brown. Remove from oven. With a spatula lift ladyfingers from baking sheets, to cool on wire cake racks. Makes 24 ladyfingers.

## A Lobster Party
### for 6

Clams on the half shell
Boiled lobsters
Hot buttered French bread
Platter of baked potato skins
Iced cucumber sticks
Melon with port wine (see p. 30)
Florentines (see p. 249)

It's easier to boil lobsters on your kitchen stove, but if you have a big grill, you could do it outside. Start the water in the house and bring it out when it's near the boiling point. If you move the party to the beach, cook the lobster in seawater, and skip the potato skins—they need an oven. To prepare hot buttered French bread, slice it diagonally every 1½ inches, not quite through the bottom. Cream ½ cup butter and spread between each 2 slices. Wrap the loaf in aluminum foil and heat in a preheated 350° oven or on the edge of the grill for about 10 to 15 minutes.

### CLAMS ON THE HALF SHELL

Count 6 clams per person. Open them or have them opened as close to serving time as possible. Arrange on plates, preferably on cracked ice, and serve with lemon wedges. Pass the pepper mill. *No red sauce.*

### BOILED LOBSTERS

6 live lobsters, about 1¾ pounds each
1 tablespoon salt

1½ cups melted butter, for serving hot, *or* mustard mayonnaise
Lemon wedges

Put lobsters in a big, 18-quart lobster pot, cover with cold water, and add salt. Cover and place over high heat; bring the water to a boil. Let boil about 5 minutes; then reduce heat to simmer gently and cook, covered, for another 15 to 20 minutes, depending on size of lobsters. Drain off water and serve lobsters hot with individual bowls of melted butter and plenty of lemon wedges. If serving cold, drain lobsters and cover immediately with cold water to stop the cooking. Serve cold lobster with mustard mayonnaise, made by adding ½ cup Dijon mustard to 1 cup mayonnaise (see p. 283).

## PLATTER OF BAKED POTATO SKINS

Scrub 6 large baking potatoes. Bake them in a preheated 375° oven for 1 hour, or until very well done, with crisp skins. Cut potatoes in half, lengthwise, and scoop out interior; reserve for another use—Roesti Potatoes, for example (see p. 15). With kitchen shears, cut potato skins crosswise into strips about ½ inch wide. Flatten them and dip into melted butter (you'll need about ¾ cup). Place on baking sheet and sprinkle with coarse salt and freshly cracked black pepper. (*May be prepared ahead to this point.*) Bake in a preheated 350° oven until you can't see the butter running off them and the skins are very crisp, about 10 to 15 minutes. Serve hot.

## ICED CUCUMBER STICKS

Peel 3 large cucumbers with a vegetable peeler, cut them in half lengthwise, and scoop out the seeds with the top of a spoon. Cut crosswise into 3-inch pieces, then into sticks. Cover with water, adding 1 tablespoon salt, and soak for 1 hour in the refrigerator. Drain on paper towels and serve—they will be very crisp.

## A Fourth of July Picnic
## for 16

Tomatoes stuffed with crab-meat salad
Meat loaf en croûte
*or* Peppered veal loaf en croûte
Baked lima beans
Cucumbers in sour cream and chives
Walnut cake
Bowl of assorted fruits

If you have ever lived in a town that has band concerts in the park on the Fourth of July, this is the kind of food you'd remember, spread out on picnic tables covered with red-checkered tablecloths. It's good backyard fare, too, homespun and hearty.

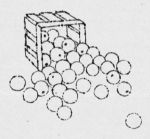

### TOMATOES STUFFED
### WITH CRAB-MEAT SALAD

16 large tomatoes               16 sprigs parsley or watercress
 2 recipes crab-meat salad
   (see p. 52)

Cut the tops off tomatoes and set aside to make lids. Scoop out seeds and turn tomatoes upside down to drain. Chill. Fill with crab-meat salad. Cut a slit in each lid and insert a sprig of parsley or watercress; place on top of salads.

## MEAT LOAF EN CROÛTE

1 recipe sour cream pastry
  (see p. 288)
2 tablespoons butter
¾ cup chopped onion
1 chopped clove garlic
3 pounds ground beef
2 beaten eggs
½ cup sour cream
½ cup chili sauce
2 teaspoons salt

1 teaspoon freshly cracked
  black pepper
¼ cup soft bread crumbs
4 strips bacon
1 egg yolk
1 tablespoon water
1 cup sour cream, optional
1 tablespoon chopped fresh
  dill, optional

Make pastry and put it in the refrigerator to chill for 1½ hours. Melt butter in a small pan and stir in chopped onion and garlic. Cook over high heat, stirring with a wooden spatula, until onion is transparent—do not let it burn. Put ground beef into a large bowl, add onion and garlic, eggs, ½ cup sour cream, the chili sauce, salt, pepper (1 teaspoon is correct), and soft bread crumbs. Mix together and shape into a loaf on a baking tray. Lay bacon strips over loaf and put it into a preheated 350° oven to bake for 35 minutes. Remove partly baked loaf from oven, discard bacon, and chill in refrigerator. Roll out three quarters of the sour cream pastry on a lightly floured board. Wrap it around the chilled meat loaf to enclose it completely. Do not wrap tightly. Seal the seam at bottom and ends with egg wash—egg yolk beaten with 1 tablespoon water—and place, seam side down, on baking tray. Roll out remaining pastry and cut leaves or flowers to decorate top. Stick the decorations on with egg wash and brush the crust all over with it. Prick pastry in 3 places with fork tines. (*Can be made ahead to this point and refrigerated or frozen.*) Place in a preheated 375° oven to bake for 45 minutes, or until pastry is done. Serve plain or topped with 1 cup sour cream mixed with the fresh chopped dill. May be served hot, at room temperature, or chilled.

## PEPPERED VEAL LOAF EN CROÛTE

Follow recipe for Meat Loaf en Croûte, substituting ground veal for ground beef, and adding 2 teaspoons (this is correct—3 teaspoons altogether) freshly cracked black pepper.

## BAKED LIMA BEANS

4 cups dried lima beans
1 tablespoon plus 1 teaspoon
 salt
1 cup cubed salt pork

½ cup dark molasses
1 teaspoon dry mustard
2 tablespoons butter

Rinse beans in cold water; then place in a bowl, cover with cold water, and soak overnight or for at least 12 hours. Drain, put in a saucepan, add 1 tablespoon salt, and cover with boiling water. Simmer, uncovered, for 1½ hours. Drain beans and place in a 2-quart buttered bean pot or casserole along with cubed salt pork. Mix molasses, mustard, and 1 teaspoon salt in 2 cups hot water and pour over beans. Dot with butter. Cover and bake in a preheated 350° oven until beans are soft, about 3 hours. Uncover the beans during last 30 minutes of cooking to brown them. *Can be baked ahead and reheated.*

## CUCUMBERS IN SOUR CREAM AND CHIVES

4 cucumbers
1 tablespoon plus ½ teaspoon
 salt
2 tablespoons finely chopped
 parsley

¾ cup sour cream
3 tablespoons finely chopped
 chives
½ teaspoon freshly cracked
 white pepper

Peel cucumbers and cut them in half lengthwise, scooping out seeds with the tip of a spoon. Slice crosswise as thin as possible, using a vegetable cutter or *mandoline*. Sprinkle with 1 tablespoon salt and place in refrigerator with a plate on top of them, to weight them; the salt and weight will work together to release moisture, which can be bitter. After 2 hours, put in a sieve and rinse off salt. Squeeze to release excess liquid. Put in a bowl, add remaining ingredients, and stir with 2 forks to mix. Chill until ready to serve.

## WALNUT CAKE

½ cup butter, plus butter to
  grease pan
1¼ cups confectioners' sugar
½ cup milk
2 teaspoons vanilla extract
½ teaspoon almond extract

2 cups lightly spooned flour
2 teaspoons baking powder
¼ teaspoon salt
5 egg whites
½ cup broken walnuts
  Frosting (recipe follows)

Butter an 11 x 7 x 1½-inch cake pan and set aside. In electric mixer bowl, cream the butter, gradually adding confectioners' sugar, and beat until very light. Add the milk and vanilla and almond extracts. Sift the flour 3 times with the baking powder and add to butter mixture, stirring until blended. Add the salt to the egg whites and beat until stiff but not dry. Fold them into the batter carefully; then very lightly fold in broken walnuts. Pour batter into prepared cake pan and bake in a preheated 350° oven for about 25 minutes, or until cake tests done. Cool in the pan, on a rack. Spread with Frosting, or, for a less rich effect, sift confectioners' sugar over the cake just before serving.

## FROSTING FOR WALNUT CAKE

1½ cups sugar
2 egg whites

¼ teaspoon cream of tartar
2 teaspoons vanilla extract

Combine ½ cup water and the sugar in a small saucepan and bring to a boil, stirring until sugar dissolves. Cook until syrup forms a soft ball in cold water (234° to 238° on the candy thermometer), about 15 minutes. When syrup is almost ready, beat egg whites until stiff but not dry; then slowly add the cooked syrup to the whites in a thin stream, beating constantly. Beat in cream of tartar and vanilla and continue beating until smooth and thick. Then place the bowl in a pan of boiling water and beat frosting with a wooden spatula until you feel the spatula grating slightly against the bottom of the bowl. Remove from heat immediately and spread over cooled cake.

## A Pool Party
## for 12

Crudités with coarse salt
Pissaladière
Stuffed eggplant
Sesame breadsticks
Melon wedges, crystallized ginger
(see p. 257)

### CRUDITÉS WITH COARSE SALT

Arrange raw vegetables on a tray or platter of ice and serve with a bowl of coarse salt. For vegetable suggestions, see p. 234.

### PISSALADIÈRE

1 package active dry yeast
¼ cup warm water (105° to 115°)
1½ tablespoons olive oil *or* melted butter
1 teaspoon sugar
1 teaspoon salt
⅔ cup warm water
3 cups lightly spooned flour

FILLING:

6 cups sliced onions
½ cup olive oil, plus oil for pan
1 1-pound, 4-ounce can Italian tomatoes
¾ cup freshly grated Parmesan cheese
1 tablespoon rosemary
2 2-ounce cans flat anchovy fillets
16 black olives, pitted and cut in half lengthwise

Sprinkle yeast into ¼ cup warm water, stir to dissolve, and let stand 5 minutes. Put 1½ tablespoons olive oil, the sugar, salt, and ⅔ cup warm water in mixer bowl; add yeast mixture. Beat in flour, 1 cupful at a time. Mixture will be very stiff. Turn dough out on a floured board and knead about 5 minutes, adding a little flour if dough sticks to the board. Put the dough in a plastic bag or a bowl to rest for precisely 30 minutes. In a saucepan, cook onions in ½ cup olive oil over high heat until they are very soft, almost a puree, and brownish yellow. In another saucepan, mash and cook tomatoes until mixture looks like a puree, about 20 to 30 minutes.

Brush a 12-inch pizza pan with olive oil (or substitute 2 6-inch flat, round pans with 1-inch-high sides). Roll out dough and fit it into the oiled pan, rolling the edge to make it thick and crusty. Prick dough all over the bottom, all the way through. Let rest at least 10 minutes. (*May be prepared ahead to this point.*) Then place in a preheated 400° oven for 10 minutes—this prebaking will ensure a crust that's completely baked. Remove from oven and sprinkle the shell with grated Parmesan. Spoon the onion mixture around the edge, the tomato mixture in the center. Sprinkle with rosemary. Arrange anchovy fillets over the filling, like wheel spokes, and place olive halves around the edge, plus 1 in the center. Return to the oven to bake for 15 to 20 minutes, or until crust is brown. Make, bake, and serve in sequence; this gets soggy if made ahead.

### STUFFED EGGPLANT

3 large (or 6 small) eggplants
¾ cup olive oil, about
3 cups finely chopped onion
1½ teaspoons finely chopped garlic
1 tablespoon salt
1½ teaspoons freshly cracked white pepper
3 tablespoons chopped parsley
6 tablespoons grated Parmesan cheese

Cut eggplants in half; cut a thin slice from the resulting bottom of each half, so it won't roll around. Dig out centers, leaving shells about ½ inch thick. Parboil the shells for 5 minutes. Chop centers roughly. Heat ½ cup of olive oil in a heavy skillet. Add onion, garlic, and chopped eggplant; stir and cook over high heat until onion is transparent. Season with salt and pepper. Spoon this mixture into parboiled shells. Drizzle with olive oil (use about 2 teaspoons per large half); sprinkle with parsley and Parmesan cheese and another drizzle of olive oil. (*Can be prepared ahead, ready to bake. Or you can bake eggplant and reheat, or serve cold.*) Place in a preheated 375° oven to bake until shells are tender, about 35 to 45 minutes.

## *A Beach Picnic*
### *for 6*

Cold cream of onion soup
Deviled eggs (see p. 70)
Pain bagna
Chick-pea salad
Pears and Gorgonzola cheese
Sangría

### COLD CREAM OF ONION SOUP

½ cup butter
6 cups sliced onion
1 chopped clove garlic
1 cup chopped celery
3 cups diced raw potato
2 cups chicken stock (see p. 278)
6 cups light cream

1 teaspoon salt
½ teaspoon freshly cracked white pepper
¼ teaspoon freshly grated nutmeg
2 tablespoons finely chopped parsley

Melt the butter in a large saucepan. When it is hot and foamy, stir in onion, garlic, celery, and potato. Cook slowly for about 15 minutes, stirring frequently—do not let them brown. Heat stock, pour onto vegetable mixture, and cook slowly for about 30 minutes; half-cover the pan. Add light cream, salt, and pepper and heat through. Check the seasoning. Puree the mixture in a blender and chill. (*Can be made the day before.*) Pack it in Thermos bottles, and just before serving flavor each portion with nutmeg and a sprinkle of chopped parsley.

## PAIN BAGNA

2  10-inch round loaves of
    French bread
½  cup French olive oil, more
    if necessary
16  lettuce leaves
6  thinly sliced tomatoes
1  cup chopped black olives
2  2-ounce cans flat anchovy
    fillets

1  large red onion, thinly sliced
½  teaspoon crushed rosemary
½  teaspoon basil
½  teaspoon salt
¼  teaspoon freshly cracked
    black pepper

Cut each loaf of bread in half, horizontally, and pull out some of the soft interior from each piece. Drizzle olive oil over the 4 hollowed-out pieces and let it soak in; you may need a little more oil. Cover the hollow of each bottom half with overlapping lettuce leaves. Then arrange tomato slices, black olives, drained anchovy fillets, and onion in circles on top of the lettuce. Sprinkle with rosemary, basil, salt, and pepper and cover each bottom half with a top half of bread. Wrap each loaf in aluminum foil and carry it anywhere. To serve, cut in wedges; have plenty of paper napkins available. *Make this the morning of your picnic, not the day before.*

## CHICK-PEA SALAD

1  15½-ounce can chick-peas
½  cup tarragon vinegar
½  cup olive oil
1  chopped clove garlic
1  teaspoon salt
½  teaspoon freshly cracked
    black pepper
¼  pound hard salami, cut in
    strips
½  cup pimento-stuffed olives,
    sliced

¼  cup finely chopped celery
¼  cup finely chopped green
    pepper
    Romaine lettuce leaves to
    line salad bowl
3  tablespoons finely chopped
    scallions
2  tomatoes, peeled, seeded,
    and diced
2  tablespoons finely chopped
    parsley

Rinse the chick-peas in cold water, dry thoroughly, and set aside. Mix vinegar, olive oil, garlic, salt, and pepper in a bowl. Add chick-peas, salami, olives, celery, and green pepper and toss to coat with the dressing. Put in a salad bowl lined with romaine and sprinkle with scallions, tomatoes, and parsley. Refrigerate under plastic wrap until ready to carry it (carefully!) to your picnic spot.

## SANGRÍA

½ cup sugar
1 thinly sliced lime
1 thinly sliced orange
1 bottle dry red wine
1 pint brandy

1 pint club soda
Ice
Lime and orange slices for
    garnish, optional

Combine sugar and 1 cup water in a small saucepan and heat, stirring, until sugar dissolves. When syrup reaches the boiling point, remove from heat and add lime and orange slices. Let macerate at least 24 hours. Take the syrup and fruit to the beach in a jar, along with remaining ingredients. When ready to serve, fill a pitcher one quarter full of ice; add syrup, wine, brandy, and club soda. Stir with a wooden spoon and serve. Garnish each glass, if you wish, with a fresh slice of lime and orange.

# *Basic Recipes*

### BEEF STOCK

2 pounds cubed lean beef brisket or shin
2 pounds raw beef bones
1 veal knuckle
1 cup sliced carrots
1 cup sliced celery, with leaves
2 medium-size peeled onions
4 whole cloves

1 cup dry white wine
1 mashed clove garlic
½ teaspoon dried thyme
1 bay leaf
3 sprigs parsley
2 tablespoons tomato paste
1 tablespoon salt
½ teaspoon freshly cracked black pepper

Put beef, beef bones, veal knuckle, carrots, celery, and onions stuck with cloves in a roasting pan and place in a preheated 450° oven for about 30 minutes, or until beef is thoroughly browned.

Stir vegetables occasionally to prevent scorching; remove vegetables when browned. Put the browned vegetables and meat and bones into a deep kettle or stock pot. Pour 1 cup water into the roasting pan and scrape up the brown bits. Pour into kettle, adding more water, enough to make 4 quarts in all. Add wine, garlic, thyme, bay leaf, parsley, tomato paste, salt, and pepper and bring slowly to a boil. Skim. Reduce heat, half-cover the kettle, and simmer gently for 4 hours.

Strain through a sieve lined with a double thickness of cheesecloth wrung out in cold water. Stock may be stored in the refrigerator for up to 1 week, if boiled every day, or frozen for up to 2 months. If recipe calls for extra strength stock, boil ordinary stock, uncovered, over moderately high heat until it is reduced by one third. Makes 2 to 3 quarts.

## CHICKEN STOCK

4 pounds chicken backs, wings, necks, and giblets, or a 4-pound whole chicken
1 cup sliced carrots
1 cup sliced celery, with leaves
4 medium-size peeled onions
4 whole cloves
1 cup dry white wine

1 mashed clove garlic
½ teaspoon dried thyme
1 bay leaf
3 sprigs parsley
2 tablespoons tomato paste
1 tablespoon salt
½ teaspoon freshly cracked black pepper

Place all ingredients (stick the whole cloves into the onions) and 4 quarts of cold water in a deep kettle or stock pot. Bring to a boil slowly. Skim. Reduce heat, half-cover the kettle, and simmer gently for 1½ hours. Remove the chicken, strip the meat from the bones, return the bones to the kettle, and simmer for another 2½ hours. (Use the meat in any recipe calling for cooked chicken.) Strain the stock through a sieve lined with a double thickness of cheesecloth wrung out in cold water. Stock may be stored in the refrigerator for up to 1 week, if boiled every day, or frozen for up to 2 months. If recipe calls for extra strong stock, boil, uncovered, over moderately high heat, to reduce by one third. Makes 2 to 3 quarts.

## VEAL STOCK

To make veal stock, follow the recipe for chicken stock, substituting veal and veal bones for the chicken.

## FISH STOCK

1 cup sliced onion
½ cup sliced celery rib
½ cup sliced carrot
2 pounds fish bones and trim-
    mings, all from lean fish

1 cup dry white wine
Bouquet garni (see p. 283)
1 teaspoon salt
½ teaspoon freshly cracked
    white pepper

Put all ingredients and 1 quart cold water into a kettle or stock pot and bring to a boil. Skim. Reduce heat, partially cover the pot, and simmer ½ hour. Strain through a fine sieve. Makes 3 to 4 cups.

## COURT BOUILLON

Court bouillon can be used for poaching or boiling any fish or shellfish, but never, never drop fish or shellfish into *boiling* court bouillon—it will toughen the fish.

2 cups dry vermouth or other
    dry white wine *or* 2 cups
    cider vinegar
½ cup chopped onion
½ cup chopped carrot
½ cup chopped celery

2 teaspoons salt
8 peppercorns
3 sprigs parsley
1 bay leaf
1 clove
½ teaspoon dried thyme

Put all ingredients and 2 quarts cold water into a large saucepan or kettle, bring to a boil, and boil rapidly for 30 minutes. Strain bouillon and cool. Makes 9 to 10 cups.

## ASPIC

2 cups strong chicken stock
    (see p. 278)
½ cup tomato juice
2 tablespoons (2 envelopes)
    unflavored gelatine
1 crushed eggshell

2 lightly beaten egg whites
2 tablespoons Cognac, brandy,
    Madeira, or white wine
1 teaspoon salt
½ teaspoon freshly cracked
    black pepper

Combine all ingredients in a saucepan and bring slowly to a boil, whisking constantly. Remove from heat and let stand 5 minutes. Strain into a bowl through a strainer lined with a double thickness of cheesecloth wrung out in cold water. Do not force liquid through; just let it drip through by itself. Hold strainer well above liquid in bowl. If not clear, pour it through the strainer again. Place in the refrigerator for 1 hour to set or make a day ahead and refrigerate. Do not freeze. Makes about 2 cups.

## MEAT GLAZE

Meat glaze is nothing more than strained beef stock reduced to a syrup. Use it whenever a concentrated beef flavor is called for.

Boil 3 quarts beef stock (see p. 277) in a large kettle for 30 minutes, or until reduced to 1 quart. Strain the reduced stock into a small saucepan and boil 30 minutes more, or until reduced to about 1½ cups. Watch carefully near the end, so it doesn't scorch. Cool about 1 hour; store in a covered jar in the refrigerator for up to 2 months. Always use a clean spoon to dip into meat glaze. Makes about 1½ cups.

## VELOUTÉ SAUCE

¼ cup butter
¼ cup flour

2½ cups chicken stock or veal stock (see p. 278 and p. 279)

Melt butter in a saucepan and stir in flour with a wooden spatula. Cook over high heat, stirring constantly, for 2 minutes. Do not let it brown. Remove from heat, change to a whisk, and add stock, whisking vigorously for 3 minutes. Return pan to high heat and cook, stirring, until sauce thickens and comes to a boil. Boil 1 minute. Makes 2 cups.

## BASIC BROWN SAUCE

3 tablespoons butter
¾ cup finely minced onion
½ cup diced carrot
4½ teaspoons flour
2 cups beef stock (see
    p. 277)
1 tablespoon minced shallot

2 minced cloves garlic
    Bouquet garni (see p. 283)
2 teaspoons tomato paste
¼ teaspoon freshly cracked
    black pepper
½ teaspoon meat glaze (see
    p. 280)

Melt butter in a small pan; add onion and carrot and cook over high heat for 5 minutes, stirring with a wooden spatula. Blend in flour with wooden spatula and cook, stirring constantly, about 10 minutes, or until nicely browned. Remove pan from heat, change to a wire whisk, and add the beef stock, beating vigorously. Add shallot, garlic, bouquet garni, tomato paste, pepper, and meat glaze. Return pan to heat, bring to a boil, reduce heat, cover the pan, and cook *very* slowly for 30 minutes or up to 2 hours, to intensify flavor. Strain through a fine sieve; taste, and adjust seasoning. Store in refrigerator up to 1 week, or freeze for up to 2 months. Makes 1 cup.

## HOLLANDAISE SAUCE

½ cup butter
3 egg yolks
2 tablespoons lemon juice

¼ teaspoon salt
¼ teaspoon freshly cracked
    white pepper

Melt butter, which should be very hot when you are ready for it. Put egg yolks and 3 tablespoons cold water in a small non-aluminum pan. Whisk them together over high heat, raising and lowering the pan to control heat—the pan must not get too hot. Whisk continuously until mixture starts to mound and is the consistency of heavy cream. Remove from heat and whisk in ¼ cup of the hot melted butter, 1 tablespoon at a time. Return pan to heat and add remaining butter in a thin stream, whisking continuously. Whisk about 5 minutes or until the mixture is thick and creamy; remove the pan from the heat if it starts to get too hot, but don't stop whisking. Add lemon juice, salt, and pepper. Hold sauce in a pan of warm water until serving time. Makes ¾ to 1 cup.

## BÉARNAISE SAUCE

½ cup butter
1 tablespoon chopped shallot
½ cup tarragon vinegar
1 tablespoon dried tarragon or
3 tablespoons finely chopped
 fresh tarragon

3 egg yolks
¼ teaspoon salt
¼ teaspoon freshly cracked
 white pepper
2 tablespoons chopped parsley,
 optional

Melt butter, which should be very hot when you are ready for it. Put shallot, vinegar, and tarragon in a small nonaluminum pan. Cook, stirring with a wooden spatula, over medium-high heat, until all liquid evaporates, about 5 minutes. Do not let the mixture burn. Take the pan off heat, add egg yolks and 2 tablespoons cold water, and whisk together until well blended. Return pan to heat and whisk over high heat, raising and lowering the pan to control heat—the pan must not get too hot. Whisk continuously until mixture starts to mound and is the consistency of heavy cream. Remove from heat and whisk in ¼ cup of the hot melted butter, 1 tablespoon at a time. Return pan to heat and, still whisking, add remaining butter in a thin stream. Whisk, raising and lowering the pan over heat, until mixture is thick. Strain sauce, if desired, before adding parsley. Season with salt and pepper. Hold sauce in a pan of warm water until serving time. Makes ¾ to 1 cup.

## FRENCH VINAIGRETTE DRESSING

2 tablespoons vinegar
½ cup oil
1 teaspoon coarse salt

½ teaspoon freshly cracked
 black pepper

Beat ingredients together with a fork, or shake in a jar. You can use red or white wine vinegar, tarragon vinegar, or cider vinegar, and French peanut oil, vegetable oil, or French, Italian, Spanish, or Greek olive oil.

## MAYONNAISE

Prepared mustard
½ teaspoon salt
1 tablespoon vinegar or lemon
   juice
¼ teaspoon freshly cracked
   white pepper
1 egg yolk
1 cup olive oil or vegetable
   oil or a mixture of the two

In a small bowl, whisk together mustard, salt, vinegar or lemon juice, pepper, and egg yolk. Whisk in ¼ cup of the oil, 1 tablespoon at a time, whisking thoroughly after adding each spoonful. Then pour in remaining oil in a thin stream, whisking constantly until mixture is thick and smooth, about 5 minutes. Makes 1 cup.

## BOUQUET GARNI

1 rib celery
1 bay leaf
¼ teaspoon dried thyme
3 or 4 sprigs parsley

Make a celery sandwich by laying herbs on half the celery rib, folding the other half over, and tying with a string. Leave one end of the string long and tie it to the handle of your pot or casserole so the bouquet garni will be easy to remove.

## DUXELLES

¼ pound very finely chopped
   mushrooms
¼ cup butter
¼ cup finely chopped shallots
1 tablespoon lemon juice
½ teaspoon salt
¼ teaspoon freshly cracked
   black pepper

Put the mushrooms in the corner of a tea towel and wring them out to get rid of excess moisture. (This step is not essential, but it will shorten cooking time.) Melt the butter in a skillet, add the chopped shallots, and cook over high heat for a few minutes, stirring with a wooden spatula, until shallots are transparent. Do not let them brown. Add mushrooms, sprinkle with lemon juice, and cook, stirring constantly with a wooden spatula, until the mushrooms look dry. This may take 15 to 20 minutes. Season with salt and pepper and cool. Can be stored in the refrigerator up to 10 days, or frozen for up to 1 month. Makes 1 cup.

### SAUTÉED MUSHROOMS

Wipe mushrooms clean with paper towels dipped in acidulated water (1 tablespoon lemon juice to 1 quart water). Trim stems and slice mushrooms vertically. Melt butter (1 tablespoon butter for each ¼ pound mushrooms) in a heavy skillet over high heat. When it's hot and foaming, add mushrooms, squeeze on a few drops of lemon juice, sprinkle with salt and freshly cracked black pepper, and toss over high heat for about 3 minutes.

### *SAUTÉED FLUTED MUSHROOM CAPS*

Follow directions for sautéed mushrooms, but leave mushrooms whole. To flute mushroom caps, cut off the stems even with the caps—don't twist the stems out, or the caps will collapse—then use a small curved knife or lemon stripper to cut grooves that spiral out from the center of each cap to the edges, all around.

### TOMATO ROSES

For each tomato rose, choose a large, red tomato. At the stem end, cut a slice *only two thirds* of the way across—this will be the base of the rose. Then place your knife so as to peel the tomato, starting from this base, in a continuous spiral ¾ inch wide and ⅛ inch thick. If you break the spiral, start over with a fresh tomato. To form the rose, start at the free end of the spiral and coil it up toward the stem base. Secure with a toothpick if necessary.

### TURNIP ROSES

For a turnip rose, cut turnip into a rose shape with a paring knife.

## BEER BATTER

Make beer batter at least 1 to 2 hours before you want to use it and let stand at room temperature. If you make it further ahead, refrigerate it—can be kept in the refrigerator for up to 3 to 4 days.

1 12-ounce can beer
1 to 1¼ cups lightly spooned flour

1 tablespoon salt
1 teaspoon paprika
½ teaspoon baking powder

Pour beer into a bowl, then flour into beer. It will foam; it thickens as it stands. Stir in salt, paprika, and baking powder. Makes about 2½ cups.

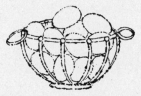

## BASIC CRÊPES

½ cup lightly spooned flour
¼ teaspoon salt
2 eggs
2 egg yolks

¼ cup vegetable oil, plus oil to film crêpe pan
½ cup milk

Put all ingredients (except oil to film pan) into a blender and blend at top speed, or whisk until smooth. Strain the batter if lumps or flour specks remain. Refrigerate batter for at least 1 hour. Before frying crêpes, thin batter, if too thick, with a little cold milk or water. Batter should be the consistency of heavy cream. Fry crêpes one at a time in a seasoned iron crêpe pan over high heat. Use a 5-inch pan for dessert crêpes, a 7-inch pan for entrée crêpes. Film pan with oil, heat it almost to the point of smoking, and, for a 5-inch pan, pour in 2 to 3 tablespoons of batter, and for a 7-inch pan, a scant ¼ of a cup of butter; quickly tilt pan in all directions to spread batter all over bottom of pan. The crêpe should be very thin. Fry 1 minute, or until the edges brown; then turn crêpe and fry on the other side for about 30 seconds. Film the pan lightly with oil before frying each crêpe. Makes 8 7-inch or 12 5-inch crêpes. Recipe can be doubled or quadrupled.

*Note:* When you fold or roll crêpes, always put the 30-second side inside.

### PÂTE À CHOUX (Cream Puff Paste)

6 tablespoons butter, at room          1 cup lightly spooned flour
   temperature                              4 eggs

Cut up the butter and add to 1 cup water in a saucepan. Bring slowly to a boil. As soon as butter melts, dump in the flour all at once and beat it with a wooden spatula until the mixture looks like mashed potatoes. Continue beating over high heat until mixture begins to coat the bottom of the pan, about 2 minutes. Remove from heat. Make a well in the mixture and have the first egg cracked and ready; drop it into the well and quickly beat it in before it scrambles. Beat in remaining 3 eggs, one at a time, beating to mix thoroughly before adding the next. Continue beating the mixture until it is shiny (do this by hand unless you have a mixer with a flat whip—mixture will clog rotary beaters). Use as directed in recipes.

### HOMEMADE PASTA

Roll and cut noodles at least 2 hours before cooking them— they need drying time. You can mix the dough the day before and store in the refrigerator. You can freeze uncooked noodles for up to 1 month or store them for 2 to 3 days in the refrigerator. This recipe makes just under 1½ pounds of noodles, or enough pasta to cut 24 cannelloni pieces.

3 cups lightly spooned flour          1 tablespoon olive or
½ teaspoon salt                              vegetable oil
3 eggs                                          2 to 3 tablespoons water

Put flour in a bowl and stir in salt. Make a well and drop in eggs and oil. Mix with your fingers. Sprinkle on water, 1 table-spoonful at a time, and mix with your hands, using a squeezing motion. Use as little water as possible; dough should hold together when it's squeezed, but it will look raggedy. Turn it out on a floured board and knead for 10 minutes; it will not get really smooth—it should still look raggedy, with cracks in it. If you got too much water in the dough, put some flour on your board and knead it into the dough. Cover dough and let it rest for 15 minutes, or wrap and refrigerate overnight.

To roll by hand: divide dough into 4 pieces and roll out each piece, in turn, like pie pastry, on a lightly floured surface. Roll it very, very thin—as thin as possible—and in a rectangular shape. Sift a little flour over the surface, spreading it with your hands to coat lightly; this will keep dough from sticking to itself. Roll it up like a jelly roll—but from the long side. Cut noodles by slicing the roll with a knife, whatever width you want noodles to be. Toss the slices high in the air to unroll the noodles, letting them fall to a floured tea towel. Spread them out loosely to dry, about 2 hours. Cook as directed, or wrap tightly in freezer wrap and freeze.

To use pasta machine: shape dough into a sausage and cut it into 8 equal-size pieces. Flatten each piece. Set machine rollers at widest setting (no. 10 on most machines) and crank dough through to flatten it. Fold dough and crank it through again. Repeat with remaining pieces. Reset rollers to no. 8 and put each piece through again—just once this time, and do not fold. Continue through settings 6, 4, 2, and 0. Pasta gets longer and thinner with each rolling. To cut noodles, remove handle from roller position to cutter position for thin or wide noodles, whichever you want to make. Roll pasta through cutters and toss the resulting noodles high in the air onto a floured tea towel. Spread them out loosely to dry, about 2 hours.

*Variation:* To make cannelloni, with a knife, cut rolled pasta into rectangles about 4 x 6 inches (or smaller if you wish).

## SANDY'S PIECRUST

| | |
|---|---|
| 3 cups lightly spooned flour | 1 cup lard |
| 1 teaspoon salt | 1 egg |
| 1 tablespoon sugar | 2 tablespoons ice water |
| ¼ teaspoon baking soda | 2 tablespoons lemon juice |

Stir together flour, salt, sugar, and baking soda. With a pastry blender or two knives, cut in lard until mixture looks like small peas. Lightly beat the egg with ice water and lemon juice. Add to flour mixture and toss with a fork to moisten evenly. Gather dough into a ball and wrap in waxed paper; refrigerate for ½ hour or until ready to roll out. (*May be made 2 to 3 days ahead and refrigerated.*) Makes 2 9-inch piecrusts.

### PÂTE BRISÉE SHELL

2 cups lightly spooned flour    ¼ cup vegetable shortening
½ teaspoon salt    3 to 4 tablespoons ice water
½ cup chilled butter

Put flour in a bowl and stir in salt. (If you use unsalted butter, increase salt to 1 teaspoon.) With a pastry blender, two knives, or your fingertips, cut or rub in butter and shortening until mixture looks like small peas. Add ice water, 1 tablespoon at a time, sprinkling it on the flour mixture while tossing mixture with a fork. Use just enough water to make dough hold together. Gather it into a ball, wrap in waxed paper, and chill for at least 30 minutes. Roll out on a lightly floured board and fit into a 9- or 10-inch flan ring (whatever your recipe calls for). Prick dough all over the bottom with a fork and chill it again in the refrigerator for at least 20 minutes. Before baking, line the shell with waxed paper and fill it with dried beans or rice. Bake in a preheated 350° oven 30 minutes. Remove beans, waxed paper, and flan ring, reduce heat to 325°, and bake another 20 to 25 minutes, or until pastry is a pale gold color. Remove from oven and cool on a wire rack.

For a partly baked shell, bake in a preheated 375° oven for 20 to 25 minutes, or until pastry is set; then remove beans, waxed paper, and flan ring. Add the filling and continue baking as recipe directs.

Pâte brisée dough can be stored in the refrigerator for up to 2 days, wrapped in foil or plastic wrap. It can be frozen for up to 1 month. Defrost frozen dough in the refrigerator before using. The shell can be frozen unbaked for up to 1 month; defrost it in the refrigerator before baking. Partly baked or wholly baked shells can be refrigerated for 2 days or frozen for up to 1 month.

### SOUR CREAM PASTRY

2 cups lightly spooned flour    ¾ cup chilled unsalted butter
½ teaspoon salt    ½ cup dairy sour cream

Put flour in a bowl and stir in salt. Cut or rub butter into flour with a pastry blender, two knives, or your fingers; mixture should look like coarse cornmeal. Add sour cream and mix with a fork. Gather mixture together (it will be soft) and knead it a few times on a lightly floured board; then form it into a ball, sprinkle it with a little flour, wrap in waxed paper, and chill in the refrigerator for at least 1½ hours. Dough can be refrigerated for 2 days or frozen for up to 1 month.

# Index

Afternoon Tea Menus, 245–249
  Elegant (8), 247
  Substantial (12), 245
Ainsworth, Sandy, Bread-and-Butter Sandwiches, 247
Ainsworth, Sandy, White Bread, 245
Alice Peterson's Chocolate Cheesecake, 71
Almond
  Apricot Marzipan Tart, 43
  Cake, Swedish, 100
  Chocolate Almond Soufflé, Cold, 171
  Orange Almond Torte, 209
  Torte, 167

Alpine Logs, 236
Alsatian cooking, 4, 95
Anchovies and Roasted Peppers, 235
Anchovy Sauce (Salsa di Alici), 238
Antipasto, 256
Apple, Apples
  and Bananas, Glacéed, 145
  Chausson, 97
  Cinnamon, Baked, 14
  Poached, with Meringue, 18
  and Potato Salad, 262
  Tart Tatin, 137
Apricot Glaze, 26
Apricot Marzipan Tart, 43

Artichokes, Stuffed, 224
Asparagus
  Roman, 131
  Soup, 101
  White, Vinaigrette, 115
Aspic Dishes
  Aspic (basic), 48, 279
  Aspic for pâté, 230
  Chaudfroid Chicken, 47; on Cold
    Capered Rice, 89
  Chaudfroid Coating, 48
  Chicken, Jellied, 261
  Mustard Ring, 154
  Pâté en Croûte, 229
  Trout, Poached, Glazed, on As-
    pic, 124
Avocado, Cherry Tomatoes Stuffed
  with Guacamole, 158
Avocado with Crab Meat, 73


Bacon
  Breakfast, 14
  Canadian, Baked, 22
  Canadian, Slices, Sautéed, 30
Baked Alaska, 200
Bananas and Apples, Glacéed, 145
Bananas (with) Meringue, 109
Barley Pilaf, 178
Basic Recipes, 278–289
Batter, Beer, 285
Bavarian Cream, 208
Bavarian Cream, Pistachio, 185
Bean, Beans
  Black, Soup with Garnishes, 85
  Fava, with Coarse Salt, 90, 265
  Lima (dried), Baked, 270
  Lima (fresh), with Black Butter,
    212
  Yellow and Green, Mixed, with
    Shallots and Butter, 86
Beard, James, 3
Béarnaise Sauce, 282
Beck, Simone, 3
Beef
  Alpine Logs, 236
  Birds, 254
  Burgundy, 178
  Coulibiac of, with Mustard Hol-
    landaise, 183

Beef (Cont.)
  Fillet of, Cold, on Horseradish-
    Buttered White Bread, 258
  Hamburgers with Green Pepper-
    corns, 66
  London Broil, 102
  Meat Loaf en Croûte, 269
  à la Mode, 187
  Roast Beef Hash, 25
  Sirloin Strip, Roast, 114
  Steak Tartare, 221
  Stir-Fried, 144
  Stock, 277
  Zucchini, Stuffed, 201
Beer Batter, 285
Beet Salad, 189
Berries (raspberries or strawber-
  ries) with Cold Zabaglione,
  134
Beverages
  for Brunch, 10
  Café au Lait, 14
  for Luncheon, 40
  Sangría, 276
  Tea, 244
  Viennese Coffee, 27
Bibb Lettuce Salad, 111; and Cu-
  cumber, 49
Biscuits, Baking Powder, Hot, 74
Blowfish, Sautéed, 197
Bouquet Garni, 283
Brandade of Trout, 234
Brandy Curls, 82
Breads, Quick Breads
  Baking Powder Biscuits, Hot, 74
  Carrot Bread, 35
  Cheese Puffs, 246
  Popovers, 20
Breads, Yeast Breads
  Brioche, 11
  Coffee Cake, Easy, 15
  Croissants, 13
  Danish Pastry, 25
  Kugelhopf, 17
  Panettone, 23
  White Bread, Sandy Ainsworth's,
    245
Breakfast Menus, 11–36
  in Bed (2), 29
  Champagne (6), 36

Breakfast Menus (*Cont.*)
  childhood memories, 9–10
  Classic Continental (any number), 11
  Country (6 to 8), 14
  Hunt (10), 34
  Morning After a Late Party (8), 28
  Weekend Guests (4), 21
  Winter, Hearty (6 to 8), 17
Brioche, 11
  Giant, 12; Stuffed with Scrambled Eggs, 32
  Individual, 12
  Kielbasa in Brioche, 69
  Slices with Mustard Butter, 28
Broccoli
  Puree, 108
  Timbales, 173
  with White Wine, 225
Brown Sauce, Basic, 281
Brunch Menus, 24–28, 31–33
  drinks, 10
  by the fireplace (6), 24
  Holiday Buffet (16), 31
  Summer, Light (4), 27
Buffet Menus, 183–213
  "Cook-in" (6 to 8), 197
  Holiday Brunch (16), 31
  Italian (8), 201
  Just Desserts (25), 203
  Lap (12), 183
  Make-Your-Own-Salad (24), 191
  New Year's Eve Sit-down (16), 193
  planning, 181–182
  Sit-down (12), 186
  Summertime Seafood (8), 210
Butter, Maître d'Hôtel, 114
Butter, Olive, 68
Buttercream, *see* Icings and Fillings, Dessert
Butterfish en Papillote with Tartar Sauce, 54

Cabbage
  Red, 96
  Red (with apples), 140
  (sauerkraut) Choucroute Garni, 136

Café au Lait, 14
Cakes and Tortes
  Almond Cake, Swedish, 100
  Almond Torte, 167
  Carlsbad Oblaten Cake, 204
  Cheesecake, Chocolate, Alice Peterson's, 71
  Ginger Roll, 65
  Gold Cake, 200
  Jelly Roll, 208
  Kugelhopf, 17
  Meringue Cake with Peaches, 74
  Meringue Torte with Chocolate Buttercream, 195
  Orange Almond Torte, 209
  Panettone, 23
  Paskha, 154
  Pound Cake, 262
  Rum Babas, 247
  Savarin, 207
  Strawberry Roll, 248
  Tourinoise, La, 206
  Walnut Cake, 271
  White Chocolate Roll, 255
Canadian Bacon, *see* Bacon
Canapés, 232
Cannelloni, 287
Capered Rice, Cold, 90
Capon with Tarragon Butter, Roast, 147
Caramel, 180
Caramel Soufflé, Cold, 226
Carlsbad Oblaten Cake, 204
Carrot, Carrots
  Bread, 35
  Chinese, 46
  and Onions, Braised, 105
  Salad, 179
  Soufflé, 198
Cauliflower and Black Olive Salad, 100
Cauliflower Covered with Broccoli Puree, 108
Caviar Barquettes, 110
Celeriac and Potatoes, Mashed, 97
Celeriac Sticks, 111
Celery, Braised, 83
Celery Victor, 128
Chaudfroid Chicken, 47; on Cold Capered Rice, 89

Cheese-Flavored Dishes
  Alpine Logs, 236
  Cheesecake, Chocolate, Alice Peterson's, 71
  Cheese Croquettes with Tomato Sauce, 64
  Cheese Puffs, 246
  Cheese Roll, Four Ways, 44
  Cheeses, Assorted, 192
  Coeur à la Crème, 58
  Eggs à la Princesse Caramon, 41
  Gnocchi à la Parisienne, 162
  Gnocchi, Russian, 188
  Gougère, 75
  Green Salad with Roquefort Cheese, 125
  Noodle Ring, 61
  Onion Crêpes, 194
  Paskha, 154
  Passatelli Soup, 78
  Pears Stuffed with Roquefort Cheese, 67
  Roman Asparagus, 131
  Roquefort Salad Dressing, 192
  Tyropita, 153
Cherry Tomatoes, *see* Tomato, Tomatoes
Chestnut
  Buttercream, 189
  Mont Blanc, 189
  Mousse, 207
  Tart, 141
  Tourinoise, La, 206
Chicken, *see also* Capon; Cornish Hens; Squabs
  with Almonds, 161
  Chaudfroid, 47; on Cold Capered Rice, 89
  Jellied, 261
  Livers en Brochette, 27
  Pancakes, Curried, with Chutney, 217
  Paper-Wrapped, 142
  Périgourdine, 60
  Pie, 93
  Stock, 278
  Suprêmes with Champagne Sauce, 120
  with Tarragon Butter, Roast, 99
  Wings, Barbecued, Cold, 70

Chick-Pea Salad, 275
Chicory Salad, 59
Chinese Carrots, 46
Chinese 5-spice powder, 143
Chocolate
  Almond Soufflé, Cold, 171
  Buttercream, 196
  Carlsbad Oblaten Cake, 204
  Cheesecake, Alice Peterson's, 71
  Leaves, 249
  Mint Soufflé, Hot, 95
  Mousse, 77
  Pastry Cream, 204
  Pudding, Steamed, with Hard Sauce, 79
  Soufflé, Cold, 205
  White, Roll, 255
Choucroute Garni, 136
Cinnamon Apples, Baked, 14
Clams on the Half Shell, 266
Cocktail Party Menus, 229–240
  Large (50), 229
  planning menu and drinks, 227–228
  Small (12), 237
Coeur à la Crème, 58
Coffee
  Café au Lait, 14
  Coffeehouse Mousse, 223
  Praline Ice Cream, 122
  Viennese, 27
Coffee Cake, Easy, 15
Confection, Chocolate Leaves, 249
Consommé Normande, 119
Cookies and Small Cakes
  Brandy Curls, 82
  Florentines, 249
  Ladyfingers, 265
  Pignolia Cookies, 249
  Sand Tarts, 62
Corn on the Cob, 176
Cornish Hens
  Glazed, 127
  à l'Orange, 166
  with Tangerines, 159
Coulibiac of Beef with Mustard Hollandaise, 183
Court Bouillon, 279

Crab Meat, 34
  Avocado with, 73
  Salad, 52
  Sautéed, 88; on Virginia Ham, 34
  Seafood Mélange, 132
Cream Puff Paste (Pâté à Choux), 286
Cream, whipped, for desserts made ahead, 7
Crème Anglaise, 213
Crème Caramel, 206
Crêpes, *see* Pancakes and Crêpes
Croissants, 13
Croquettes, Cheese, with Tomato Sauce, 64
Croquettes, Polenta, 20
Crostini, Salsa di Alici, 238
Crudités with Coarse Salt, 272
Cucumber, Cucumbers
  Balls, Marinated, 109
  and Bibb Lettuce Salad, 49
  (and) Endive, and Mushroom Salad, 185
  in Sour Cream and Chives, 270
  Sticks, Iced, 267
Curried Chicken Pancakes with Chutney, 217
Custards
  Bavarian Cream, 208; Pistachio, 185
  Crème Anglaise, 213
  Crème Caramel, 206
  Riz à l'Impératrice, 115

Danish Open-face Sandwiches, Assorted, 80–82
Danish Pastry, 25
Dessert Omelette, 87
Desserts, *see* Cakes and Tortes; Coeur; Cookies and Small Cakes; Custards; Frozen Desserts; Icings and Fillings; Meringue Desserts; Mousse; Pastry Desserts; Pies and Tarts, Dessert; Pudding; Sauce, Dessert; Soufflé; *see also* names of fruits

Dinner Menus, 93–180
  Adult Birthday (4 to 6), 177
  Alsatian, Informal (6), 135
  with an American Flavor (8), 158
  Autumn, with an Alsatian Touch (6), 95
  Chinese (6 to 8), 141
  Christmas, Hearty (8), 149
  Cooking Lesson Show-off (8), 168
  Duckling (6), 104
  Early, Before a Gala (8), 161
  Easter, Unusual (8), 151
  Formal (6), 116
  Formal, Rich and Delicious (8), 113
  Formal, on the Terrace (6), 129, 253
  Formal, on a Winter's Evening (8), 110
  for Frogs' Legs Lovers (6), 163
  Game (6), 138
  Informal (8), 101; (6), 107
  Old-Fashioned Shore (8), 174
  Potluck (4), 93
  for Special Friends (6), 155
  Spring, Chic (8), 165
  Summer (8), 132
  Summer, Elegant (6), 123
  Summer, Formal (8), 126
  Sunday Night, Relaxed (6), 98
  for Sweetbread Lovers (6), 172
  Thanksgiving (8), 146
  Winter (6), 119
Dinner party planning, 91–92
Duckling, Broiled, 104
Duck Pâté, 239
Duxelles, Mushroom, 284

Eggplant, Stuffed, 273
Eggs
  Hard-Cooked
    Andalouse, 152
    Deviled, 70
    à la Princesse Caramon, 41
  Omelette, Dessert, 87
  Scrambled, 32

Endive, Belgian
à la Crème, 114
(and) Mushroom, and Cucumber Salad, 185
and Watercress Salad, 42
English Muffins, Toasted, and Strawberry Jam, 246

Fava Beans, see Bean, Beans
Fennel, Braised, 102
Fettuccine with Pesto Sauce, 202
Field, Michael, 3
Fillings, Dessert, see Icings and Fillings
Fillings, Entrée, see Stuffings and Fillings
Fish, see also names of fish
Chowder, 258
en Croûte, 45
Stock, 169, 279
Stuffed, Baked, 174
Florentines, 249
Flounder Paupiettes Stuffed with Fish Mousse, Poached, 210
Flour, measuring, 5
Forcemeat for pâté, 230
Freezer use, 6
French Dressing, 192
French Onion Soup, Gratiné, 29
French Toast, Double-Dipped, 22
French Vinaigrette Dressing, 282
Frill for bone of Gigot, 194
Fritters, Mushroom, 33
Frogs' Legs Provençale, 164
Frozen Desserts
Ice, Raspberry, with Cassis, 56
Ice Cream, Coffee Praline, 122
Ice Cream, Vanilla, Homemade (with Strawberries), 176
Oranges, Stuffed, 218
Fruit, see also names of fruit
and Champagne, 89
Fresh, Bowl, 28
Glazed, 31
Macédoine of, 61

Garnishes
Mushroom Caps, Fluted Sautéed, 284

Garnishes (Cont.)
Tomato Roses, 284
Turnip Roses, 285
Garniture Bourgeoise, 188
Gâteau Saint-Honoré, 179
Gazpacho, 260
Giblet Sauce, 150
Gigot Provençale, 193
Ginger Roll, 65
Ginger Sauce, 22
Gnocchi à la Parisienne, 162
Gnocchi, Russian, 188
Gold Cake, 200
Goose, Roast, with Giblet Sauce, 149
Gougère, 75
Grand Marnier Soufflé, Cold, 112
Grape Tart, 205
Green Mayonnaise, 53
Green Salad with Roquefort Dressing, 125
Green Salad, Tossed, 195

Ham
Baked in Paper, Jo Klein's, 259
Melon and Prosciutto, 47
Mushroom-Ham Stuffing, 121
Rolls, Individual, 32
Roulade with Lemon Butter Sauce, 77
Roulade with Mustard Sour Cream, 36
Scallops and Prosciutto, 210
and Turkey-Breast Paupiettes, 107
Hamburgers with Green Peppercorns, 66
Hard Sauce, 79
Hash, Roast Beef, 25
Herbs, dried and fresh, 6
Holiday Menus
Christmas, Hearty (8), 149
Easter, Unusual (8), 151
Fourth of July Picnic (16), 268
New Year's Eve Sit-down Buffet (16), 193
Thanksgiving (8), 146
Hollandaise Sauce, 281
Hominy, 34
Hominy Soufflé, 35

Hors d'Oeuvres
  Alpine Logs, 236
  Antipasto, 256
  Artichokes, Stuffed, 224
  Brandade of Trout, 234
  Canapés, 232
  Caviar Barquettes, 110
  Cheese Roll, Four Ways, 44
  Cherry Tomatoes Stuffed with Crab Meat, 234
  Cherry Tomatoes Stuffed with Guacamole, 158, 234
  Clams on the Half Shell, 266
  Crostini, Salsa di Alici, 238
  Crudités with Coarse Salt, 272
  Duck Pâté, 239
  Eggs Andalouse, 152
  Lentil Salad, 135
  Meat Balls, 240
  Melon and Prosciutto, 47
  Mushroom Flan, 53
  Mushroom, Onion, and Sausage Flan, 163
  Mussels en Brochette, Béarnaise, 155
  Mussels Marinière, 186
  Olive Butter, 68
  Oysters, Fried, 237
  Oysters Rockefeller, 117
  Pâté en Croûte, 229
  Peppers, Roasted, and Anchovies, 235
  Quenelles de Brochet, 168
  Radishes with Olive Butter, 84
  Salami Cornucopias on Pumpernickel, 63
  Scallops and Prosciutto, 210
  Seafood in Strudel, 238
  Shad Roe, Poached, Hollandaise, 165
  Shrimp Maison, 235
  Shrimp, Puffed, 142
  Smoked Salmon with Caviar, 149
  Tomatoes Stuffed with Crab-Meat Salad, 268
  Trout Amandine, 138
  Trout, Poached, Glazed, on Aspic, 124
  Vegetables, Raw, with Olive Butter, 234

Icings and Fillings, Dessert
  Apricot Glaze, 26
  Caramel, 180
  Chestnut Buttercream, 189
  Chocolate Buttercream, 196
  Chocolate Pastry Cream, 204
  Filling for Coffee Cake, 16
  Frosting for Walnut Cake, 271
  Pastry Cream, 180
  Praline Powder, 123
  Vanilla Water Icing, 27

Jelly Crêpes, 30
Jelly Roll, 208
Jerusalem Artichoke Soup, 146
Jo Klein's Baked Ham in Paper, 259

Kartoffelklösse, 140
Kielbasa in Brioche with Assorted Mustards, 69
Klein, Jo, Baked Ham in Paper, 259
Kugelhopf, 17

Ladyfingers, 265
Lamb
  Crown of, Béarnaise, 110
  (leg) Gigot Provençale, 193
  Leg of, Orange, en Croûte, 170
  (leg) Roast, with Soubise, 130
  Noisettes with Veal Mousse, 118
  Rack of, with Green Peppercorns, 198
Leeks Mornay, 199
Leeks Vinaigrette, 94
Lemon Butter Sauce, 77
Lemon Tart, 103
Lentil Salad, 135
Lettuce
  Bibb, and Cucumber Salad, 49
  Bibb, Salad, 111
  Lemon-Dressed, 88
  Oak-Leaf, with Sour Cream Dressing, 257
  Romaine, Salad, 58
Lima Beans, *see* Bean, Beans
Livers, Chicken, en Brochette, 27

Lobster, Lobsters
  Boiled, 266
  Halves, Truffled, Cold, Vinai-
    grette, 129
  Thermidor, 219
London Broil, 102
Lucas, Dione, 2, 3
Luncheon Menus, 39–90
  Celebration (12), 59
  Country-Kitchen (6), 83
  Danish Open-face Sandwich
    (12), 80
  Elegant (8), 44
  Formal (8), 53
  Holiday Season (6), 77
  Informal (8), 66
  Ladies' (8), 41
  Late, on a Wintry Day (8), 75
  Light and Delicate (6), 51
  Light, Easy-to-Prepare (4), 86
  Low-Calorie (4), 88
  Pleasant and Inexpensive (12 to
    16), 63
  Quick and Tasty (8), 56
  Robust, After Tennis or Golf (8),
    68
  Summer, Formal (12), 47
  Summer, for Ladies and Chil-
    dren (4 and 8), 70
  Summer, Refreshing (6), 72
  Summer, at Tables under a
    Shade Tree (8), 89
  Winter (12), 84


Macédoine of Fruit, 61
Maître d'Hôtel Butter, 114
Marzipan, Apricot Marzipan Tart,
  43
Mayonnaise, 283
Mayonnaise, Green, 53
Meat Balls, 240
Meat Glaze, 280
Meat Loaf en Croûte, 269
Meats, *see* Bacon; Beef; Ham;
  Lamb; Pork; Sausage; Veal;
  Venison
Melba Rounds, Toasted, 42
Melba Toast Fingers, 236

Melon
  with Port Wine, 30
  and Prosciutto, 47
  Wedges, Crystallized Ginger,
    257
Meringue Desserts
  Apples, Poached, with Meringue,
    18
  Baked Alaska, 200
  Lemon Tart, 103
  Meringue Bananas, 109
  Meringue Cake with Peaches, 74
  Meringue Torte with Chocolate
    Buttercream, 195
  Mont Blanc, 189
  Salzburger Nockerln, 106
Mincemeat Roll with Hard Sauce,
  150
Mont Blanc, 189
Mornay Sauce, 157
Mostarda, 68
Mousse, Cold
  Chestnut, 207
  Chocolate, 77
  Coffeehouse, 223
  Spinach, 51
Mushroom, Mushrooms
  Broth Garnished with Mush-
    room Rounds, 51
  Caps, Fluted Sautéed, 284
  Duxelles, 283
  (and) Endive, and Cucumber
    Salad, 185
  Flan, 53
  Fritters, 33
  -Ham Stuffing, 121
  (and) Onion, and Sausage Flan,
    163
  Salad, Raw, with a Dressing of
    Sour Cream, Caraway, and
    Chives, 78
  Sauce, 175
  Sautéed, 284
  Soup, Cream of, 99
Mussels
  en Brochette, Béarnaise, 155
  Marinière, 186
  (and) Oysters, and Shrimp,
    Fried, with Tartar Sauce, 225

Mustard
  Hollandaise, 183
  Mayonnaise, 267
  Ring, 154
  Sour Cream, 36

Noodle Ring, 61

Olive, Black
  Butter, 68
  and Cauliflower Salad, 100
  and Red Onion Salad, 67
Olney, Richard, 3
Onion, Onions
  and Carrots, Braised, 105
  Crêpes, 194
  (and) Mushroom, and Sausage
    Flan, 163
  Pie, 85
  Red, and Black Olive Salad, 67
  Rings, Deep-Fried, 85
  Soubise, 130; Filling, 157
  Soup, Cream of, Cold, 274
  Soup, French, Gratiné, 29
  Stuffed with Onions, 69
Orange, Oranges
  Almond Torte, 209
  Grand Marnier, 84
  Leg of Lamb en Croûte, 170
  Stuffed, 218
Outdoor Menus, 253–276
  Back Porch Supper (8), 259
  Beach Picnic (6), 274
  Formal Dinner on the Terrace
    (6), 129, 253
  Formal Picnic (8), 263
  Fourth of July Picnic (16), 268
  Lobster Party (6), 266
  Picnic in the Woods (8), 256
  Pool Party (12), 272
  Summer Luncheon at Tables un-
    der a Shade Tree (8), 89
  Tailgate Picnic (8), 257
Oyster, Oysters
  Fried, 237
  Rockefeller, 117
  (and) Shrimp, and Mussels,
    Fried, with Tartar Sauce, 225
  Stew, Hot, 75

Pain Bagna, 275
Palm, Hearts of, Salad, 171
Pancakes and Crêpes
  Chicken Pancakes, Curried, with
    Chutney, 217
  Crêpes, Basic, 285
  Jelly Crêpes, 30
  Onion Crêpes, 194
Panettone, 23
Paskha, 154
Passatelli Soup, 78
Pasta
  Cannelloni, 287
  Fettuccine with Pesto Sauce, 202
  Homemade, 286
  Noodle Ring, 61
Pastry, Basic
  Barquettes, 49
  for Orange Leg of Lamb, 171
  Pâte Brisée Shell, 288
  Pâte à Choux (Cream Puff
    Paste), 286
  for pâté molds, 230
  Piecrust, Sandy's, 287
  Sour Cream Pastry, 289
Pastry Desserts
  Gâteau Saint-Honoré, 179
  Mincemeat Roll with Hard
    Sauce, 150
  Strawberry Barquettes, 49
Pastry Entrées and Hors d'Oeuvres
  Alpine Logs, 236
  Caviar Barquettes, 110
  Coulibiac of Beef with Mustard
    Hollandaise, 183
  Duck Pâté, 239
  Fish en Croûte, 45
  Gougère, 75
  Meat Loaf en Croûte, 269
  Orange Leg of Lamb en Croûte,
    170
  Pâté en Croûte, 229
  Seafood in Strudel, 238
  Tyropita, 153
  Veal Loaf en Croûte, Peppered,
    269
Pastry Cream, *see* Icings and Fill-
  ings
Pâte Brisée Shell, 288

Pâte à Choux (Cream Puff Paste), 286
Pâté en Croûte, 229
Pea
    Pod Soup, 216
    Potage Saint-Germain, 221
    Roulade, 55
Peaches, Fresh, with Champagne, 36
Peaches in Port, 46
Pear, Pears
    Baked, with Heavy Cream, 21
    Poached, in Cassis, 162
    Poached in White Wine, 165
    Stuffed with Roquefort Cheese, 67
    Tart, Fresh, 132
Pecan Pie, 161
Pennsylvania Scrapple, 19
Peppercorns, green, 66, 198
Peppered Veal Loaf en Croûte, 269
Pepper, Green, Salad, 65
Peppers, Red, Roasted, and Anchovies, 235
Pesto alla Genovese, 202
Peterson, Alice, Chocolate Cheesecake, 71
Picknicking, packing up, 251–252
Picnics, see Outdoor Menus
Piecrust, Sandy's, 287
Pies and Tarts, Dessert
    Apple Chausson, 97
    Apricot Marzipan Tart, 43
    Chestnut Tart, 141
    Grape Tart, 205
    Lemon Tart, 103
    Pear Tart, Fresh, 132
    Pecan Pie, 161
    Raspberry Tart, 128
    Tart Tatin, 137
Pies and Tarts, Entrées and Hors d'Oeuvres
    Chicken Pie, 93
    Mushroom Flan, 53
    Mushroom, Onion, and Sausage Flan, 163
    Onion Pie, 85
    Pissaladière, 272
Pignolia Cookies, 249
Pike, Quenelles de Brochet, 168

Pilaf, see Barley; Rice
Pineapple, Glazed, in Kirsch, 24
Pissaladière, 272
Pistachio Bavarian Cream, 185
Polenta, 19
    Croquettes, 20
    Ring Mold with Sautéed Fluted Mushroom Caps, 83
Pommes Parisienne, 255
Popovers, 20
Pork, see also Bacon; Ham; Sausage
    Choucroute Garni, 136
    Fresh Ham, Roast, 152
    Rack of, 95
    Scrapple, Pennsylvania, 19
    Spareribs, Barbecued, 143
Potage Saint-Germain, 221
Potato, Potatoes
    and Apple Salad, 262
    and Celeriac, Mashed, 97
    Kartoffelklösse, 140
    Pommes Parisienne, 255
    Roesti, 15
    Skins, Baked, 267
    Soufflé, 119
    Steamed, with Caraway and Melted Butter, 137
    Straw, 127
    Sweet, Whipped, 160
Poultry, see Capon; Chicken; Cornish Hens; Duck, Duckling; Goose; Squabs; Turkey
Pound Cake, 262
Praline Powder, 123
Provençale Sauce, 164
Pudding, Chocolate, Steamed, with Hard Sauce, 79

Quenelles de Brochet, 168

Radish, Radishes
    Black, Salad, 222
    Black, Slices, Vinaigrette, 76
    with Olive Butter, 84
Raspberry, Raspberries
    with Chilled Framboise, 90
    Ice with Cassis, 56
    Tart, 128

Reheating, 6

Rice, *see also* Wild Rice
Brown, Pilaf; 167; with Almond Slivers, 111; with Pine Nuts, 105
Capered, Cold, 90
Fried, 144
Risotto, 57
Riz à l'Impératrice, 115

Ris de Veau, Velouté Sauce, 172
Risotto, 57
Riz à l'Impératrice, 115
Robbins, Ann Roe, 3
Roesti Potatoes, 15
Romaine Salad, 58
Roman Asparagus, 131
Roquefort Dressing, 192
Rum Babas, 247
Russian Dressing, 192
Russian Gnocchi, 188

Salad
Apple and Potato, 262
Asparagus, White, Vinaigrette, 115
Avocado with Crab Meat, 73
Beefsteak Tomatoes and Chives Marinated in Sour Cream Dressing, 176
Beet, 189
Bibb Lettuce, 111; and Cucumber, 49
Black Radish, 222; Slices Vinaigrette, 76
Broccoli with White Wine, 225
Carrot, 179
Cauliflower and Black Olive, 100
Celery Victor, 128
Cherry Tomatoes Vinaigrette, 173
Chick-Pea, 275
Chicory, 59
Crab-Meat, 52
Cucumber Balls, Marinated, 109
Cucumbers in Sour Cream and Chives, 270
Cucumber Sticks, Iced, 267
Endive, Mushroom, and Cucumber, 185

Salad (*Cont.*)
Green Pepper, 65
Green, with Roquefort Cheese, 125
Green, Tossed, 195
Hearts of Palm, 171
ingredients, 192
Leeks Vinaigrette, 94
Lentil, 135
Lettuce, Lemon-Dressed, 88
Mushroom, Raw, with a Dressing of Sour Cream, Caraway, and Chives, 78
Oak-Leaf Lettuce with Sour Cream Dressing, 257
Red Onion and Black Olive, 67
Romaine, 58
Tomato, 87
Tomatoes with Chives, 73
Tomatoes Stuffed with Crab-Meat Salad, 268
Watercress, 122; and Belgian Endive, 42; with Cherry Tomatoes and Chives, 162

Salad Dressing
French, 192
Mayonnaise, 283
Mayonnaise, Green, 53
Roquefort, 192
Russian, 192
Tartar Sauce, 55
Vinaigrette, French, 283

Salami Cornucopias on Pumpernickel, 63
Salmon, Smoked, with Caviar, 149
Salzburger Nockerln, 106
Sand Tarts, 62

Sandwiches
Bread-and-Butter, Sandy Ainsworth's, 247
Fillet of Beef, Cold, on Horseradish-Buttered White Bread, 258
Ham, Baked, in Paper, Jo Klein's, on Mustard-Buttered French Bread, 259
Open-face, Danish, Assorted, 80–82
Pain Bagna, 275

Sandwiches (*Cont.*)
 Turkey, Cold Roast, on Sandy
  Ainsworth's White Bread, 246
Sandy Ainsworth's Bread-and-But-
 ter Sandwiches, 247
Sandy Ainsworth's White Bread,
 245
Sandy's Piecrust, 287
Sangría, 276
Sauce, *see also* Sauce, Dessert;
 Salad Dressing
 Anchovy (Salsa di Alici), 238
 Béarnaise, 282
 Brown, Basic, 281
 Giblet, 150
 Hollandaise, 282
 Lemon Butter, 77
 Maître d'Hôtel Butter, 114
 Meat Glaze, 280
 Mornay, 157
 Mushroom, 175
 Mustard Hollandaise, 183
 Mustard Mayonnaise, 267
 Mustard Sour Cream, 36
 Pesto alla Genovese, 202
 Provençale, 164
 for Quenelles de Brochet, 169
 Shrimp, 211
 Soy Dipping, 142
 Tartar, 55
 Tomato, 64
 Velouté, 281
Sauce, Dessert
 Crème Anglaise, 213
 Ginger, 22
 Hard, 79
 Strawberry, 106
 Zabaglione, 203; Cold, 134
Saucepans, heavy, for high-heat
 cooking, 6
Sausage
 Kielbasa in Brioche with As-
  sorted Mustards, 69
 (and) Mushroom, and Onion
  Flan, 163
 Salami Cornucopias on Pumper-
  nickel, 63
Savarin, 207
Scallops, Bay, Sautéed, 86
Scallops (sea) and Prosciutto, 210

Scrapple, Pennsylvania, 19
Seafood Mélange, 132
Seafood in Strudel, 238
Shad Roe, Poached, Hollandaise,
 165
Shrimp
 en Brochette, 57
 Maison, 235
 (and) Oysters, and Mussels,
  Fried, with Tartar Sauce, 225
 Puffed, 142
 Sauce, 211
 Seafood Mélange, 132
Sirloin Strip, Roast, 114
Skewered Dishes
 Chicken Livers en Brochette, 27
 Crostini, Salsa di Alici, 238
 Mussels en Brochette, Béarnaise,
  155
 Shrimp en Brochette, 57
Sorrel Soup, Cold, 253
Soubise, 130; Filling, 157
Soufflé, Cold
 Caramel, 226
 Chocolate, 205
 Chocolate Almond, 171
 Grand Marnier, 112
Soufflé, Hot
 Carrot, 198
 Chocolate Mint, 95
 Hominy, 35
 Salzburger Nockerln, 100
 Violet, 212
Soup, Cold
 Gazpacho, 260
 Onion, Cream of, 274
 Sorrel, 253
 Tomato and Dill, 126
 Vichyssoise, 263
 Watercress, 191
Soup, Hot
 Asparagus, 101
 Black Bean, with Garnishes, 85
 Consommé Normande, 119
 Fish Chowder, 258
 Jerusalem Artichoke, 146
 Mushroom Broth Garnished with
  Mushroom Rounds, 51
 Mushroom, Cream of, 99
 Onion, French, Gratiné, 29

Soup, Hot (*Cont.*)
  Oyster Stew, 75
  Passatelli, 78
  Pea Pod, 216
  Potage Saint-Germain, 221
  Watercress, 191
Sour Cream
  Dressing, 176
  Pastry, 288
Soy Dipping Sauce, 142
Spareribs, Barbecued, 143
Spatula, wooden, 6
Spinach Mousse, Cold, 51
Spinach Timbales, 121
Squabs, Glazed, 127
Squabs à l'Orange, 166
Starch for thickening, 6
Steak Tartare, 221
Stew, Oyster, Hot, 75
Stock
  Beef, 278
  Chicken, 278
  Fish, 169, 279
  Veal, 279
Strawberry, Strawberries
  Barquettes, 49
  in Fresh Orange Juice, 27
  over Homemade Vanilla Ice
    Cream, 176
  Roll, 248
  Sauce, 106
Straw Potatoes, 127
Stuffings and Fillings
  Forcemeat for Pâté, 230
  Mushroom Duxelles, 284
  Mushroom-Ham Stuffing, 121
  Soubise Filling, 157
  Stuffing for Beef Birds, 254
Supper Menus, 216–226
  After Theater, Ballet, or Opera
    (8), 216
  Election Night (10), 224
  Late Night Champagne (6), 218
  Robust, for Poker Players (12),
    220
Swedish Almond Cake, 100
Sweetbreads, Ris de Veau, Velouté
  Sauce, 172
Sweet Potatoes, Whipped, 160

Tartar Sauce, 55
Tea, 244
Toasts
  English Muffins, Toasted, and
    Strawberry Jam, 246
  French Toast, Double-Dipped,
    22
  Melba Rounds, 42
  Melba Toast Fingers, 236
Tomato, Tomatoes
  Beefsteak, and Chives Marinated
    in Sour Cream Dressing, 176
  Cherry Tomatoes
    with Coarse Salt, 265
    Stuffed with Crab Meat, 234
    Stuffed with Guacamole, 158,
      234
    Vinaigrette, 173
  with Chives, 73
  and Dill Soup, Cold, 126
  Grilled, 33, 35
  Roses, 284
  Salad, 87
  Sauce, 64
  with Soubise, Baked, 184
  Stuffed with Crab-Meat Salad,
    268
Tortes, *see* Cakes and Tortes
Tourinoise, La, 206
Trifle, 208
Trout
  Amandine, 138
  Brandade of, 234
  Poached, Glazed, on Aspic, 124
  Poached, with Hollandaise Sauce,
    113
Turkey
  Breast and Ham Paupiettes, 107
  Roast, Cold, Sandwiches, 246
  with Tarragon Butter, Roast, 147
Turnip Roses, 284
Turnips, Braised, 150
Tyropita, 153

Vanilla Ice Cream, Homemade
  (with Strawberries), 176
Vanilla Water Icing, 27

Veal
  Birds with Brown Sauce, 133
  Breast of, Stuffed with Pâté, 264
  Loaf en Croûte, Peppered, 269
  Orloff, 156
  Rack of, Béarnaise, 124
  Stock, 279
  Sweetbreads, Ris de Veau, Velouté Sauce, 172
Vegetable, Vegetables, *see also* names of vegetables
  Crudités with Coarse Salt, 272
  Garniture Bourgeoise, 188
  Raw, with Olive Butter, 234
Velouté Sauce, 280
Venison Bourguignonne, 139
Vichyssoise, 263
Viennese Coffee, 27
Vinaigrette Dressing, French, 283
Violet Soufflé, Hot, 212

Walnut Cake, 271
Watercress
  and Belgian Endive Salad, 42

Watercress (*Cont.*)
  Salad, 122; with Cherry Tomatoes and Chives, 162
  Soup, 191
Whisk, 6
Wild Rice Ring, 148
Wine-Flavored Dishes
  Beef Birds, 254
  Beef Burgundy, 178
  Beef à la Mode, 187
  Broccoli with White Wine, 225
  Chicken Suprêmes with Champagne Sauce, 120
  Fruit and Champagne, 89
  Melon with Port Wine, 30
  Peaches in Port, 46
  Pears Poached in White Wine, 165
  Sangría, 276
  Venison Bourguignonne, 139

Zabaglione, 203; Cold, 134
Zucchini, French-Fried, 134
Zucchini, Stuffed, 201